AF605833

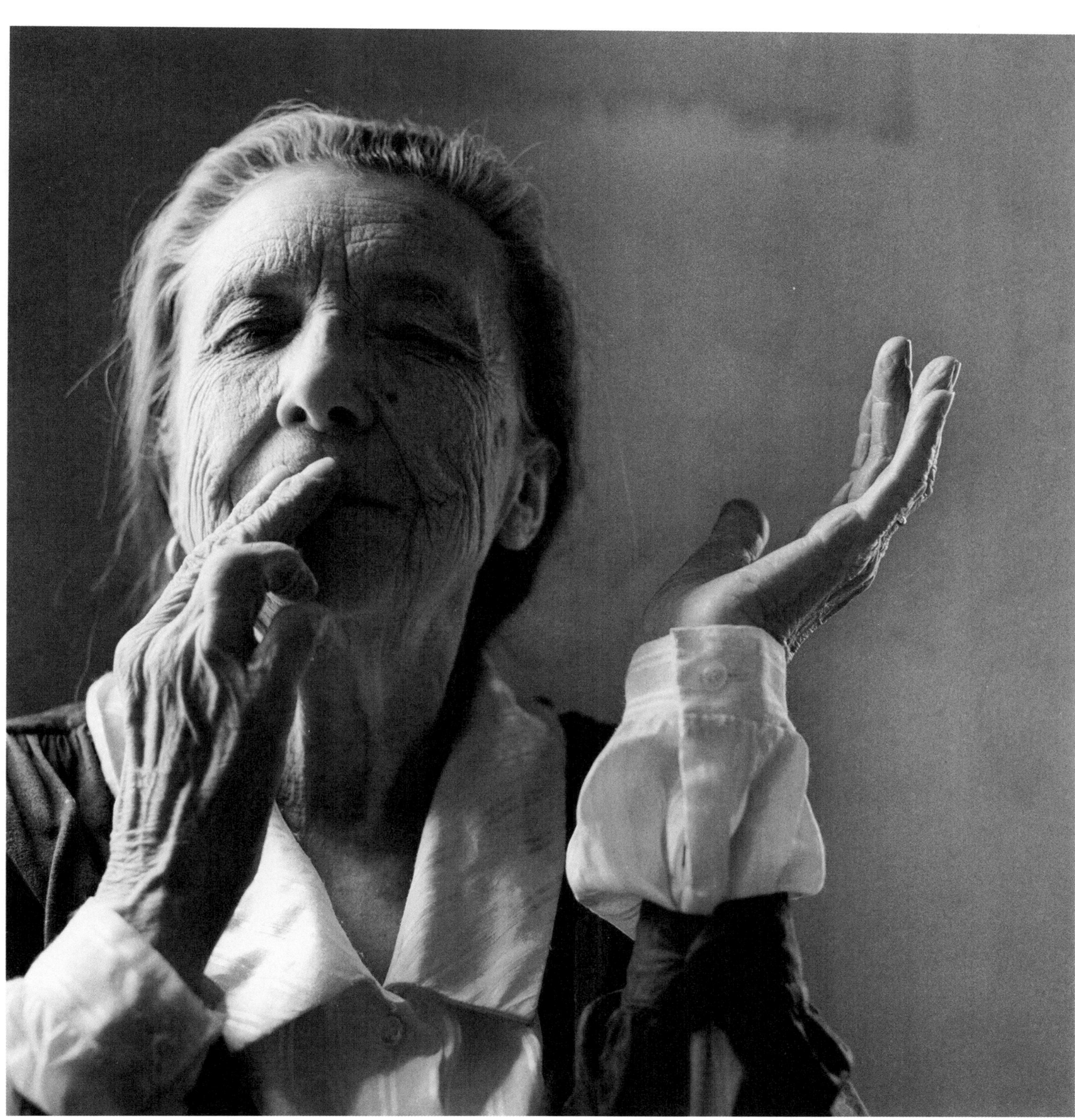

The Art Gallery of New South Wales acknowledges the traditional custodians of the Country on which it stands, the Gadigal of the Eora Nation.

LOUISE BOURGEOIS

opening page:
Louise Bourgeois, 1990, photo: Yann Charbonnier

following spread:
Louise Bourgeois *Maman* 1999 (detail) at the
Art Gallery of New South Wales, with partial view
of Karla Dickens *To see or not to see* 2022

EDITED BY
JUSTIN PATON

WITH
CONTRIBUTIONS BY
JANE CAMPION
CHRIS KRAUS
PHILIP LARRATT-SMITH
JUSTIN PATON
JAMIESON WEBSTER

LOUISE BOURGEOIS

HAS THE DAY INVADED THE NIGHT OR HAS THE NIGHT INVADED THE DAY?

ART GALLERY OF NEW SOUTH WALES

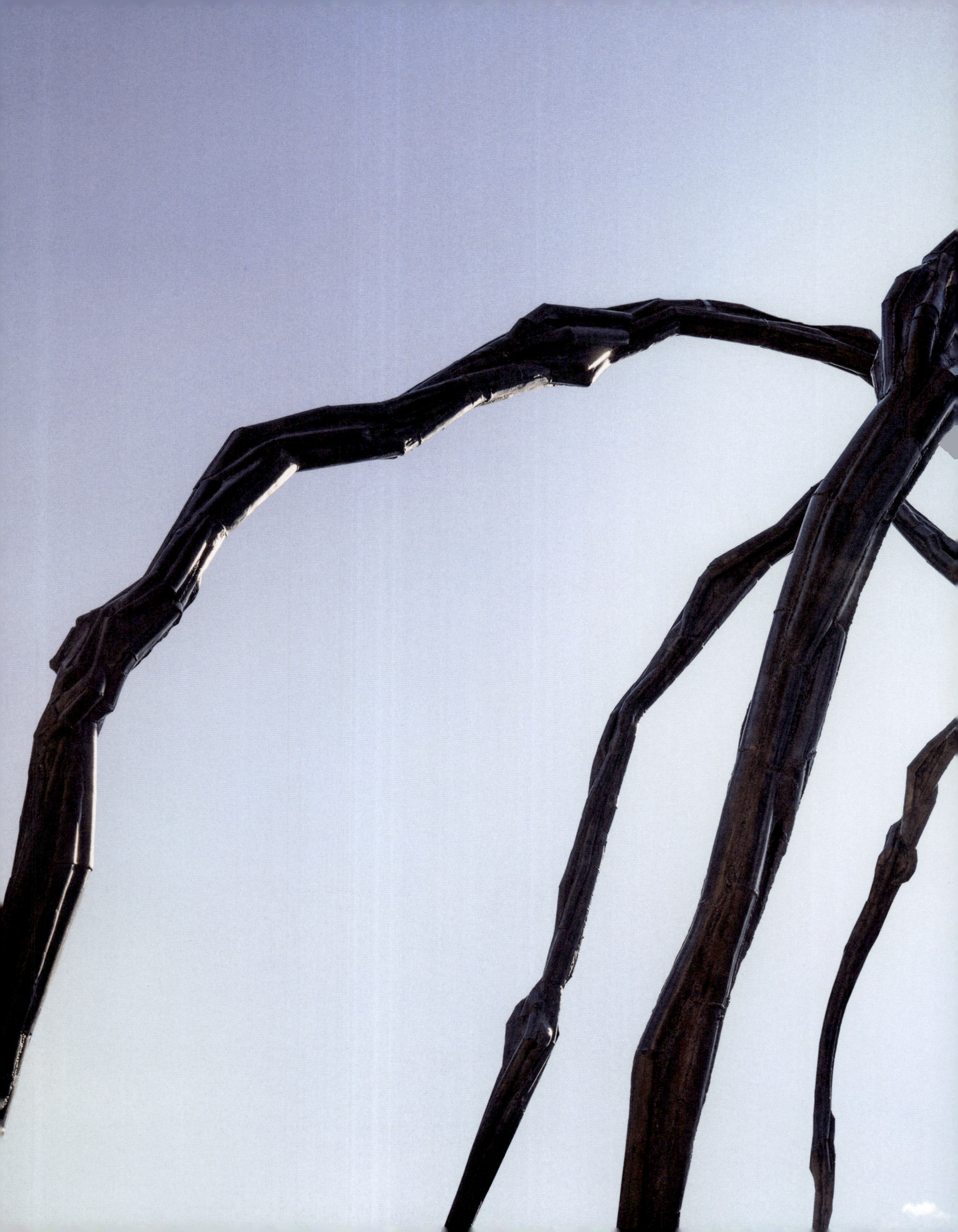

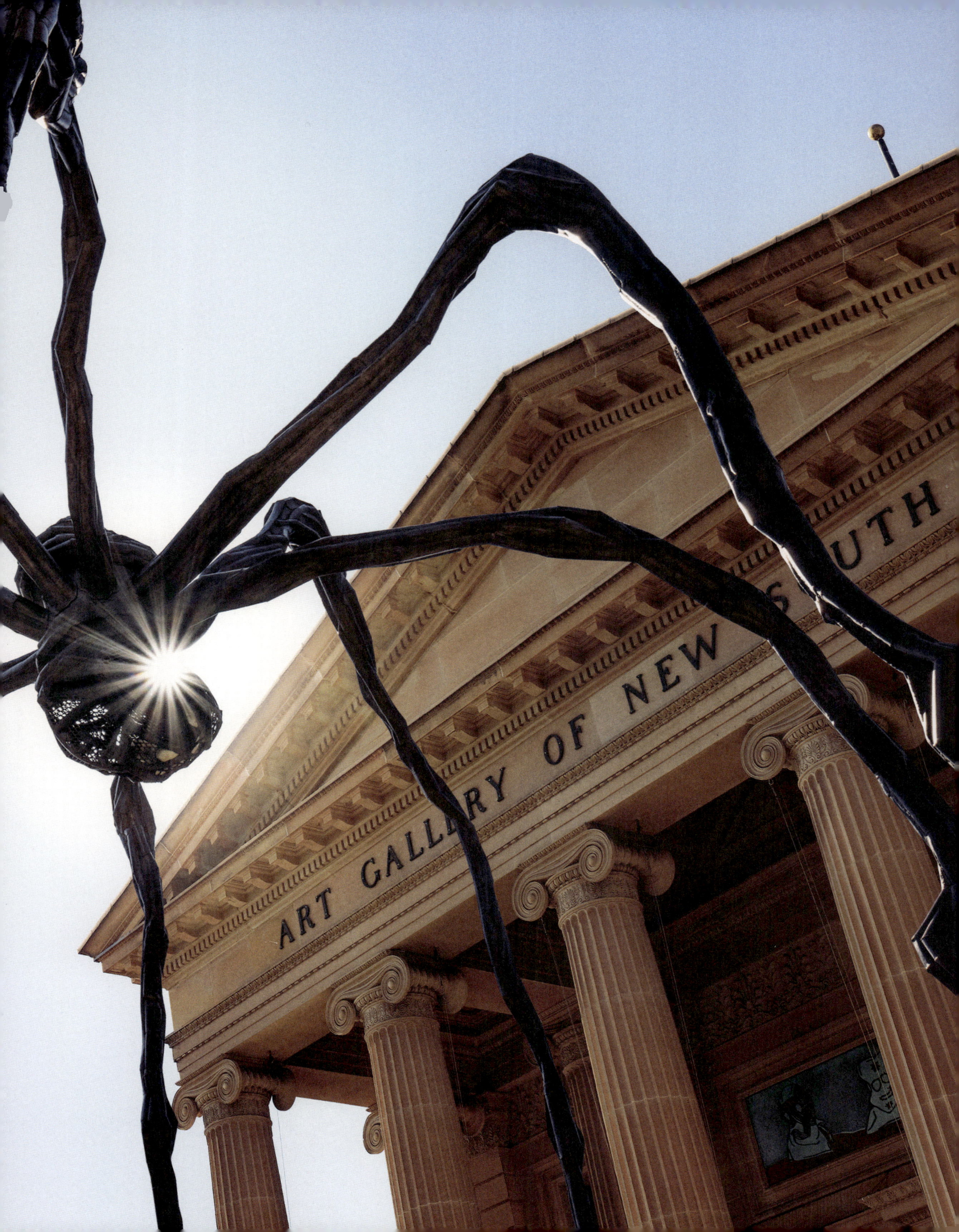
ART GALL RY OF NEW S UTH

MESSAGE FROM THE MINISTER

On behalf of the NSW Government, it is my great pleasure to welcome you to the Art Gallery of New South Wales for the Sydney International Art Series exhibition *Louise Bourgeois: Has the Day Invaded the Night or Has the Night Invaded the Day?*

From sculptures and installations to printmaking, fabric works and painting, Louise Bourgeois experimented with many mediums and pushed the boundaries of artistic expression to become one of the most influential artists of the past century. The largest presentation of Bourgeois's work ever seen in Australia, this exhibition is also unique in the way it is displayed across dramatically different gallery spaces to explore the powerful emotional tensions which are central to Bourgeois's practice.

This exhibition is part of the Sydney International Art Series – a collaboration between the NSW Government's tourism and major events agency, Destination NSW; the Museum of Contemporary Art Australia; and the Art Gallery of New South Wales.

Securing exceptional exhibitions of this scale for the Sydney International Art Series drives visitation to our city and reinforces its reputation as a global artistic and creative hub.

I am sure you will be fascinated and moved by Louise Bourgeois's life and work, and I invite you to take some time to explore our beautiful city and its unique combination of vibrant cultural precincts and natural wonders.

The Hon John Graham MLC
Minister for Jobs and Tourism
Minister for the Arts
Minister for Music and the Night-time Economy

DIRECTOR'S FOREWORD

The opening of the new Art Gallery of New South Wales building in December 2022 marked the completion of an immense project. It also marked the beginning of an exciting new chapter, in which our art museum will share an expanded view of the art of the world from our place on Gadigal Country in Sydney. Accordingly, I am delighted that the first major solo exhibition in our new SANAA-designed building takes as its subject the great French–American artist Louise Bourgeois (1911–2010) and the moving and mysterious works she created across seven decades.

The first encounter Bourgeois had with Australians occurred in an unusual setting. In a reminiscence of her work as a docent at the Musée du Louvre in Paris in the 1930s, Bourgeois recalled that 'The Australians would say, "Gorgeous! Gorgeous!" I'd never heard that word before.' It is fitting, as we launch the most comprehensive exhibition of Bourgeois's work ever presented in Australia and indeed the larger Asia-Pacific region, to acknowledge a tradition of local interest in her work that began with the acquisition of *C.O.Y.O.T.E.* 1947–49 (pp 96–97) for the National Gallery of Australia by then director James Mollison in 1980–81. This continued through focus exhibitions organised in 1995–96 at the National Gallery of Victoria (which also travelled to the Museum of Contemporary Art in Sydney) and in 2013 at Heide Museum of Modern Art, Melbourne.

Spanning two major exhibition spaces and including more than 120 works, this exhibition – *Louise Bourgeois: Has the Day Invaded the Night or Has the Night Invaded the Day?* – demonstrates the Art Gallery's commitment to revealing the depth and complexity of the artistic careers we explore. It also demonstrates our commitment to the work of women artists in our collections and exhibitions.

The foremost reason for presenting Bourgeois's art in depth – as head curator of international art Justin Paton elaborates in his lead essay – is its combined emotional intensity, searching intelligence, and ceaseless exploration of life's extremes: light and darkness, love and rage, solitude and togetherness, conscious order and unconscious desire.

Bold artists inspire art museums towards new approaches, and I am proud that Bourgeois's art has inspired an exhibition that is itself exploratory. Beginning with an introductory journey through Bourgeois's career in the elegant white rooms of the Ainsworth Family Gallery, the exhibition continues in a very different key downstairs in the darkness of the spectacular Tank, a Second World War fuel bunker repurposed by SANAA. This presentation uses the varied spaces of our new building to offer two very different ways of experiencing Bourgeois's art, and in the process opens up questions about survey exhibitions and how they frame artists' lives and creations.

This exhibition is an outcome of a conversation that began in 2016 with the acquisition of Bourgeois's *Arched Figure* 1993, cast 2010 (p 81), through the financial support of the Art Gallery of New South Wales Foundation – a sculpture that has since played a part in a number of our exhibitions. For his steadfast support and matchless understanding of Bourgeois's art, we extend our thanks to Jerry Gorovoy, president of The Easton Foundation and Bourgeois's deeply valued assistant across the last three decades of her life; and to Philip Larratt-Smith, curator at The Easton Foundation, for the deep knowledge and essential counsel he has shared in his role as advising curator. Jerry and Philip's colleagues at The Easton Foundation and the Louise Bourgeois Studio in New York have been unstinting with their help as we organised a many-faceted exhibition.

Here in Sydney, I congratulate Justin Paton, who championed Bourgeois's work for our collection and has, with the support of assistant curator Emily Sullivan, realised an exhibition like none presented here before. Senior exhibitions manager Danielle Earp and senior registrar Lauren Parker also deserve special mention for their key roles among the large Art Gallery team that is acknowledged fully by Justin later in this publication. For lending important and beautiful works by Bourgeois, I offer sincere thanks to public and private collectors, and Hauser & Wirth as representatives of the artist's estate; above all, I acknowledge The Easton Foundation and Louise Bourgeois Trust for sharing the core of exceptional works around which this exhibition has been organised. I also thank the marvellous family of benefactors and supporters, listed in full later in this publication, whose support has made possible both an ambitious exhibition and the presentation in Australia for the first time of the mighty sculpture *Maman* 1999. From that family, I must extend particular gratitude to John Grill AO and Rosie Williams for their extraordinary support as principal exhibition patron.

One thing became immediately evident to me after this exhibition was announced – the excitement felt by many contemporary artists for whom Bourgeois is a longstanding inspiration. That admiration can be felt in the contributions to this catalogue by Jane Campion, Chris Kraus and Jamieson Webster, remarkable women artists and writers who celebrate Bourgeois's rigour, determination, vulnerability and power. This respect and fascination is further evident in contributions to the exhibition from two extraordinary women artists of subsequent generations: the first is Jenny Holzer, who has orchestrated scrolling projections of Bourgeois's psychoanalytic writings for the Tank; and the second is Kali Malone, who has created a subtle sonic response to Bourgeois's work for viewers to listen to as they look. Their contributions are homages to an uncompromising and deeply influential artist, whose work we are honoured to introduce to new generations in Sydney.

Michael Brand
Director
Art Gallery of New South Wales

CONTENTS

‘Has the day invaded the night or has the night invaded the day?’ Louise Bourgeois’s unending search

Justin Paton

1 (A DOUBLE-EDGED KNIFE)

Night and day. Two times, two states, two conditions in opposition. But bound together, impossible to separate, each unimaginable without the other. When we say that two people are like night and day, we mean that they could not be more different. And when we say that someone works at something night and day, we mean they pursue it incessantly, excessively.

Louise Bourgeois (1911–2010) is an artist of night and day in both senses. She is, first, an artist of extremes, of opposed yet intertwined impulses – an artist obsessed with the complicated and contradictory truth of our feelings towards ourselves and others. Self-knowledge was what she desired above all. She was the question her art sought to answer. And she spoke time and again of the tensions that defined her, and of their vexing, generative power. She was, she said, a double-edged knife, and a pendulum swinging from one extreme to the other. She was torn between being a woman of emotion and a woman of rationality. She expressed tenderness while feeling violence inside and expressed murderousness while feeling intense love. She made, destroyed, repaired, made again; attacked, sought peace, regathered. And she 'refused to choose'. She lived with and worked with her polarities. Tension is energy held. By capturing tensions in her art, she sourced and channelled tremendous vitality.[1]

Bourgeois is also an artist of night and day in her determination and round-the-clock persistence. There is no rule that says that artists are obliged to keep asking the most difficult questions. Indeed, there is an abundance of art that contents itself with doing otherwise. But questions of love, loss, mortality and conflict have not gone away. And there remains, correspondingly, a need for artists who would never think of not confronting those matters. Bourgeois, every day (and many nights) of her seven-decade career, was one of those artists. She intersected with many of the major artists and movements of New York's mid twentieth-century art scene (émigré surrealists and dadaists, the first generation of abstract expressionists) but outlasted them all and lived and worked on into the late twentieth and early twenty-first century, a mischievous and fearsome heroine to new generations. As the achievements of many 'modern masters' settled into popularity and familiarity, her own work maintained – and still delivers – a charge of intimacy, urgency and piercing peculiarity. Far from being a distant and admirable monument, Bourgeois comes to us as a contemporary – someone working through unfinished business about womanhood and selfhood today. It's amazing, the number of people (and not just artists) one meets for whom her independence and tenacity mean everything.

This exhibition seeks to share the day(s) and night(s) of Louise Bourgeois's art: the enthralling intensity of her search and its affecting longevity. It does so by starting with a question, an appropriately long and looping one: 'Has the day invaded the night or has the night invaded the day?' The question first appears, written in pencil, in Bourgeois's diary on Tuesday 7 February 1995 (also on that day: her long-time assistant Jerry Gorovoy is in Helsinki, and curator Lynne Cooke is visiting at 11am; see p 26).[2] Bourgeois will use it in several artworks, including one that we'll come to. But even, or especially, in this workaday setting, the question gets at something essential. A chronic insomniac, Bourgeois had good reason to think of night and day competing; for the sleepless person, each new night or day arrives in debt to the one preceding. But it's more than that. The question places something insoluble at the core of existence. For 'night and day' is always a metaphor for all the nights and days we are given. The experience of waking and sleeping is one of the frames through which we comprehend existing and dying. But *invaded* – it's such a loaded word for a cycle usually thought of as natural. Bourgeois once said of the huge bronze spiders she sculpted that they had an 'invading power'.[3] And to speak of the day invading the night which also invades the day is to posit a turbulent energy, a chasing at the heart of things to which we have no answer – or to which the only answer, between two options, is a paradoxical 'yes' (the 'yes' of rigorously discontented acceptance).

Surveying a career that works in this way is like trying to measure a rope while it is being knotted. Indeed, the bureaucratic tone of words like 'survey' and 'career' feels unsuited to Bourgeois, whose mission in the studio, as Jerry Gorovoy once said, was not to 'make shows' but to make it through the day.[4] To survey is to take stock and make sense, dividing a life's work into legible chapters. But there is a danger, in committing to the form of the survey, of finding only the logic that surveys look for. As the life's work is arranged in sequential rooms and patiently explicated in wall labels, the risk is of knowing the artist not wisely but too well. The liveness in the life's work is muffled. There's no space for productive madness in the method. This issue does not irk as much when the artist in question 'develops' steadily and conventionally. But it looms when the artist, like Bourgeois supremely, sets no store by steady 'progression'. A hyperintelligent child whose classical education equipped her with formidable skills of observation, explication and analysis, Bourgeois also knew, from the earliest, the wrecking emotional effects of war and the destabilising power of her own inner conflicts. The art she made reflects her existential sense of a world without reassurances and guarantees. This art searches, circles, interrupts itself. It comes back, and back again, to the problems. It spurns consoling fictions of improvement in favour of unsettling self-knowledge. It works seven days a week and it does not sleep easily. It moves up and down, in and out, and back around on itself incessantly.

The question, then, is how to capture this restless searching movement in an exhibition. Our answer in Sydney – provisional, as it must be – is an exhibition that itself moves 'up and down', circling between a space of 'day' and another evoking 'night', in our new (one-year-old) building. In conceptualising this exhibition physically, we have taken heart and inspiration from Bourgeois's own openness to suggestions from 'below' – in this case, from the museum's own architectural unconscious. Upstairs, a selective seven-decade survey unfolds through our major exhibition gallery, with regular cuts, interruptions and chronological 'back-stitches' to agitate the story. Here the days of Bourgeois's working life are staged in broad sequence through clean and well-lit rooms. But this daylit narrative exists in permanent tension with a counter-story or anti-narrative, which is discovered by descending a spiral staircase to an immense space of 'night' below. This is the Tank, the vast Second World War fuel bunker gallery that lies beneath the Art Gallery's new building, and one is tempted to say that it has been waiting for these works – or perhaps they've been waiting for it. With its time-stained walls, wartime echoes, raw formwork and deep shadows, the Tank is the dark twin of the white cube gallery above – and a fitting 'host body' for the works of an artist who once said 'I know how to make lairs. I can make them subterranean.'[5] Here, among a forest of tall columns, many times and moments in Bourgeois's art dream furiously together.

Spiralling down the stairs from 'day' to 'night' or spiralling back up from 'night' to 'day', what emerges is a single exhibition whose two halves are constantly pursuing (perhaps invading) each other. The tensions that crackle in individual works and bodies of work (between inside and outside, conscious and unconscious, male and female, and so on) also define the exhibition. Perhaps it is best described as two exhibitions in one, facing in two directions like Bourgeois's *Janus fleuri* 1968 (left and p 240) – the split yet strangely peaceful hanging bronze, her favourite among all her sculptures, which she named after the two-faced Roman god of beginnings and considered a kind of self-portrait.[6] How do you navigate an exhibition that looks both ways? You must start somewhere. Let's begin with 'day'.

2 (DAY)

Bourgeois was born in Paris in 1911 into a situation both comfortable – her parents ran a prosperous tapestry repair business – and volatile. She was hypersensitive to the frictions she perceived between her father and mother, Louis and Joséphine, and these anxieties mingled in her young mind with the shocks and losses of the First World War. Her father's beloved brother died and Louis himself was wounded in the infantry; Bourgeois carried potent memories of visiting her father in hospital as a four-year-old in 1916 with

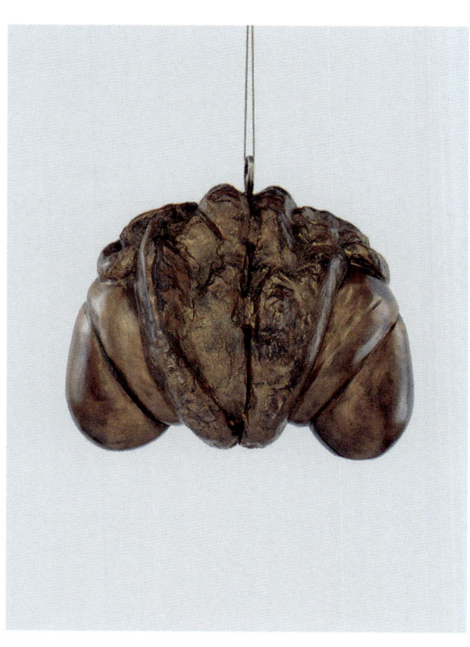

Janus fleuri 1968

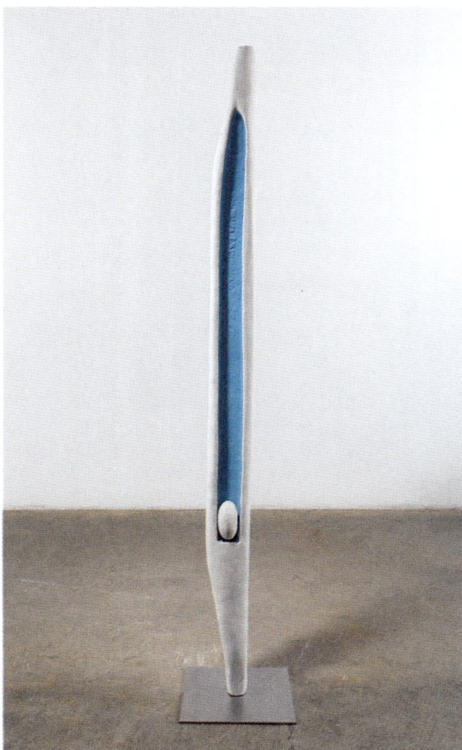

Untitled 1947–49

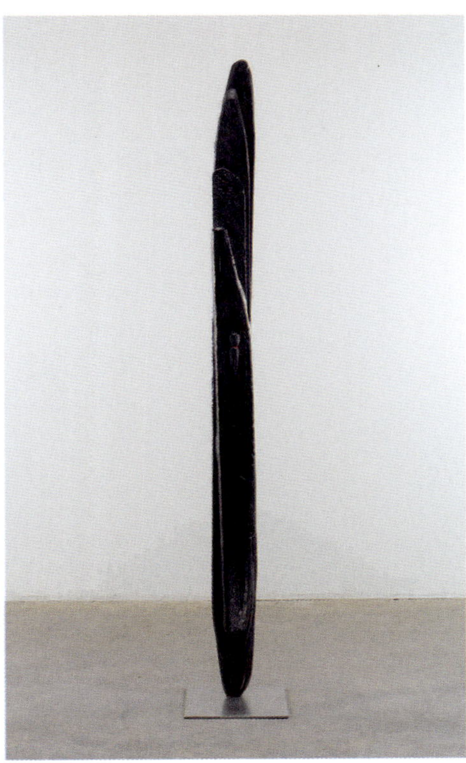

Dagger Child 1947–49

her distraught mother. The favourite child, and an honorary 'boy' among her siblings (an older sister and younger brother), Bourgeois longed to please but also registered acutely the confounding irrationality and injustice of the adult world: her father's infidelities and teasing; her mother's stoic tolerance and maddening need. When Joséphine became ill with what was probably Spanish influenza, Bourgeois assumed increasing responsibility for her care through the 1920s and early 1930s – the daughter nursing the person who had nursed her. Her mother's death in 1932, when Bourgeois was twenty, triggered a suicide attempt (she tried to drown herself in the Bièvre river) and lingering depression that ultimately precipitated a defining life decision – to end her education in mathematics at the Sorbonne and take up artistic studies. No longer consoled by the certainties of solid geometry and differential calculus, Bourgeois sought another way of coming to grips with her world. The decade's end brought another fateful decision: to move to New York with art historian Robert Goldwater. Three weeks after meeting in Paris, they were married; one month later, she arrived in New York.

This is the artist we meet at the start of this exhibition in the first room of 'Day', in a small painting that is also the earliest work on show. *Self-portrait* c1939 (p 79) is a modest study that makes a viewer feel not just seen but *considered*. From a handsome face that is barely brushed in, the blue eyes meet us sidelong but fixedly, inaugurating a central theme for Bourgeois: the charged relationship between one and others. The painting tallies emotionally with Bourgeois's description of herself as 'the runaway girl', working in 'exile and alienation' far away from a family she feared she had abandoned.[7] In her late twenties here, Bourgeois was about to enter a decade defined by war in the world at large and by her experience of motherhood in a new country (she arranged to adopt her oldest son Michel in 1939, and gave birth to Jean-Louis and Alain in 1940 and 1941 respectively). She bodies forth the complexity of her feelings during this period in the haunting family of sculptures called the Personages (left and pp 83, 89–92, 94–95).

Abstract in their carving yet sized to evoke her family, cousins and friends, the Personages were first shown in Peridot Gallery, New York, in 1949 and again in 1950 as a gathering that viewers could move through – a formally radical presentation with a profound psychological payoff.[8] The balance of oneness and otherness, togetherness and loneliness, shifted constantly in relation to viewers' movements. Encountered together in the first major room of this exhibition, the Personages still induce a kind of nervous quiet. Standing on their narrow points, they appear permanently apprehensive about toppling. Their tiny apertures and openings – like windows in fairytale towers – suggest that these bodies are also dwellings which shelter watchful inner selves. Some of the Personages hold precious egg-like cargo

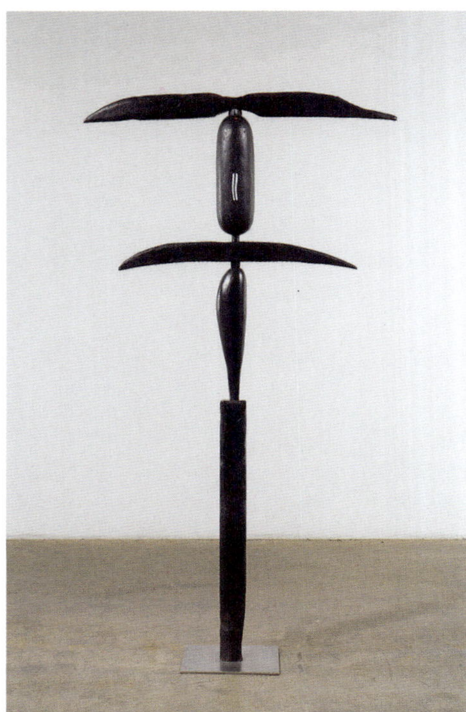

The Winged Figure **1948**

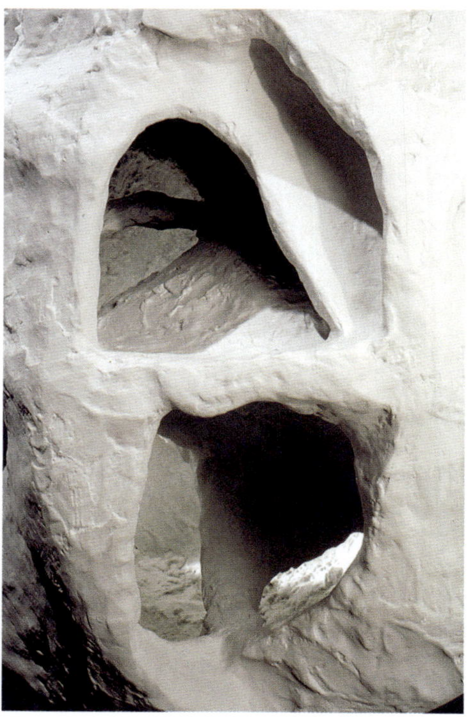

Fée couturière **1963, cast 2010 (detail)**

(*Untitled* 1947–49, p 15) or bear maternal burdens (*Woman with Packages* 1949, p 92). Some watch you solemnly (*Observer* 1947–49, pp 91, 266) while others appear to have sharpened defensively on hearing you approach (*Dagger Child* 1947–49, p 15; *Knife Couple* 1949, p 89; *Needle Woman* 1947–49, p 90). *Portrait of C.Y.* 1947–49 (p 94) has been spiked with nails, like a slender Saint Sebastian. Several of these works are painted black, which Bourgeois said reflected 'the deep mourning of the war'.[9] She also referenced 'the tension of their relations', summing up much to come.[10]

Guilt and homesickness plagued Bourgeois at this time, along with the responsibilities of motherhood and the vicissitudes of marriage. There was also the loss of her father, who had been a figure of reverence yet anger and anxious fixation in Bourgeois's emotional life – at once charming, selfish, seductive and domineering. When Louis died suddenly in Paris in 1951, after a decade in which they corresponded regularly but saw each other infrequently (in part due to the Nazi occupation of France), Bourgeois was spun into an incapacitating depression. She clawed her way back to a provisional equilibrium, not through art (she stopped making sculpture for a decade) but through psychoanalytic analysis and writing. Her diaries and loose notes from this time are frighteningly honest dredgings of her unconscious mind, often written in the middle of the night or when she woke in the morning, and sometimes rising to a poetic pitch that parallels the Personages at their most ominous: 'she talks with a hatchet – / when he talks it smells of semen – / when she talks or cleans it is a killing process –'.[11] Fittingly, the works she made as she emerged from these ten years of self-scrutiny (pp 98–112) have a birthed, almost coughed-up, appearance: lumpy, coiled, abject, fleshy and temptingly tactile. Lairs become a favourite form: places someone, or something, can take refuge in or attack from (*Lair* 1962, p 98). So do labyrinths: spiralling structures with the potential to lure or ensnare us (*Labyrinthine Tower* 1962, p 99). A heavy sensuality pervades the works, sometimes grisly and sometimes drowsy. *Le regard* 1963 (p 103) is an eye-like orifice made from latex and cloth, with a dank, almost clammy interior. As Joan Acocella remarked of this object, 'We feel we shouldn't be looking.'[12] *Le Trani Episode* 1971 (p 103), meanwhile, is a tactile fantasy of coupling – one breast-like yet penile form draped sleepily over another; maleness and femaleness trading properties. Though such works do not represent figures traditionally, they are of and from the body, expressing a sense of being, sheltering, fearing, desiring and surviving 'from the inside out' (the phrase is the title of Lucy Lippard's important article on Bourgeois from 1975).[13] Marble, which Bourgeois began working with in Italy in the late 1960s, and which is so often used to heroically elevate bodies, expresses anti-classical vulnerability. *Clamart* 1968 (pp 106–07) is a shrouded huddle of white growths whose ceremonial quality is partly explained

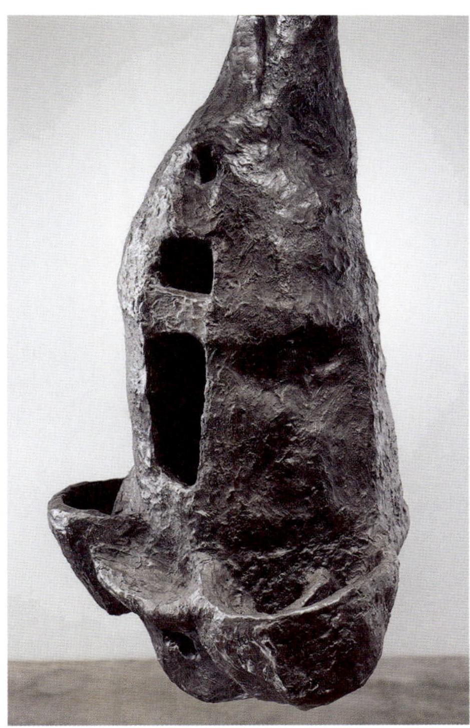

The Quartered One 1964–65 (detail)

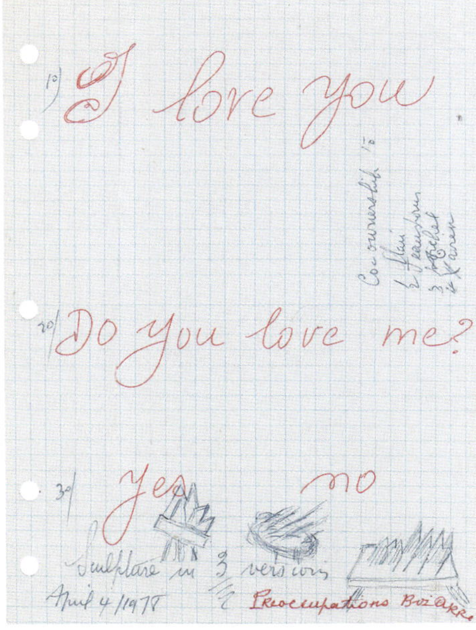

I Love You 1987

by its title, which refers to the town where the family tomb is located and where her parents and grandparents were buried. And while some works hunker, others hang – a physical state Bourgeois associated with ambivalence. *Fée couturière* 1963 (opposite and p 109) is a suspended white labyrinth with irregular holes and internal layers that refer to the nests of the *fauvette couturière*, or tailorbird, which are built from scavenged household and organic materials (and stitched together using spider webs).[14] *The Quartered One* 1964–65 (left and p 226) is a dark hanging carcass with pits and grottoes that suggest defensive habitation. The two works encompass 'an ambivalence of feelings that goes from pleasure to fear'.[15]

Bourgeois called sculpting a fight to the finish; she loved the way the material resisted.[16] A combative spirit is also present in her work more broadly throughout the 1970s. The Museum of Modern Art survey that would vault her to prominence in 1982–83 was still far off, even though feminist artists and curators had, in a co-signed letter from 1973, implored the museum to give Bourgeois an exhibition.[17] A sense of sharply focused frustration comes through in small works from the early 1970s that charge images of femininity with aggression: a startlingly fragile mother and child pierced with rusty pins (*Mother and Child* 1970, p 160); and a pudendum-shaped wooden form likewise pierced (*Femme pieu* c1970, p 115). Bourgeois's talent for combining violence and vulnerability is also evident in a black-and-white video from 1975, in which Bourgeois – who had lost her husband Robert Goldwater two years earlier – is seen in her home cradling the marble sculpture called *Femme couteau* 1969–70.[18] Sharp-tipped but curvaceous, the sculpture in her arms looks at once like a sword and a vulnerable child. This aesthetic of shapely threat intensifies through the 1980s.

Sensuality is spiked in these works (pp 114–27). Breasts hold blades – be careful what you're attracted to. As well as echoing the ambivalent violence in the work of modern women poets (consider Sylvia Plath's poem 'Totem': 'There is no mercy in the glitter of cleavers'), such sculptures resonated with the works of younger feminist artists using their own bodies provocatively and politically (the young performance artists Ana Mendieta and Hannah Wilke were among the attendees at a 1979 dinner party in Bourgeois's honour).[19]

Shredder 1983 (pp 50, 120–21), a vast wooden reel poised to crush a female mannequin, is exemplary in its directness and refusal to console. At a stretch, it could be read as an attack on the tired stereotype of femininity embodied in the mannequin, or possibly as an image of female endurance in the face of patriarchal violence (Bourgeois once observed that 'a woman has no place as an artist until she proves over and over that she won't be eliminated').[20] But it is just as plausible to see in the work an expression of personal aggression and murderous rivalry. At the very least, we must recognise a dark elation in the work – Bourgeois unleashing trouble without reassurance. It falls to us, in the path of this punk anti-monument, to make what sense we can of its unabashed antagonism. Also handed to us, in a series of mischievous works in red ink on paper from 1987, is the obligation to declare our affections (p 17). 'I love you do you love me?' these works ask passive-aggressively (one of them adds, for good measure, 'put a circle around your answer', p 116, while another is inscribed with the image of a knife and the words 'le suicide threat', p 118). In her marble sculptures of the time, Bourgeois relished the 'extremes of tenderness and aggression' she could achieve through polishing and hacking.[21]

Colour plays an essential part in Bourgeois's world of tensions and oppositions. Across the colour wheel from her violent reds, Bourgeois cultivated a world of blue – a distanced and desireless place of 'peace, meditation and escape' (pp 128–37).[22] The wild emotional weather in Bourgeois's work almost always occurs indoors. She regarded clouds and skies, by contrast, like the solid geometry she once studied, as something 'very positive, very calming, and very verifiable'.[23] *My Blue Sky* 1989–2003 (p 80), which we encounter in the introductory room of 'Day', offers a glimpse of calm after emotional storms, though the promise is qualified by the remoteness of the sky, which we see through a broken window. *Clouds and Caverns* 1982–89 (opposite and pp 128–29), an anchoring work in 'Day', is her grandest articulation of this blue world. Here, the menacing geometry of *Shredder* yields to consolingly regular curves. Soft, scrubbily brushed 'clouds' of blue float down in front of 'caverns' of tin. It's like a stage set for an actor-less play in which conflict never emerges. Figures embrace in the forest of steel rods that constitutes *The Couple* 2002 (pp 132–33), and their embrace is sheltered and made special by the blue glass beads that are threaded on the rods – an embellishment that calls to mind the story of Bourgeois's father saving a pebble for every 'beautiful moment' he experienced.[24] *Topiary IV* 1999 (p 110) is a small sculpture of a woman who has become an aged tree, scarred by experience (one of her legs has been amputated) but with topaz flowers blooming on her branches in defiance of mortality. The textile suite *The Waiting Hours* 2007 (pp 134–35), made from Bourgeois's old scarves and blouses, is a particularly poignant addition to this group of blue and solacing works, for its twelve sections describe a fading from day into night (and death) that is accepting rather than melancholy. The horizon rises, falls and tips as if seen from a moving vessel. Night claims more of the daytime sky as the journey progresses. But those skies express, even as they darken, the consolations of geometry and restoration. The eight triangular sections that form each sky create a radial, web-like structure, recalling the reparative work of the spider-mother that becomes such a presence in her late work. There is even, in the last two sections of the suite, a hint of the spider herself in the darkness, her body and legs suggested by the white moon and the eight seams radiating from it.

The mood of serenity and forgiveness in these works threads through the central section of 'Day', which brings together textile-based works from the last two decades of Bourgeois's life. Having identified primarily with her father for the first five decades of her career, from 1990 Bourgeois, as Philip Larratt-Smith has observed, transferred her imaginative allegiance to her mother.[25] In a wonderful daytime memory, she recalled Joséphine's happiness as she embroidered or mended in the sun.[26] As Bourgeois herself attained an age her mother never reached, she felt that impulse towards reparation ever more deeply (pp 155–69). *Ode à la Bièvre* 2007 (pp 164–67) is a twenty-five-page fabric book in which Bourgeois the 'shredder' becomes a repairer and rememberer – piecing together the garments of a lifetime in homage to the river of her childhood where fabrics were washed and dyed. *Spider* 1997 (pp 36, 161–63), with its sac of three glass eggs wrapped in hosiery, is a mighty homage to maternal protection and power. The creature presides over a cell of memory that is webbed in steel mesh, furnished with a tattered throne, and partly shrouded in tapestry fragments. In the early 2000s Bourgeois created soft fabric stacks that recall her mother's stacked tapestry samples, friendly 'endless columns' that celebrate domestic ordering and offer gentle stays against chaos.[27] And her attraction to cadence and regularity is evident also at this time in her return to making illustrated books, a form she first explored in the parable-like pairings of text and image in *He Disappeared into Complete Silence* 1947 (pp 84–88). In contrast to night, when we get lost in our own thoughts, day is when we talk with others, and the illustrated book *Sublimation* 2002 (pp 176–83) is a grand example of Bourgeois as daytime narrator. Across fifteen spreads that incorporate mesmerising drawings, she tells a tale of a resourceful child transforming hurt into symbolic action. As his parents argue savagely in a public setting, the boy retrieves a broom from a closet and starts intently sweeping. We realise, as we read, that Bourgeois is offering an allegory of her own late practice. The boy is using a sculpture-like object to calm himself and reroute destructive energy into something reparative.

It is a fine reminder of the role of bodies as carriers of emotion in her last two decades. Love and fear, trust and chaos, protection and abandonment – she pursued these polarities through sculpted figures in many mediums. And as we see in one of the later rooms in 'Day', she returned with poignant obsessiveness to images of hands and embraces (pp 139–53). Hands come together in a moment of tabletop reassurance in *Untitled (no. 7)* 1993 (p 140), or they sit apart anxiously in the scene of instruction and expectation that is *Cell (Glass Spheres and Hands)* 1990–93 (pp 141–43). Two suspended figures try to maintain their embrace as a coiling form binds and

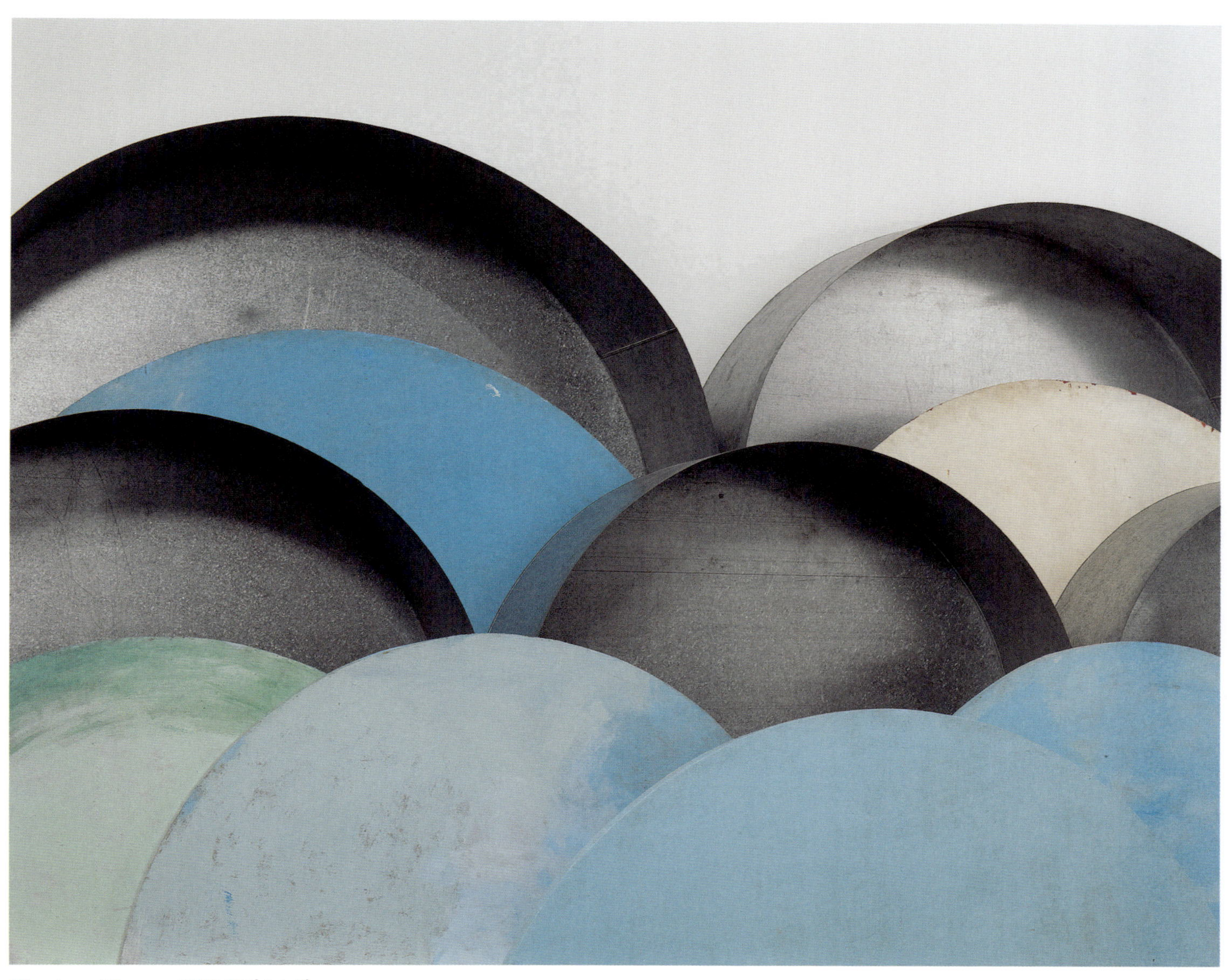

Clouds and Caverns 1982–89 (detail)

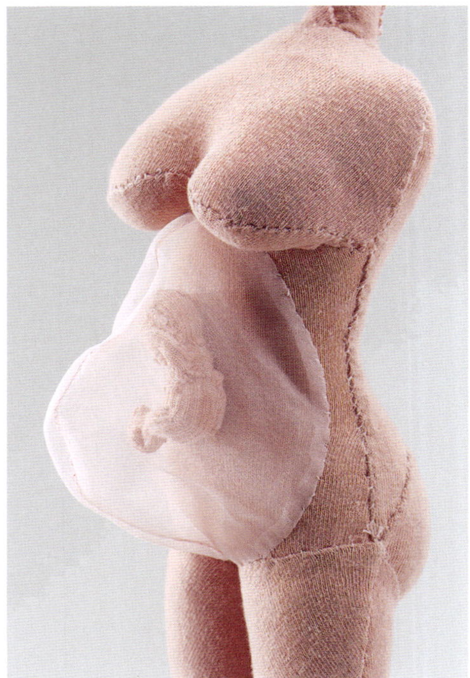

Umbilical Cord 2003 (detail)

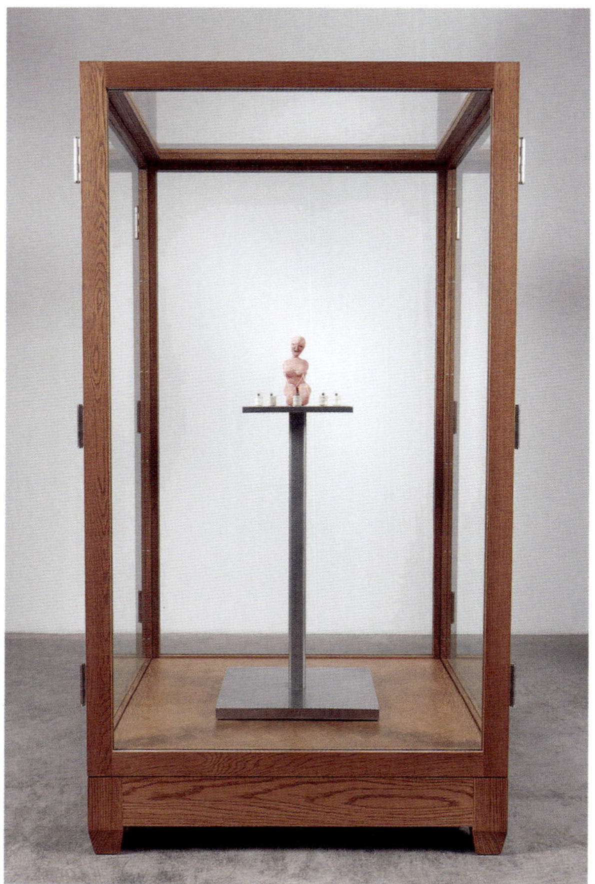

The Good Mother 2003

blinds them (*The Couple* 2003, p 145). And in a small textile, she commemorates the metaphorical holding that takes place when one person looks intensely at another: 'I held his eyes within my gaze' (p 144). Though Bourgeois spoke much more openly about her childhood than her emotional life and relationships in old age, she acknowledged the loneliness of growing old without her husband and the stabilising force that was her studio routine.[28] The most tender of her late works acknowledge the presence in her daily world of her longtime assistant and 'éminence grise' Jerry Gorovoy, whose arms meet the artist's in *Untitled (no. 7)* and, almost forty times over, in the suite *10 AM Is When You Come to Me* 2007 (that being the time Gorovoy arrived each morning and set the day's activities in motion; see pp 148–53).

The final room of 'Day' contains sculptural bodies with a special place in Bourgeois's universe of polarities – works that generate particularly personal and protective responses among viewers. Largely from the 2000s, these are works that deal with motherhood and parenting: bodies inside bodies (*Umbilical Cord* 2003, left and p 189), bodies emerging from bodies (*The Arrival* 2007, p 190), bodies separate yet still connected (*The Found Child* 2001, pp 192–93). Often created at the size of dolls, which are the sculptures we start out with, they invite us to lean close and 'feel along' (as Leo Steinberg puts it) with their physical and psychological situations. The knit fabric often makes the figures look swaddled in their own skins. And tiny grace notes of texture and gesture communicate their predicaments. Looking at *Umbilical Cord* with a friend, I mentioned the gentleness of the detail of the gauze stomach containing the baby. 'But she has no arms,' she objected. 'It's like she's been taken over and can't alter it; I remember that feeling.' In *The Found Child*, mother and baby appear separate but each is the other, as we realise when we see how an apron of fabric connects the two bodies. The novelist Rachel Cusk might be describing this work in her memoir of motherhood, *A life's work*, when she recounts, with loving anxiety, the experience of first being handed her newborn baby to feed:

> In this moment I realise that a person exists who is me, but who is not confined to my body. She appears to be some sort of colony. What she needs and wants will vie with, and often take priority over, what I need and want for the foreseeable future.[29]

Cusk also remarks that the maternal experience should move even those who haven't been through it, because we recognise in it the primal version of *all* experiences of separation from others. Looking at these sculptures, vicariously holding them in our minds, is a way towards that recognition.

Let's end, then, with *The Good Mother* 2003 (left and p 202–03), a small monument to maternal ambivalence. This figure's talent for care is evident from the constancy with which she feeds out her threads of milk. But she's also tied eternally to this place by her life-giving powers. It is a remarkable image of the demands of motherhood but also of the bind of being an artist, tempted by the dream of completion yet constantly tethered to the work you will be making next.

3 (NIGHT)

Bourgeois wrote and talked about her own works with devilish charm and vividness. There's an irresistibly quotable comment for almost every moment in her career. But as we exit 'Day' and prepare to enter 'Night', her more private thoughts feel suggestive, particularly the passages in her psychoanalytic writings that conjure scenes of darkness and abyssal depths.

The sound of a pebble falling into the black
and distant water of a well.
the unconscious memories that are reborn (1959)

... What can one do before a
void so deep and so black, one lets oneself fall in it
one lets oneself fall ... (1961)

Chaos the night the dark as large
as the whole room as long as a whole night ... (1963)[30]

Hold those words in mind and follow me down the corkscrew stairs into the exhibition's underside in the Tank. The voice you hear singing as you descend is Bourgeois in old age, recalling the lullabies of her childhood. The words scrolling up the Tank's concrete walls come from Bourgeois's psychoanalytic writings, selected by the American word artist Jenny Holzer (b1950) and projected in light like poems from the depths (pp 214, 228, 258). Stepping from the stairs into the vastness of the Tank, you enter a landscape of the unconscious – an open space where many different moments from Bourgeois's career coexist with no regard for chronological ordering (pp 210–63). Sculptures hang from the high concrete ceiling. An egg-like object glows on the floor. A macabre family dinner glows red in the distance, while a mechanical 'twosome' fucks itself in the corner. Hundreds of glass vessels stand in fragile defiance. A fabric woman carries and comforts her partner in mid-air (left). Paintings soaked in red gouache evoke the enormity of a child's need and a mother's giving. Creation, destruction, rapture and remembrance all cohabit without denying each other. The corridors of columns run in every direction. The web extends from wherever you are.

There are echoes in this reverberant space of places in Bourgeois's life. Chief among these are the studio spaces she kept in her home in Chelsea and in industrial Brooklyn. In the 1960s and 1970s, her primary workspace was located at the garden level of her Chelsea townhouse, which could be accessed from

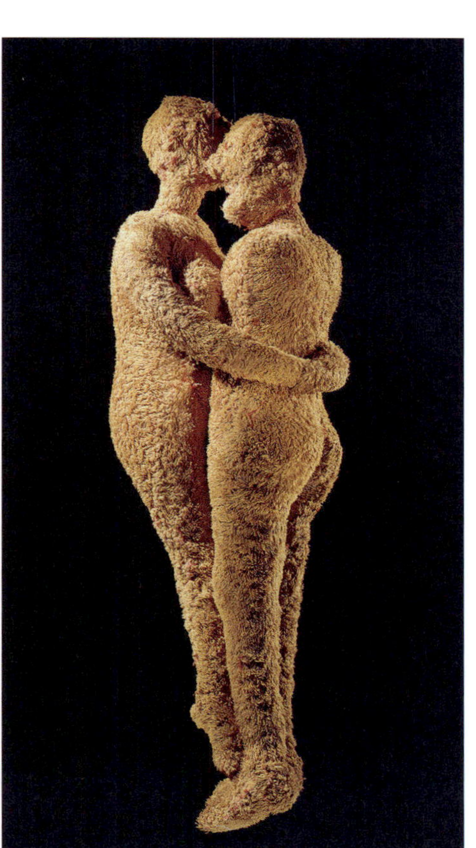

Couple 2001

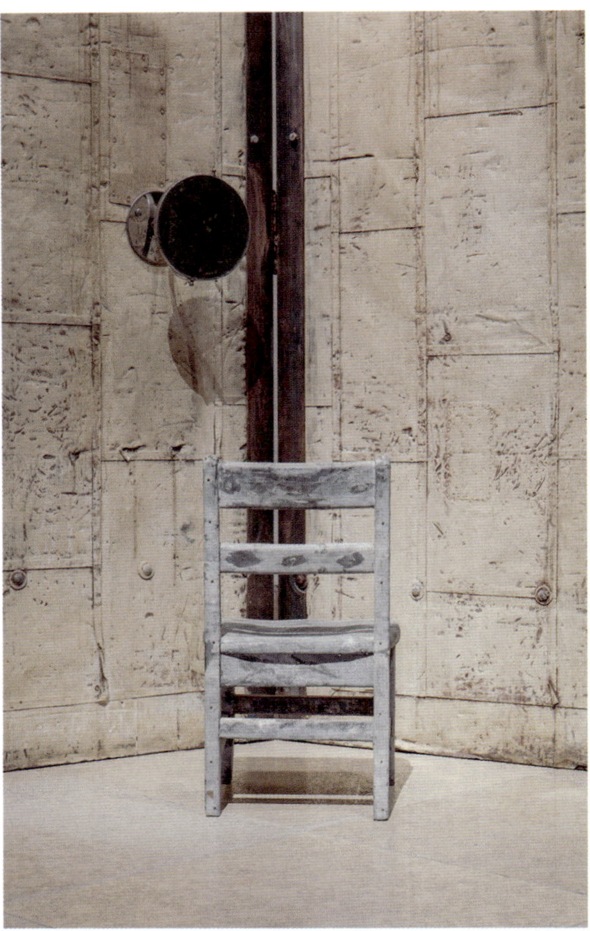

Culprit Number Two 1998 (detail)

the parlour floor by a spiral staircase.[31] Here she carved her hanging plasters and cast her latex works of the 1960s. In 1974, in the cellar or sub-basement of the house, she made *The Destruction of the Father* (pp 222–25), and, throughout the years, kept a cluttered depot of past sculptures that she described as a compensation for other abandonments: 'I never left them, the way I left my family.'[32] The much larger space in Brooklyn, acquired in 1980, was a former garment factory rich in remnants and traces of industrial labour, where Bourgeois made (and unmade, and remade) her sculptures amid the offcuts and evidence of her own increasingly ambitious practice. This was the space to which she began bringing industrial cast-offs for sculptural reuse: 'If I were more clever, I would save souls, but I save other things.'[33] And it was also, like the making space at the ground level of her home, a space of deep and silent contentment – a realm preceding the attentions of museum and market that she termed 'the space of the spell'.[34] Bourgeois was, as Gorovoy attests, never happier or less anxious than when working. Work was not a distraction from the unconscious and its insights but the royal road towards it.

As well as recalling the practical spaces where Bourgeois made and stored art, the Tank echoes emotionally charged spaces from earlier in her personal history. There was, for instance, the bare-floored and high-beamed attic where her father hung yet-to-be-upholstered chairs – a 'very pure' space that impressed the young Bourgeois and became 'the origin of a lot of hanging pieces'.[35] Or there are the caves at Lascaux, which Bourgeois visited in 1953 and cited as an inspiration for her sculptural lairs.[36] Then there are the smaller dark spaces that loom large in her psychological history, such as the closet she recalled her mother asking her to wait in during their visit to her father in the war hospital – perhaps so that the separated parents could achieve intimacy, or perhaps to save her from seeing injuries.[37] The contemporary portal for these unbidden memories in the Tank is the sculpture *The Hidden Past* 2004 (pp 32, 213), which consists of a pink textile head hung upside down in its own narrow wooden closet (in fact a salvaged Parisian elevator cabin). Resembling an insect's nest hanging from an eave or a side of meat hooked in a butchery window, the head has a strange white valve near its temple – perhaps to listen to, or whisper into. The psychoanalyst Adam Phillips once urged readers, instead of struggling to understand difficult modern poetry, to try *listening in* on it. The same advice could be applied to *The Hidden Past* and the other memory sculptures in the Tank.[38] Notable among these is the installation *Culprit Number Two* 1998 (left and p 239), an enclosure formed of vast fire doors within which sits a child's chair, placed face-in as if for punishment, beneath a suspended sphere of red glass. The work pertains to several early memories, among them an incident in which Bourgeois exposed her father as the culprit in a minor accident.[39] But the title implies a

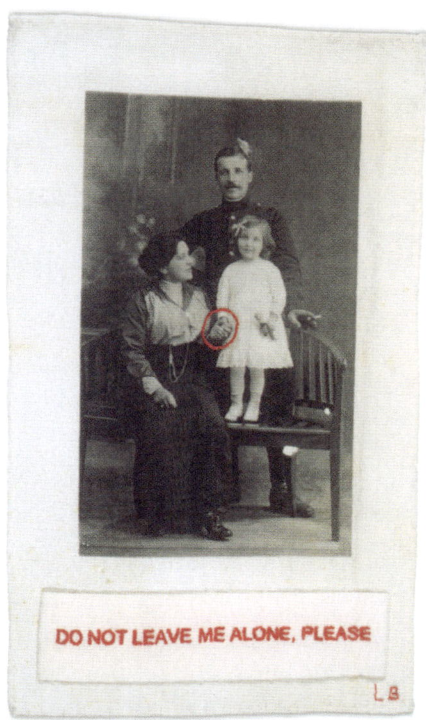

The Trauma of Abandonment 2001 (detail)

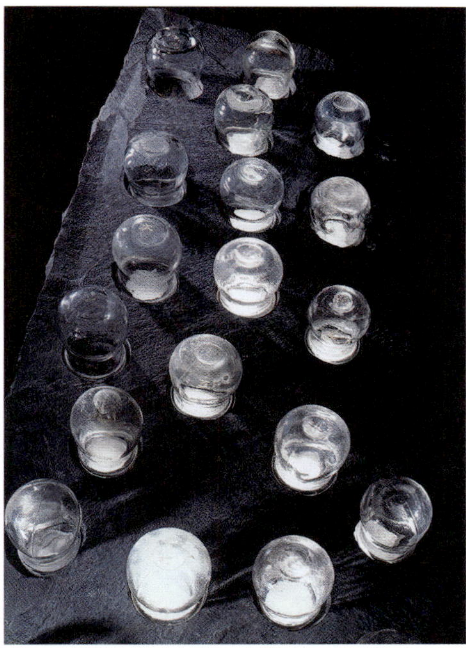

Ventouse 1990 (detail)

further layer of complicity and blame (was Louise herself the culprit in her father's shaming?), as does the child's chair with its adjacent 'rear view' mirror. Like the echoes that roll through the Tank, the questions prompted by the work ramify. Are the fire doors, salvaged from demolished New York buildings, keeping someone in or out? Who fired the arrows lodged in the walls? Where *Culprit Number Two* leads us interpretatively is as important as where it comes from. Lean closer; listen harder.

Among the spaces and sensations that 'come back' in the Tank, the most significant are of war and its damages. The Tank itself is a structure of war, built in haste in 1942 to fuel Allied ships in the Pacific. And its presence now, in the lowest reaches of a beautiful new museum building, summons another vivid memory related by Bourgeois – of the staff lunchrooms under the Musée du Louvre in the 1930s. It was here, while working as a docent giving museum tours, that Bourgeois encountered 'a hell of people with amputated limbs, people who had been wounded in the war' – there being a rule at the time that official positions should go to those who had suffered injuries. 'I walk in and look,' she recalled, 'and a leg is cut off or an arm is gone and they are all in that basement eating their lunch.'[40] It would be difficult to conjure a more vivid image of the repressed truth of the human toll of war, unseen beneath the objects on view in the treasure-house above. The scene is proof of Walter Benjamin's famous 1940 statement that 'There is no document of civilisation which is not at the same time a document of barbarism.'

The one-legged fabric figure *Untitled* 1999 (p 249) seems to look up at us from such a netherworld, a modern Man of Sorrows stitched in the colour that Bourgeois identified as 'the black of the war'.[41] Recall again the four-year-old Bourgeois trying to understand her uncle's death and her father's wounding, and how the latter event unlatched seemingly uncontrollable fear and need in her mother. In the red-stitched fabric book *The Trauma of Abandonment* 2001 (above left), she writes, 'The trauma of abandonment began when my father enlisted in World War I.' And recall that Bourgeois herself nursed her mother in the late 1920s and early 1930s, as Joséphine approached her death from lung disease. This caring is re-enacted with heartbreaking formality in *Ventouse* 1990 (left and pp 218–19), which incorporates glass cupping jars like those Bourgeois used therapeutically on her mother, but applied to a slab of black stone that could be a solemn altar or, as Larratt-Smith suggests, a coffin.[42] One could object, of course, that Bourgeois seldom referred directly to war in her art – far less often than recognised 'artists of war' such as Max Beckmann and Pablo Picasso. But gender played its part in this; direct artistic commentary on war was usually men's business. Bourgeois's response to the wars that men make is all the more piercing for being unofficial and filtered through the personal. She is an artist of internalised conflict. She examined the war within.

Again, it must be stressed: Bourgeois does not reassure or preach. She's more interested in channelling her conflicts, dragging them into form, than teaching or convincing anyone. Being a 'truth seeker', as she sought to be, meant not denying what she called 'the beast in me'.[43] In an art world where male aggression was regularly valorised (whether in the painterly 'attack' of abstract expressionism or the 'muscularity' of minimalist sculpture), Bourgeois discovered how to harness female anger as a creative power and critical metaphor. The artist who witnessed human damage beneath the Louvre performed her own precise violence on classical traditions, including in *Nature Study* 1984–94 (p 113), a work in pink marble that symbolically beheads a sculpture of a hunting dog (the plaster original was discovered in a dumpster near her foundry), and which in turn recalls antique marble sphinxes in the collection of the Louvre.[44] From these works in marble and bronze, a shadow museum or sculpture court starts to form, populated by a hanging prosthetic leg made in memory of her sister (*Henriette* 1985, p 238), an arm that blindly implores (*Untitled (with Hand)* 1989, pp 210–11), and shape-shifting, zoomorphic creatures. Resembling a bronze Egyptian sarcophagus cat that has grown a fifth leg, the feline *Self-portrait* 2007 (pp 250–51) demonstrates Bourgeois's gift for sending jolts of strangeness through traditional forms. Like the dog in *Nature Study*, which Bourgeois also described as a self-portrait, it slyly propagates confusion about the gender of the self in question. This female cat, in common with the heavy-breasted marble dog in *Nature Study*, has male genitalia.[45]

This channelling of trouble attains full force in *The Destruction of the Father* 1974, which glows like a furnace in the shadows of the Tank. In 1973 Bourgeois suffered another grievous loss when Robert Goldwater died of a heart attack. *Destruction* emerged in the year of loneliness and creative rejuvenation that followed. Not a commentary on Goldwater but rather on the damaging complacency of patriarchs generally (Goldwater emerges from Bourgeois's recollections as a supremely calm and supportive husband), *Destruction* is a red-lit chamber within which something unnamed yet frightening is occurring. Polyp-like characters recalling those in *Clamart* have gathered in a shrouded interior, where body parts (cast from chicken legs and lamb shoulders) lie on a table that could also be a bed. In the characteristically vivid narrative that Bourgeois spun alongside this work, a mother and her children finally run out of patience with the father's dinnertime pontificating. 'Once too often, he has said his piece' – they tear him up and devour him.[46]

Here again are echoes of Plath and her poem 'Daddy', with its final image of the father stabbed and trampled.[47] And there are affinities with the sharp-edged domestic critiques of younger feminist artists such as Ana Mendieta and Martha Rosler.[48] But Bourgeois's *Destruction* is singular for the relish of its violence and also its odd equanimity. Even as we shudder, we can't help noticing the ceremonial tone of it all – how the lumps and polyps gather like attendants round a table very much like an altar. As Chris Kraus notes later in this book, cannibalism is also homage. Bourgeois's critique of authority is powerful precisely because she declares her own love of (her taste for, her desire to consume) the thing she knows she must obliterate. Standing in front of this work, which also looks like a mouth and a gut, we too feel we might be consumed. And lest mothers seem spared in Bourgeois's fascinated appraisal of parental responsibility and authority, *Destruction* has apt accompaniment in the Tank in the form of footage of a performance Bourgeois created, with Suzan Cooper in a starring role, to accompany another installation piece, *Confrontation* 1978, at Hamilton Gallery of Contemporary Art, New York (also discussed by Kraus, pp 42–53). As Cooper stalks the crowd in high heels and a latex sheath dress (pp 49, 221), she sings 'she abandoned me' and declaims 'that one was a mother' with an anguish that oscillates with elation. Like Cooper (who once dressed as Bourgeois's own mother at the costume party thrown in the artist's honour; see p 269), Bourgeois loved accessing the high emotional registers in which opposed feelings disclose their affinities.[49]

This seductive instability of meaning is present everywhere in the Tank. Nothing is only itself. A 'metamorphic energy' (Robert Storr's phrase) runs through everything.[50] Forms hang, turn, split and repeat (*Janus* 1968, p 245, *Hanging Janus with Jacket* 1968, p 215). The artist–caterpillar spins her silver cocoon (*Untitled* 2004, p 220). A phallus ripens or rots on its hook (*Fillette (Sweeter Version)* 1968–99, p 244). Legs lose their structure and stretch out queasily (*Legs* 1986, p 248). A spider seems to scutter up the wall (*Spider IV* 1996, pp 216–17, 273), while the self-portrait cat waits to lead us somewhere. *Sleep II* (pp 227, 267), a remarkable marble from 1967, enacts the change of state we all undergo nightly. Its plump head, so often called phallic, drops forward into slumber – but as happens in sleep, what seemed definite discovers itself as something different. For the phallic form could as plausibly be seen as clitoral or breast-like. And the hardness of marble yields, to use a description of Bourgeois by the late sculptor Phyllida Barlow, to 'an intoxication of dreamy rapture which creates a peaceful recognition of deep sex'. With the directness of one great woman sculptor addressing another, Barlow describes these qualities of metamorphosis and instability as 'the sneeze of Louise': 'the sexual charge in her sculpture, unpredictable in how, where and with what it will direct itself'.[51]

Barlow would surely have identified that charge in the two largest works in the Tank: the baroque monster that is *Crouching Spider* 2003 (pp 232–33) and the vast mechanical work *Twosome* 1991 (opposite and pp 256–57). The spider, a thrashing and thick-muscled form, stands tensed among the columns of

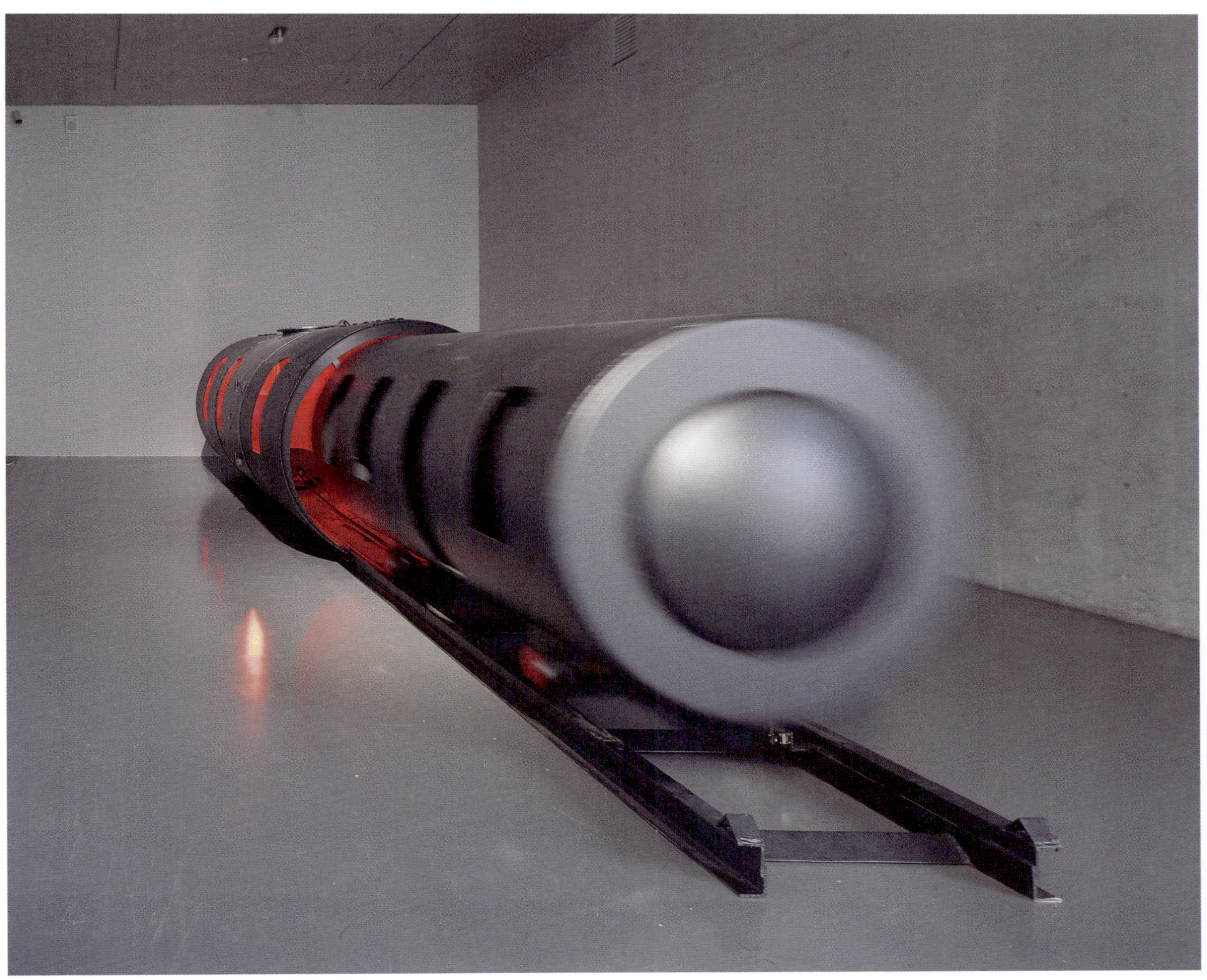

Twosome 1991

the Tank. The tips of its legs are sharp as bayonets; it's threatened and ready to stab. A mother and protector, it's been turned by our arrival into a 'stinger, a killer'. Fear and the consequent impulse to attack have made it into an awesome presence. It is, in this sense, a self-portrait by an artist who once wrote, 'When I do not "attack" I do not feel myself alive.'[52] And it's a thrilling projection of the predicament of monumental sculpture by an artist who was always skeptical of authority. Unlike most huge bronzes, which assume and want an audience, this one recoils from us. Art, Bourgeois reminds us, has no obligation to like us back. It may even want to menace us for interrupting its labours.

Meanwhile *Twosome* shunts back and forth through a corridor of columns. Made from disused fuel tanks, it is a fitting arrival in an underground gallery where oil was once stored. As a work that *works*, it is also a fitting image of the blind desires that drive human culture and conflict above ground. As the smaller tank grinds in and out of the larger one, and a red light whips round inside them, *Twosome* accounts for all the fundamentals: eating, excreting, having sex, giving birth, leaving home, coming back, being buried, re-emerging. Bourgeois, in an interview with Storr, elaborated further on this 'in and out': 'in and out of trouble, in and out of faith, in and out of time, in and out of synch, in and out of focus, in and out of bounds'. Despite its technical complexity, *Twosome* gave Bourgeois unusual satisfaction – the satisfaction she derived whenever she found inarguable form for 'unconscious motivations'.[53] Sex machine, birth machine, life and death machine: *Twosome* is the engine of her night-time imagination.

4 (TO INFINITY)

It's not that 'Night' is exclusively frightening, or that 'Day' is exclusively restorative. Solace and nurture have their place in the Tank, just as anxiety and rage have their place upstairs. It is rather that each space haunts the other without a determined conclusion. The feelings and experiences attached to each polarity are always moving back and forth.

On the page of her diary where Bourgeois first wrote 'Has the day invaded the night or has the night invaded the day?', she also sketched a form like a coiling snake alongside the words 'comes back' (left). This form does what the question does: it loops back around on itself. And the sculpture which takes that question as its title places *us* inside the loop (opposite and p 229). Standing in front of this giant mirror with its reversed strip of glowing blue lettering, we're loomed over and made small, like children in an adult dressing room. Bourgeois knew how to put her viewers on the spot existentially – to set the scene and then say, *your move*.

So follow the loop, take the stairs again, move between 'Night' and 'Day'. Notice how forms encountered in one space appear in the other and vice versa.

FEBRUARY 7 TUESDAY
1995 38th day – 327 days follow

Diary entry, 7 February 1995

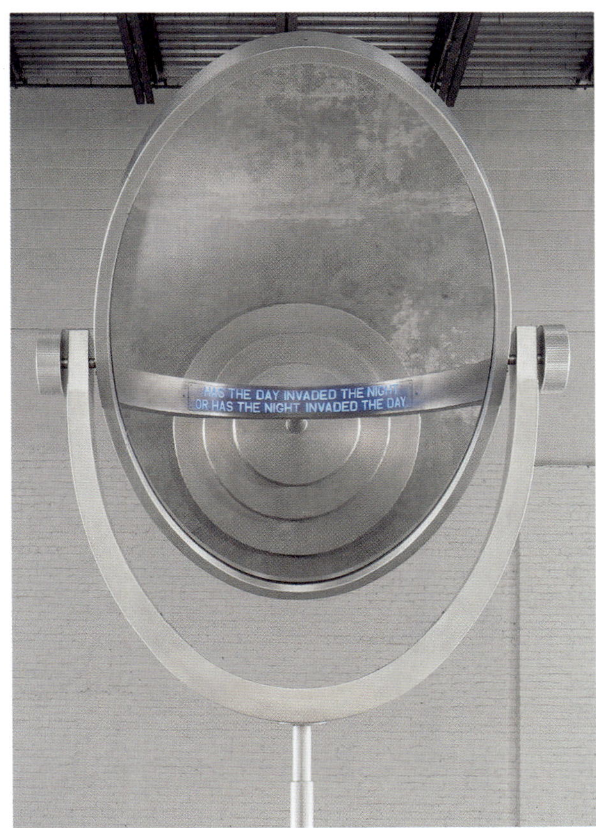

***Has the Day Invaded the Night or Has the Night Invaded the Day?* 2007 (detail)**

Le Trani Episode, fashioned in latex and plaster in 1971, is reborn in illuminated alabaster twenty years later. *Fée couturière* 1963, as mentioned earlier, finds its dark descendant in *The Quartered One* 1964–65. The four-faced knitted Janus head upstairs (*Untitled* 2009, p 185) is countered below by the supplicating red head of *Cell X (Portrait)* 2000 (pp 246, 259). The protective *Spider* 1997 has its night-time cognate in the muscular *Crouching Spider* 2003, which waits, a threatened and threatening presence, on the darkened outskirts of the Tank. The tiny locket mirror within the cell for *Spider* re-emerges as the vast standing mirror downstairs. These are not instances of the 'formal development' that survey exhibitions often plot. They are churnings, repetitions and returns that have a more driven character – as if the artist needed not to solve the problem but re-experience its contours (artists repeat themselves, Bourgeois once said, because they cannot find a cure).[54]

Part of the pleasure of spending time with Bourgeois's protean art is deciding which works *we* return to (art viewers too may be incurable: they keep coming back for more). For me, two works from above and below call out at the end of our walkthrough, and it is no coincidence that both works deal with matters of ending and continuing. The first, which forms a frieze around a room upstairs, is the suite of sixteen large etchings, embellished with pencil and paint, called *À l'infini* 2008–09 ('to infinity'; pp 28, 194–201). Here Bourgeois portrays herself as a child and an adult travelling unclothed through spaces both womb-like and cosmic. Forms resembling umbilical cords, veins, intestines and scars stream through the linked space of these painted prints, looping together the experiences of conception and death from opposite ends of a life. It's intimate and immediate; you feel the physical movements of the artist in her nineties as she embellishes the works on her parlour table. Words float through – '*un bébé*', '*amour*', '*rouge*' – and then unspool. The mood of welcomed dissolution and visceral acceptance makes *À l'infini* exceptional. At the end of a life of pursued resistance, Bourgeois finds a grammar for letting go.

The second work, which appears in the centre of the Tank downstairs, is the suspended polished bronze *Arch of Hysteria* 1993 (p 29, pp 242–43). This body descends out of darkness on its umbilical wire as if dropped from a height and stopped suddenly – the whole figure bending back in that instant to form an arch, a strange bracelet, of emotion. The absence of the head feels less like violence than an expression of the body's intelligence in extreme situations. Hysteria is when the body says what the person is not allowed or able to express. Is this body expressing agony as it holds this pose and almost touches its heels with its fingertips? Don't bodies sometimes spasm in this way when they're poisoned and the powerful back muscles contract? Is it rather a physical rapture, the ecstasy of release almost attained? Is there even something embryonic in this image?

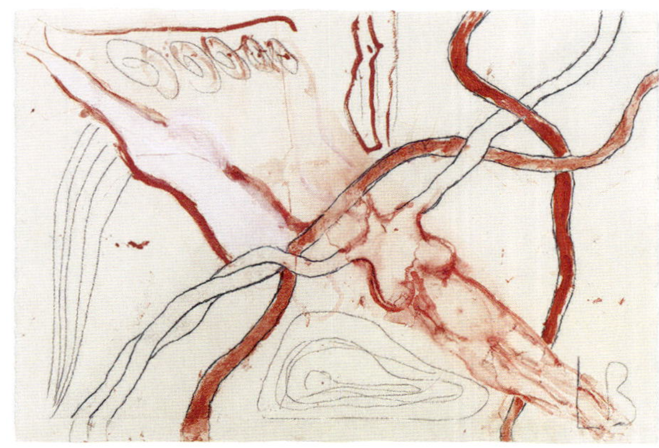

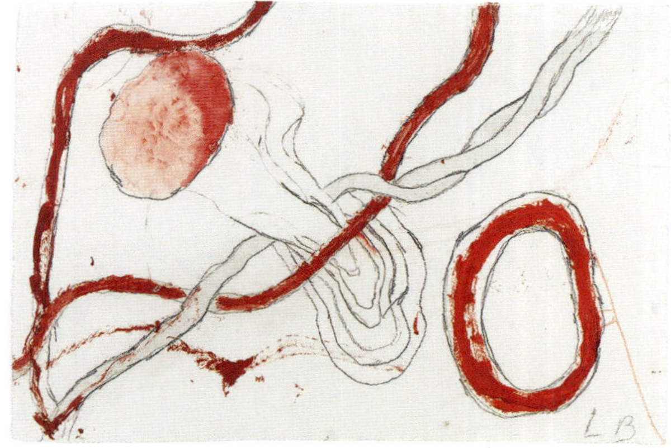

À l'infini 2008–09 (details)

The sculpture is a circle that turns on its thread, and these questions circulate with it. You might say the sculpture *is* the question. You feel it in your own spine and fingertips.

In their different ways, these two late works offer portraits of human lives in time. *À l'infini* threads creation and oblivion together across almost thirty metres. *Arch of Hysteria* fuses hurt and energy in one indelible object. Both bring into view a fundamental but so far unacknowledged opposition: the one that exists between mortal bodies and durable artistic form. Let us consider one of the writings that rises into and then passes from view on the walls of the Tank. In it, Bourgeois, aged around forty-five, writes movingly about the existential paradox of being a human with one body and limited time. 'My life is a succession of / quarters of an hour which are spent / in a succession of square meters', she begins, and goes on to say (in an image conflating footprints and souls) 'You only occupy two soles / of the earth except when you sleep / you occupy 6 feet.' We're defined by absence, she asserts, because we're missing from every other place and time in the universe. And this loneliness is made even stranger by the fact that we're never not with ourselves. 'I've schlepped Louise Bourgeois around with me / for more than 40 years,' she writes, concluding that 'every day brought / its wound and I carried my wounds cease / lessly.' It is a rousingly stoic conclusion, complete with a premonitory image of the artist as a 'hide perforated beyond hope of repair'. But what I'm drawn to is an earlier moment in this reverie, almost lost in the onrush of thoughts, where she writes, 'I would / rather say that we live more by the intensity of our / affects than by time or by the space / in time.'[55]

An intensity of affect that defies time and space – this is a fine definition of what ambitious art delivers. The artist transfers life force into a finite object which then projects it beyond the moment and place of its making.[56] As *À l'infini* and *Arch of Hysteria* prove, Bourgeois lived – and still lives – by that intensity.

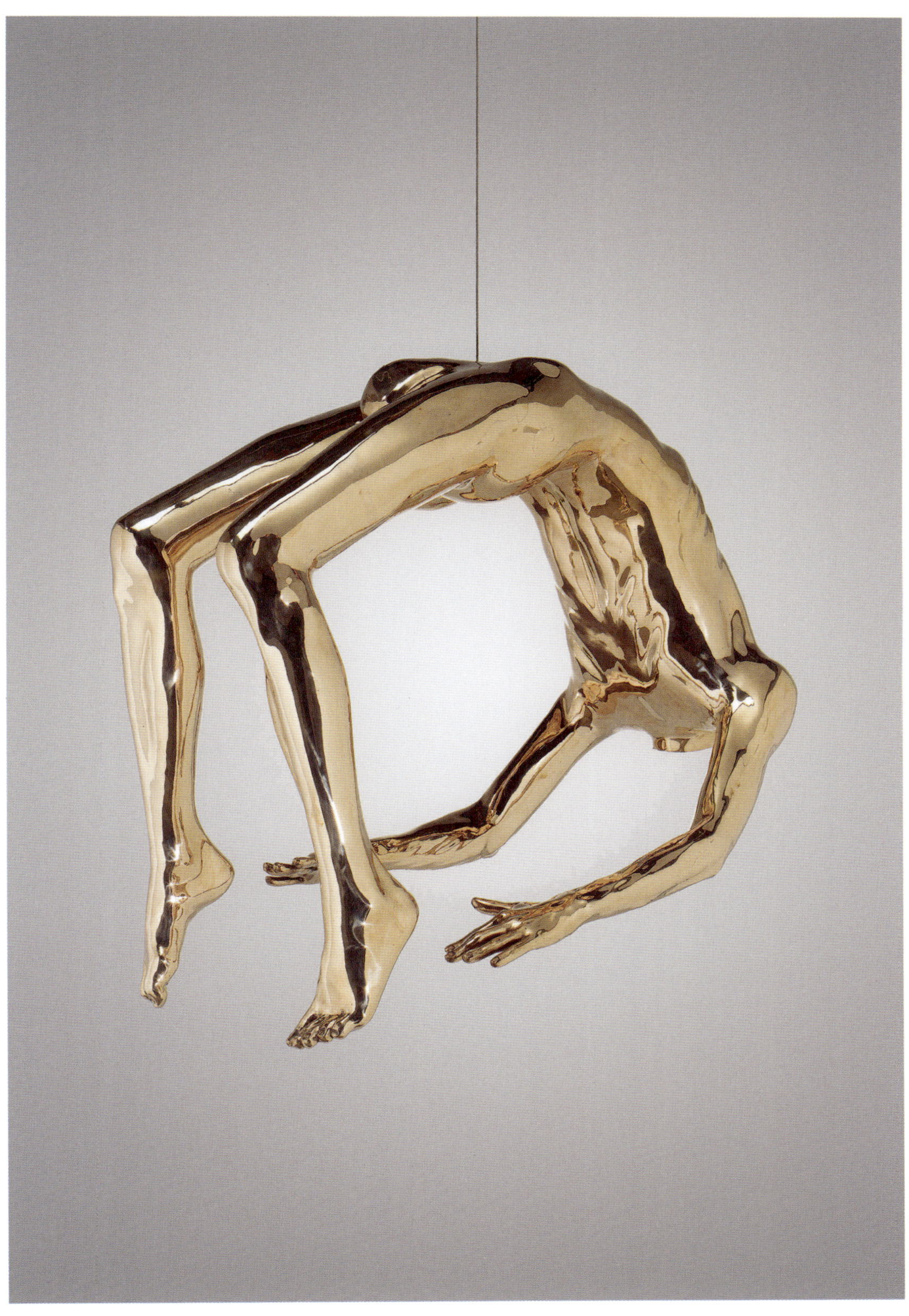

Arch of Hysteria 1993

‘It comes back again and again’ On Louise Bourgeois and psychoanalysis

Jamieson Webster

The verbal is too easy and makes me anxious. To talk does not constitute a catharsis. It's the actual doing. A work of art is successful for me when it removes anxiety. The price we have to pay ... The work is only an acting out, trying to get rid of things. The work of art is limited to an acting out, not an understanding. If it were understood, the need to do the work would not exist anymore ... Art is a guaranty of sanity, but not liberation. It comes back again and again.
– Louise Bourgeois, in conversation with Jerry Gorovoy, 1992[1]

Psychoanalysis has a lot to learn from Louise Bourgeois, who turns some well-worn Freudian ideas on their head. She reminds us of the importance of psychoanalysis as a way of working with patient's lives, as against the mere study and theorisation of the psyche – psychoanalysis as an act of doing, making, working and reworking that she often speaks of in relation to the making of art. Bourgeois views psychoanalysis, founded by Sigmund Freud as a treatment for neurosis in the late nineteenth century, with admiration but an important degree of scepticism too, calling it 'a jip', 'a duty', 'a joke', 'a love affair', 'a bad dream', 'a pain in the neck' and 'my field of study', among other things.[2] Many of her thoughts on psychoanalysis, detailed in diaries and hundreds of loose sheet writings, speak to her very long analysis with European émigré and Freudian psychoanalyst Dr Henry Lowenfeld (from 1952 until 1966 and then less intensely until his death in 1985), and we can see in her notes that she worked with psychoanalytic ideas all her life.

Being an artist who worked outside the field, Bourgeois was able to convey her experience in psychoanalysis and the impact it had on her – what it was in psychoanalysis that allowed her to work well as an artist. Her psychic suffering could bring her work as an artist to a halt. Her analysis could bring her back to the making of art. On her relationship to psychoanalysis, she said she was:

deeply involved in the subject, not through books but my own experience. NOT through jargon of writers or teachers, through my unfortunate own experience. It may be idiosyncratic – but it is not literary.[3]

This idiosyncrasy is the singularity of each of us. I don't think it is a stretch to say that psychoanalysis saved Bourgeois's life. After a suicide attempt, extreme anguish following the deaths of her mother and father, and difficulties with her varied roles as a mother, wife and artist, she was eventually able to work powerfully and relentlessly, which she did until her death at the age of 98. I consider her work a testimony to the importance of psychoanalytic treatment.

The testimony of patients is quite rare. Some famous testimonies stand out: the American poet Hilda Doolittle's *Tribute to Freud* about her analysis with Sigmund Freud in 1933–34; French writer Marie Bonaparte's childhood 'copybooks' with her and Freud's notes on them through the lens of her analysis with Freud; and Brazilian writer and psychoanalyst Betty Milan's account of her psychoanalysis with

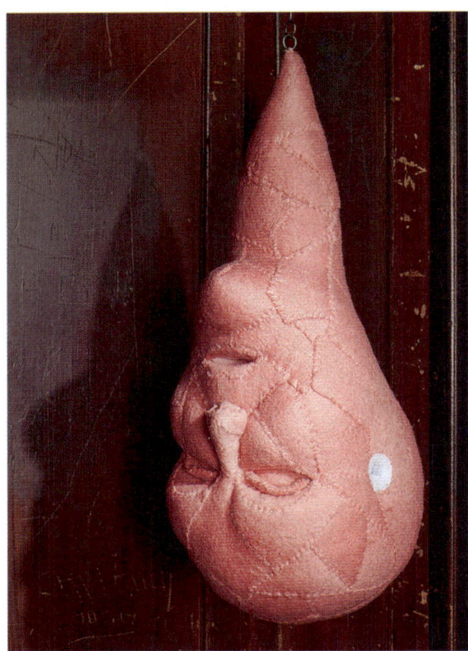

***The Hidden Past* 2004 (detail)**

Jacques Lacan, Freud's renegade French disciple, in the 1991 biographical novel *The Parrot and the Doctor*. Interestingly, all three of these testimonies involve art. Doolittle's poetry brackets her analysis, which took place after a period of severe writer's block, and after which she wrote vehemently until the end of her life. Bonaparte chose to work with Freud on her childhood copybooks, which are filled with drawings and stories she produced between the ages of seven and ten in the years between 1889 and 1892. And Milan's memoir is cast as a novel. Why do these testimonies take the form of art?

Bourgeois is instructive. 'I do, I undo, I redo' was as much a life mantra as it was the title of her monumental three-tower installation for the Tate's Turbine Hall in 2000. As she says to her assistant Jerry Gorovoy, she does not trust the verbal and its purported end goal of 'understanding'. Nor does she trust the ideal of liberty which would make it all go away. If that were so, Bourgeois says, the need to make art would also disappear. Rather, what interests Bourgeois is the 'actual doing', art as an 'acting out', a way of continuing to 'get rid of things', especially anxiety, which gives a momentary feeling of sanity.

This sanity is felt despite the insanity of the fact that 'it' – by which I think she means the elements of psychic life, one's history, one's pain – comes back again and again. There 'it' is, a fabric head hung like a garment or weighted bag in a wooden elevator cabin in *The Hidden Past* 2004 (left and p 213), a sculpture whose open front ensures the past is not so hidden. It could be a reworking, in physical form, of a passage from a 1995 writing by Bourgeois:

I opened the closet, upstairs, and the smell made me shake like a leaf
there's always a silver lining (the expected seamstress didn't show up)
The discovery of an unconscious collection: dozens
The total disappearance of the brassieres, not a single one. <u>*unconscious*</u>
The Repetition, ad infinitum *of the* <u>*non-accomplished*</u> *action.*
The perpetual Restart. The myth of Sisyphus
still an instant of happiness
the Devil *is my own intensity*[4]

She lives a palpable Freudian truth, her own myth of Sisyphus, since nothing in the unconscious can be destroyed. Freud's repetition compulsion, revisiting again and again that which troubles us to achieve mastery over it, is synonymous with what it means to live. The devil is her own intensity and Sisyphean will. Every day she opens the closet of the past and seeks to discover its elusive burdens – her rock – only to confront that weight again in her 'instant of happiness' when she opens the closet again the next day.

Bourgeois thus delivers important correctives – first, to the fantasy that analysis can rid us of parts of ourselves; and second, to the wish to interpret or understand it all away. She refutes the fantasy of self-reinvention in which the subject gets better by digesting what is restorative and permanently

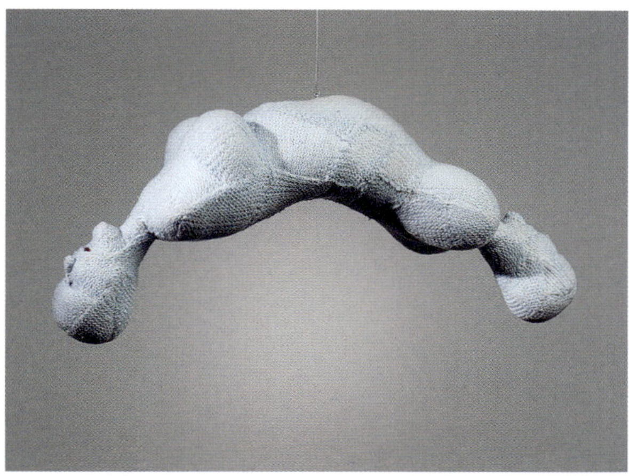

Arch of Hysteria 2004

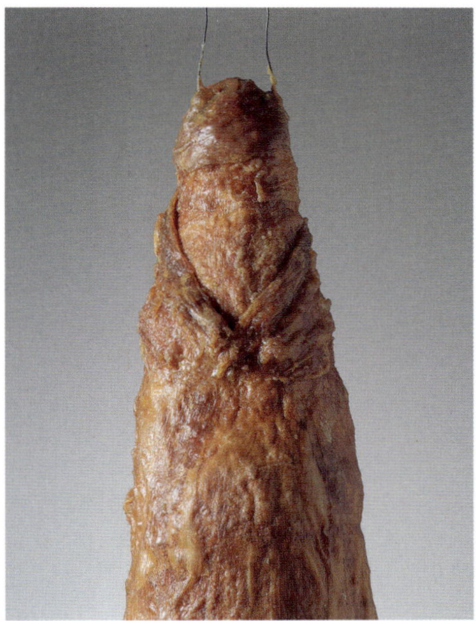

Fillette (Sweeter Version) 1968–99 (detail)

expelling what is difficult. Bourgeois offers another vision of what it means to be cured, which involves taking on all aspects of oneself and becoming even more who one is. The key point is this: you have to find the way to make something of what will never leave you, namely your history and the difficult, endlessly conflictual feelings engendered by it. She shows us a way of looking after one's conflicts and neurotic insolubilities as material – material which, when it is re-approached and reshaped (rather than repressed), provides a form of vitality, if not immortality: witness the tremendous energy held in her successive variations on the form of the hysterically arched body (*Arch of Hysteria* 1993, pp 242–43; *Arch of Hysteria* 2004, left and pp 254–55). Importantly, this capacity to act and rework and twist, and even to memorialise and embody, is a truth that psychoanalysis discovered from its work with hysterical women at its very origin.

•

Bourgeois's relationship with post-Freudian psychoanalysis is fascinating. Not surprisingly, she turns most often to her compatriots, the French psychoanalysts. She thought Jacques Lacan (1901–81) was a bit of a fraud, 'a fake, a joke': a macho intellectual and father figure who was not to be trusted – a certain kind of Frenchman she knew all too well.[5] At the same time, she noted how much she and Lacan had in common. They were both French Catholics born after the turn of the century, who drew so much from the Jewish psychoanalysts, whether Freud or Dr Lowenfeld, or any of the analysts (among them Anna Freud and Melanie Klein) she read so closely.[6] Both she and Lacan loved and married Jewish partners, felt saved by these marriages, and, as she put it, 'took something from them'.[7] And Lacan's final explorations of the spatial or 'topological' qualities of psychic life are, Bourgeois notes, where she begins.[8] For Bourgeois, the exploration of surfaces, cuts, voids, space, edges and boundaries, in works such as *Fée couturière* 1963, cast 2010 (pp 16, 109) and *Fillette (Sweeter Version)* 1968–99 (left and p 244), is connected to the experience of having a body, an experience she associates with being a woman (*Fillette*, though profoundly phallic at first glance, has a title which translates as 'little girl' and a cloaked appearance that complicates a reading of its gender). It amuses me that neither Bourgeois nor Lacan – in their psychoanalytic, political and aesthetic sensibilities – were attracted to an idea of liberation, finding in psychoanalysis a kind of stoicism regarding what is possible and the limits of human rationality. Both lived through two world wars.

Bourgeois wants, so she says, to 'dress' Lacan 'down', as she wanted to with all overbearing and complacent father figures, notably including the surrealists.[9] She wants to demystify Lacan and those like him whose work does not proceed from a place of personal urgency. As she investigates her own psychic life, both in psychoanalysis and in the studio, she refuses to allow it to be generalised or become abstract, unlike 'all those crazy Frenchmen' who did not dare to speak about themselves or *make* anything.[10] She says:

> *The name of Bachelard has been mentioned. But the intensity ... comes from something which is happening today. For instance your visit today. How I am ... depends on the affect you ... have on me. When you come to this room I know what it does to me. The things which move me on are very real tangible things ... Bachelard follows the opposite. He or Lacan, all these crazy Frenchmen, start from the abstractions, from the ideas. I do not. I start from the very immediate present, if immediate present makes me terribly upset I go little by little back on my own track. It comes from me going back to my remote past whilst Bachelard's method is the opposite. The difference is whether you go from the particular to the general or from the general to the particular. I want to go back in time, to discover reasons ... and with Bachelard everything is like everything else ... instead of being analytical his approach is synthetic. The other method, characteristic equally of Pascal and Kant, and from which I also come, is scientific investigation about the particular, investigation of everything in its own right.*[11]

This is one of the most important lessons of psychoanalysis: to stay with what is happening immediately in the analysis, give attention to the particular and then move only backwards or outwards ('I held his eyes within my gaze', runs the phrase on a handkerchief-sized textile from 2002; p 144). Psychoanalysis must reinvent itself with every new patient, and always be wary of applying abstract ideas to a particular person's life. Bourgeois's translation of her life into unique works of art is a lesson for the psychoanalyst and his intellectual pretensions.

But there is as much reverence as contempt towards Lacan and these other fathers, and this is a conflict, a knot, that also requires reworking. We can see and hear in Bourgeois's work and writings a valuing of certain concepts from the psychoanalytic fathers, such as repetition compulsion, the life/death drive, the unconscious and, importantly with respect to Lacan, the idea of lack – the hole, the lost object of desire. Bourgeois, despite her protests, was attracted to Lacan's ideas of loss. She hears in those ideas a description of out-of-placeness and the intimation of a kind of 'atopia' – somewhere that cannot be seen from one's usual perspective because it is always outside. This leads her in turn to the idea of trying to give this loss, or quality of lostness, a place.

Bourgeois knows the importance Lacan attributed to repetition in his reading of Freud, and in her notes she acknowledges Lacan's notion that repetition is always repetition with a difference. Crucially, this brings an element of creativity and creation to psychoanalytic work, taking it beyond scientific or empirical validation. When repetition occurs, when 'it comes back', there is always new work to be done. Returning to the studio, to favoured motifs, Bourgeois was not just witnessing her history and her losses, but working and reworking them. Thus in 1991 there appears a new version of the 1971 sculpture *Le Trani Episode* (opposite and pp 103, 230–31) –

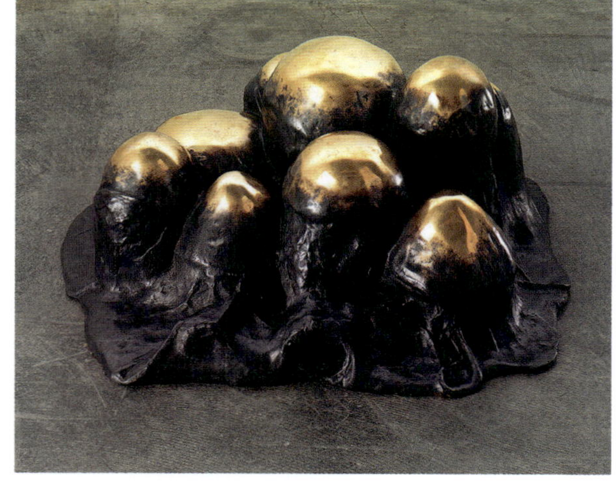
Unconscious Landscape **1967–68, cast 2010**

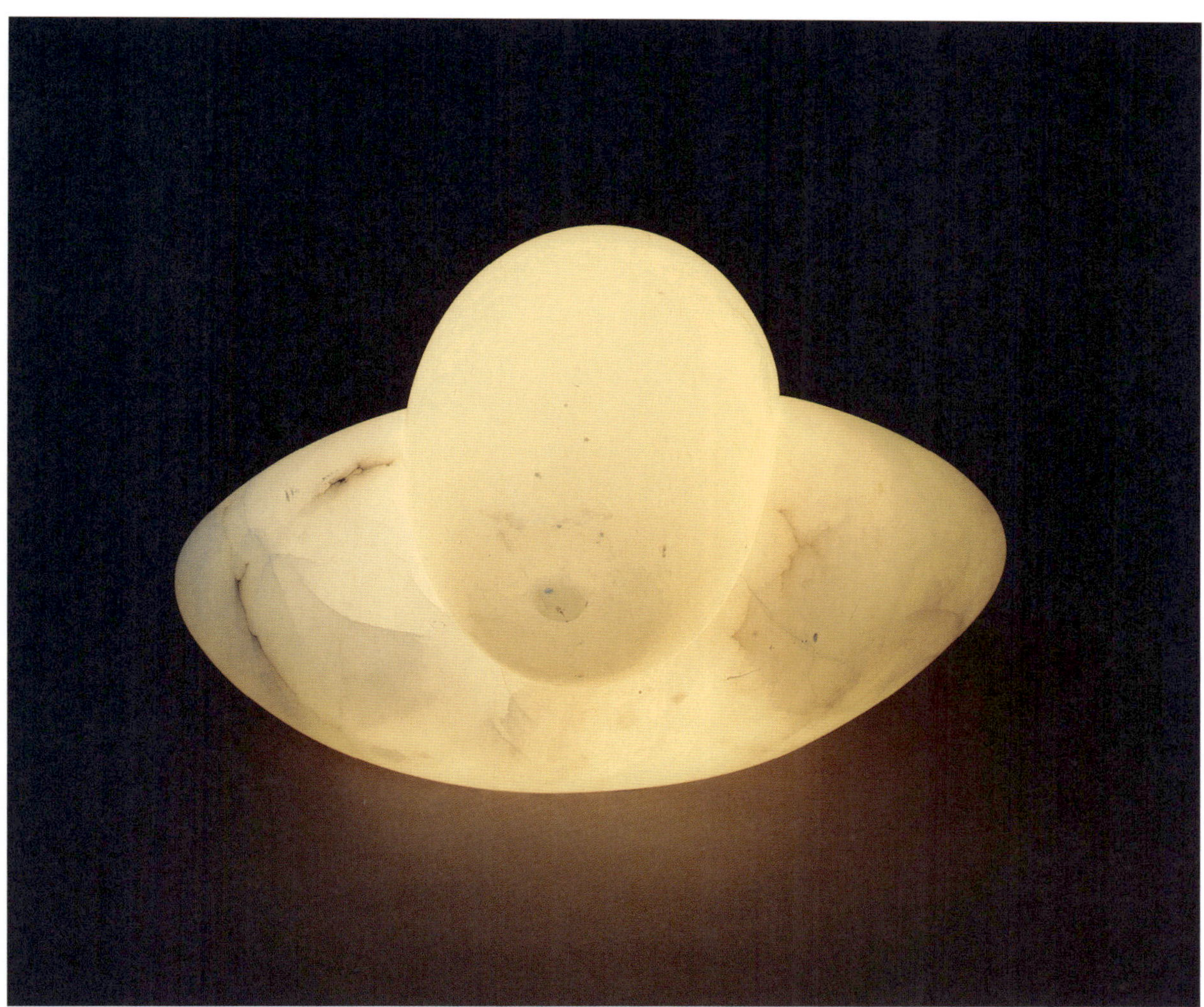

Le Trani Episode 1991

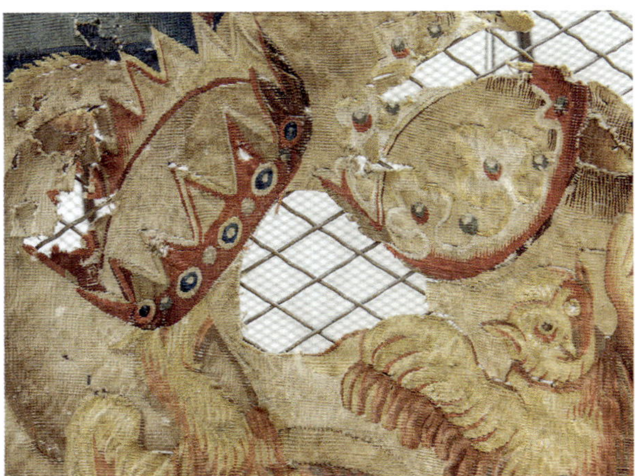

Spider 1997 (detail)

a reworking in alabaster that glows with electric light. According to art museum conventions, these are, of course, two different sculptures from two times. But they could be described psychoanalytically as the same sculpture thought differently at different moments in its creator's life.

This brings us close to the centre of the knot. The space of loss, the atopia, the missing solution, the lack that Bourgeois describes when she writes of '*the Repetition*, ad infinitum *of the non-accomplished action*' – this becomes the place from which a creative and devilish power can be born. Part of the way both she and Lacan turn Freud on his head is to show that the woman, the 'hysteric', in being closer to what is missing – due to her disempowered position in patriarchal society and the 'penis envy' she feels in reaction – is closer to this truth, this non-place from which work will spring. Freud learned of the unconscious, the meaning of dreams and symptoms, and the importance of sexuality from listening to hysterical women at the turn of the century. As if recalling those women a century later, Bourgeois, in a 1995–96 notebook, powerfully evokes the actions of 'sisters' who are working with a hole that is as important as what fills it:

I am deprived
You are deprived (lie)
He is deprived "
She is deprived poverty
We are deprived
You are deprived
They are deprived
They are deprived of knowledge, charm
means
Poor sisters how do you put up with the absence of . . .
absence of the other, absence of means, absence of ideal
absence of interest; an absence is a well that must
be filled an empty stomach that must be filled
a hole without water – a river dried out.
There must be ways to fill . . . that empty
sac – that lack –
The lack is much more important than the filled
One can even take care of it and play to fill it then
empty it. Children digging a hole in the sand, at
the beach – The tide fills the hole with water then
goes out then comes in eternally – Penelope weaves it and un
weaves it[12]

I love this image on which she ends: the hole that is filled and then unfilled eternally, as linked to the figure of Penelope from Homer's *Odyssey*, weaving and un-weaving to keep her suitors at bay. I love it especially because of Bourgeois's family history of mending tapestries that had come undone. Quite Lacanian, this is an image of life as the situating of one's lack so that you can 'take care of it' and even play with it, seeing what fills and fulfils it, and allowing it to be emptied out again and again. The more one does this, the less anxiety and fear there will be. In a detail from the monumental work *Spider* 1997 (opposite and pp 161–63), a hole in one such tapestry even bears a crown, as if the lack (which the artist herself may have perpetrated with scissors) is being revered.

Interestingly, the question of space, empty space, was key to one of Bourgeois's symptoms, namely the experience of extreme vertigo and fear. She wrote about it often and found in the work of Marie Bonaparte (1882–1962), the French psychoanalyst, some important clues concerning the connection of these spatial fears to femininity (notably, Bonaparte was Lacan's nemesis). Bourgeois is drawn to Bonaparte's theories of feminine sexuality and so she pulls together numerous threads, including the girl-child oscillating between blaming father and blaming mother for her 'condition', the association between the vagina and the unseeable reproductive organs, and fears of feelings of emptiness that are distinctively female. These threads are interwoven with her own intense resentment of the roles that women are forced into. She writes:

> I do not have to live in an empty world
> world of vacuum (Marie Bonaparte) I can create
> my own, artist world of omnipotence + fantasy
> I have to control space because I cannot
> stand emptiness
> emptiness is a space the edge of which you do
> not know and you are not sure of – like falling
> into space or like being dizzy.
> *This question of space is perhaps sim*
> *ply based on the fear of falling –*
> *When Pierre was born Maman said – Louise got*
> *up and she walked. Maybe I was just*
> *afraid to fall at that moment – Vertigo and*
> *great fear on balconies (roof at* 18th St)
> Pull yourself together. Do not try several things
> just so that one will pull you away from the
> one before – Be modest and tight knitted
> *Always go back to the work you have on hand –*
> *Perfect and revisit again.*[13]

The final sentence is a reference to French poet Nicolas Boileau-Despréaux in *L'art poétique* (1674): '*Vingt fois sur le métier remettez votre ouvrage*' or 'Twenty times upon the anvil, put your work back'. The solution to vertigo is perfection through repetition of work. What emerges in this passage by Bourgeois is the idea of the constant manipulation of space as a way of mastering the terror of emptiness, and of rage at the mother for being likewise 'empty' or 'castrated'. This mother, not being able to give you everything you want, leaving you lacking, leaving you to a world that is unjust to women and mothers, is shown as the beginning of sculptural production and imagination. One has to get up, leave the mother, and walk unto death. This is the path that lies ahead for the unacknowledged child in the 'bad mother' sculptural element from Bourgeois's *I Undo* (one of the three towers from the Tate's Turbine Hall installation), 1999–2000. This child must escape the 'vacuum' of the bell jar it inhabits (pp 205–06) and shape spaces of its own.

Perfectionism is often seen as being a feminine compulsion, especially when it concerns the body. There is an important link here to sculpture in particular, as an exploration of the emptiness whose edges one does not know. The girl-child's curiosity about her sexual organs, and her wondering about the interior of the mother's body as a place where she came from but has no memory of, are the impetus for the imagination and exploration of space. Sculpture is the most concrete equivalent of this desire and Bourgeois, from *Woman with Packages* 1949 (p 92) to *Nature Study* 1984–94 (p 113) to *The Found Child* 2001 (pp 192–93) and beyond, takes the added step of making sculpture into an art about women and their relationships to their bodies and desire.

One might characterise this work with the body, perfecting it in the form of an object, as a compulsion. Bourgeois certainly did, but she adds that what is repeated infinitely must also be 'eternally magical'.

The characteristic of the compulsive object is that:
repeated, repeated, repeated, repeated ad infinitum
and eternally magical
meaningless to others, strange, never let
go of. *best as we can ...*

shake <u>*hands*</u> *with the adult*, nothing
will make me release it
<u>The hand</u>

The resistance is against
progress, help of any kind

against pleasure sex
to deserve not —[14]

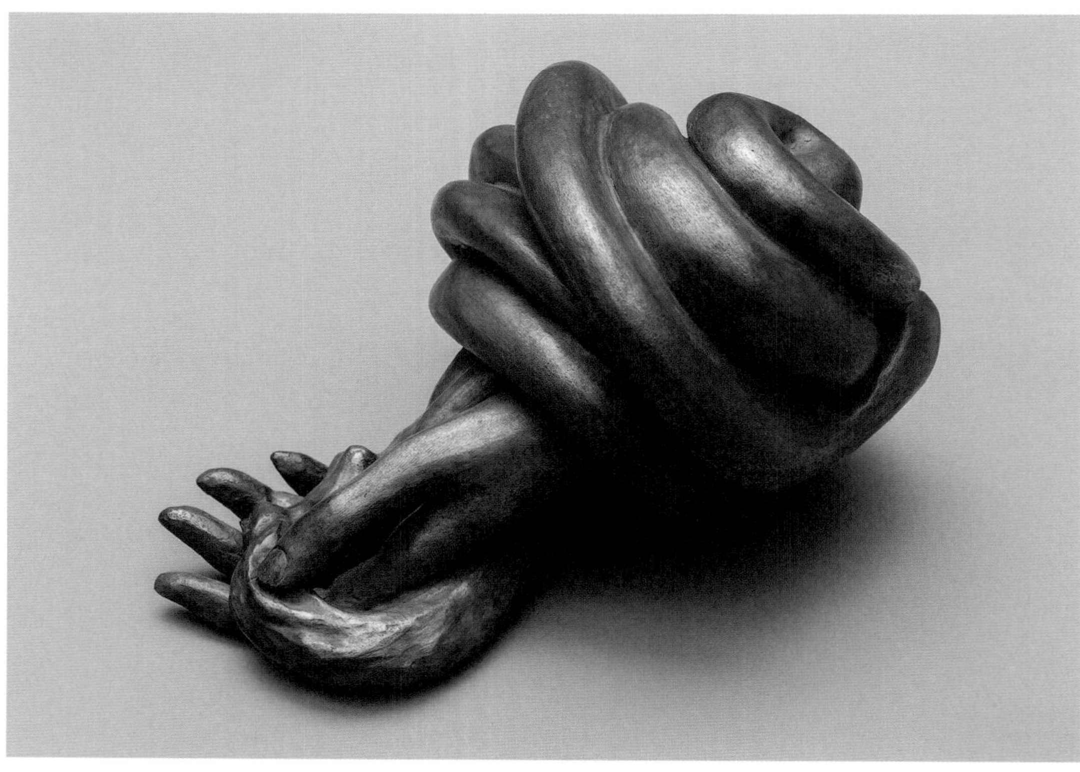

Nature Study 1986

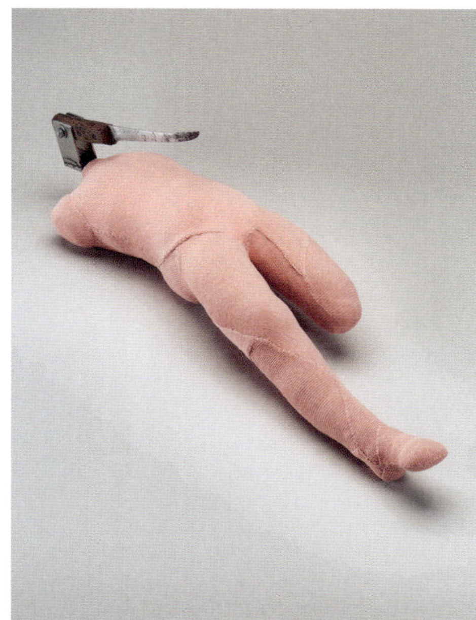

Knife Figure 2002

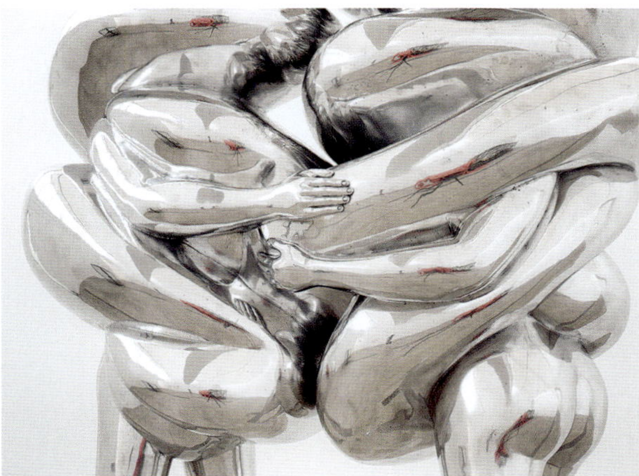

The Couple 2003 (detail)

What one wants to repeat will be meaningless to others. One's compulsions always look a bit crazy, like Bourgeois's hoarding of fabrics and clothing in her upstairs closets, or sleeping in a room with a single bed, surrounded by art in progress, books, boxes and recording devices, writing notes on the wall, her life practically a sculpture. This is her way of not letting go of the magic, a magic that she knows is close to pleasure, sex.

Playing with the body as a surface folded around a series of holes is how psychoanalysis conceives of the meeting between being born human with an unconscious and drives and having to confront sexuality in real time in our intimate relationships, and, importantly, in the wider culture. The way this peculiar life of the body is rendered in Bourgeois's work, showing its transformation into forms of psychic suffering but also creativity, I think accounts for a large share of her art's power and attraction in a time when we have the contradiction of greater equality existing alongside continued licence to attack women. We are so close here to Freud's definition of the value of true sublimation: showing how one can really live with desire, even when thwarted. Bourgeois demonstrates this 'again and again' throughout her decades of investigating, especially in her pieces on the question of the mother, motherhood and the cycle of life. It continues 'to infinity' in her late series *À l'infini* 2008–09 (pp 28, 194–201), where the woman is both adult and childlike in a space that is bodily yet ethereal.

Far from giving up compulsions, then, I think we exacerbate them into a style – if we are following Bourgeois. 'Nothing will make me release it,' she writes in the 1988 diary entry quoted above; 'never let go'. Psychoanalysis, terminable and interminable, as Freud wrote about it in one of his last papers, also never lets go. It is a work that is unending, but it is the unendingness that one learns to embrace in the end, even after one has stopped seeing one's analyst. One might remember that Bourgeois saw her analyst until he died. She never let go until forced.

Any survey of Bourgeois's work shows an oeuvre that makes of life an ouroboros knot. Life and work eat into each other, merge as infinite reworkings of each other. She redoes her relationships, her history, her suffering, in sculptures, drawings and paintings, again and again. She went as far as she could go, never changing course in what came to be a long life, but also dug as far into herself as she could, as if she wished to hit bottom. The themes these works investigate are repeated *ad infinitum* with no resolution. The hand and body won't be untangled in *Nature Study* 1986 (opposite and p 139). *Twosome* 1991 (pp 25, 256–57) persists in its movements. *Knife Figure* 2002 (above left) is ever threatened, ever defensive. This repetition without resolution is perhaps clearest in her many suspended works, such as *The Couple* 2003 (left and p 145), which turn continuously around their own centres, turn without going anywhere.

It is this act of raising herself up as an object, again and again, to which Bourgeois gives a kind of dignity. There is no shame in coming back to the same problem over and over. There is no shame in life, in misfortunes, in incapacities, in hating even as one loves, or in our wildest symptoms, even as they all engender intense shame. Resist the idea of progress. These objects, these revelations, accumulate and could prove immortal, archived in human history, reaching out to so many others. As she writes in 1985, *'it's an* act *of blind love, he who can do the most can do the least'*.[15] Let me conclude with these words from Bourgeois, written on the back of an exhibition announcement from 1947:

I know you do not
see that I am talking to you
I know that you do not
hear my voice and that you
do not know my 2
languages french and
english because you
would have too much to do to
understand all the
languages of all the countries
but I know you will under-
stand my statue,
because it does not make
any noise, it does not
bother you, it does not smell
bad, it is not
possible that it bothers you
or offends you –
If I make one, two, three,
four statues in one
series it is because I
must repeat myself, to be
sure *that my message*
reaches you, if you want
ten of them I will make ten, a hundred
an infinity I will never
tire, we will have an
accumulation of
statues like the grains
of sand on the shore.[16]

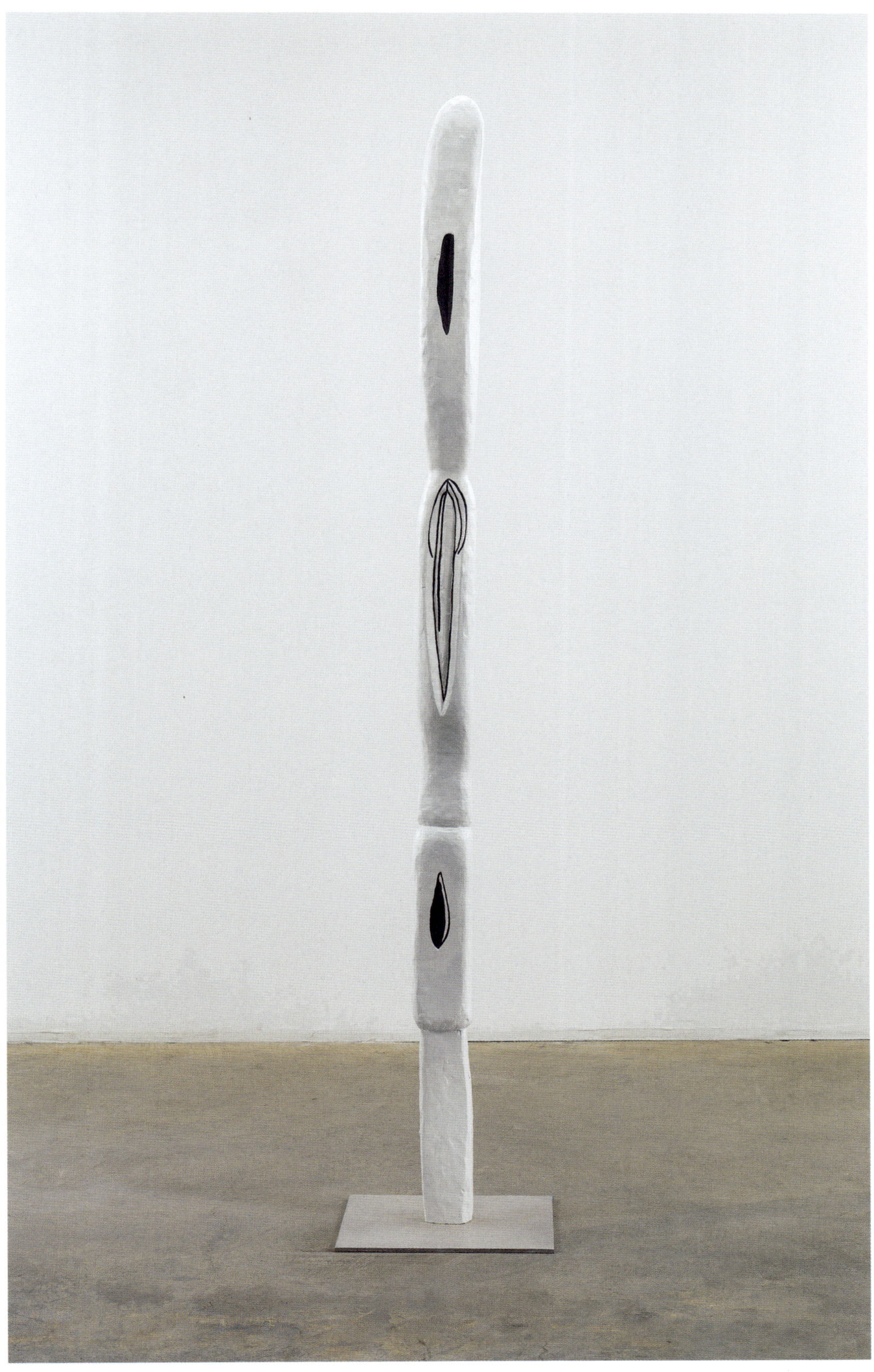

Untitled 1947–49

The heart of something
An interview with Chris Kraus

Justin Paton

Justin Paton: I'd like to ask you about Louise Bourgeois then and now: about the artist you met in the late 1970s and the artist as you see her today, forty-five years later. What comes to mind when you recall your early relationship?

Chris Kraus: It was a relationship between Louise, my late friend the performer Suzan Cooper (1952–2023) and me. Louise 'adopted' Suzan and by extension me in 1978, the year of her *Confrontation* installation. She 'directed' another crazy performance we did together; she invited us over for cocoa at 4am after our topless bar shifts. I saw her deploy Suzan's drunken abandon at social gatherings of staid art-world people, including the *New York Times* head critic. She was obviously, in her mid to late sixties, needing to inhale something about being young in New York at that time. She saw where she wanted to be, annexed to late punk in New York City – and she went for it.

JP: How did her art strike you, in the context of other art being made and shown in the city at that time?

CK: Neither Suzan nor I were very much in the visual art world. We were doing performance, theatre, hanging round with people in bands, with St Marks Poetry Project. It's not as if I was coming to Louise's work with any particular knowledge of art. But I definitely responded to it. I felt very comfortable with Louise's work.

JP: Which works of hers did you see at the time?

CK: I remember her *Femme maison* paintings and some related prints from the 1940s. I saw these at her house very early on and delivered some of them to her gallery on my bike and, though I knew very little then, was touched.

JP: That is a wonderful image, of now-famous works being delivered by you by bike. It brings a very different art world into view.

CK: I think Louise had just begun working with Xavier Fourcade Gallery. Fourcade wanted the work brought up and for whatever reason the gallery didn't organise an art-moving company. Louise was resentful or miffed about that. I was topless dancing by then, but one of my many jobs in New York had been as a bike messenger and I still rode my bike because it was cheap and fun. So she made me pretend. She kept saying, 'You are a licensed bonded messenger.' She said it over and over. Maybe she was trying to stick it to Xavier Fourcade, because a licensed bonded messenger I was not. I was this skinny art girl on a beat-up bike.

JP: You use the word 'comfortable' to describe your feelings about Louise's work. It's not the first word many people would use of her art. Why did you feel at home with it?

CK: Because it was so direct. You didn't have to worry, 'How should I be seeing this? What should I be thinking? What is this really about?' It was direct, but not simple – subtle and deep. In that sense it felt performative, with qualities we maybe look for more often in literature than visual art. Her work carried a complex and rich immediate experience with an afterlife you can never quite sum up.

JP: There's a *Femme maison* painting in this exhibition (p 207) of a darkened building, a woman house, that is leaping in fright or exultation, I can never decide which ...

CK: The answer would be both, of course. It's not the woman house's physical reaction that hits me first in this painting. It's the access, the staircase leading up to the hole. The staircase is so public. The whole world can walk up. And the little windows at the top – are they there for her to observe, or is she being observed there as well? There's a cacophony of reactions, a feeling of being invaded, being filled by anything that comes off the street. Which was very much like real life.

JP: And what about Louise herself? What kind of impression did she make at this time?

CK: I watched the 2008 documentary *The spider, the mistress and the tangerine* recently and her relation to the interviewer and filmmaker Amei Wallach brought back a lot about Louise. If you have the idea that she was a friendly, maternal mentor figure to us, that was really not the case. She was not nice.

JP: Expand on 'not nice'.

CK: It was very clear that anything that transpired was transpiring for its usefulness and interest to Louise. There was no bland altruism at work. There was a purpose to everything. There's nothing wrong with that. Her engagement with us was transparent. And she was just so interesting and stimulating to be around. It was wonderful to go through the door of her townhouse in Chelsea into this musty and antiquarian world, crammed with stuff. She always sat in front of those bevelled glass doors to the kitchen. She wore these French *ouvrier* [worker] clothes, a blue smock over these blouses with little Peter Pan collars. I think she'd just turned sixty-six when we first met. And the way that she was using her age was just so badass. There were very few women

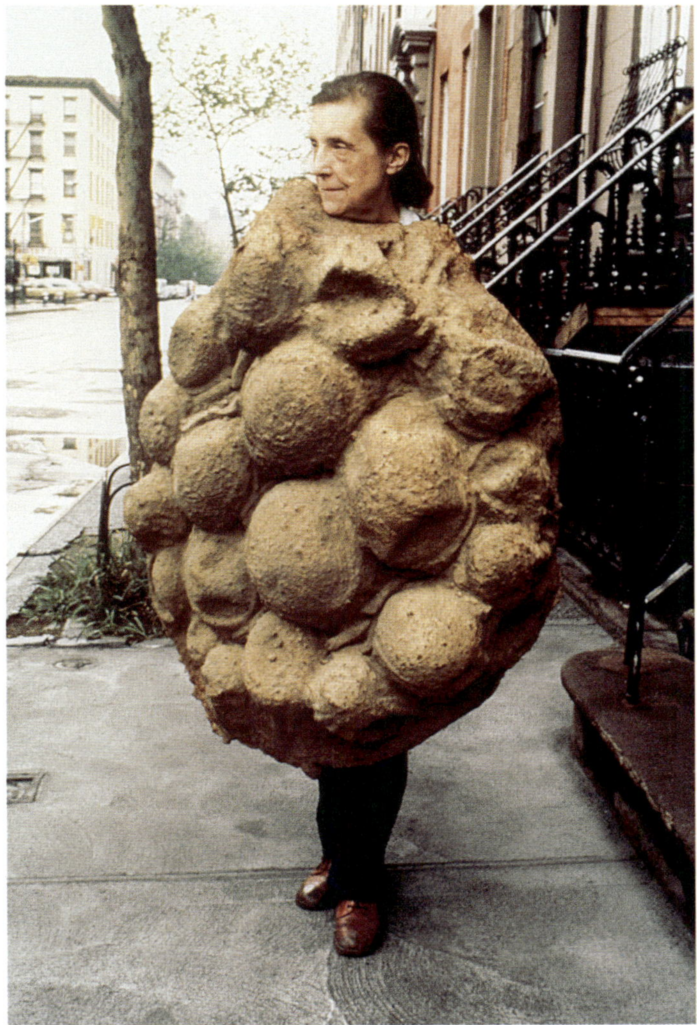

Louise Bourgeois wearing the latex sculpture *Avenza* 1968–69, which became part of *Confrontation* 1978, in front of her home on 20th Street, New York, 1975

wielding any power in the art world at all, and then for it to be an old woman, and a different kind of old woman from an art-world grande dame like Louise Nevelson. This was an old woman who acted like a punk girl.

JP: You and Suzan were young punks too, in your twenties at the time. How did you all connect?

CK: I met Suzan the year before the *Confrontation* installation, in 1977, when we were both in a summer school program with director and performance theorist Richard Schechner and The Performance Group. Richard was absolutely intrigued by Suzan. She was such a disruptive influence. Crazy, brilliant, extremely abrasive and confrontational. Tits in your face all the time, very sexual, weaponising her sexuality whenever possible. Meanwhile, I – recently arrived from New Zealand via London – was the polar opposite. I was reticent, thoughtful, surveying everything, thinking about it. Suzan and I distrusted each other, and Richard found that fascinating. He proposed that if we wanted to work together on a show, he'd direct it and present it at The Performing Garage. How could we say no? Suzan and I, these bad twins, were thrown together by this big opportunity.

JP: 'Thrown together' could almost be a Louise Bourgeois title. How does she come in?

CK: In the spring, after we'd been working on the show for half a year, Suzan met her mother for lunch at MoMA, as they often did when her mother came in from East Orange, New Jersey. On her way out, Suzan saw an older woman artist in the lobby and mistook her for Louise Nevelson, who was famous at the time, much more so than Louise Bourgeois. Suzan ran up to her and said, '*Louise!*', and of course, Louise was offended when she realised that Suzan mistook her for Nevelson. But she saw something in Suzan and they became friends from then on. Suzan adored her – her Frenchness, her shrewd wisdom, and her availability at that time. She was thrilled, and brought me to meet Louise, too.

JP: The bad twins visit ...

CK: Yes, Louise had the same take as Schechner did, receiving us together. Louise recognised my intelligence and diligence. There was a kind of collegial understanding, younger and older, between us. But there was a much more emotional bond between her and Suzan. Louise was just beginning to work explicitly with the material on her own family and father, and she found that Suzan had a similar story. A sophisticated father, hip and educated, who kept an apartment in Manhattan, and a mother who was left behind. There was a bad divorce early on, and she maintained an admiring and adversarial relationship with her father. Suzan was financially supported by her family, but money is never free, there are always conditions attached. Suzan talked a lot about this with Louise, and I think being close to that – a family drama that was so fresh and unprocessed – was triggering, in a good way, for Louise. She liked to show us the slides that she'd show publicly later on, of her family home, and the tapestries. She and Suzan looked at these images many times, and Louise talked about them with us often. She was really working through that.

JP: So there was give and take?

CK: Yeah, there was a kind of quid pro quo. She used to send us to Key Food on Eighth Avenue; Chelsea was nothing special then. She cooked a lot. She had an old-fashioned pressure cooker and she'd make these gigots. We often ate there. She taught me manners. I was very eating-phobic at the time; it was hard for me to eat in front of people. She said: 'No, you're insulting people when you do not eat their food.' She would always tell you the straight shit. That's something I learned from Louise that I've continued in my own work as a teacher. To just put it all on the table, to say everything you see and you know, and let people work with that.

JP: She also designed the flyer for your show at The Performing Garage in 1978, yes? The one pinned to the wall in photos of her dining room?

CK: Yes, that was her favour to us: designing the flyer (below). The performance was called *Scenes from an almost socialist marriage*. Suzan was Suzan Socialist and I was Chris Class. We put our hearts and souls into the show for nine months. It was the most important thing in the world. And seeing that kind of drive in an older person was amazing. But she had this house and this set-up, she was able to host. She was the spider. Come into my web.

JP: It does sound entangling – Louise processing her feelings as a daughter through two new daughters. People sometimes talk about her being rediscovered by the art world in the early 1980s, but she emerges from all you're saying very much as an orchestrator and an agent in her realm. It's not happening to her. She's making it happen.

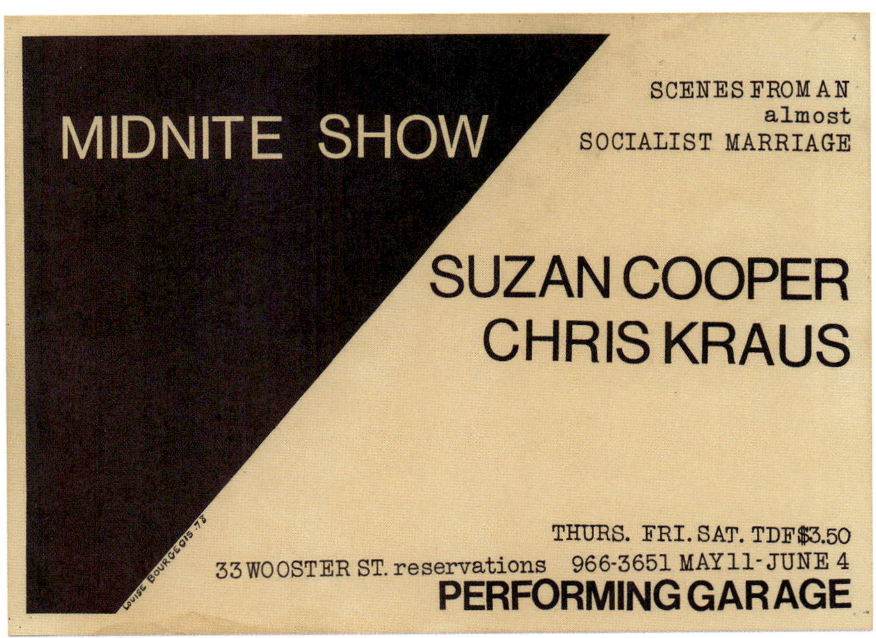

Bourgeois's poster for *Scenes from an almost socialist marriage* by Suzan Cooper and Chris Kraus, Performing Garage, New York, 1978

CK: Louise always knew what she was doing; she had the most strategic intelligence I've ever seen. She'd draw Suzan into these difficult, somewhat dangerous situations, where Suzan could be relied on to get drunk and high and shock everyone in the room. My job was the caretaker: to make sure Suzan got safely home after Louise drew her out. Suzan and I thought we were effecting a symbiosis … that our polarities combined added up to one complete person. It got a little out of control. And Louise amplified that.

JP: There's an extraordinary document of this time in a video clip of Suzan in *A Banquet / A Fashion Show of Body Parts*, the performance Louise orchestrated in her installation *Confrontation* at the Hamilton Gallery of Contemporary Art in 1978. I was amazed to learn you had not seen this clip, even though you are there in the crowd supporting Suzan. Tell me what seeing this brought back, because the best director in the world could not conjure a more perfect time capsule. It's so redolent.

CK: Seeing it now, I remembered the photos I used to look at back in New Zealand of this exciting and glamorous world in New York and London that I longed to be a part of. It didn't feel that way that night, of course. Suzan was nervous, Louise was relying on Suzan to perform, and it was just one more thing we had to get through.

JP: Something happens though when Suzan leans into her song …

CK: That was a punk song Suzan wrote as the opening act for one of our productions. The song was called 'The mother' and it went, 'She abandoned me. She abandoned me … She was a mother. That one was a mother.' It was perfect for Louise's show.

JP: She's quite blazing. She really storms through the artifice and awkwardness.

CK: She's completely fabulous. Suzan passed away early in 2023, aged 71, but seeing this reminds me that part of her genius was being a great truth-teller. She always saw exactly what was going on under the surface. And she had no problem calling it out. She always did that, always. Suzan appeared in a film Sylvère Lotringer and I made together in 1985 called *Foolproof illusion*. In it, she wears bondage regalia and 'lectures' to Sylvère's Columbia students about the French writer Antonin Artaud (1896–1948) telling stories about her 'relationship' with Artaud and reaching an essence of madness that eludes most Artaud scholars. Louise had that same madness,

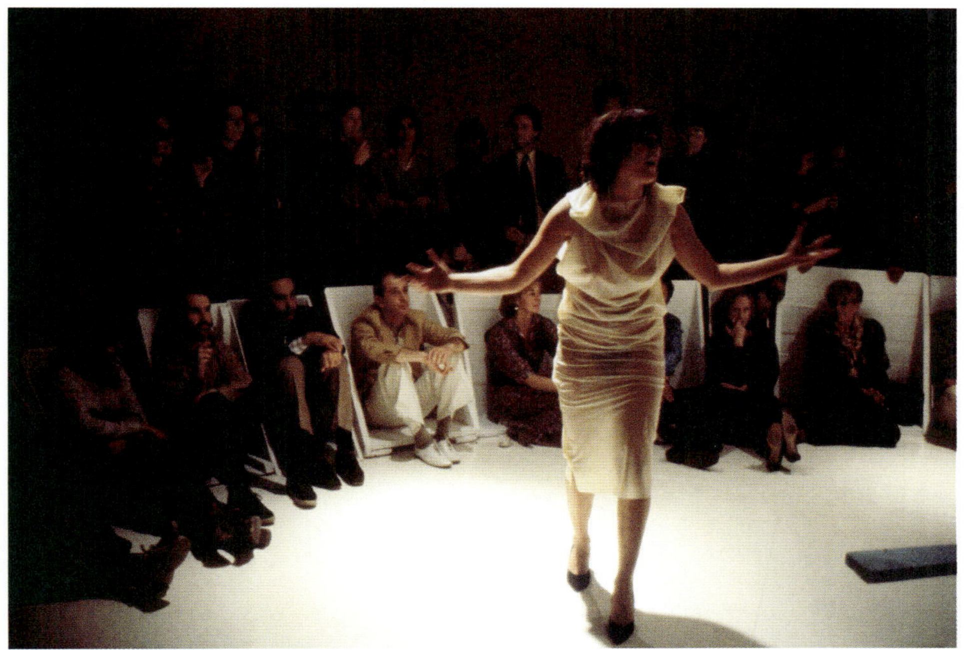

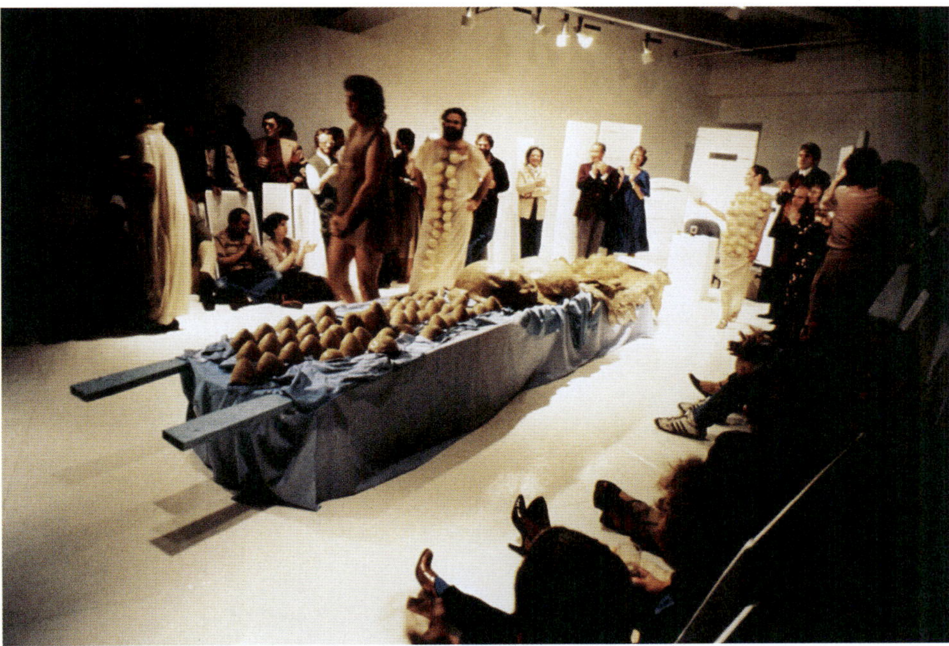

Bourgeois's performance *A Banquet / A Fashion Show of Body Parts*, featuring Suzan Cooper (top), staged in the installation *Confrontation*, Hamilton Gallery of Contemporary Art, New York, 21 October 1978

an ability to access the heart of something. Years later, Sylvère and I invited her to participate in an evening celebrating the 2001 publication of *Hatred of capitalism*, the Semiotext(e) anthology. Louise filmed a woman's hand wielding a hammer to smash a hard ball, shouting *dada – daddy – daddy!* She didn't attend but had Robert Storr introduce it. And he did, in the most high-minded way, almost a parody of a museum curator. So when the film started, the infantilism of it was shocking. A real dada performance.

JP: As well as being drawn to the two of you in 1978, was Louise gravitating to something that was in the air culturally in that late punk, No Wave moment? Or had the culture just arrived where she already was? A work like *Shredder*, which was made a little later, in 1983 (below and pp 120–21), strikes me as very punk, in its directness and feeling of blunt threat.

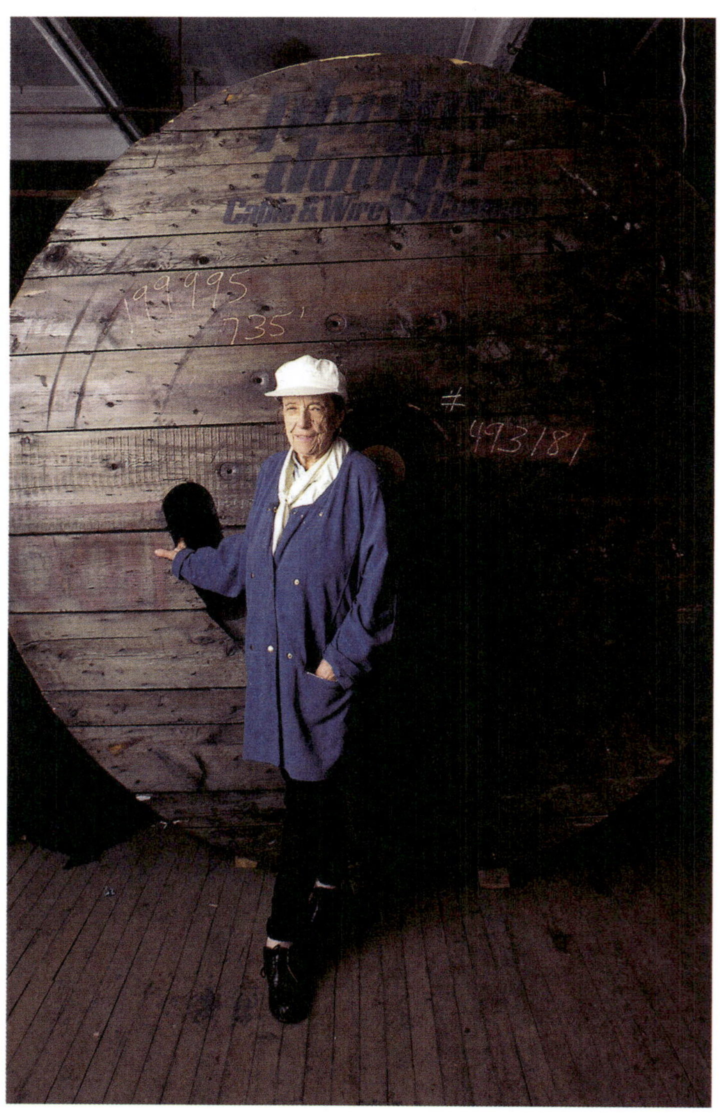

Bourgeois with an element from the sculpture *Shredder* 1983 in her Brooklyn studio, New York, 1995

CK: I think it was Louise's rigour that made her seem punk. She wasn't a floaty hippy like the previous generation we all hated. She was absolute, uncompromising and tough. You see that in the documentary, the way she challenges Amei. Amei offers an anodyne prompt about men and women and Louise is enraged: 'I did not say that; that's not a quote, why would I even say it, it's so obvious.' I've been reading Proust's *Sodom and Gomorrah* and I think there's a similarity between his mania for precision and Louise's rigour. To keep going at something, parsing it further, identifying all the things it is not until you finally reach the essence of what it is – that can be a very cruel process. I couldn't have articulated it at the time, but I think that's what I responded to.

JP: What was at stake for Louise in this rigour? By the time of that documentary, the art world was looking her way. A different artist might have relaxed into the admiration. What was the end game? Why be so accurate and demanding and uncompromising?

CK: It's an ethos that people often have when they're young and then lose with age. In your early twenties, you believe in art as the channel for every thought, every feeling. And then, with some success and some age, people look for a compromise between art and life. That fierce desire softens, becomes blended with other things. Louise was so punk in her desire to define things precisely. She talks in the documentary about striving for accuracy. Years later, when I finally started writing, I came to a similar point: 'I may not be a great writer,' I thought, 'but at least I can try to be accurate.'

JP: This is so interesting, because it puts paid to any idea that the transformations and metamorphoses in her works are fantastical or 'free' and somehow unbeholden. This term 'accuracy' implies a model of truth-telling – there is something in the world or in the self or in relationships that the artist is seeking to honour.

CK: Yeah, it's reaching down for something very deep, externalising it, giving it a form and turning it into play. That's what she was doing.

JP: Tell me what you see and value in Louise's art from the perspective of now?

CK: I often think it's so easy to be an artist. You need only one idea every ten years, and then there's the making of it. But Louise's work always involved the manifestation of a psychic process. Something very internal being externalised, which could move between things in a surprising and unpredictable way. She created a kingdom in a way that very few people ever have.

JP: Is this something you miss in contemporary culture?

CK: Frances Morris says something great in the documentary: in Louise, she saw twentieth-century modernism and contemporary art combined. She'd never seen that in the same person. There's an undertow of twentieth-century modernism in Louise's work that you can't expect to see now. It's not even something you can regret, because it's not in the world.

JP: What are you referring to there? You mean the sense of existential high stakes?

CK: Yes – taking one's internal process so seriously. Not as an ego revelation, or an anecdote, but an exhaustive investigation of one's own unconscious. Which feels like a non sequitur today. People pull things from life, but the reality of what constitutes an internal world now is so different.

JP: Do you see anyone building kingdoms in ways comparable to Louise?

CK: More in literature than in art, maybe. I think of Clarice Lispector, Gary Indiana, Constance Debré, Marie Darrieussecq, Nathalie Léger ... But these are all writers.

JP: The commitment is daunting. The search begins again each day without any promise of resolution. Again one might ask: Why dig so deep, why hurt so much, why unearth so much?

CK: I saw Louise in the late 1970s going back to her childhood story over and over again and at the time I didn't understand it. This woman is sixty-six years old, why is she obsessed with something that happened when she was four? But it's like trauma work – people hang on to early trauma, because paradoxically it's the thing that makes them feel most alive, even while it makes them dead to the present.

JP: Fascinating. And it's fascinating how this cuts across sentimental conceptions of how art deals with problems. This idea of art museums as public spaces where artists surface problems so that we can all triangulate our opinions and be wiser. I'm as invested in this idea as the next curator, but Louise isn't reassuring me ...

CK: No, she's going for something witchier. A dark mystery that's pulling you deep down.

JP: That's wonderfully put. As you know, in Sydney the exhibition has a 'deep down' in the form of a darkened oil tank where works like *Twosome* 1991 (pp 25, 256–57) and *The Destruction of the Father* 1974 (pp 222–25) will glow and grind away. These very red, aggressive pieces in a kind of landscape of the unconscious.

CK: That piece, *The Destruction of the Father*, is an act of cannibalism. But cannibalism is always a tribute and an act of violence at the same time. You're taking something into yourself of the enemy, tearing something apart but, at the same time, becoming it.

JP: And then perhaps the spider comes in at a later moment in this cycle, pulling or extruding her creation from her belly.

CK: The spider is very efficient. She's more admirable than frightening. Look at all those legs, doing her bidding! It's like a spider machine.

JP: It's so interesting, this question of needing the problem, feeding off it, being fuelled by it, imbibing it, taking it into yourself. Acting as if you want a solution, when actually it's the problem that's generative, and a solution may be the last thing you want. There's a remarkable line of hers from very late in her life: 'Never let me free from this burden that will never let me be free.'[1]

CK: Yes, yes, that line is so brilliant. Because that's the most vibrant part. That's where the mystery is. That's the witch's kitchen.

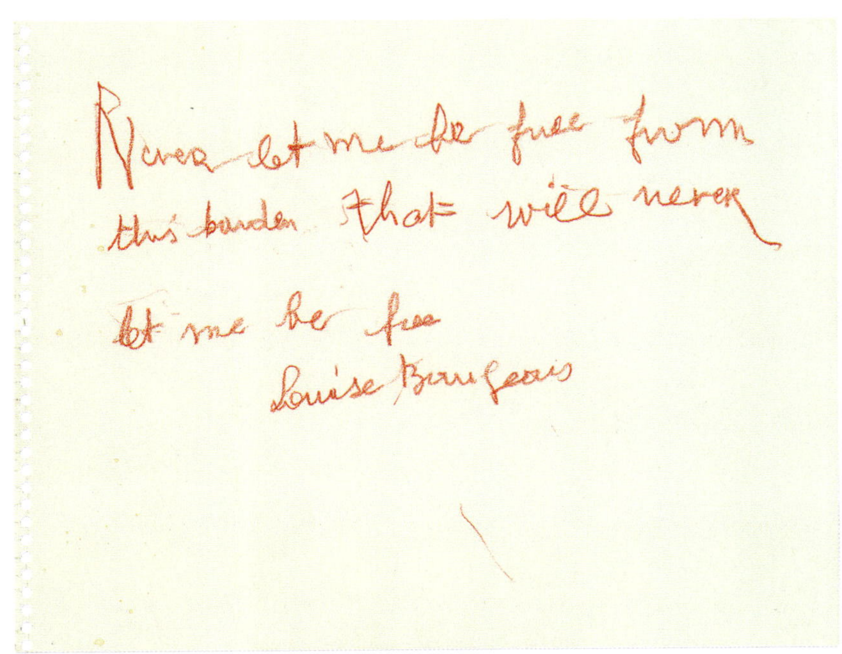
Never let me be free from this burden that will never let me be free
Louise Bourgeois

Louise Bourgeois, loose sheet of writing, c2008 (LB-0516)

To the depths
About me and Louise

Jane Campion

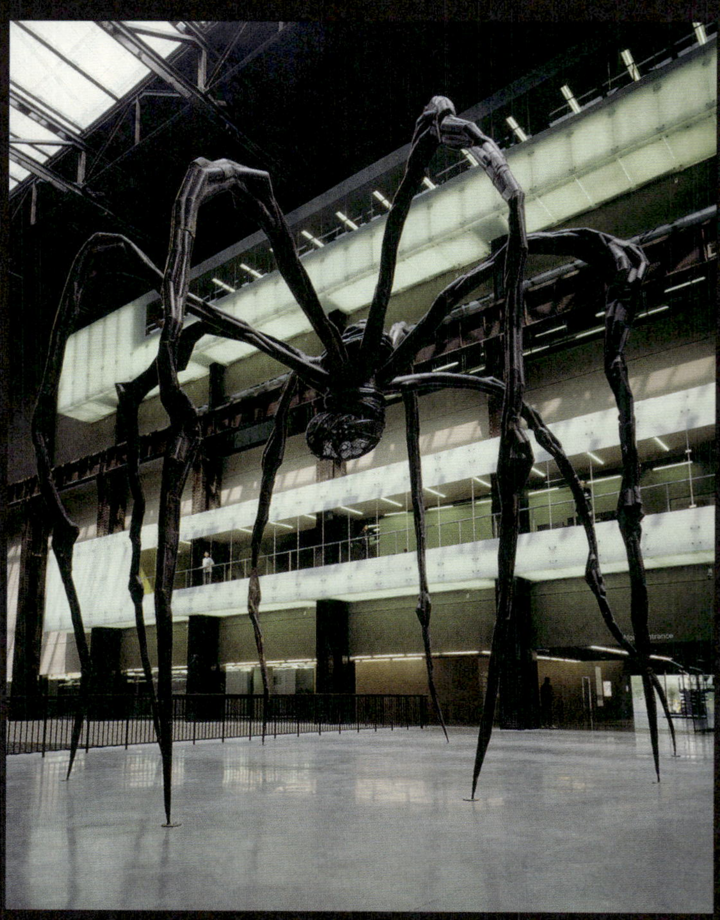

Installation view of Louise Bourgeois's *Maman* 1999 in the Turbine Hall at Tate Modern, London, 2000

I believe it was in 2000, at the new Tate Modern, that I glimpsed Louise Bourgeois's *Maman*. Sidled past it, hurrying to catch a plane, but the deed was done. It was my first encounter with Louise, and I never forgot that audacious creation, that boldness, the aliveness of the provocation. It was stamped into my psyche like fairytale images. Red Riding Hood, Bluebeard, Snow White. Once heard as a child they are never forgotten.

The spider is huge, and there is a paradox with its size. The spider is the size a human would appear to a spider. It goes further, like an echo chamber, because, while even the largest spider is relatively small, there is a creepiness to them that is writ large in our fear and horror, and that fear is writ large in the size of the spider Louise has made. So it becomes the psychic spider.

The image of the vast female spider plays with the fear of women, of their supposed unpredictability, their lack of rationality, and their desire to entrap. Men especially, but children too, feel that fear of the grasping mother and the web of need she spins. Somehow, Louise herself plays into this story, like a fairytale godmother possessing otherworldly powers that can help you. Louise is not a good witch or a bad witch, she's an art witch. She's out for herself, which I like, and she shares in an enormously personal way. For me that's where the love is. She shows herself; nothing is hidden. Her life is lived for art and her art is her – the mystery, pain and wild impulses of being her.

Louise is important to me. I recognised her as my art idol, my female icon. Broken, mysterious, wounded, angry, deep, powerful, *mine*. She led me to the female web like it was a playground full of glories and stories and pungency. In so many ways, I felt seen by Louise, understood by her creations. Her use of her own clothes, for example. Sometimes when I can't sleep, I lie in bed and remember all my important clothes. My brown velvet mini dress with embroidery and a matching bonnet from when I was fifteen. A mauve long-sleeved shirt that matched a deeper mauve maxi skirt that was laced up the side. The shoes I always bought too small because I thought my feet were too big, especially a pair of brown patent leather lace-ups with a trainer heel. My own heels bled. I didn't care; I put plasters on them.

And Louise's mending. As a thirteen-year-old, wearing dull brown stockings to school, I'd get a little hole in the knee and then I'd stretch it. I'd use brightly coloured cottons to darn across the hole, to make a beautiful woven patch, something I tried to do very perfectly. More than anything, I remember the shame of wanting to be admired, to be chosen, to be loved. Without a man loving me in some important way, I was orphaned, I didn't exist, I couldn't be free. This web of my own thinking and female thinking in general was exquisitely painful. Filmmaking, telling stories, was my release.

I do believe that Louise shows you the paradigm and the way out. I recognised myself, my sister, my mother in Louise, but her power was in her willingness to confess, to meet the shadowy painful wounds of the psyche and befriend them, to be curious and even, literally, to bandage them. I can recall feeling that the secrets of girlhood formed a true and rich territory – not known to men, not discovered in cinema. Rather than compete with the boys at film school for the cranes and the rigs, I thought, 'Let them have them, I'll go underground into the world of memory and secrets and explore that.' I was in my twenties and extremely energised because I had cracked the mirror of the false self and crossed over to the true self, the psyche. In this world I was very free, very confident. I knew it was real, I knew it had power, and I could trust it.

When you're in touch with the psyche, you're not flinching, you're not performing for anyone, you're not trying to be liked or loved. It's such an attractive space to be in, such a solid place, and so full of surprises. You don't know what's in there, and in you, until you start looking. Dreams are a way to begin. Nightmares are gifts from the psyche. They prepare you for things not working out. No one's prepared for the unhappily ever after. Another way to reach the solid place is to go over things you remember. Why is this thing, of all things, held in my mind forever? Didn't Louise say that she kept watch over her memories, that she needed them?

I do find objects very powerful. The piano in *The piano* (1993) is a metaphor for civilisation and expression. When Ada pulls out one of the keys, it's like she's beginning to unravel. After her finger has been cut off, we see she has begun wearing a silver prosthetic finger. It's beautifully made but it also shows the injury. It remembers the attempt to control her.

In *The power of the dog* (2021) I was very aware that the rope, which is the murder weapon, is made from the hide of an animal raised on the ranch, and that the process of creating it was also the means by which Phil, the victim, became friends with Peter, the murderer. And that when Peter placed the rope under his bed, it also had erotic value. Louise understood this so well – the way the same object can carry and knot together different meanings.

When I was writing *Bright star* (2009) and thinking about Fanny Brawne and her sewing, I went to the Portobello Market in London and bought a small Regency period chemise, because the stitches were so unbelievably small and perfect. I pinned it to the wall in front of me while I was writing to remind me of

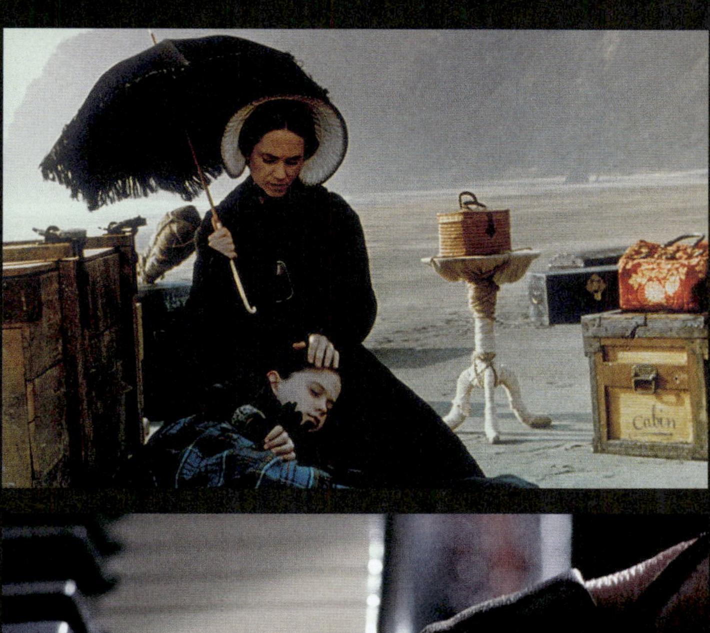

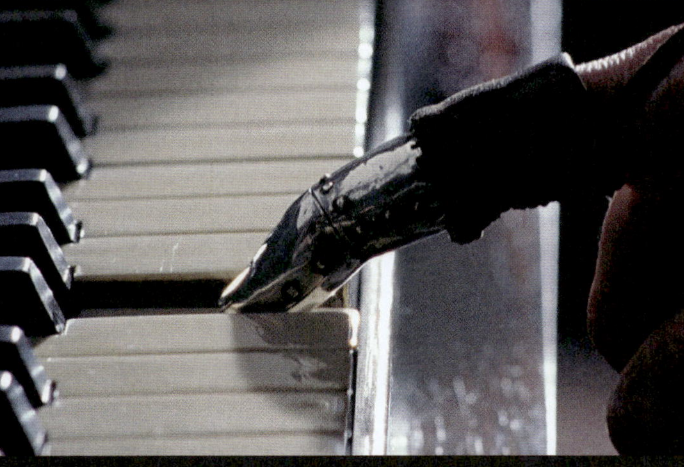

Stills from Jane Campion's *The piano* (1993): (top) Ada McGrath (Holly Hunter) and daughter Flora (Anna Paquin); (bottom) Ada's prosthetic finger

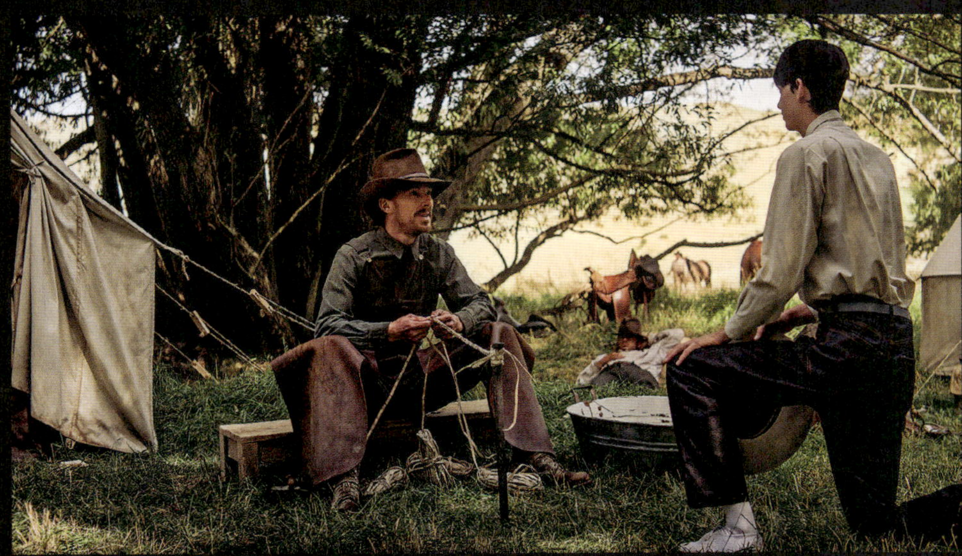

Still from Campion's *The power of the dog* (2021), featuring Benedict Cumberbatch as Phil Burbank and Kodi Smit-McPhee as Peter

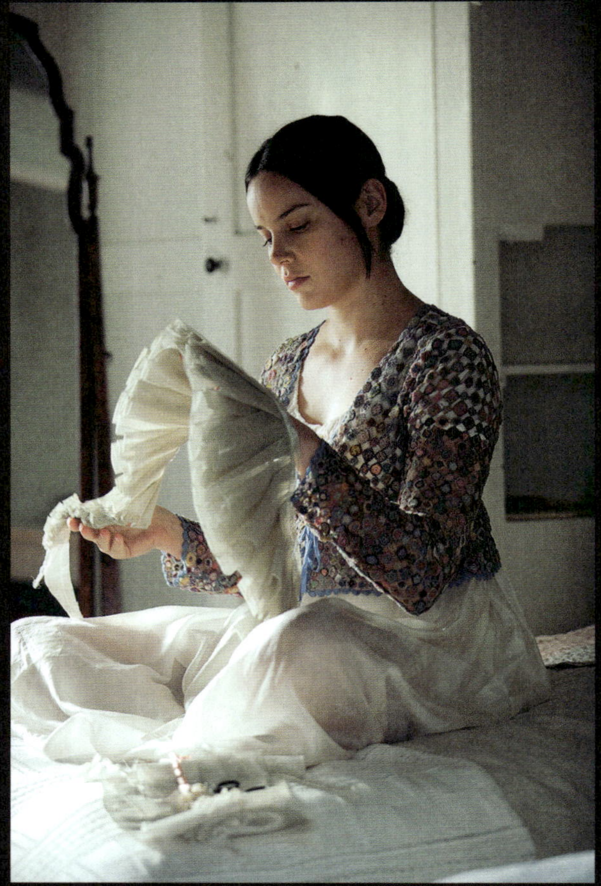

Still from Campion's *Bright star* (2009), featuring Abbie Cornish as Fanny Brawne

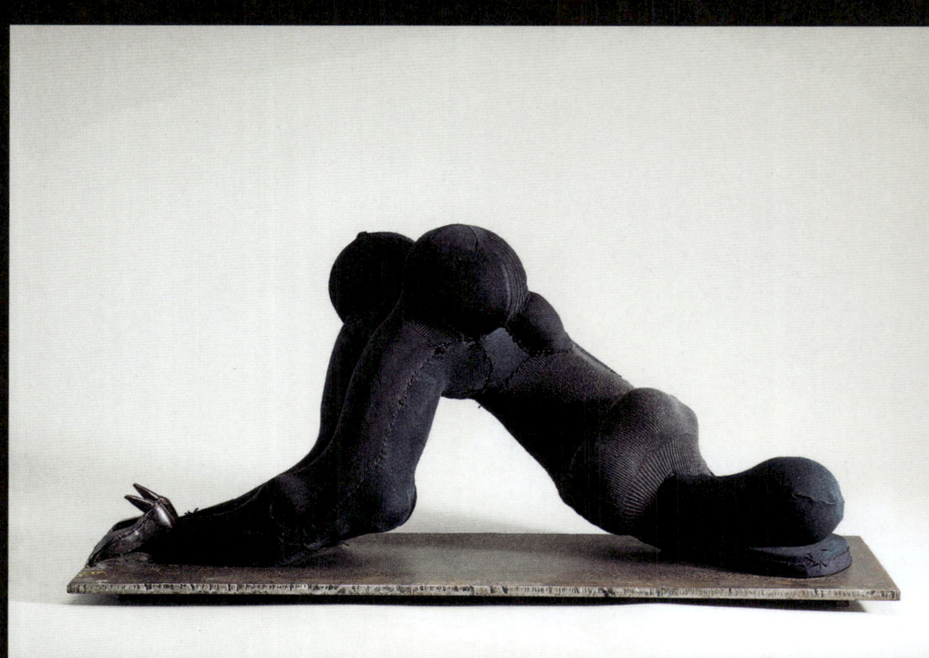

Louise Bourgeois *High Heels* 1998

what Fanny could make, her absorption in that world of sewing. Like Louise, who loved her mother's talents as a repairer, I have an overwhelming respect for women of that period and their creations, which few people value but which have hours and hours of work in them.

I love in Louise how the fabric figures are made. They're not perfect. They look bandaged. Everything is reduced to just what's needed. Everything that's there is important. One image that really gets me is the little metal high-heels on the kneeling textile figure, in *High Heels* 1998 (opposite). They're so neat and decorous in the sex act. They say something unsayable. Or the fabric couples, with their dark embraces and strange passions, which break me on the inside. Someone said to me Louise hands us problems to resolve. But it's not that, it's more personal. It's like she's birthed the problem for us, and we get to see that child. Like Janet Frame or Emily Dickinson, she makes things that have a desire to be. How do you discuss someone like that? You don't want to diminish their achievement by so-called understanding them.

My guides are mostly female. Dickinson, Frame, the Brontë sisters, Lina Wertmüller, Liliana Cavani. All are women with skin in the game. They all searched for the true life over the false life. But no one is as vivid and monumental as Louise. Nothing compares with her uneasy mix of beauty, truth-sharing, dark hidden memories, pain, shame and comedy. She's gone to the depths. She will lead you there and keep you there. You will be needing a thread to lead you back. It's like an umbilical cord. You may not want to cut it.

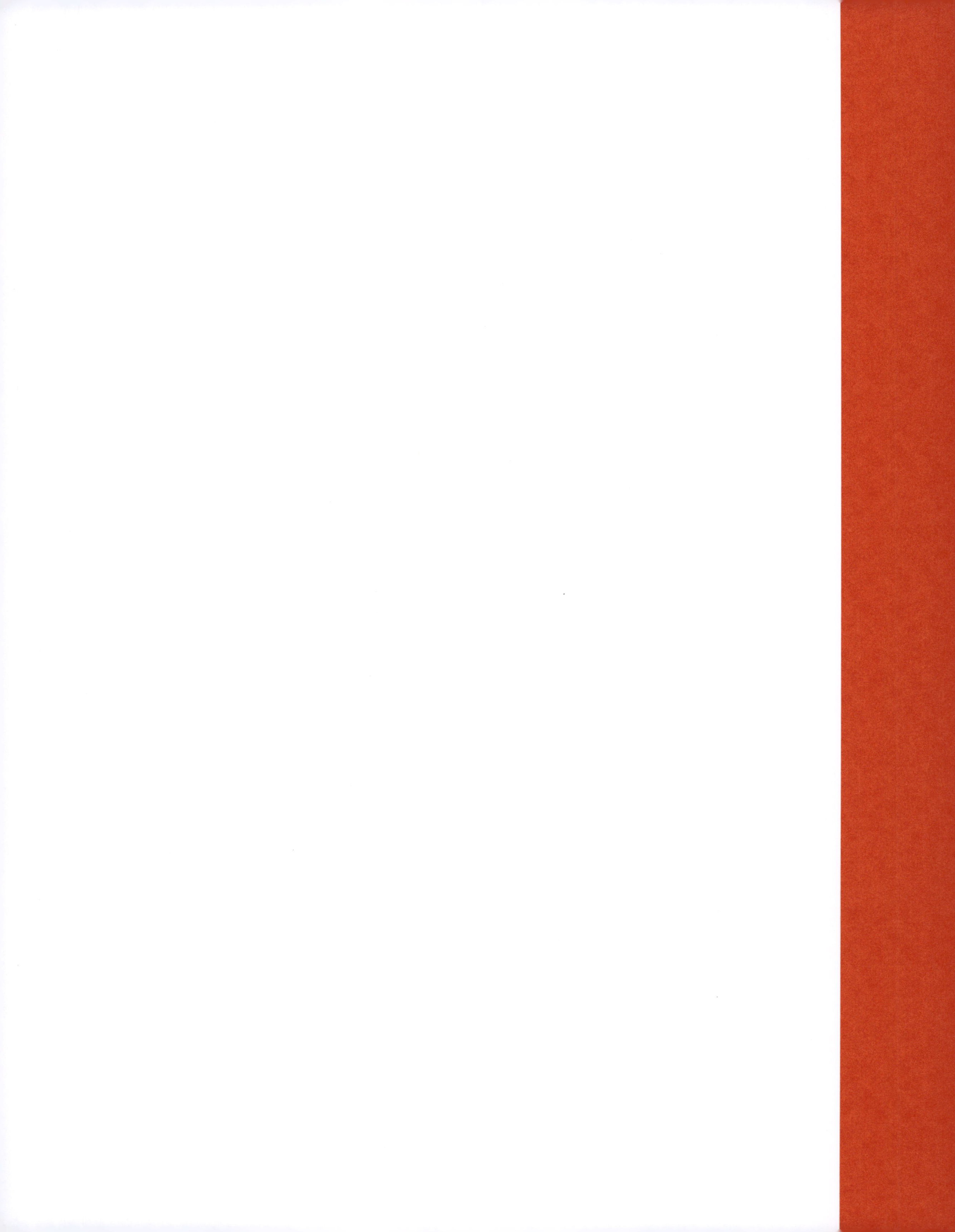

Night mind
Louise Bourgeois's dream recordings

Selected by Philip Larratt-Smith

In a 1998 interview with American art critic Donald Kuspit, Louise Bourgeois drew a fine distinction between the dream and the spell:

> I have never mentioned the word *dream* in discussing my art, while [the surrealists] talked about the dream all the time. I don't dream. You might say I work under a spell, I truly value the spell. [...] The spell and the dream are not the same. The spell is more friendly than the dream. The 'spell' is acted out on a physical level; it's not a passive state, like a dream. The dream blinds you; the spell does not. It is a friendly process.[1]

Bourgeois consistently maintained that her work had nothing in common with the surrealists, whose depiction of dream imagery, she felt, was narrative and illustrative. Instead, her emphasis was laid squarely on the physical dimension, in keeping with her belief in the primacy of the body – its distempers and dysfunctions – as the instrument by which unconscious disturbances manifested themselves. The dreamer's 'passive state' is contrasted with the active process of the artist working under a 'friendly' spell. Bourgeois sought the resistance of the material rather than the talking cure; formal invention rather than literary content. With its cathartic function, the working out in sculpture of her repressed wishes, fears and fantasies is equivalent to the psychoanalytic goal of making the unconscious conscious.

Perhaps more than any other artist of the twentieth century, Bourgeois produced a body of work that consistently and profoundly engaged with psychoanalytic theory and practice. In 1951, following the death of her father, the artist entered analysis, first briefly with Dr Leonard Cammer (1913–79) in late 1951, and then with Dr Henry Lowenfeld (1900–85), whom she seems to have seen intensely from 1952 to 1966 and then in an off-again, on-again fashion from 1966 until his death. At the same time, she became widely read in psychoanalytic literature, including Sigmund Freud, Marie Bonaparte, Melanie Klein, Anna Freud, Karen Horney, Otto Rank, Carl Jung, Wilhelm Stekel, Françoise Dolto, Jacques Lacan, Ernst Kris, Susanne Langer, Jacob Moreno and Bruno Bettelheim, among others. Bourgeois's encounter with psychoanalysis transformed her art-making, to the point where it is difficult to say where one activity ends and the other begins.

Late in Bourgeois's life, a cache of writings came to light in her Chelsea home. Consisting of process notes, dream recordings, notes on sculptures, and so forth, these documents – most of them handwritten on loose sheets of paper – bear witness to a strong and lasting ambivalence towards psychoanalysis. In one typewritten sheet from 1952, she lashes out at 'analysts' who 'think that they are gods'; later, she contends that their teachings and diagnoses have nothing to offer the artist, whose condition, she believes, is tragic and incurable.[2] (Her critique of the limits of psychoanalysis inevitably calls to mind Freud's admission that 'before the problem of the creative artist, psychoanalysis must, alas, lay down its arms'.) The artist is condemned to a life of repetition, and her entire production is a symbolic reenactment of the originary trauma. Yet, she is also blessed with unusual access to the 'deeper perceptions of the unconscious' and the gift of sublimation.

The dream recordings constitute a subgroup within Bourgeois's psychoanalytic writings, and the years 1952–66, from which the present selection has been culled, is particularly rich. In this period of deep depression and withdrawal, her artistic production slowed and at times seems to have ceased altogether, with the work of analysis taking the place of art-making. (The long time lag between the imagery of her dreams and her subsequent sculptural output testifies perhaps to the timelessness of the unconscious.) Bourgeois's dream life became particularly intense, revealing a psyche in conflict with itself and in search of equilibrium. As she returned to making sculpture, however, the frequency of her dreaming seems to have greatly diminished; by the early 1990s, she could claim that 'it's very strange, but I never dream' and that the 'direct connection with the unconscious comes not through the dream but through real life'; that is, through the encounter with the work or with the Other.[3]

These nine dream recordings were selected specifically for this project with a view to manifesting the continuity between conscious and unconscious, between the night mind that dreams the dream and the day mind that records them. Like Bourgeois's sculpture, the formation of dreams has a logic all its own, operating by means of the psychic mechanisms of condensation and displacement. The discipline of finding words in the morning to pin down the traces and fragments of a lingering dream from the night before sharpened her awareness of these mechanisms, the coded meanings they produced, and the ongoing life of the past within the present. At the same time, it gave Bourgeois insight into the parallel process of symbol formation in her art, which emerged from the eccentric landscape of her 'volcanic unconscious'.[4]

Note to reader: In the following extracts of Bourgeois's writings, italics denote text originally written in French; punctuation and line breaks have been retained as closely as possible. Translations from French to English are by Richard Sieburth and Françoise Gramet. All writings are Collection Louise Bourgeois Archive, The Easton Foundation, New York.

December 3.1951.After sending my notr to Dr.C.lwalk back home from the 23d street post office.Lfeel exausted butwell lenjoy breathing the coldair deeply and am proud to be "healthy " l walk slowly and carefully and lobserve the traffic and the faces of people .l notice that no one pays the least attention to me and l feel at ease and content.

when l get homelavoid R. go to the back and put away things inthe kitchen after eating my diner aligator pear,Leek soup and apple sauce that is still hot.As l go to the front lam suddenly aware of a kind of peur.lt ls a common thing in France(in my youth).

Les enfants ont peur, il ne faut pas avoir peur,Pierre a peur ,Paul n'a pas peur .Turemne avait peur mais il a dit." Carcasse,tu tremble mais tu tremblerais bien davantage si tu savais ouèje vais te mener. Turenne a vaincu sa peur.C'est un fait historique ,That kind of fear makes you put your head under the covers,makes you run or shiver or walk very loud from the station to the house,lt is accepted,mentionned. most of the time,it is vaincue.lused to be very peureuse but my fathr "taught"me.During the summer we had diner in the garden and the dark would come before we were through.We talked without seeing each other Then one day he said "l am going to teach you and your brother not to be afraid;you go to the house and bring me some thing l do not remember what.Challenged lbraced myself and started throuh the blackness the sky could not even be seen because the trees met over the lane.

THat fear has come back,l cannot go on.l cannot read what l have written. My back hurt and so does the back of my legs as if l had walked 10 miles.am going to bed at least Robert is there.

December 3 7 PM.Veryvery tired day besause of the dream.

That dream about my mother was a horror l am anxious to pin it down where can it come from andwhat can it mean,

ldremt that l was going to find something ina dream that the fight was going to be terrific and that Robert had (atany cost)to get the meaning.there is a secret and l cannot get at it.l want to reach it. L amout to pry lt The angoisse is great because lknow that lwill not succeed.Robert who haes constantly let me down (see previous day) Robert is the only person of which l have the help because the revelation is to come during the night through the dream.l am prepared facing Robert who is asleep when the dreamcomes lam going to poundn on lis chest with my fists and cry :ther it is écatch it . every thing is set.the angoisse is horrible.and it comes:it is my mother l call come come and lpound on Robert she is going away.and he does not wake up.Then in asurhuman effort knowing that he fails to answe l call her and try to reach her again,and suddenly l reach a climax and satisfaction in a long kiss .lam surprised to see that l wanted it.and she leaves in my mouth an object like an almond.which was in her mouth. l take it out inmy fingers and think that is strange,l notice that it does not move.l notice also that it is ah hard enoug to resiste the pressure of evenmy thumb nail."it is harder than soap l think that marble is harder.Then lwant to put it away for examination ."may be it is not the truth but it may be a form of truth, you know so little ,you have to try evrything you can to learn how to read aroud youAt a level above mother and the almond.L amworried about R. not hearing and answering the signal.Lam going to loose my truth .now that l hold it ,lam going to lose it .Lpoud again onhis chess howling :maman. maman.this time againl am exausted when l force myself to hear .my own voice wakes me up .Robert actually hears hears it and answers.From then on l talk without control but aloud.

3 DECEMBER 1951

December 3. 1951. After sending my note to Dr. C.[1] I walk back home from
the 23d street post office. I feel exhausted but well I enjoy breathing
the cold air deeply and am proud to be "healthy" I walk slowly and
carefully and I observe the traffic and the faces of people. I notice
that no one pays the least attention to me and I feel at ease and
content.
when I get home I avoid R.[2] go to the back and put away things in the
kitchen after eating my dinner alligator pear, Leek soup and apple sauce
that is still hot. As I go to the front I am suddenly aware of a kind
of *fear*. It is a common thing in France (in my youth).
*Children are afraid, should not be afraid, Pierre is afraid, Paul
is not afraid. Turenne was afraid but he said. "Carcasse, you're trembling now
but you'd be trembling far more if you knew where I am leading you.
Turenne has overcome his fear.*[3] *It is a historical fact,* That kind of fear
makes you put your head under the covers, makes you run or shiver or
walk very loud from the station to the house, it is accepted, mentioned.
most of the time, it is *defeated.* I used to be very *fearful* but my father
"taught" me. During the summer we had dinner in the garden and the dark
would come before we were through. We talked without seeing each other
Then one day he said "I am going to teach you and your brother not
to be afraid; you go to the house and bring me some thing I do not re
member what." Challenged I braced myself and started through the blackness
the sky could not even be seen because the trees met over the lane.

That fear has come back, I cannot go on. I cannot read what I have written.
My back hurt[s] and so does the back of my legs as if I had walked 10
miles. am going to bed at least Robert is there.

December ~~3~~4 7 PM. Very very tired day because of the dream.
That dream about my mother was a horror I am anxious to pin it down
where can it come from and what can it mean,
I dreamt that I was going to find something in a dream that the fight
was going to be terrific and that Robert had (at any cost) to get the
meaning. there is a secret and I cannot get at it. I want to reach it.
I am out to pry it The *anxiety* is great because I know that I will not
succeed. Robert who has constantly let me down (see previous day)
Robert is the only person of which I have the help because the reve
lation is to come during the night through the dream. I am prepared
facing Robert who is asleep when the dream comes I am going to pound
on his chest with my fists and cry : there it is catch it. every
thing is set. the *anxiety* is horrible. and it comes: it is my mother
I call come come and I pound on Robert she is going away. and he does
not wake up. Then in a surhuman effort knowing that he fails to answer
I call her and try to reach her again, and suddenly I reach a climax
and satisfaction in a long kiss. I am surprised to see that I wanted
it. and she leaves in my mouth an object like an almond. which was in
her mouth. I take it out in my fingers and think that is strange, I
notice that it does not move. I notice also that it is hard enough
to resist the pressure of even my thumb nail. "it is harder than soap
I think that marble is harder. Then I want to put it away for exami
nation." maybe it is not the truth but it may be a form of truth,
you know so little, you have to try everything you can to learn how
to read around you At a level above mother and the almond. I am worried
about R. not hearing and answering the signal. I am going to lose my
truth. now that I hold it, I am going to lose it. I pound again on his

chest howling: *maman. maman.* this time again I am exhausted when I force myself to hear. my own voice wakes me up. Robert actually hears it and answers. From then on I talk without control but aloud.

Loose sheet of writing (LB-0454)

1 Dr Leonard Cammer (1913–79), a psychiatrist specialising in depression. Louise Bourgeois saw Cammer nine times in late 1951 before switching to Dr Henry Lowenfeld in 1952.

2 'R' is shorthand for Bourgeois's husband Robert Goldwater (1907–73), an American art historian and museum director.

3 Henri de La Tour d'Auvergne, Viscount of Turenne (1611–75), one of the most successful generals of King Louis XIV. Bourgeois was fond of quoting this line attributed to Turenne, in which he addresses his horse Carcasse before his final battle in 1675.

29 SEPTEMBER 1955

the young husband is asleep
then wife gives him a push and
she says; wake up, you look
dead. I do not want to be accused –
the husband says all right, he
gets up, gets dressed, and goes to his
desk to write a letter.

he talks like a bottle of glue –

she talks with a hatchet –

when he talks it smells of semen –

when she talks or cleans it is a killing
process—

3 15.AM. olives, radishes with salt +
butter
I would like to eat some anchovies for something salty

Previous box - coffin terror came at the
last, menstrual upset, around 3 weeks ago
to be exact around 7 of september
packing + sending of crates, *congest
ion of statues and trunks for
the ship* – I don't care about the
weight the emphasis is on the size
anger at J.L.[1]
instead of being an agent of
death, sometimes I think of a box as a[n]
agent of refuge withdrawal + peace –
but of course sometimes children die
in the womb or are asphyxiated in
a hiding place (Paulson[2] during the
war)

Loose sheet of writing (LB-0126)

1 Bourgeois's son Jean-Louis (1940–2022).
2 Herbert 'Paul' Paulson, a friend of Bourgeois's. Paulson's recollection of a London bomb shelter being 'blown to bits' during the Second World War made a strong impression on Bourgeois, and she mentions it in several writings.

4 APRIL 1956

Glowing *cochineal* light of
the room from the red silk
shade of lamp –
A very tidy + pulled down
night gown, pulled all the way
to my heels, the door is
behind me, and some voices (2)
come in –

apartment at 174[1] [...]
– not very cosy or warm
but unafraid, awake and comfortable.

The man takes my two ankles
in his hands (enormous) and
fondles me from heel to head
I am lying on my stomach
strong response until I fear his
two hands at my neck to strangle
me. terror wakes me

Notebook excerpt, page 1 (LB-0495)

1 Bourgeois's father had a tapestry gallery at 174 Boulevard Saint-Germain, Paris, and kept a small apartment in the back. In 1938 he allowed Bourgeois to cordon off part of the front space and open a small gallery of her own, where she sold rare books and prints.

18 APRIL 1958

The dream of the pregnant Rabbit –

In the hay I find a rabbit lying
on her side, somebody younger than me
maybe Alain[1] *accompanies me I tell him*
another sick animal just like Champ
fleurette[2] *it is better not let yourself be taken*
it is always more care and sometimes these
animals just die on you
next to her half hidden in the hay
the rabbit has made small bundles that she tries
in vain to hide. Alain
opens one and says = but it's a small one so
I say: ah hold its hind legs
we are going to help her deliver the others – He
says no I do not like that this disgusts me.
I say to myself: OK do not insist –
she delivers by herself I do not look
Alain says. OK she's empty now
thank god, anyway the last one is dead
before being born I say to myself it is just as well it
will be less complicated – anxiety
following day – same night *erotic dreams*

where Jeacques[3] *& Robt are rivals the latter is*
definitely *more* successful –
upon waking up recall of terror, *constant and dull*
of the fear of being impregnated by B. *in the years*
of the twenties *after Henriette's wedding 1927.*[4] *Need*
to leave the house. Fear of getting closer to
look at him
The fear of verdigris dated from several years
before, epoch Suzanne Lamoine[5] *in the*
beautiful and clean room small copper bed, red
ceramic tiles, golden yellow rug, velvet curtains, the
sunlight seeping through in the afternoon. around 1926.
with Sadie[6] *Statue with Kiss salon d'automne*
The guilt *of* Oedipus *came from Him not from* society
It is the guilt toward the mother that torments me. I think
that I do not want to have Catherine Havens[7] *here*
because she hated her mother – the proof is
that she does not want children.
Anxiety today is obnubulating I try
to be indulgent (a good mother to Michel and
to Jean-Louis.[8] *I also try to clean*
(please the mother, appease her)
cleaning all day in the evening blunders ok. I
monitor anger hatred of the day after that
I cannot explain to myself. Tenacious insomnia. when
I manage to fall back to sleep in the large bed I
dream of the street intense sun traffic workers
accident a man (sickly) is "electrocuted" and
remains sitting + twisted in his body and in his face for
everybody to see – I go back + forth a dozen of
young men, Cannes, unaware of any danger

but not happy just busy *The men are*
gorgeous but I do not look at them. Suddenly
Jeacques Jean a nail in the hand tries to
drive it in the top of my cranium. Very
swift I duck *and say to myself "it is a* frame up"
they want my hide. next time they will get me = *awakening*

Loose sheet of writing (LB-0487)

1 Bourgeois's youngest son Alain (b1941).
2 Champfleurette was the Bourgeois–Goldwater family cat.
3 Bourgeois's cousin Jacques, who lived with the Bourgeois family after his father, Désiré, was killed in the First World War. Bourgeois harboured a long-lasting crush on Jacques, who became a successful architect.
4 Bourgeois's older sister Henriette (1904–80), who married Georges Bonnotte in 1927.
5 Suzanne Lamoine worked in the Bourgeois family atelier.
6 In 1922, Sadie Gordon Richmond was hired as the Bourgeois children's English tutor. She lived on and off with the family for almost ten years, during which time she and Bourgeois's father, Louis, had an affair.
7 A friend of the Bourgeois–Goldwater family.
8 Michel (1936–90), a French orphan, was Bourgeois's adopted son. Jean-Louis (1940–2022) was her oldest biological son.

10 OCTOBER 1958

Atrocious Dream
travel in Switzerland and by train +
car[1] – a suite of women including
Sadie with a fox fur from head to knee
[...]
a tan fox around her neck[2] *sends me*
into a rage and I reproach my father for having
made me unfit for married or profes
sional Life – he is shocked at my
mentioning sex and I realize that he
is unconscious of the harm he has done –
I feel sorry for him and ashamed of my
accusation
I turn to suicide in my need for being loved
at least that way I would make him
care – Champfleurette disguised as a little
very little yellow fox comes in, she is
dying – he says, *Poor little animal it's too*
bad – I think that maybe, I could obtain
as much sympathy as it does if I died
2 very bad day[s] after this.
irritation painful + *exciting at*
the same time leads to the realization
of a desire to urinate standing up. The Penis
envy so very difficult to realize is
present. *Proof –*

What is Penis envy
How does one prove it

---

after First Monday – terror of being abandoned
I am a bad deal   Nobody care[s] – Reassured
then
Second *Monday* – I am being jipped
[...]
Third *Monday* – No violence – I am
being jipped *Dream where* Sadie + my father
do jip me   it is a fact, *Sadie's*
jealousy appears faintly; immediately followed
by suicide. *because I cannot do anything* complete
impotence (*the word impotence is followed by the*
castration terror)
If he does not know a good thing when he
sees one, then I cannot help and I do not
care (I feel a little stronger

Loose sheet of writing (LB-0449)

1 The Bourgeois family visited Interlaken, Switzerland, in 1929.
2 Bourgeois's father once bought her a fur coat, which she refused to wear.

15 JANUARY 1959

Before falling asleep I read Sartre 10PM
The Wall and The Room[1]
I cannot fall asleep I lie
awake until 2 hours 30. then *take*
an aspirin. I dream of a family
scene where life is calm The
mother is very tall corseted formidable
but nothing unpleasant ever
occurred –
All of a sudden a person (servant
type) asks do you know what
a symbol is – it is something that
pretends to be something else.
You know this woman that you call your
mother – she really is "Death" her
body is like a wicker basket
underneath her dress – I am atrociously
flabbergasted to have lived so long
without knowing and Thank God without
being in conflict with her – I am so
frightened in retrospect *the entire next*
day that I rush through
all the errands that Robt has asked me
to run pay all the checks I am
afraid to be at fault – I am
also sad and a little disillusioned. [...]

Loose sheet of writing (LB-0257)

1 Jean-Paul Sartre (1905–80), existentialist philosopher, novelist and dramatist. 'The wall' and 'The room' were first published in the short story collection *The wall* (1939).

c1961

what he did for his son harvard[1]
what he did to his son. Pierre.[2]
cannot forgive the bad father how am I
supposed to grow up well with such a
father /vs with such a father I am sure
to go on safely – nobody could fail under
such advice and supervision – to own a
good father enables you to forgive the
bad one – If my father is good I do
not have to fear him or defend
myself against him – Could I maybe
begin to relax and fall asleep –
It depresses me to meet a father figure who
collects curiosas – obviously a person like
this presents a certain danger – If so
you must be on the defensive – To be on
the defensive makes you afraid
Relief of anxiety is achieve[d] through
activity
When activity is seen as negative
(relief of) instead of positive to an end or
a return there is outburst of resentment
at being gipped
[...]

going back to bed *at* 6AM – dream –
a huge standing up man in the
middle of a room is carrying in
his left hand a naked 15 inches
long baby girl – between the
palm and thumb of his hand
considering it – From an observer
I *identify* suddenly with the new
born + *realize* the possible danger of *inex*
pert or neglectful hands – wake in terror
do not go to L[3] – a toy in fathers hands

Loose sheet of writing (LB-0236)

1 Bourgeois's son Jean-Louis attended Harvard University at this time. Her husband, Robert Goldwater, earned his master's degree there.
2 Pierre Bourgeois (1913–60), Bourgeois's younger brother. Pierre was diagnosed with schizophrenia in 1945 and died in a mental institution in Villejuif, Paris, in 1960.
3 'L' is Bourgeois's shorthand for psychoanalyst Dr Henry Lowenfeld (1900–85), with whom Bourgeois was in analysis from 1952 until 1985.

c1964

floating mattress from
ad (wonderful feeling
of *comfort*)
Robt + I are in bed
we are floating on the
floating mattress – I
smile to myself and
touch him to see if he
does float – Turning my
head to look at him, I
discover that he does
float lightly but does

not talk or move –
then I suddenly discover
that he is dead –
Instead of calling for
help I think that
I am going to get a
good look at it
I *dive* under water
and am surprised, very
surprised, almost
shock[ed] to realize that
he is not straight,

that is to say horiz
ontal like a floating
boat but hanging
down from the
shoulder and upper
torso. very specially
his arms are hanging
down – film
of a murder
the corpse is dumped
in the water but
comes back to the
surface in that posi

tion, probably because
of the air in the lungs –
There is no fear of
being accused.
fear appear[s] <u>after</u>
the dream
he went dead
on me
because I don't excite him
any more

Loose sheet of writing (LB-0479)

c1964

I have this little baby *like a*
bath doll.
I am very proud of it it is godsend
Yvonne[1] *is jealous. people appreciate me*
a whole army is here with the king and
queen reviewing the troops.
Here I am breastfeeding the child
and people look at me
waiting and the orchestra even
stops playing –
the child has grown, he needs to be changed
he urinates in a blanket and
it makes me hysterical *I run around*
I panic I want to stop him but
he urinates anyway, I am scared
I press his body – I do not know
where to put him I am afraid of strangling him
I have to entrust him to someone
else – I cannot be trusted
do you know what happen[s] then
he shoots straight out of my
hands and disappears towards
the wall down the baseboards

I am flabbergasted but gone he is and he
certainly could get a revenge for
my treating [him] badly – I had it coming –
through a peep hole I see a rock
and dozens of exquisite *lizards*
pink blue yellow white frolicking
in frantic happiness suddenly
(feeling my eyes on them) they disa
pear in a split second – then the
mother['s] rear end reveal[s] itself
moving it is a piece of an enormous
monstrous snake – I am
surprised but that is the way of
things and who am I to have any
comment.

Loose sheet of writing (LB-0442)

1 Yvonne worked for the Bourgeois family.

Day

1
My own voice wakes me up

Self-portrait c1939

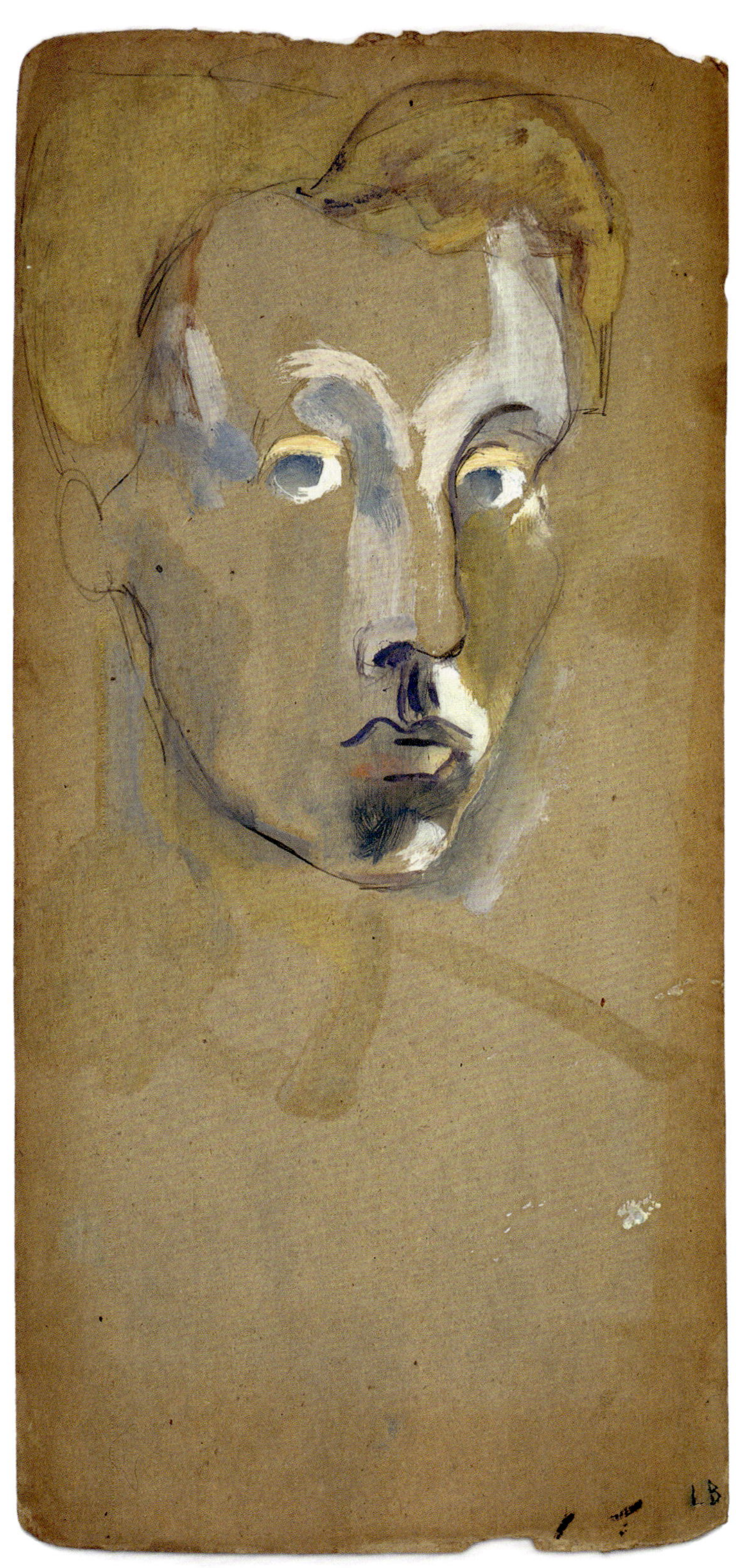

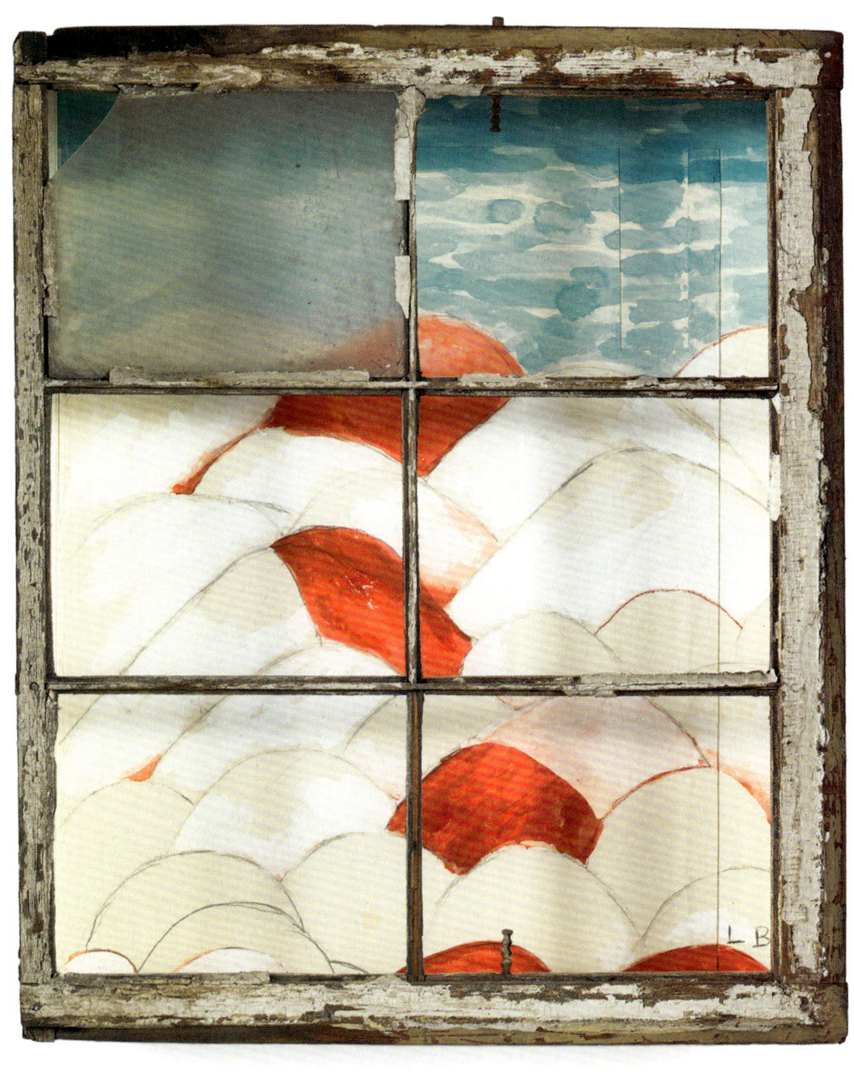

My Blue Sky 1989–2003
Arched Figure 1993, cast 2010

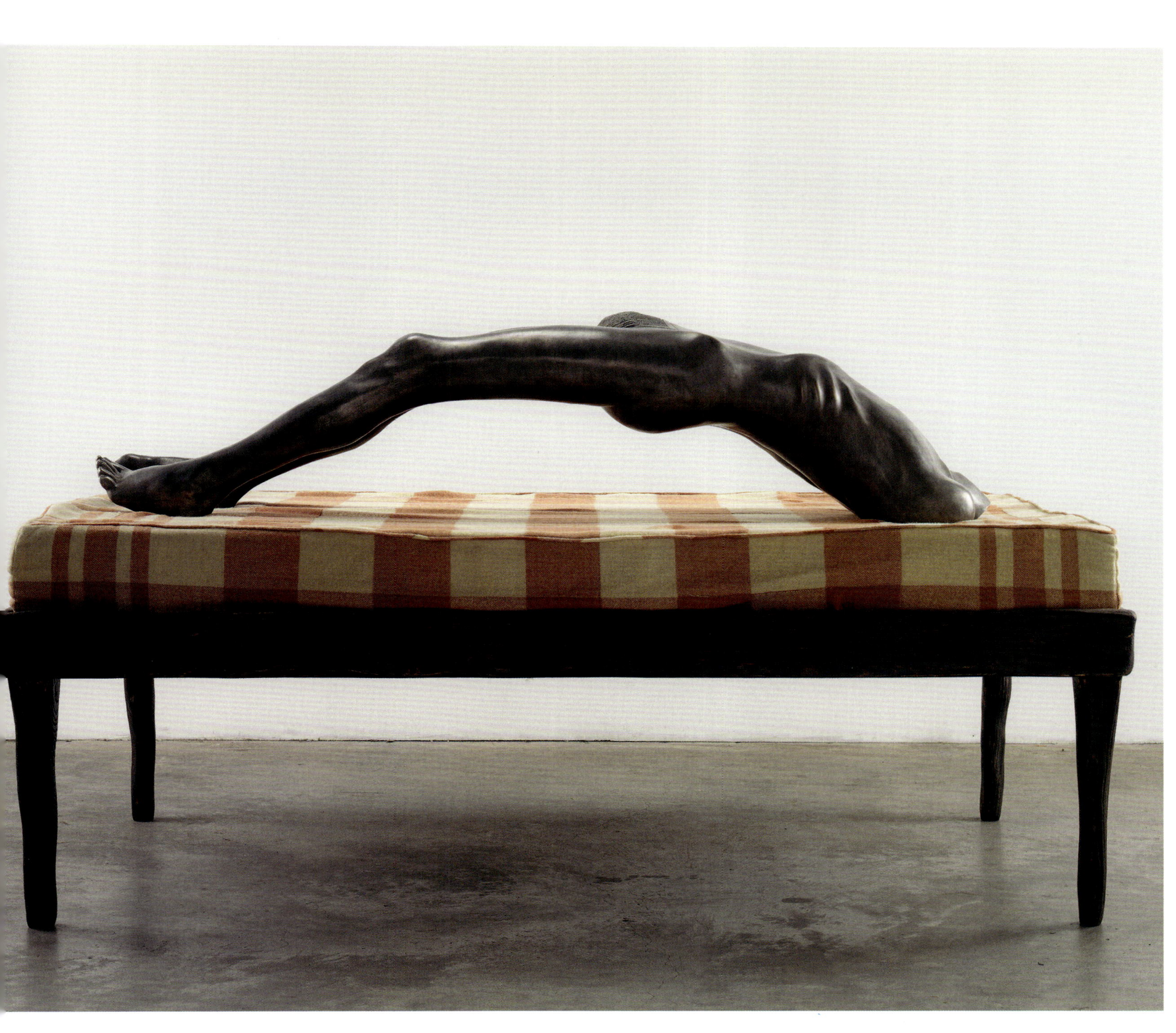

2
One and others

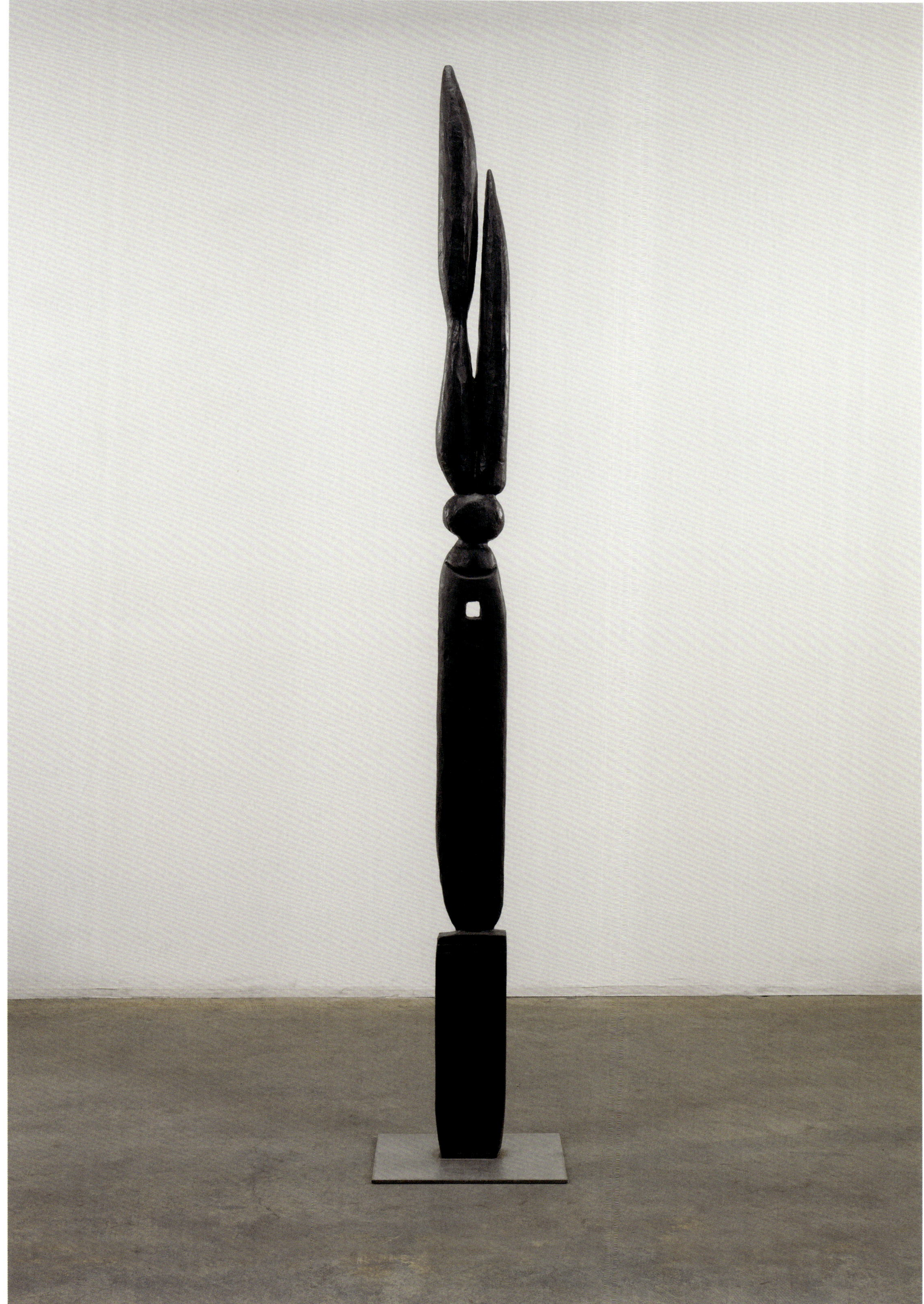

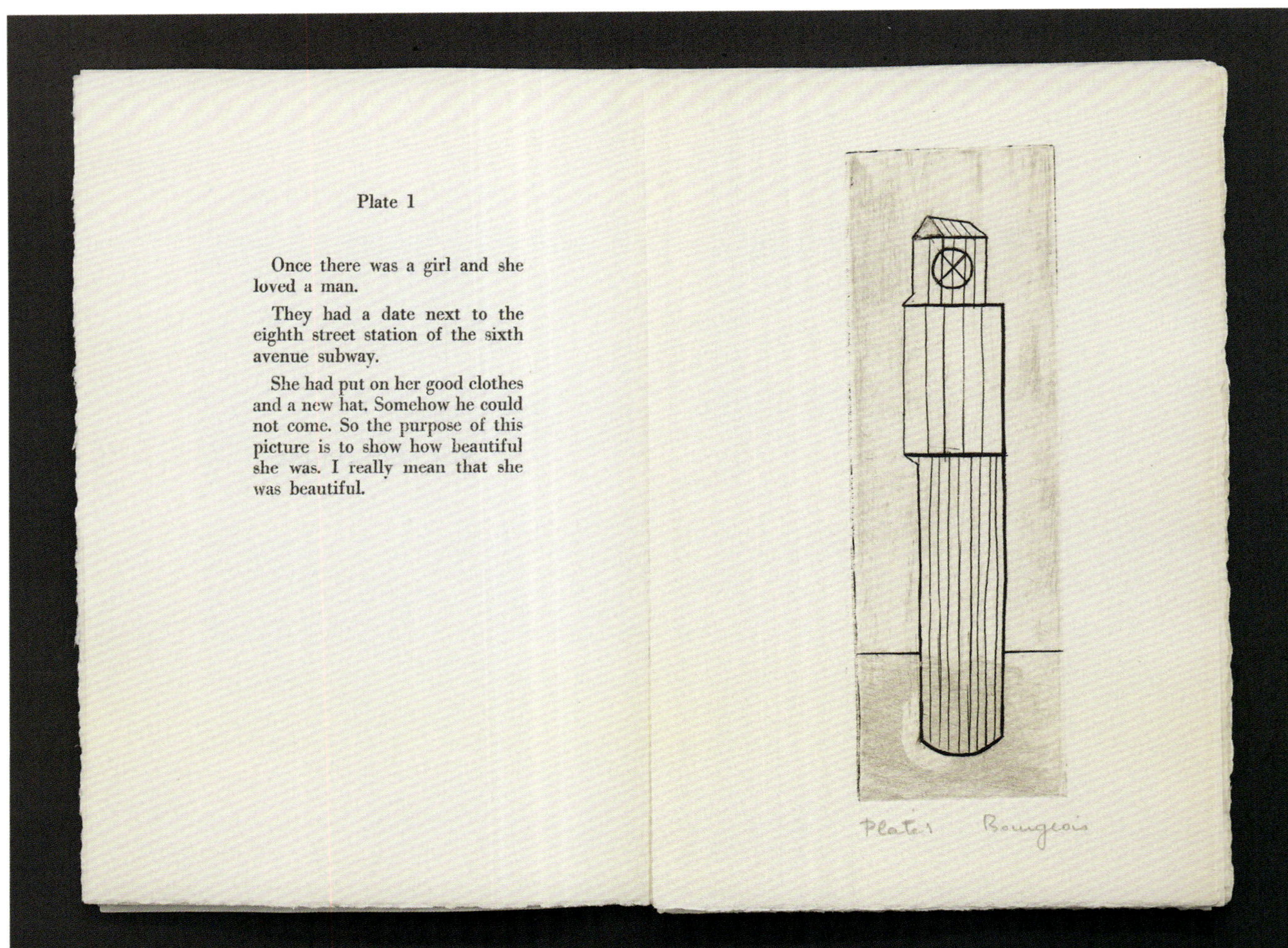

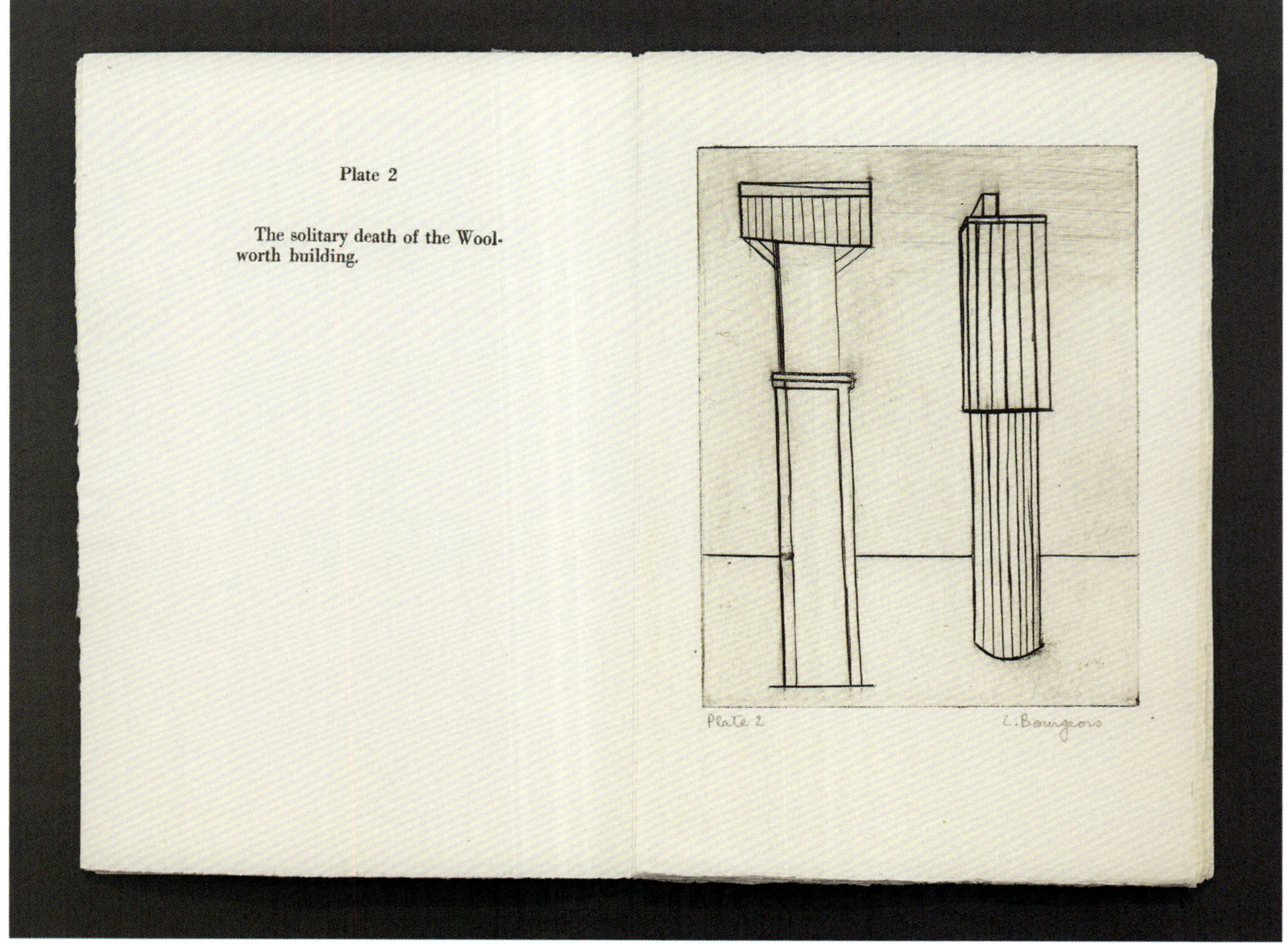

this spread and following pages:
He Disappeared into Complete Silence 1947

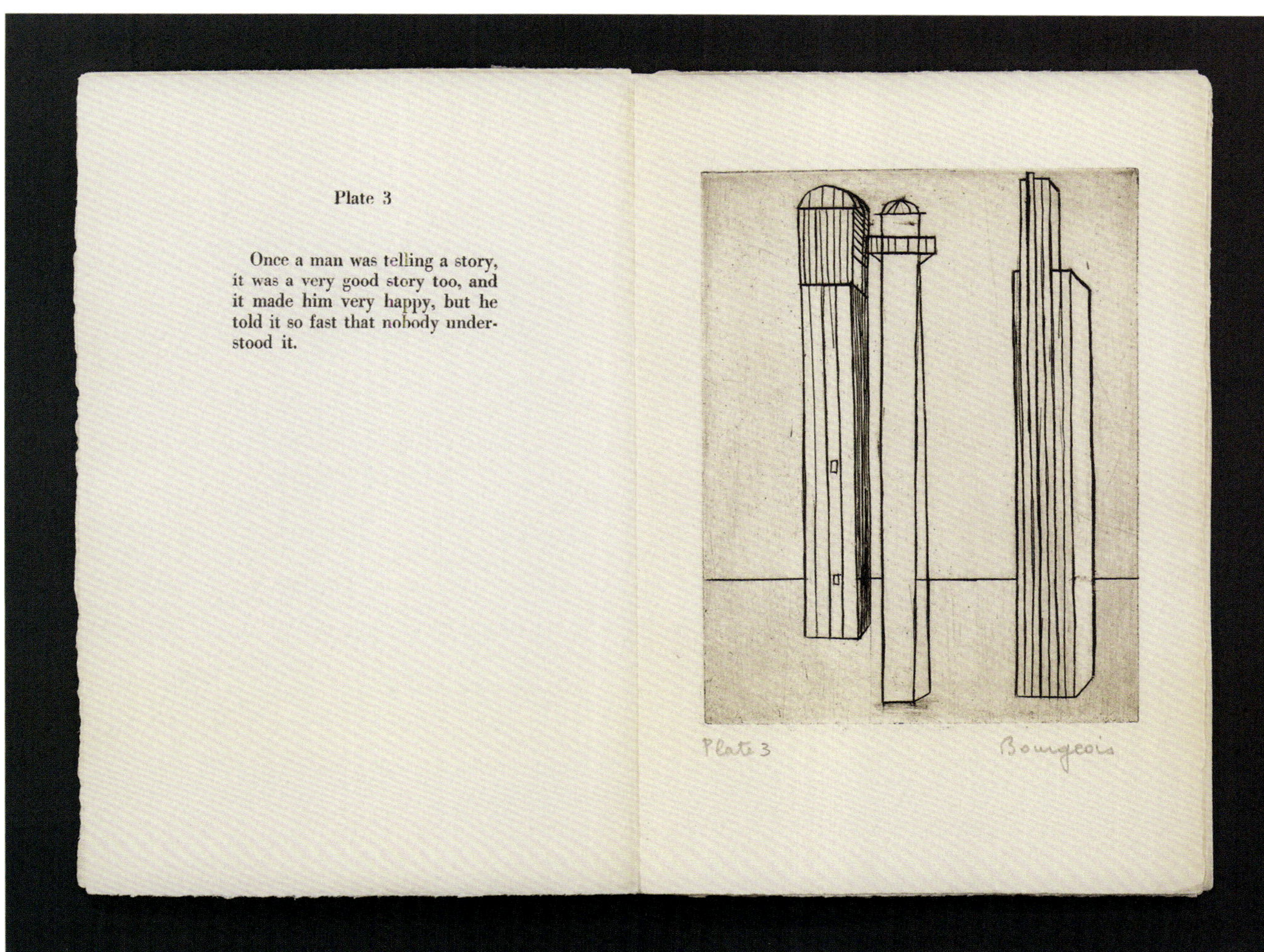
Plate 3

Once a man was telling a story, it was a very good story too, and it made him very happy, but he told it so fast that nobody understood it.

Plate 3
Bourgeois

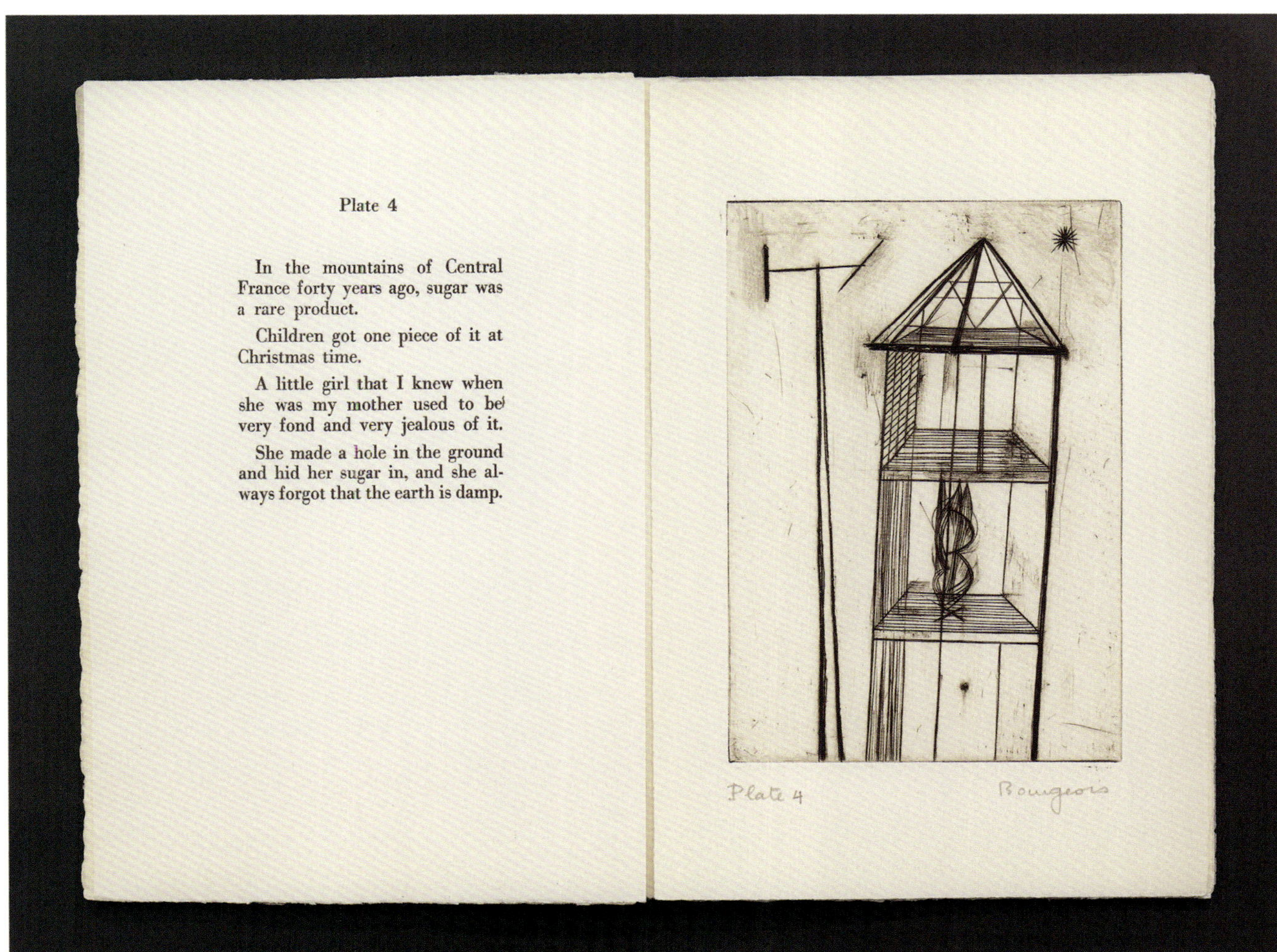
Plate 4

In the mountains of Central France forty years ago, sugar was a rare product.

Children got one piece of it at Christmas time.

A little girl that I knew when she was my mother used to be very fond and very jealous of it.

She made a hole in the ground and hid her sugar in, and she always forgot that the earth is damp.

Plate 4
Bourgeois

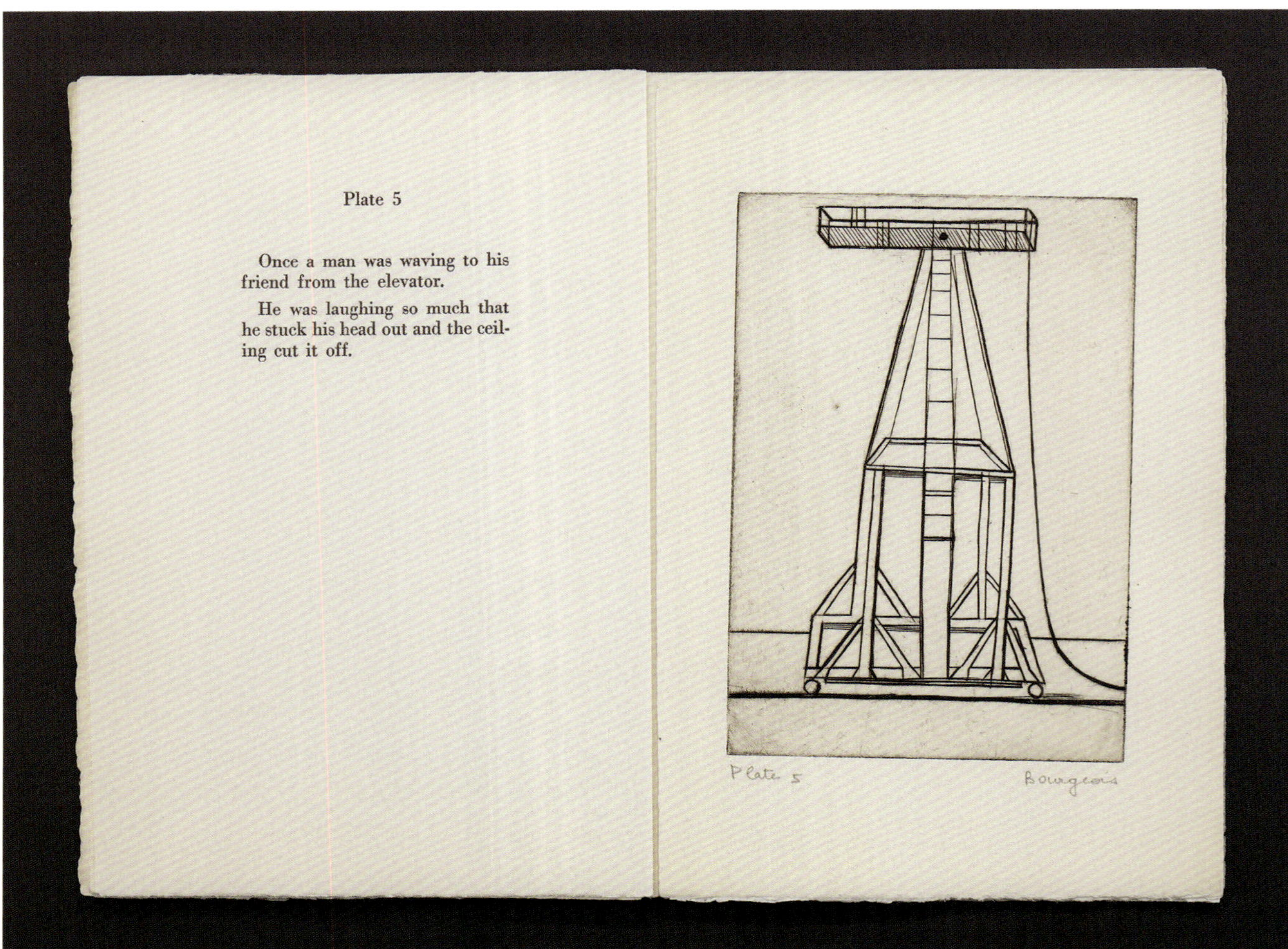

Plate 5

Once a man was waving to his friend from the elevator.

He was laughing so much that he stuck his head out and the ceiling cut it off.

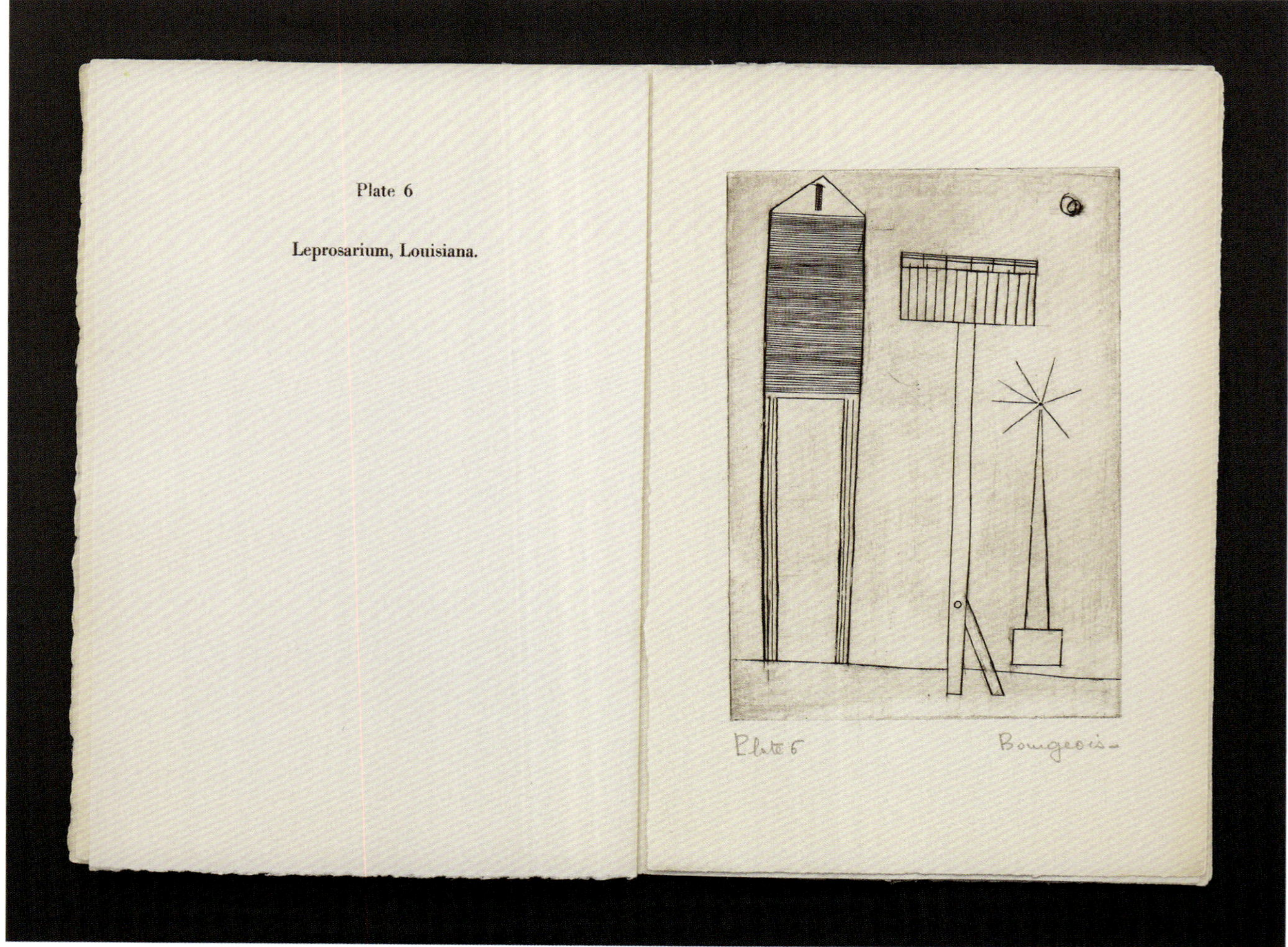

Plate 6

Leprosarium, Louisiana.

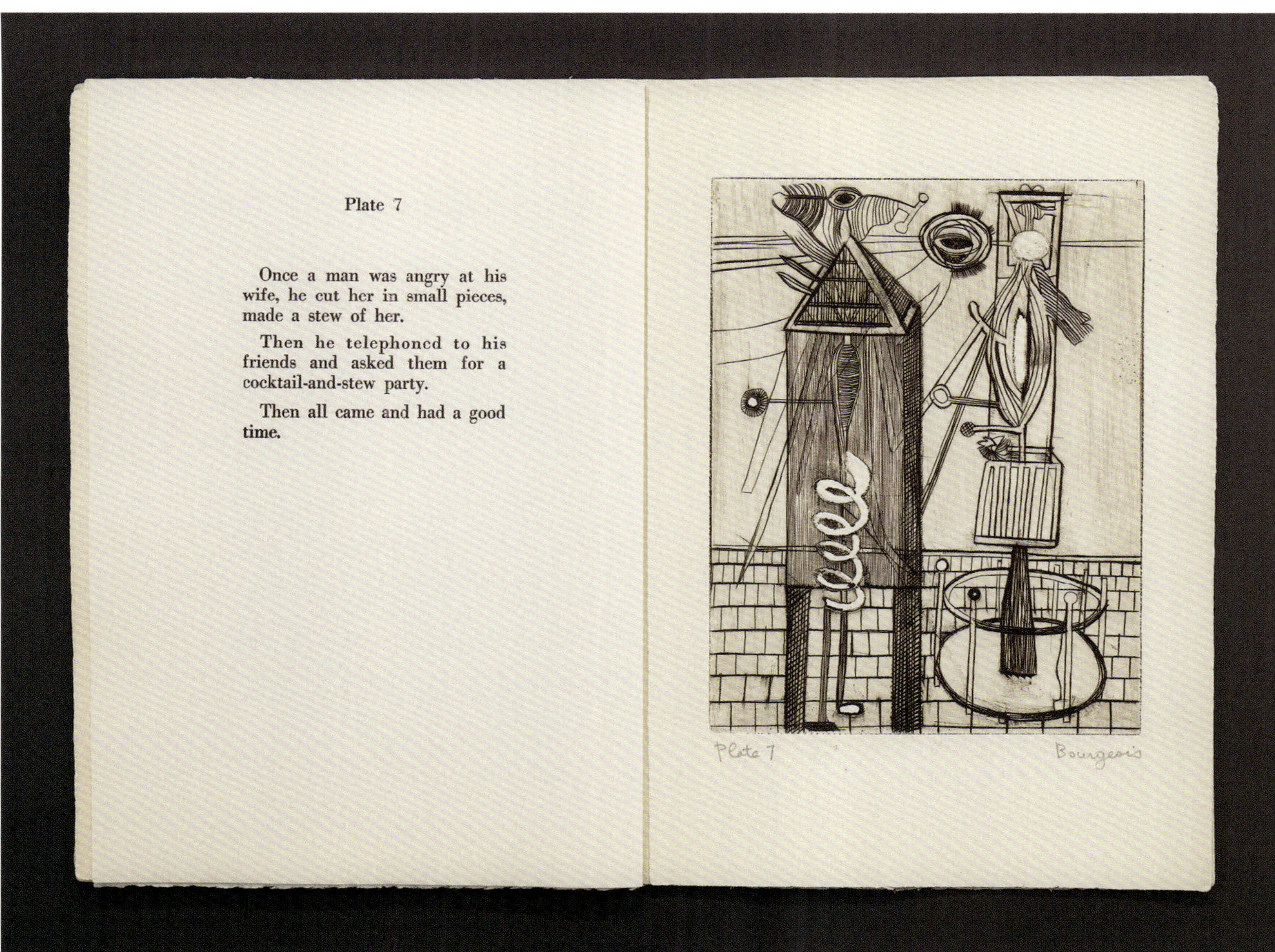

Plate 7

Once a man was angry at his wife, he cut her in small pieces, made a stew of her.

Then he telephoned to his friends and asked them for a cocktail-and-stew party.

Then all came and had a good time.

Plate 7 Bourgeois

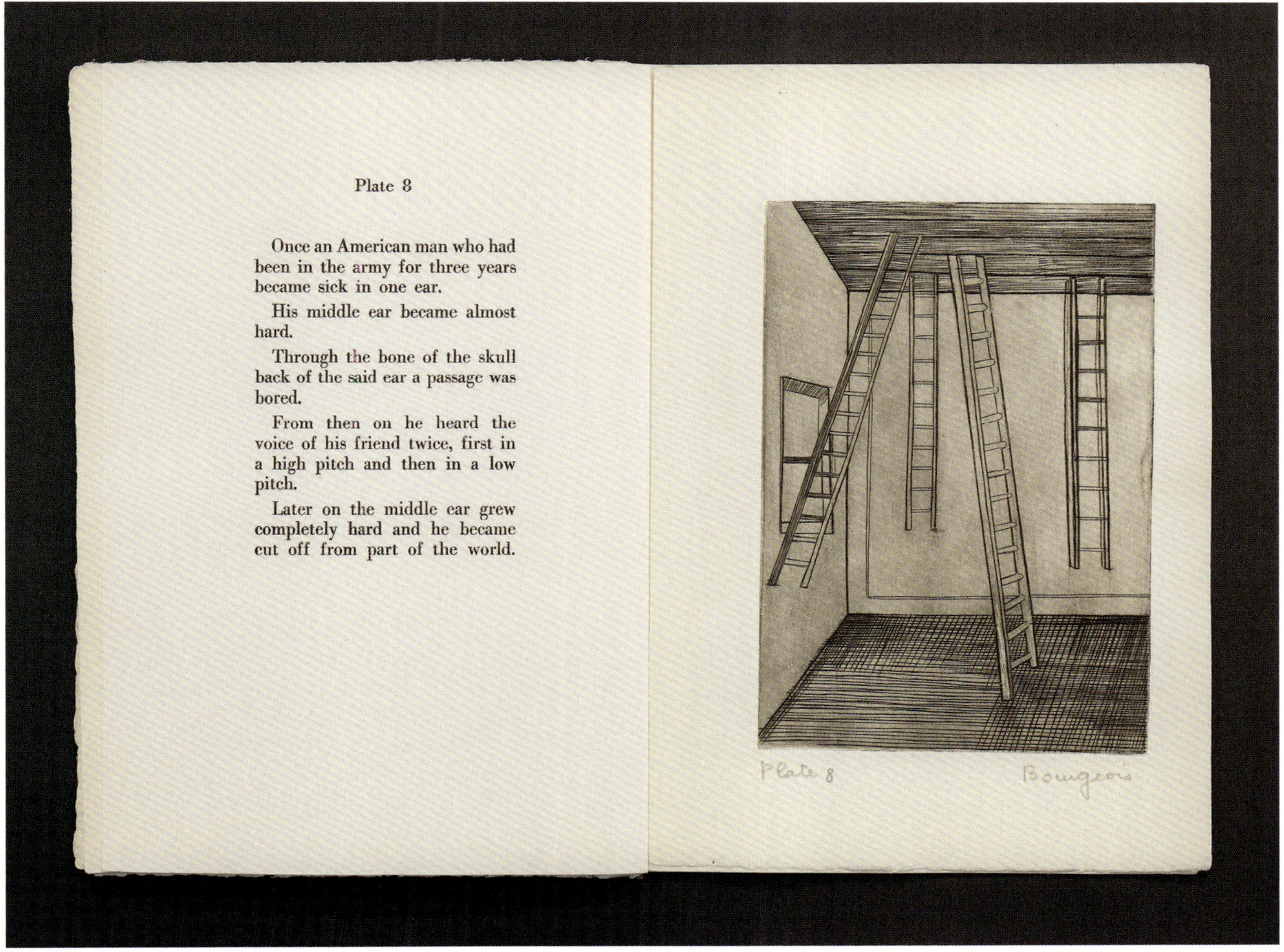

Plate 8

Once an American man who had been in the army for three years became sick in one ear.

His middle ear became almost hard.

Through the bone of the skull back of the said ear a passage was bored.

From then on he heard the voice of his friend twice, first in a high pitch and then in a low pitch.

Later on the middle ear grew completely hard and he became cut off from part of the world.

Plate 8 Bourgeois

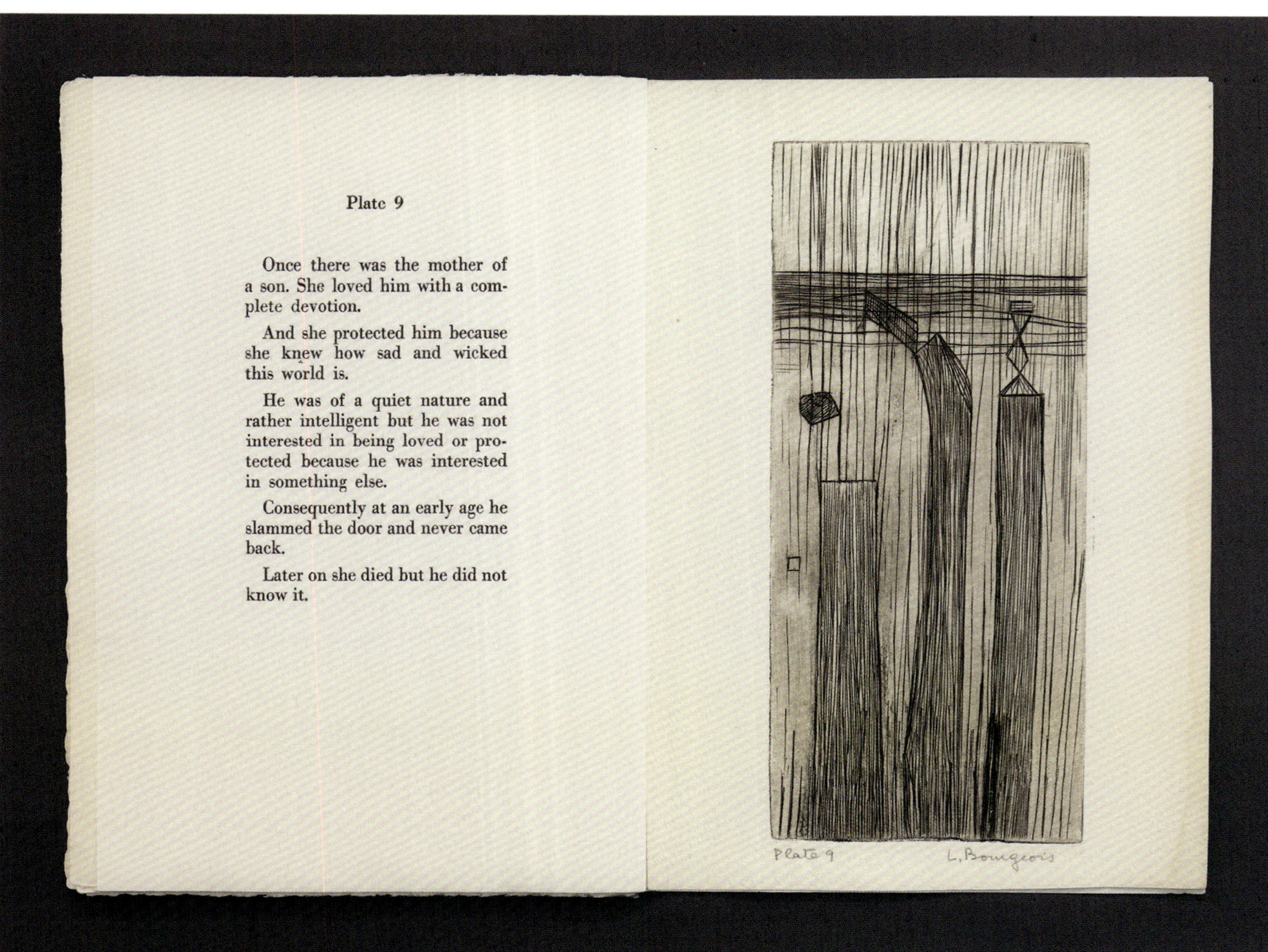
Plate 9

Once there was the mother of a son. She loved him with a complete devotion.

And she protected him because she knew how sad and wicked this world is.

He was of a quiet nature and rather intelligent but he was not interested in being loved or protected because he was interested in something else.

Consequently at an early age he slammed the door and never came back.

Later on she died but he did not know it.

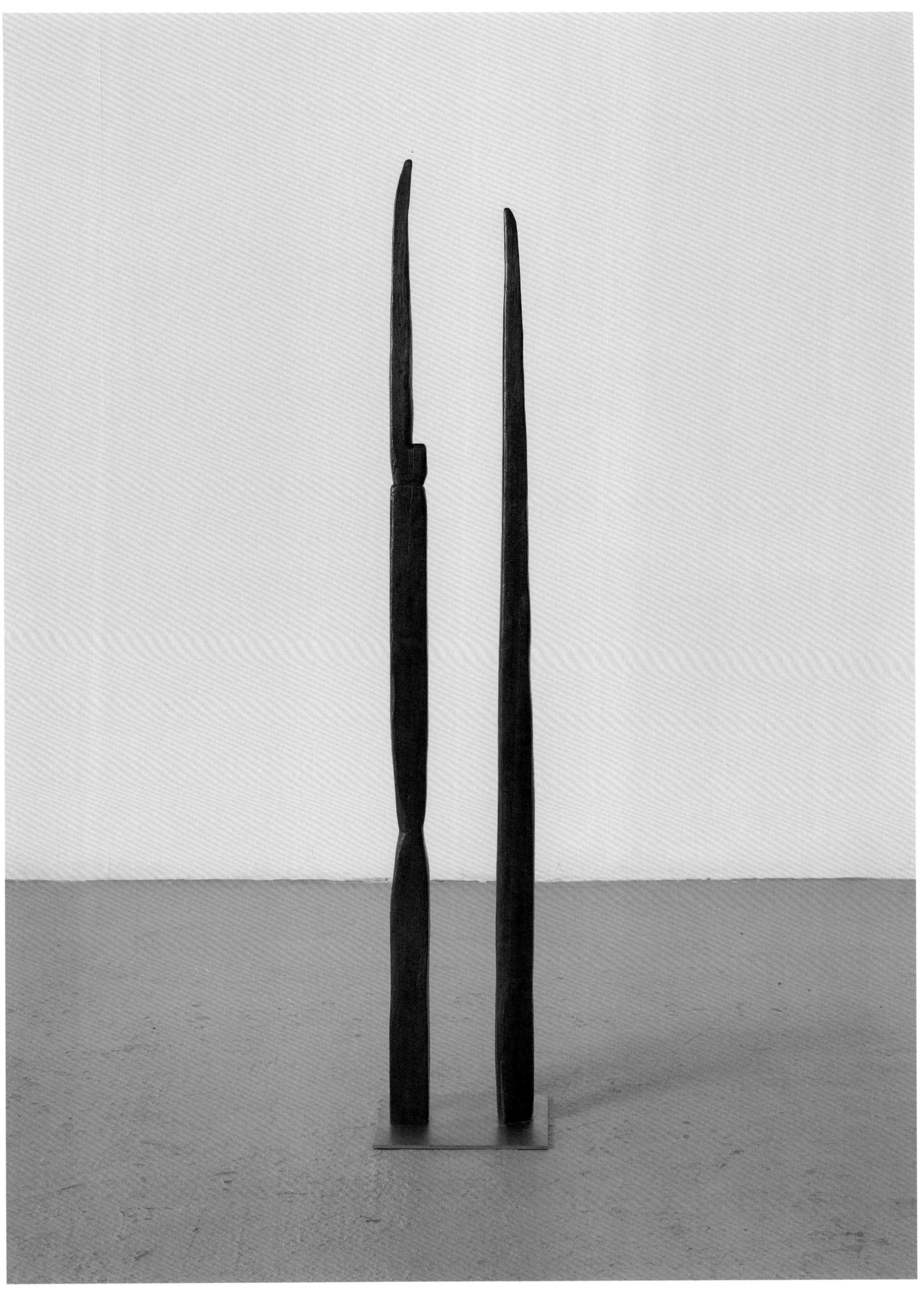

89 *Knife Couple* 1949

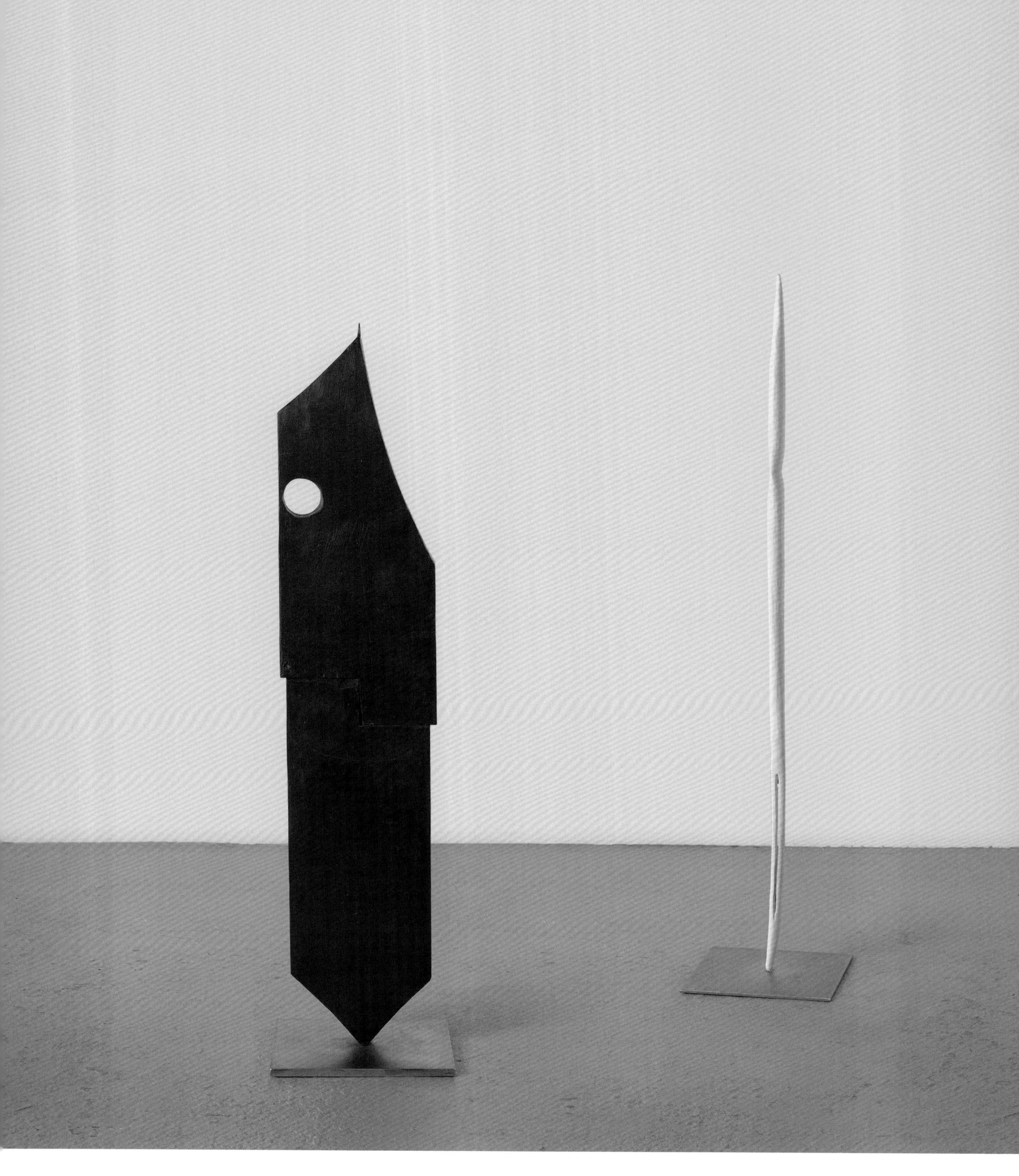

Quarantania III 1949
Needle Woman 1947–49

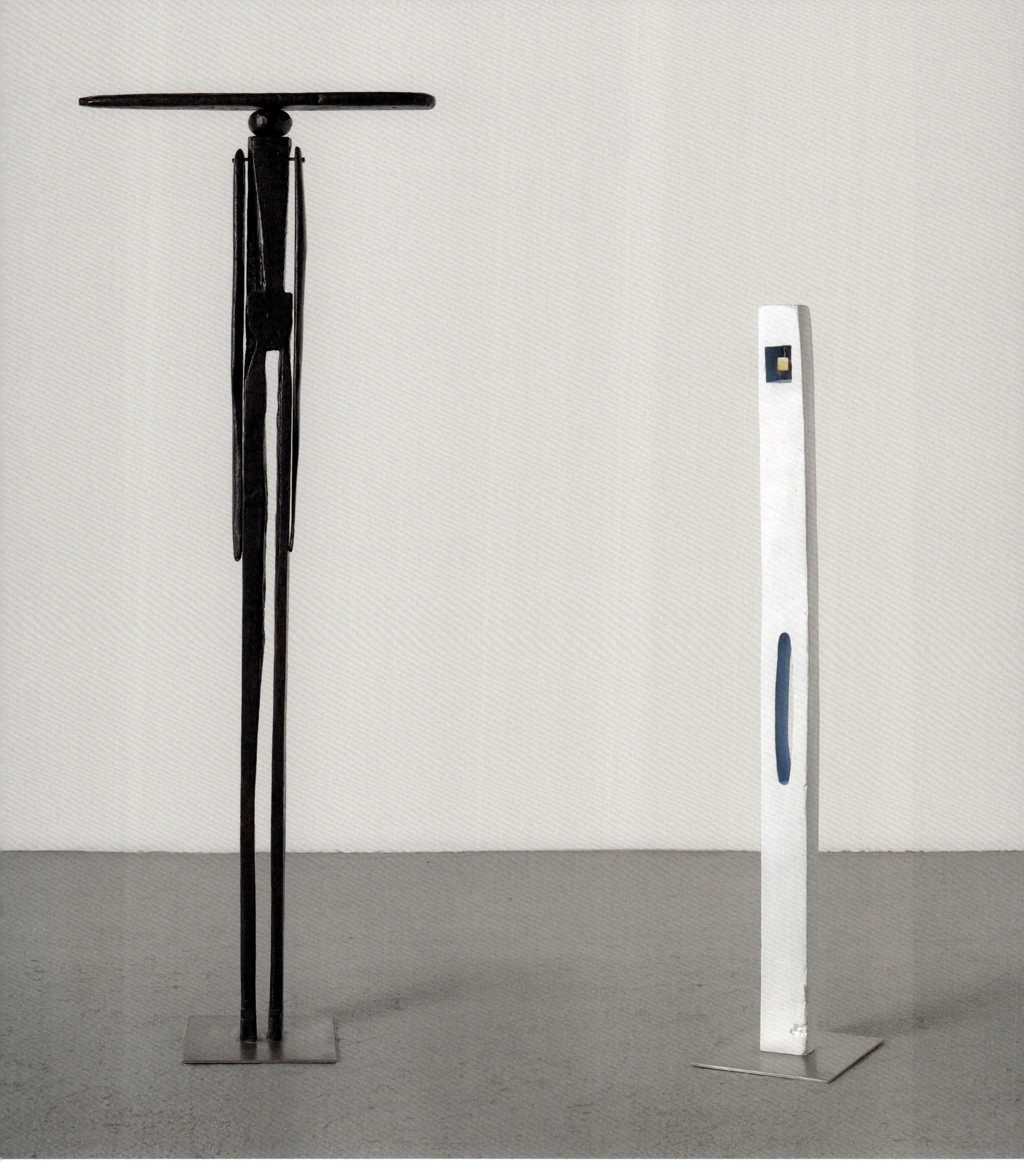

Observer 1947–49
Pillar 1947–49

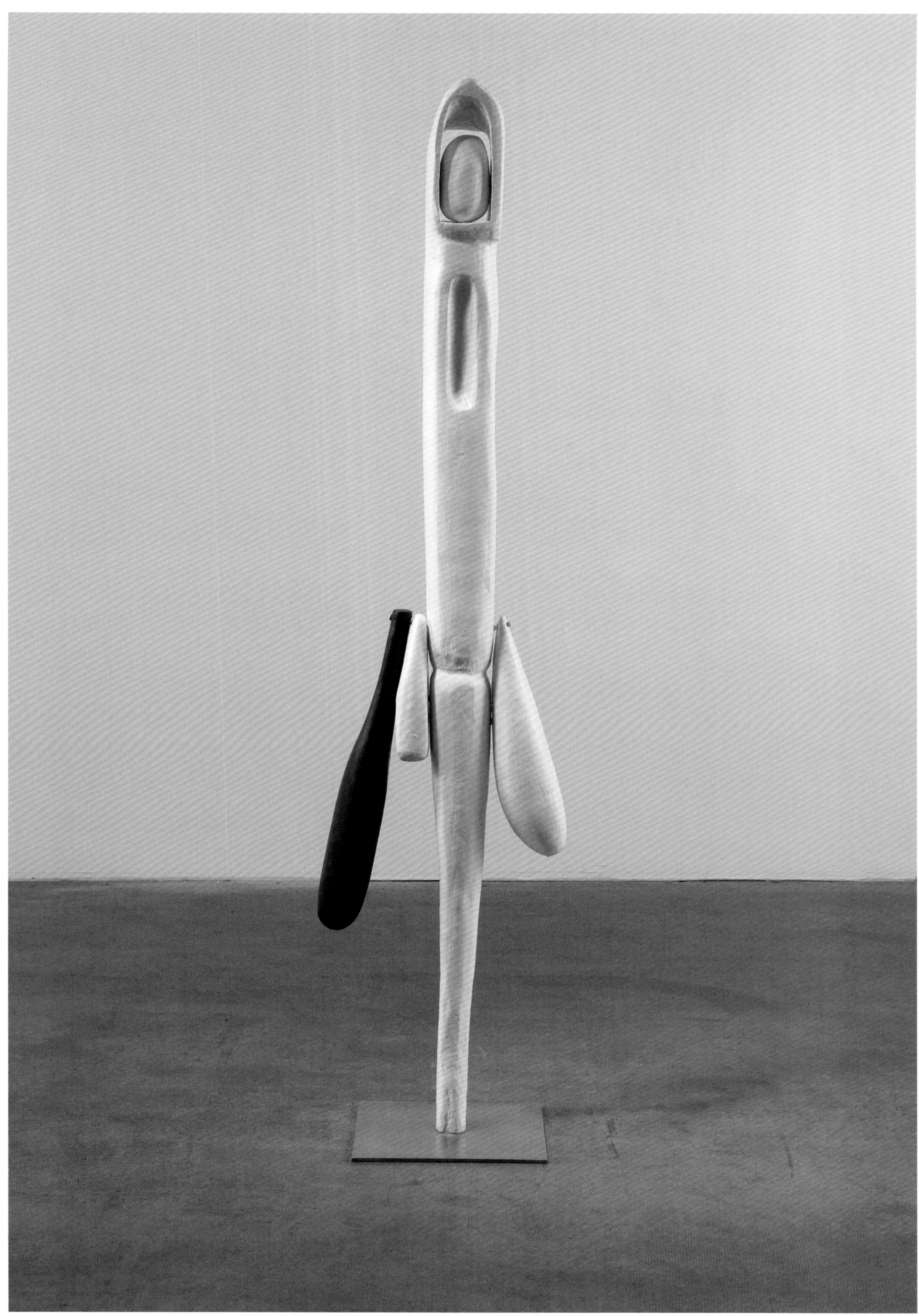

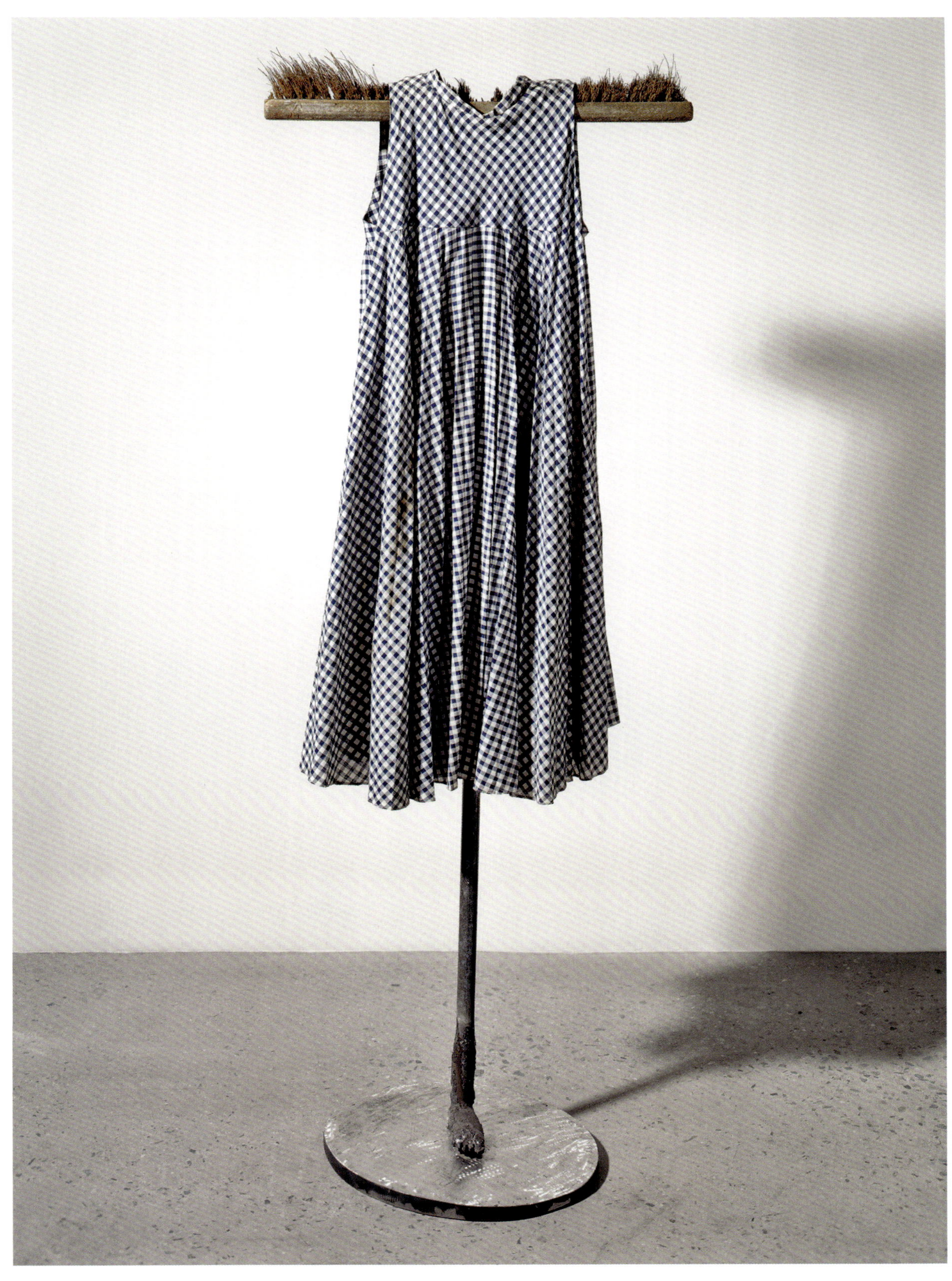

Woman with Packages 1949
Untitled (Broom Woman) 1997

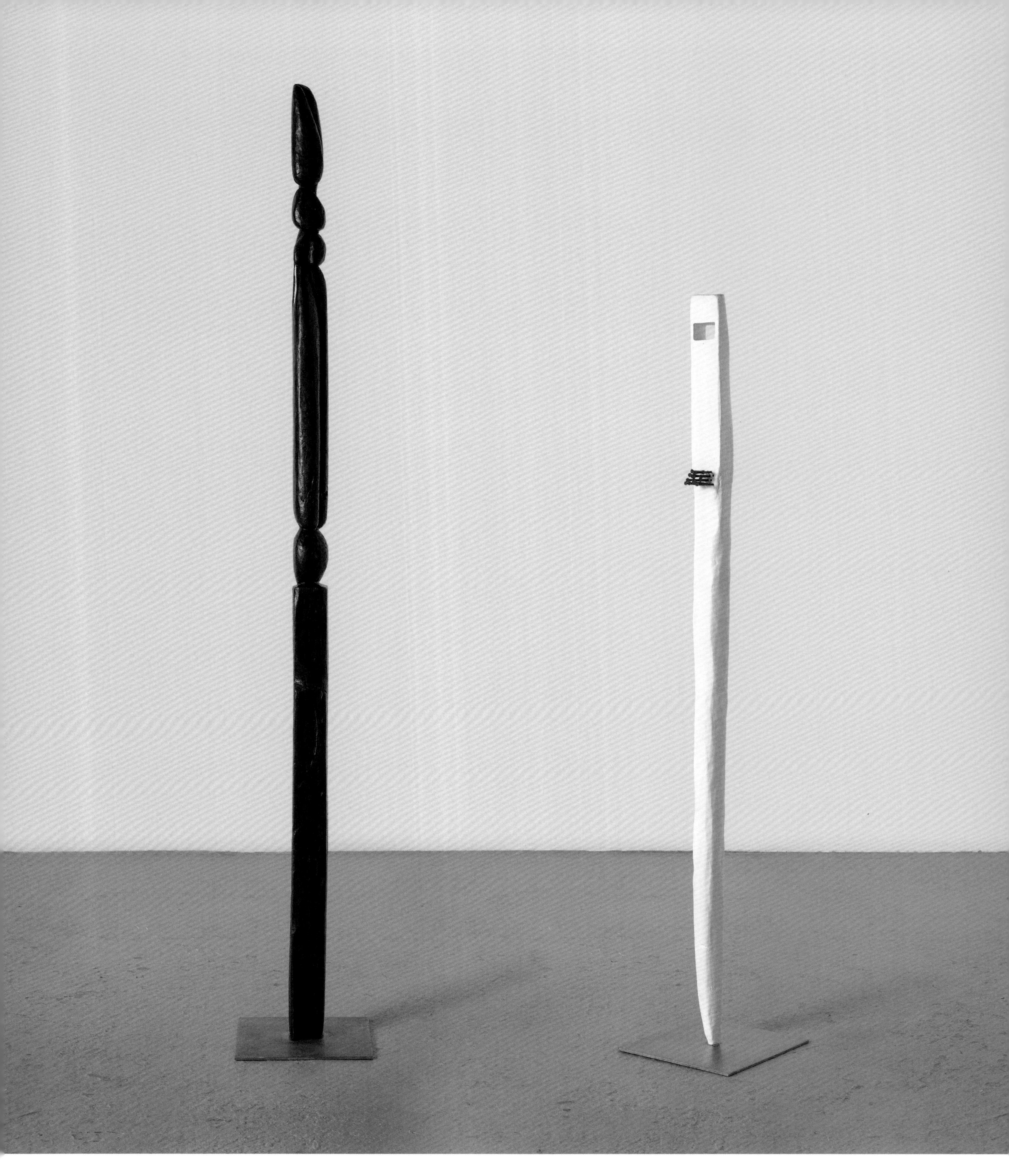

Corner Piece 1947–49
Portrait of C.Y. 1947–49

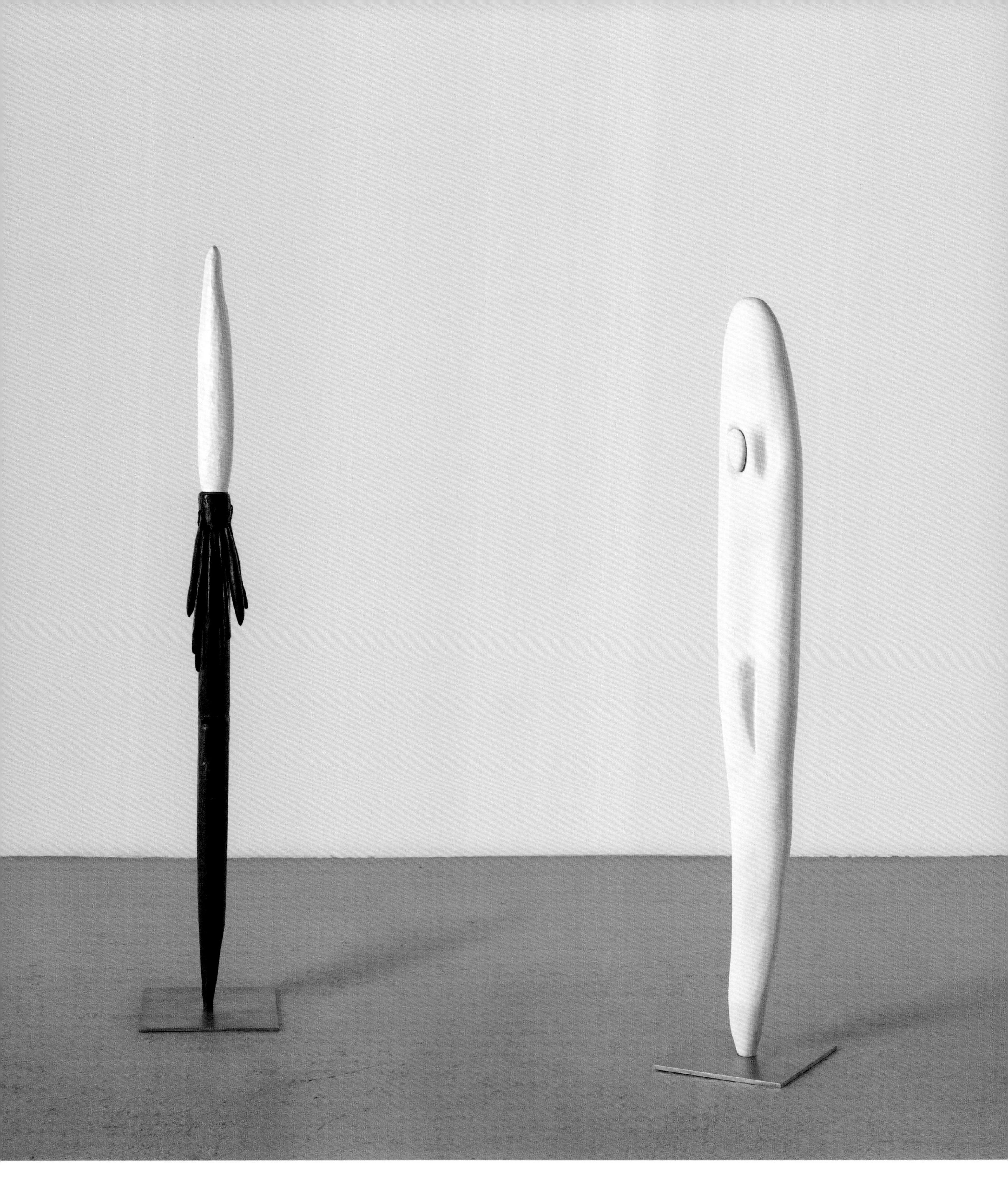

Persistent Antagonism 1946–48
Woman in the Shape of a Shuttle 1947–49

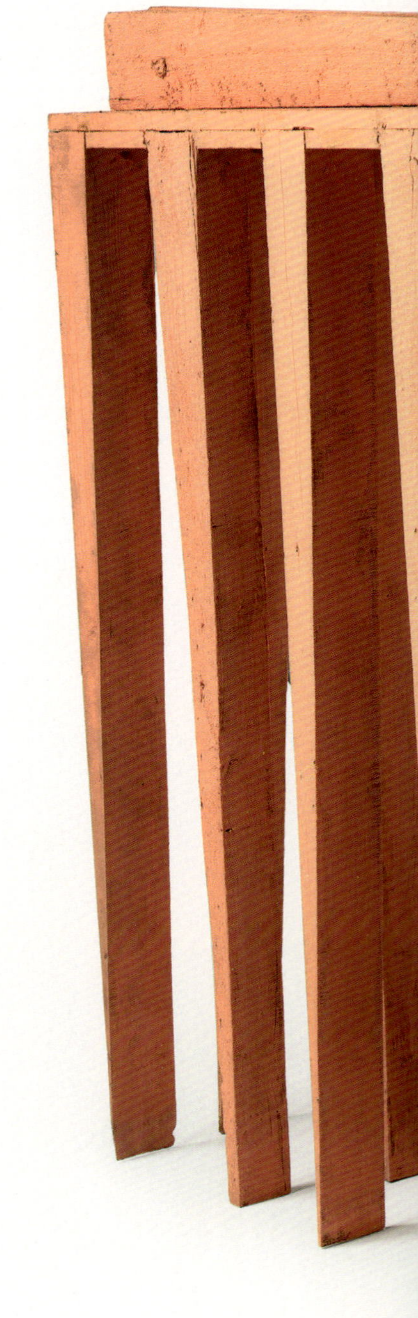

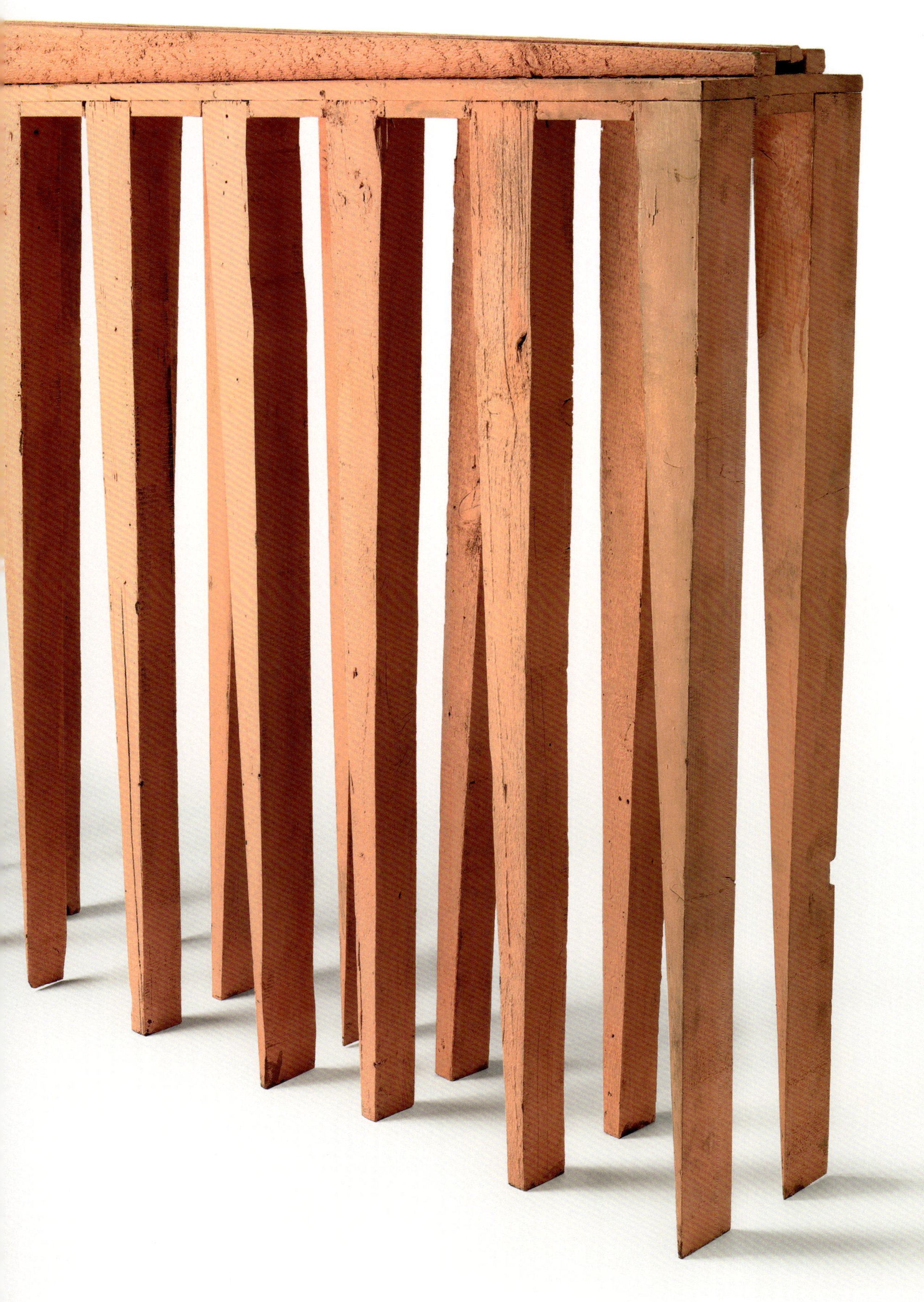

3 Lairs and labyrinths

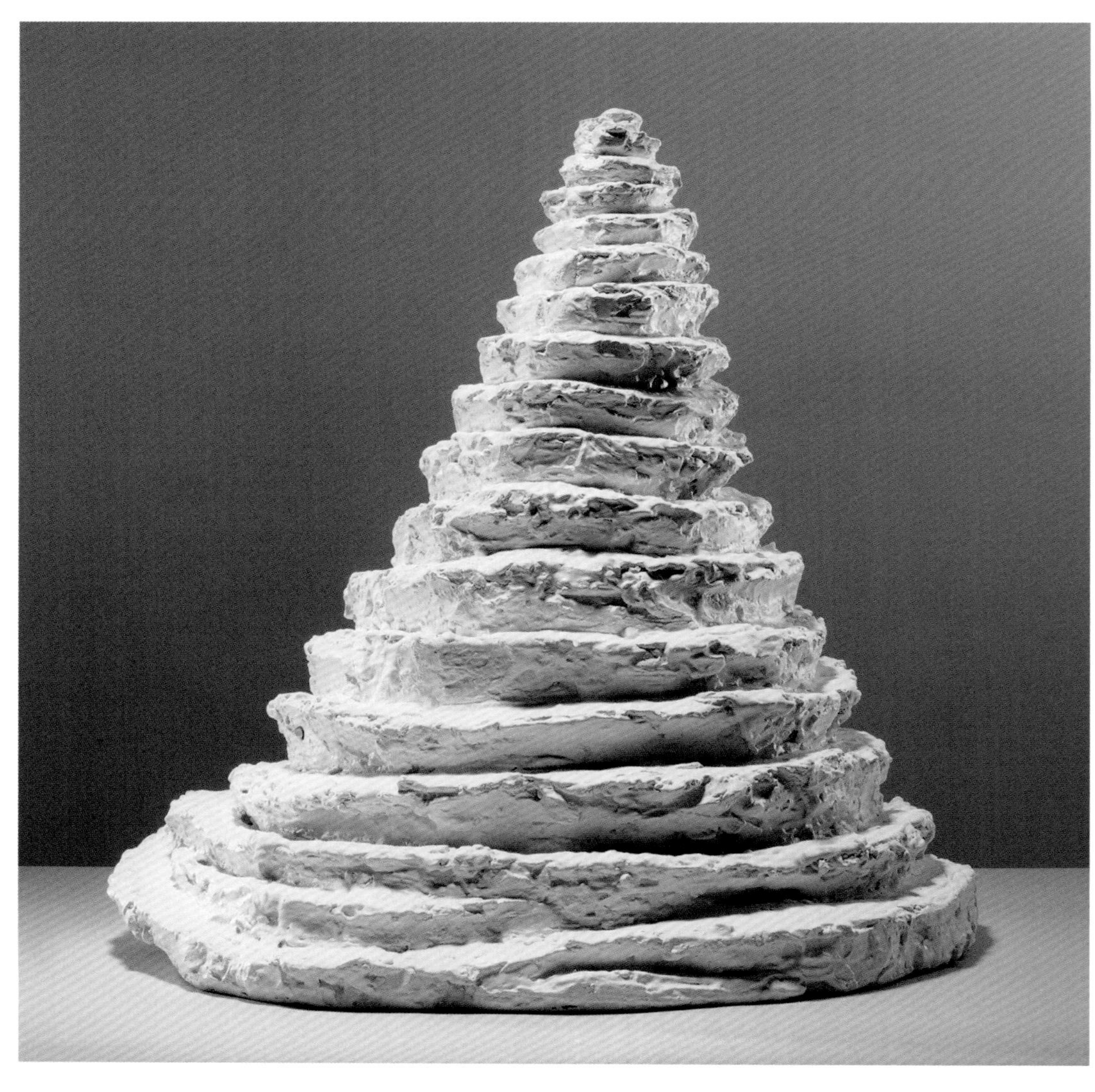

 Lair 1962, cast 2004

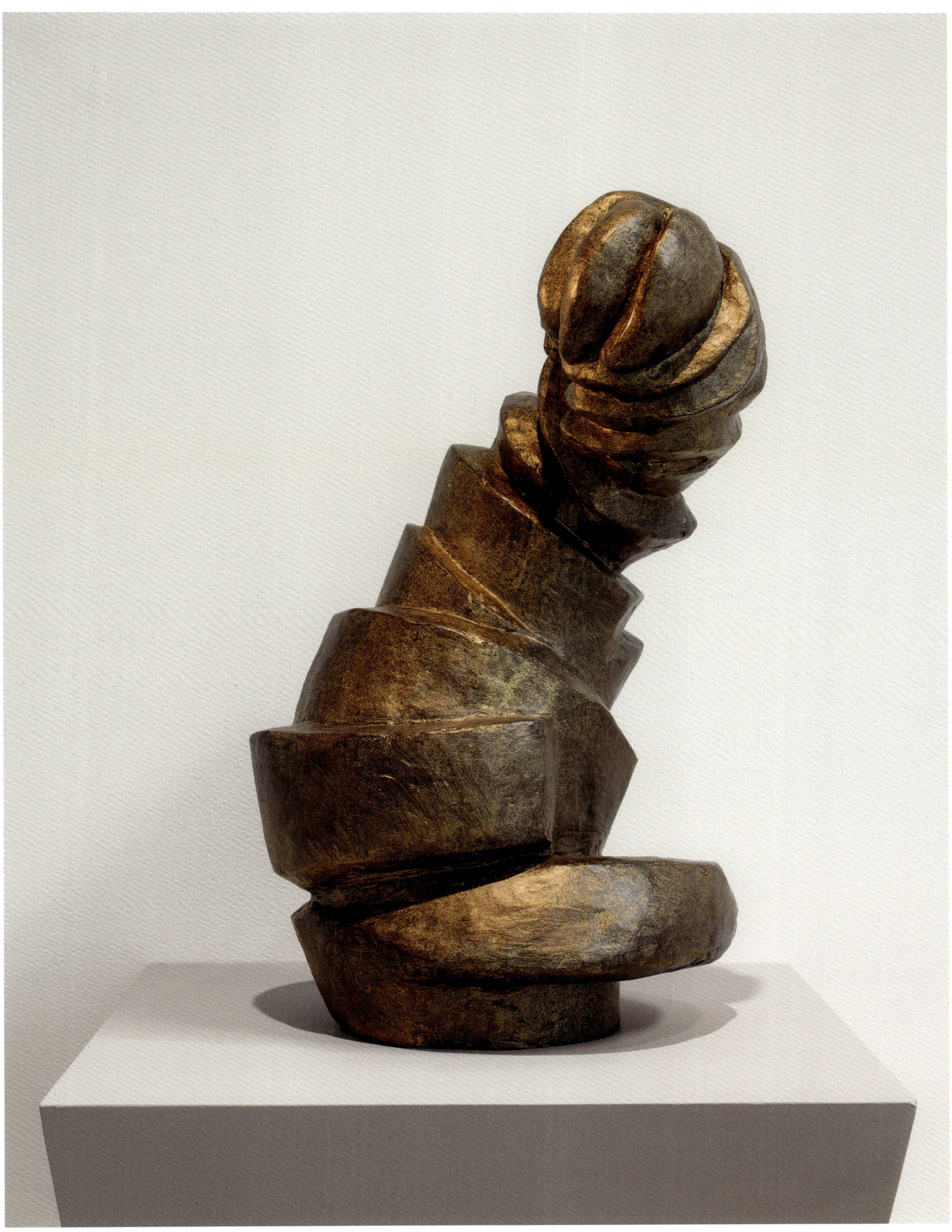

 Labyrinthine Tower 1962, cast 2003

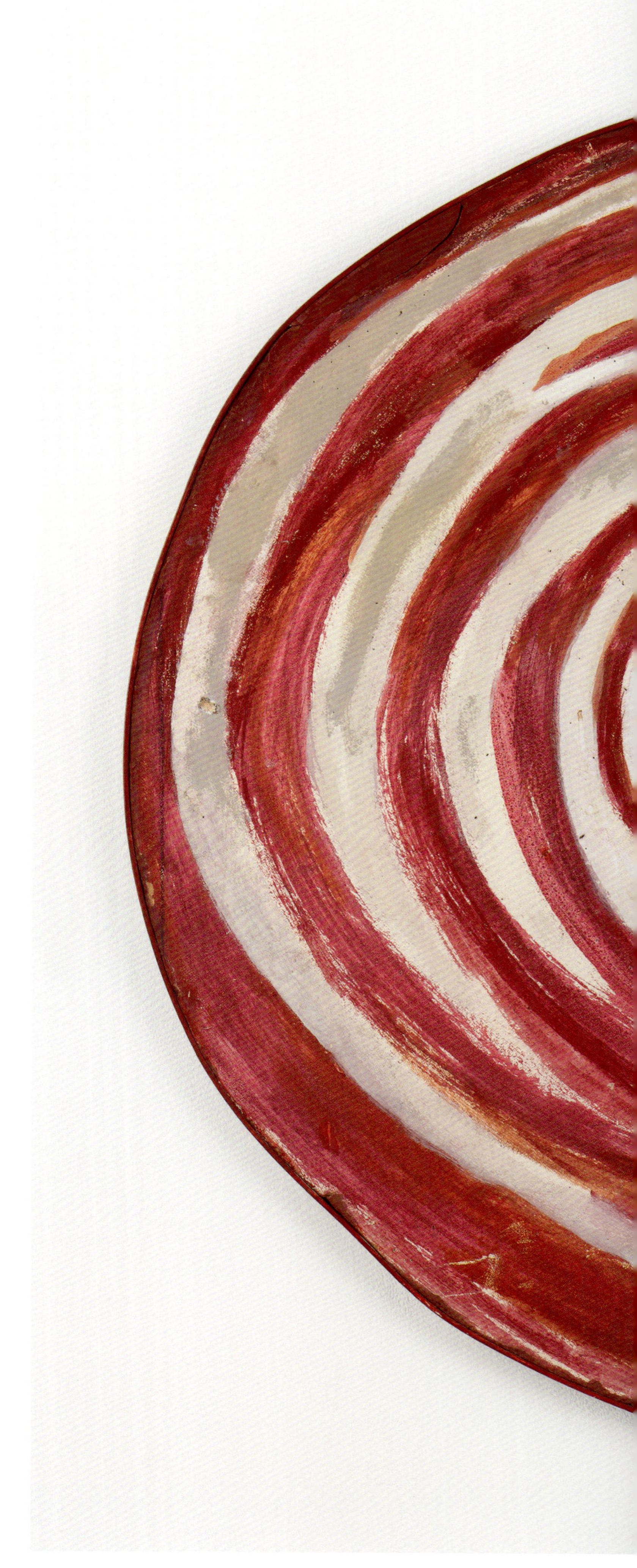

 Untitled c1970

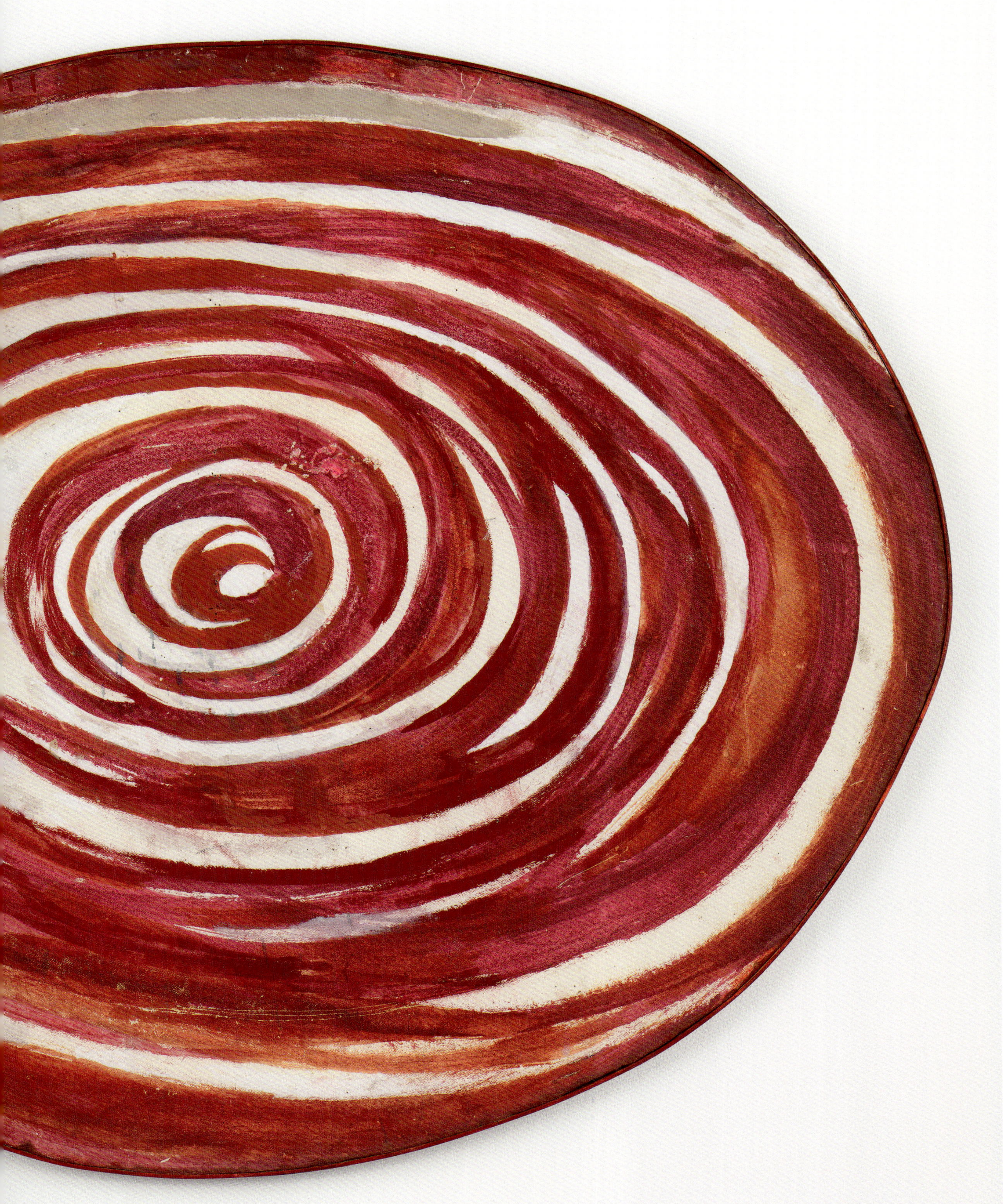

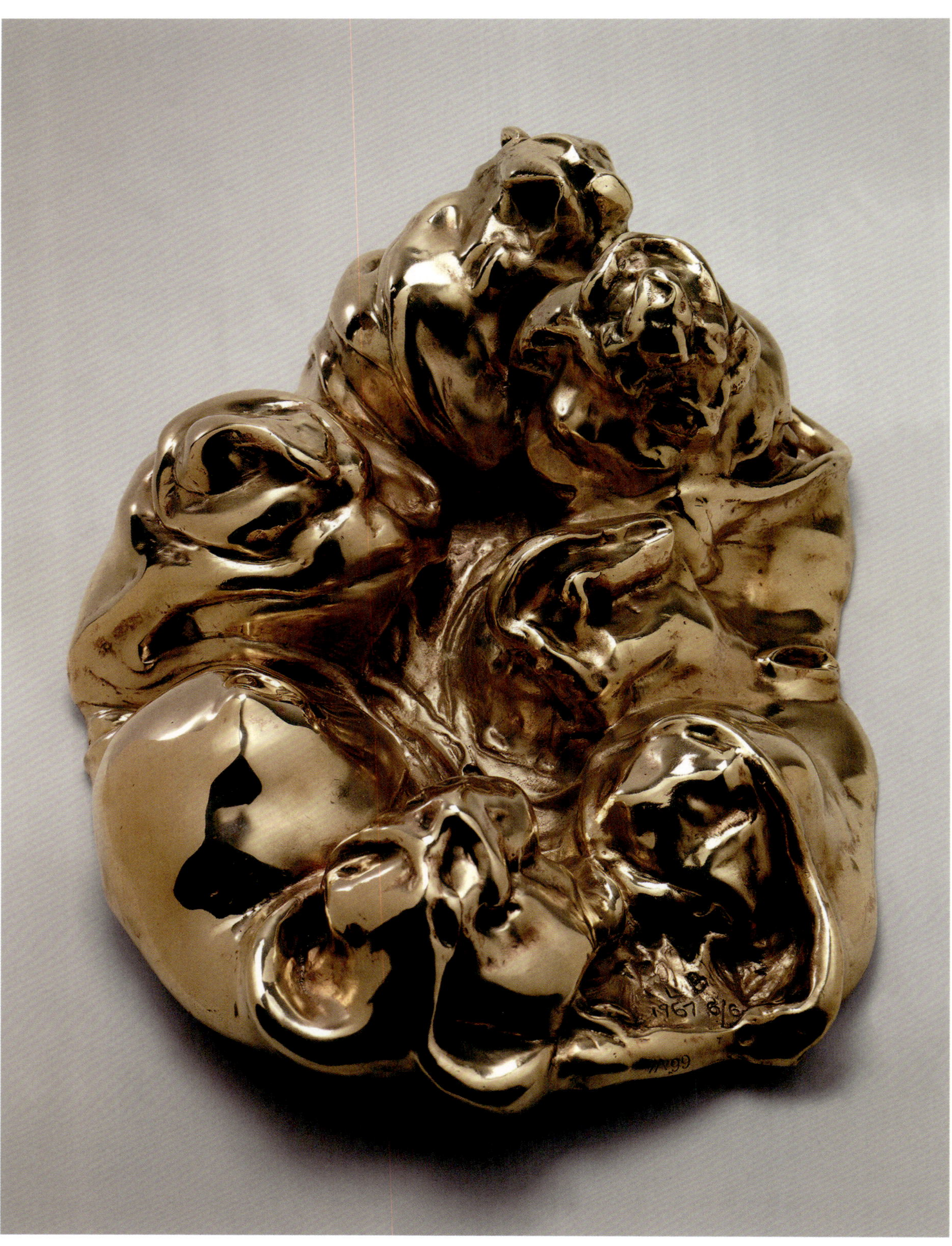

 End of Softness 1967, cast 1999

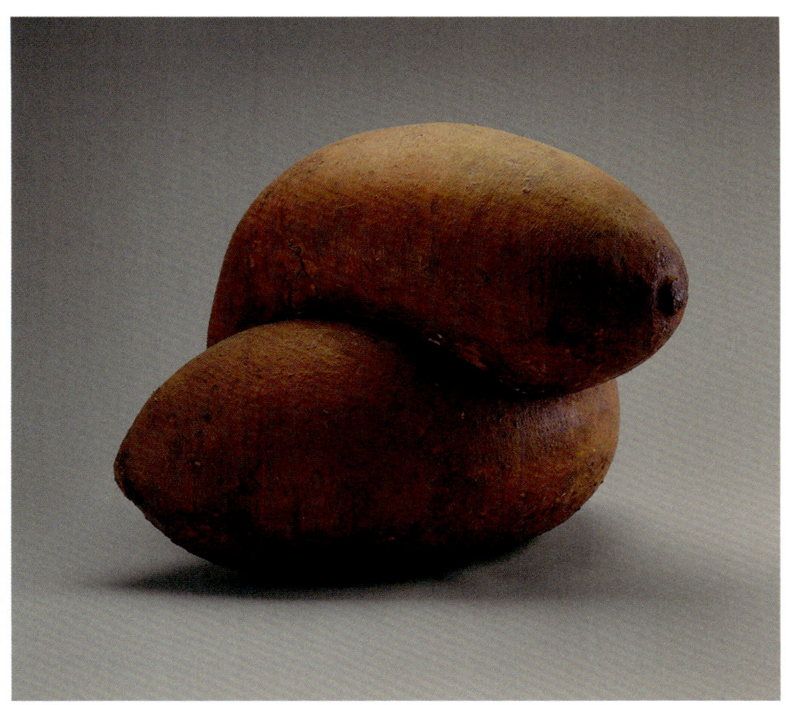

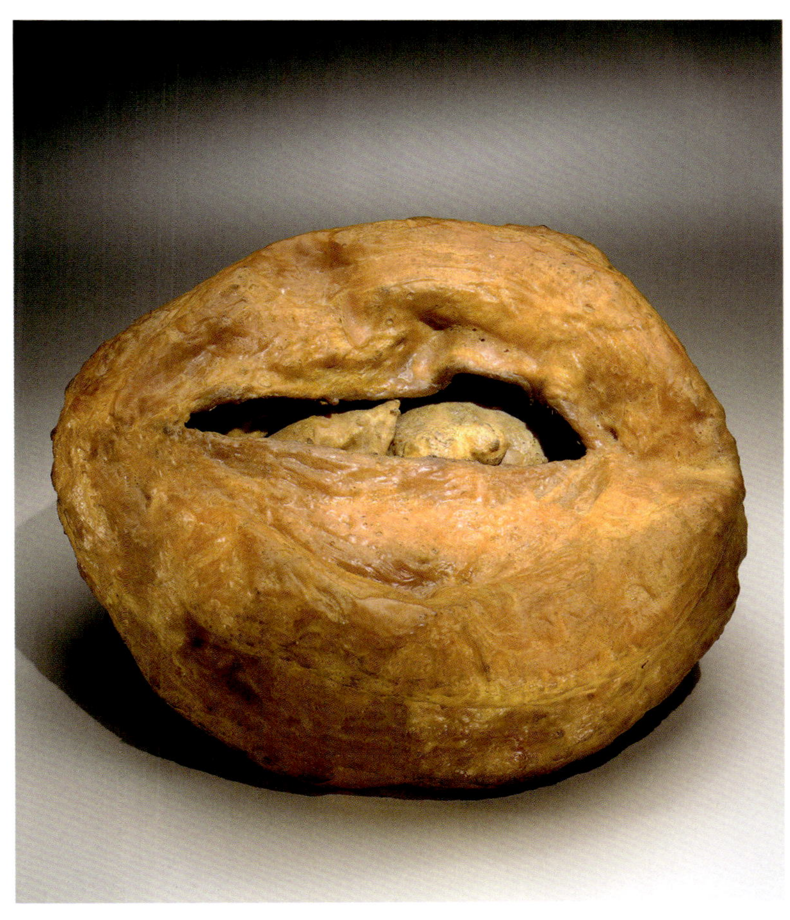

Le Trani Episode 1971
Le regard 1963

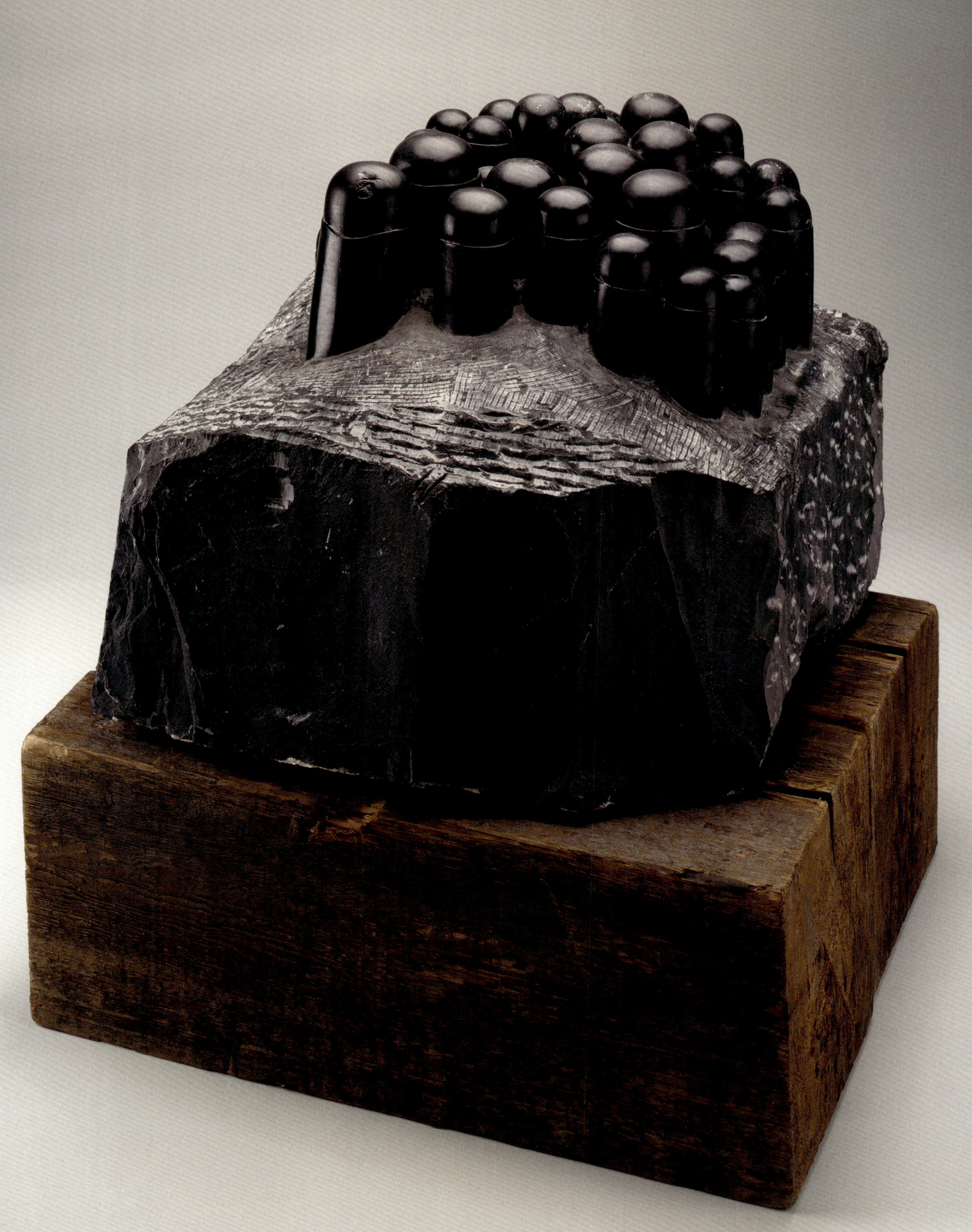

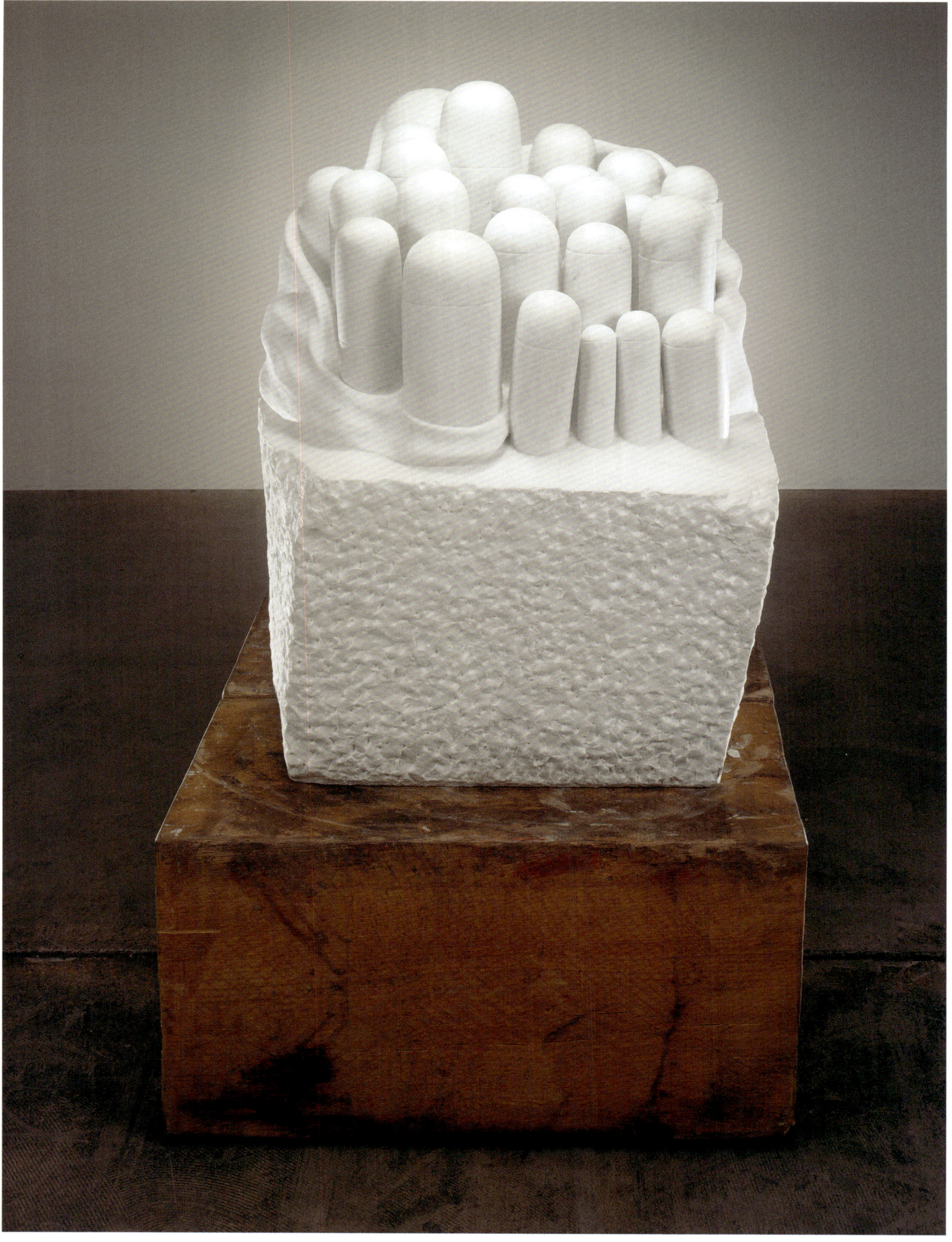

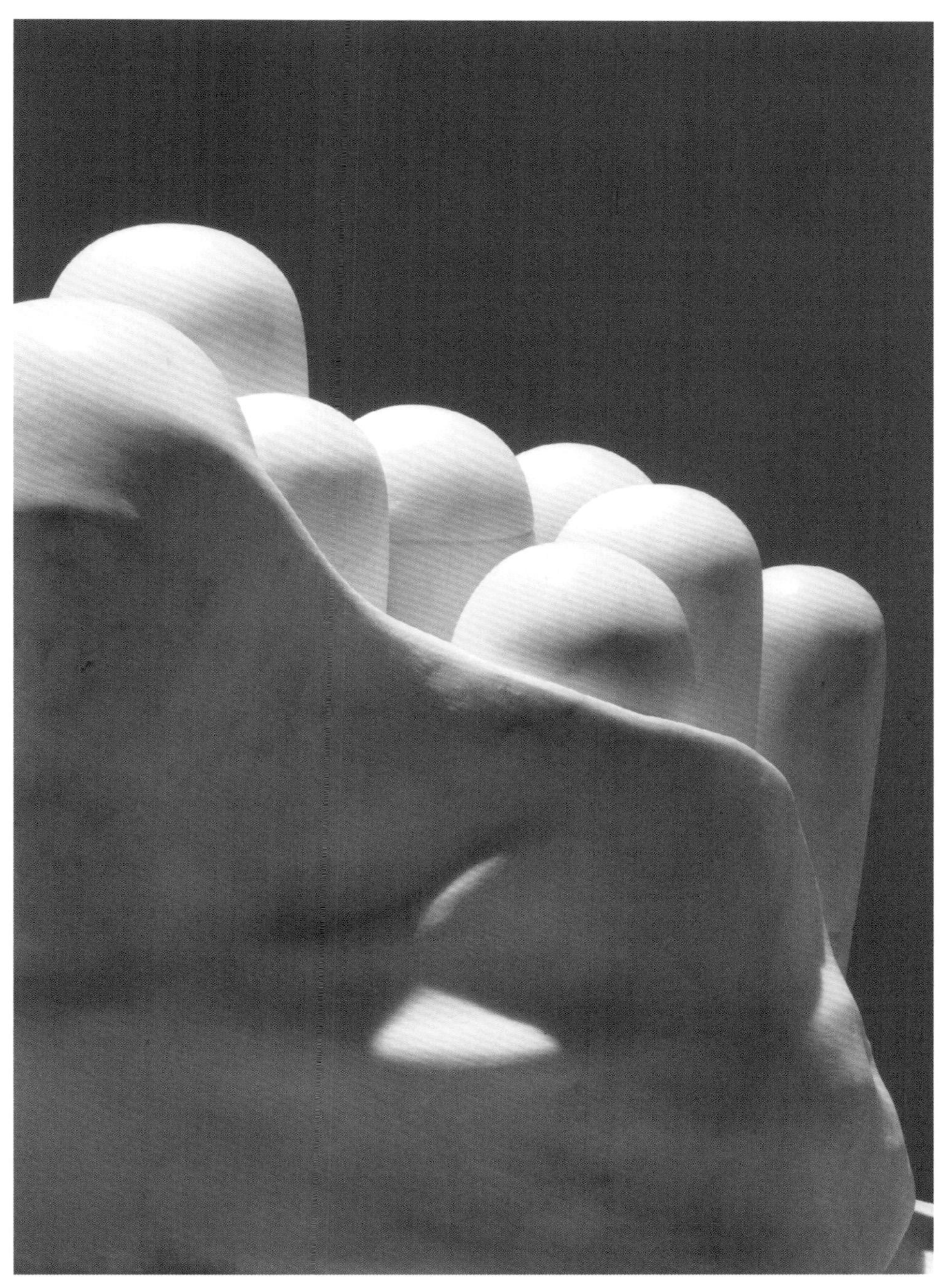

Fée couturière 1963, cast 2010

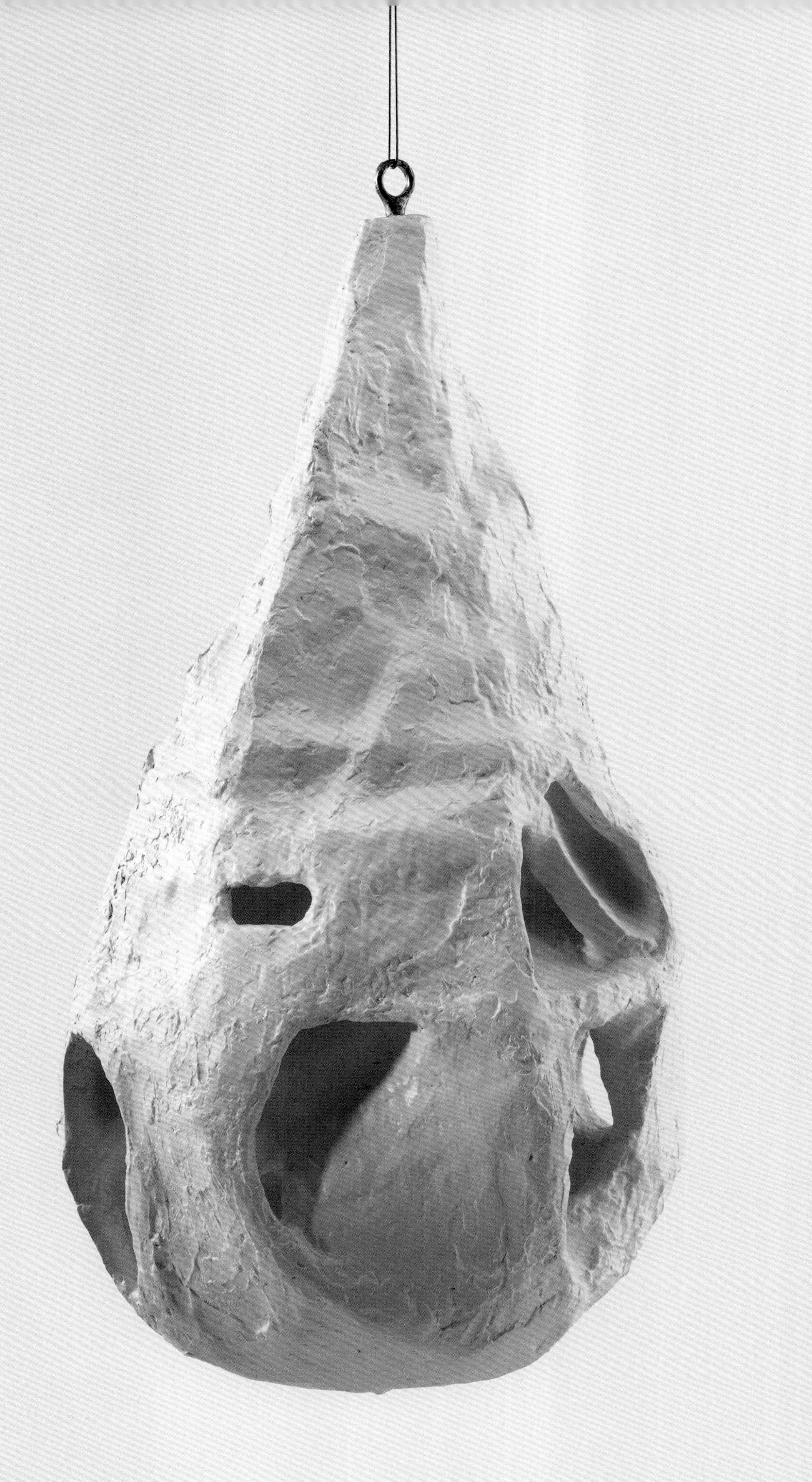

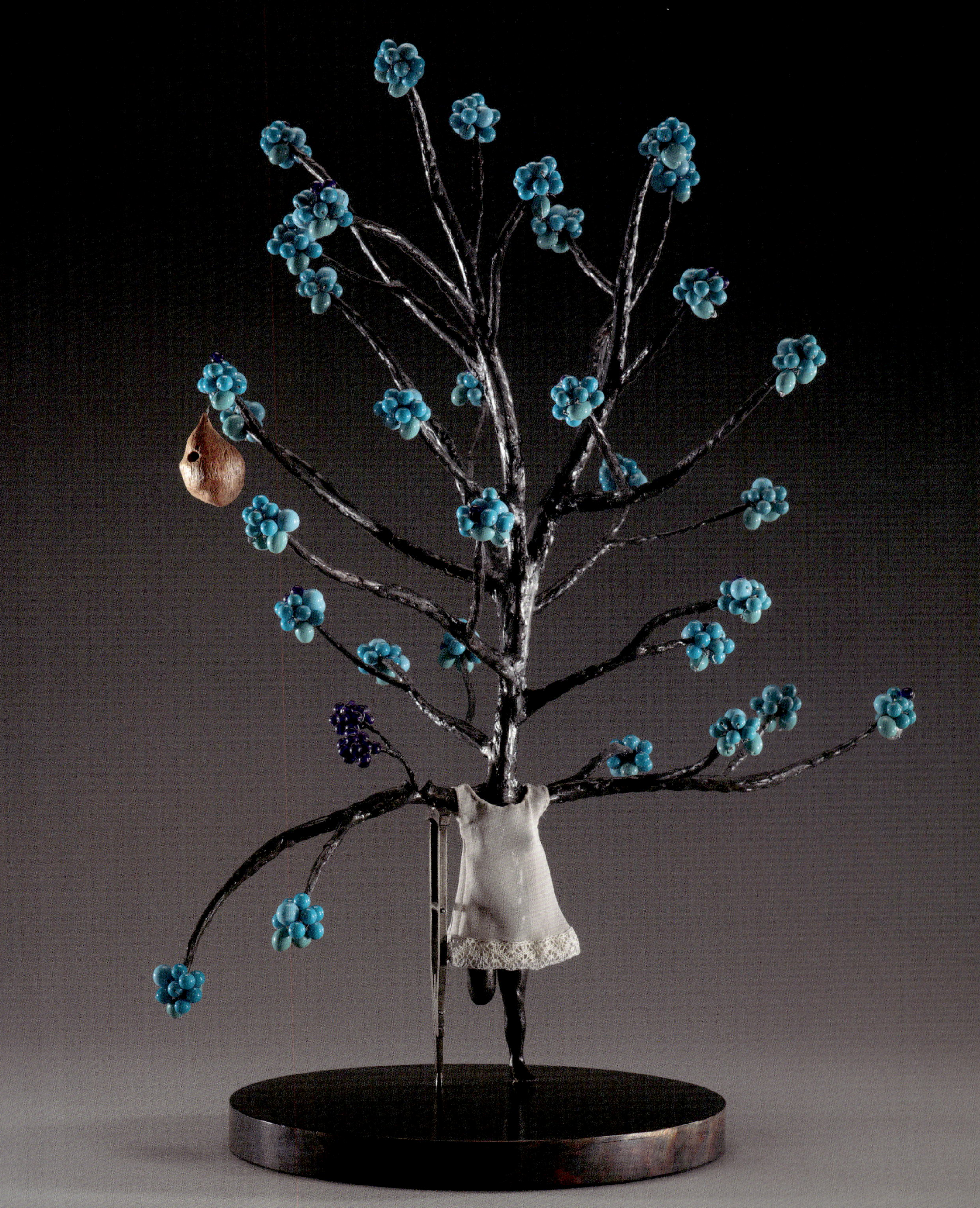

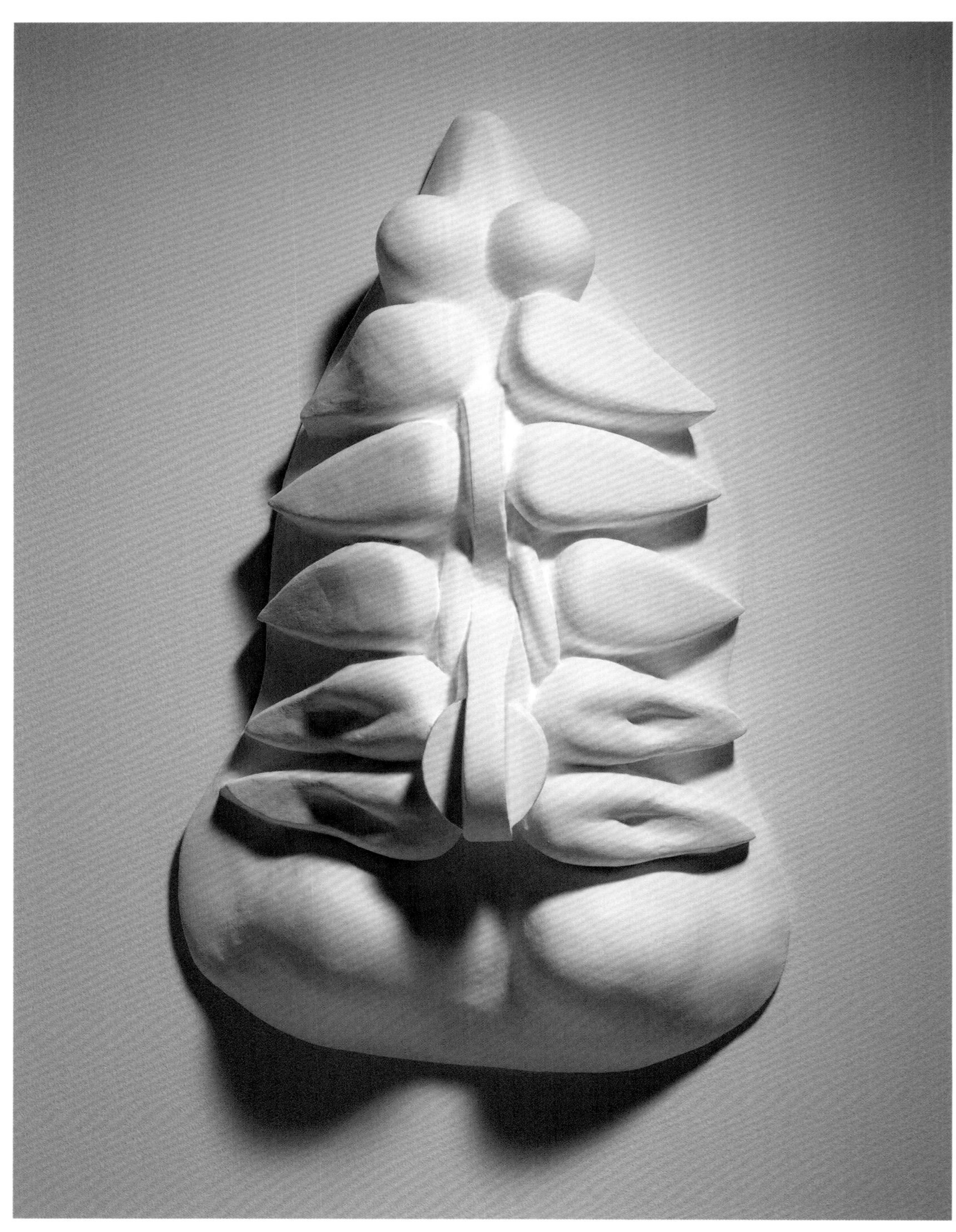

Torso, Self-portrait 1963–64, cast 1999
Nature Study 1984–94

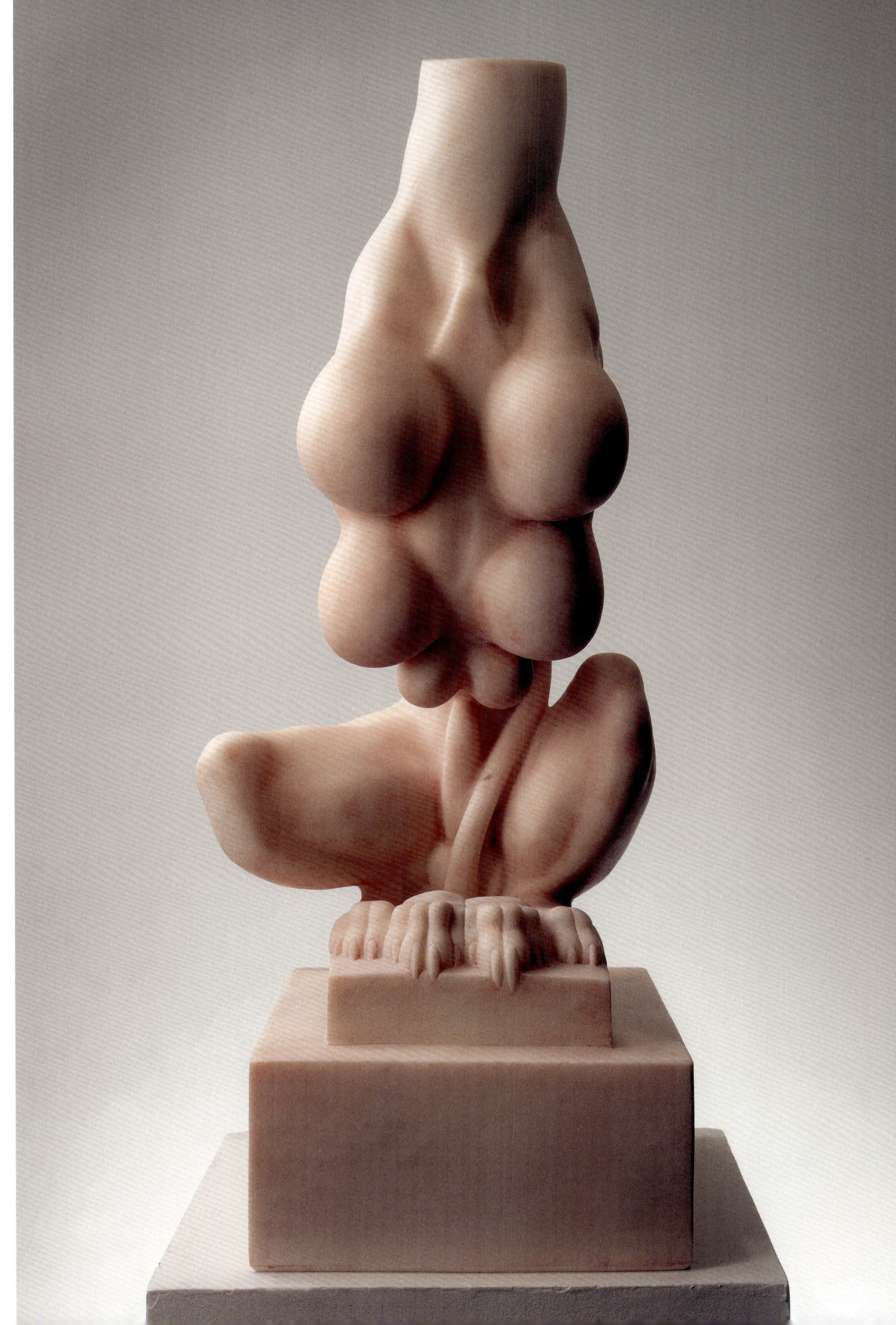

4
I love you do you love me

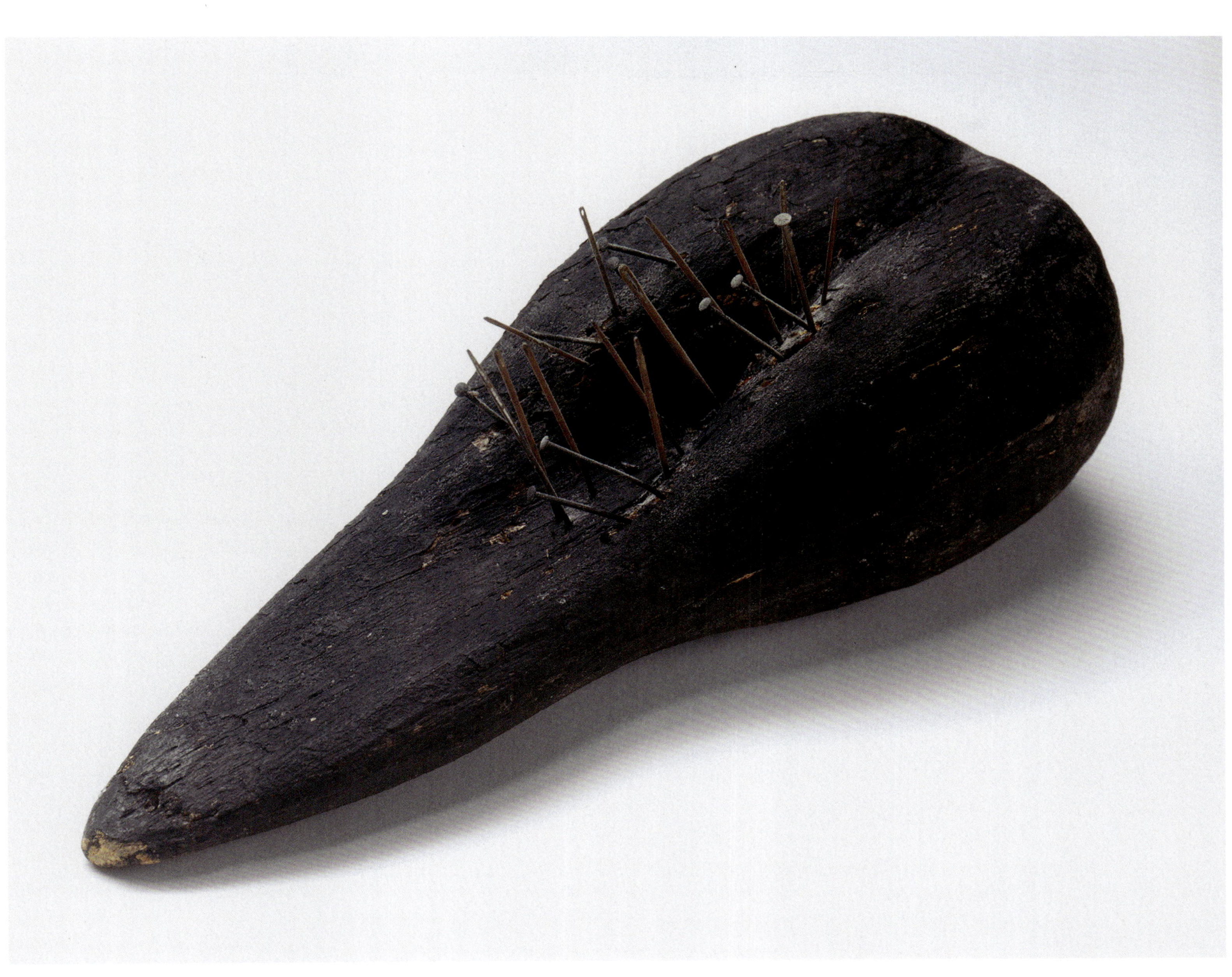

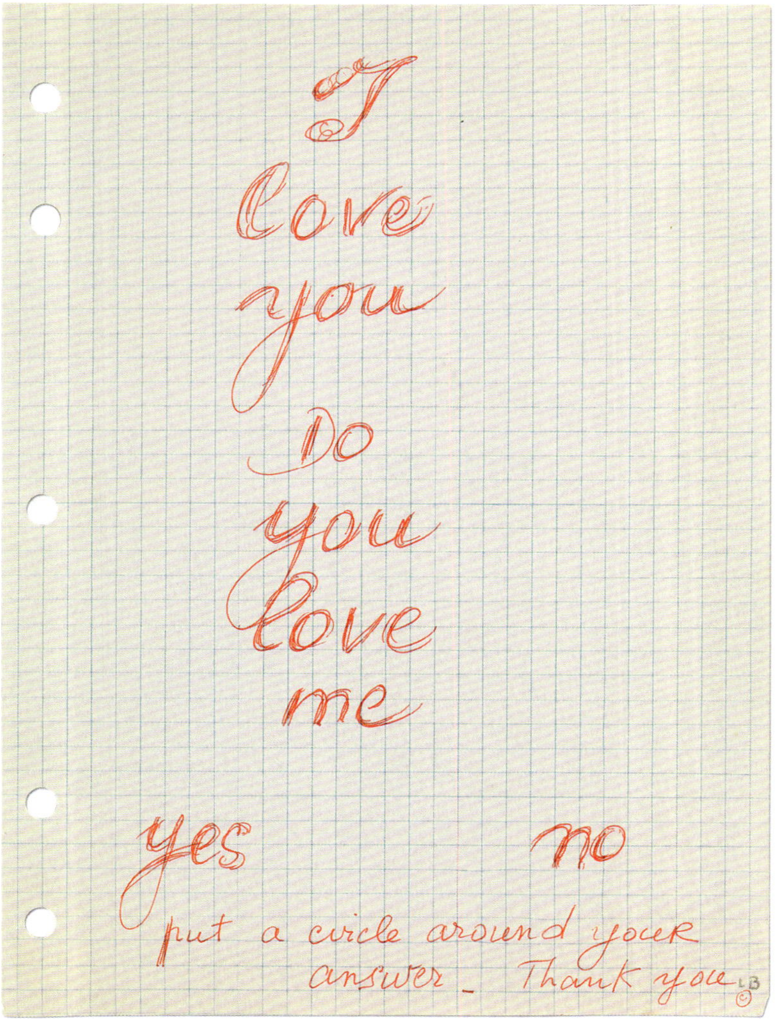

I
love
you
Do
you
love
me

yes no

put a circle around your
answer – Thank you LB ©

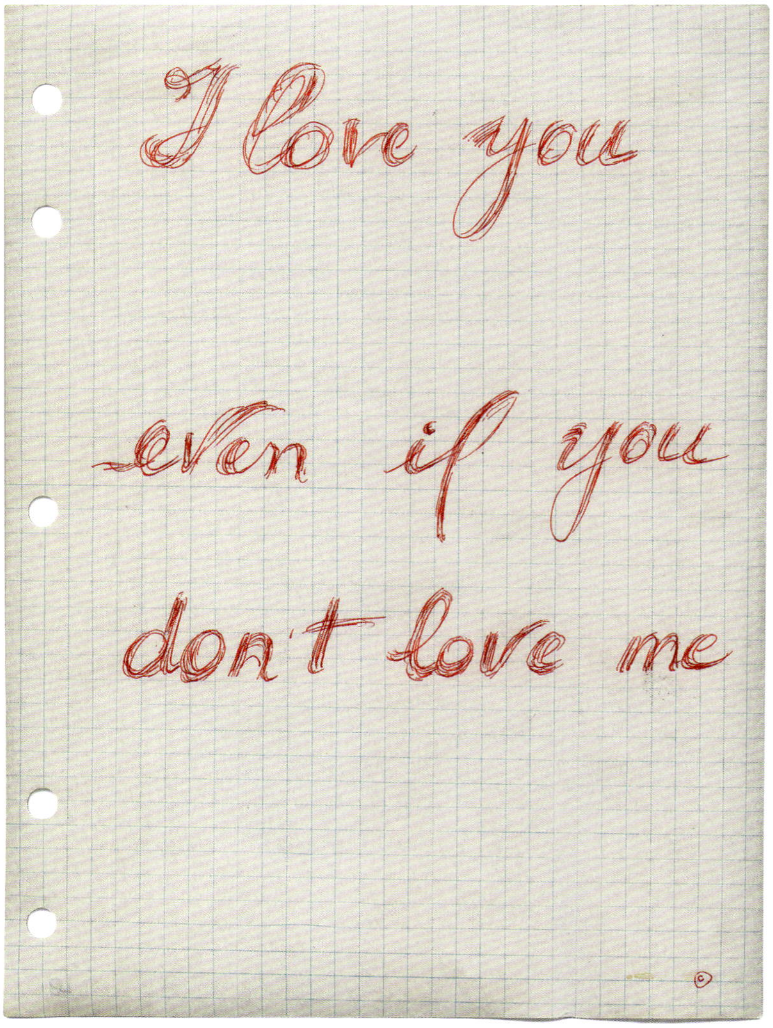

I love you

even if you

don't love me

©

I Love You Do You Love Me 1987
I Love You Even If You Don't Love Me 1987

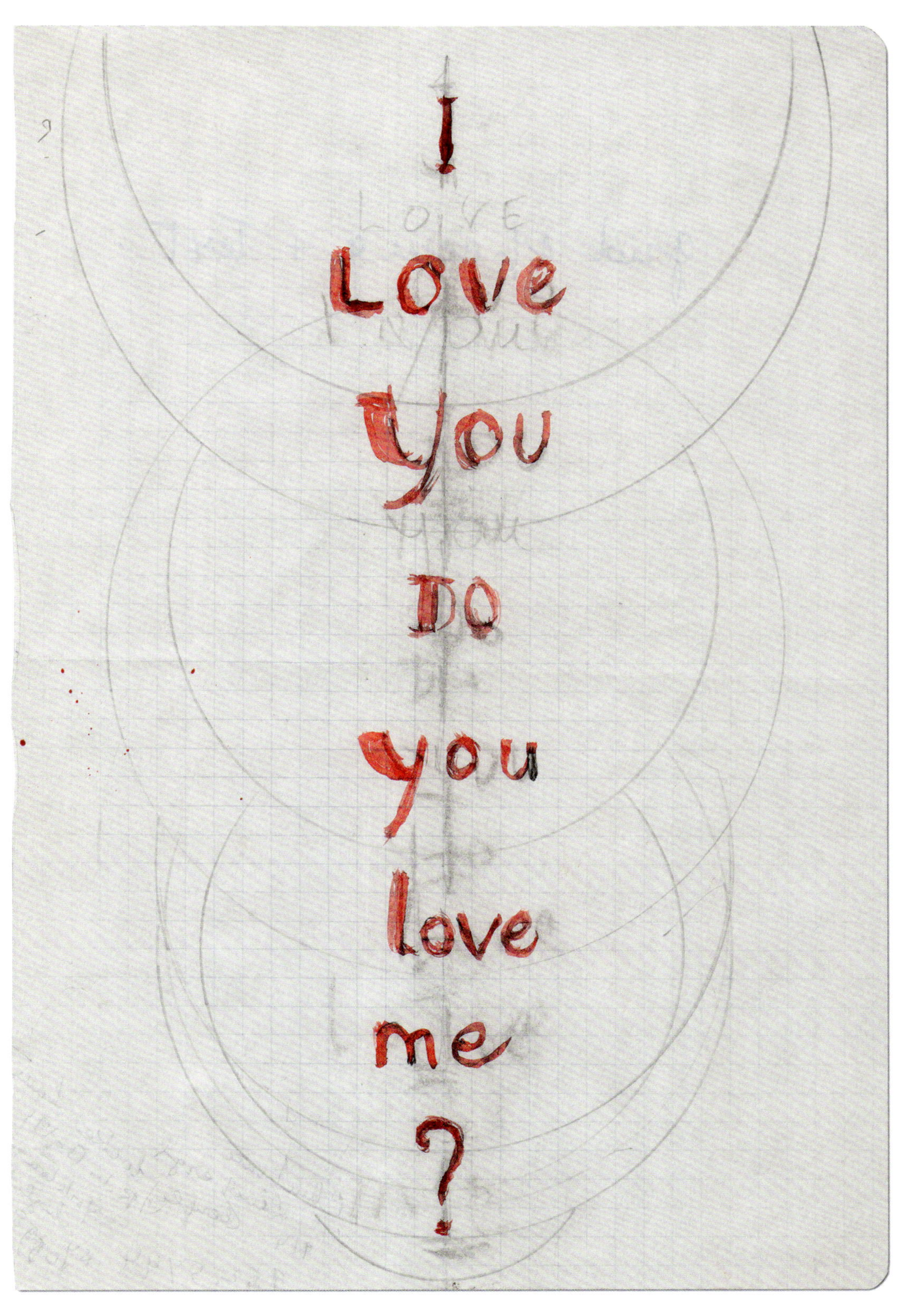

 I Love You Do You Love Me? 1987

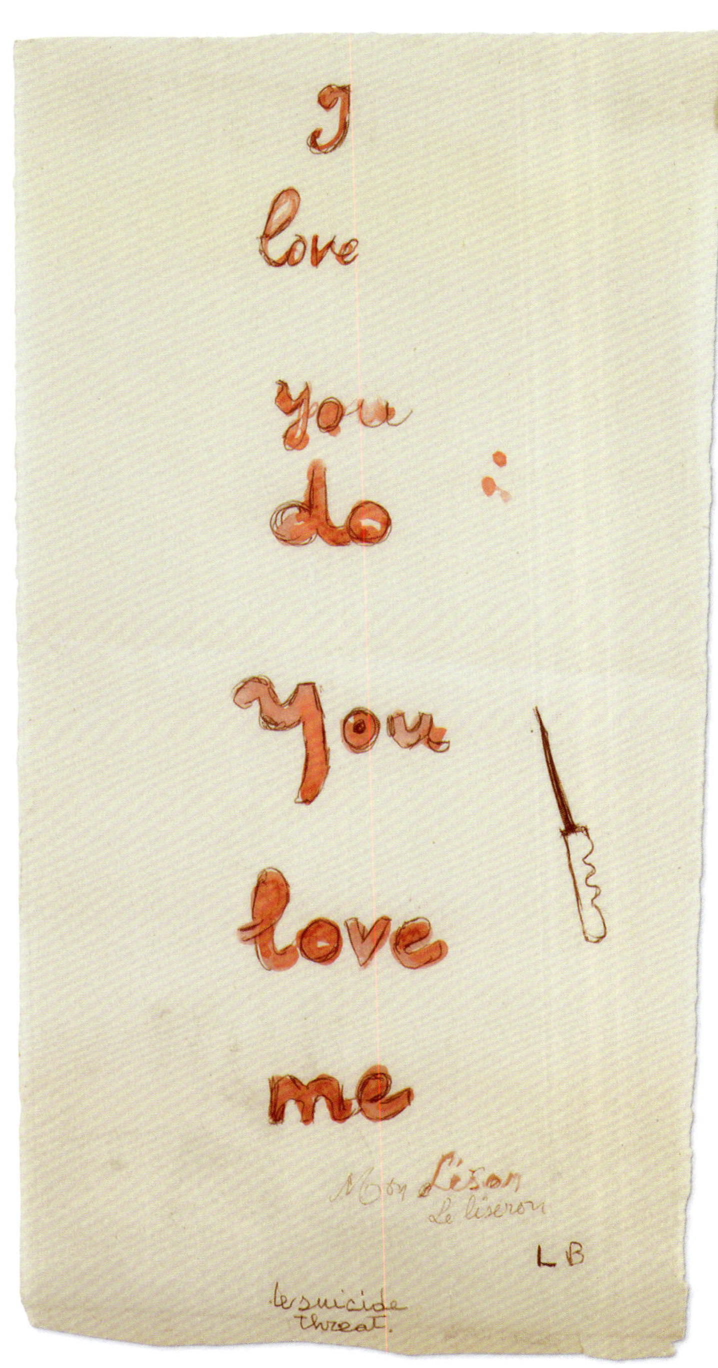

Le Suicide Threat 1987
Breasts and Blade 1991

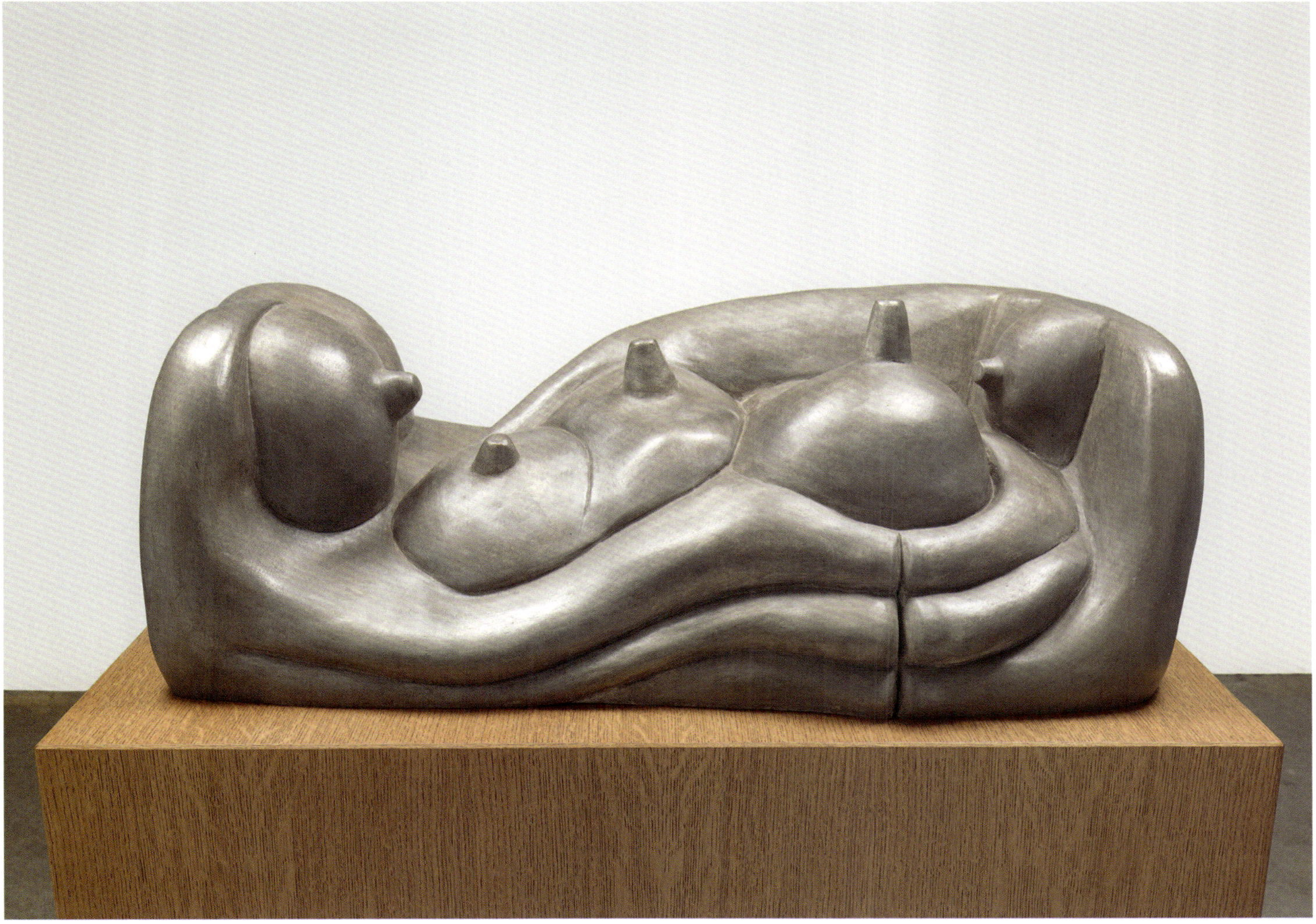

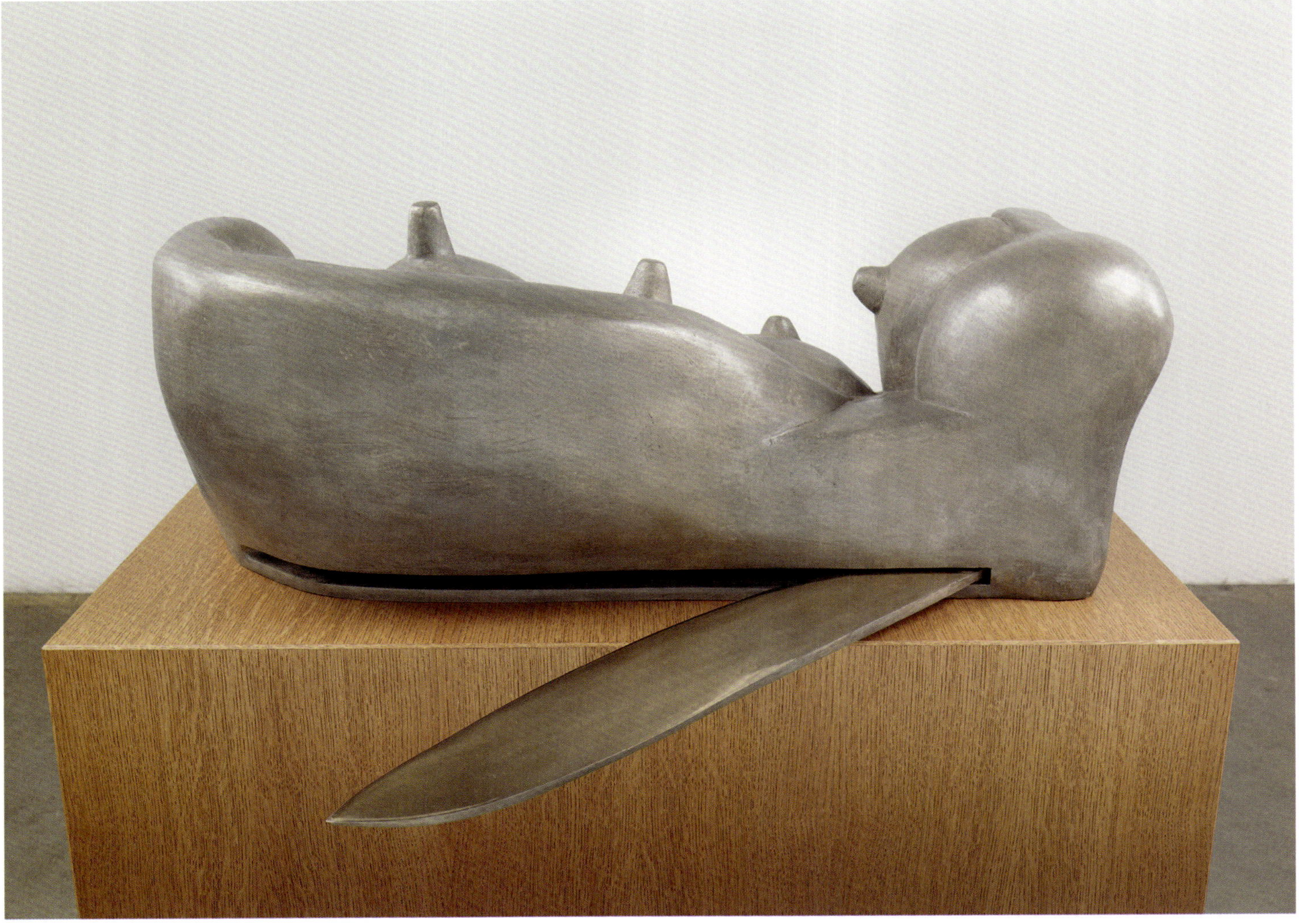

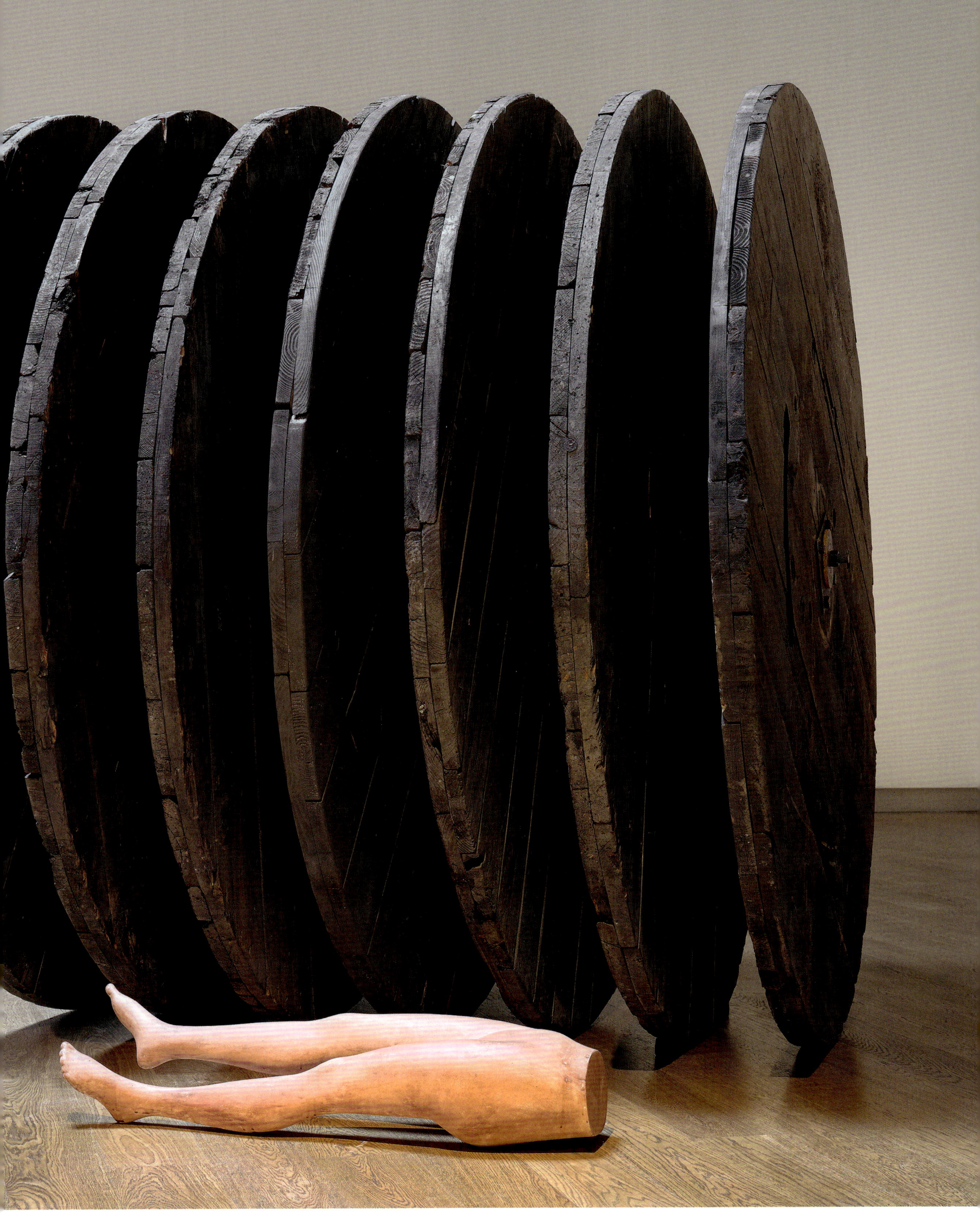

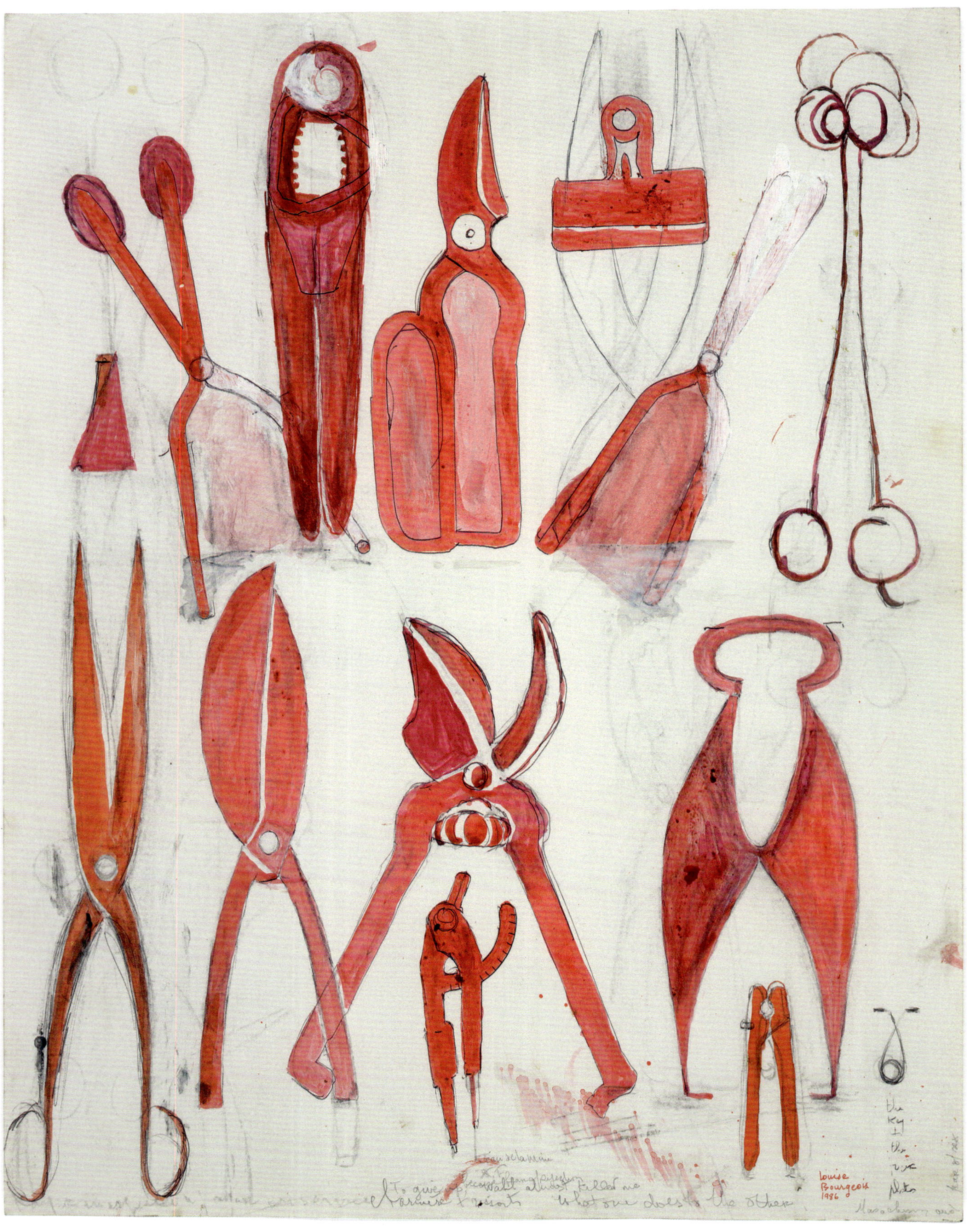

 Untitled 1986

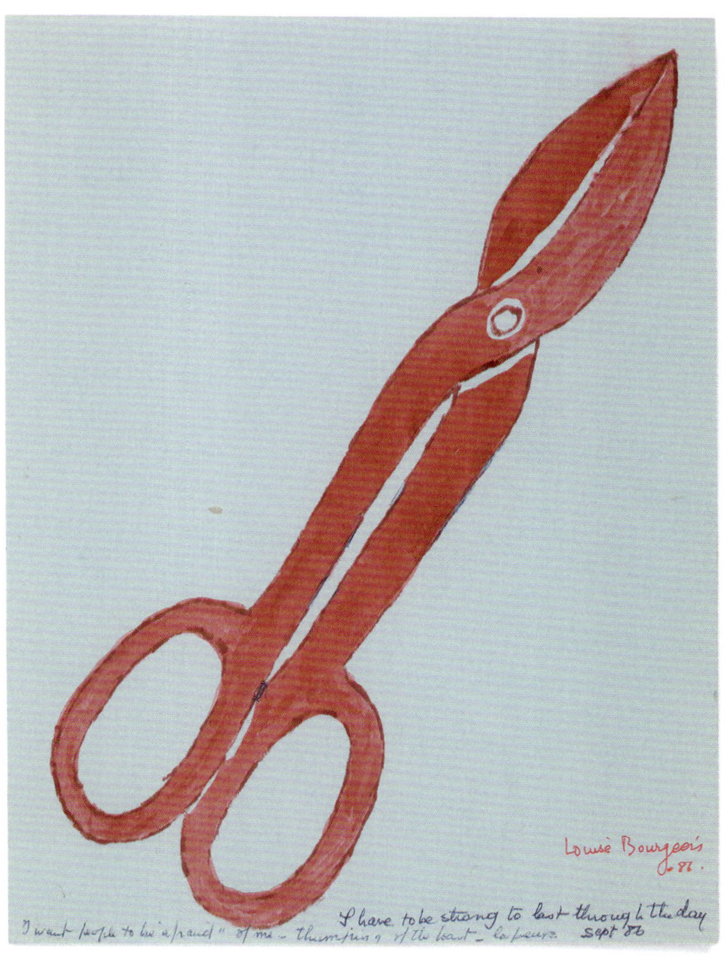

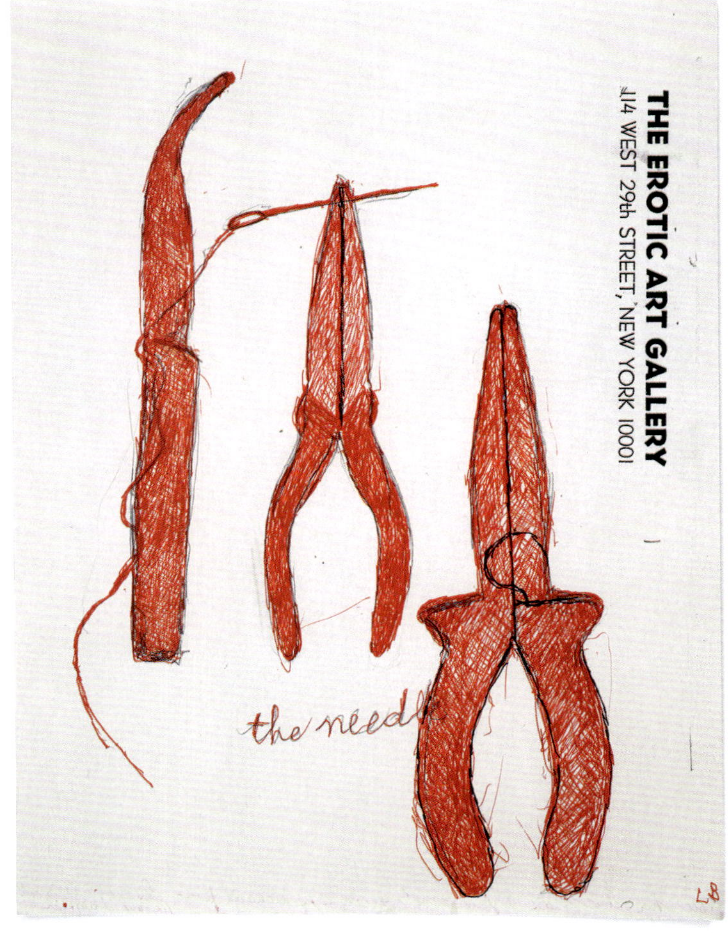

Untitled (Scissors) 1986
The Needle 2001

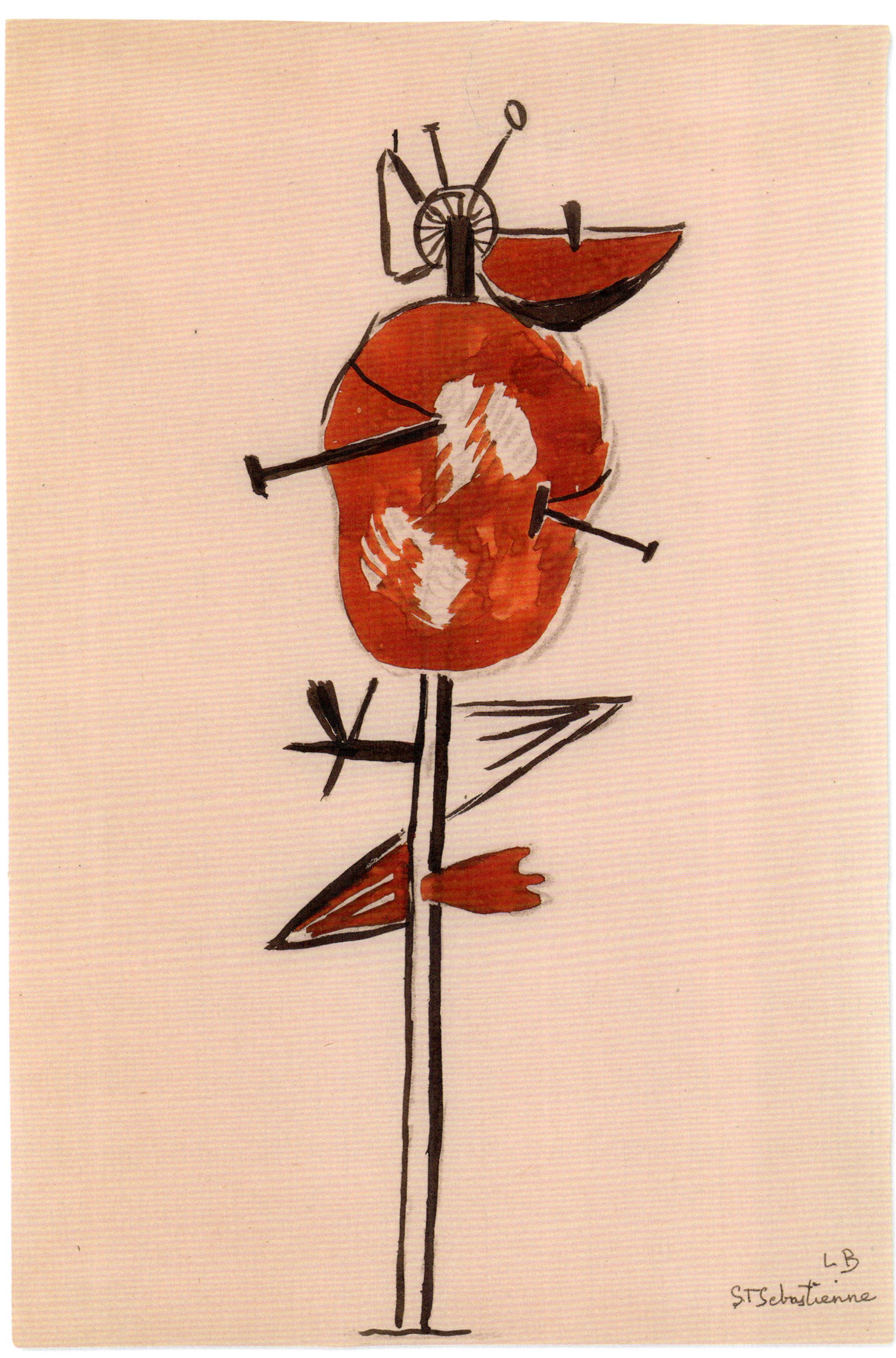
LB
ST Sebastienne

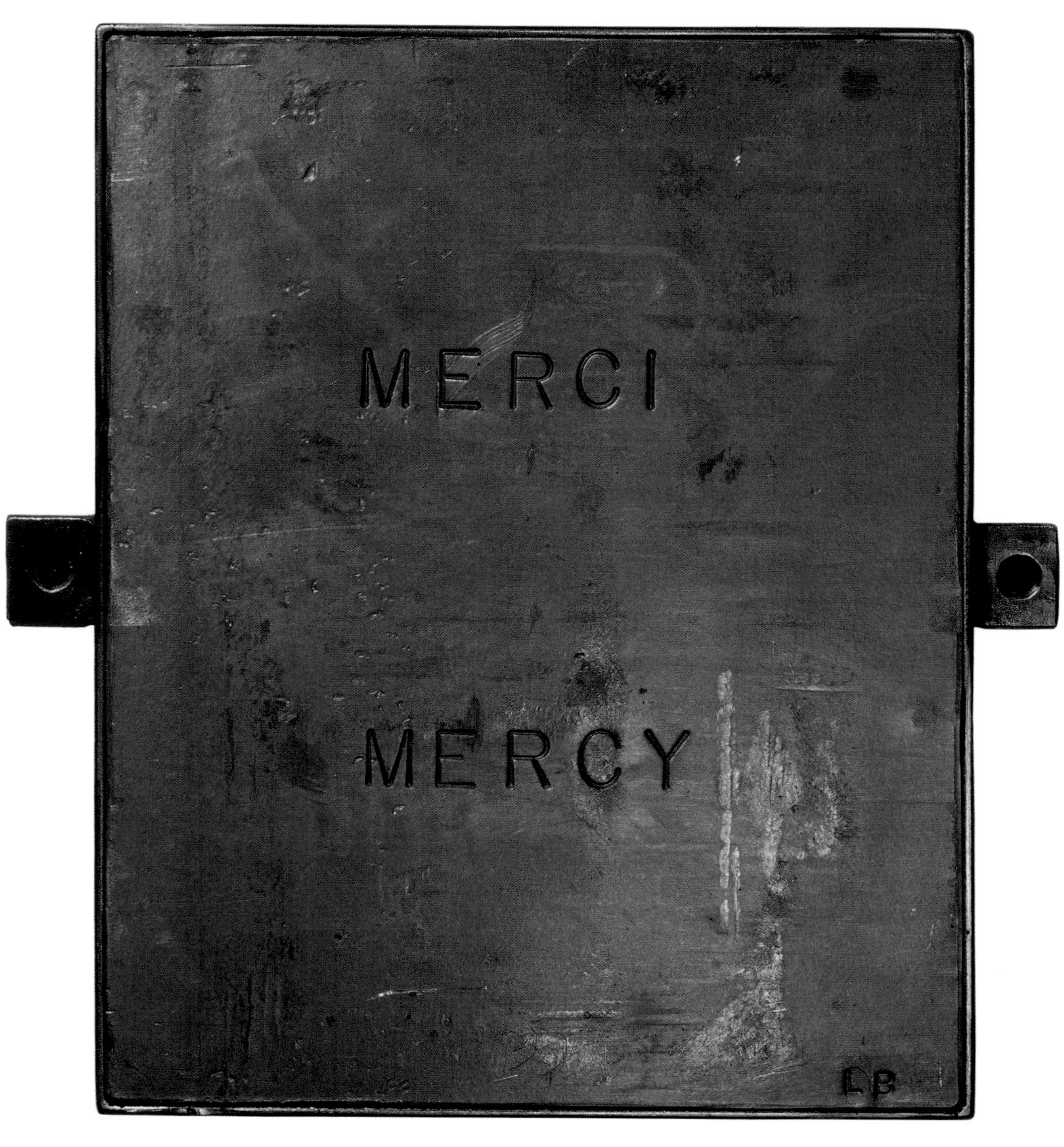

Merci Mercy 1999
Heart 2004

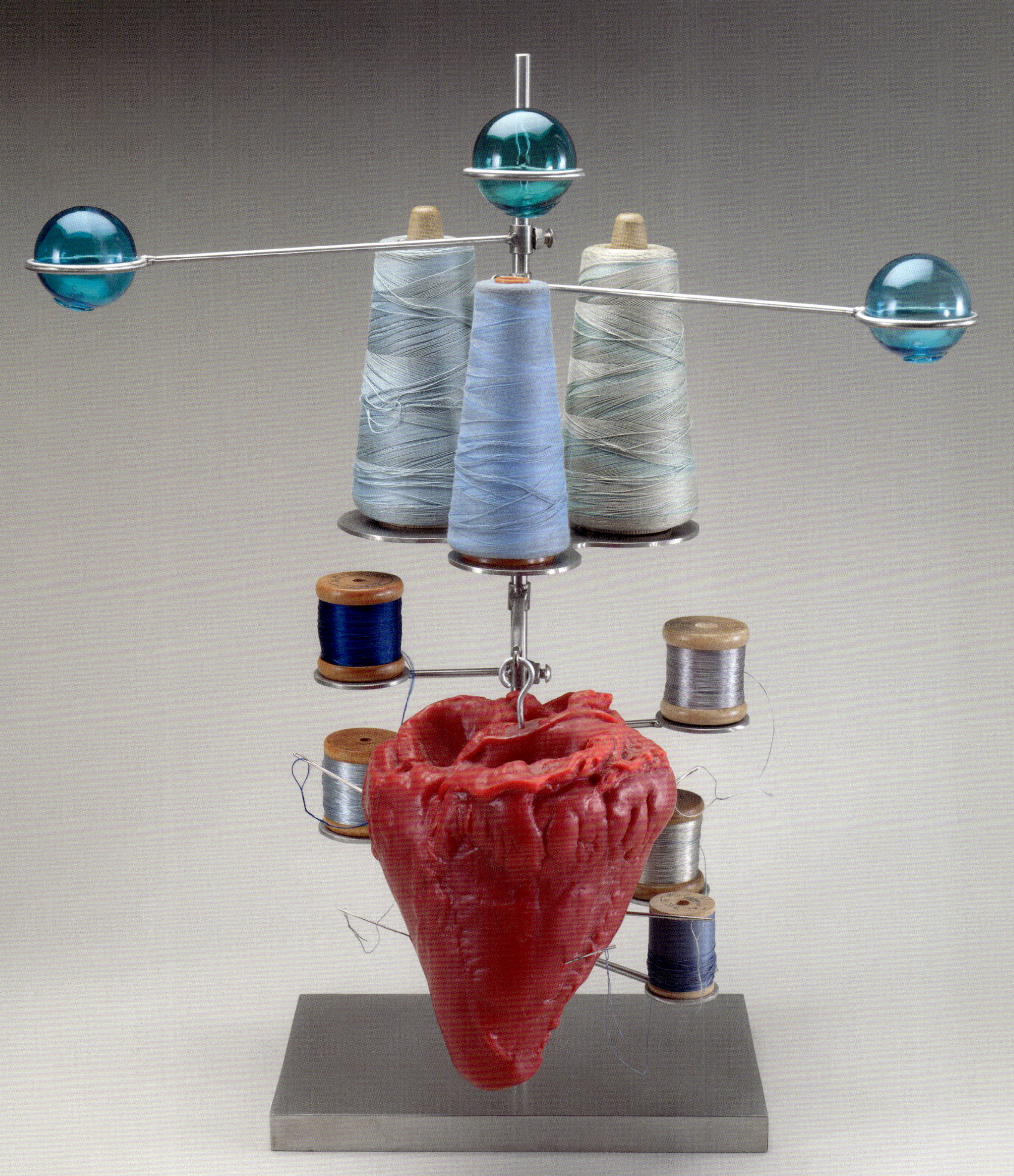

5
Clouds and caverns

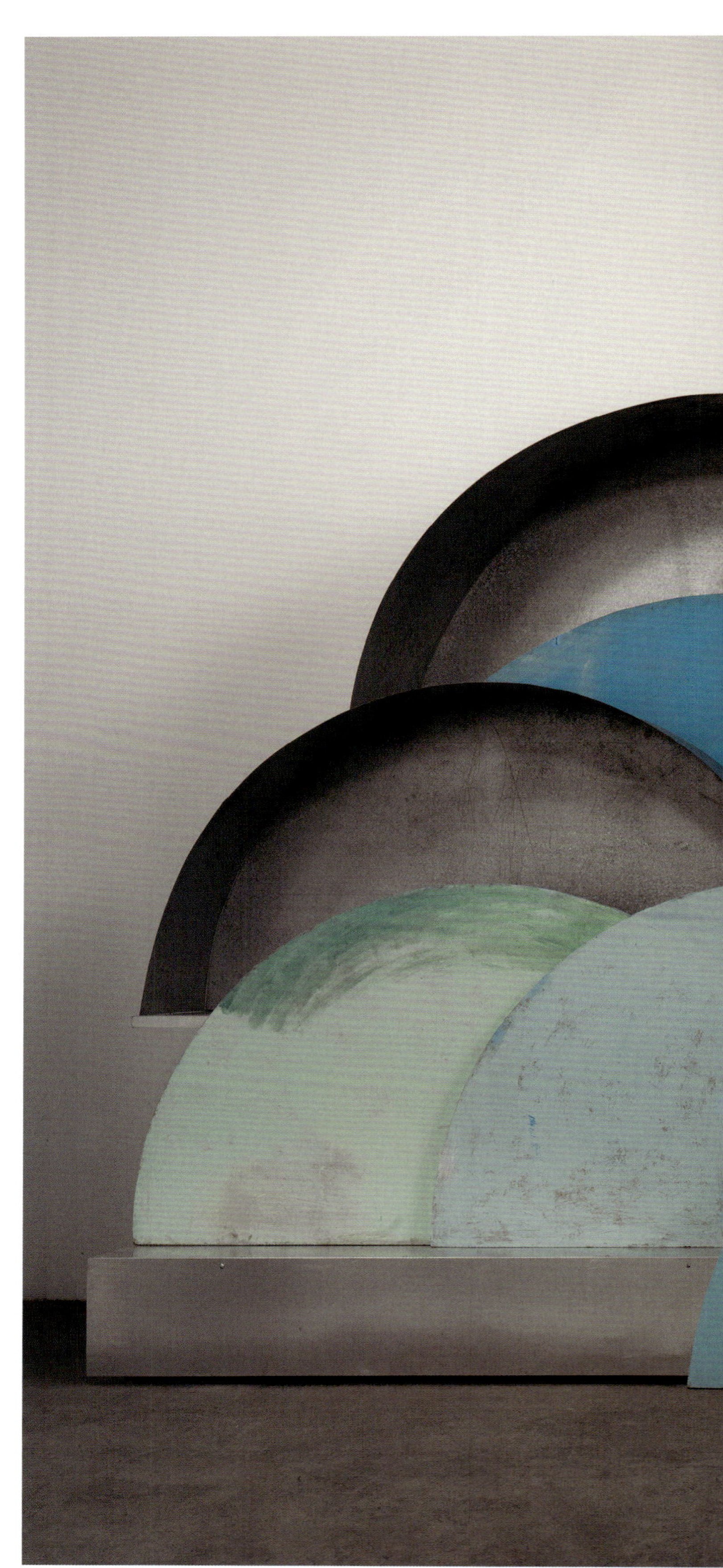

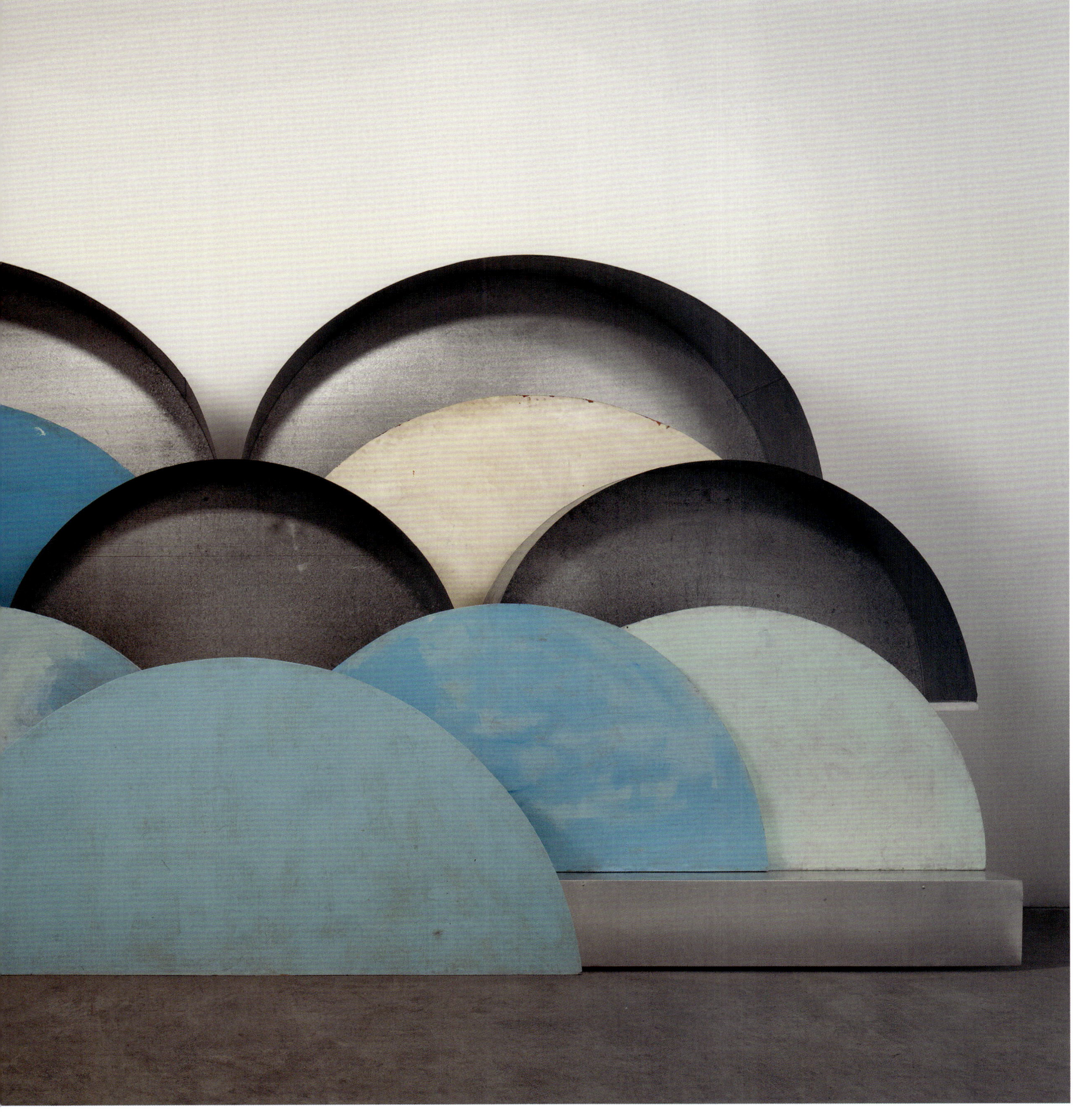

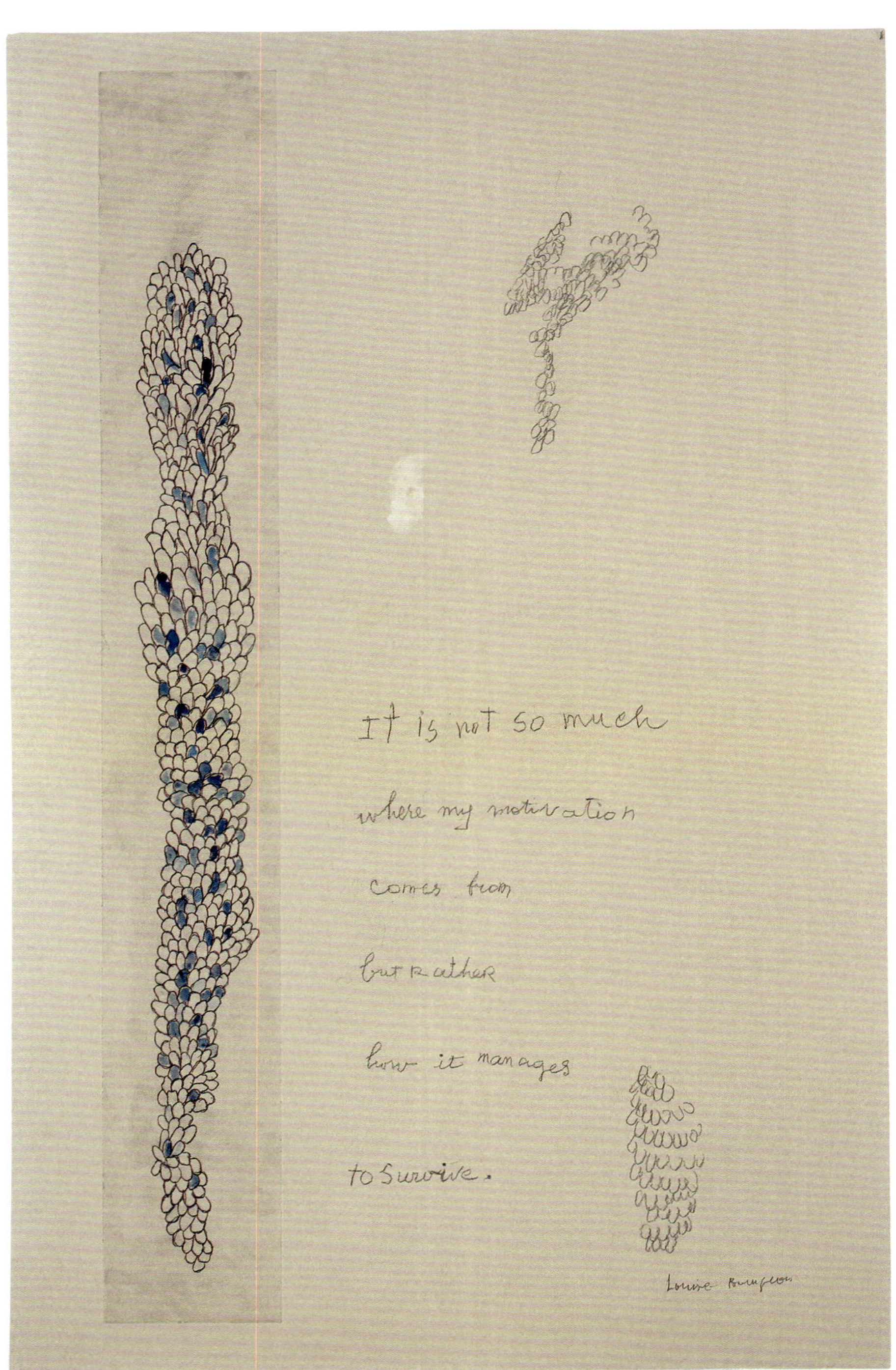

Where My Motivation Comes From 2007
Poids 1992

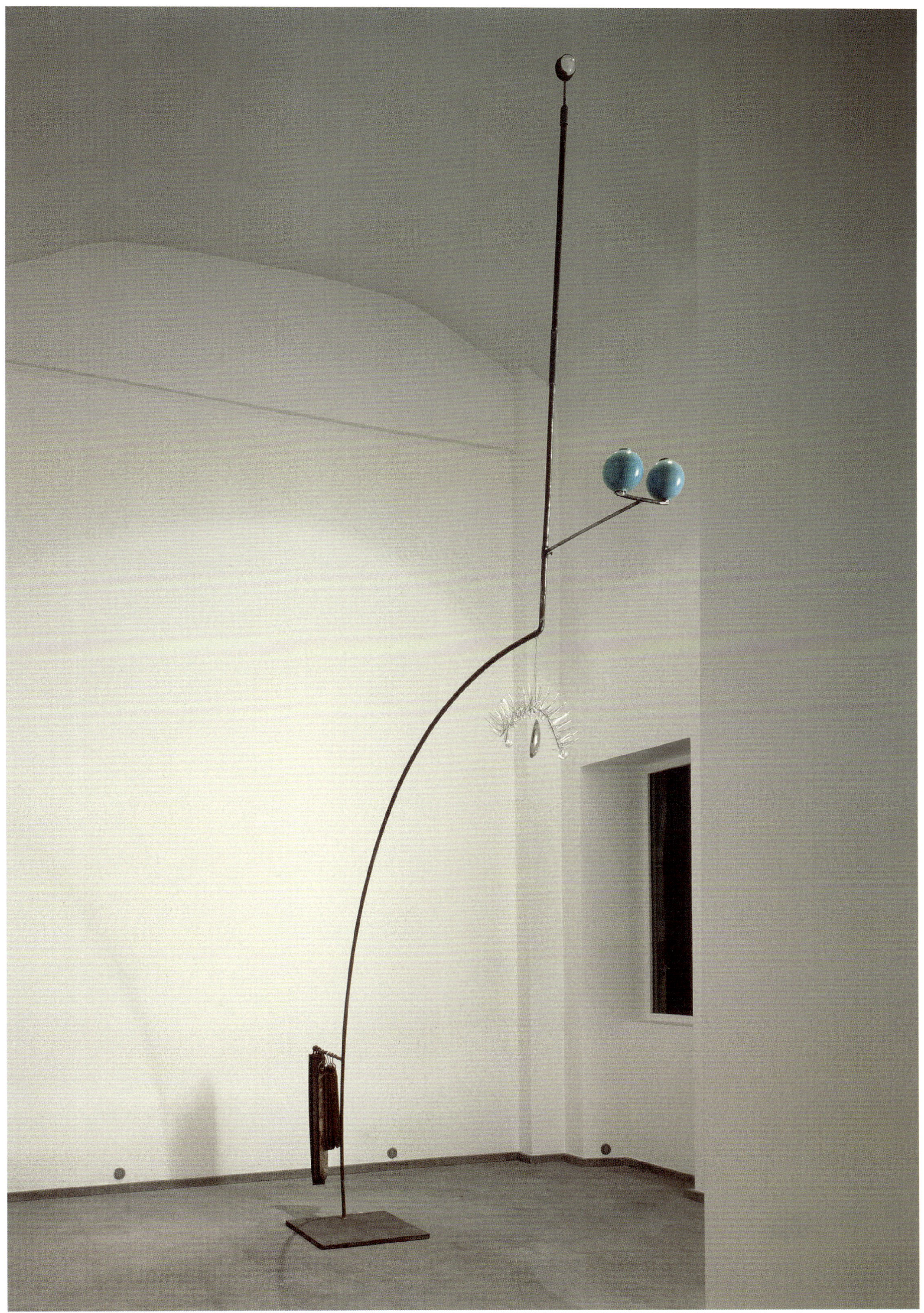

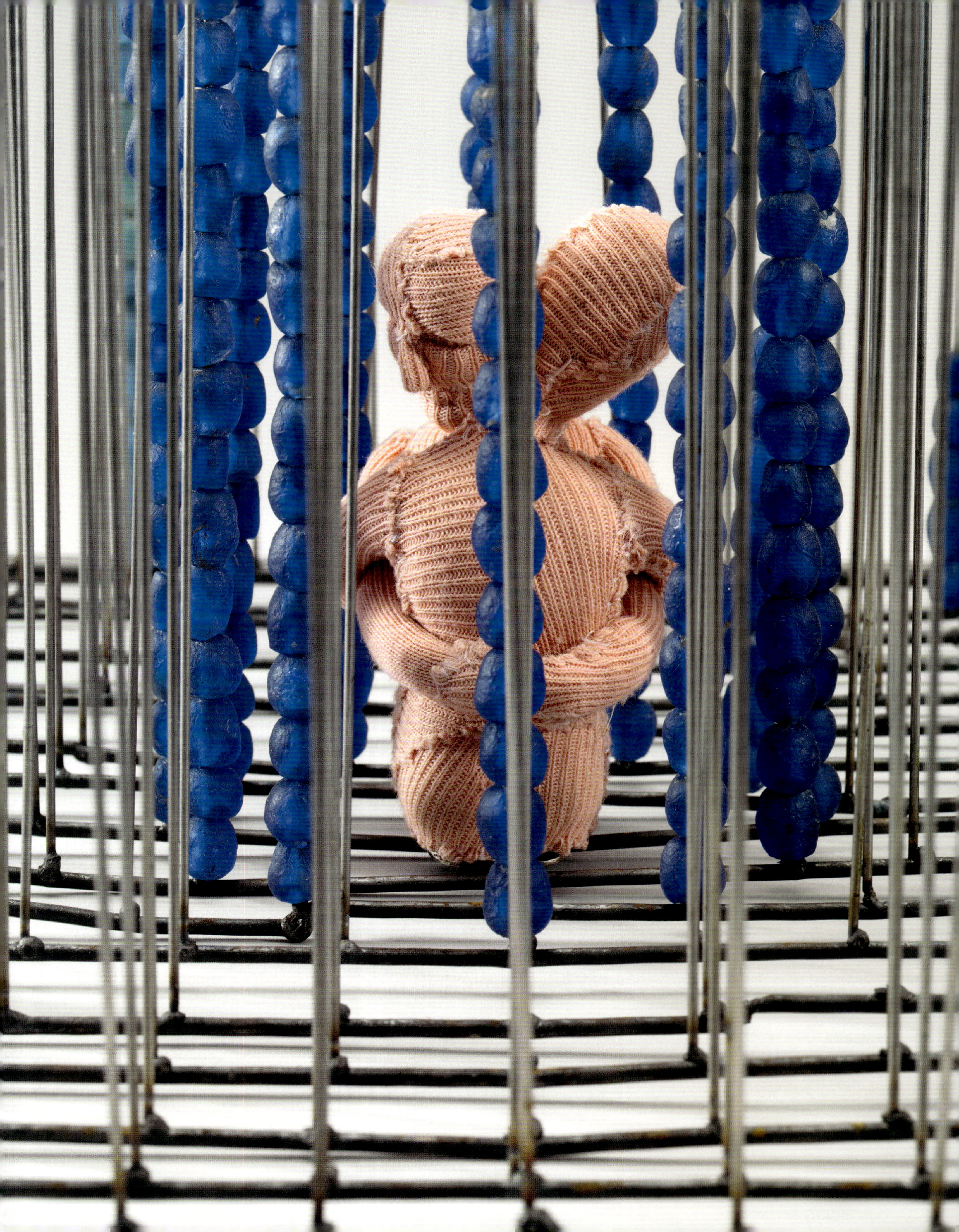

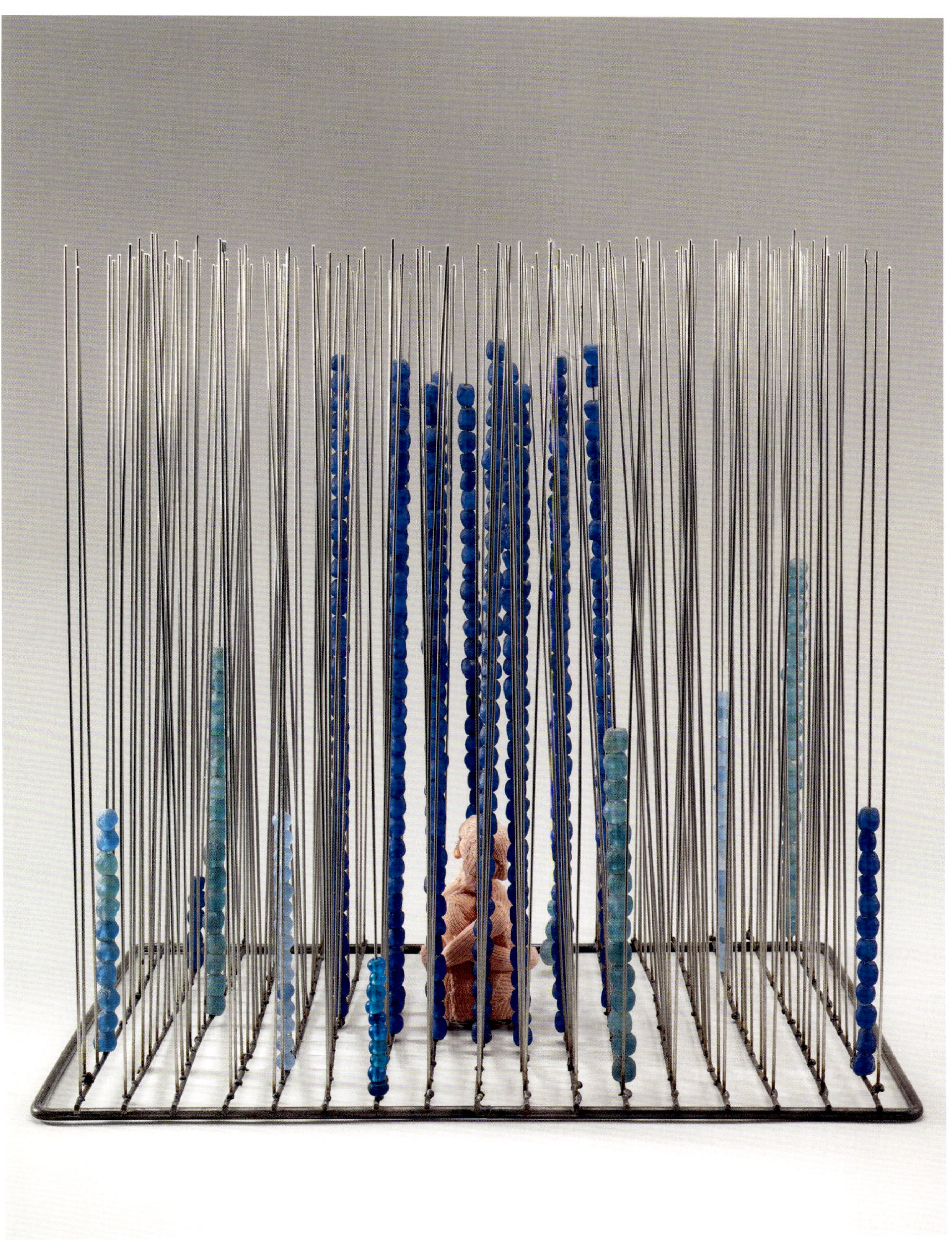

 The Couple 2002

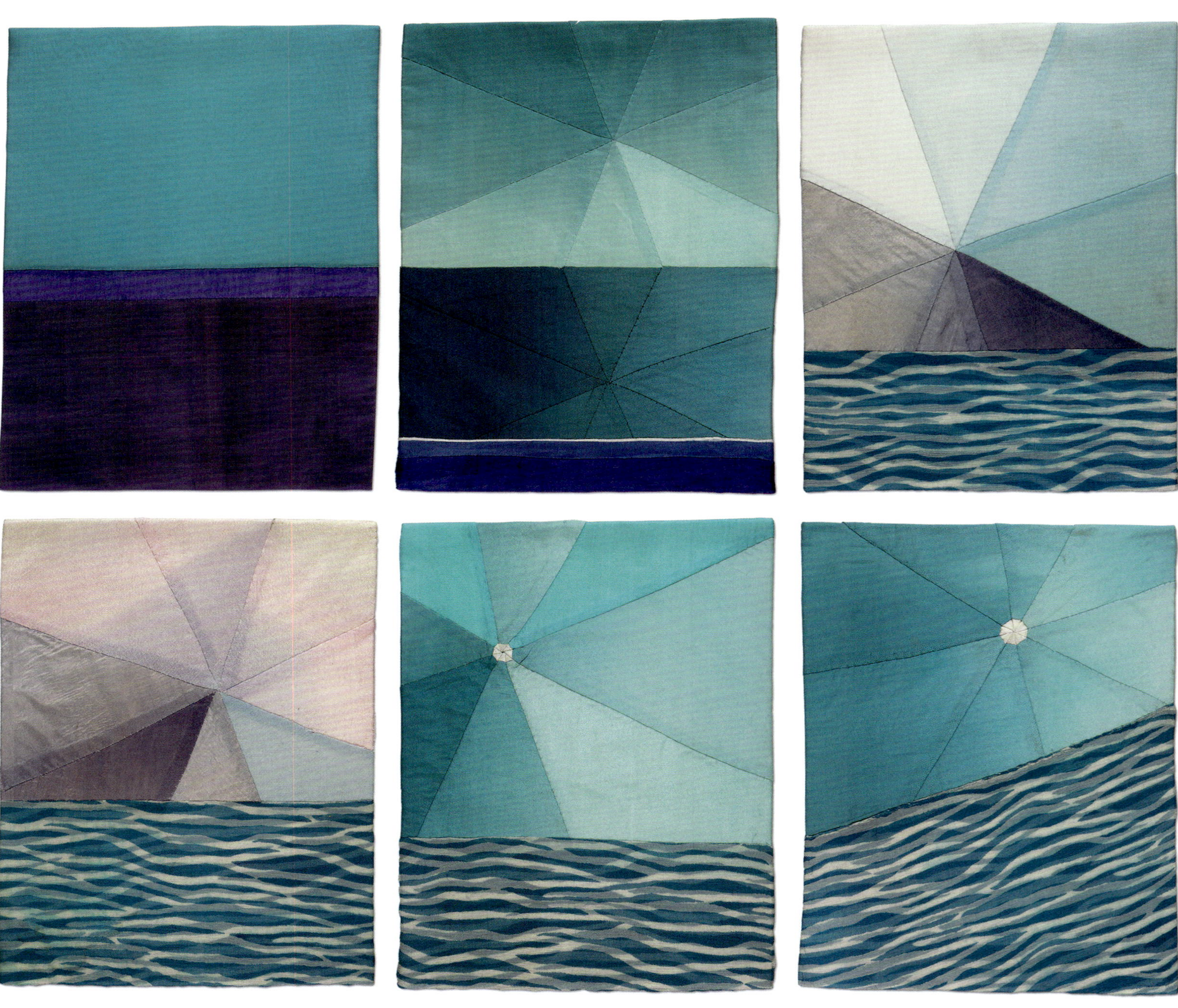

 The Waiting Hours 2007

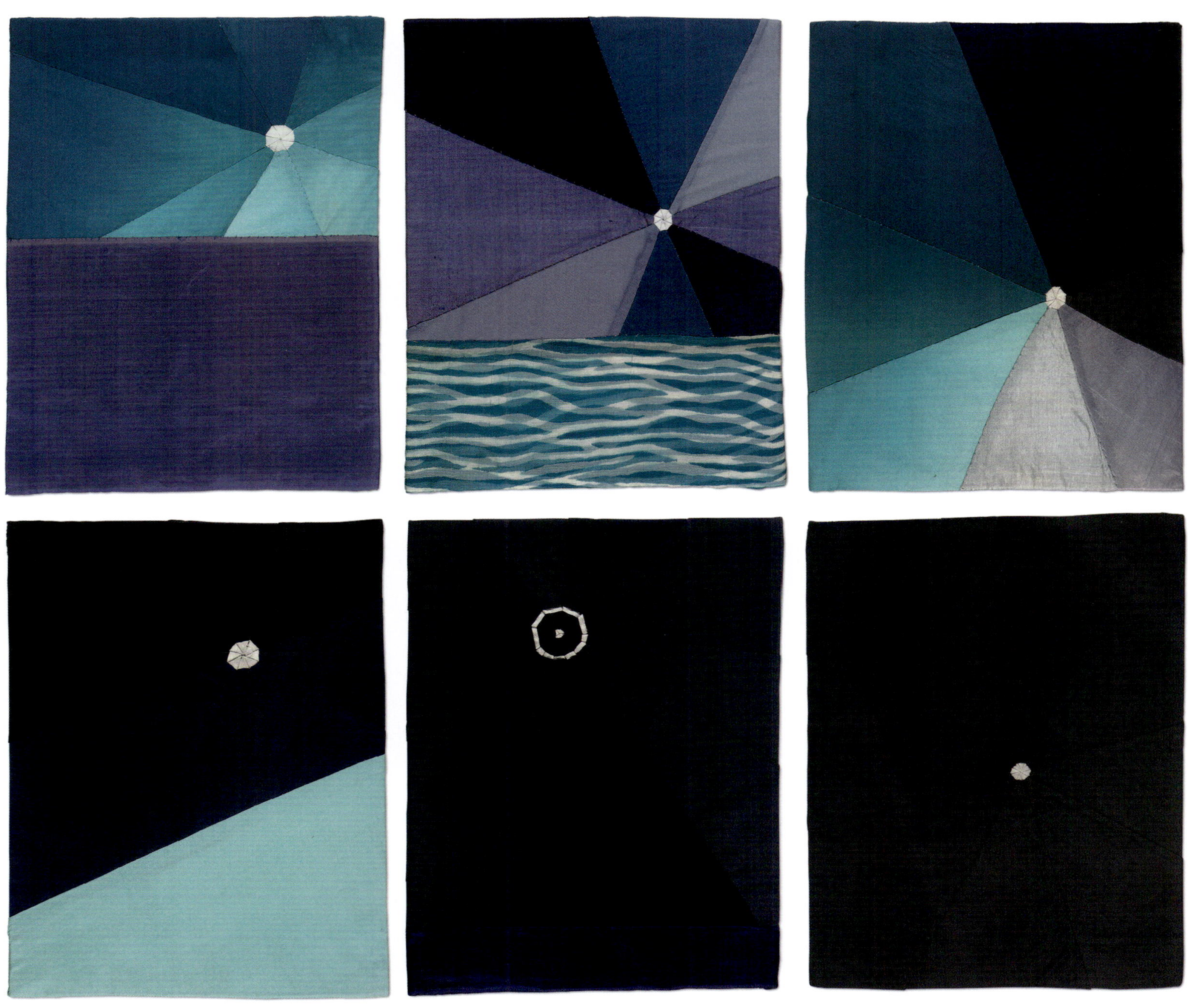

I was always conscious of a
possibility of silence falling like the
lid of a tomb and engulfing me
for ever and ever.
The silence invaded the room
and I was afraid to hear my heart
beat. this danger was coming from within
and that only this incessant flow of
words could keep it at bay if not
master it
to hear chaos, a cascade –
the Marne locks – Beethoven
a river that carries
rocks and trees
The thunder rolling
by.

Loose sheet of writing, c1958 (LB-0513)
Conscious and Unconscious 2008

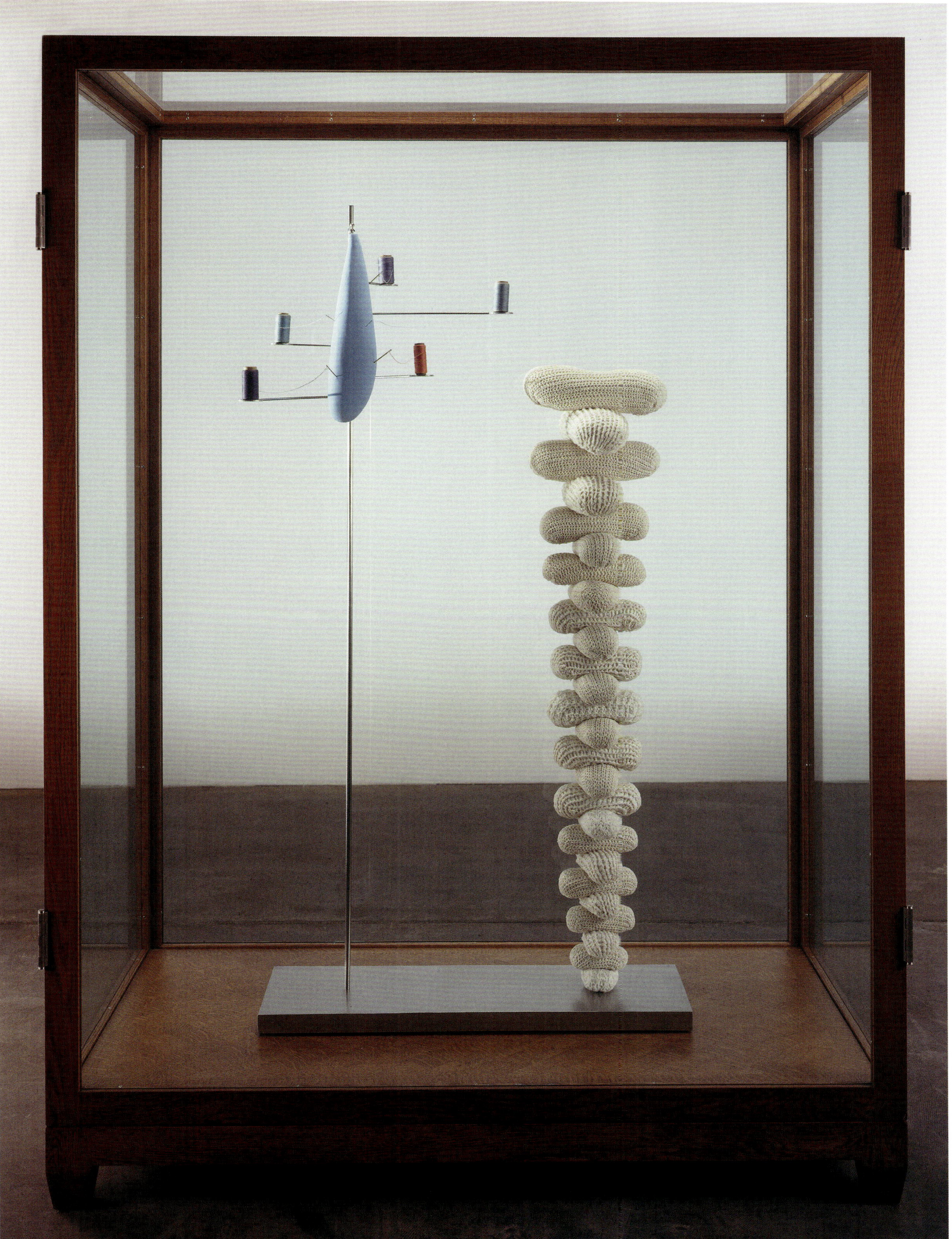

6
When you come to me

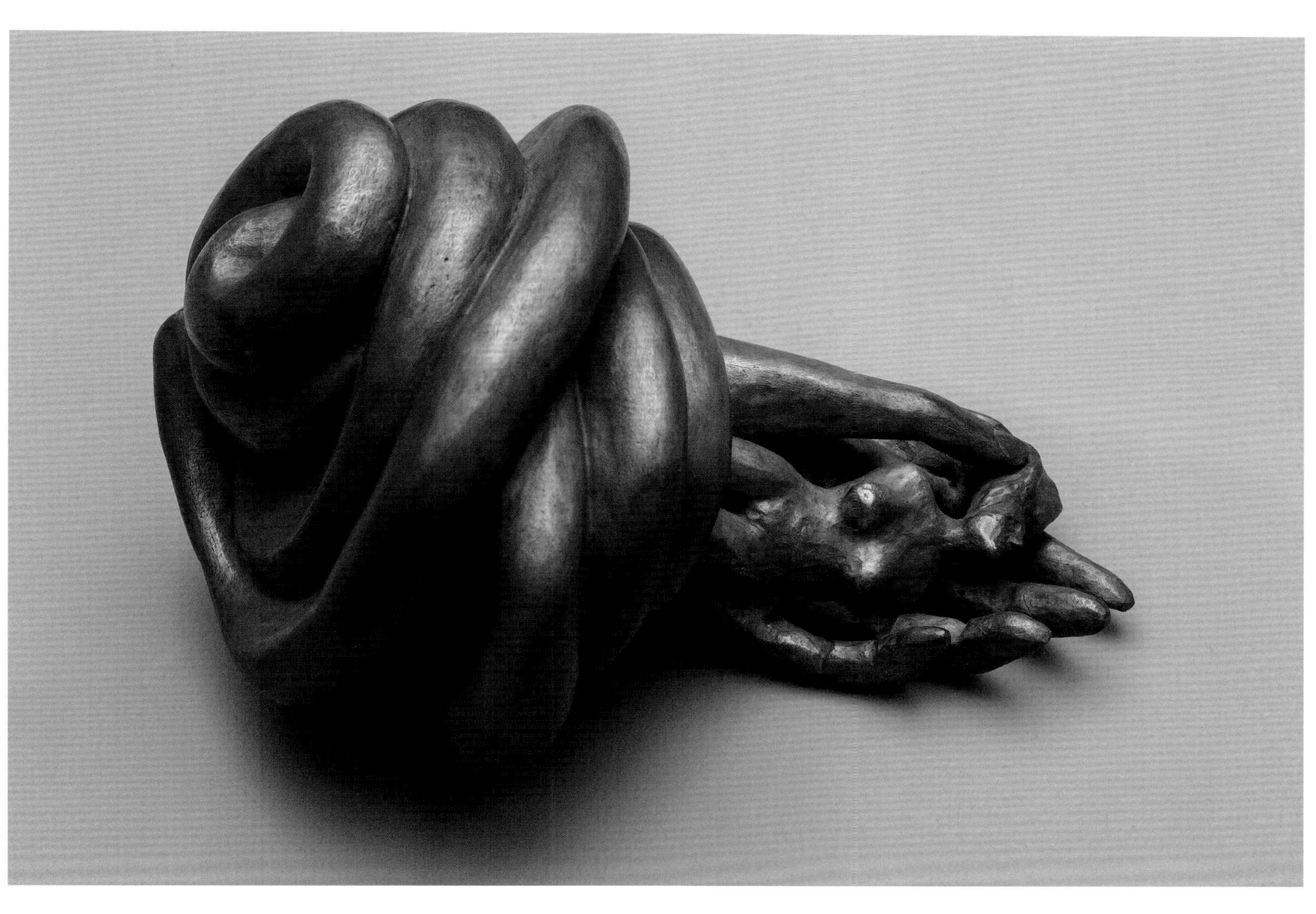

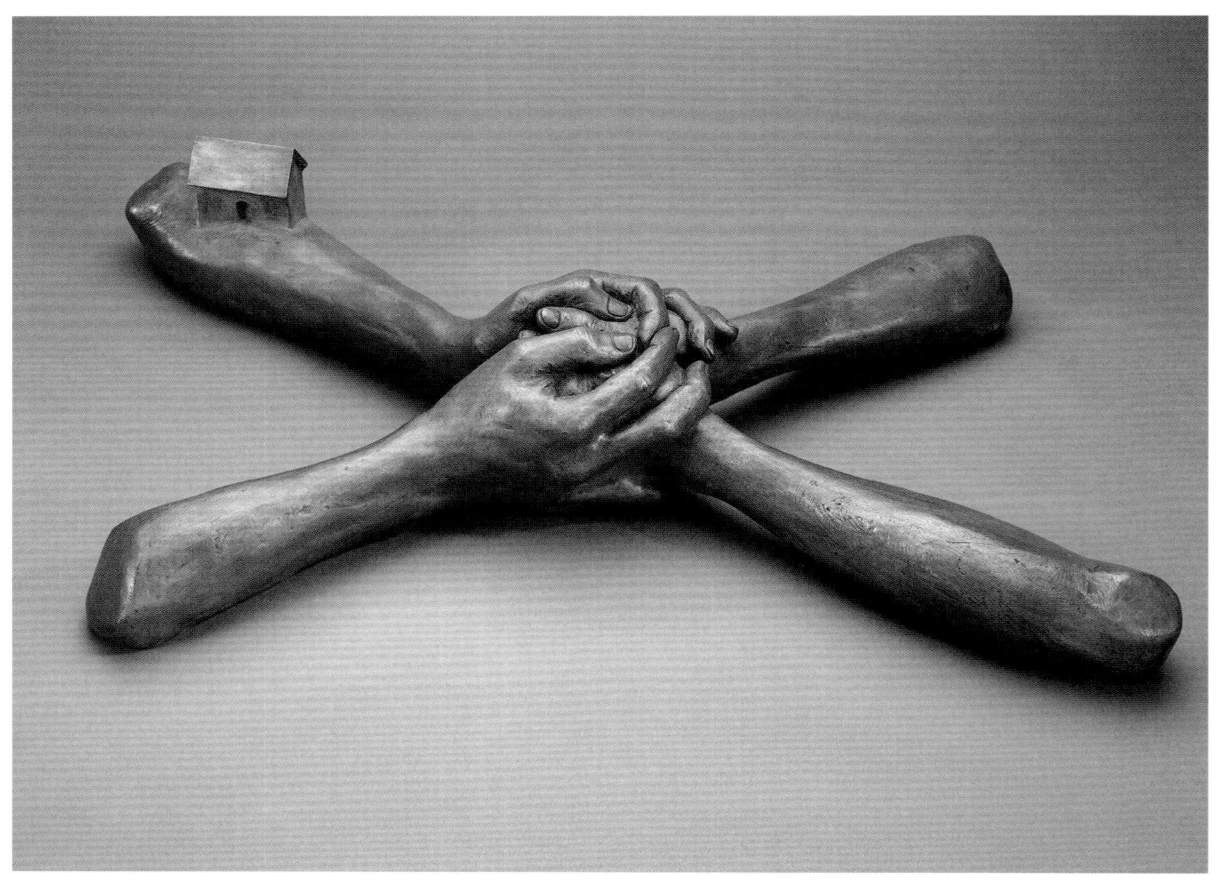

 Untitled (no. 7) 1993

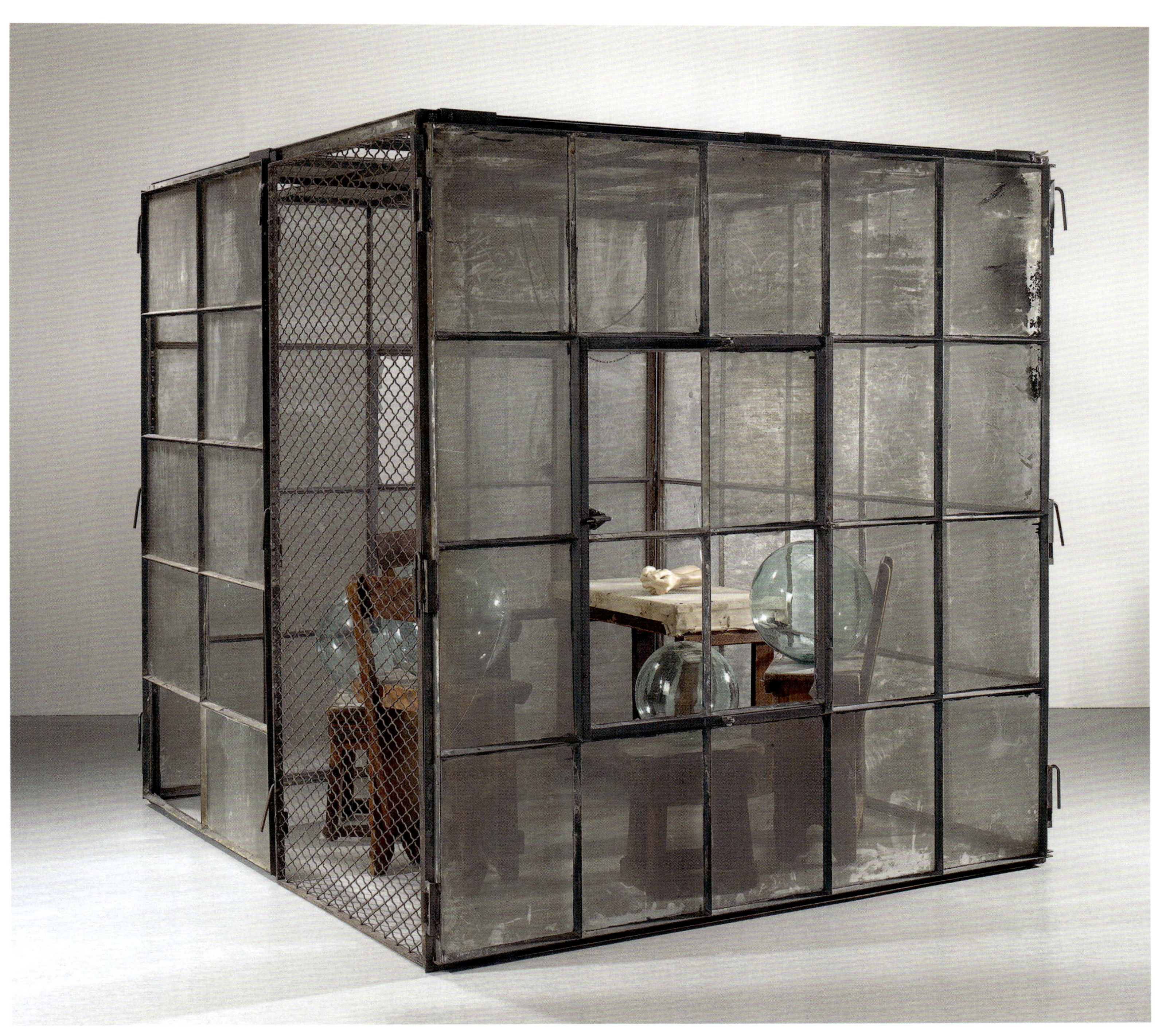

this page and following spread:
Cell (Glass Spheres and Hands) 1990–93; (detail)

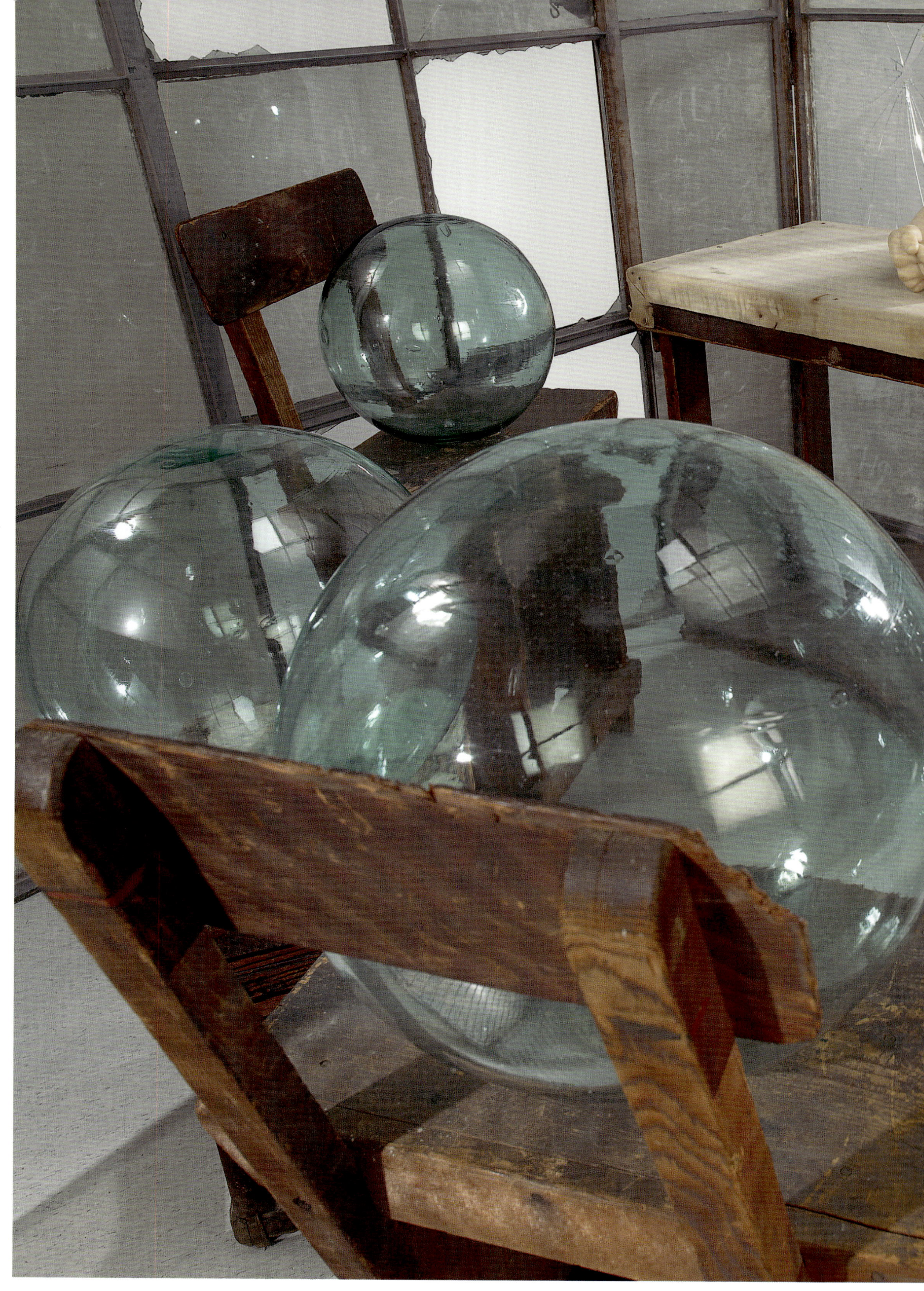

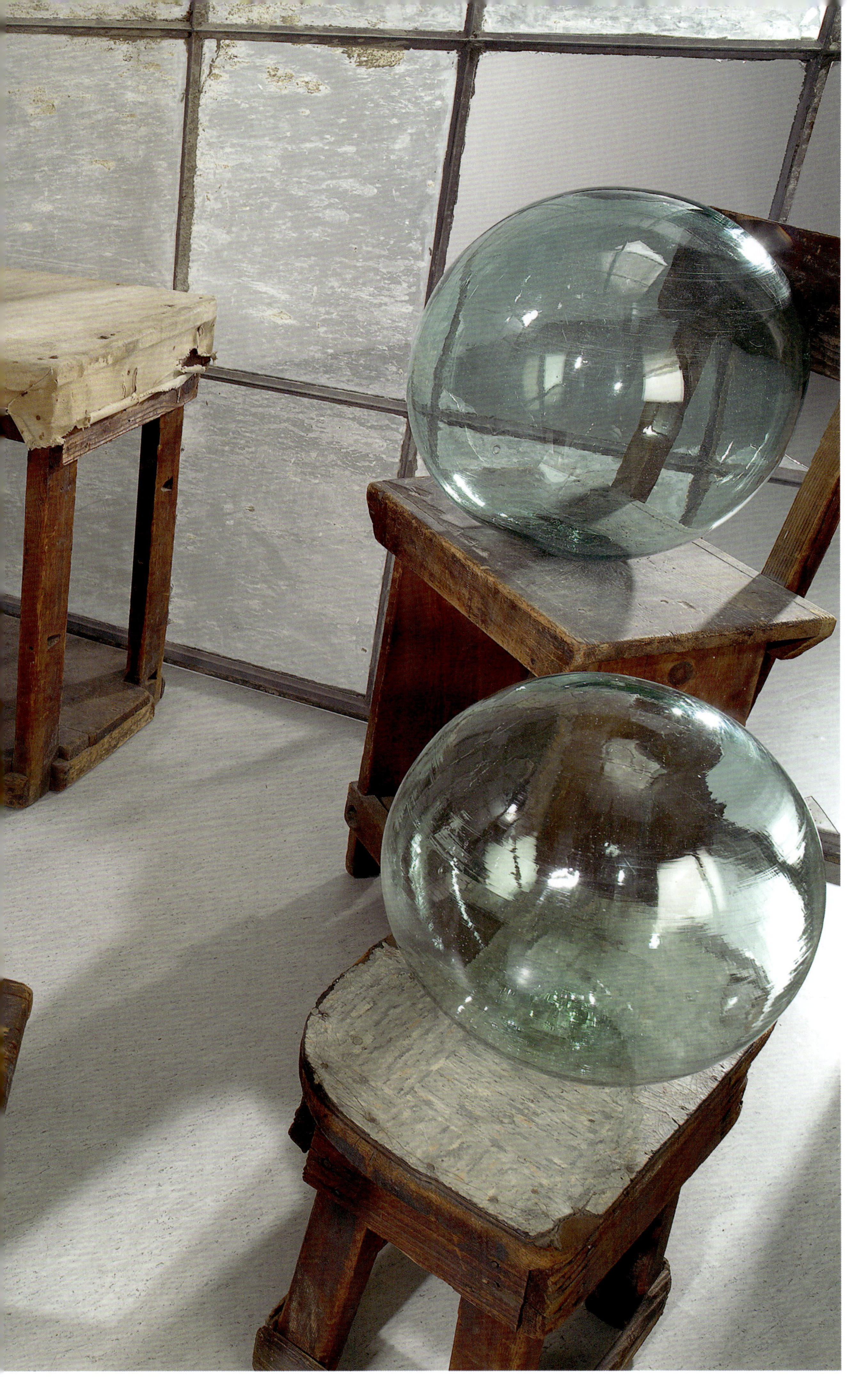

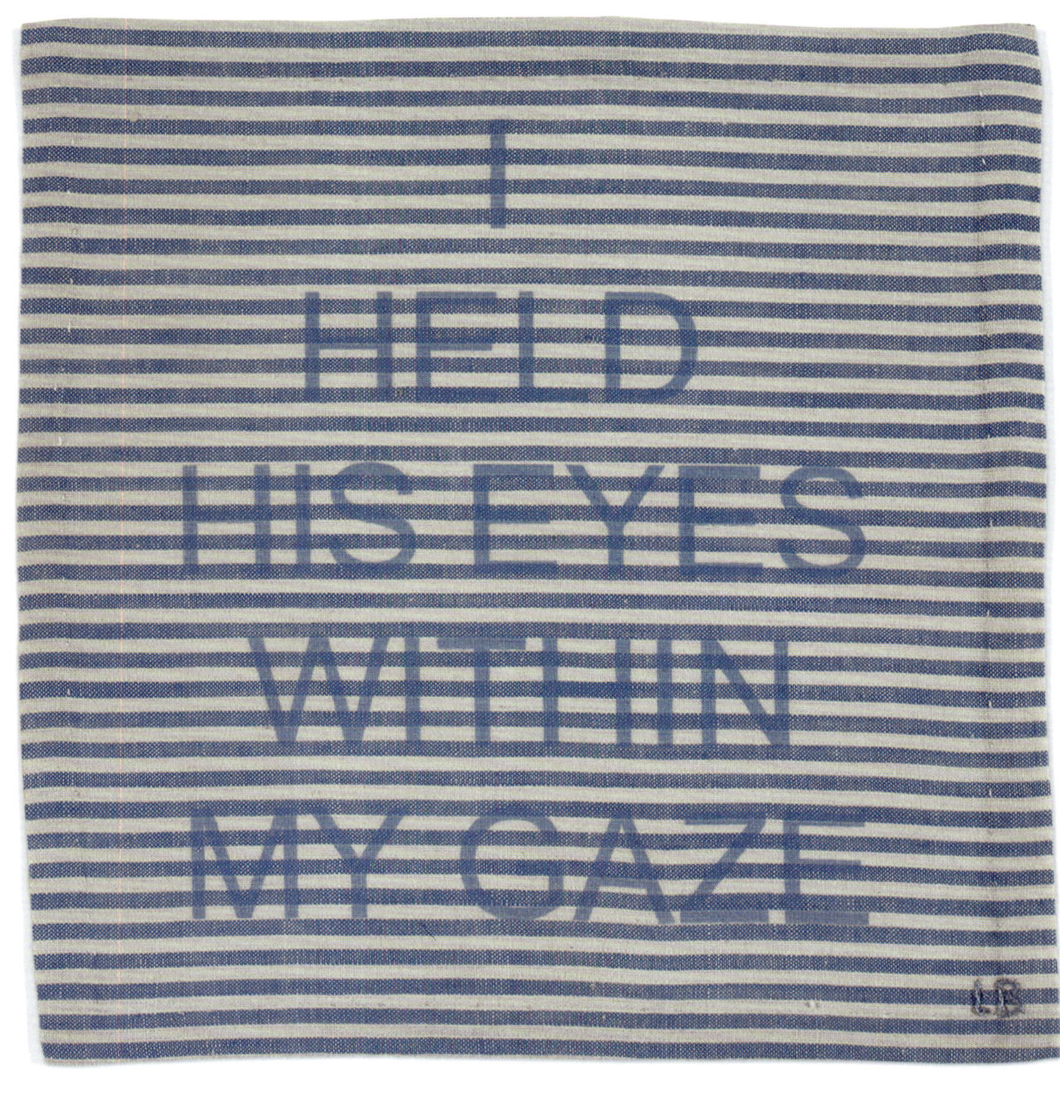

I Held His Eyes within My Gaze 2002
The Couple 2003

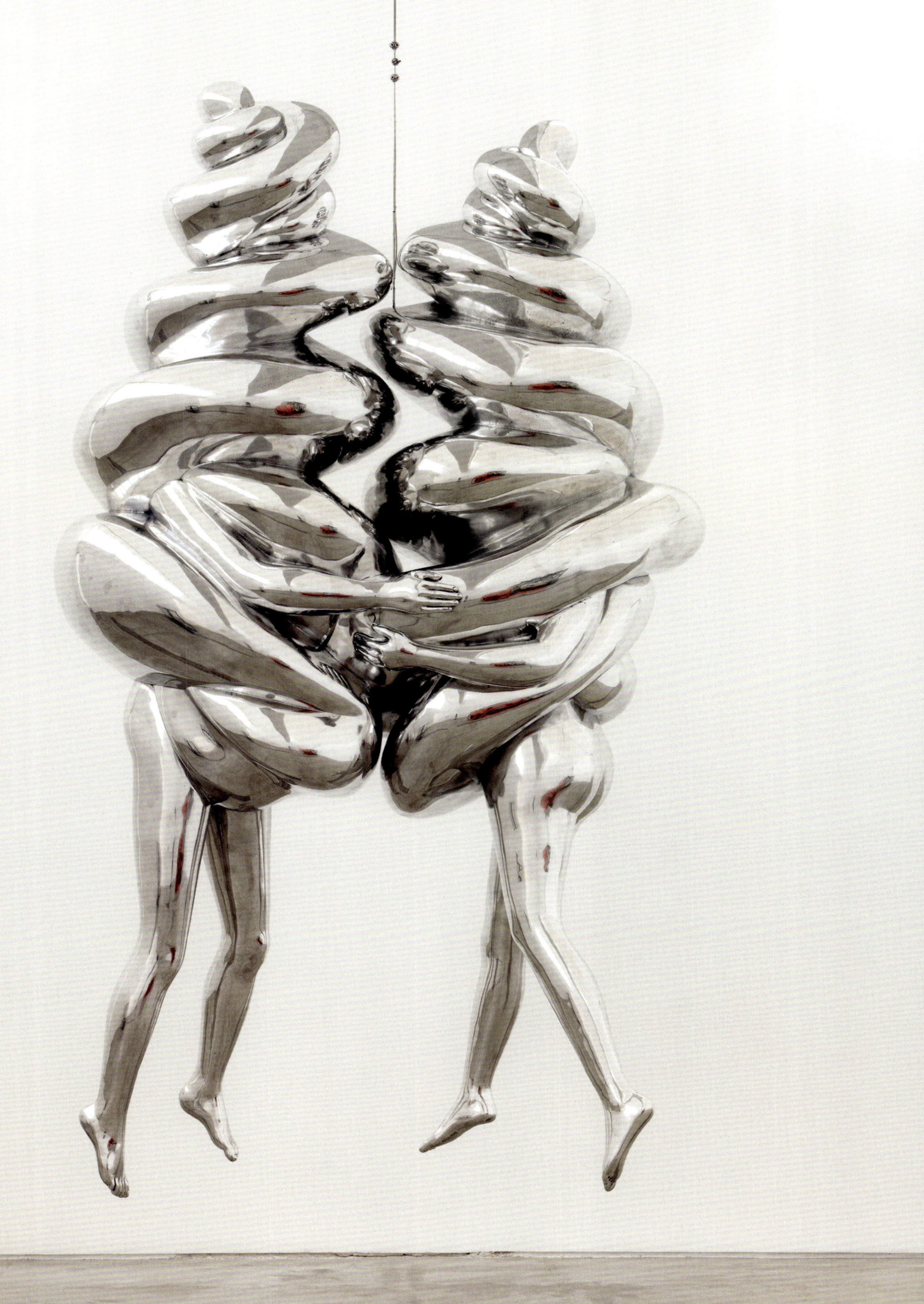

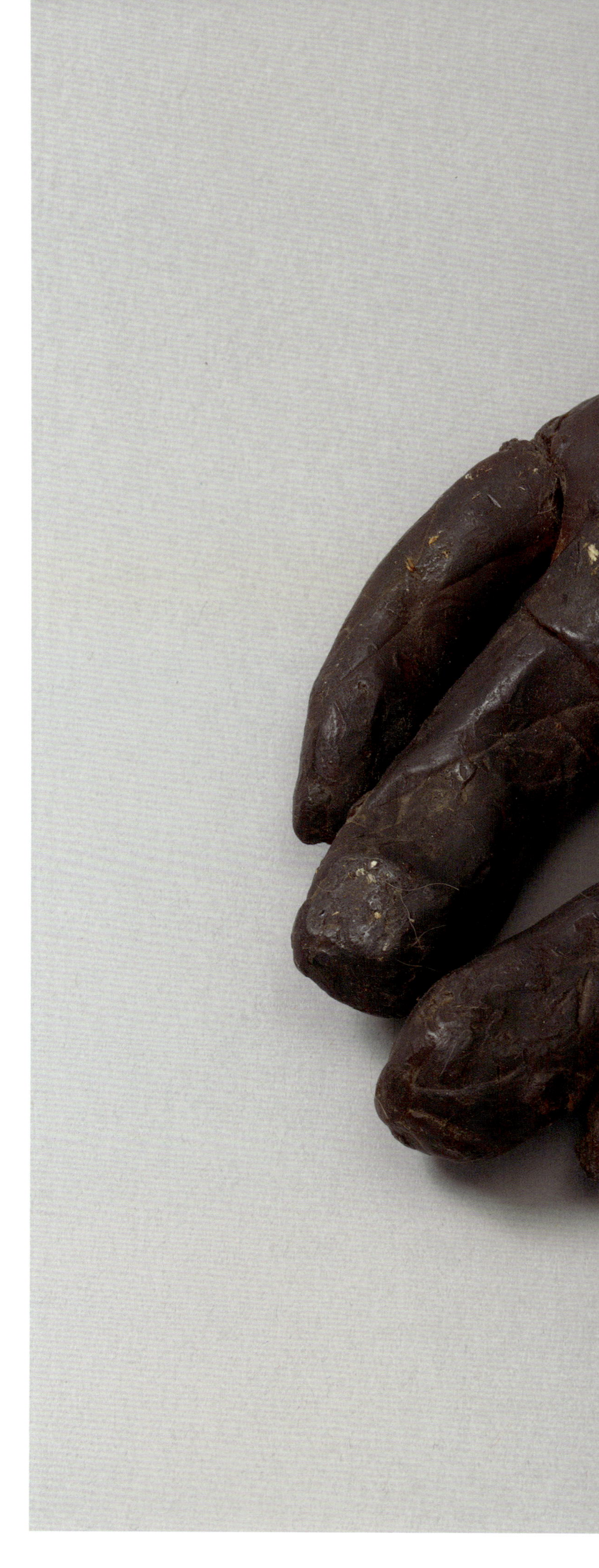

 Untitled (Hand) 1970

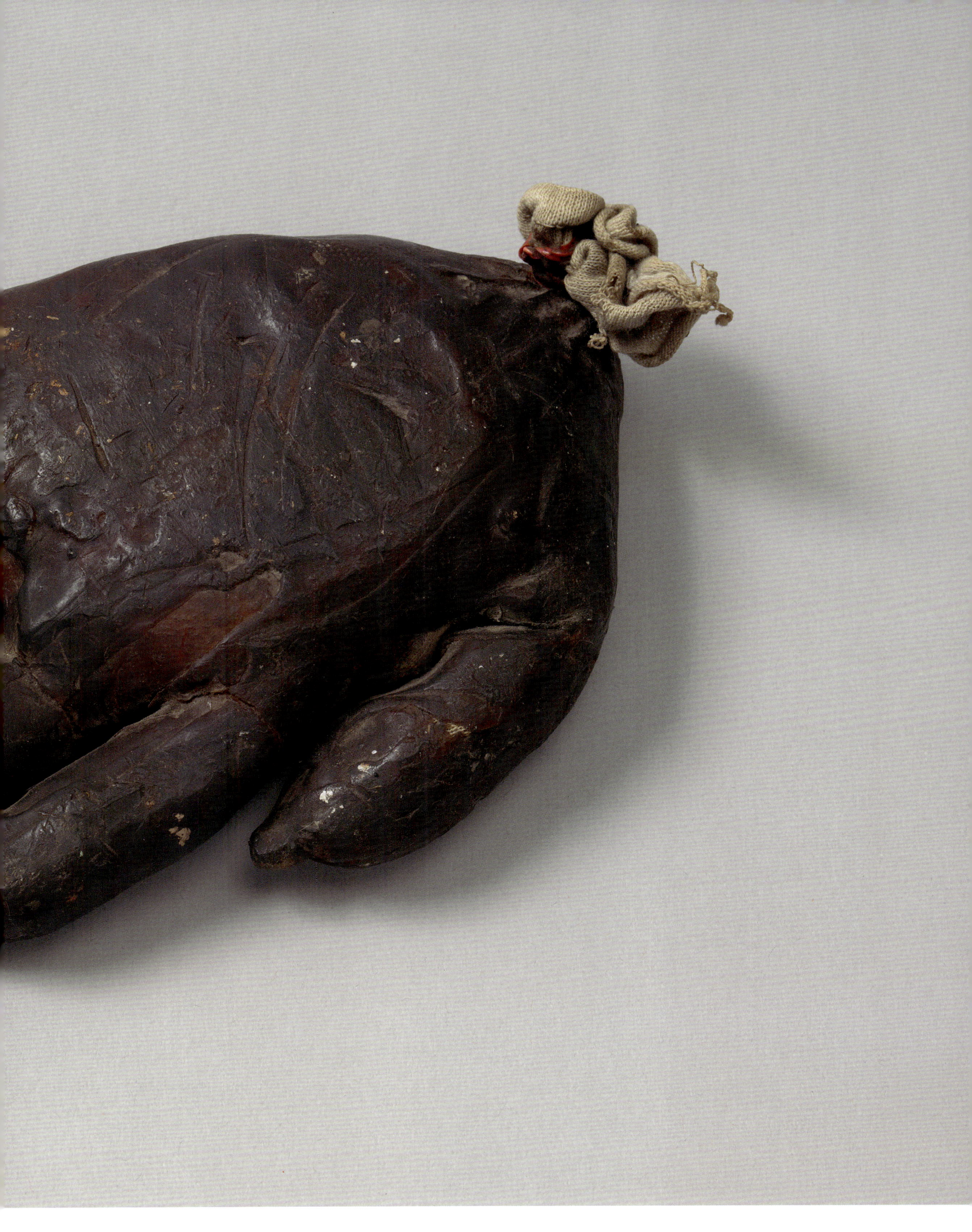

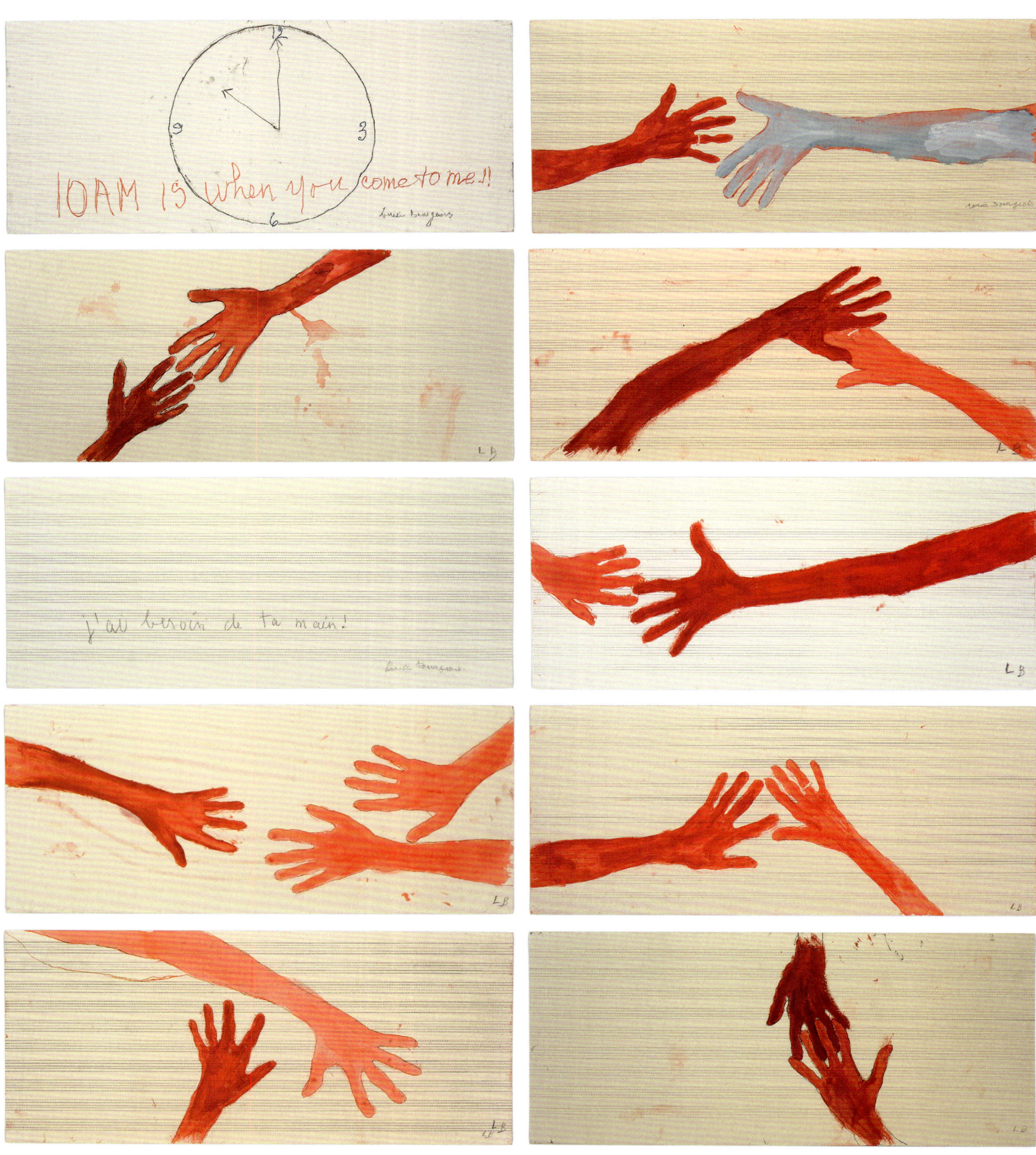

this spread and following pages:
10 AM Is When You Come to Me 2007; (detail)

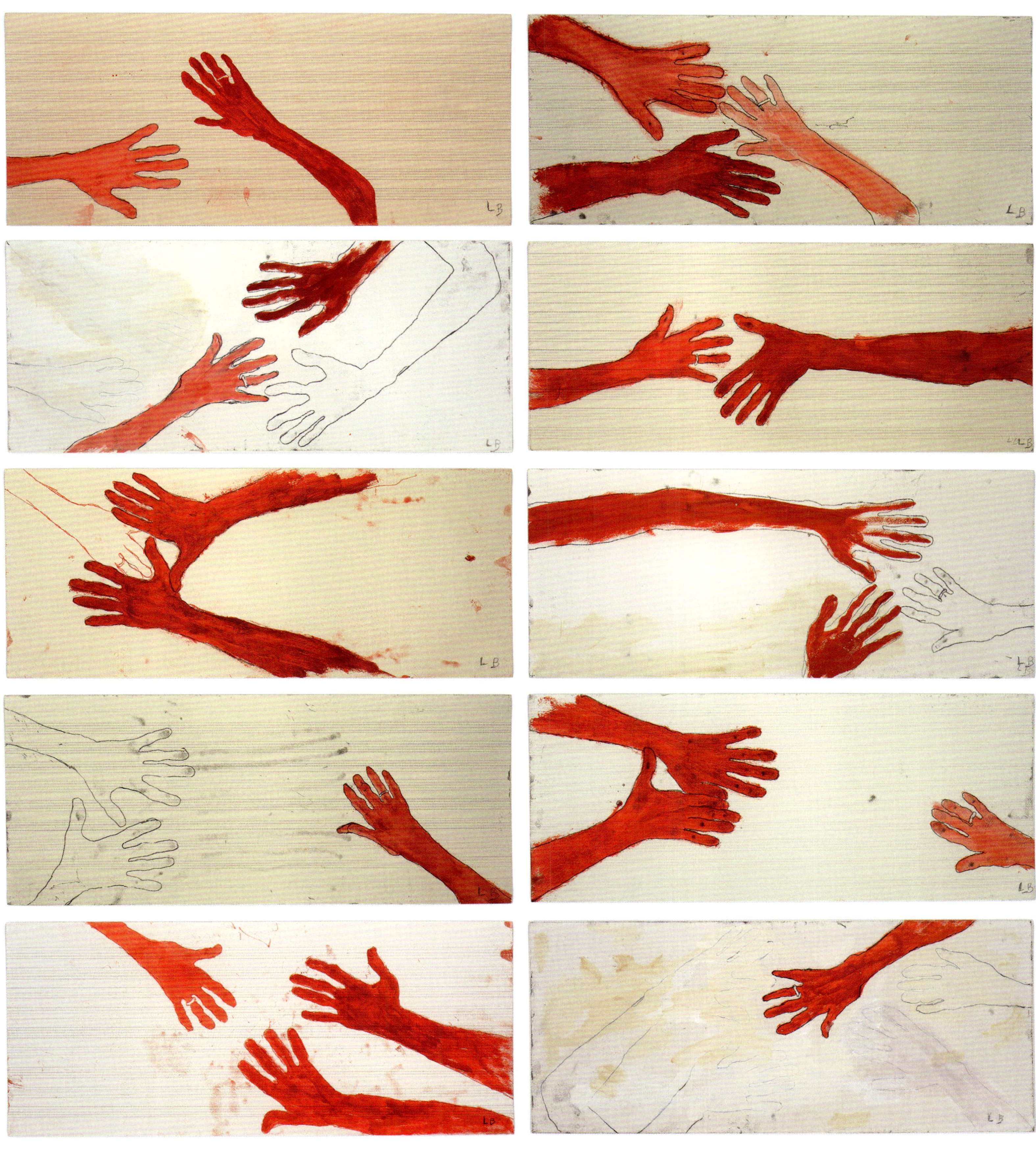

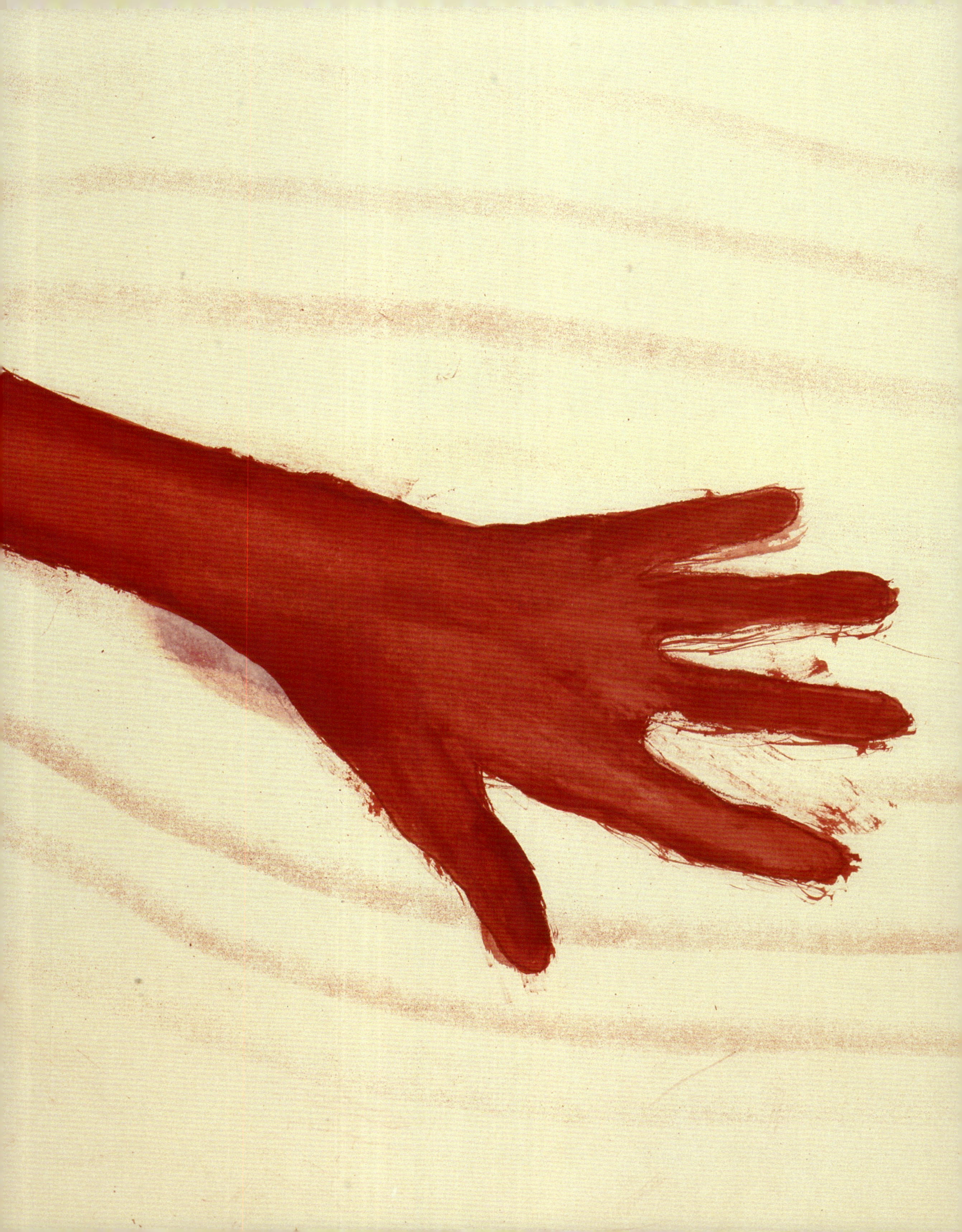

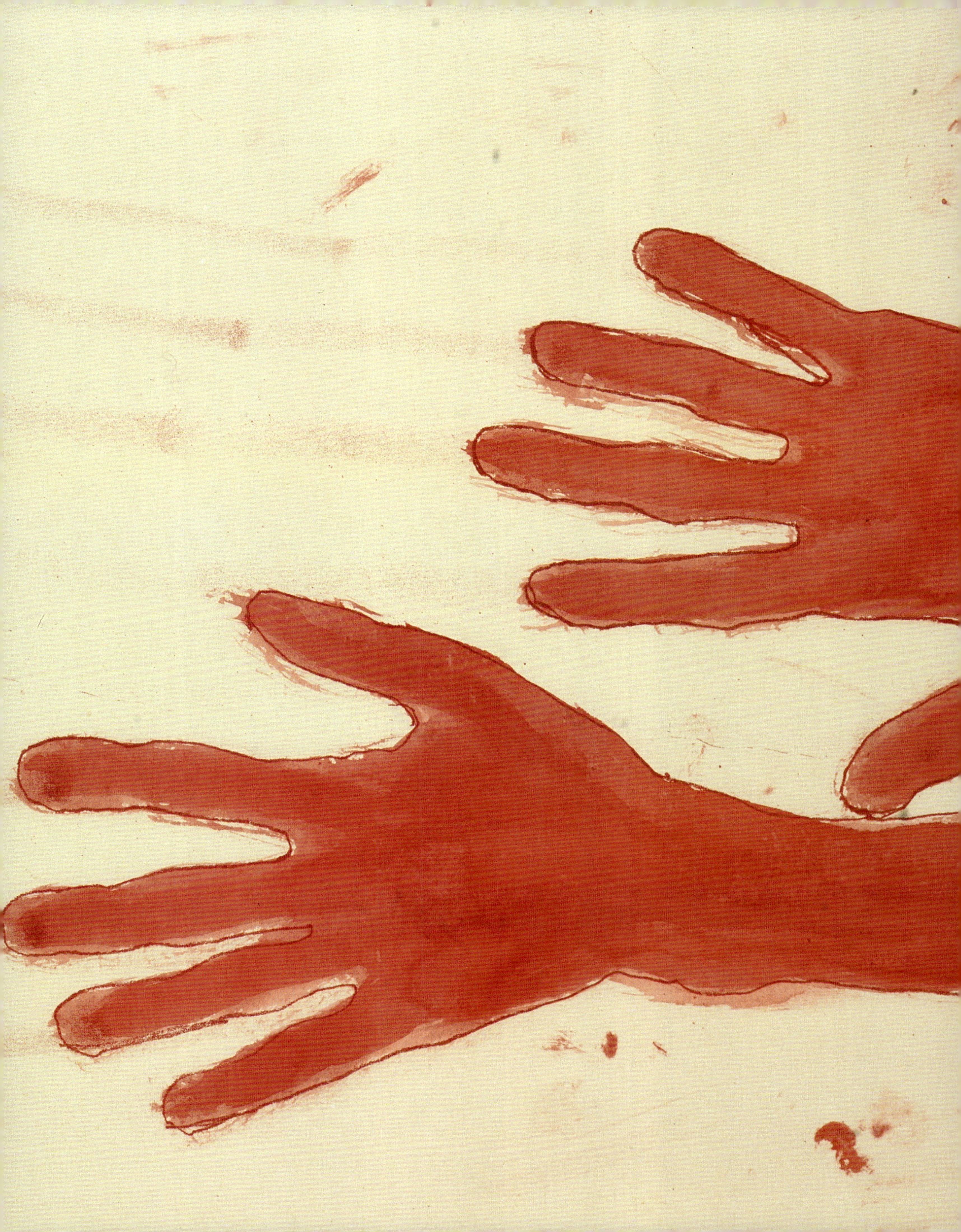

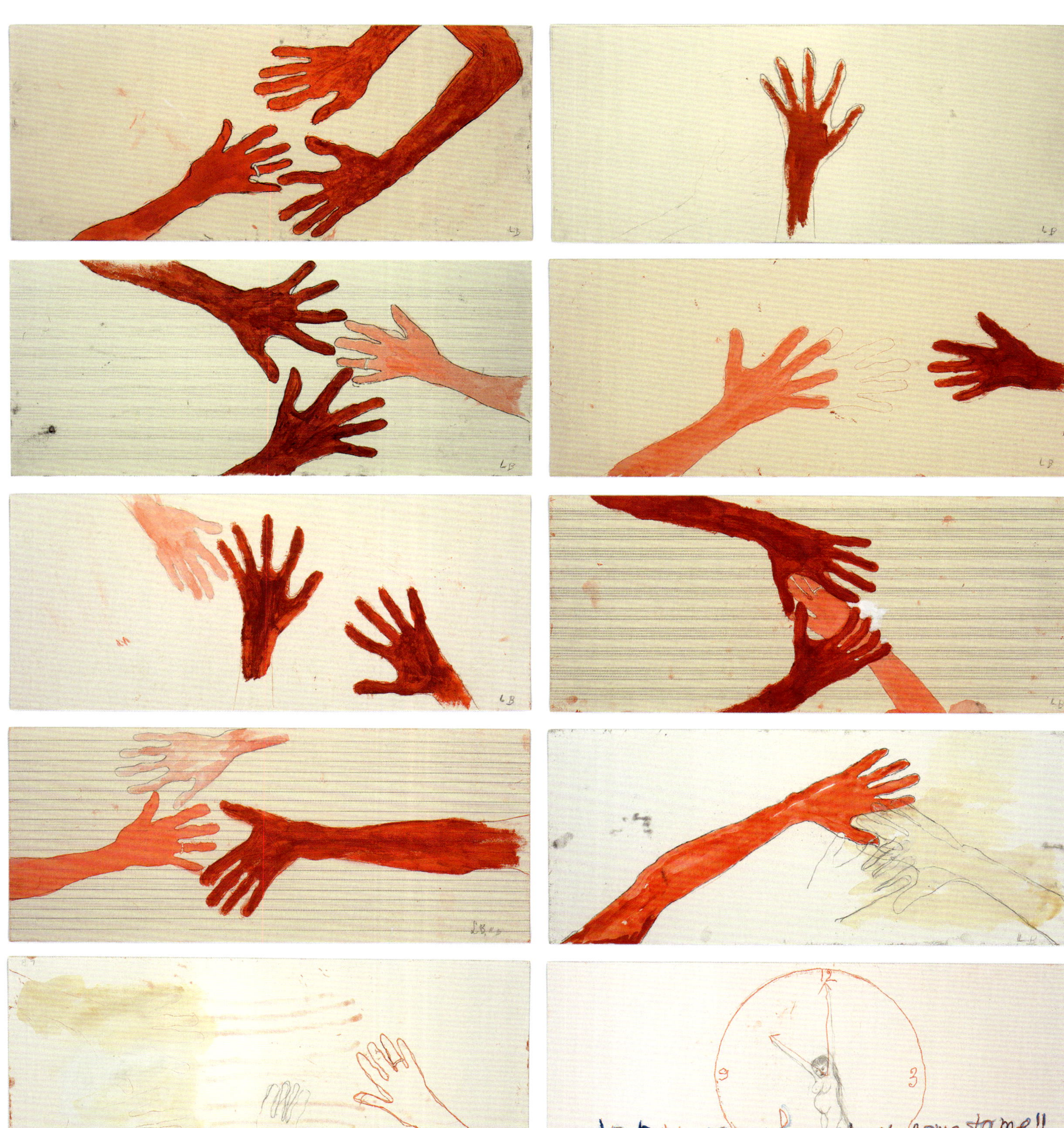
12
9
3
6
10AM IS when you come to me!!

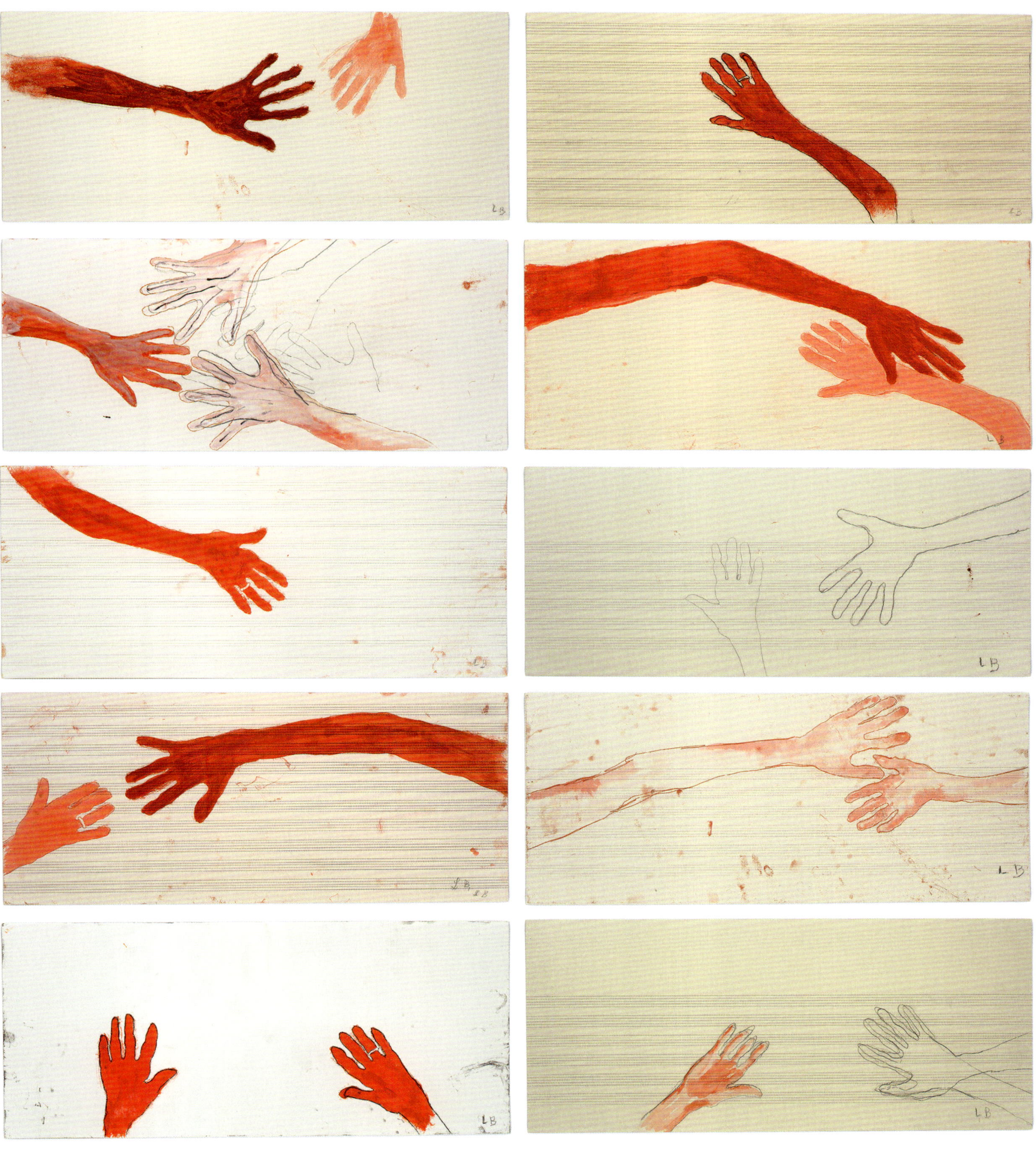

7
I undo, I redo

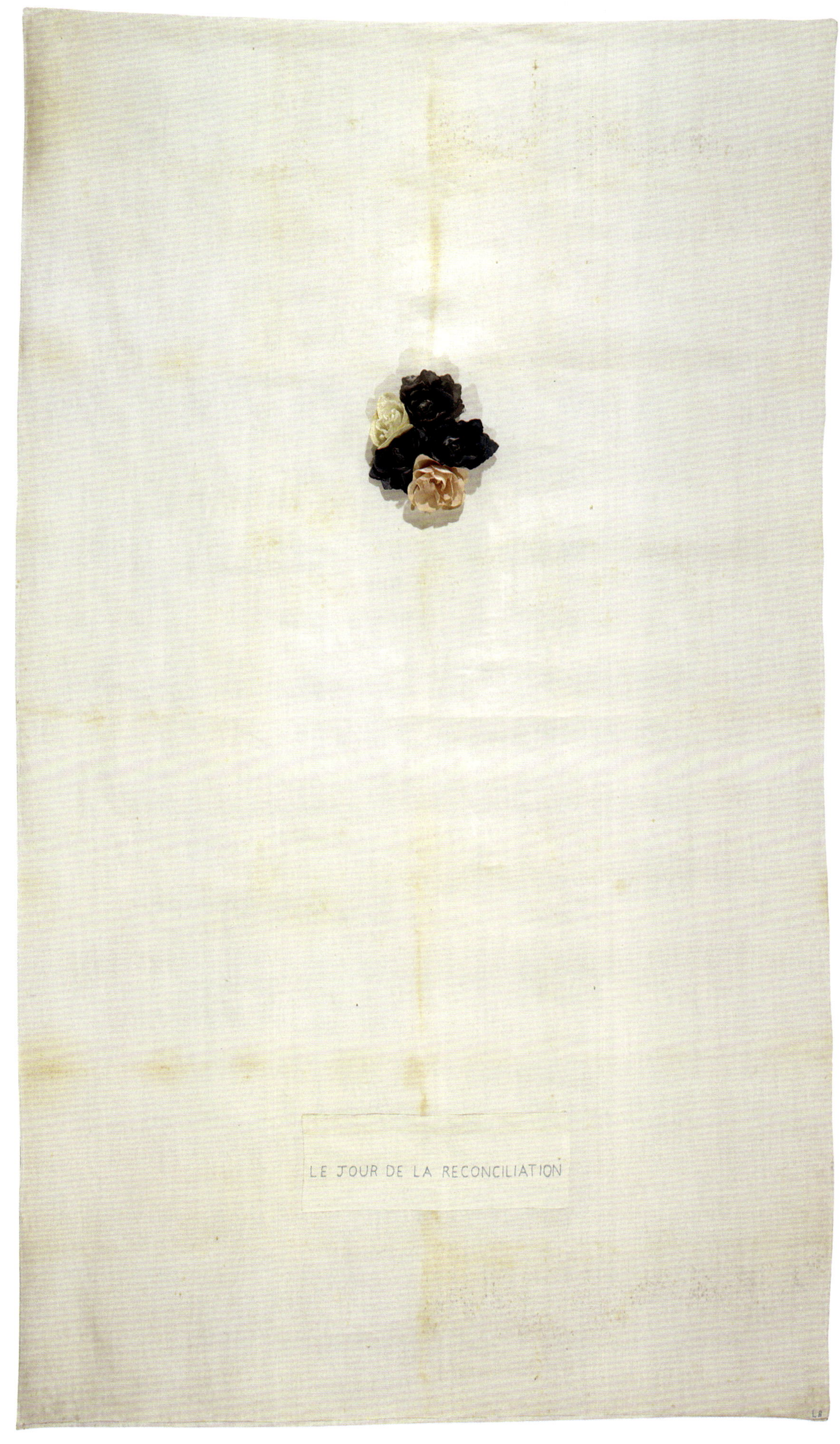
LE JOUR DE LA RECONCILIATION

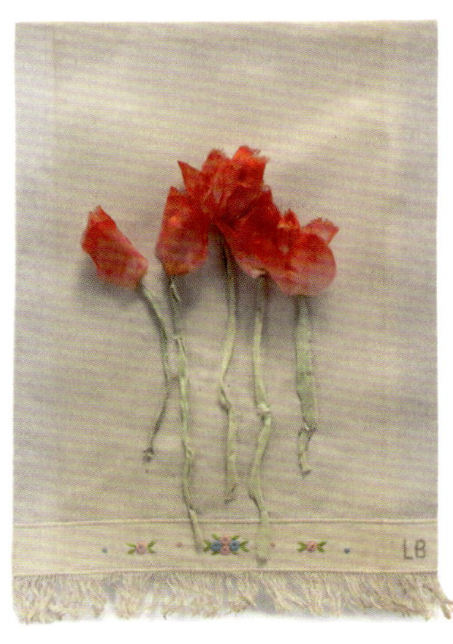

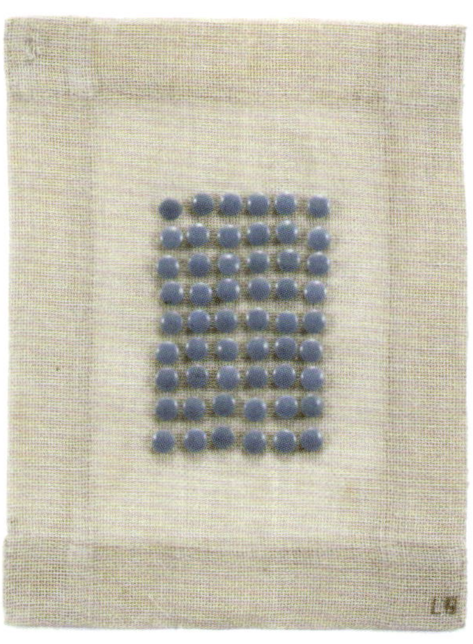

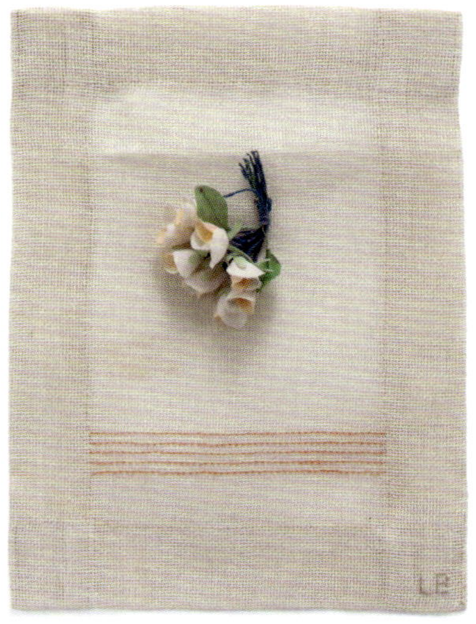

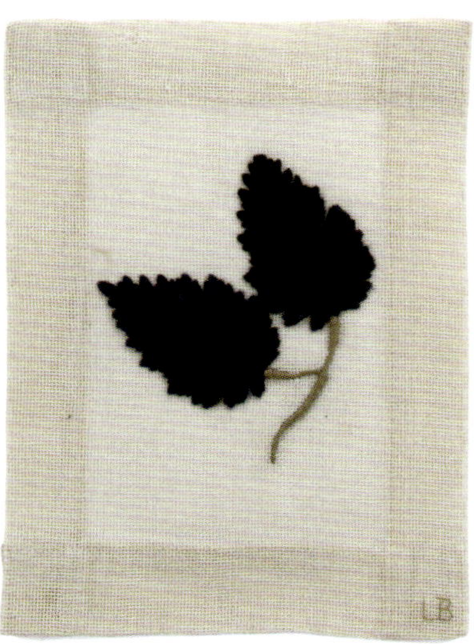

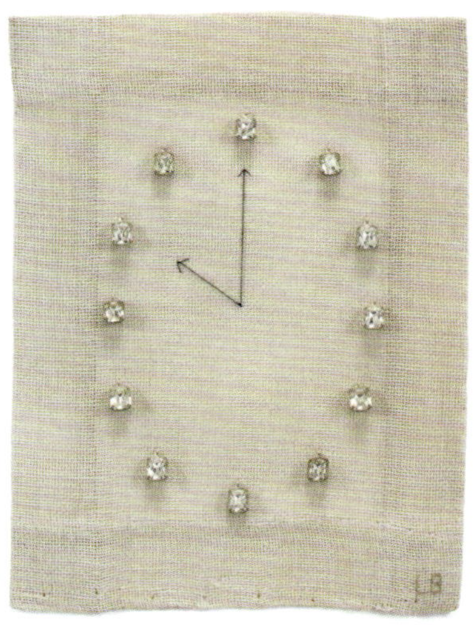

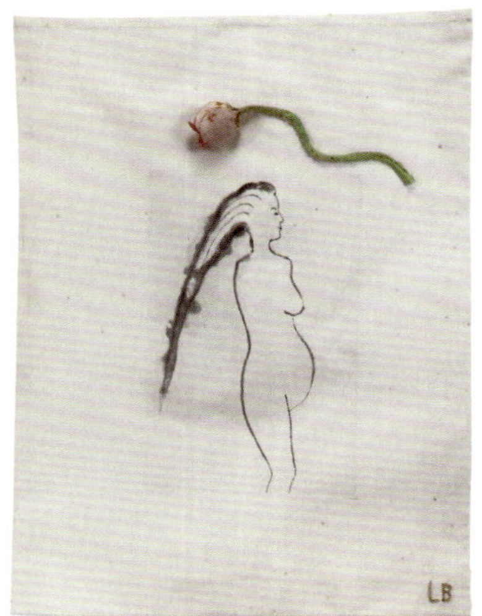

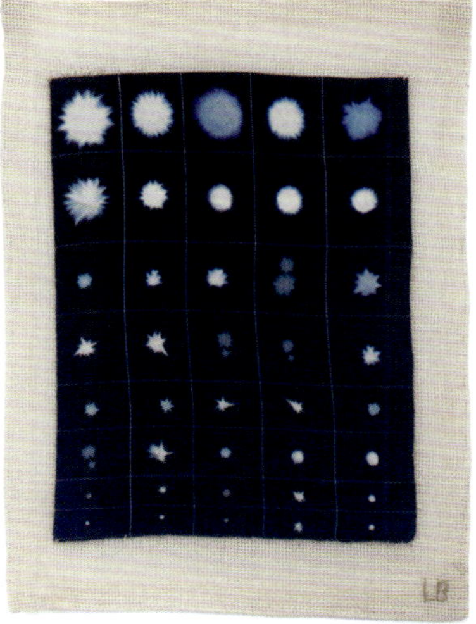

this spread and following pages:
Eugénie Grandet 2009; (detail)

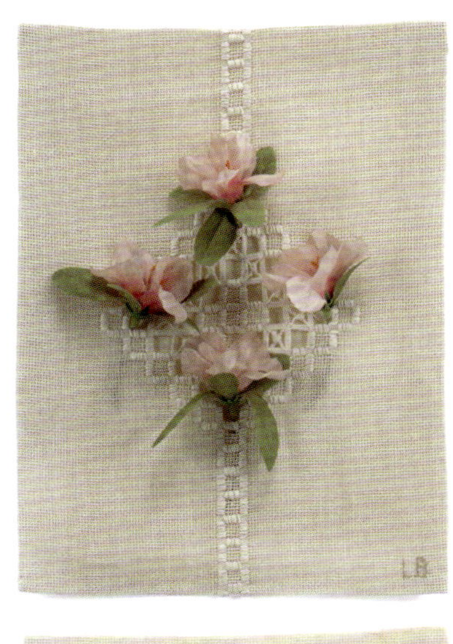
LB

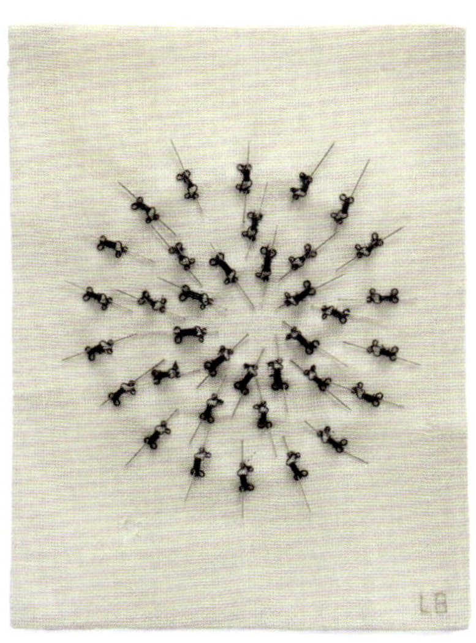
LB

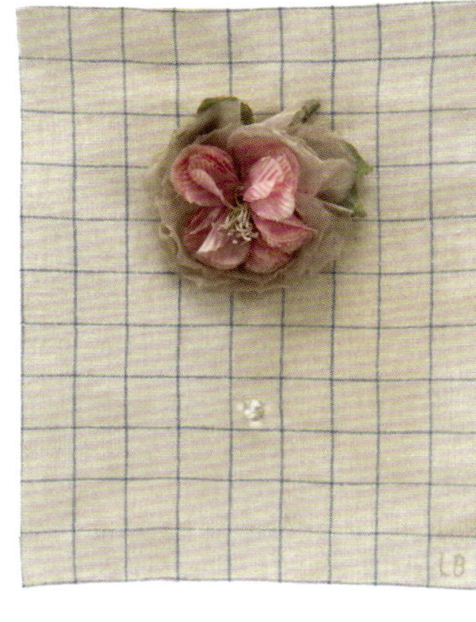
LB

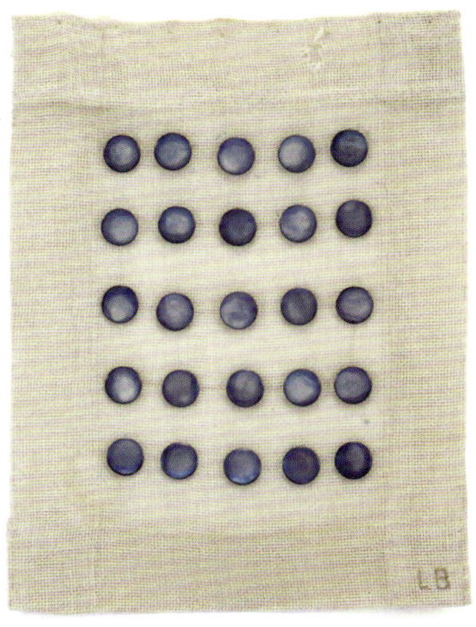
LB

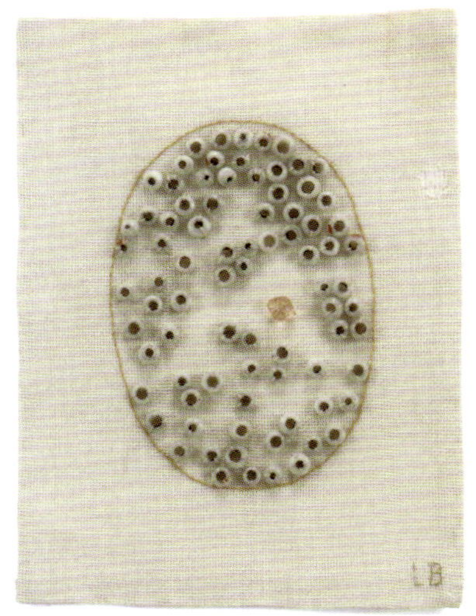
LB

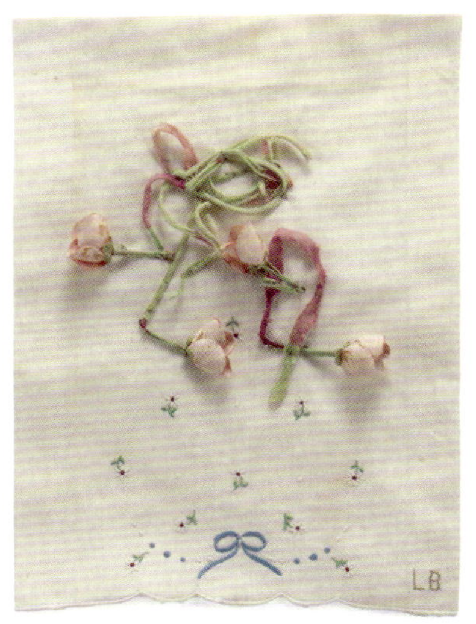
LB

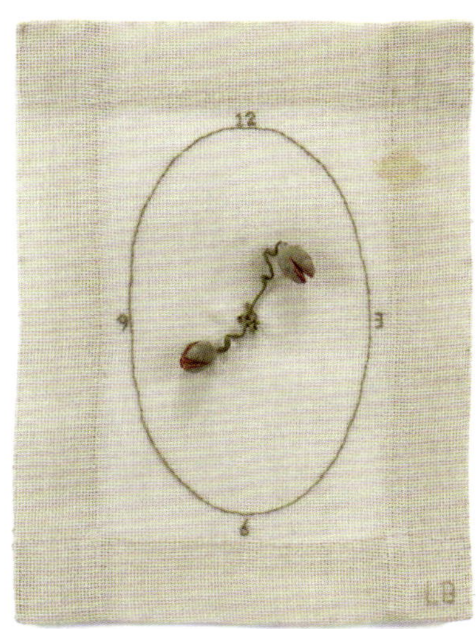
12
9
3
6
LB

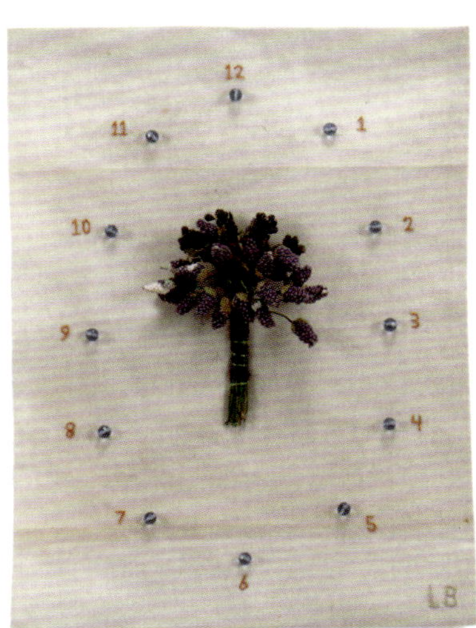
12
11
1
10
2
9
3
8
4
7
5
6
LB

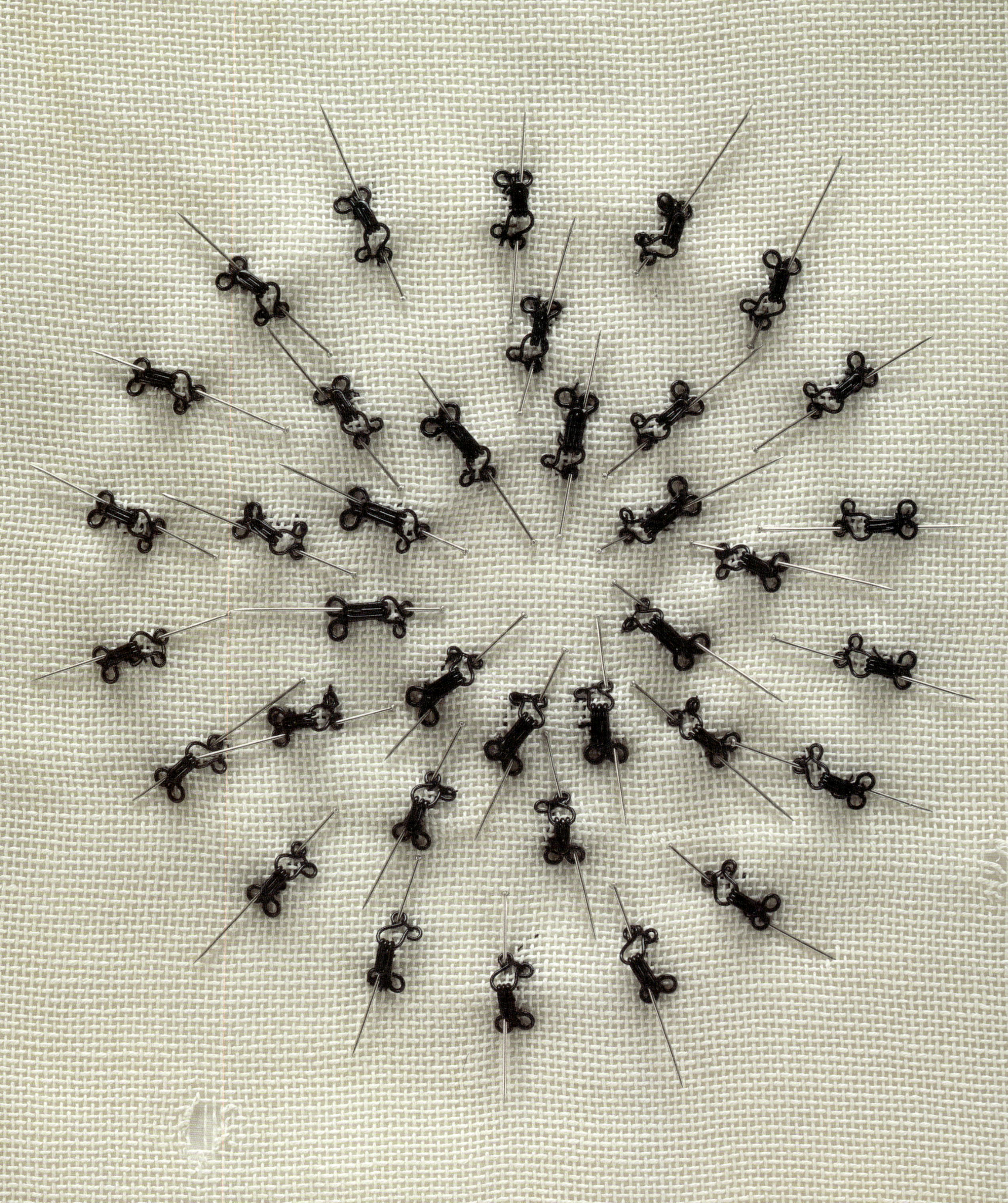

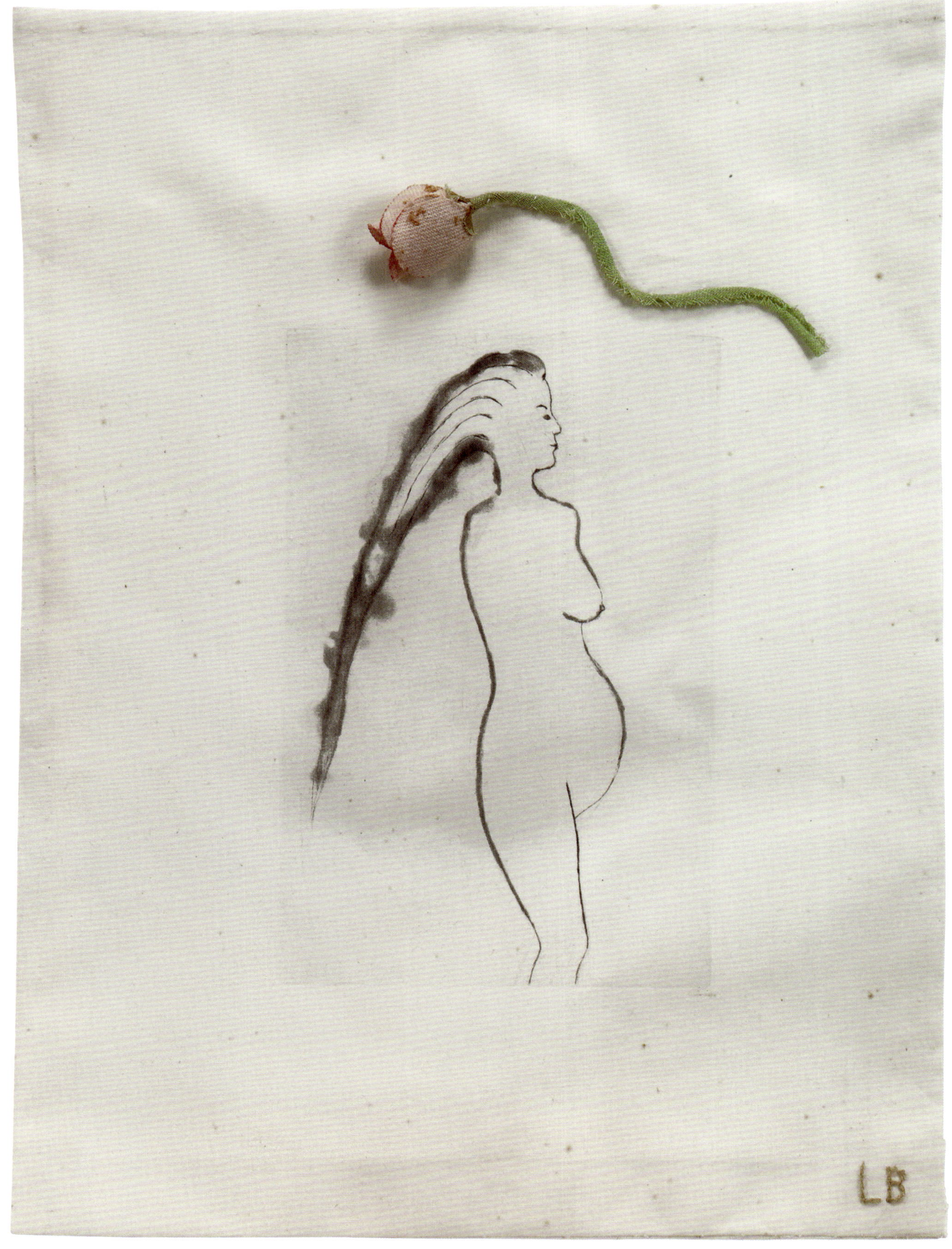
LB

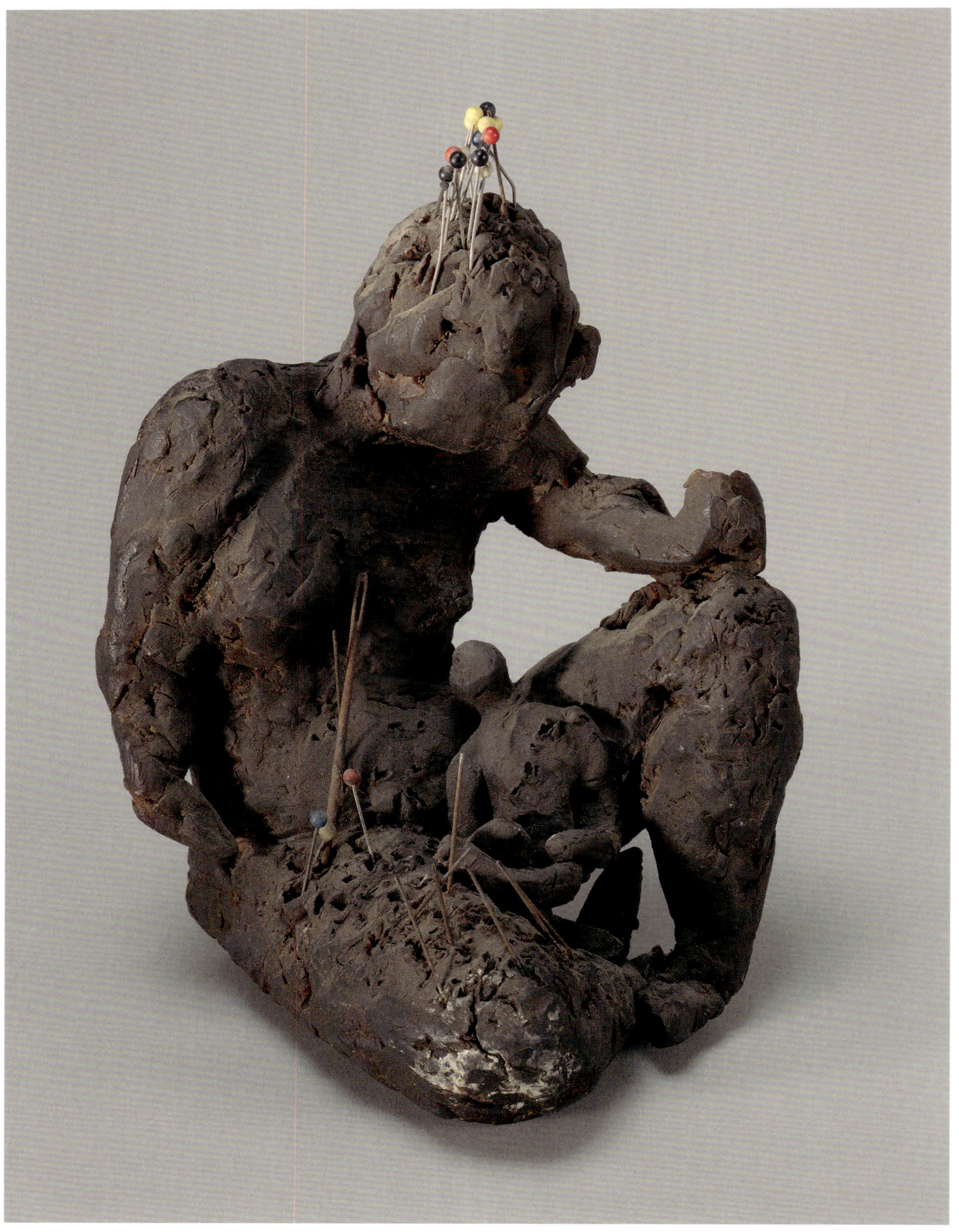

 Mother and Child 1970

opposite and following spread:
Spider 1997; (detail)

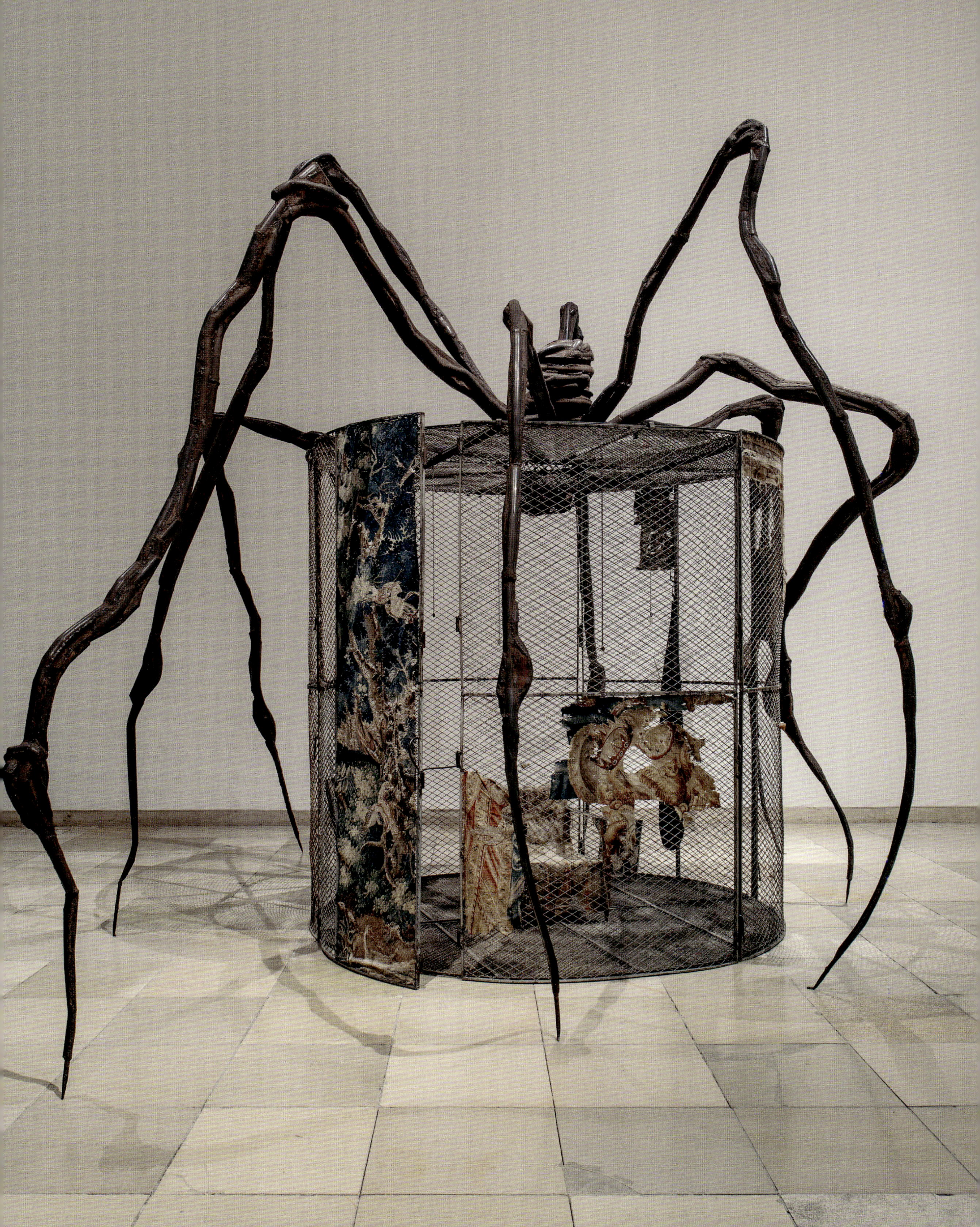

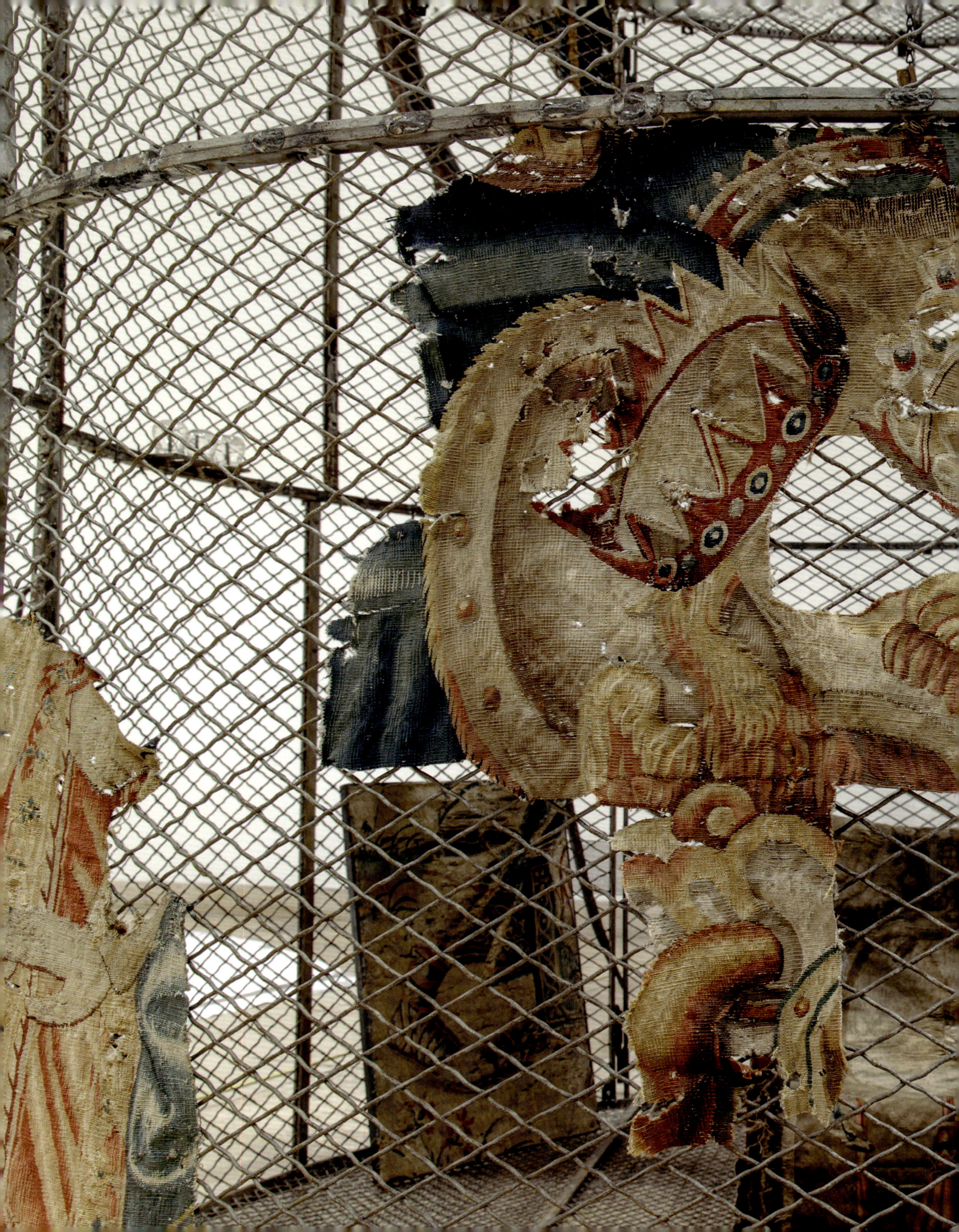

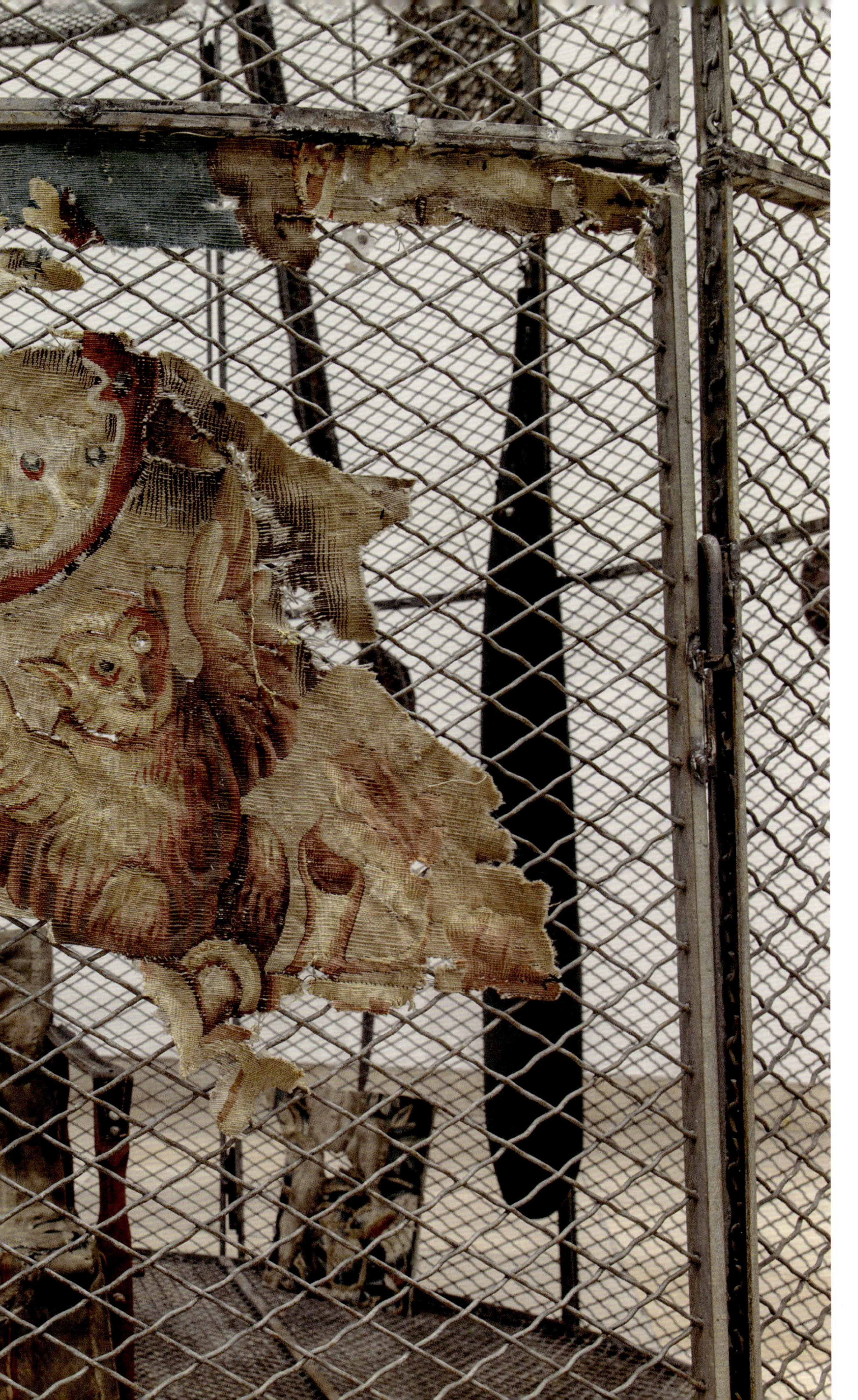

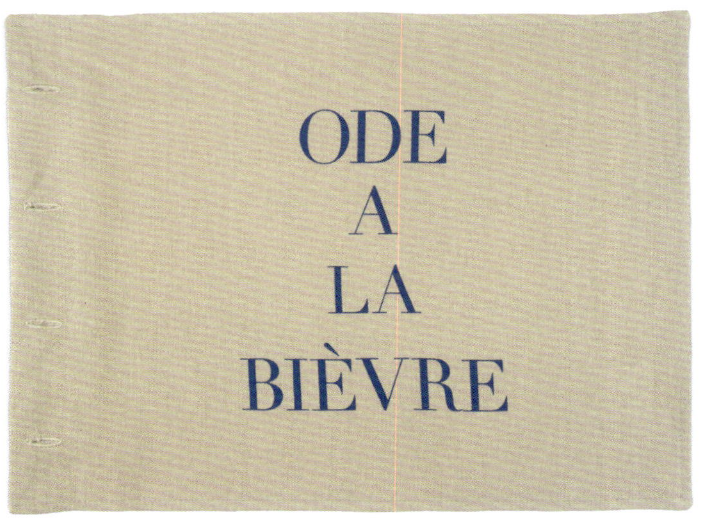

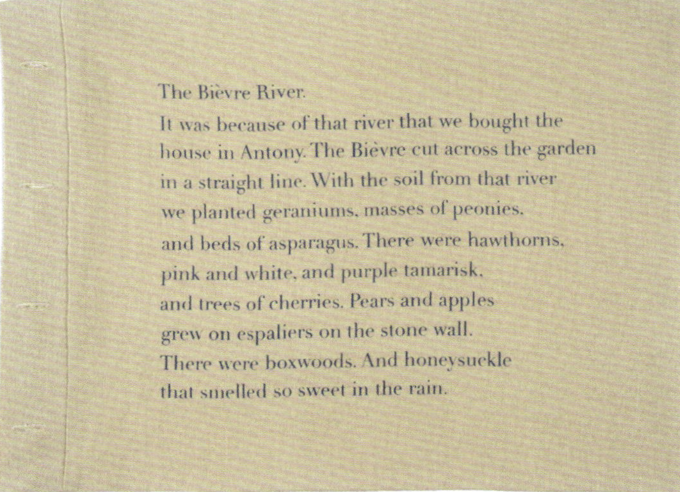

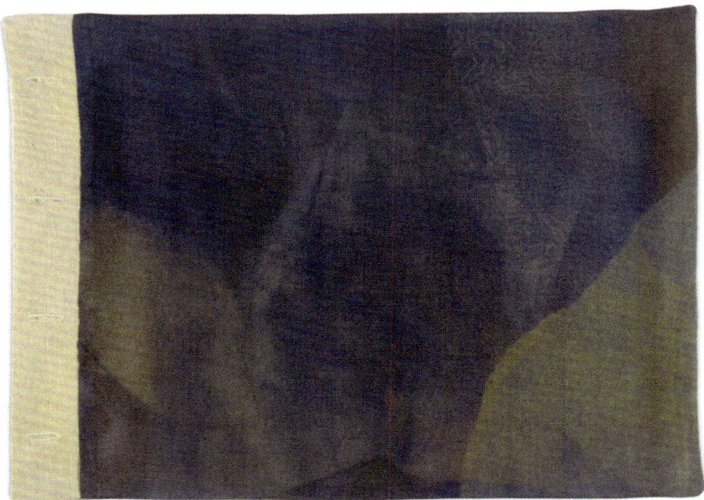

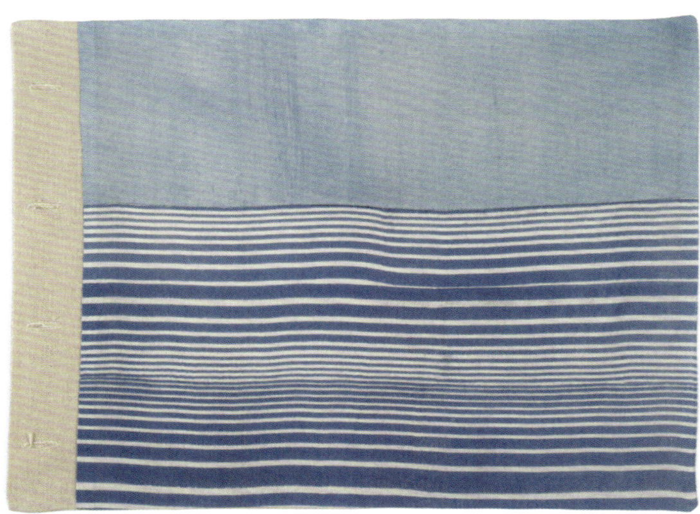

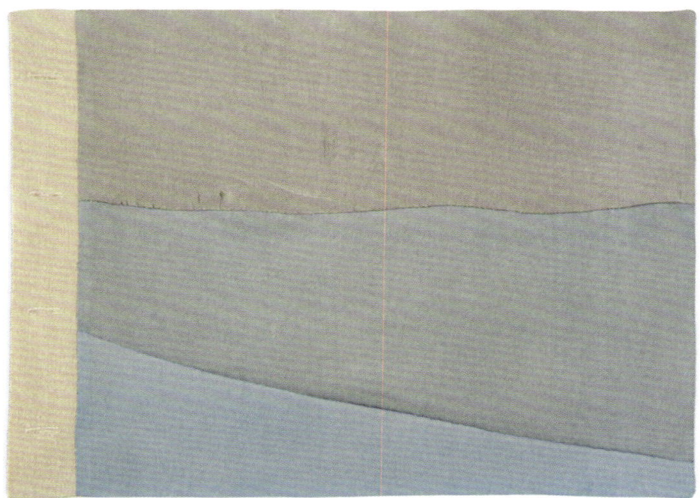

this spread and following pages:
Ode à la Bièvre 2007

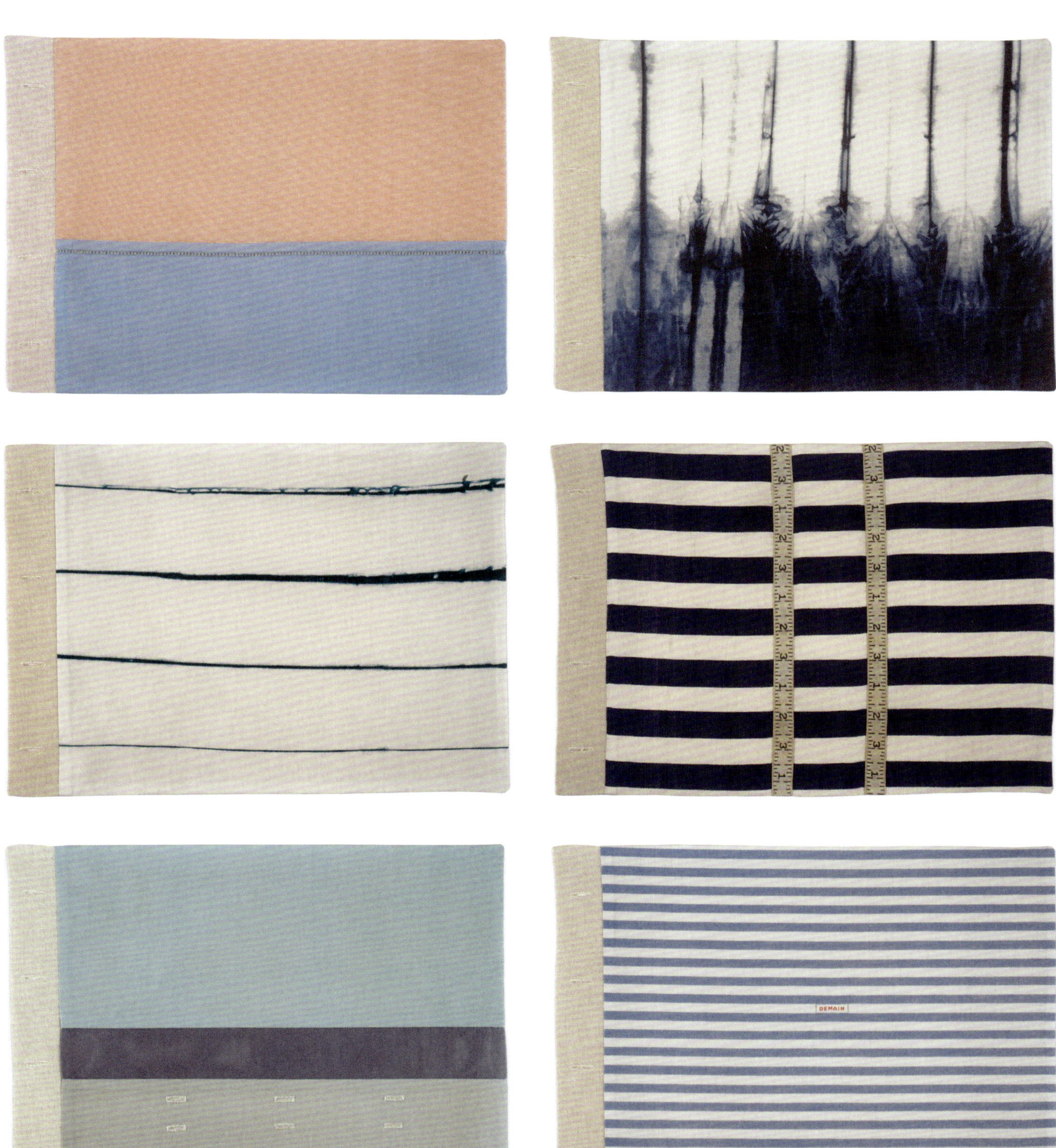
DEMAIN

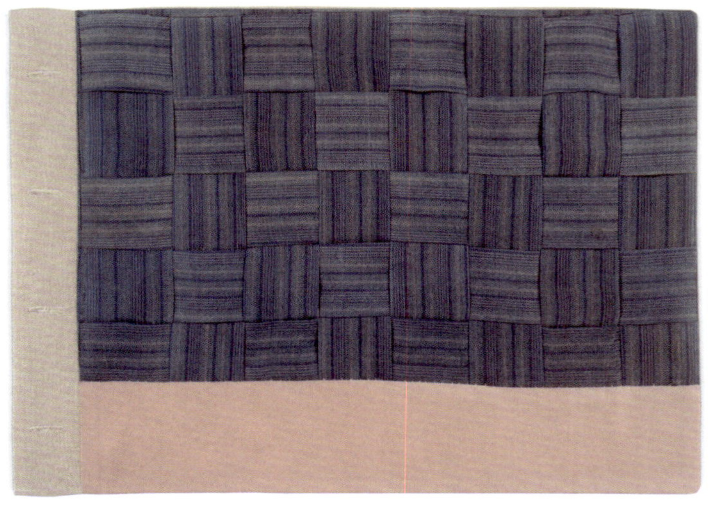
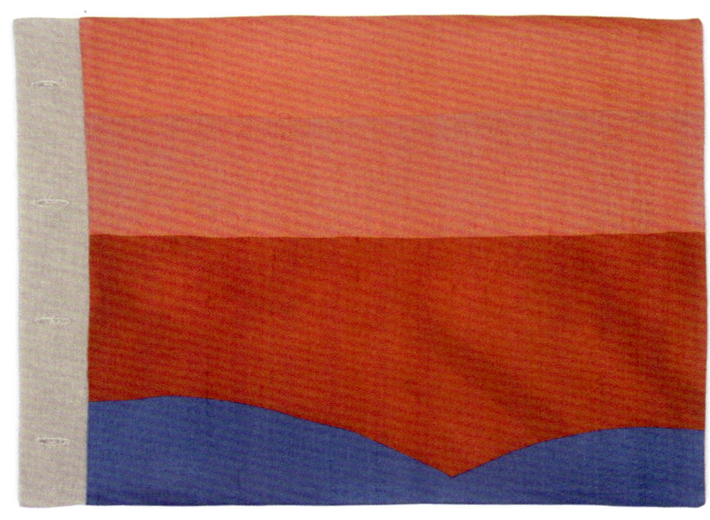
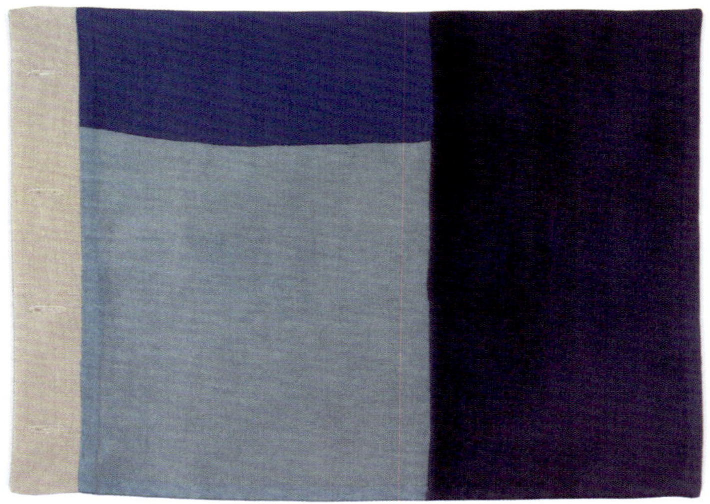
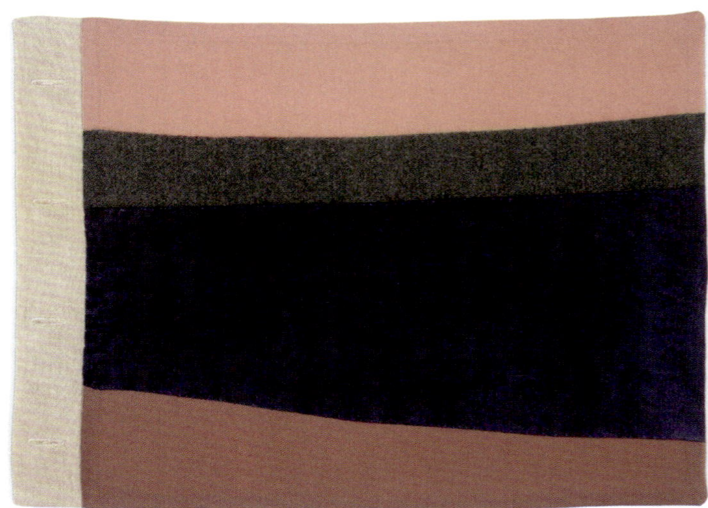
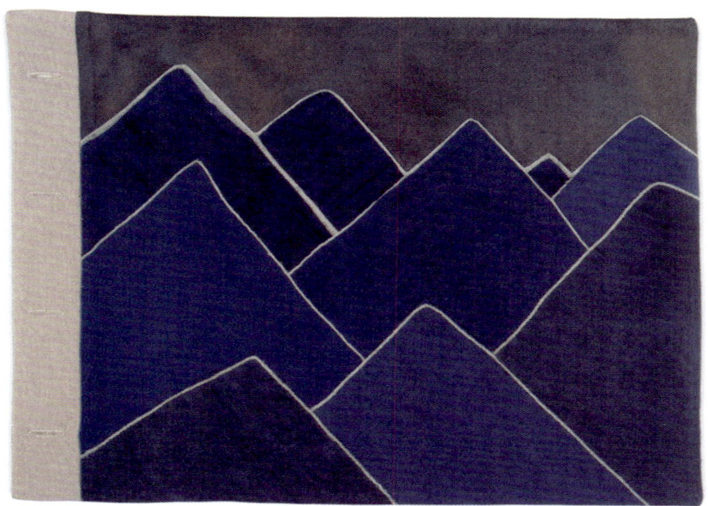
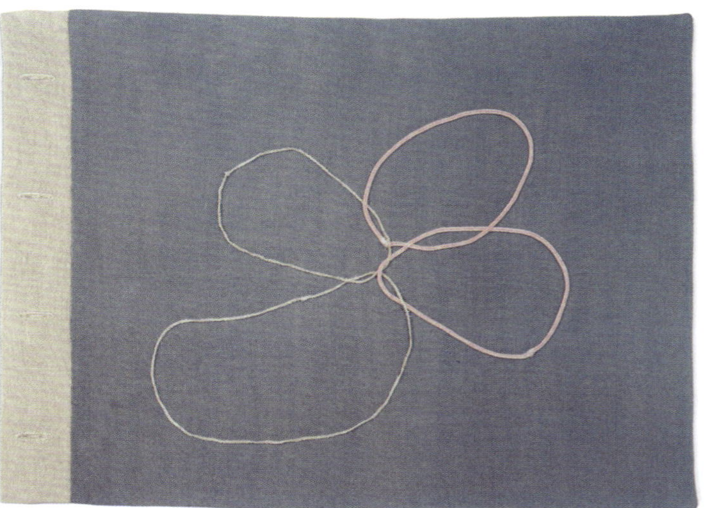

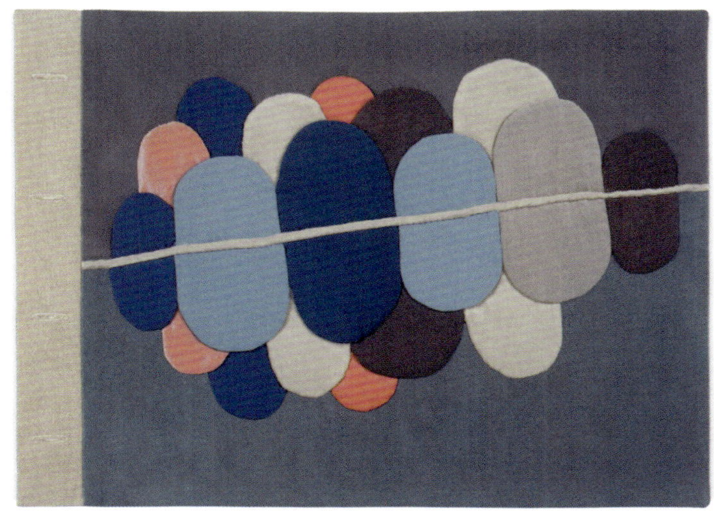

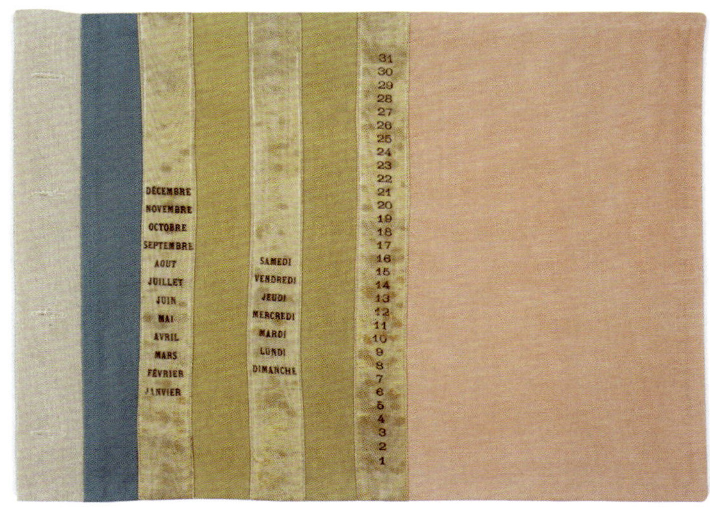

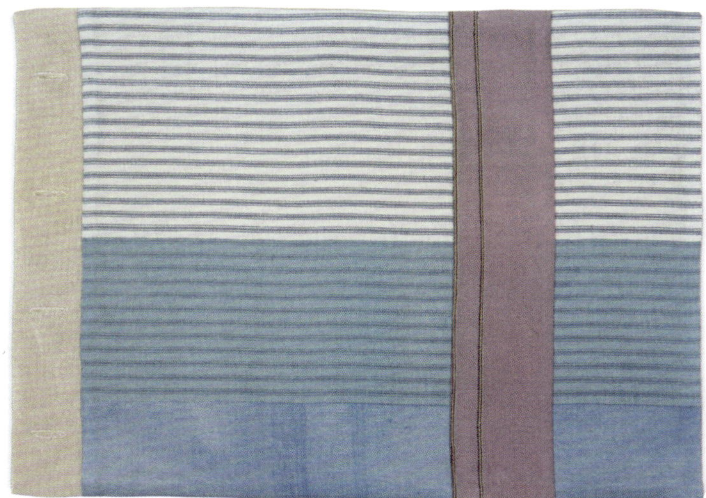

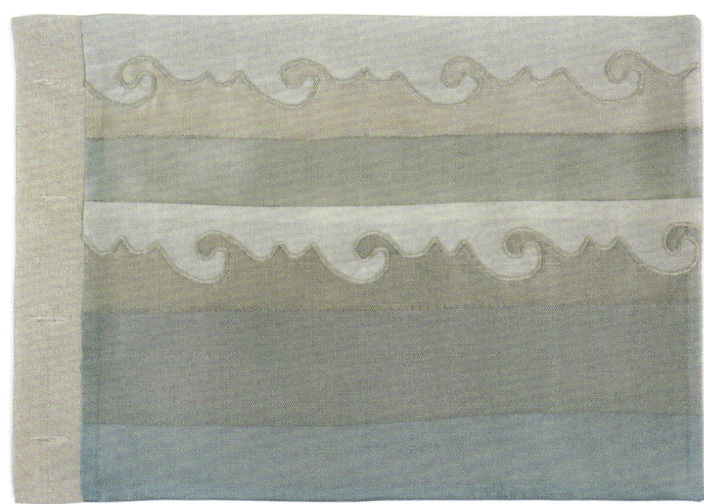

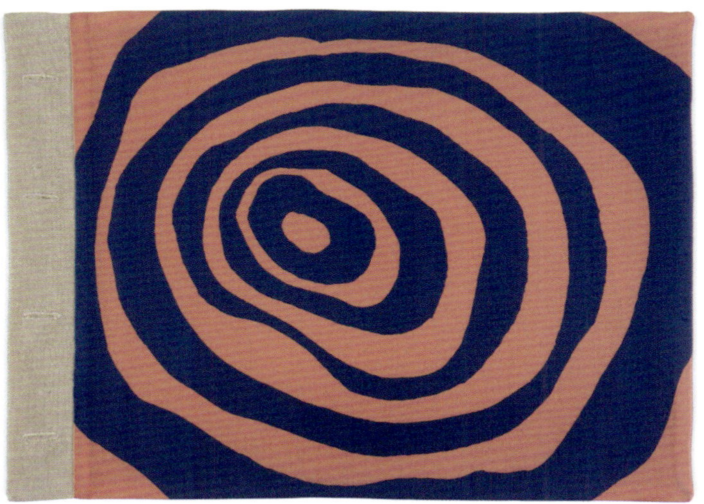

I had gone back to
Antony with my children
to see the house where I had grown up
and where the river Bièvre flowed
through the backyard.
But the river was gone.
Only the trees
that my father had planted
along its edge
remained as a witness.

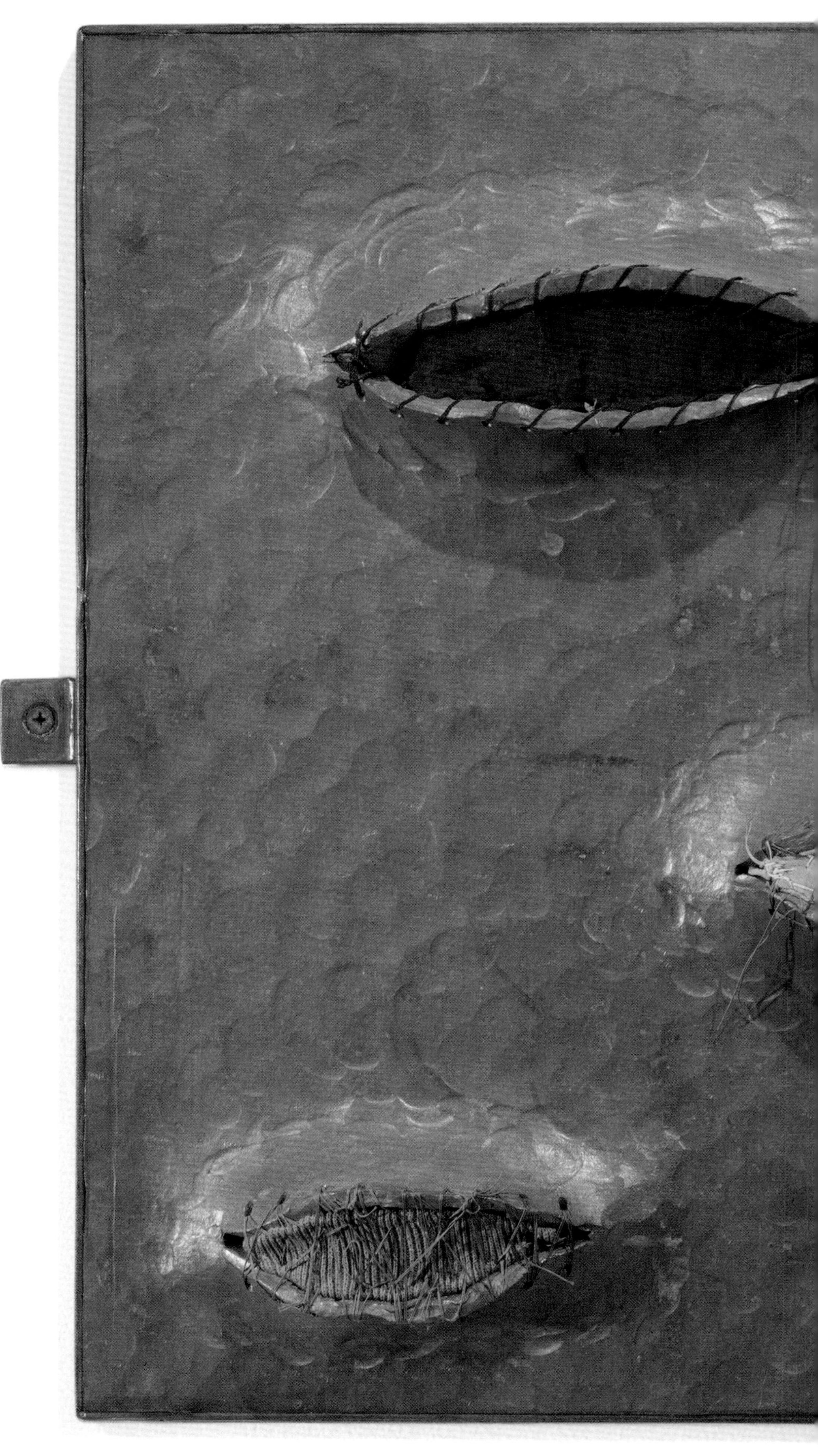

 Repairs in the Sky 1999

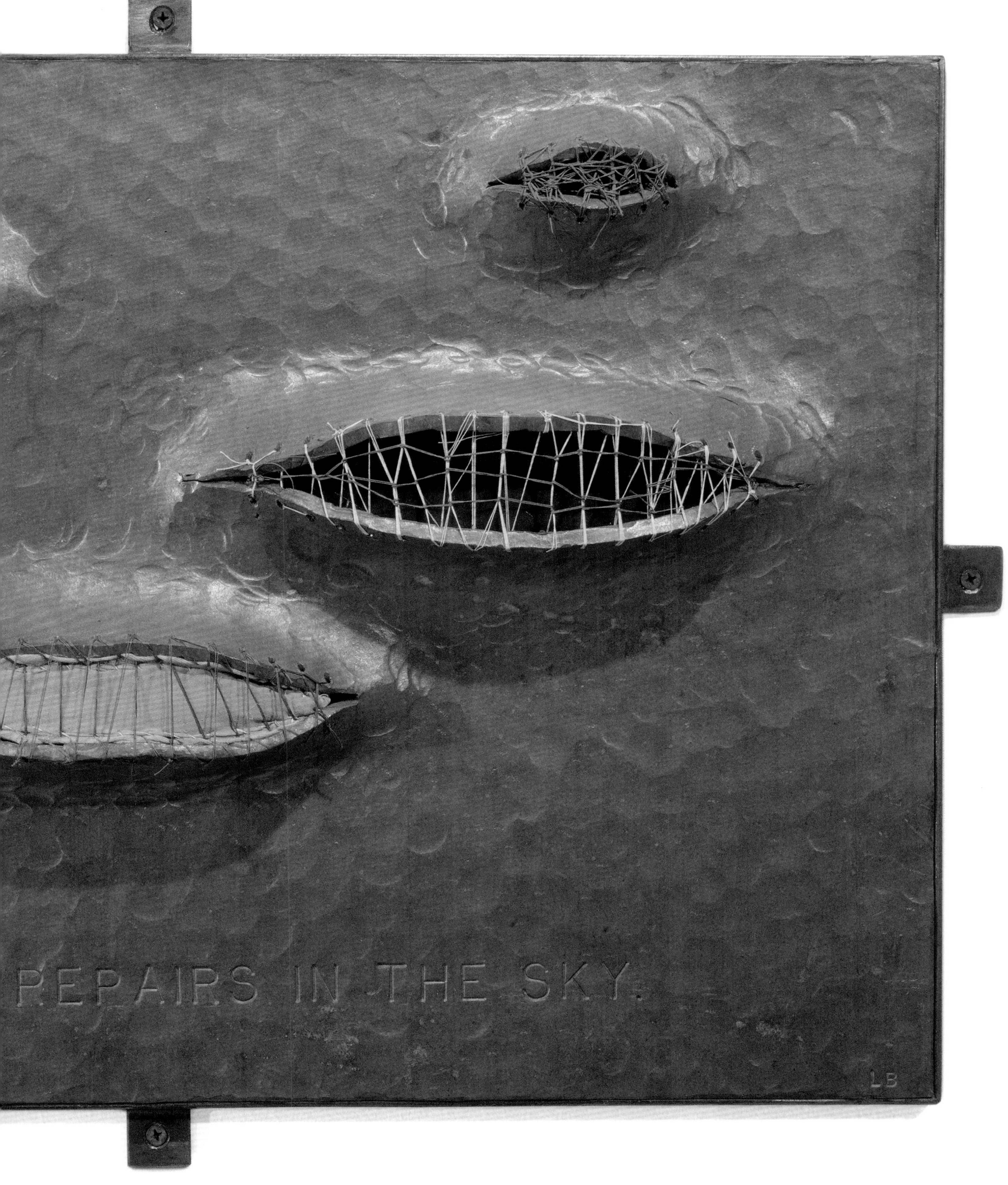
REPAIRS IN THE SKY
LB

8
The controlling of chaos

The Cold of Anxiety 2001

following spread:
Untitled 2005
Untitled 2000

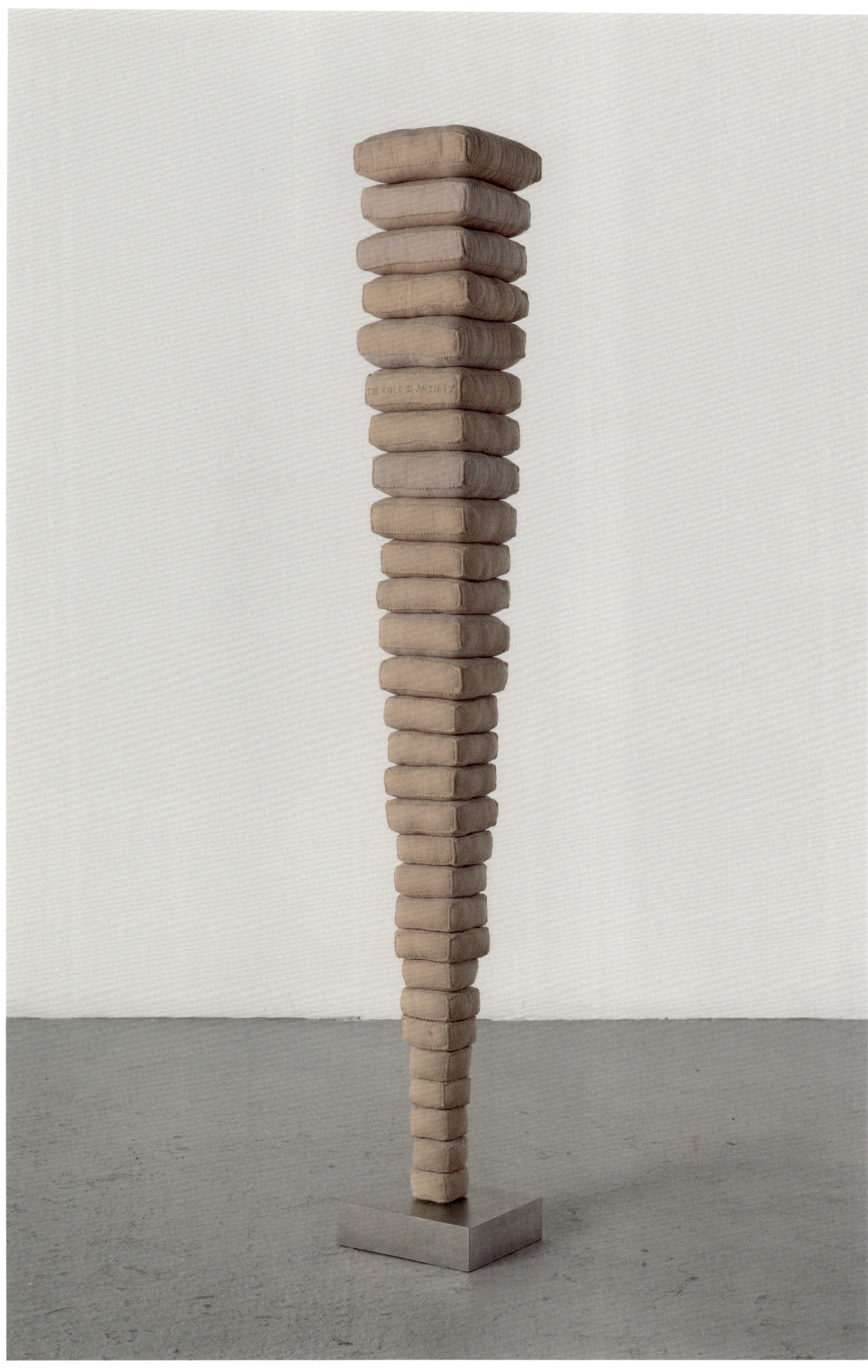
THE COLD OF ANXIETY

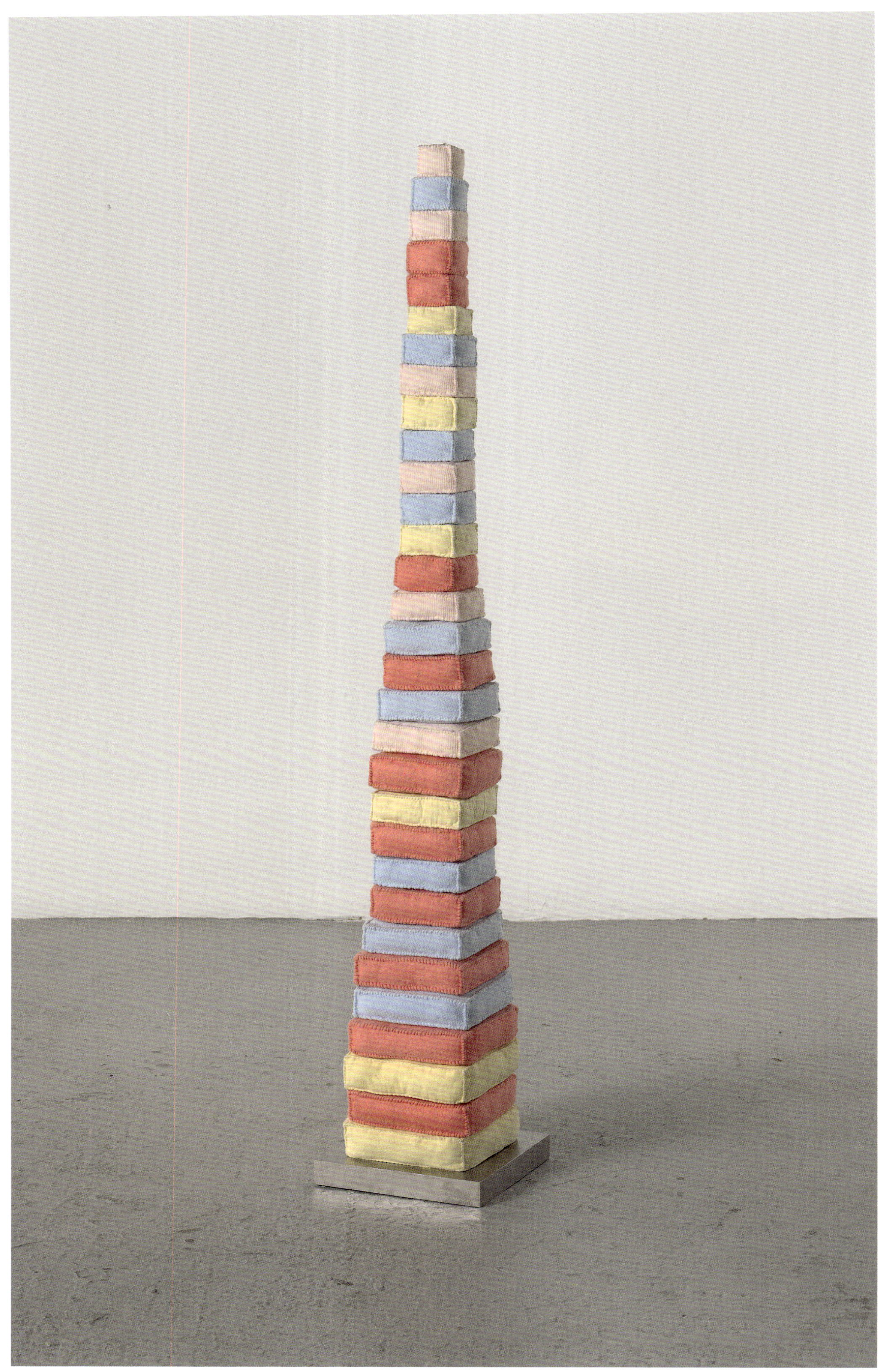

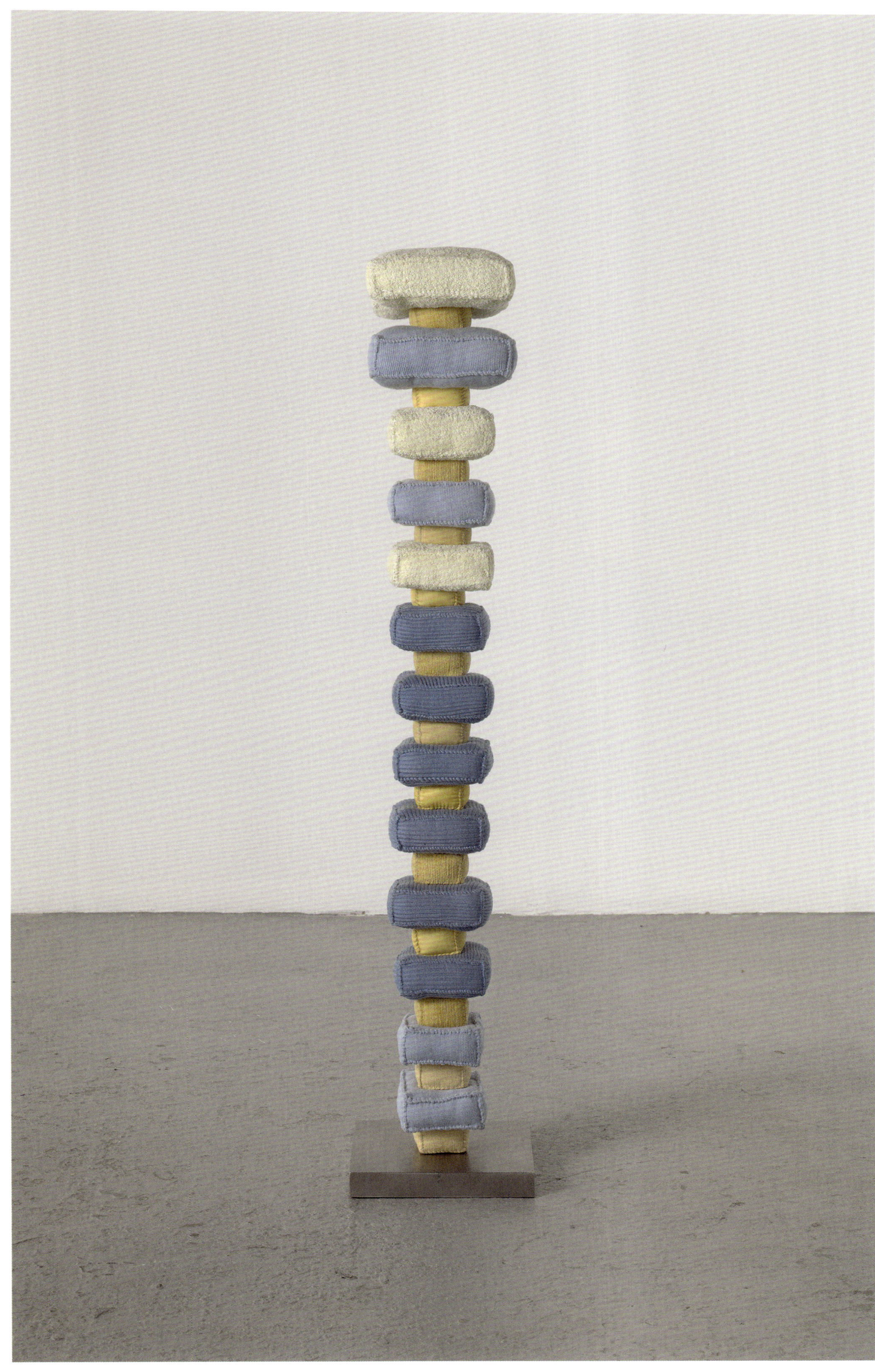

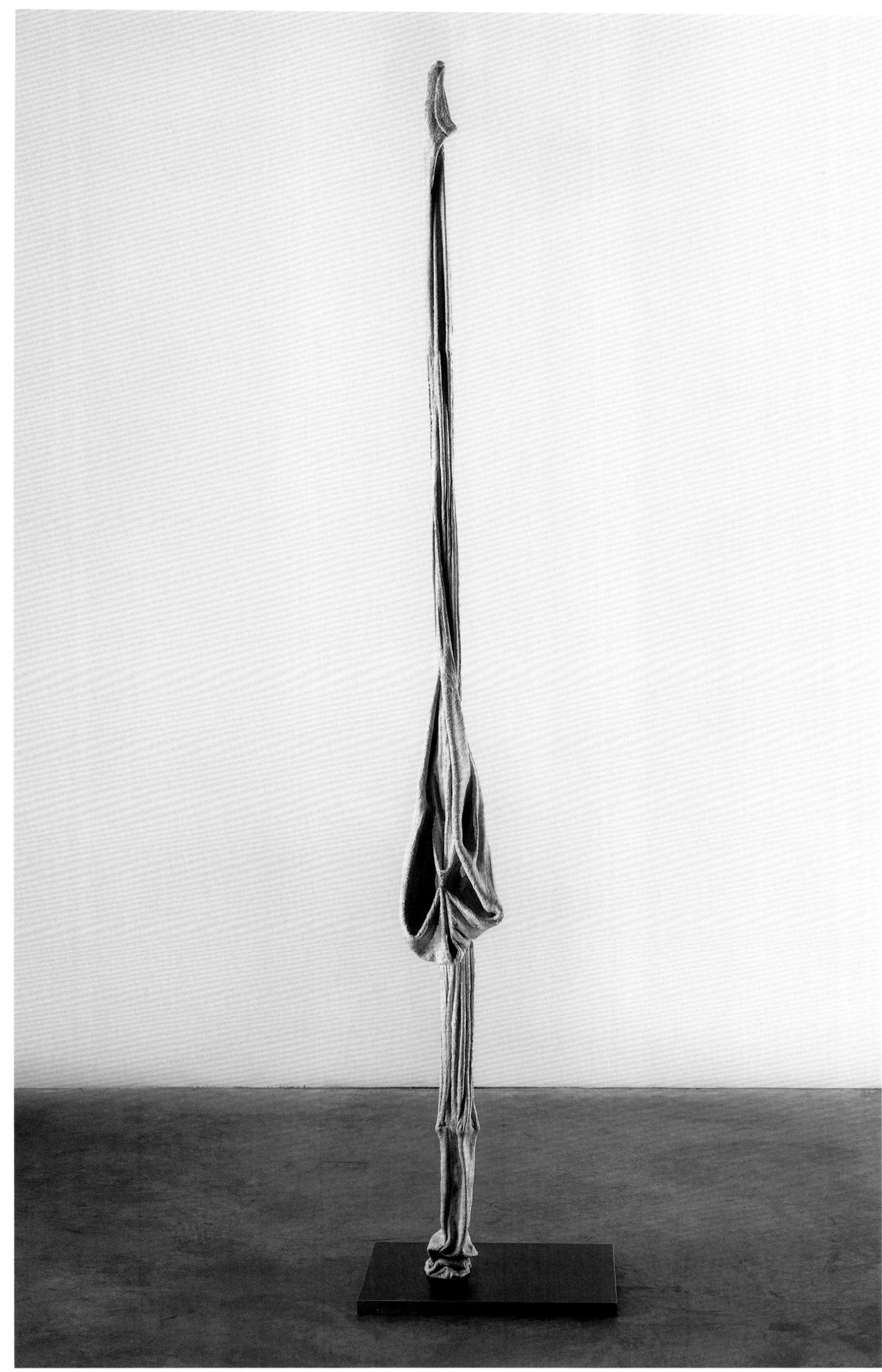

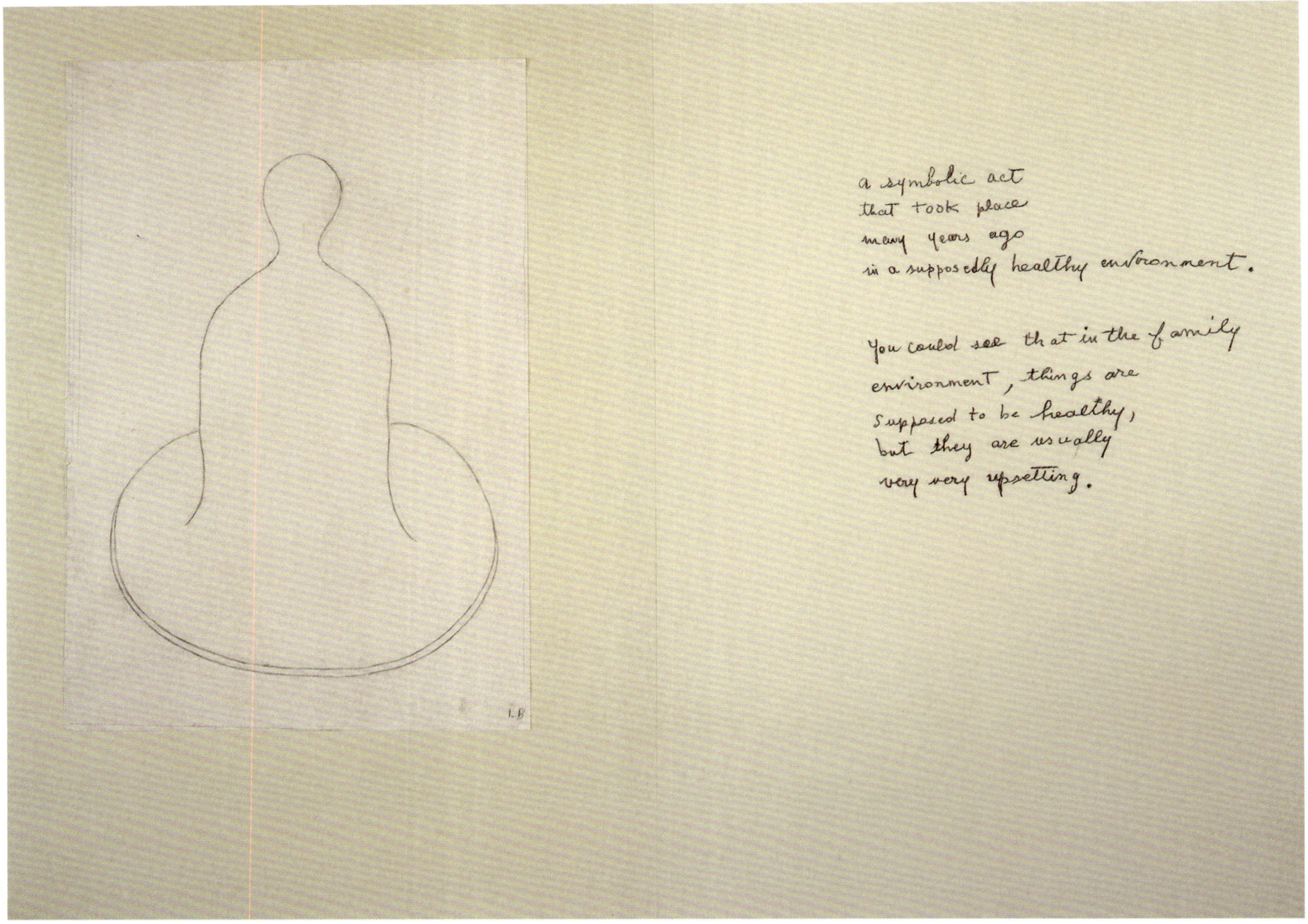

a symbolic act
that took place
many years ago
in a supposedly healthy environment.

You could see that in the family
environment, things are
supposed to be healthy,
but they are usually
very very upsetting.

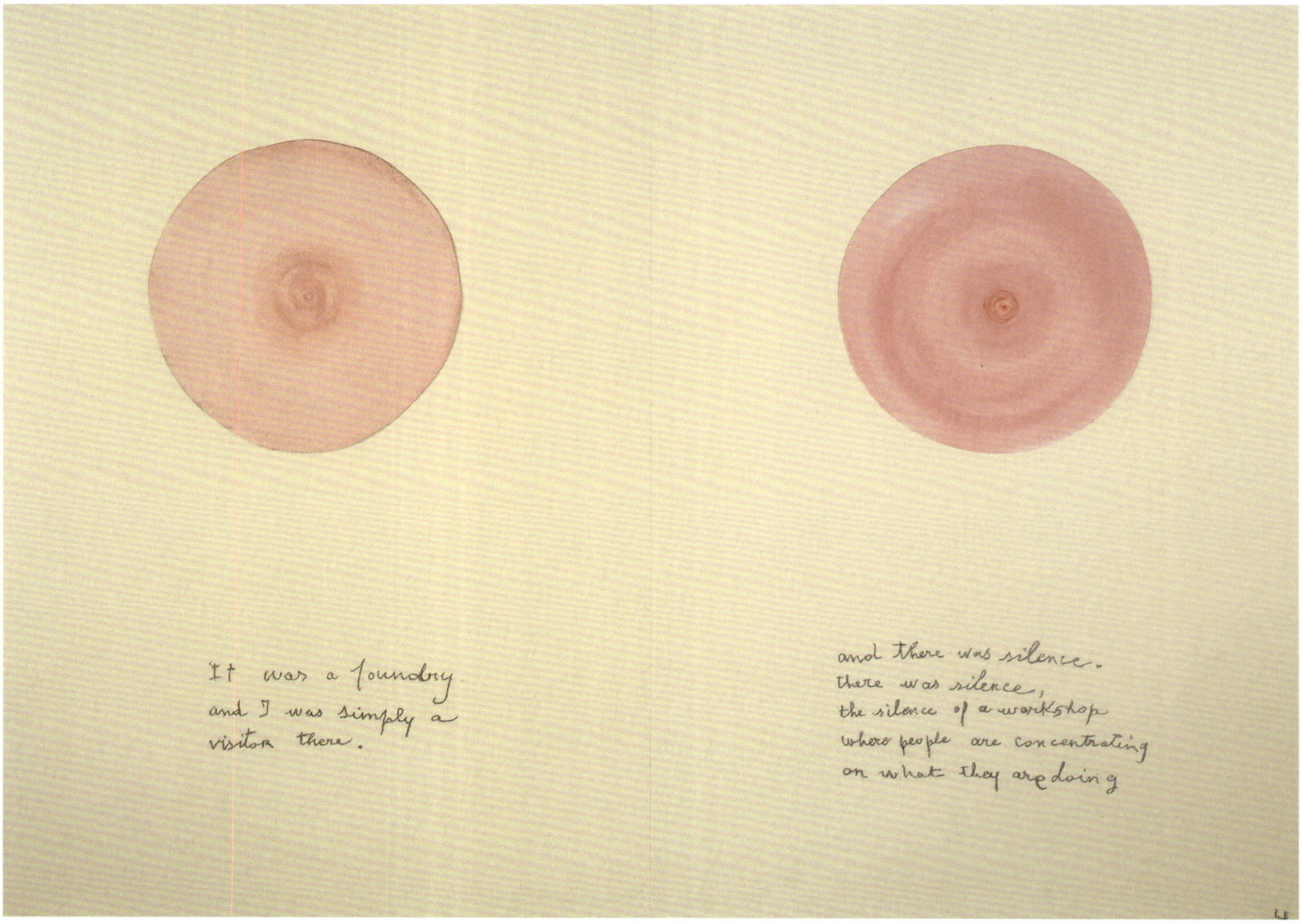

It was a foundry
and I was simply a
visitor there.

and there was silence.
there was silence,
the silence of a workshop
where people are concentrating
on what they are doing

this spread and following pages:
Sublimation 2002

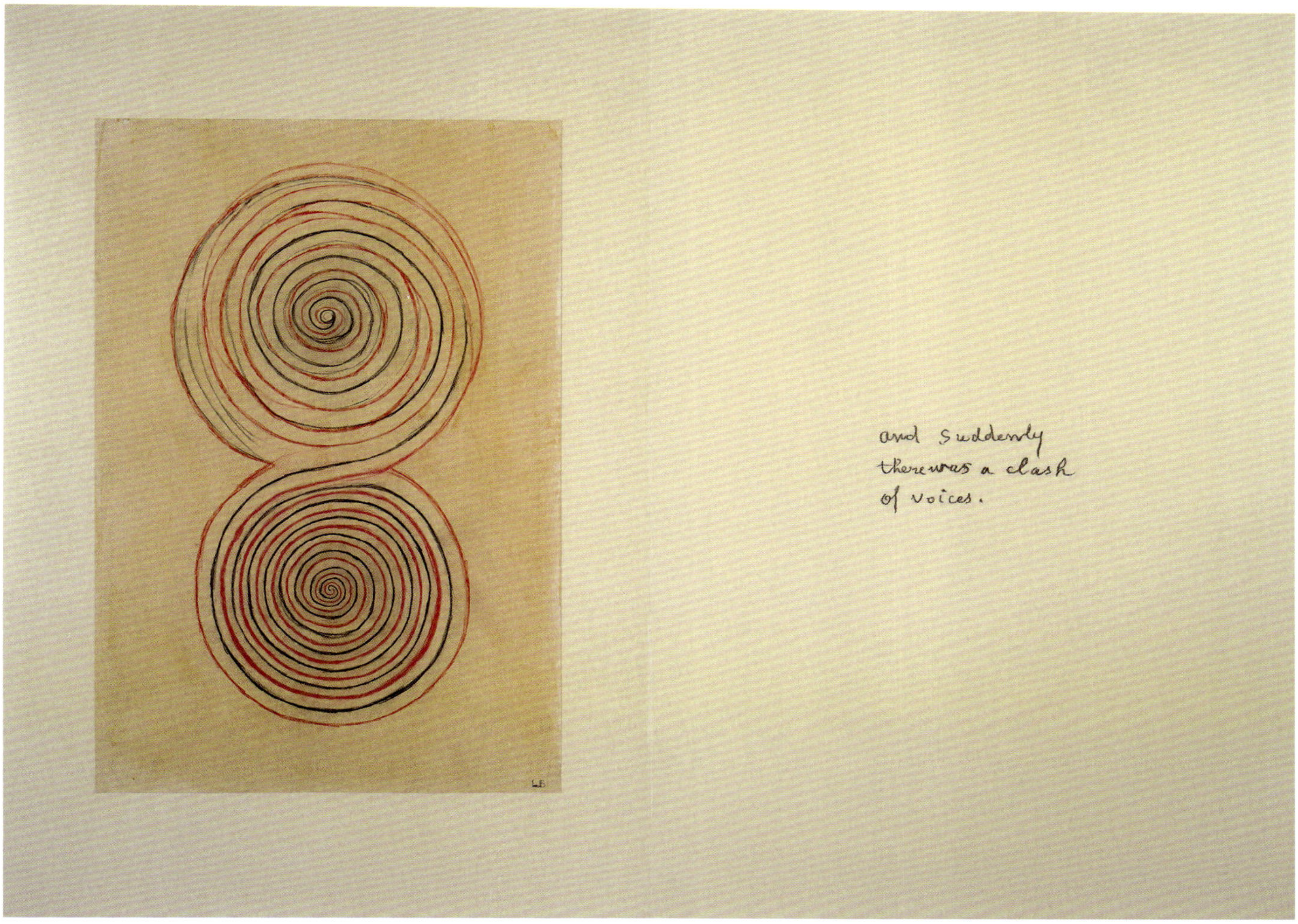

and suddenly
there was a clash
of voices.

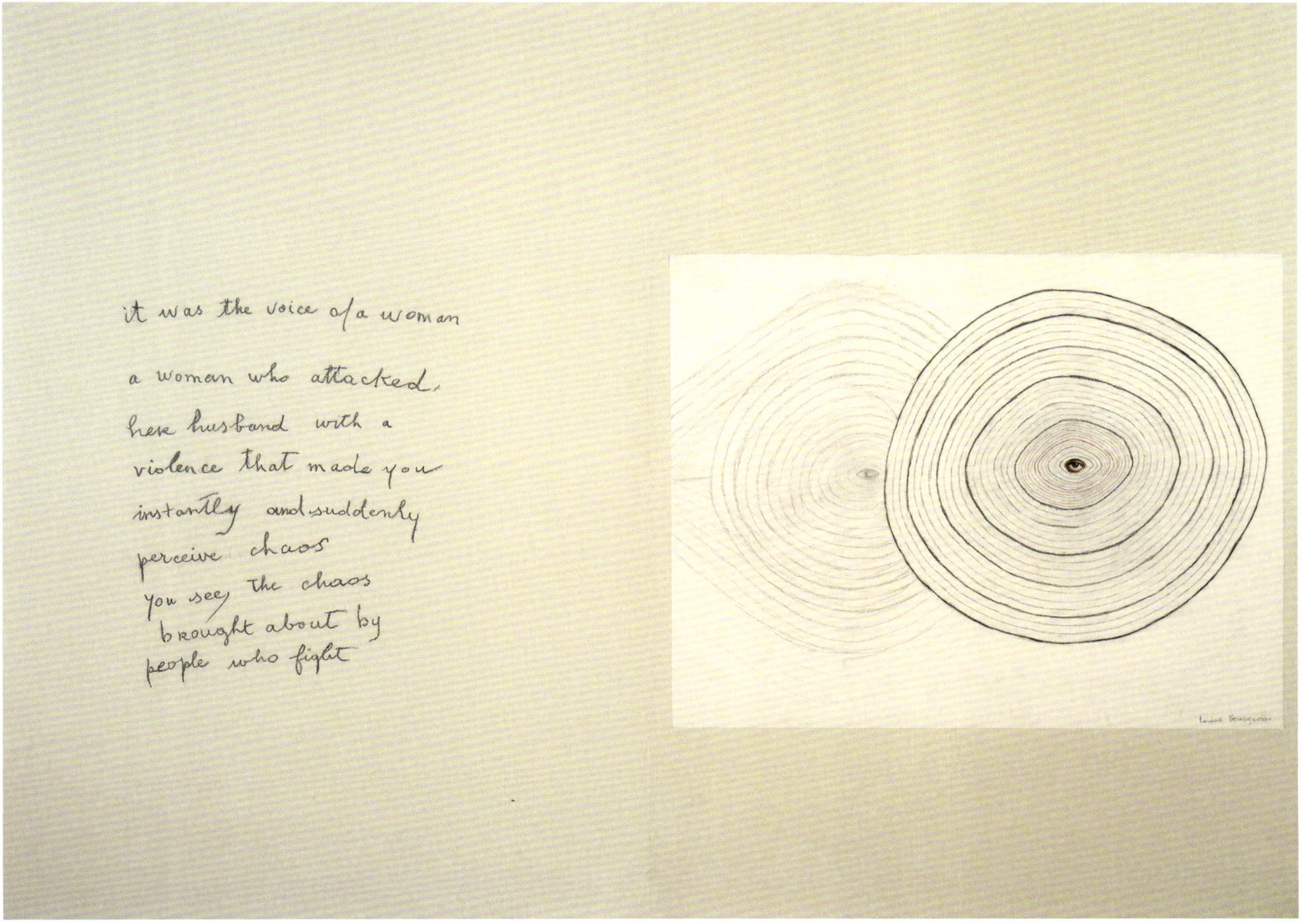

it was the voice of a woman

a woman who attacked
her husband with a
violence that made you
instantly and suddenly
perceive chaos
you see the chaos
brought about by
people who fight

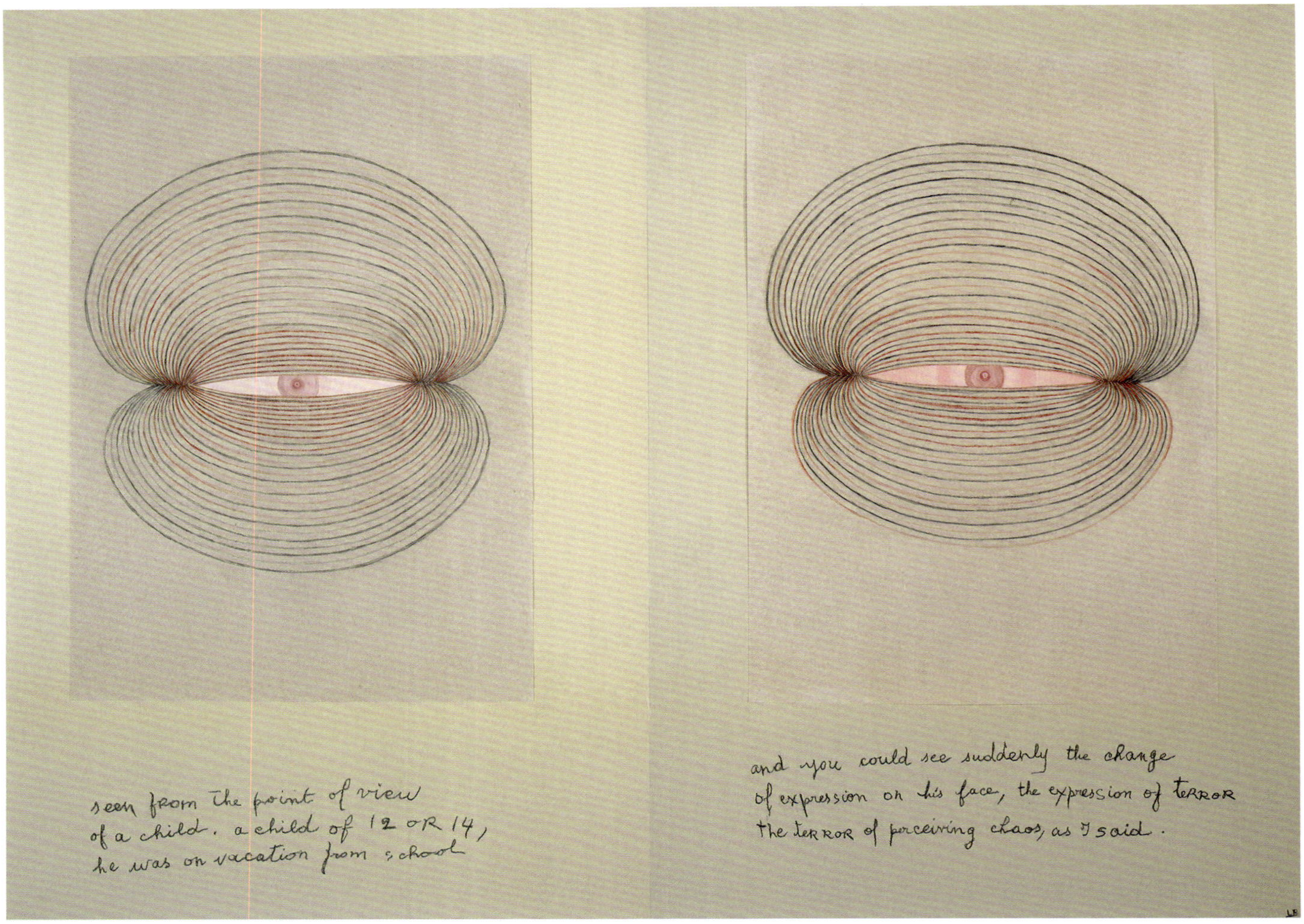

seen from the point of view
of a child. a child of 12 OR 14,
he was on vacation from school

and you could see suddenly the change
of expression on his face, the expression of TERROR
The TERROR of perceiving chaos, as I said.

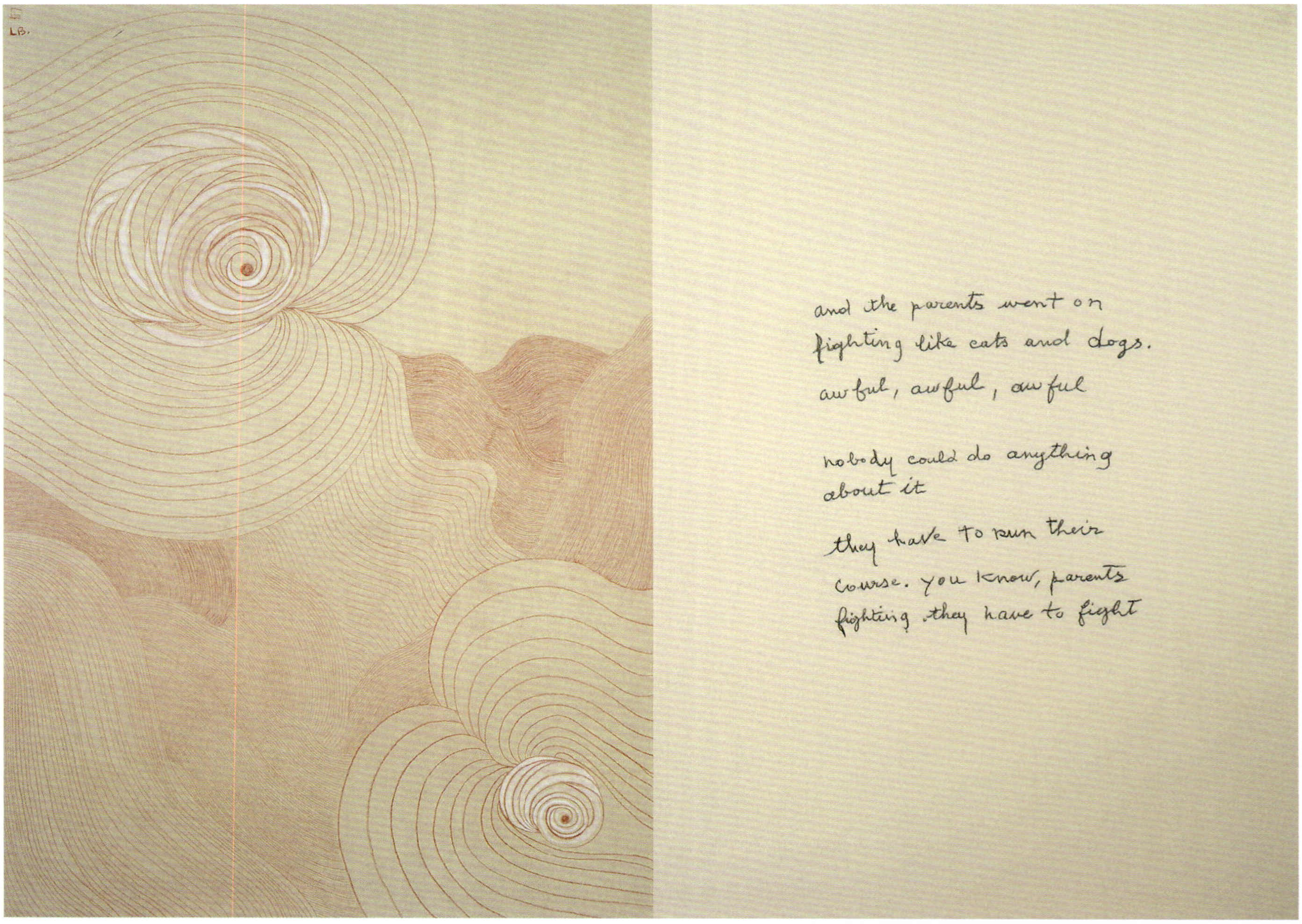

LB

LB.

and the parents went on
fighting like cats and dogs.
awful, awful, awful

nobody could do anything
about it

they have to run their
course. you know, parents
fighting. they have to fight

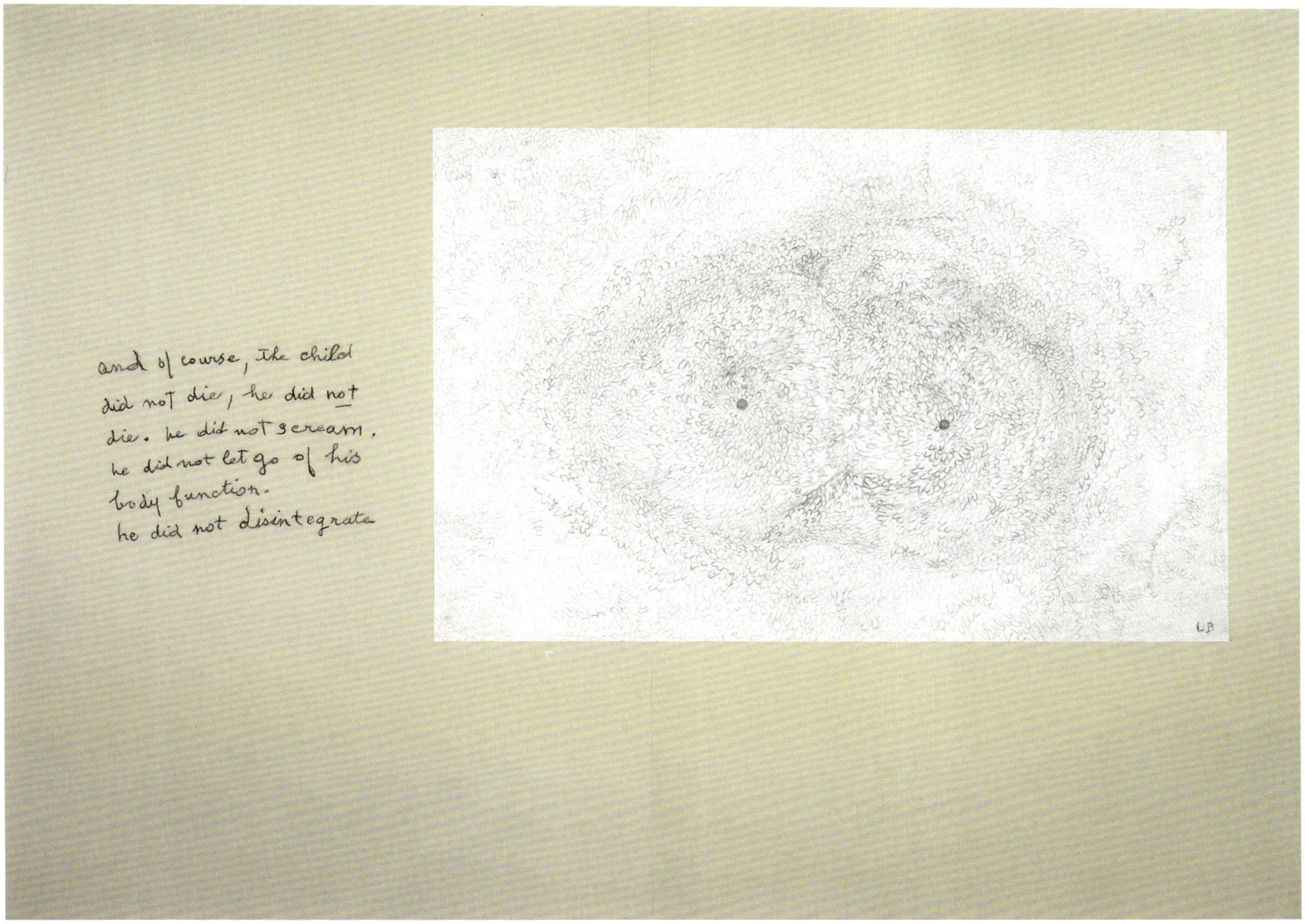

and of course, the child
did not die, he did not
die. he did not scream,
he did not let go of his
body function.
he did not disintegrate

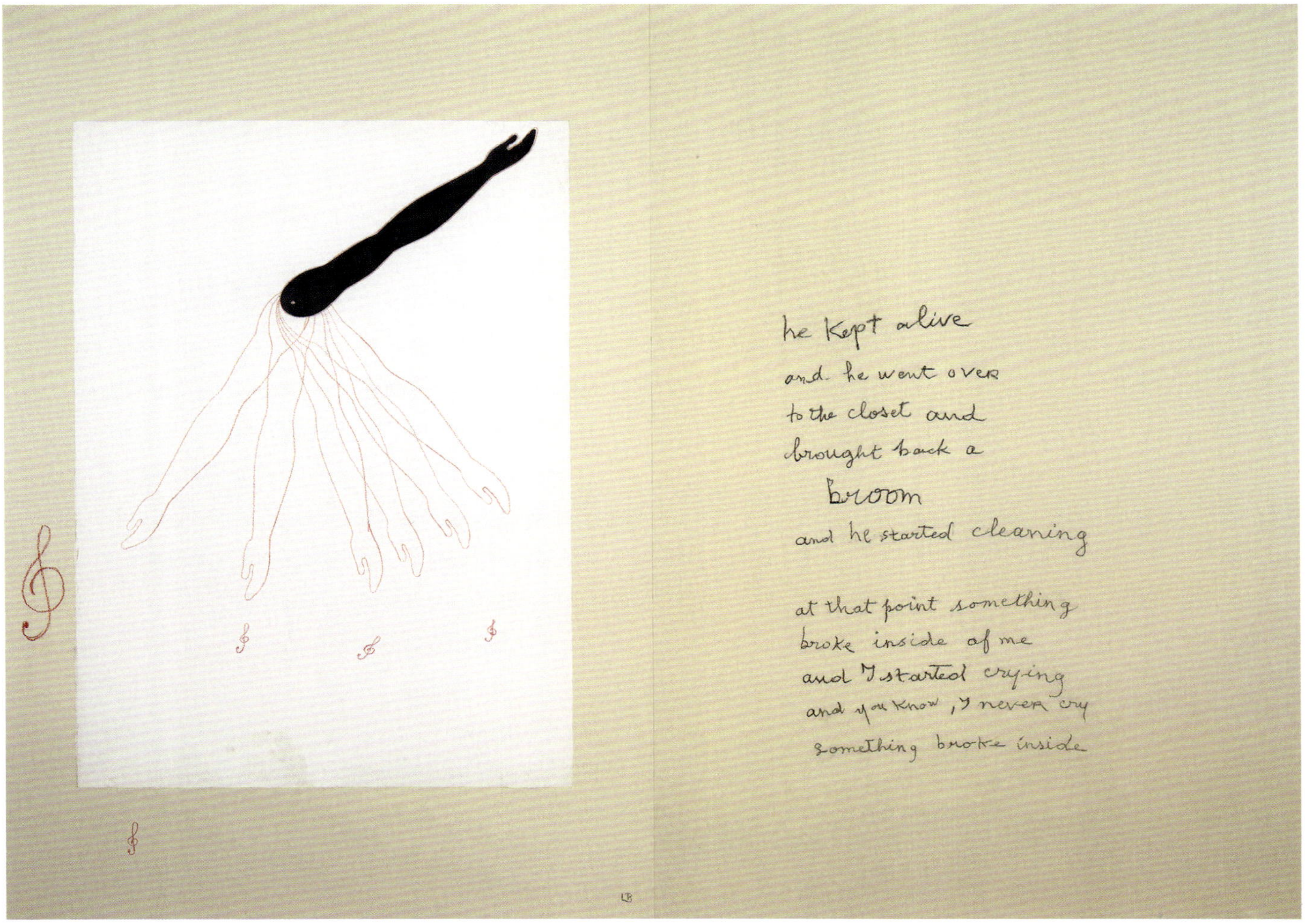

he kept alive
and he went over
to the closet and
brought back a
broom
and he started cleaning

at that point something
broke inside of me
and I started crying
and you know, I never cry
something broke inside

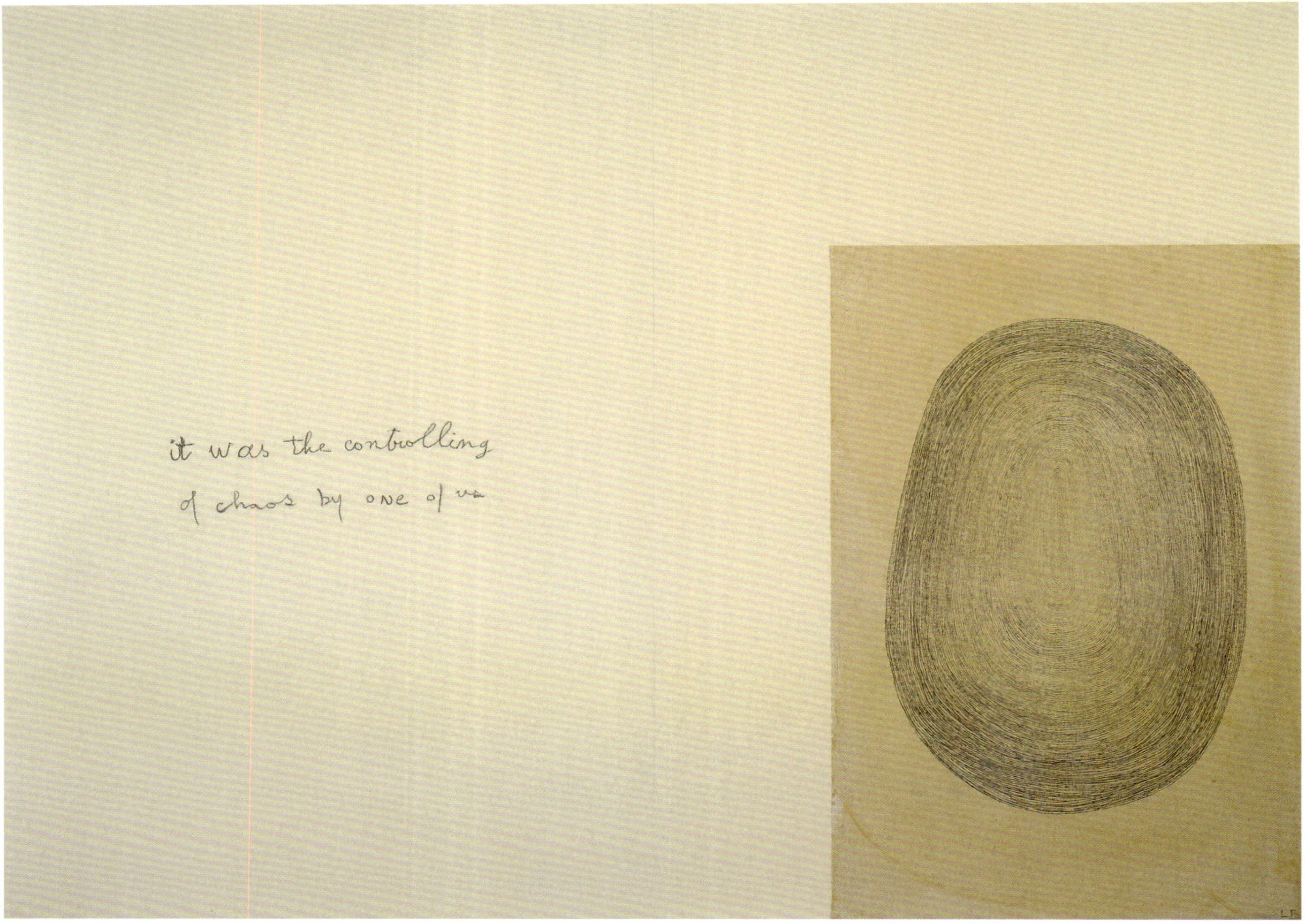

it was the controlling
of chaos by one of us

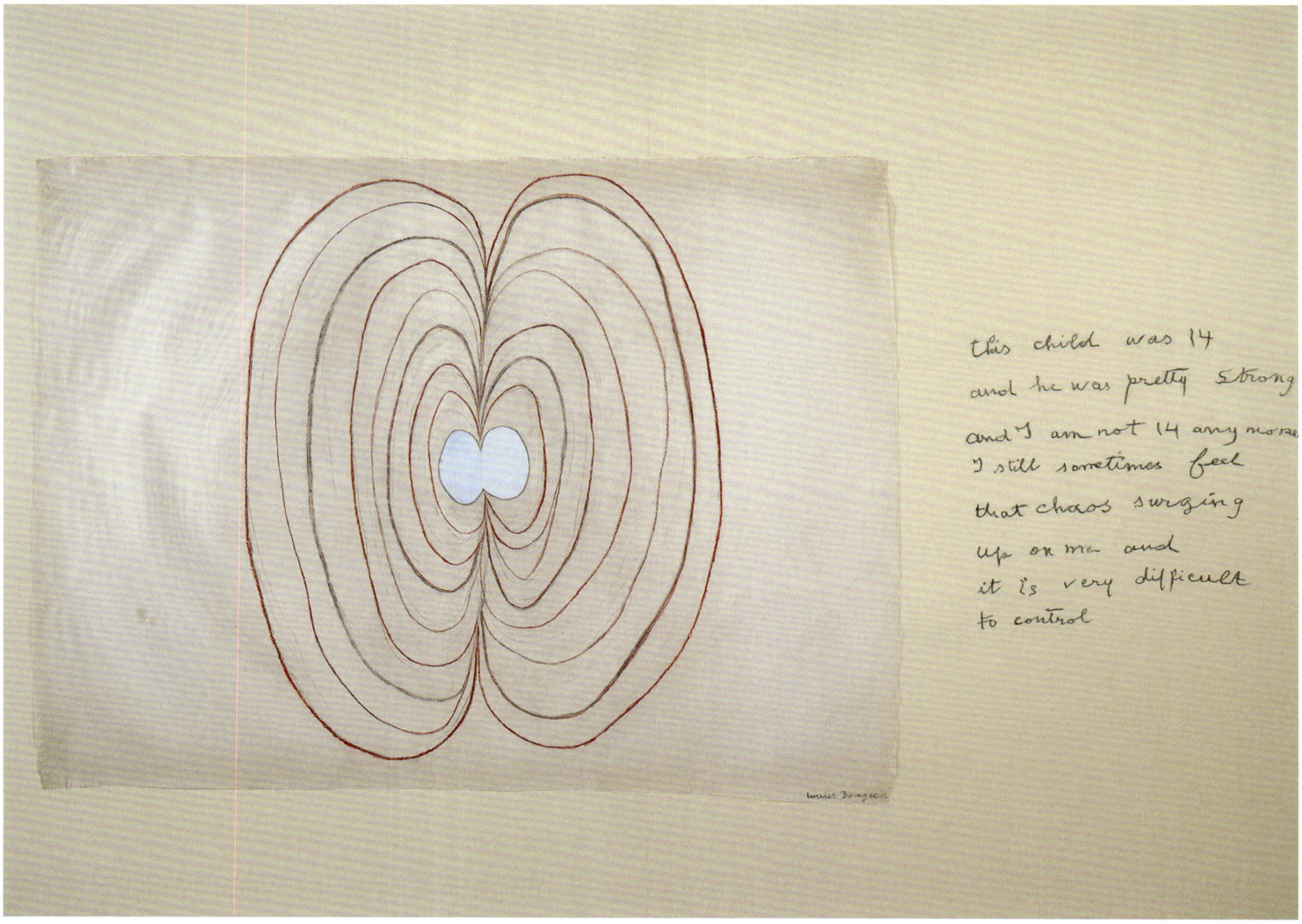

this child was 14
and he was pretty strong
and I am not 14 any more
I still sometimes feel
that chaos surging
up on me and
it is very difficult
to control

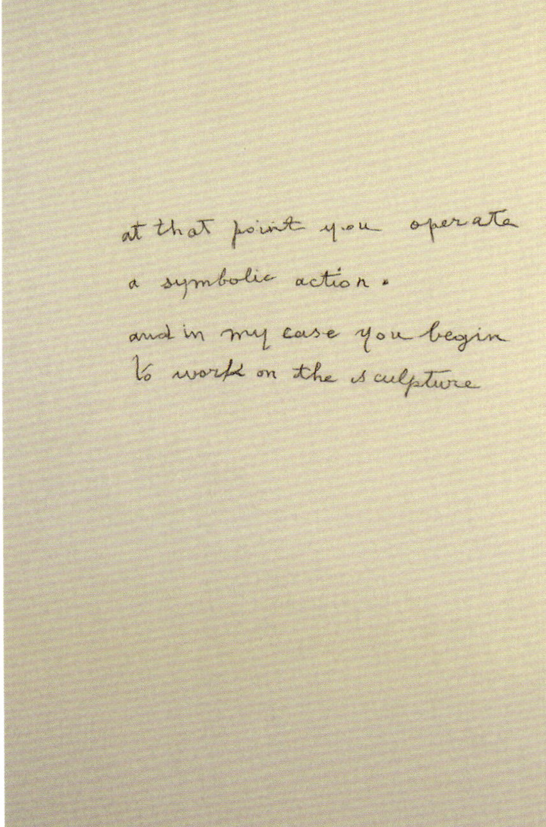

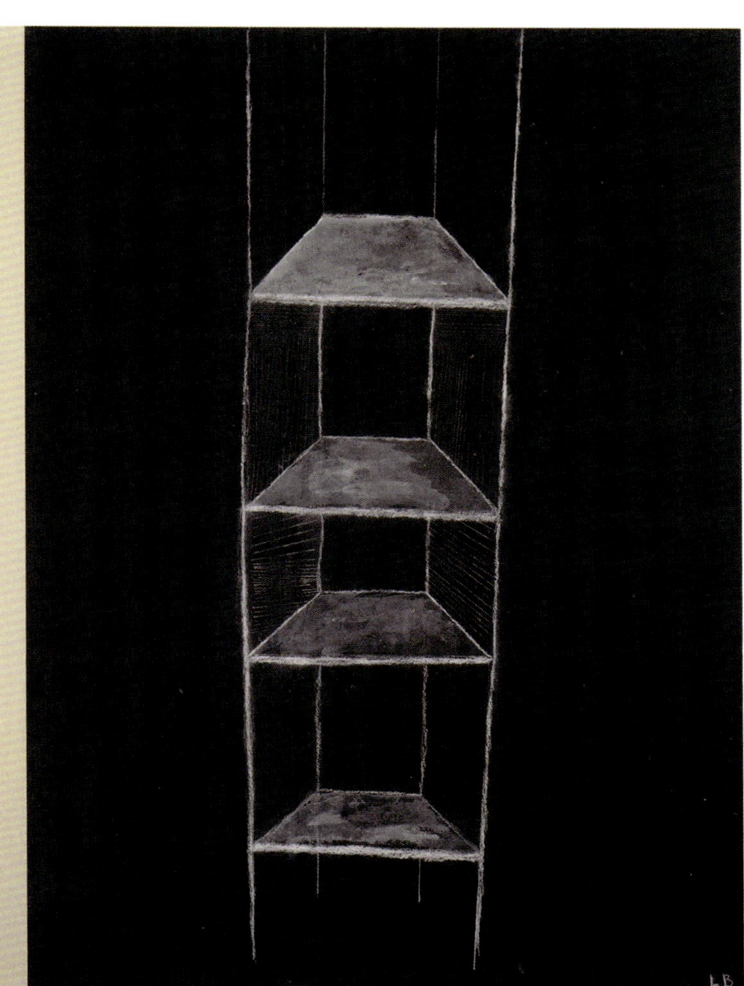

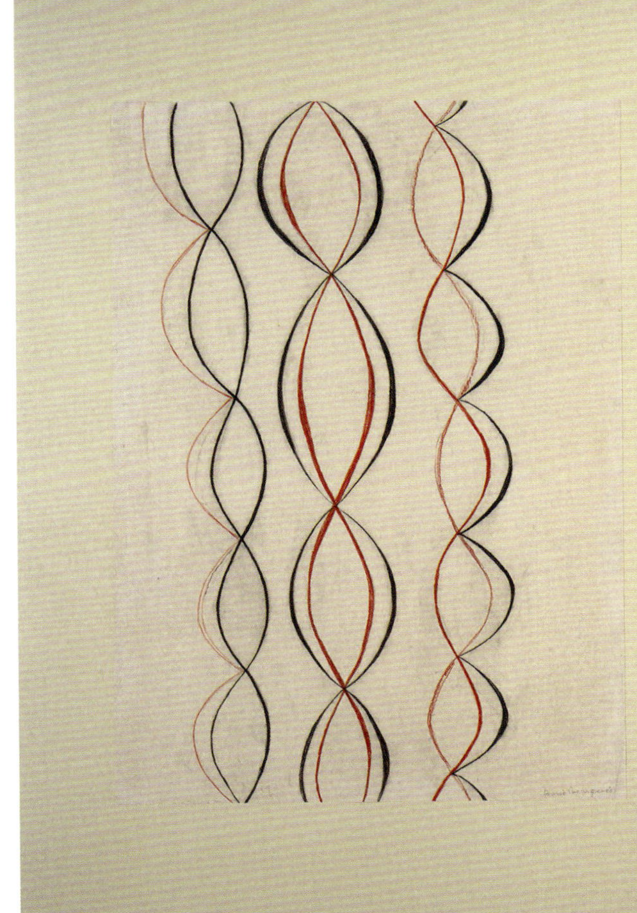

the symbolic action
can take many many
forms. Some people will
become perfectionists in
whatever they are doing
or they can write
they can write a story
or they can work on
the house

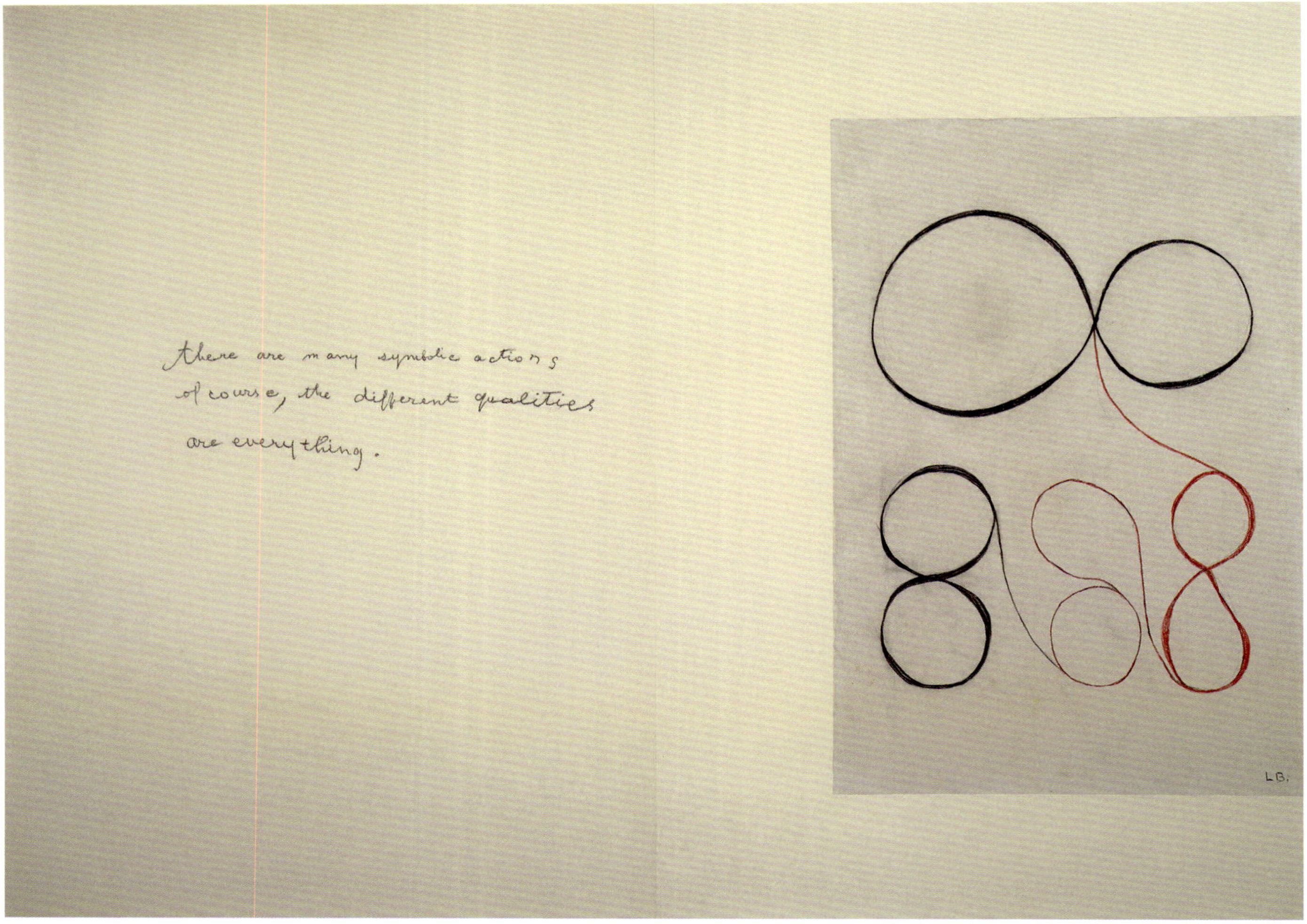

There are many symbolic actions
of course, the different qualities
are everything.

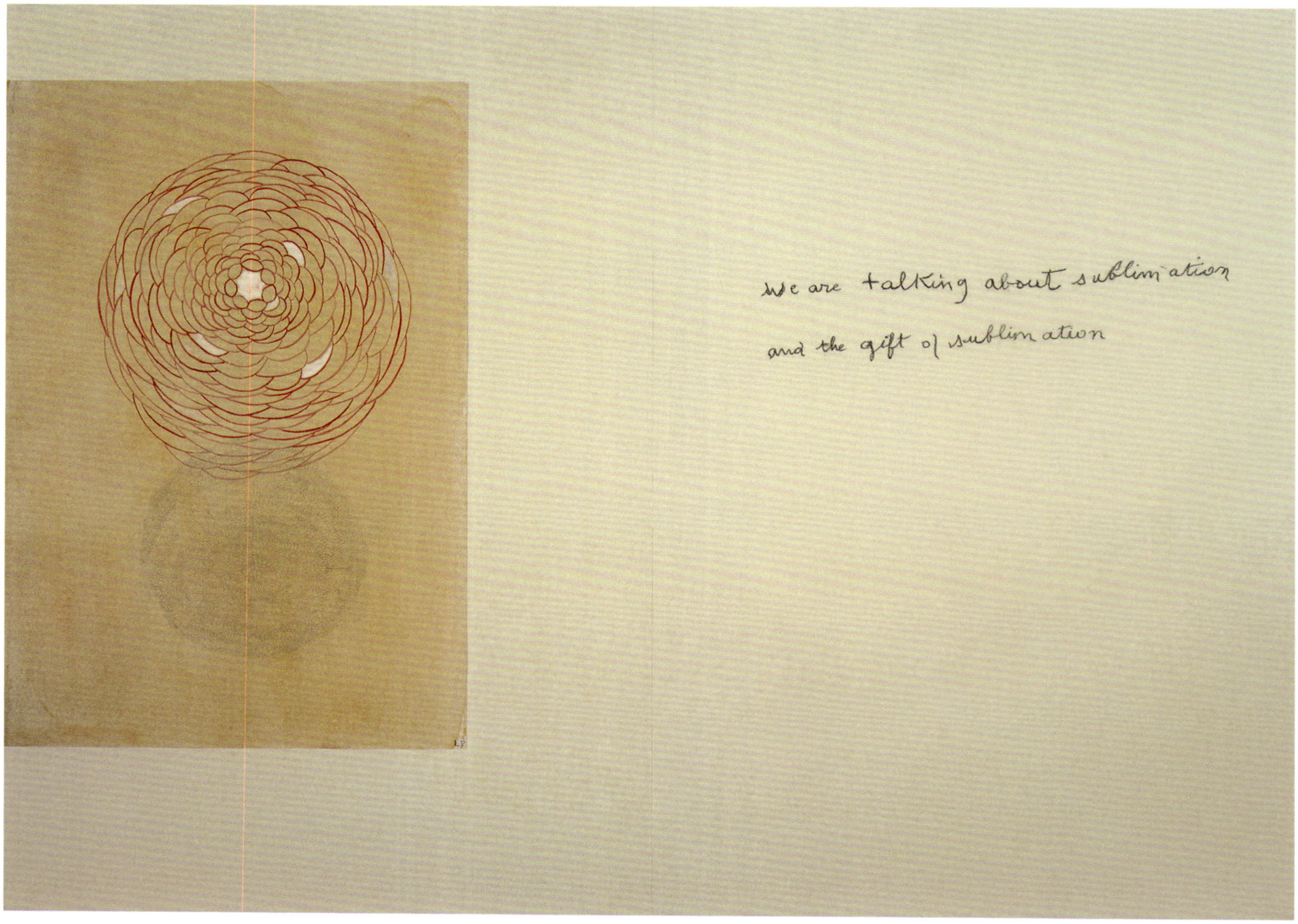

LB.

We are talking about sublimation
and the gift of sublimation

I feel that if we are able
to sublimate, in any way we do,
that we should feel thankful.

I cannot talk about any other
profession, but the artist is
blessed with this power.

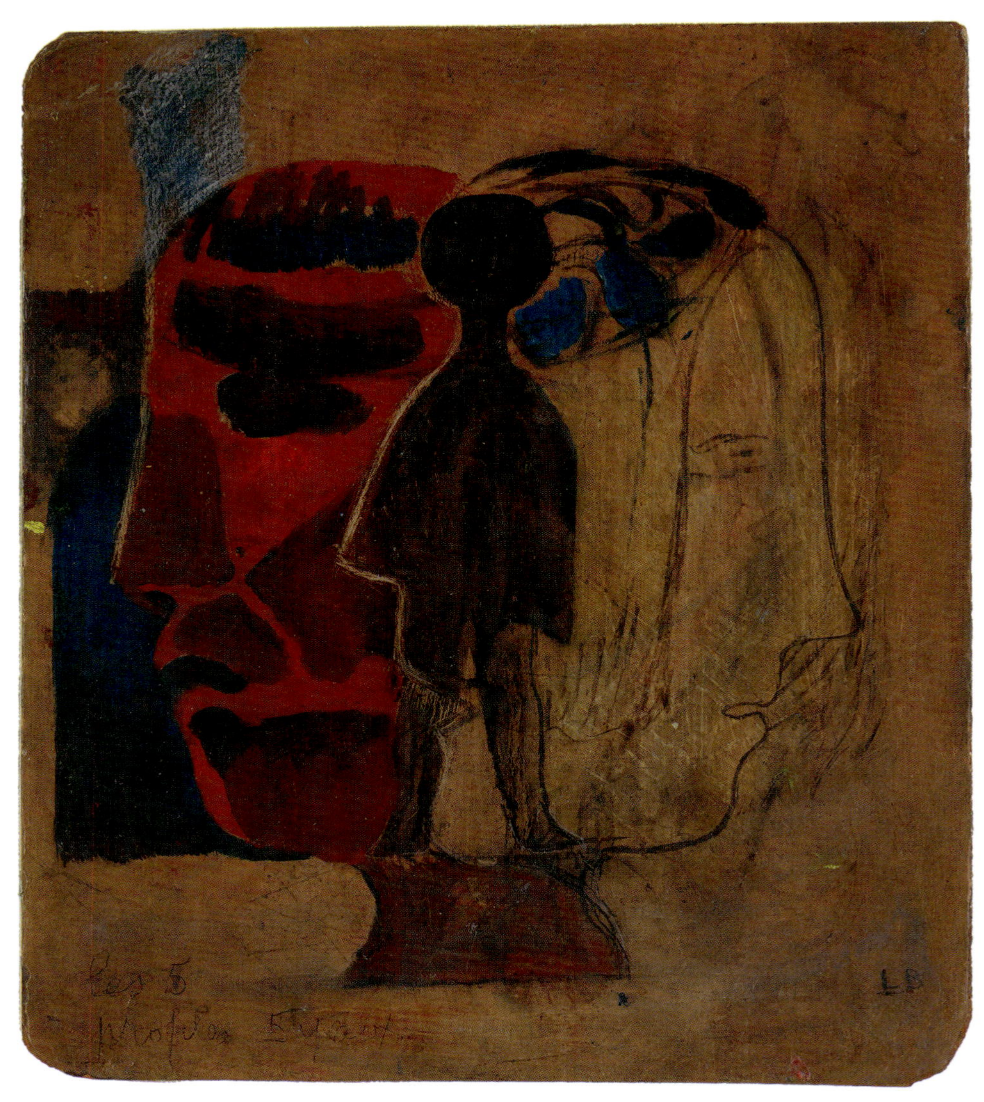

Untitled 1940
Untitled 2009

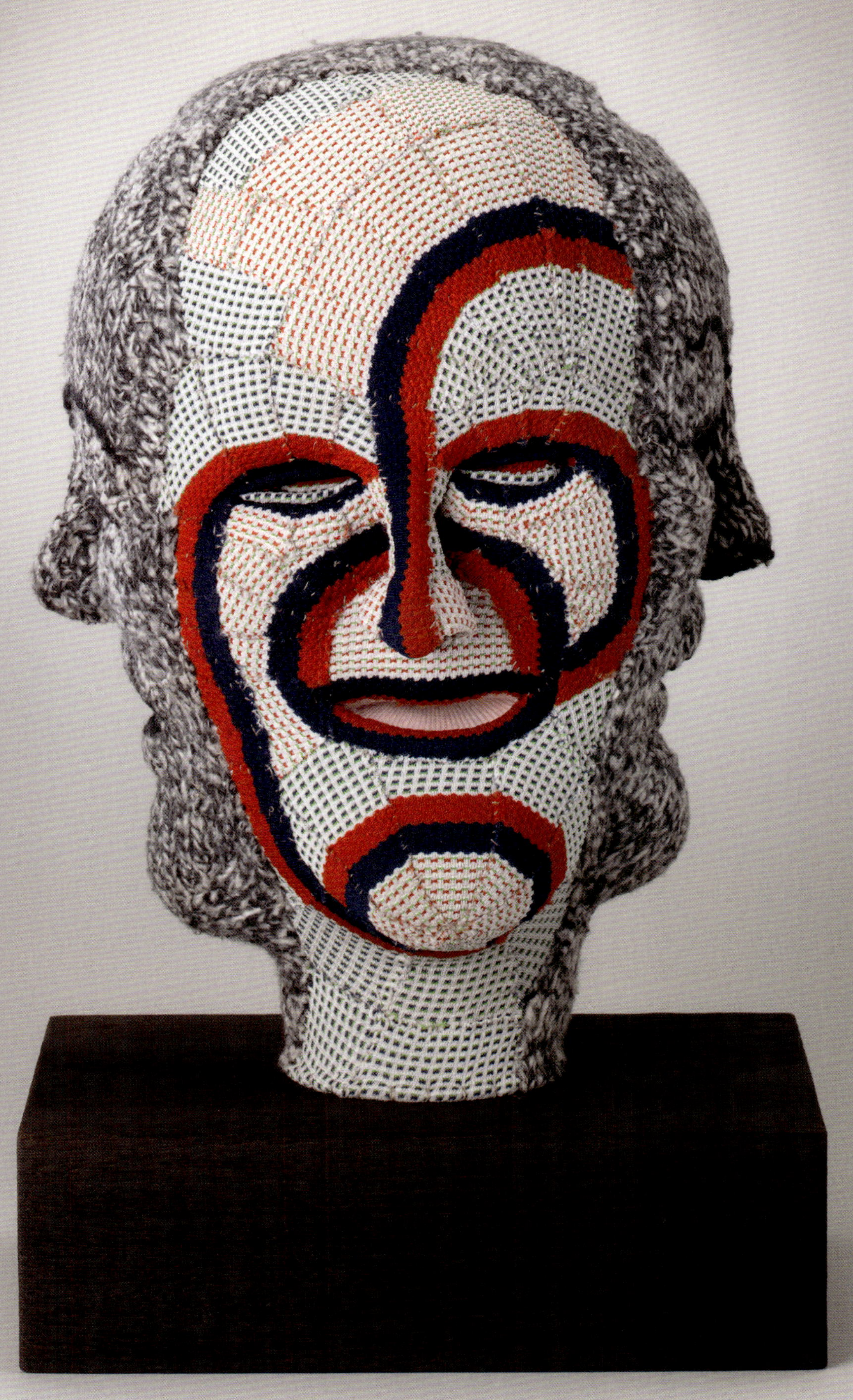

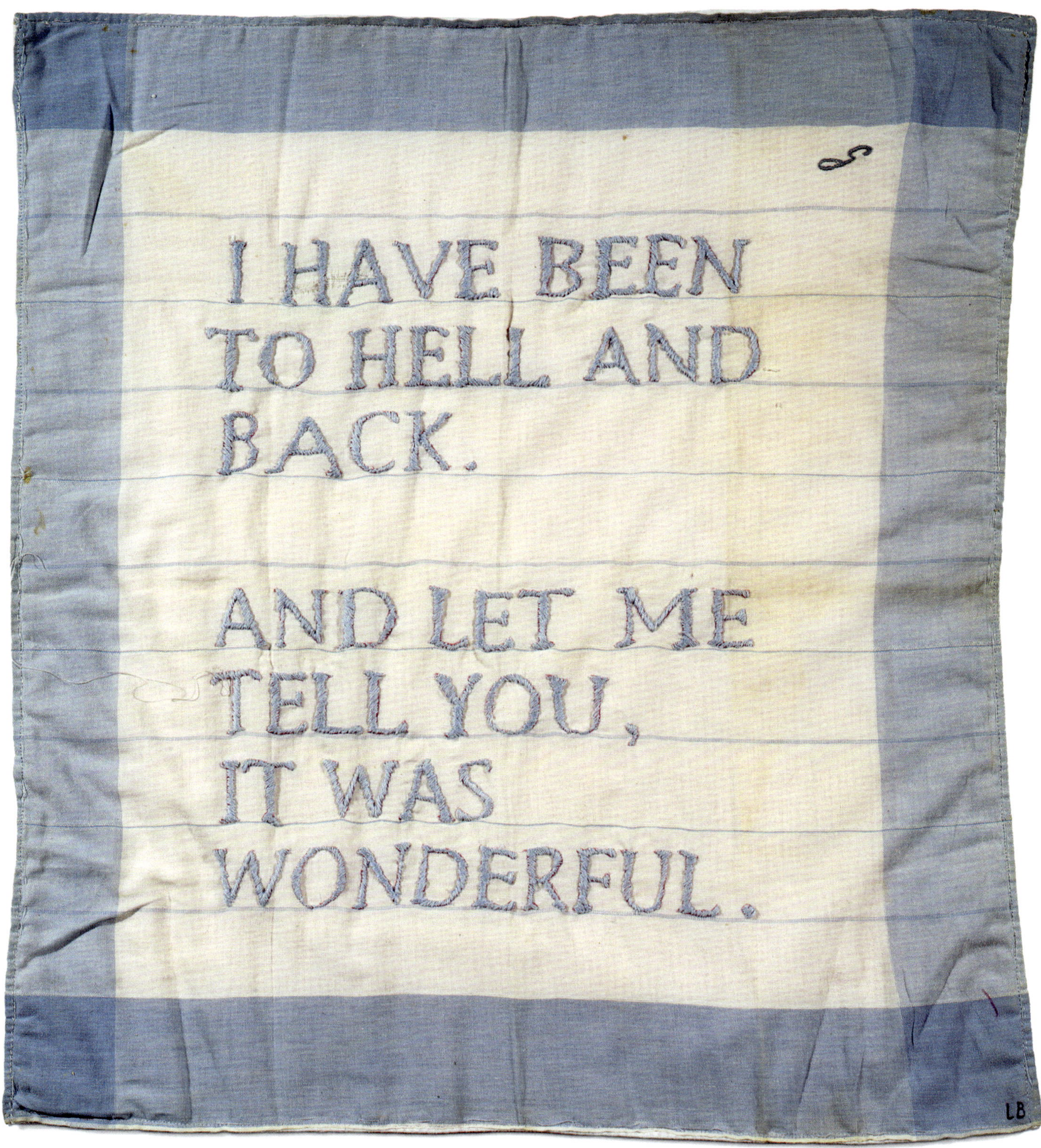
I HAVE BEEN
TO HELL AND
BACK.
AND LET ME
TELL YOU,
IT WAS
WONDERFUL.
LB

9
Good mother, bad mother

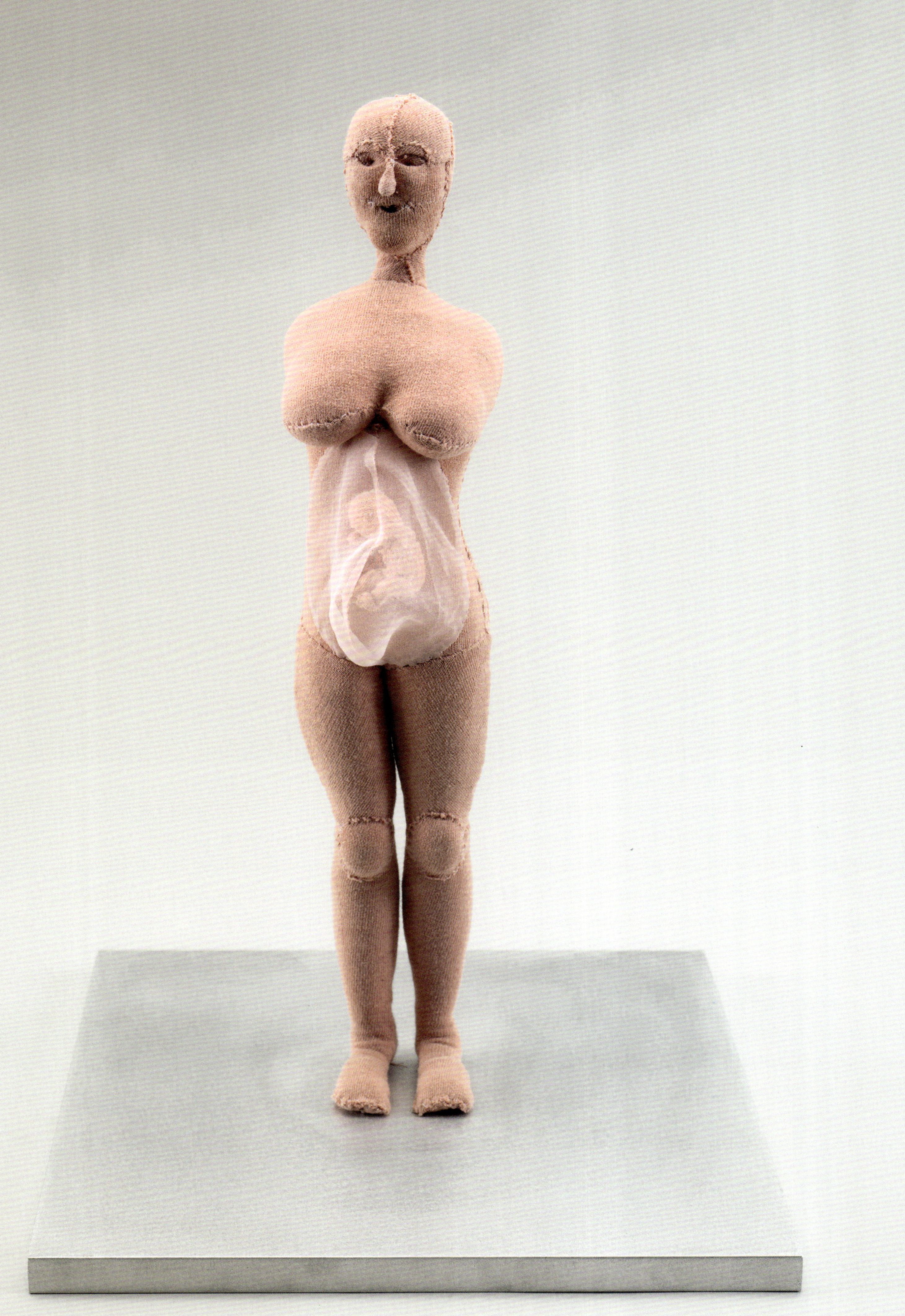

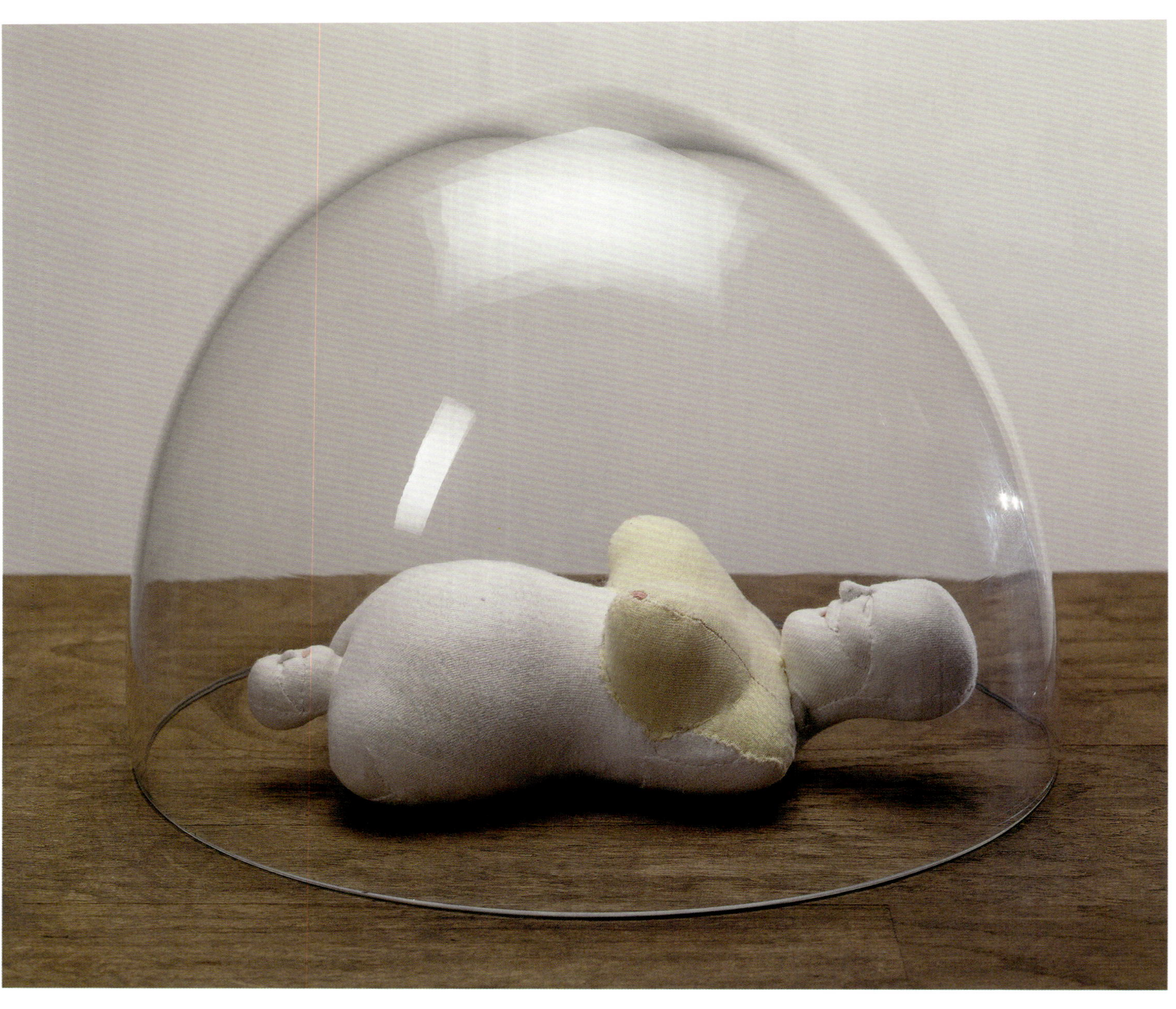

The Arrival 2007
The Woven Child 2002

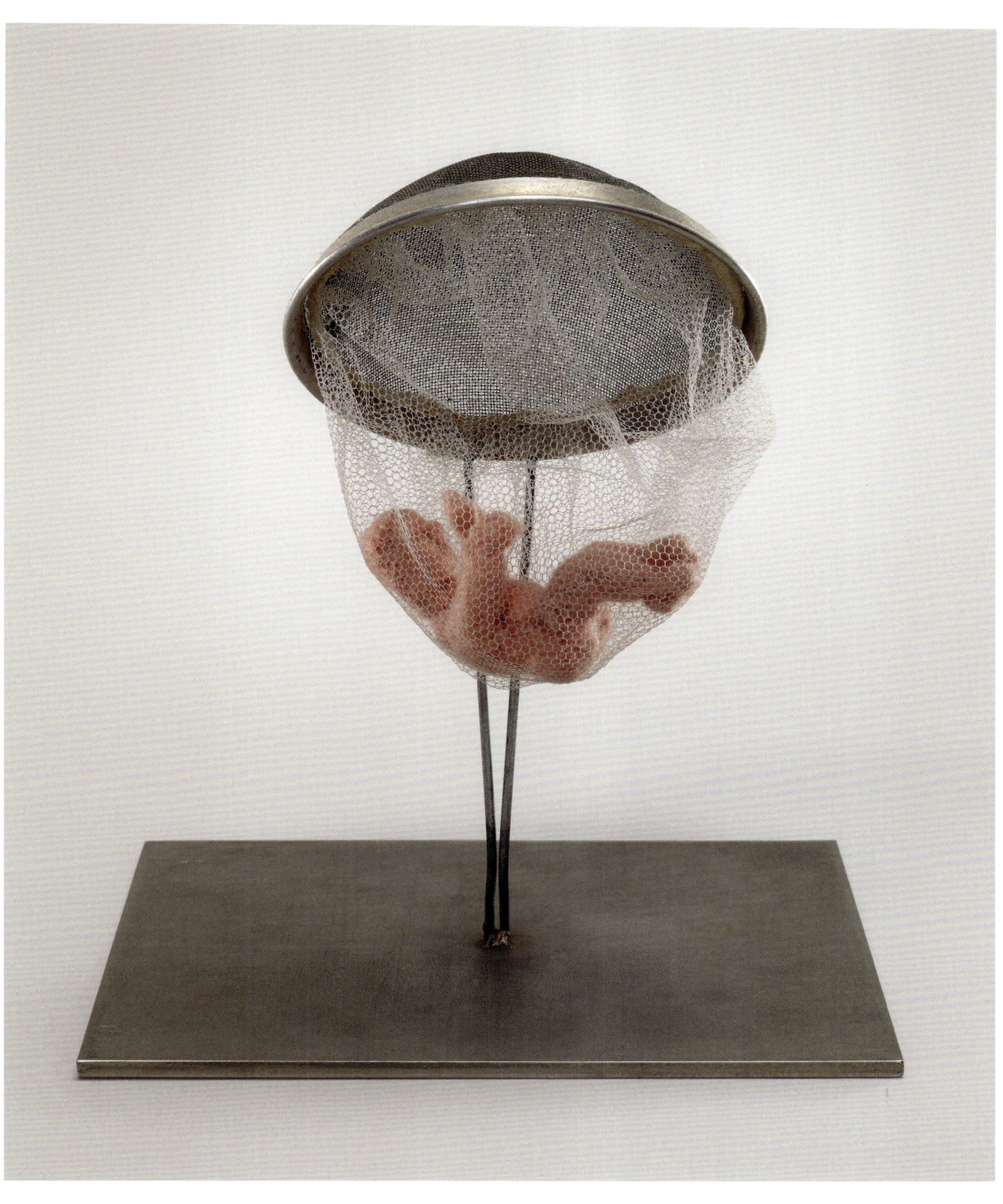

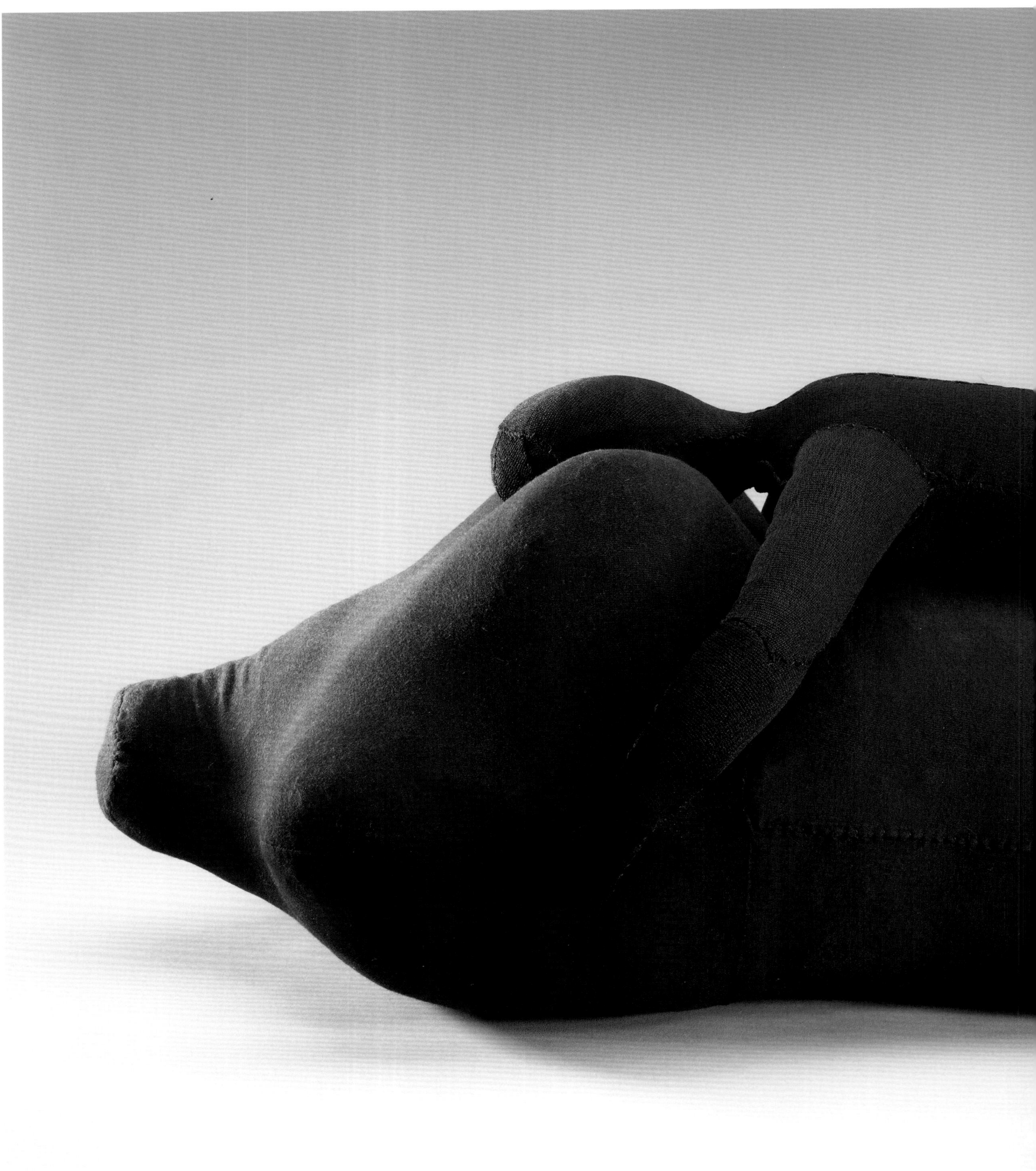

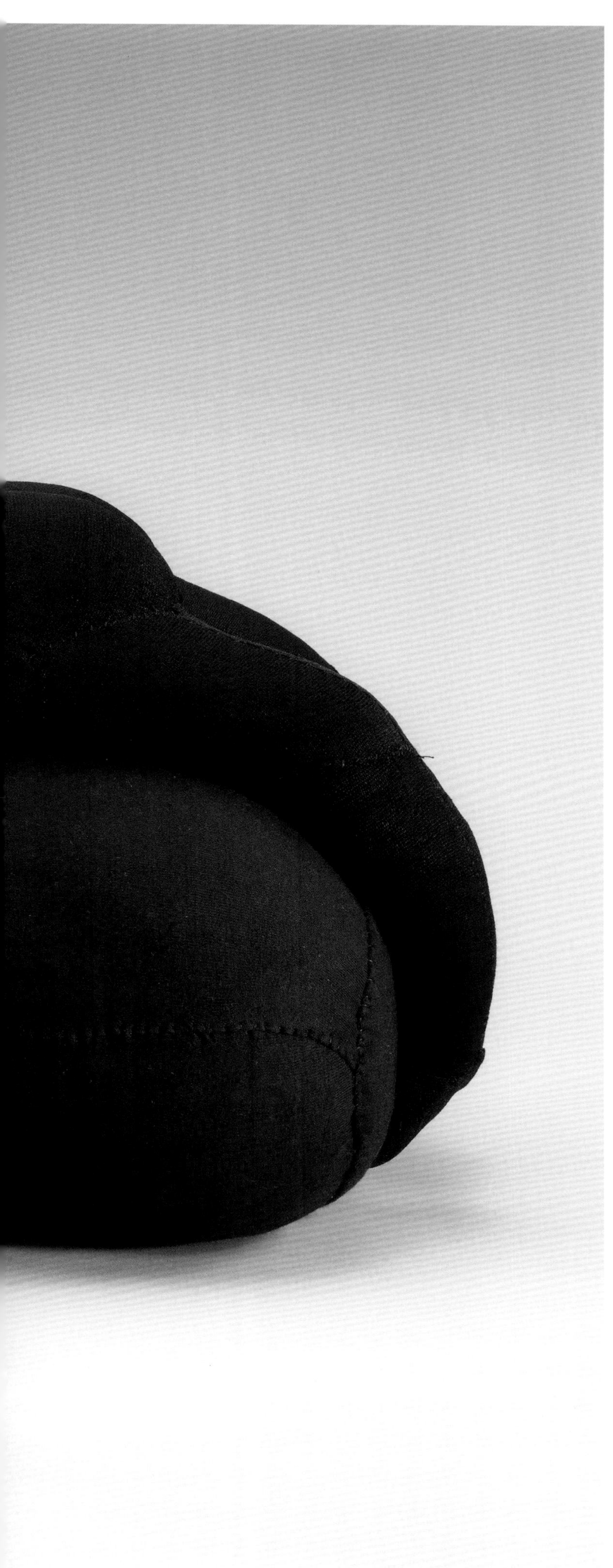

The Found Child 2001

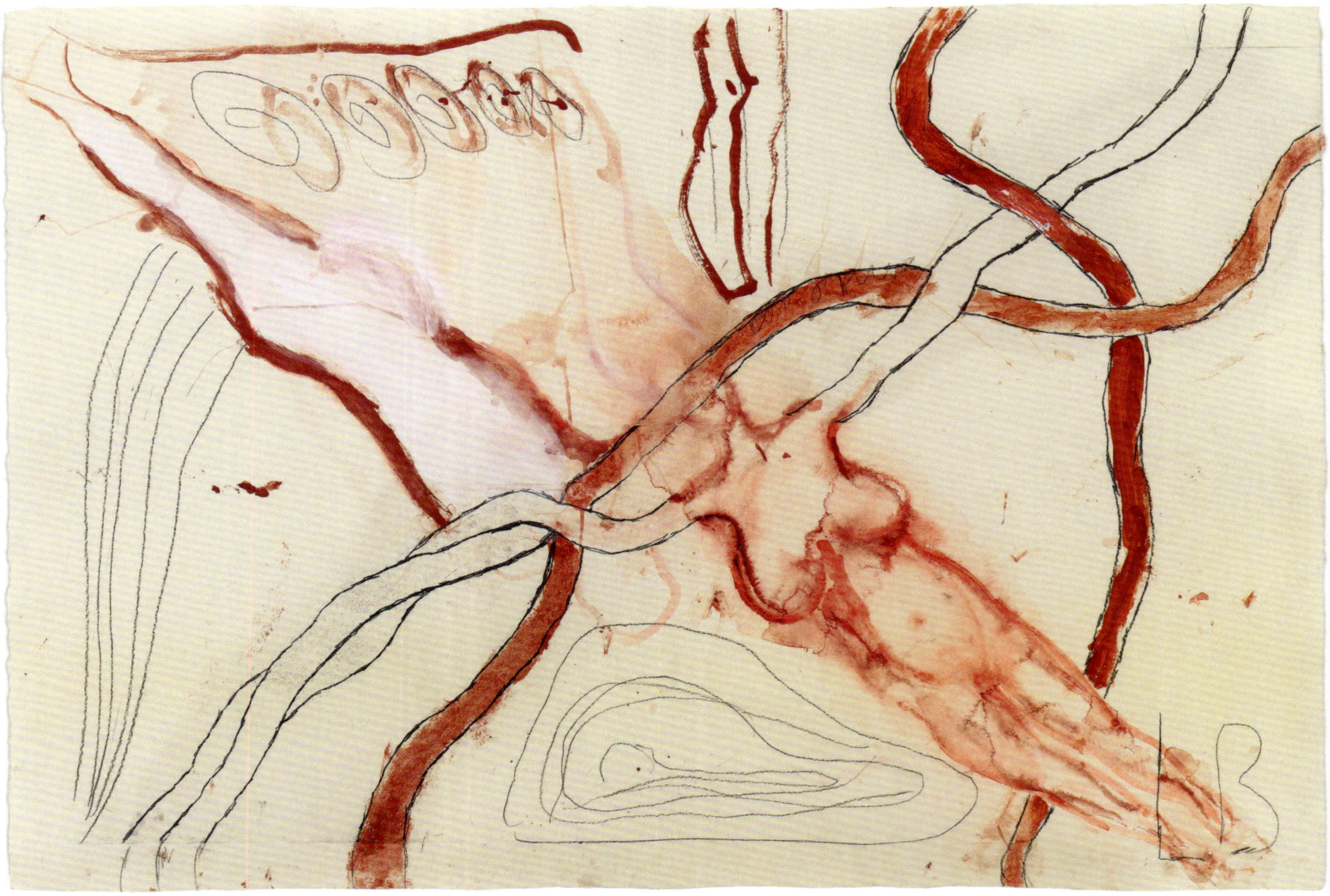

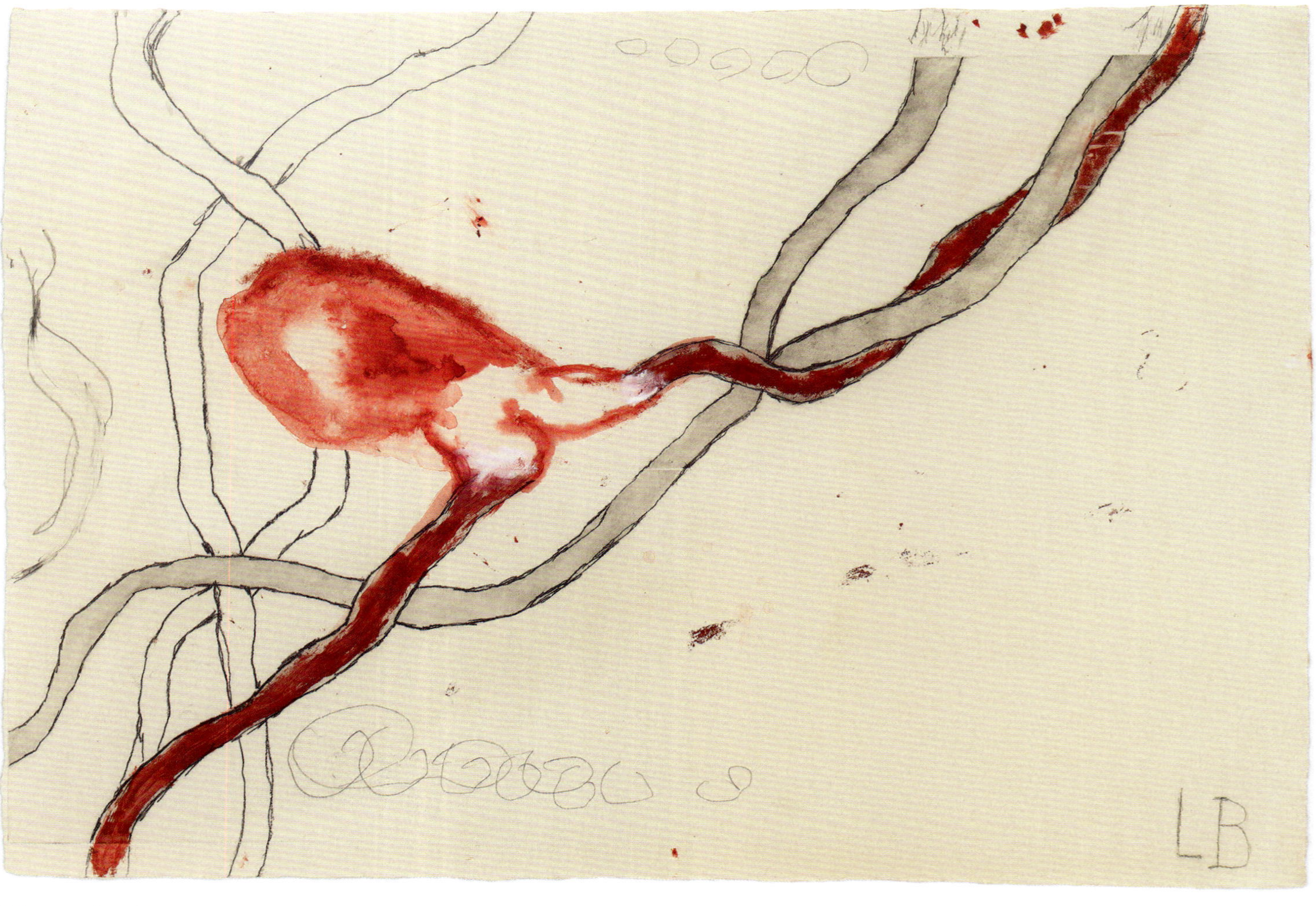

this spread and following pages:
À l'infini 2008–09

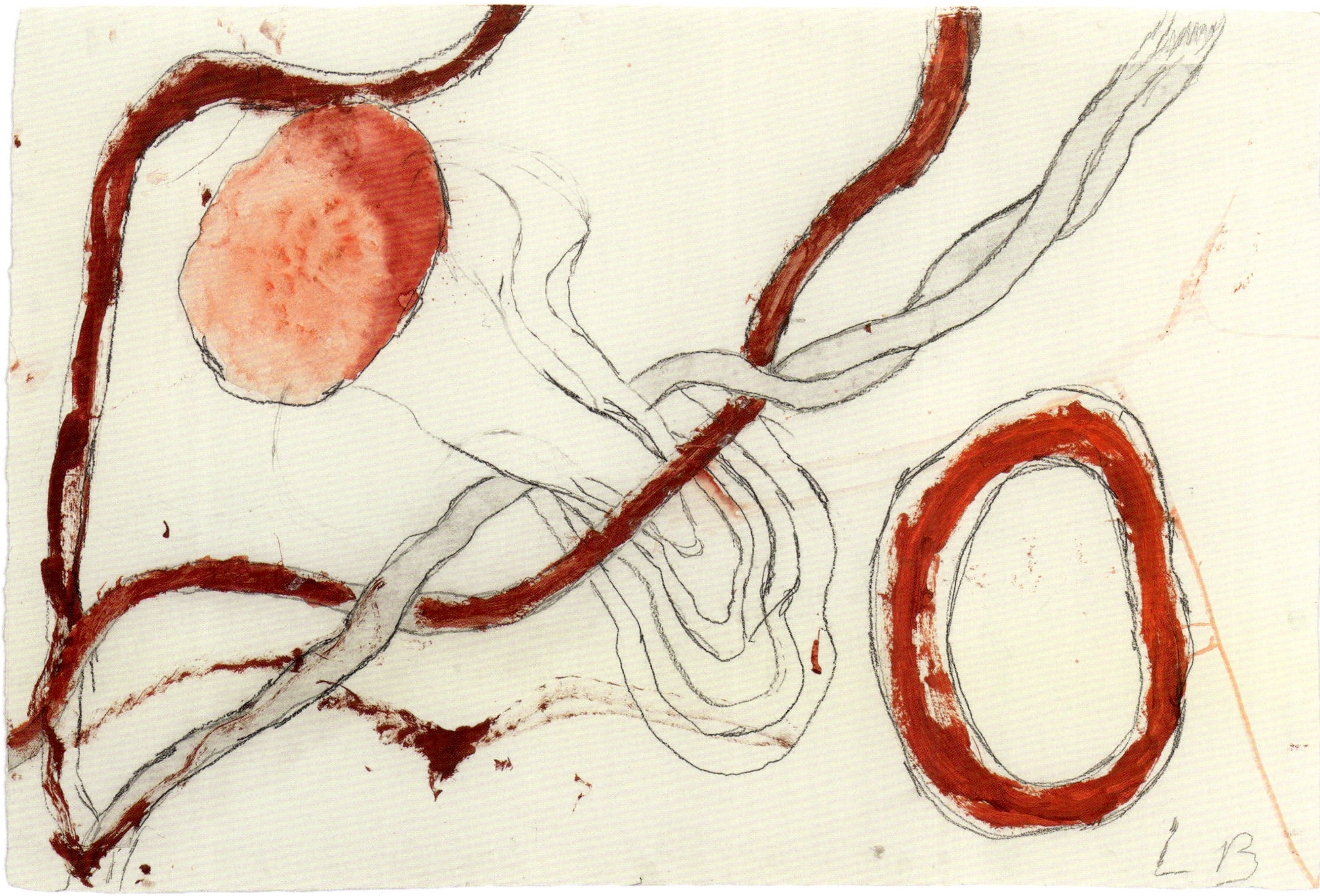

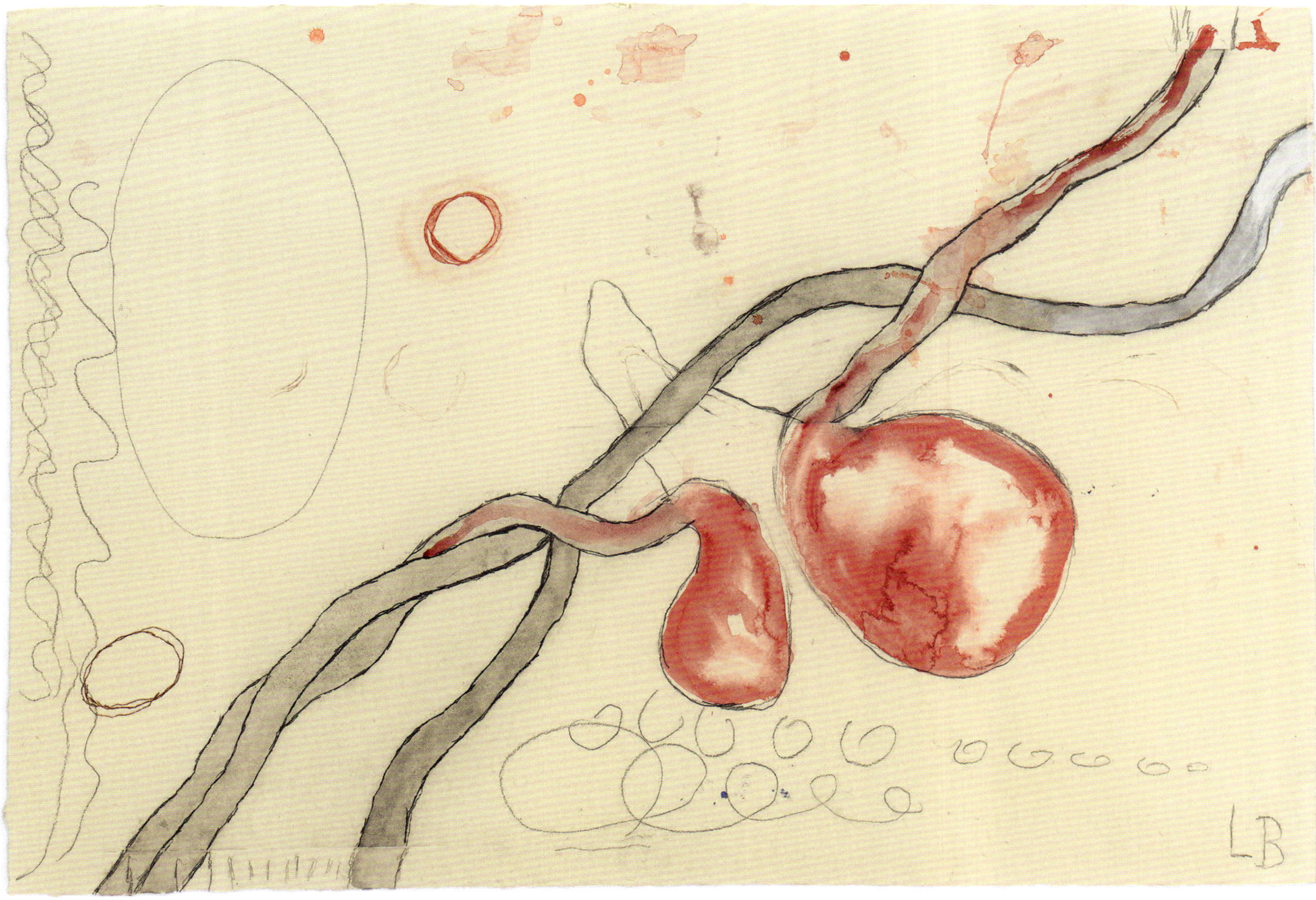

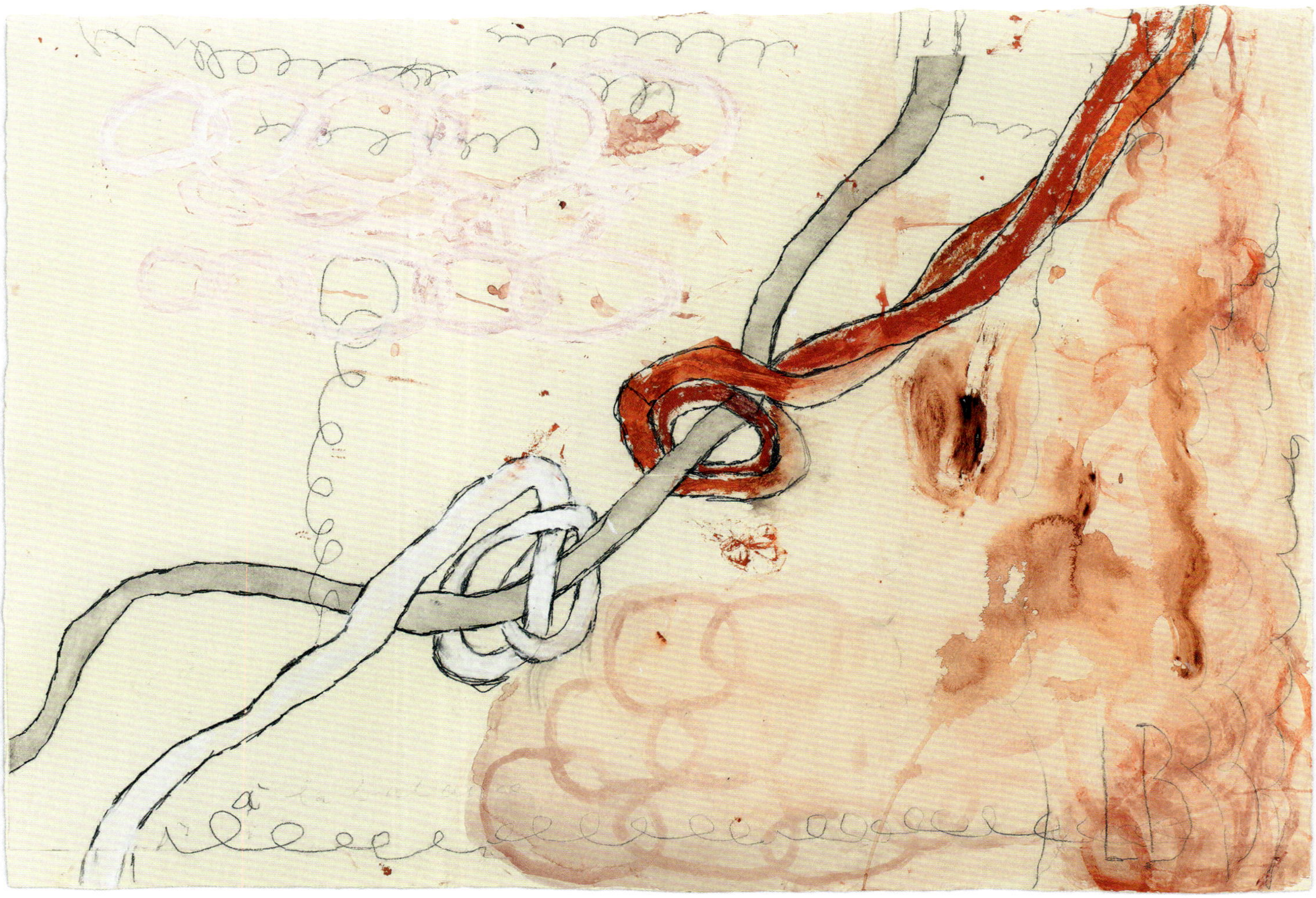

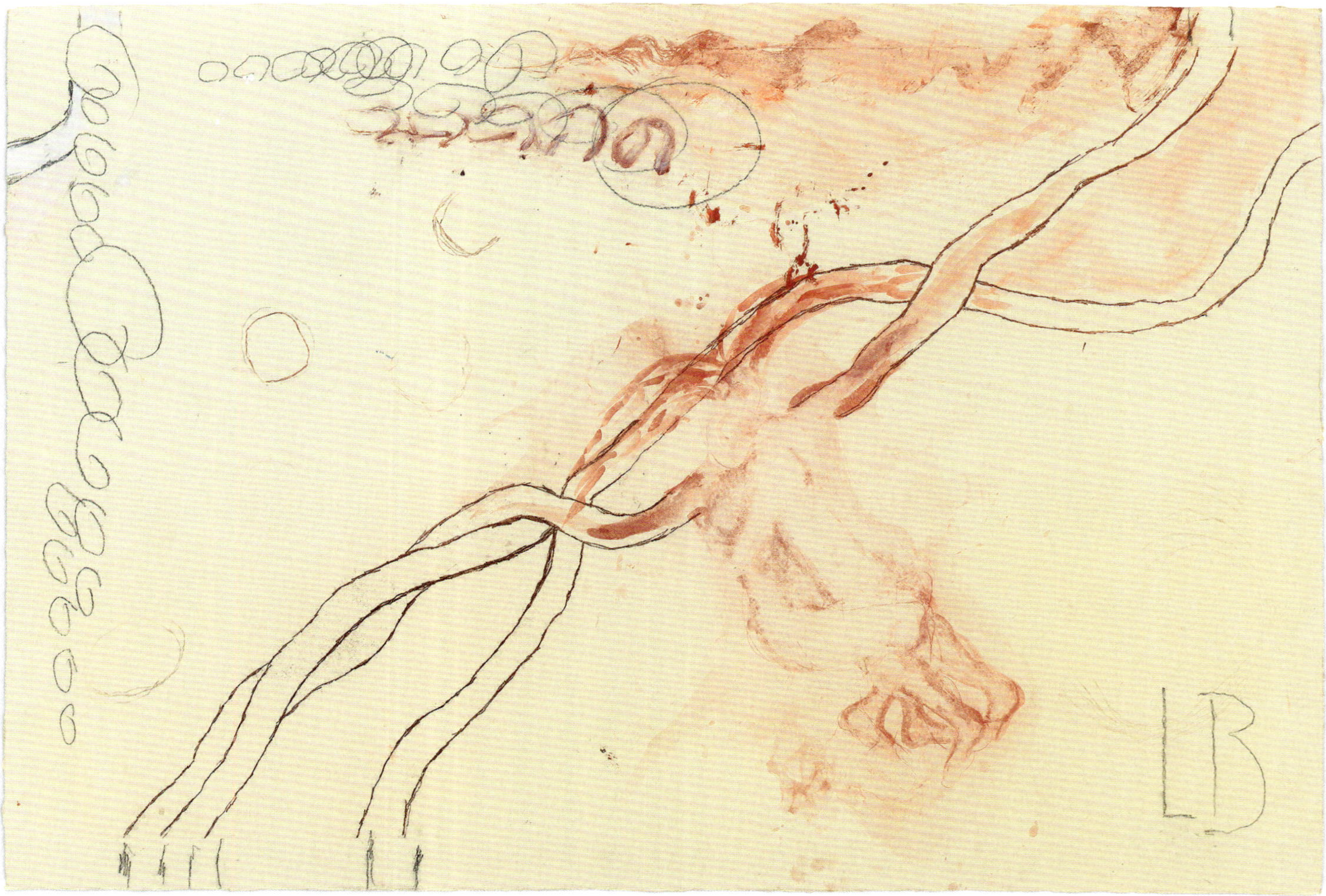

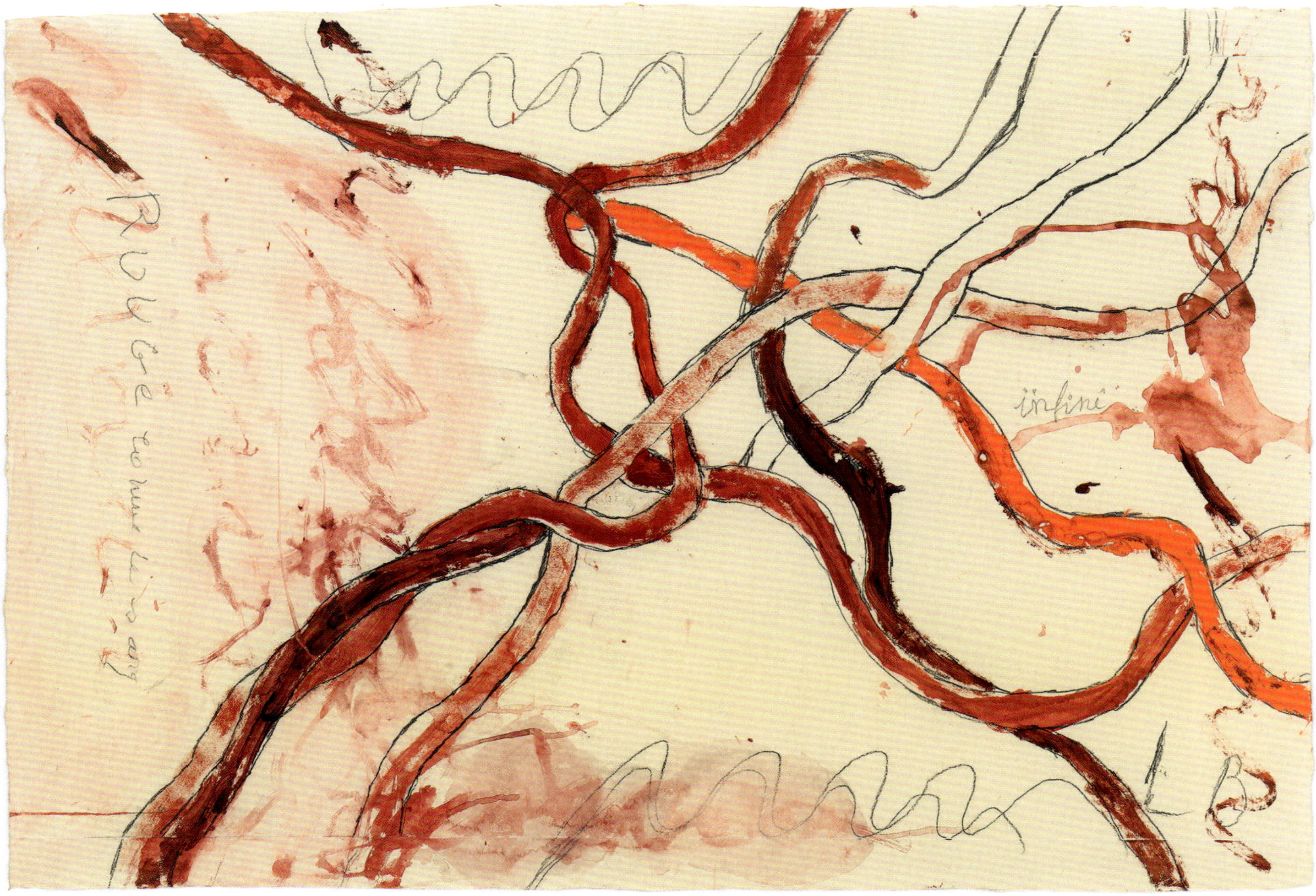

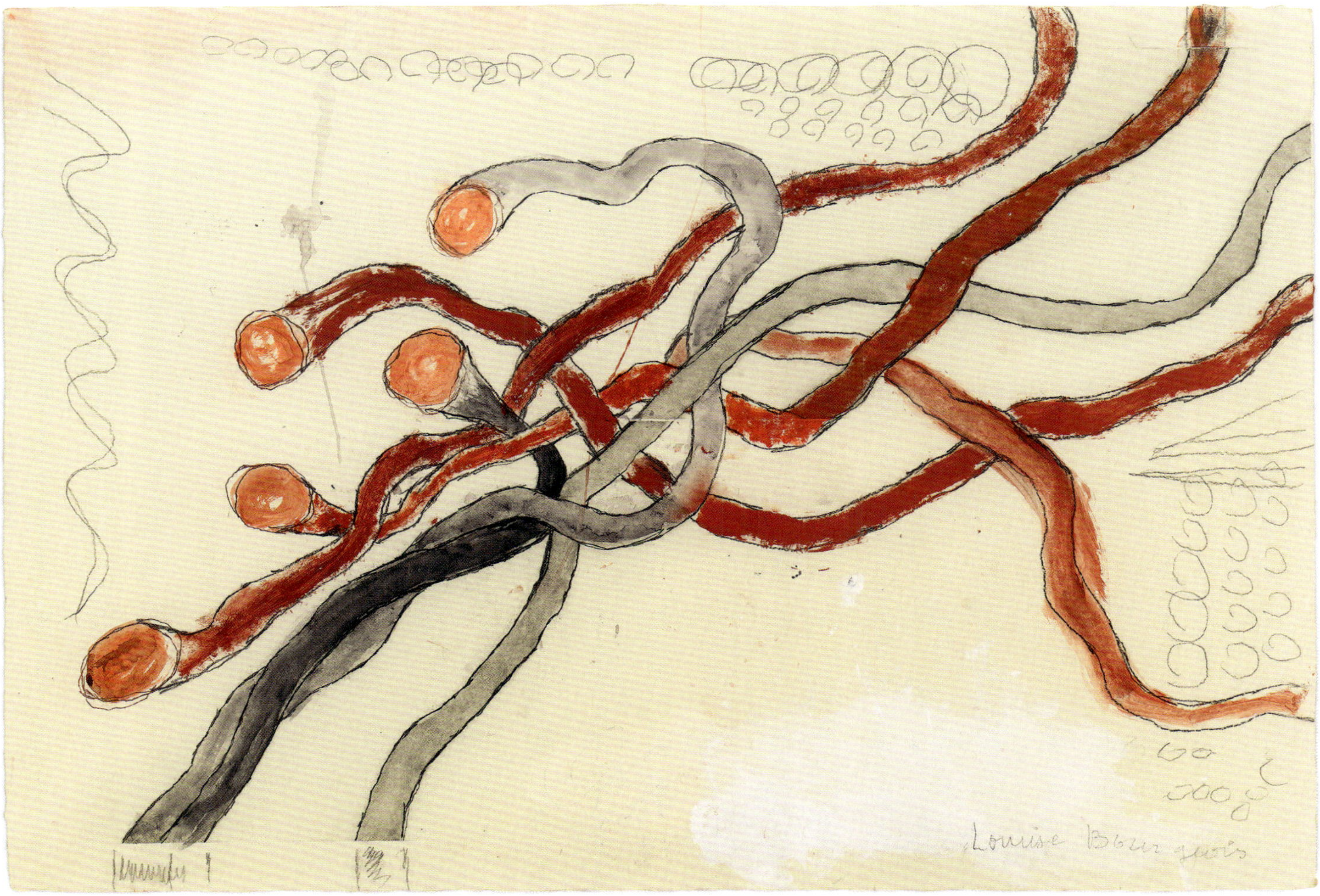

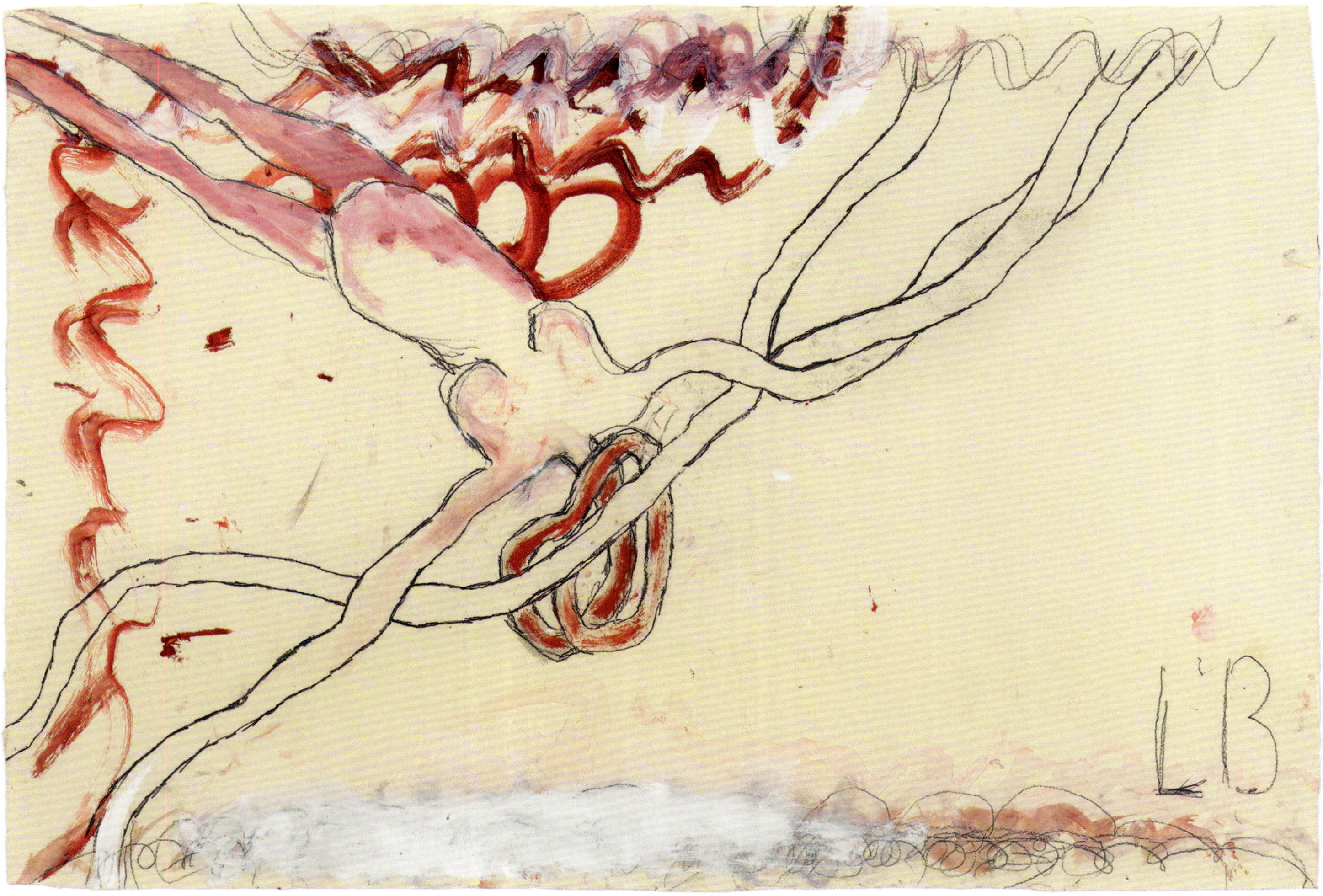
LB

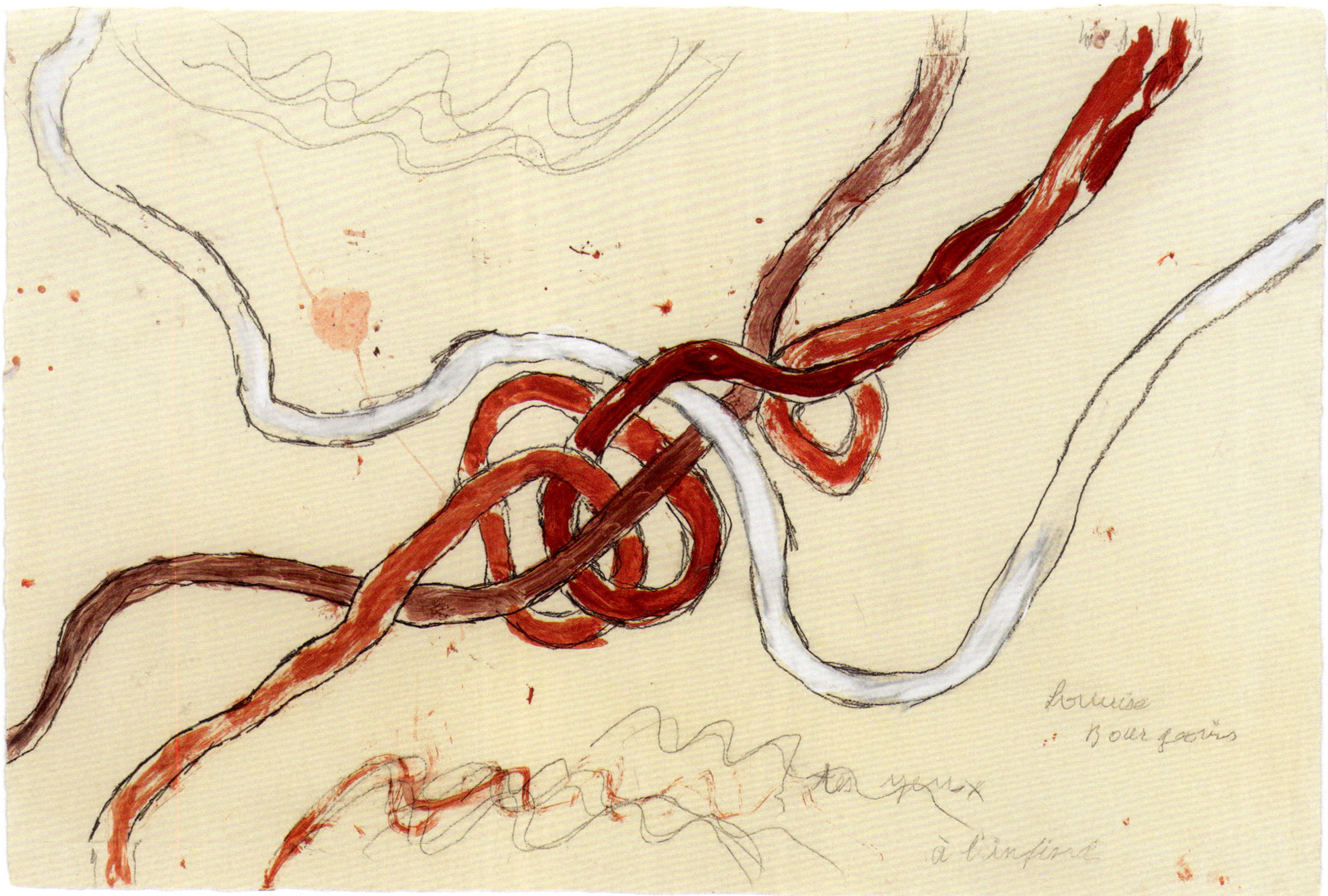
Louise
Bourgeois
tes yeux
à l'infini

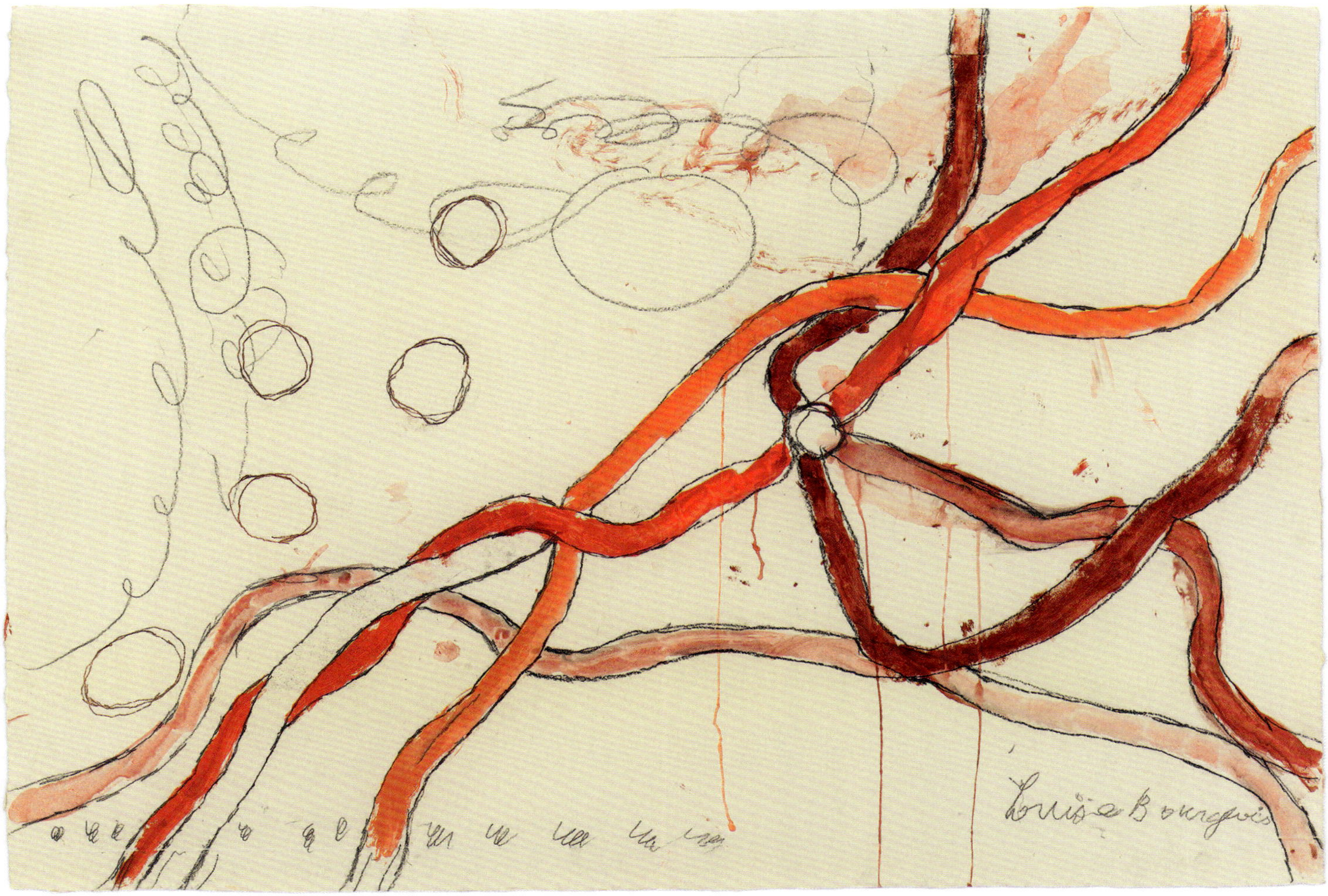

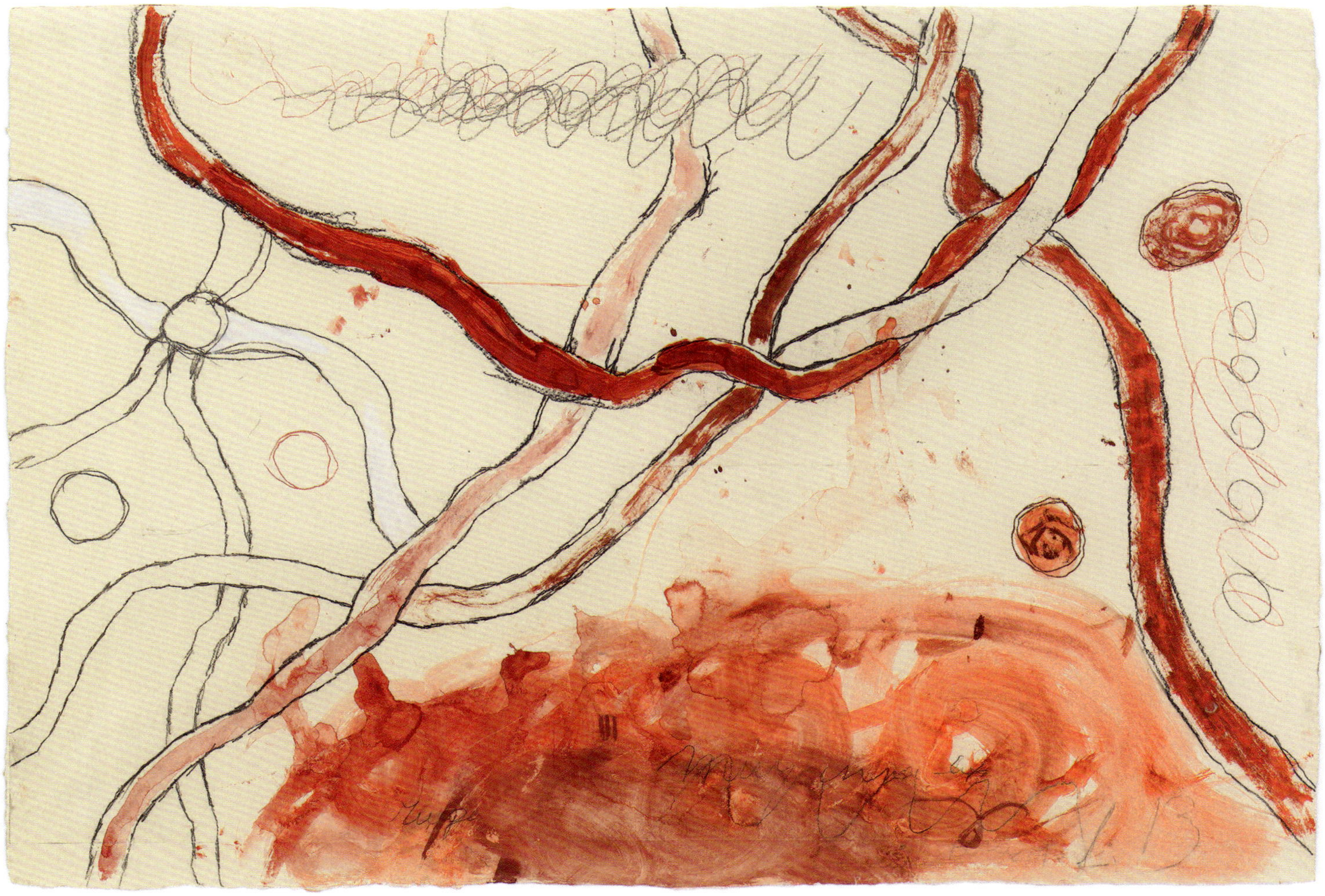

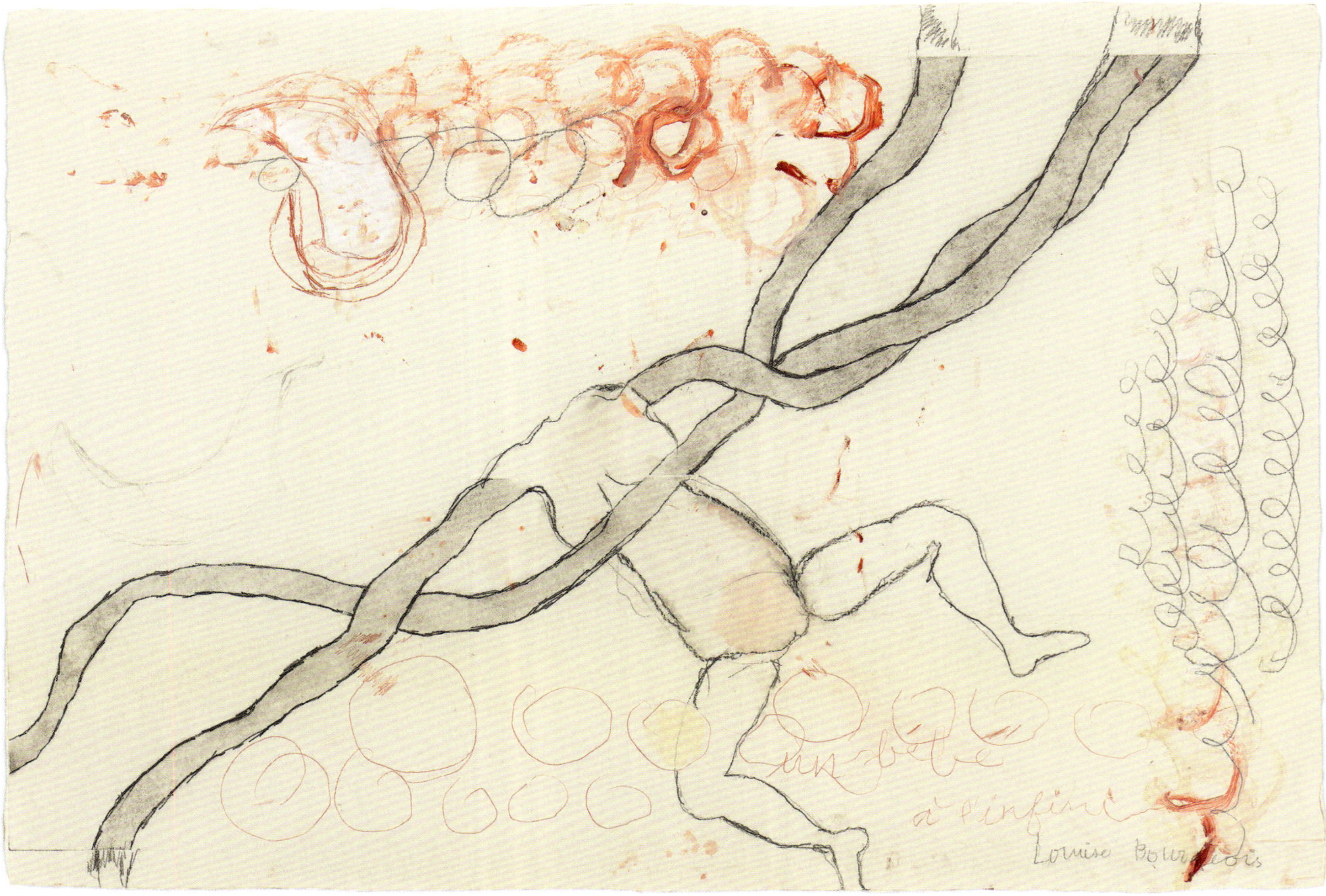

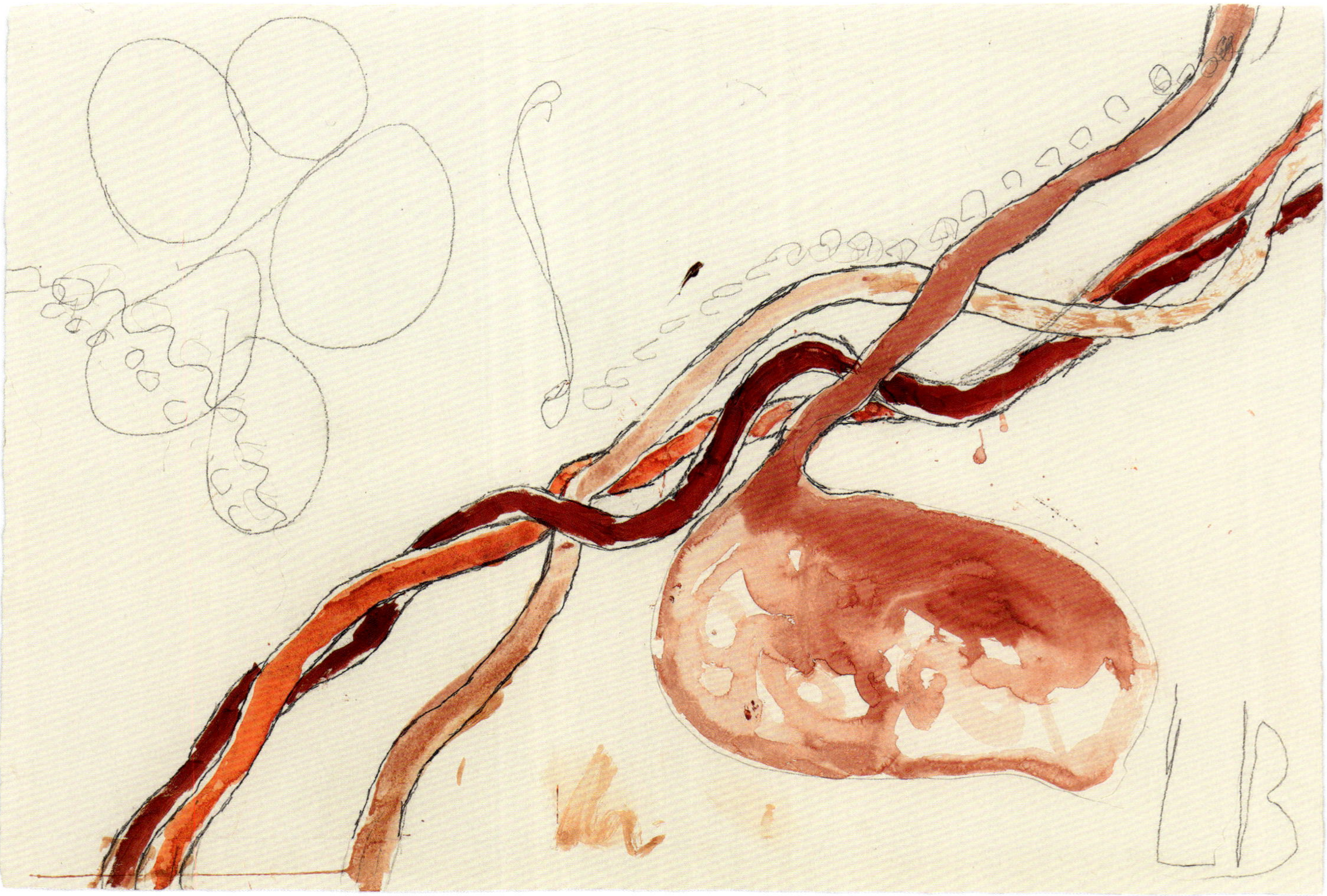

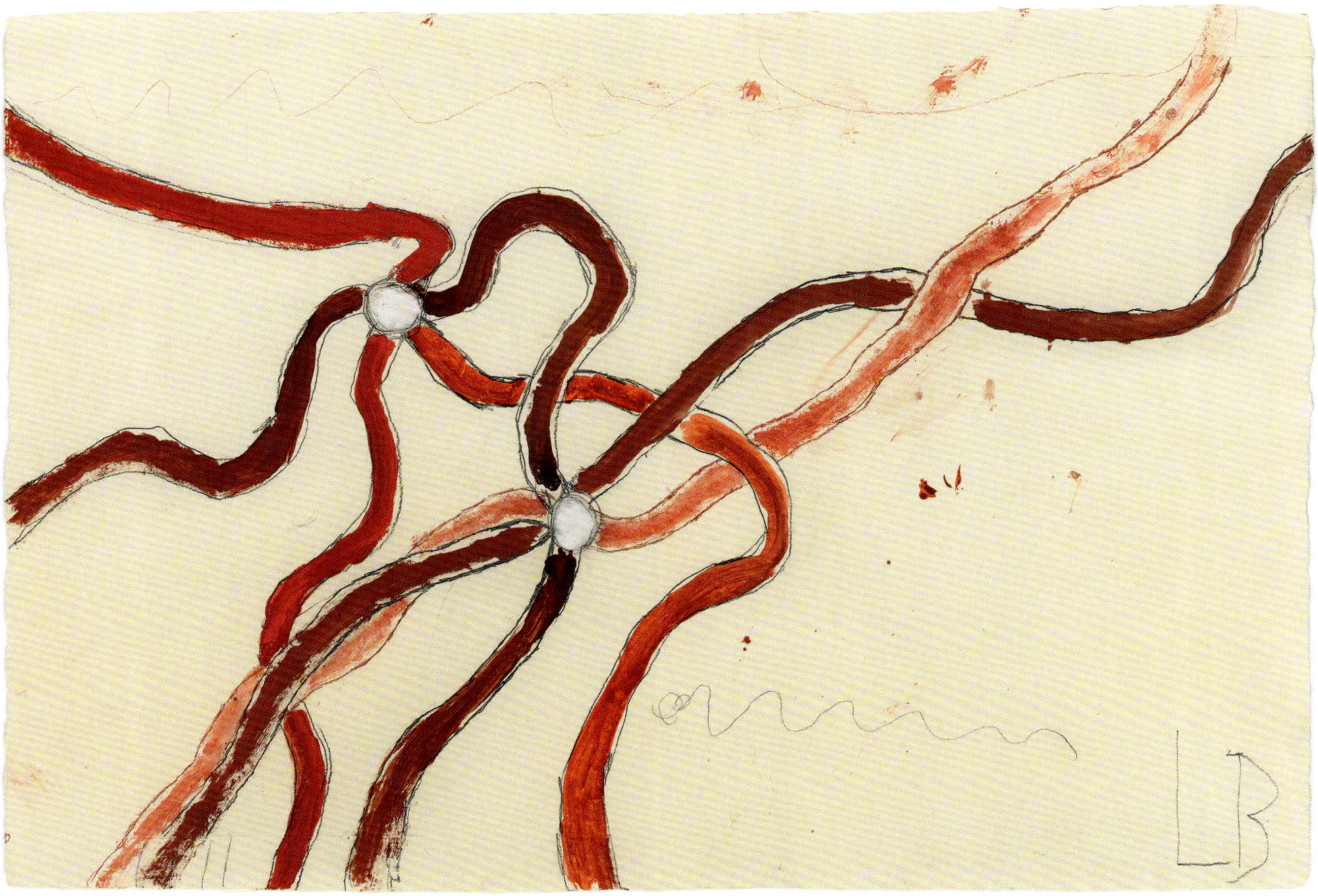
LB

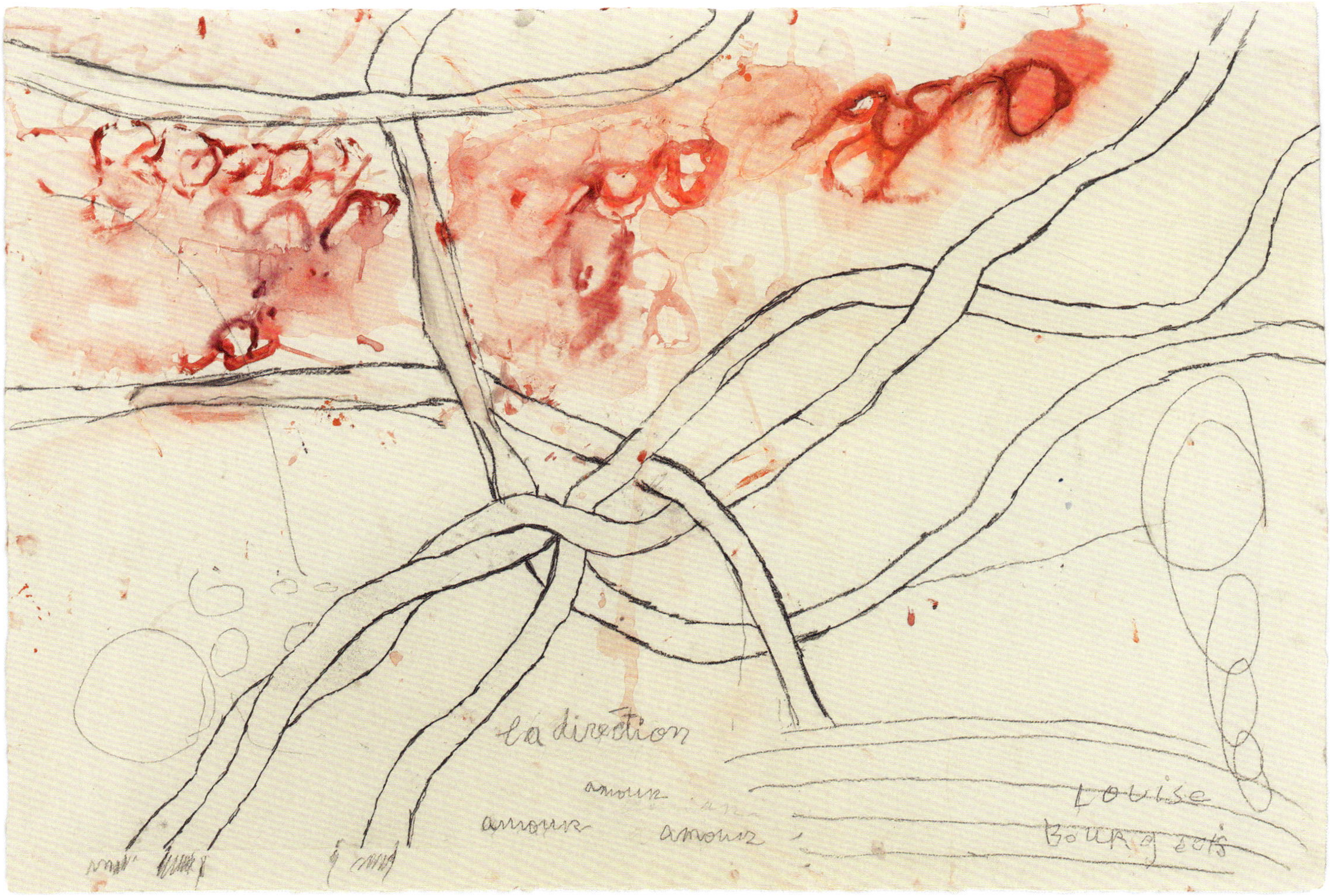
la direction
amour
amour
amour
Louise
Bourgeois

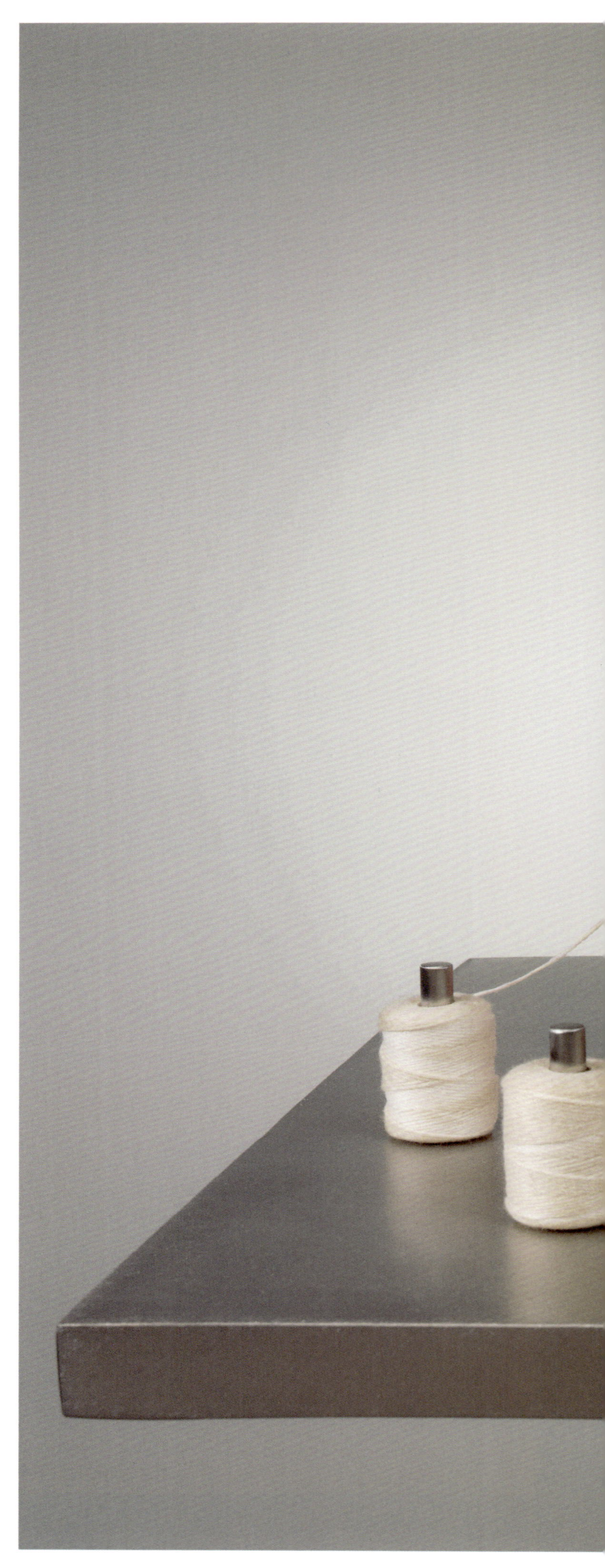

 The Good Mother 2003 (detail)

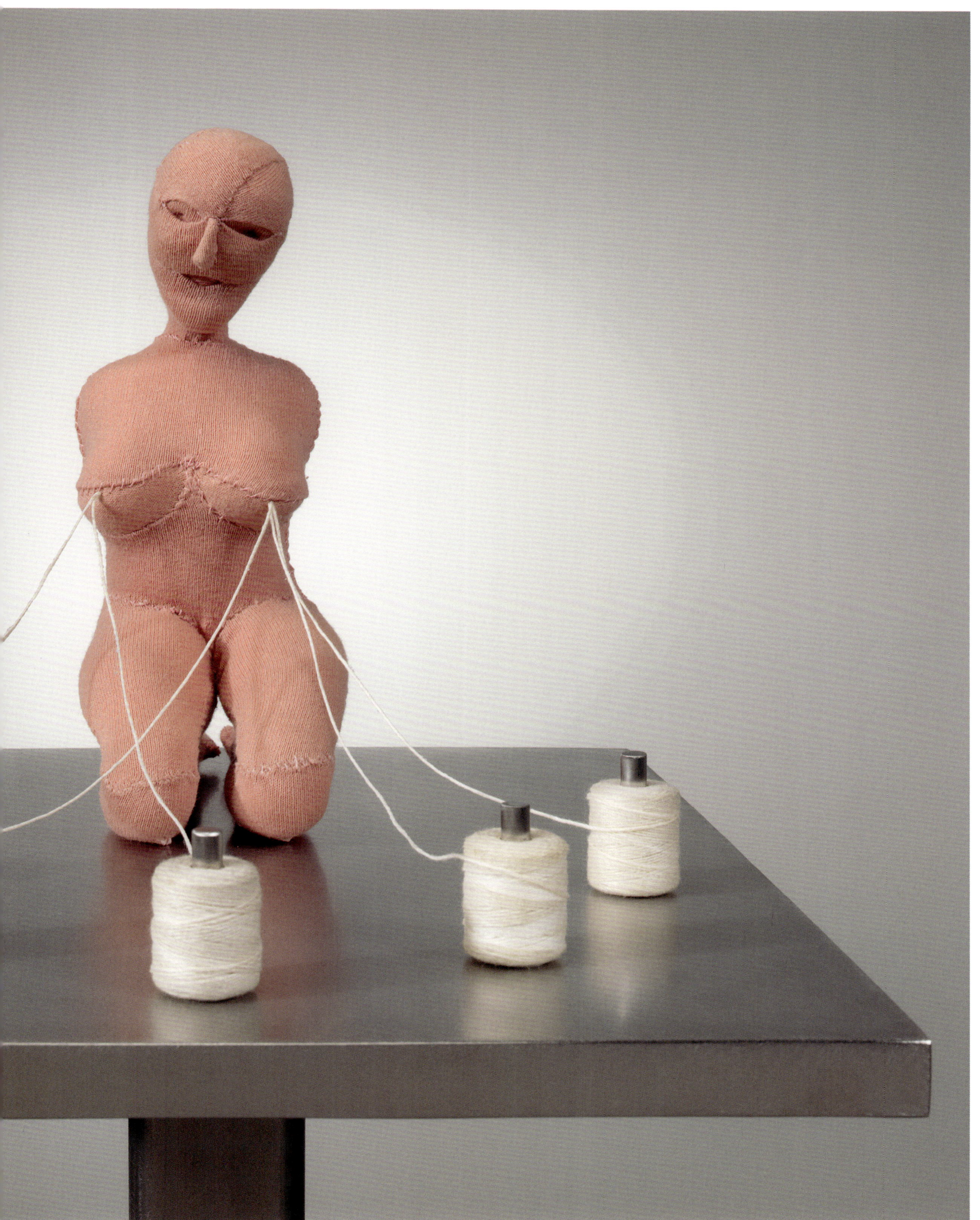

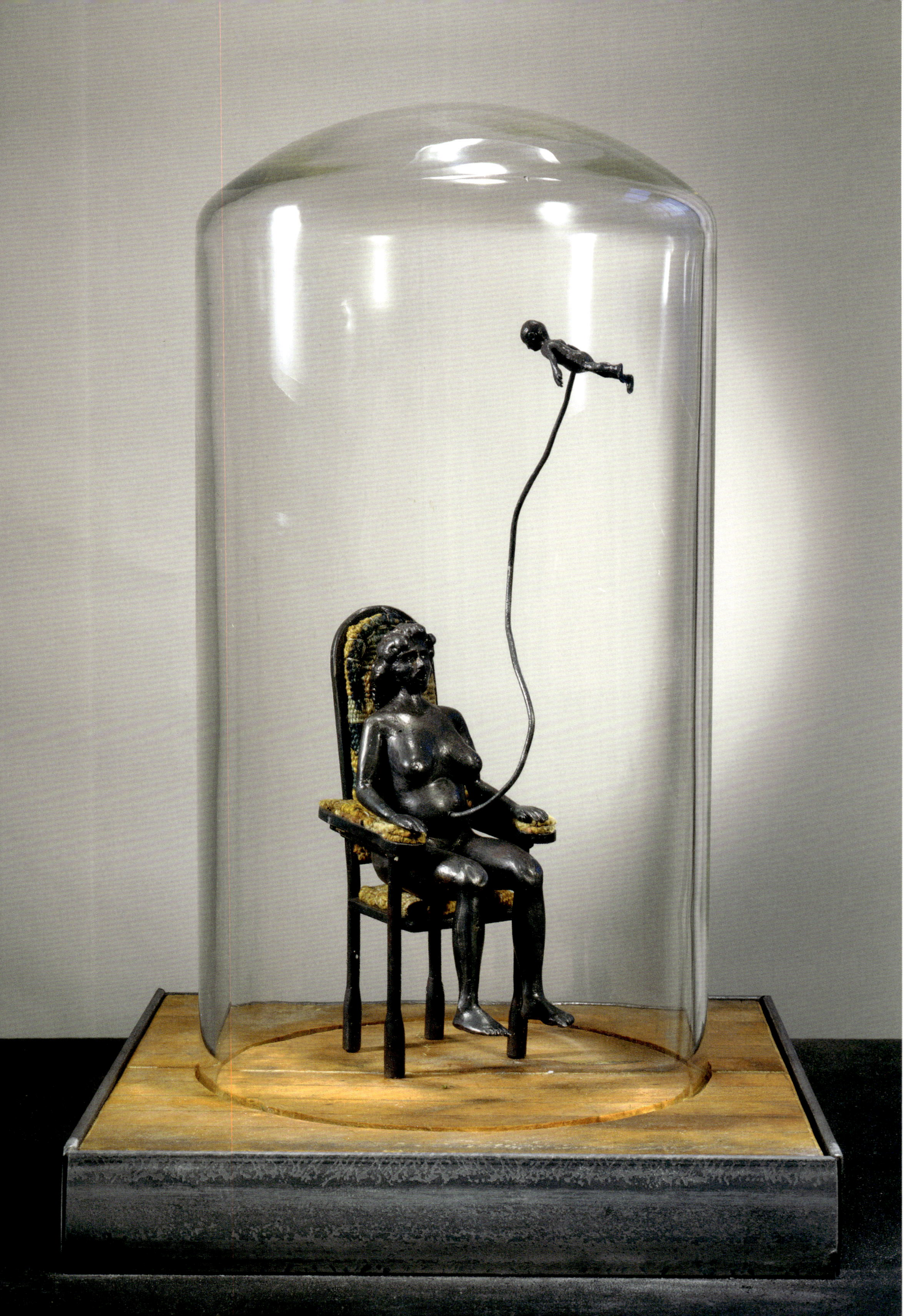

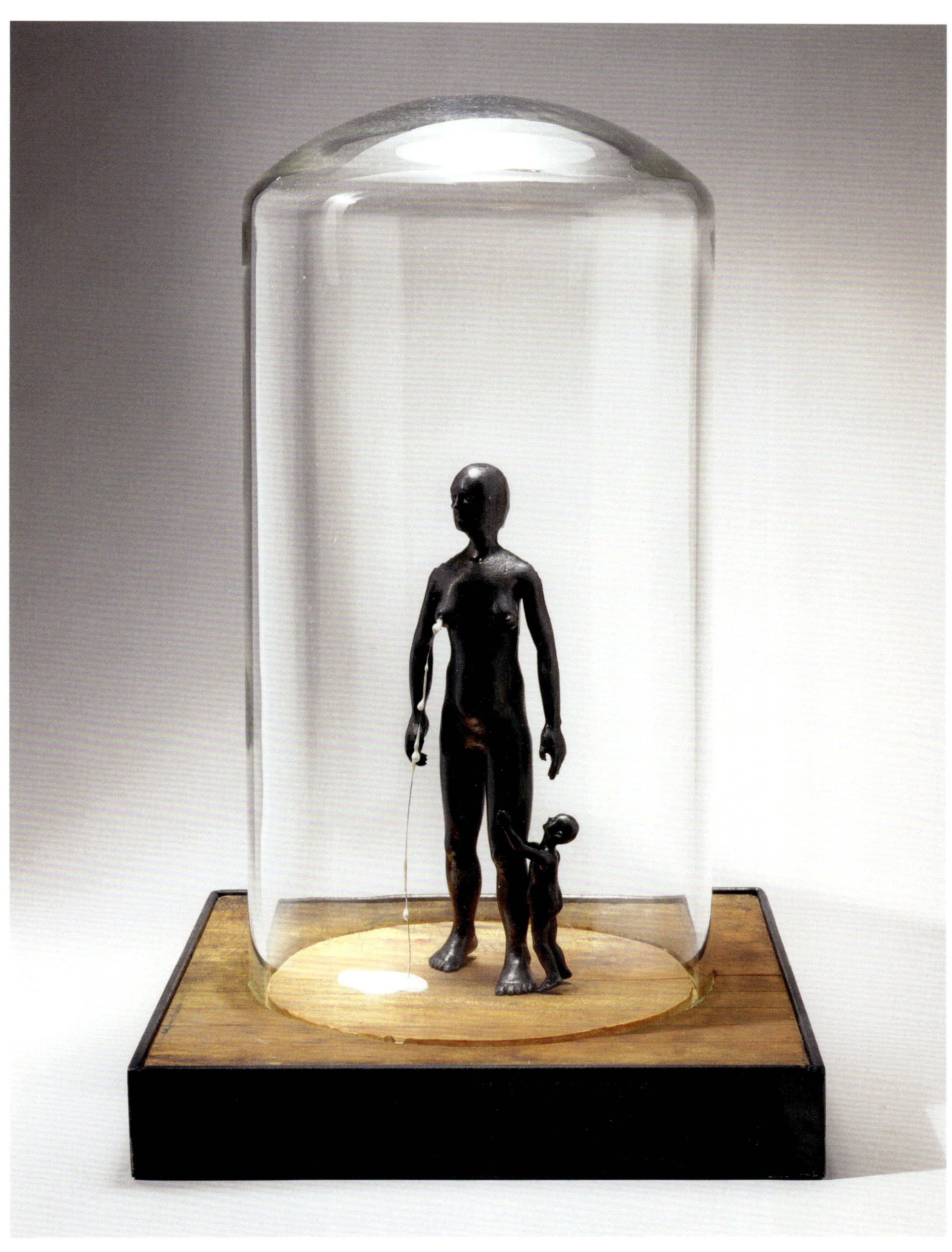

I Redo (interior element) 1999–2000
I Undo (interior element) 1999–2000

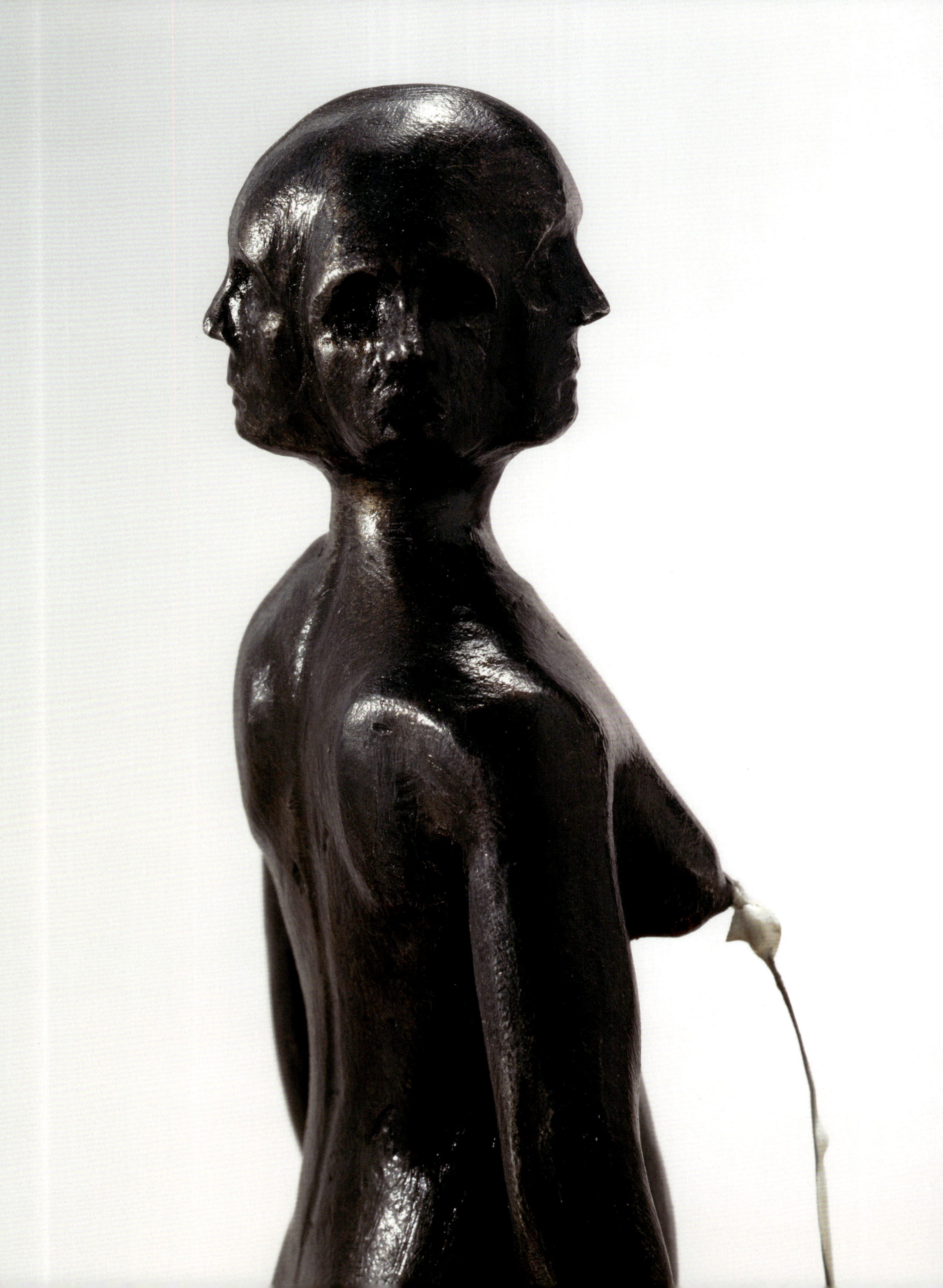

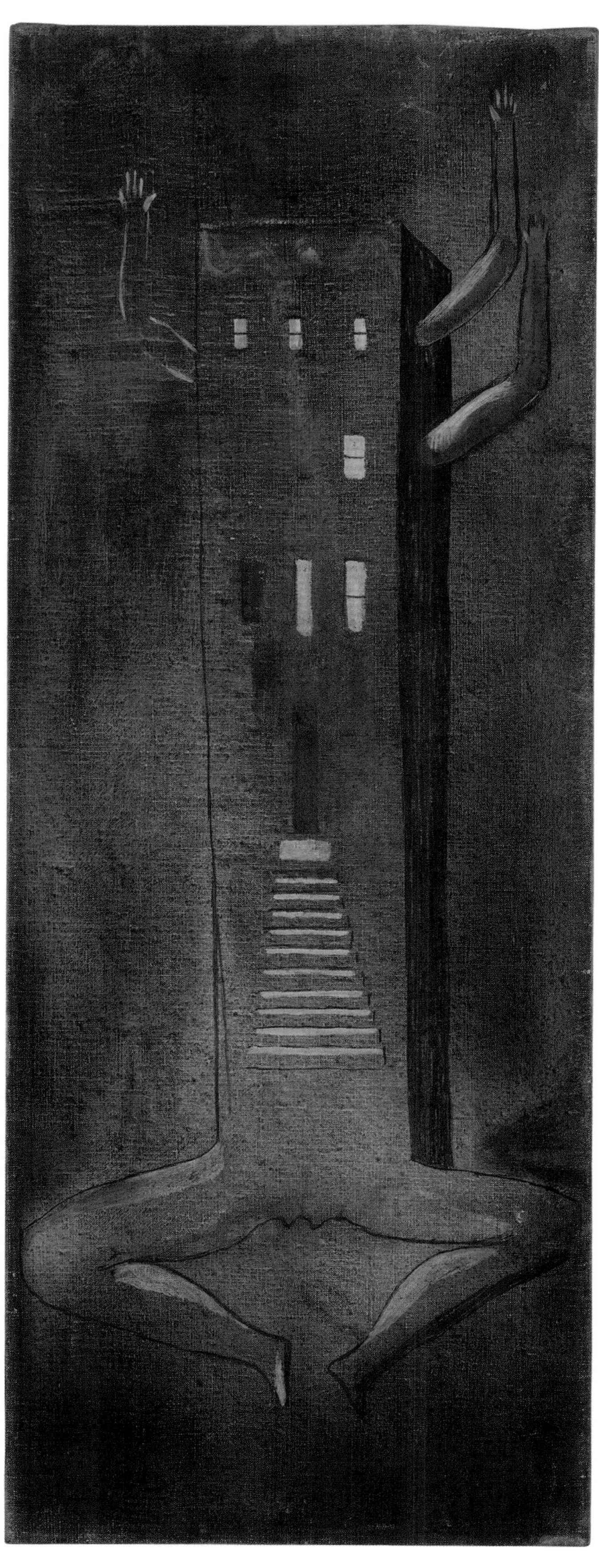

I Undo (interior element) 1999–2000 (detail)
Femme maison 1946–47

Night

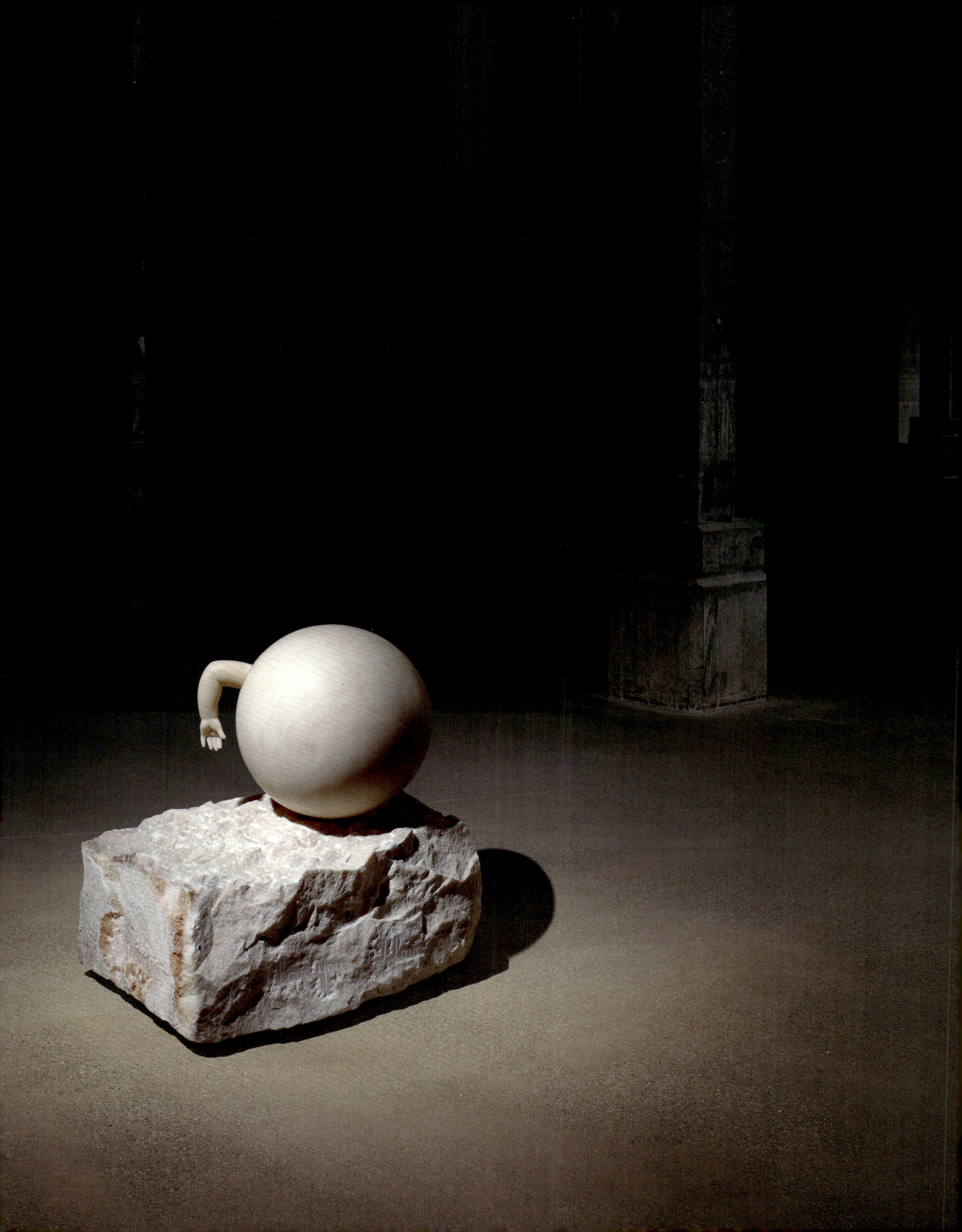
I love you

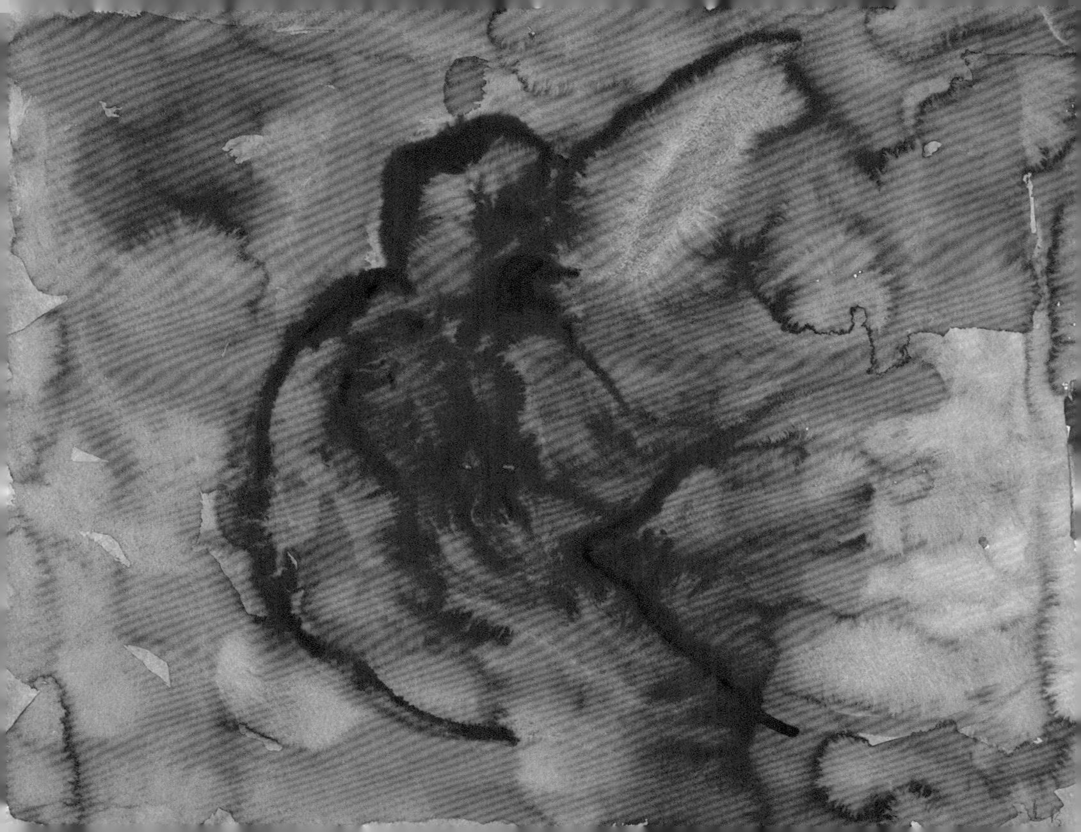

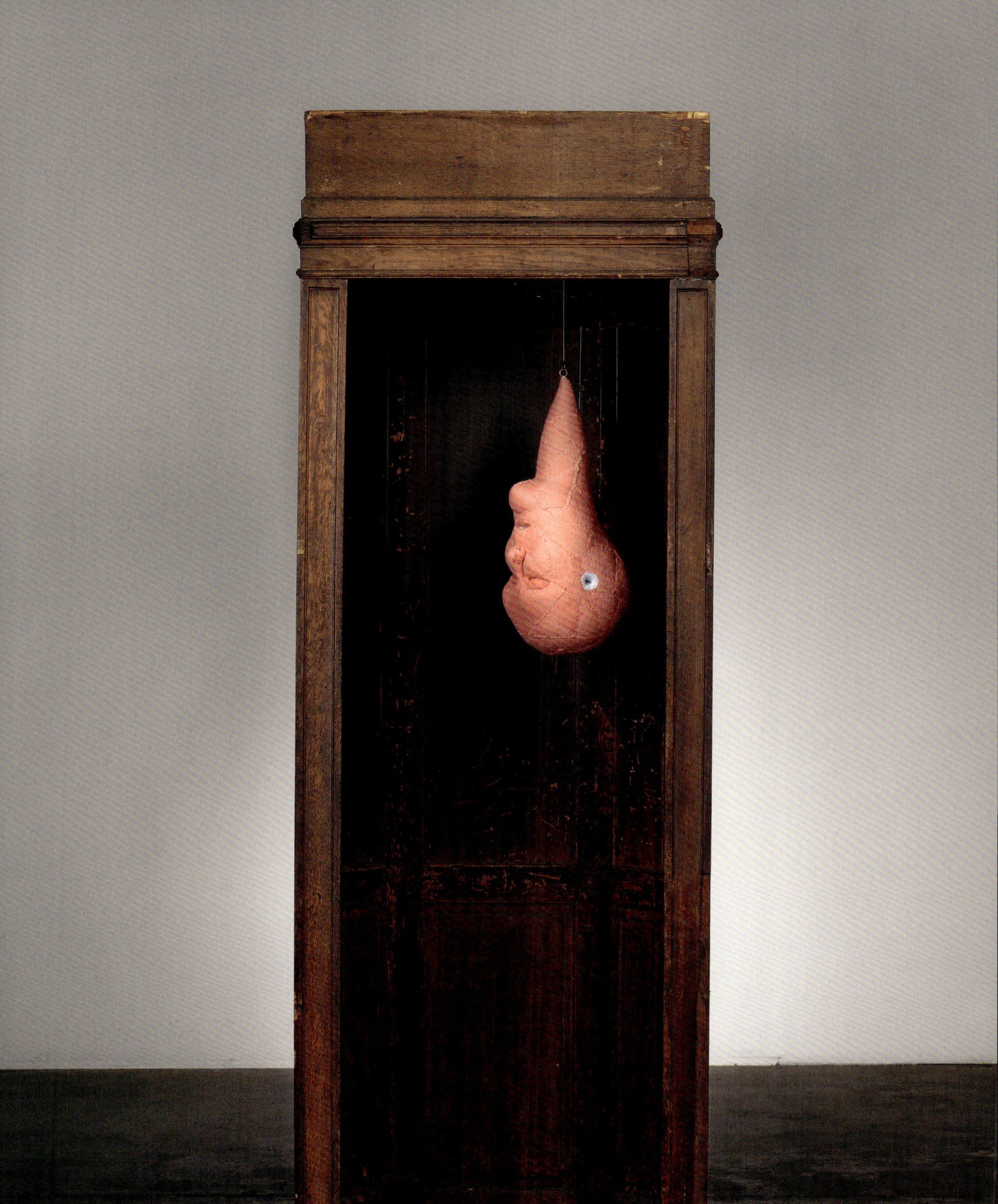

the back of the neck
the back between
the shoulder blades
the base of the ribs
the solar plexus
the stomach
the esophagus
the throat
the intestines
the anus
the pelvis bones
the joints
the legs
thighs

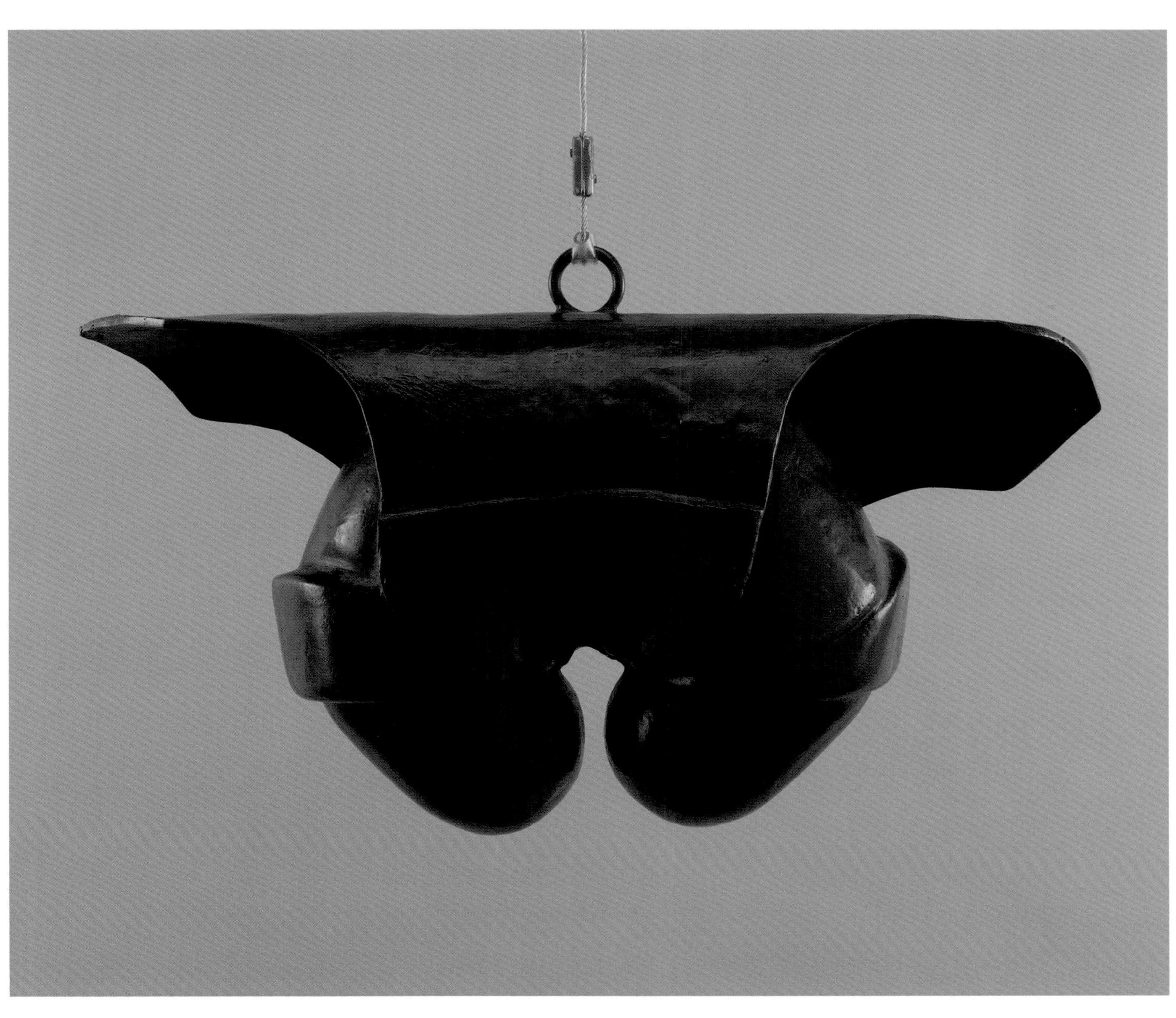

Jenny Holzer *Bourgeois X Holzer Projections* 2023
in the Tank
Hanging Janus with Jacket 1968

following spreads:
Spider IV 1996 in the Tank
Ventouse 1990

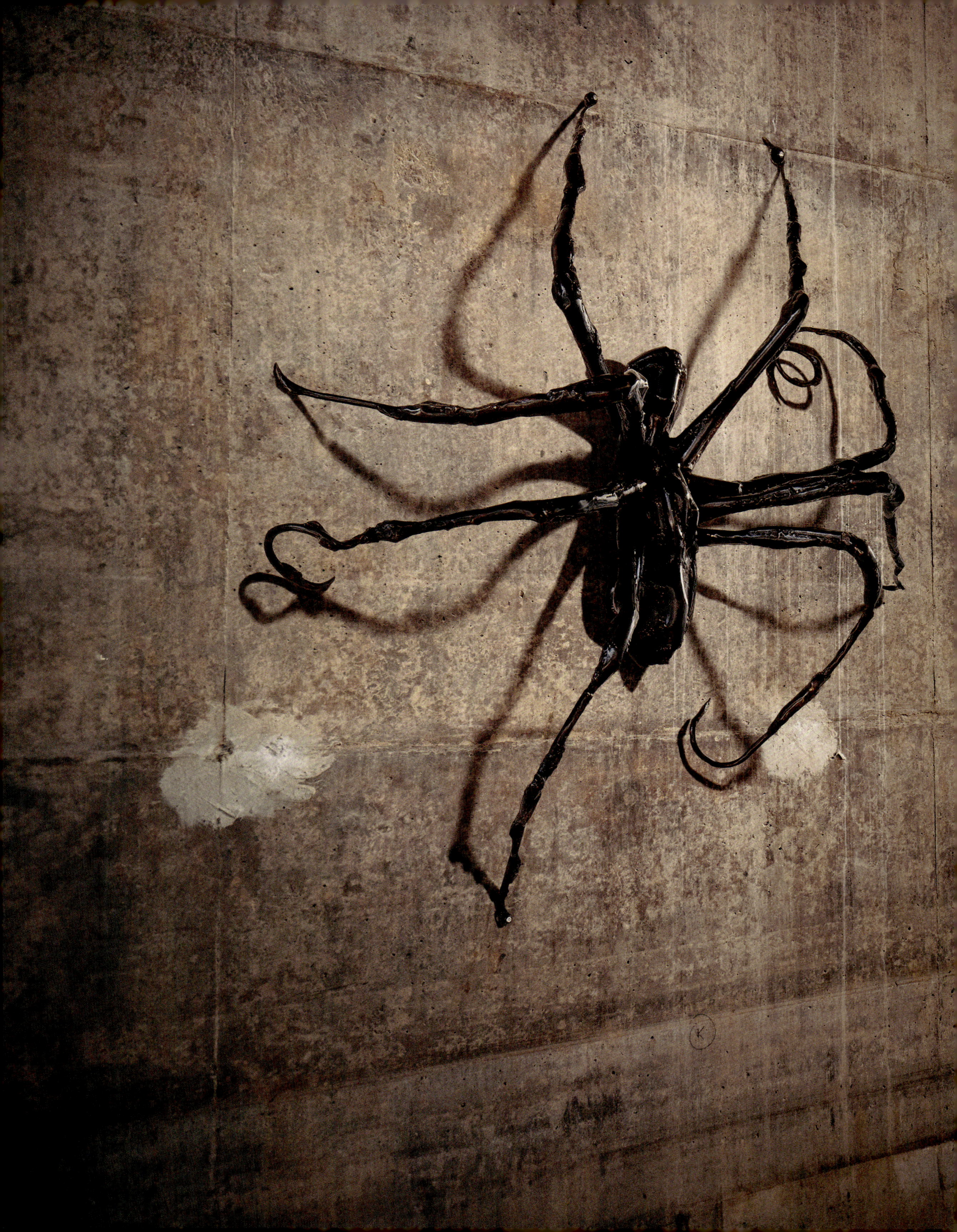

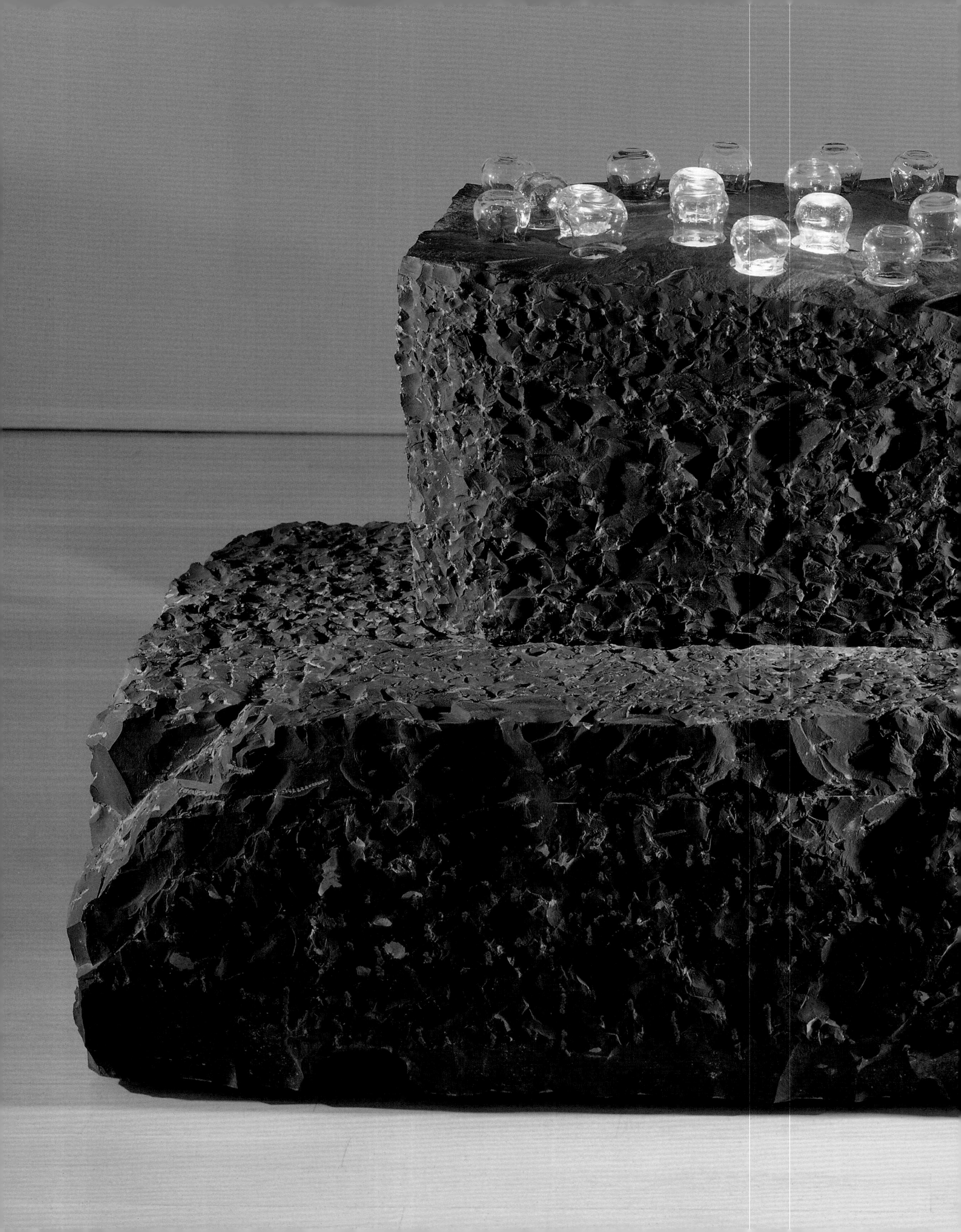

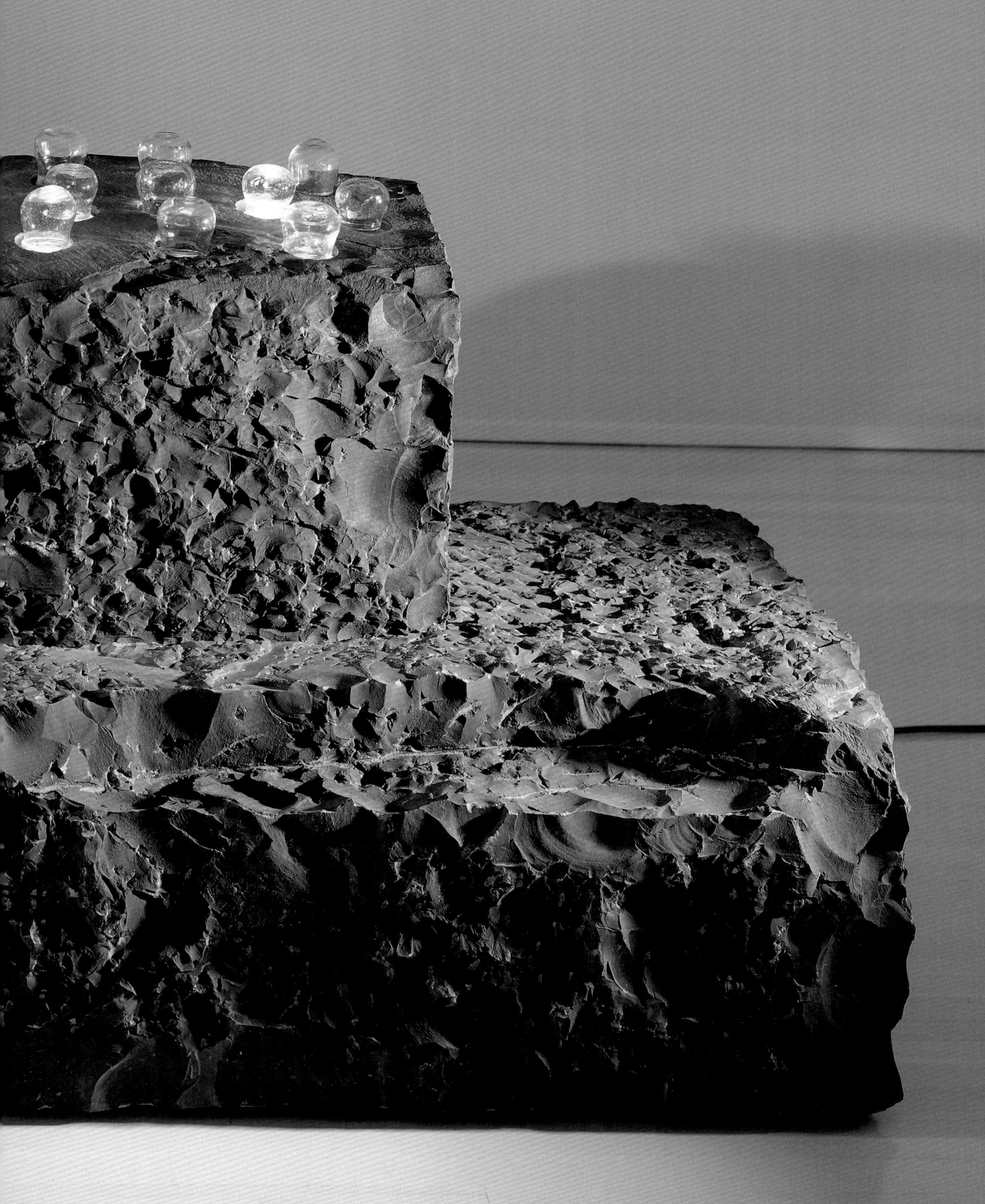

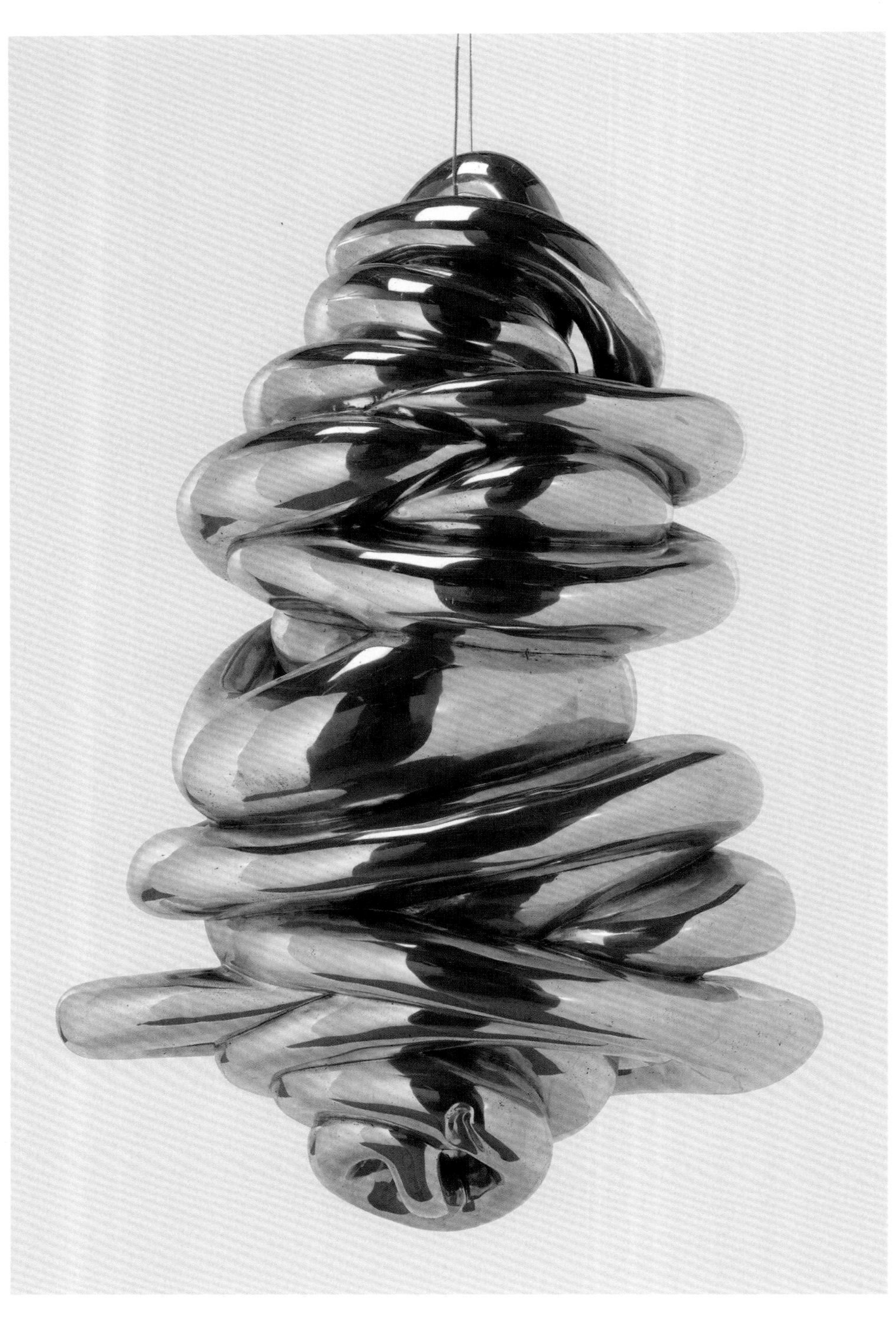

Untitled 2004
Suzan Cooper performing in Bourgeois's *A Banquet / A Fashion Show of Body Parts* 1978 projected in the Tank

following spreads:
The Destruction of the Father 1974 in the Tank; (detail)

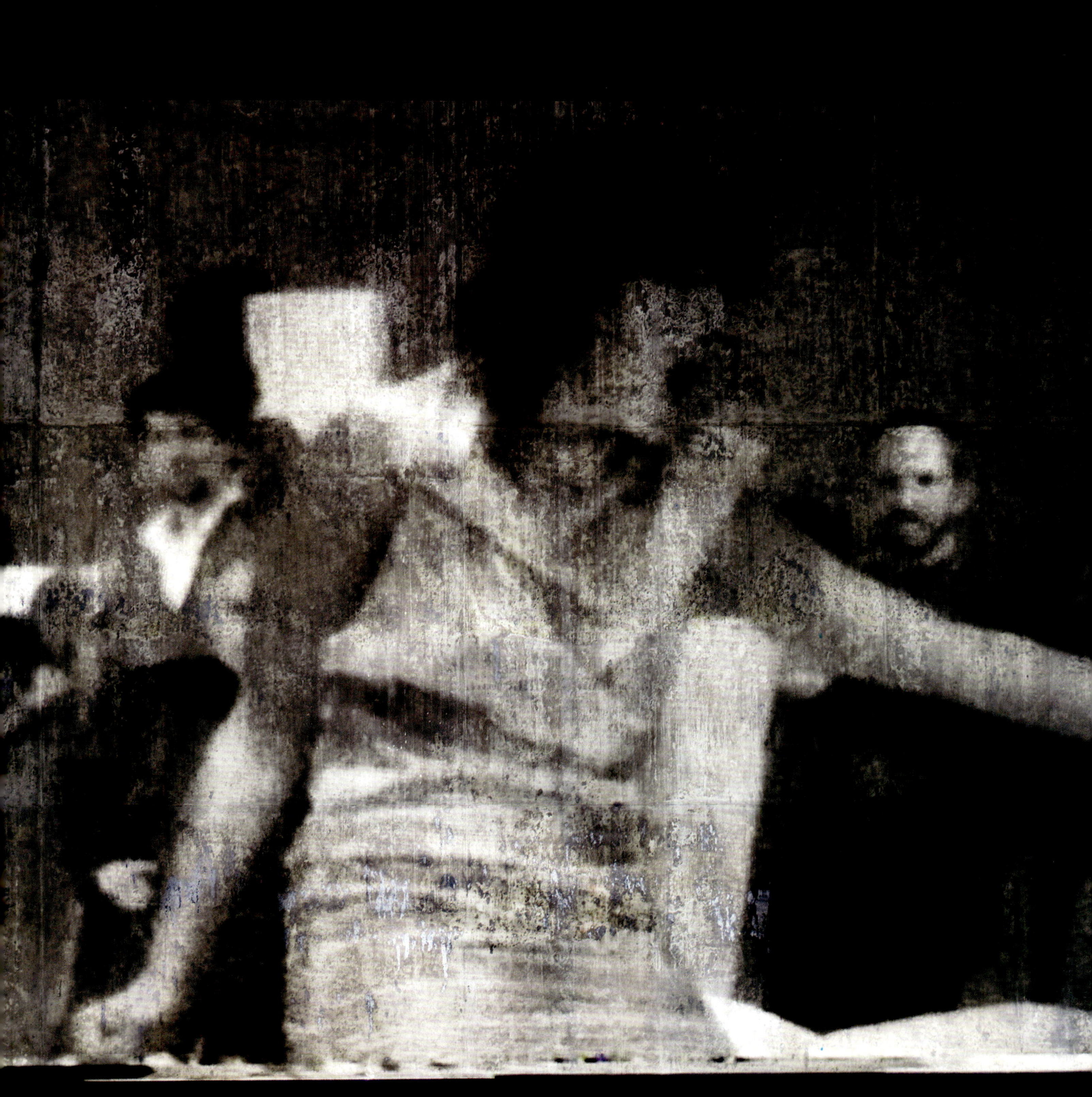

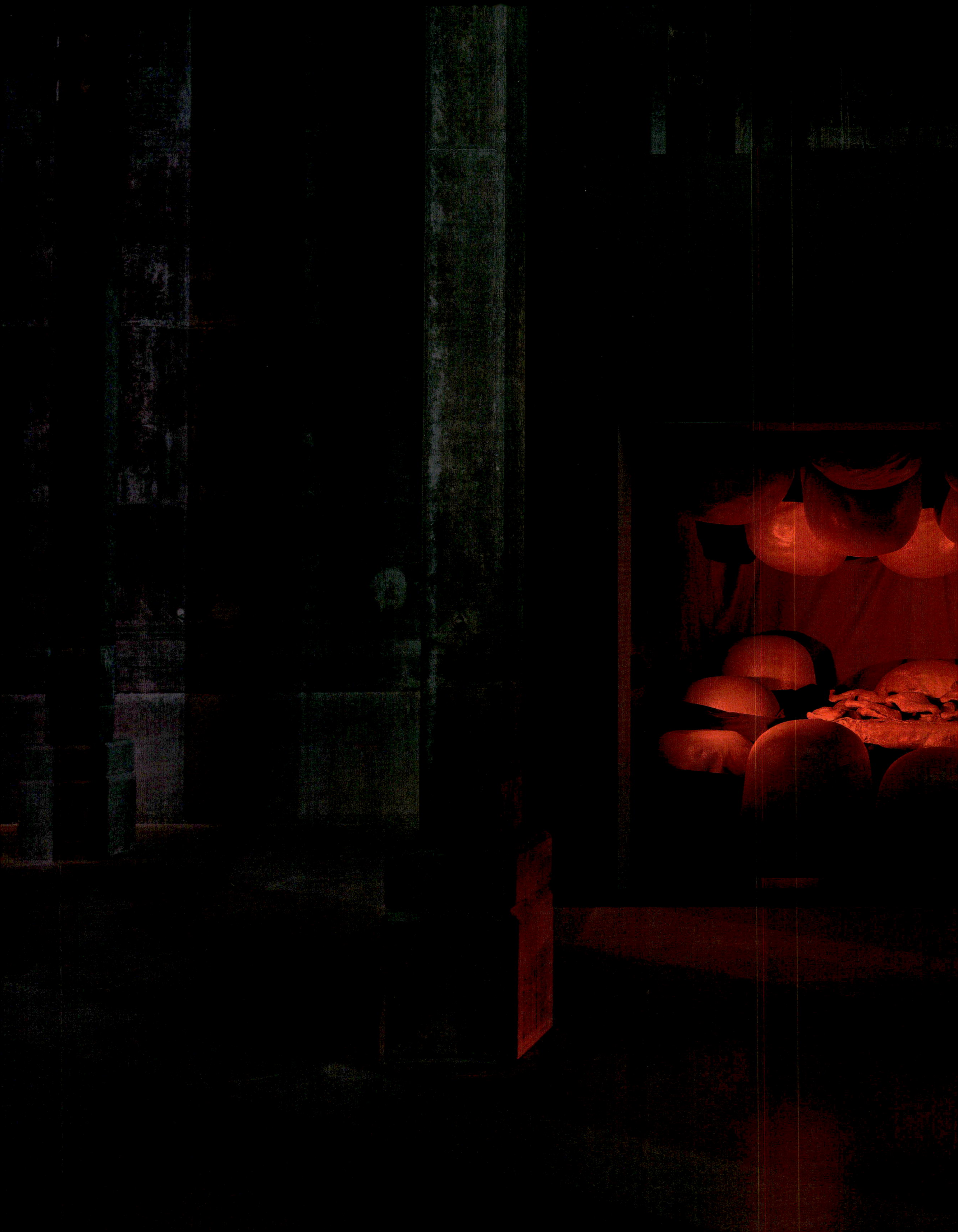

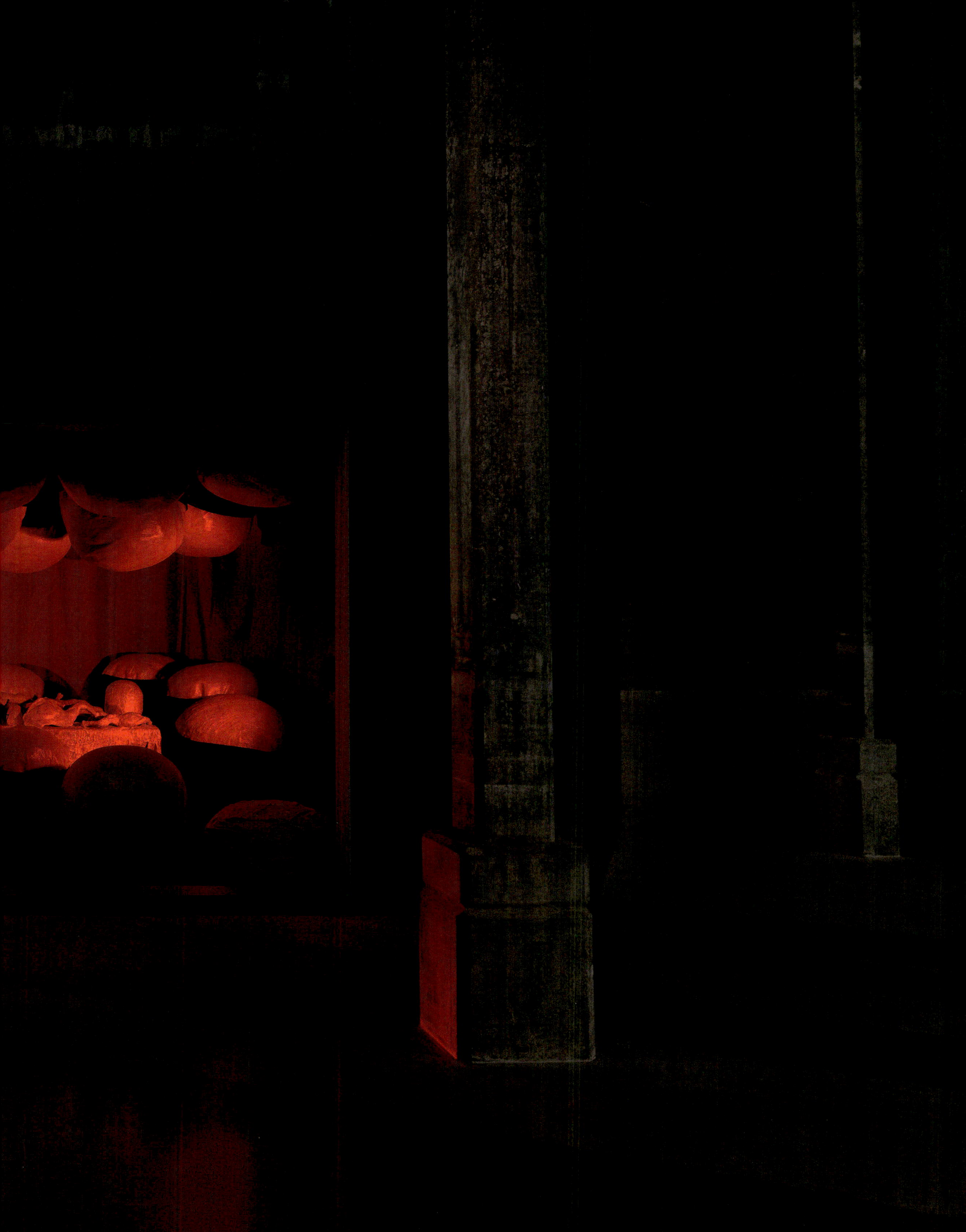

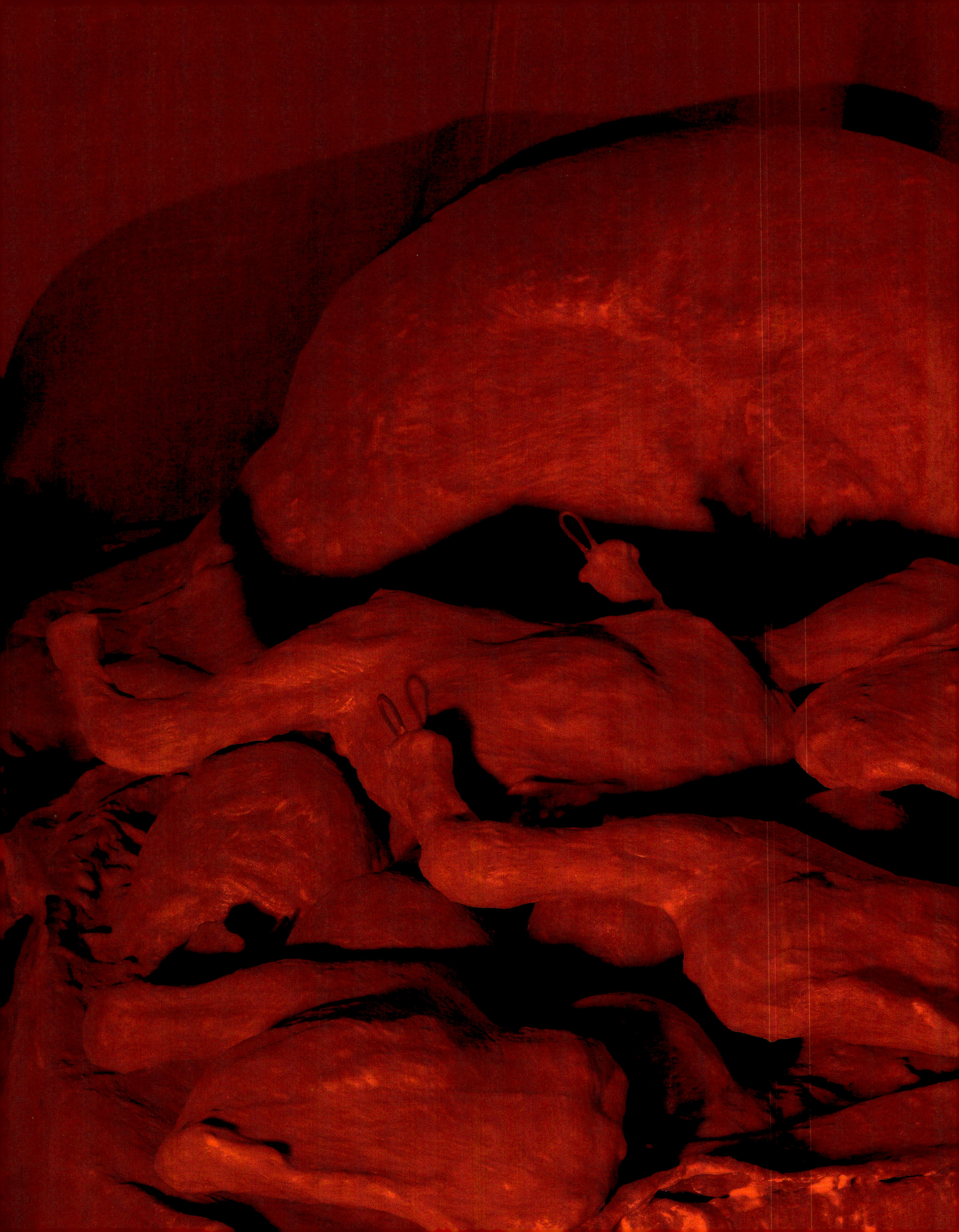

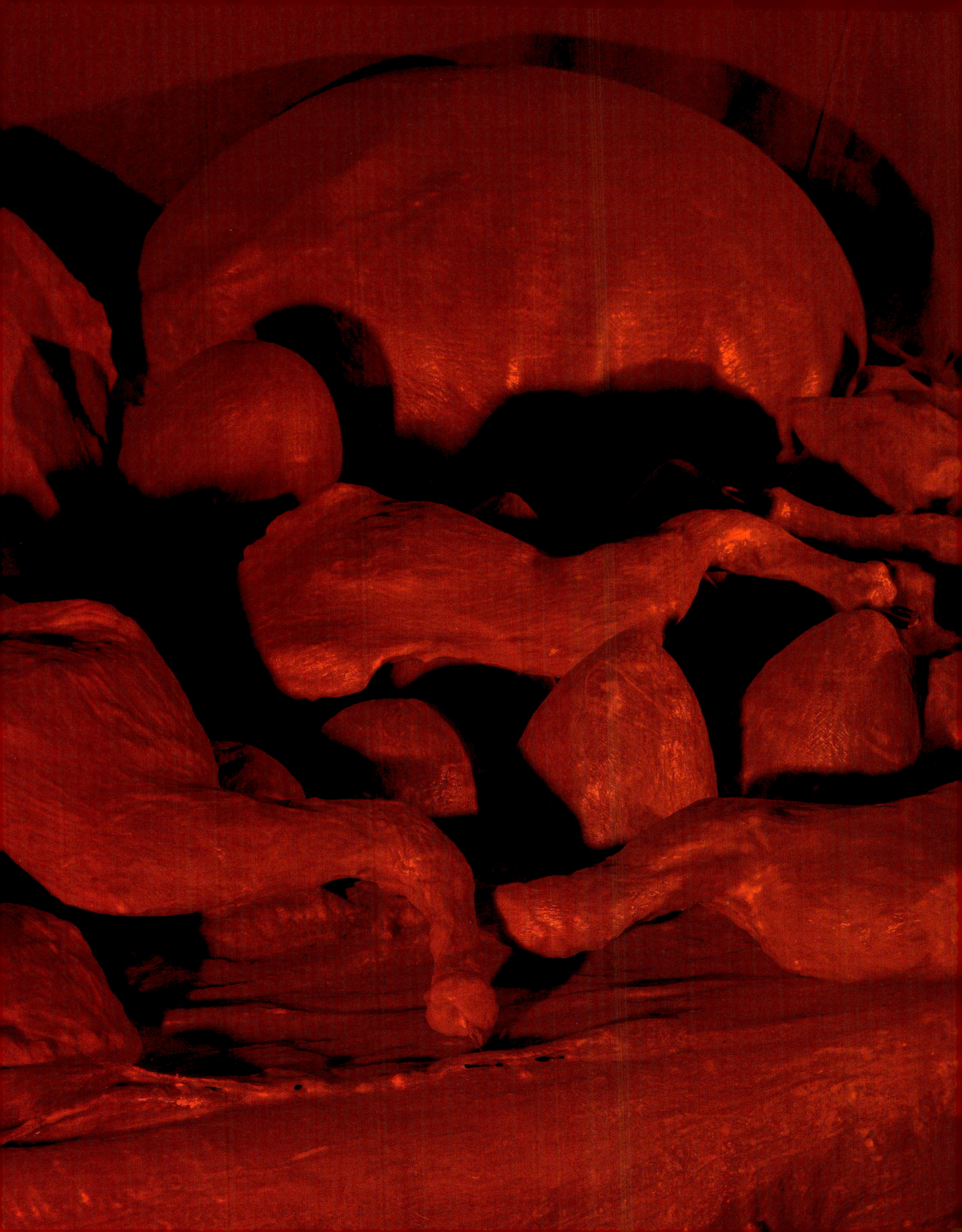

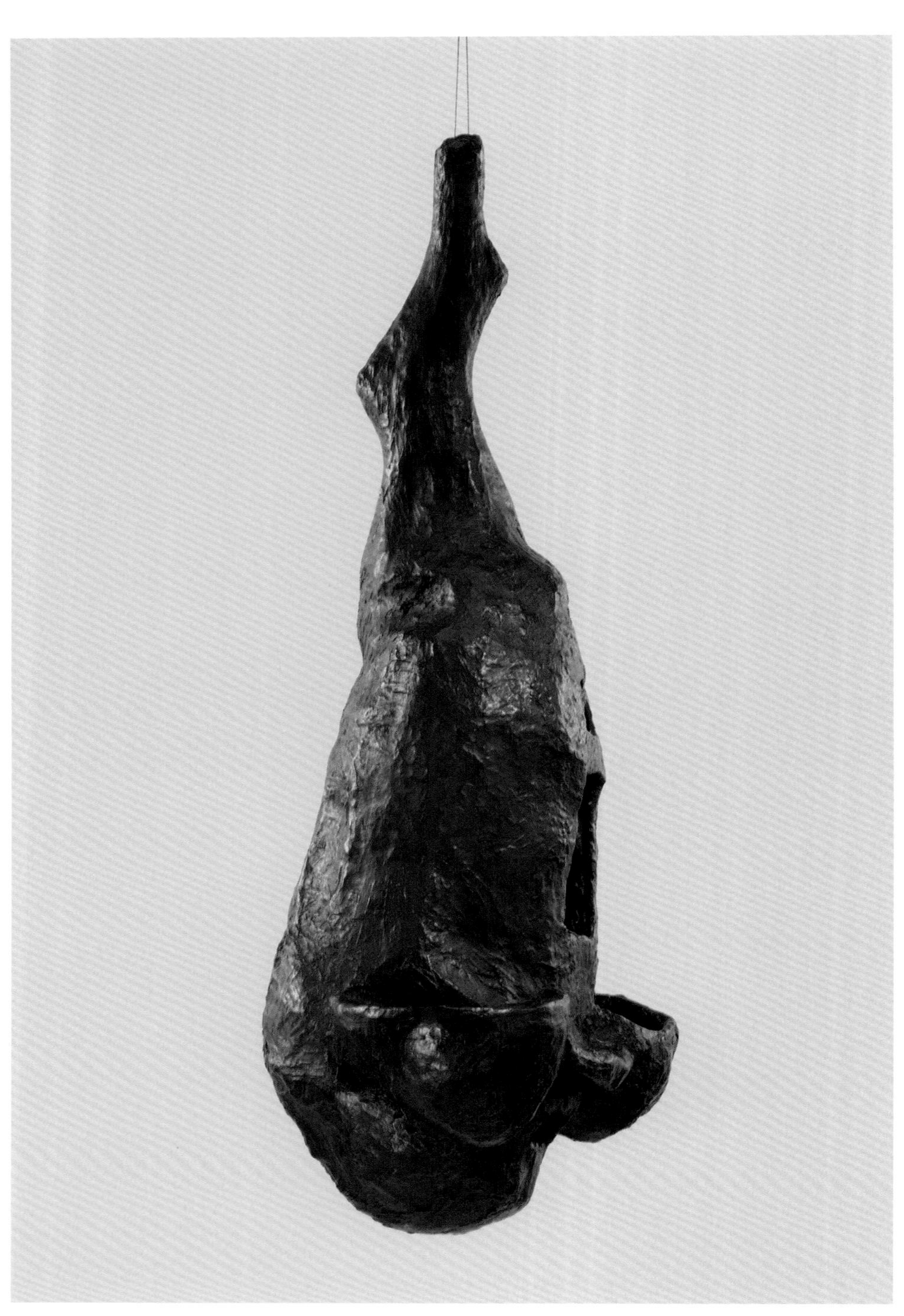

The Quartered One 1964–65, cast 2010
Sleep II 1967

following spread:
Jenny Holzer *Bourgeois X Holzer Projections* 2023 in the Tank
Has the Day Invaded the Night or Has the Night Invaded the Day? 2007

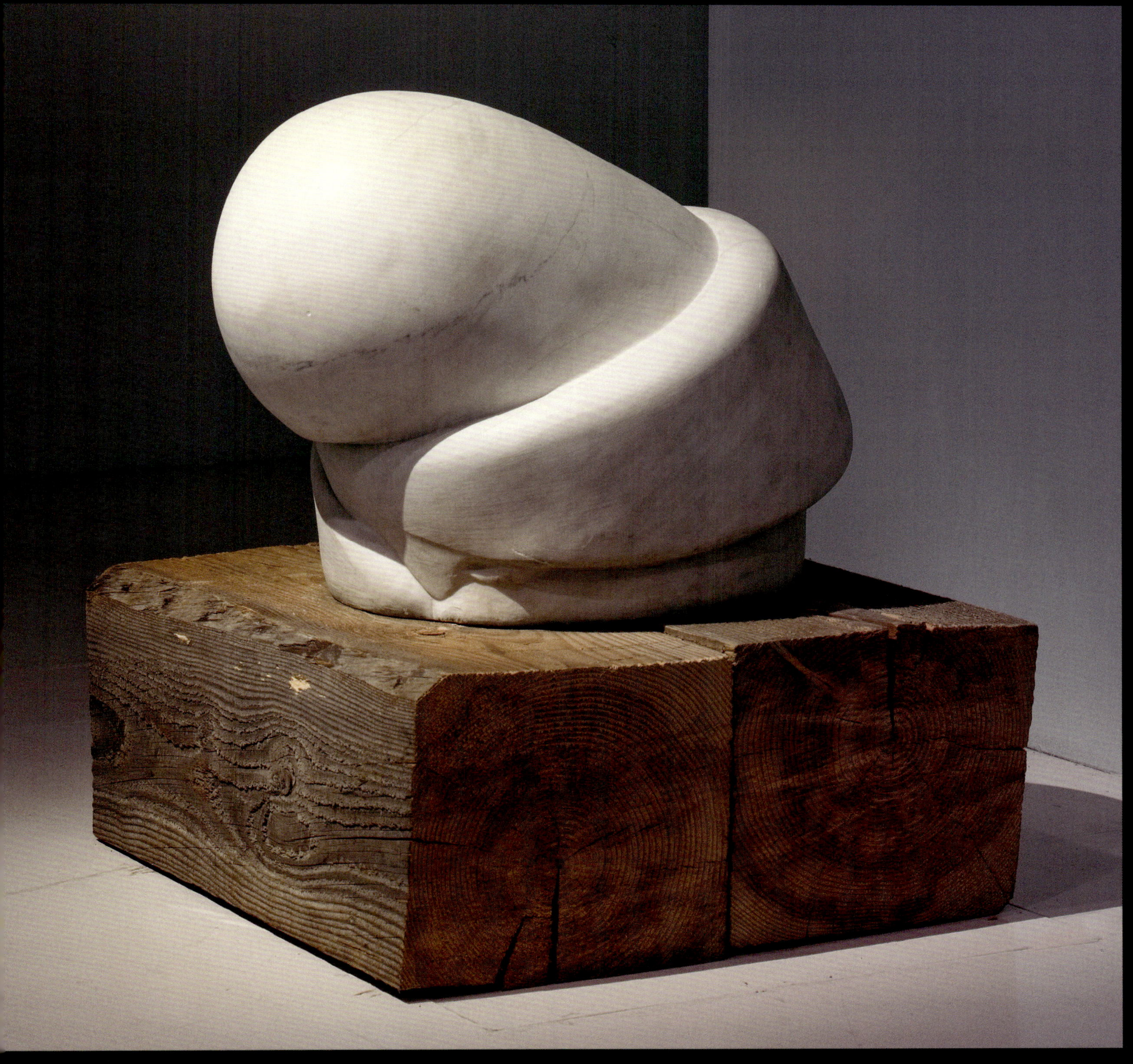

the young husband is asleep
then wife gives him
a push and she says;
wake up,
you look dead.
I do not want
to be accused -
the husband says all right,
he gets up,
gets dressed,
and goes to his desk
to write a letter.

he talks like a bottle of glue -

she talks with a hatchet -

when he talks
it smells of semen -

when she talks or cleans
it is a killing process-

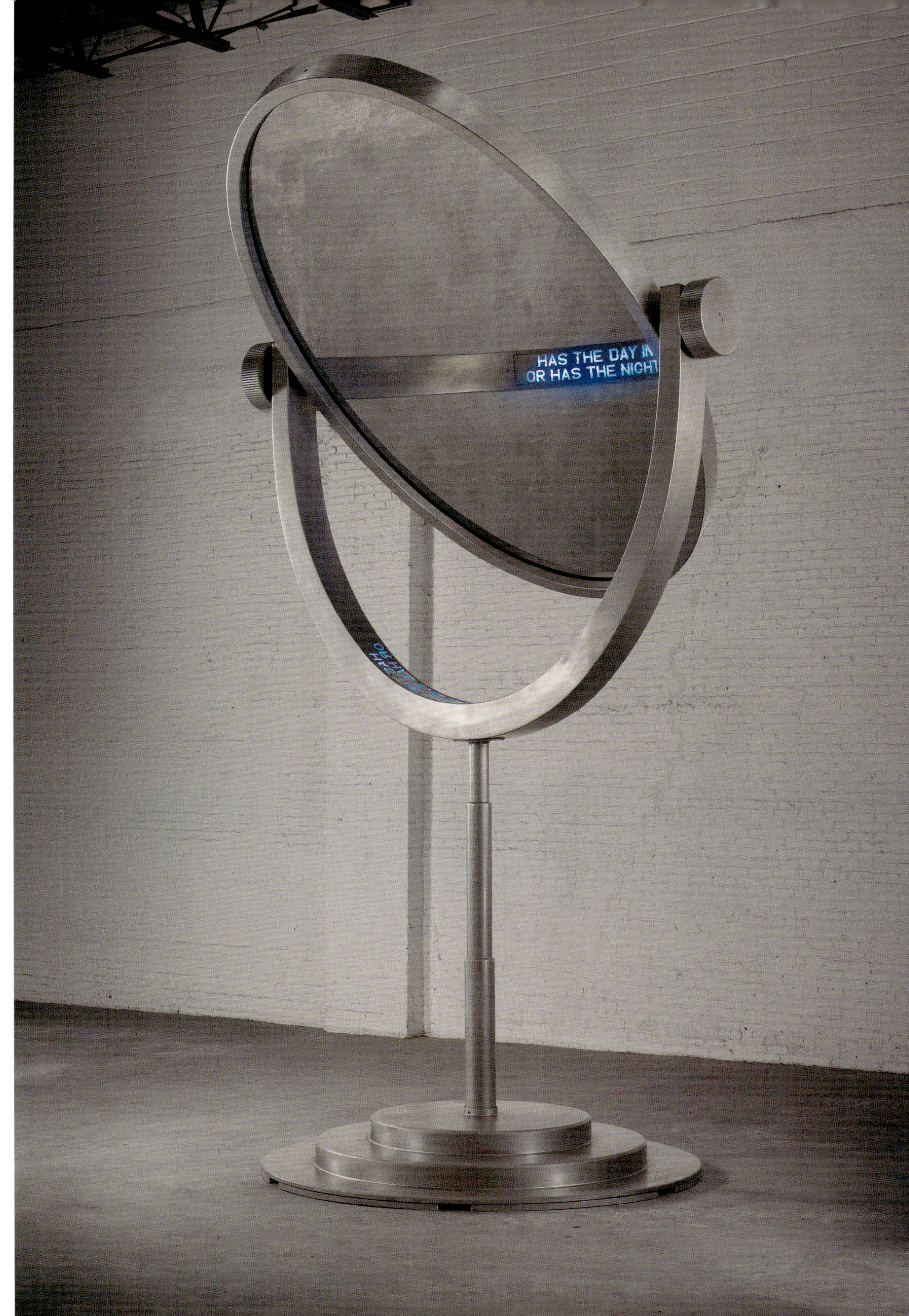
HAS THE DAY IN
OR HAS THE NIGHT

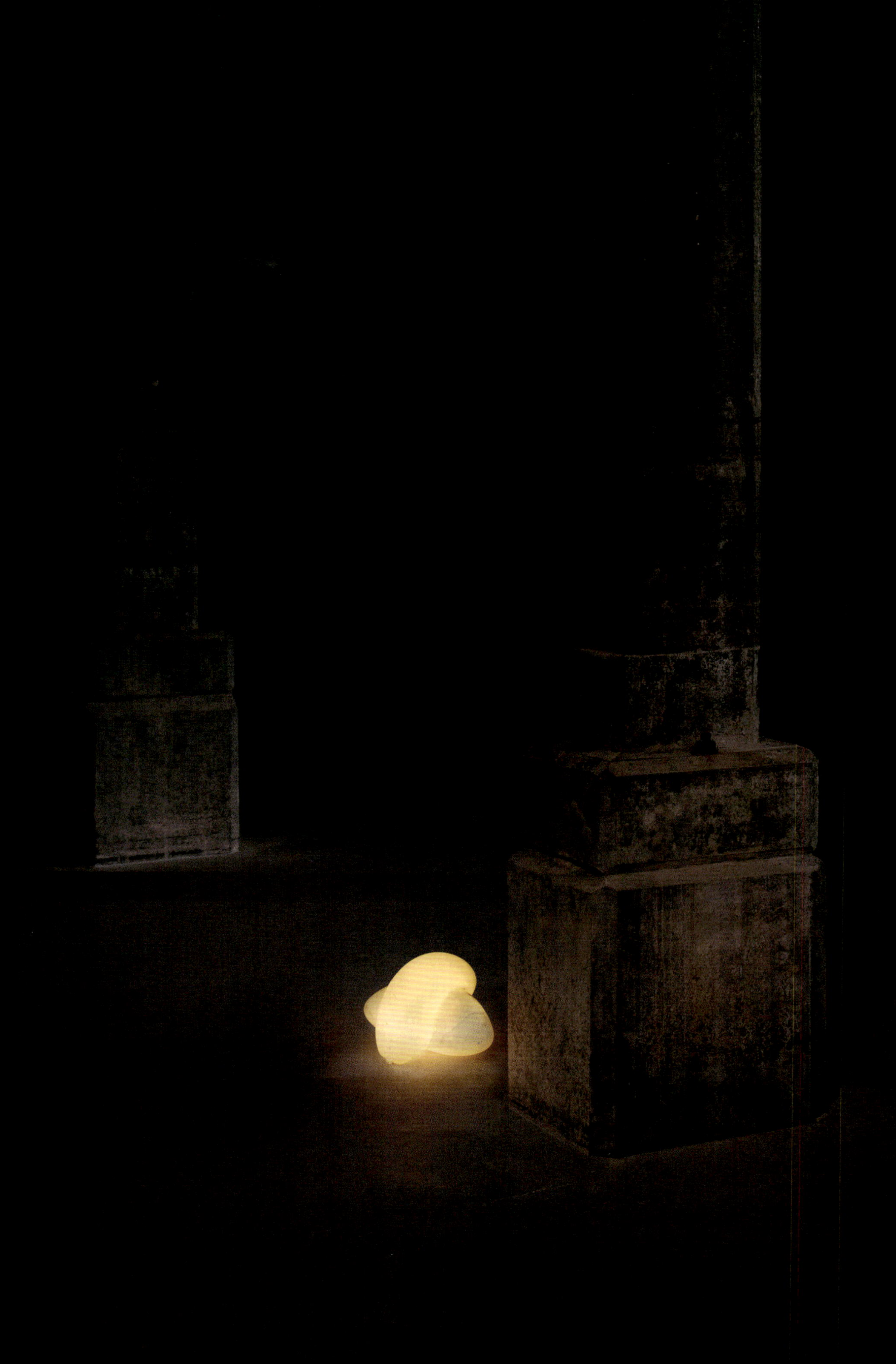

previous spread:
Le Trani Episode 1991 in the Tank

Crouching Spider 2003

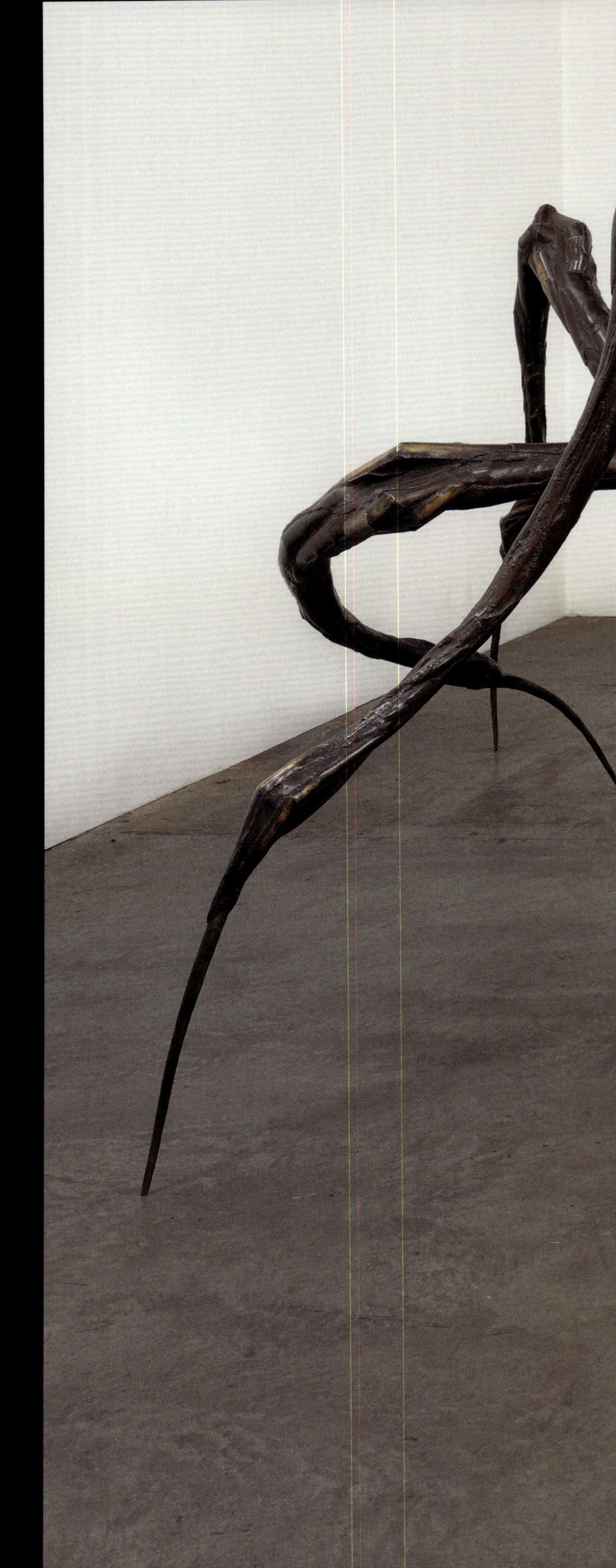

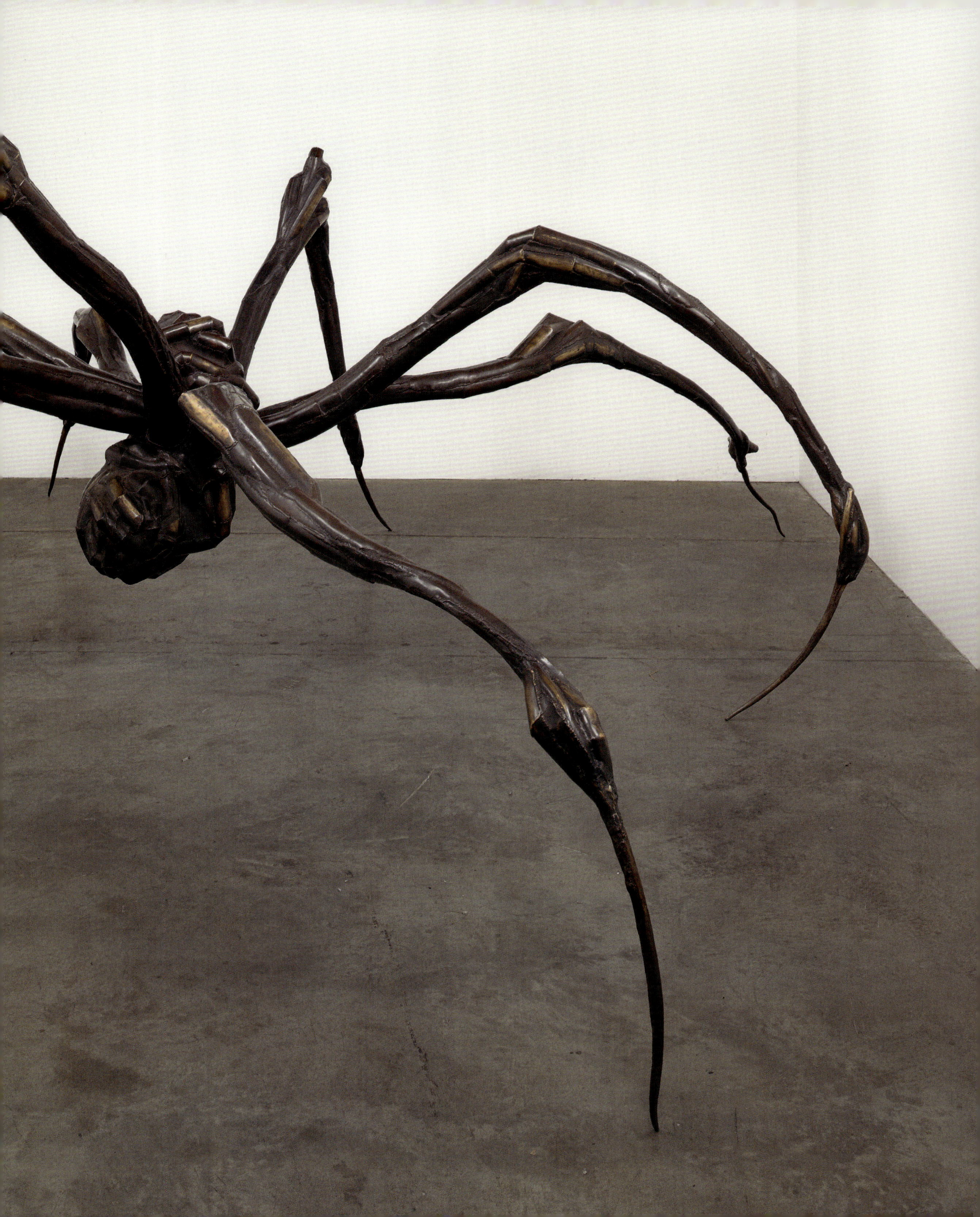

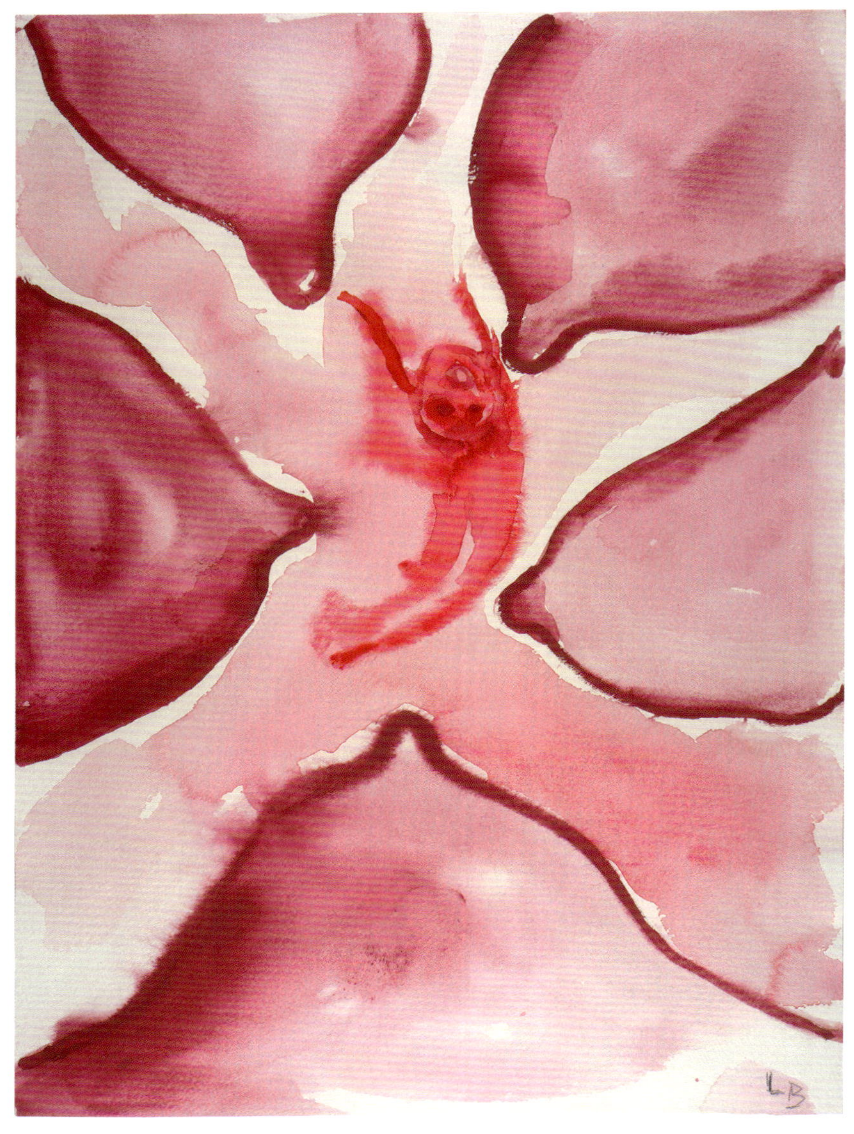

The Feeding 2007
Hysterical 2001

following spread:
Le défi II 1992 in the Tank

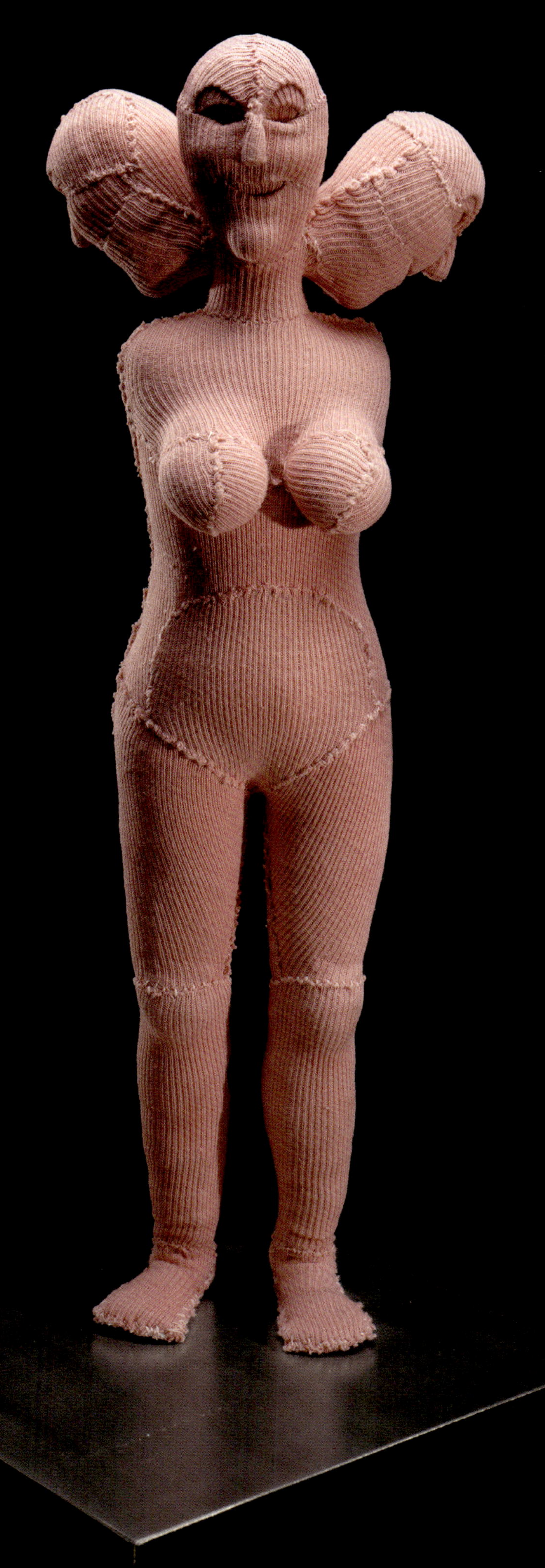

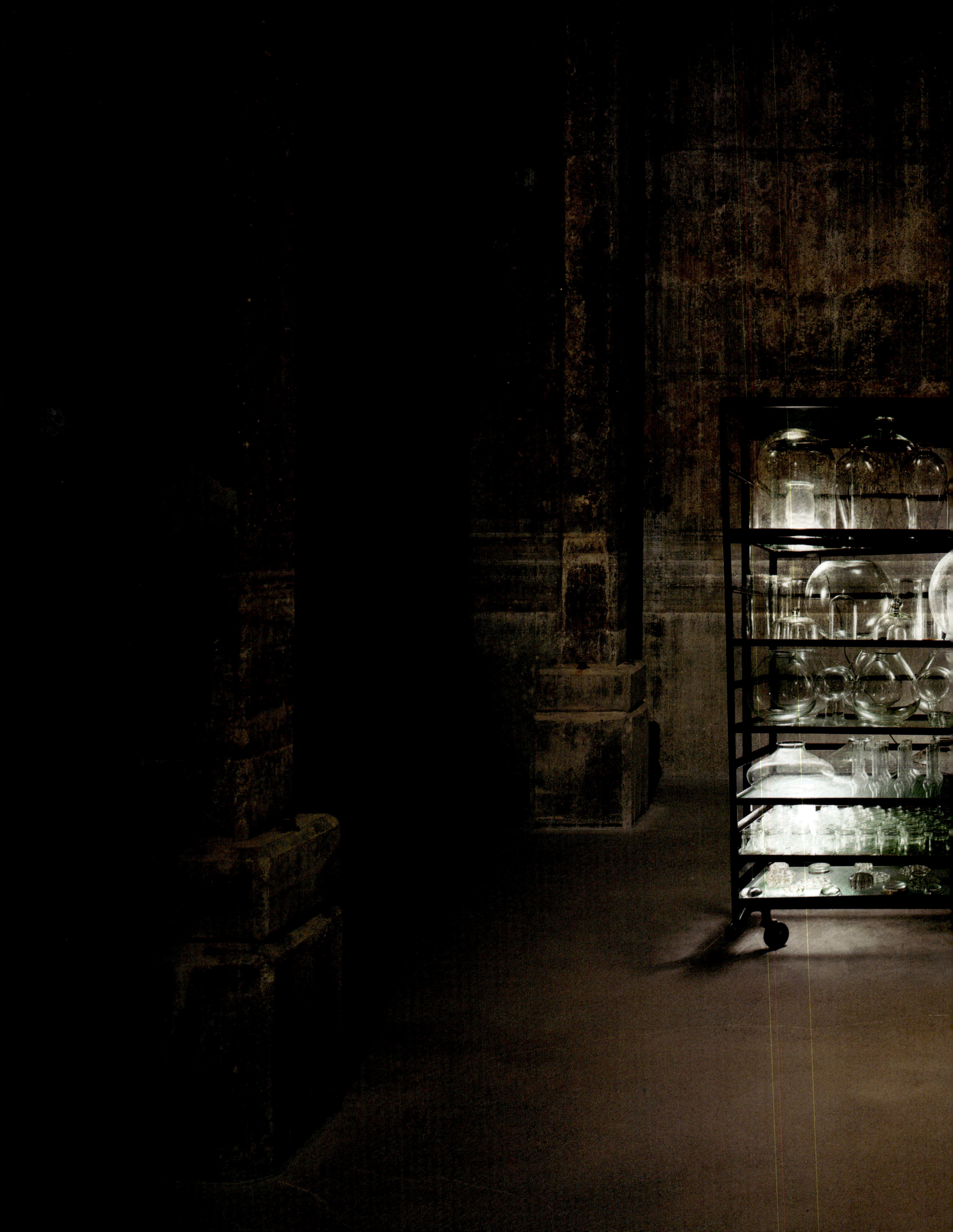

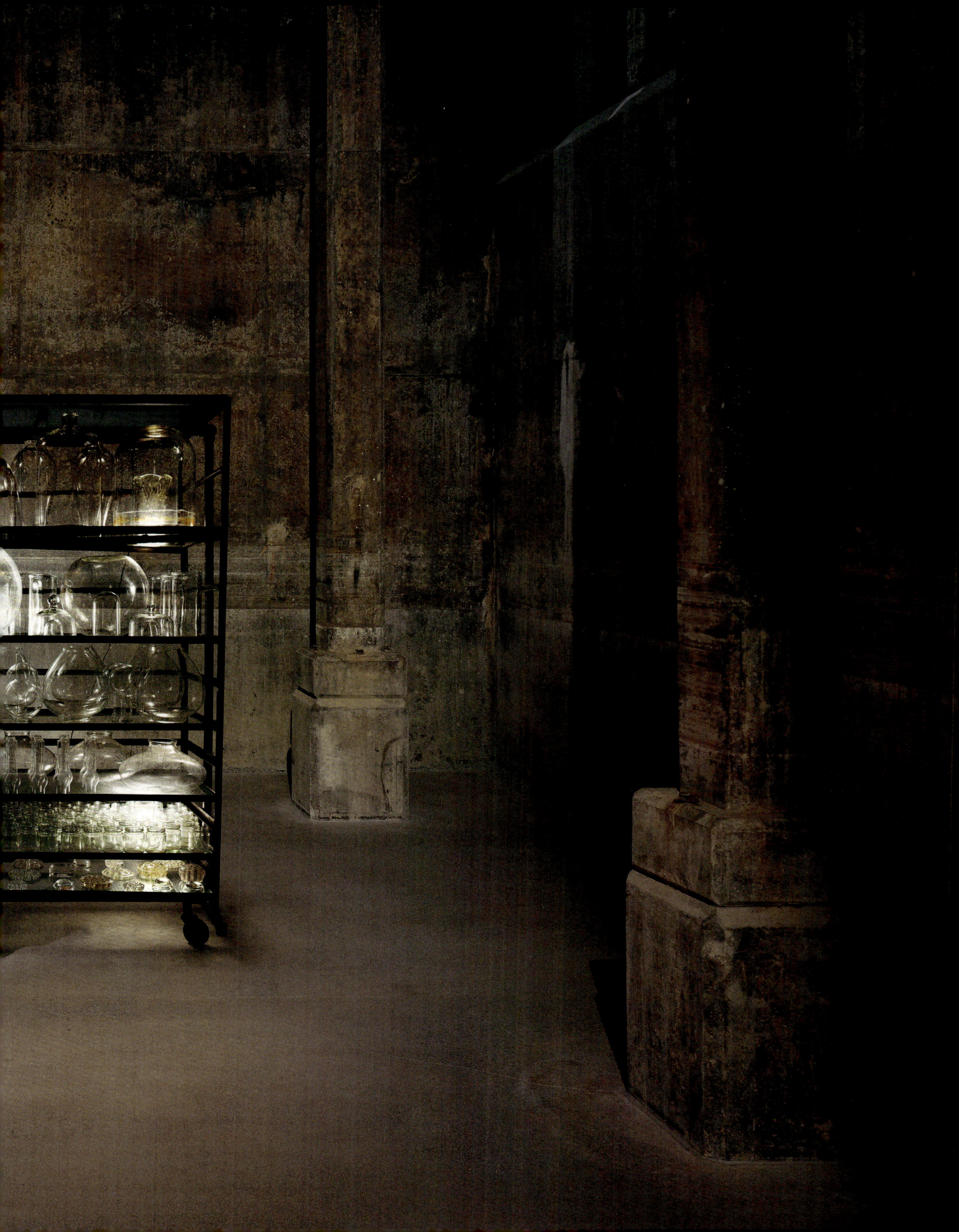

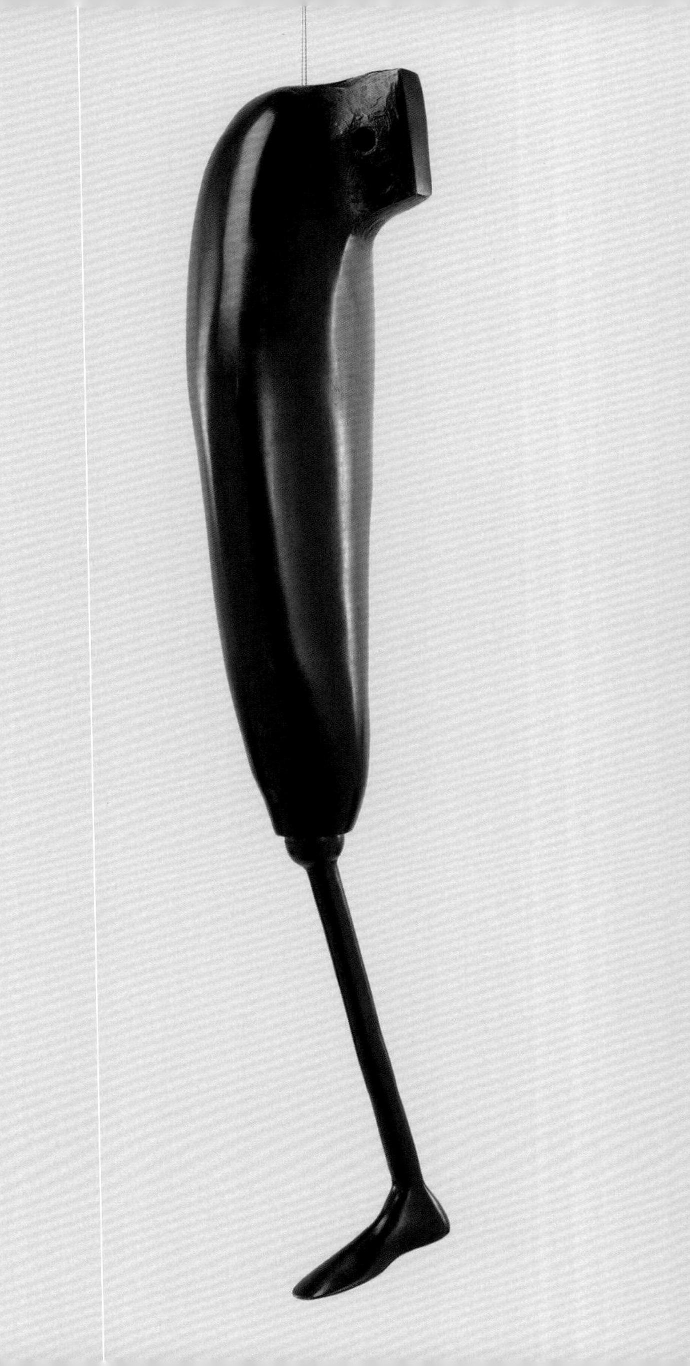

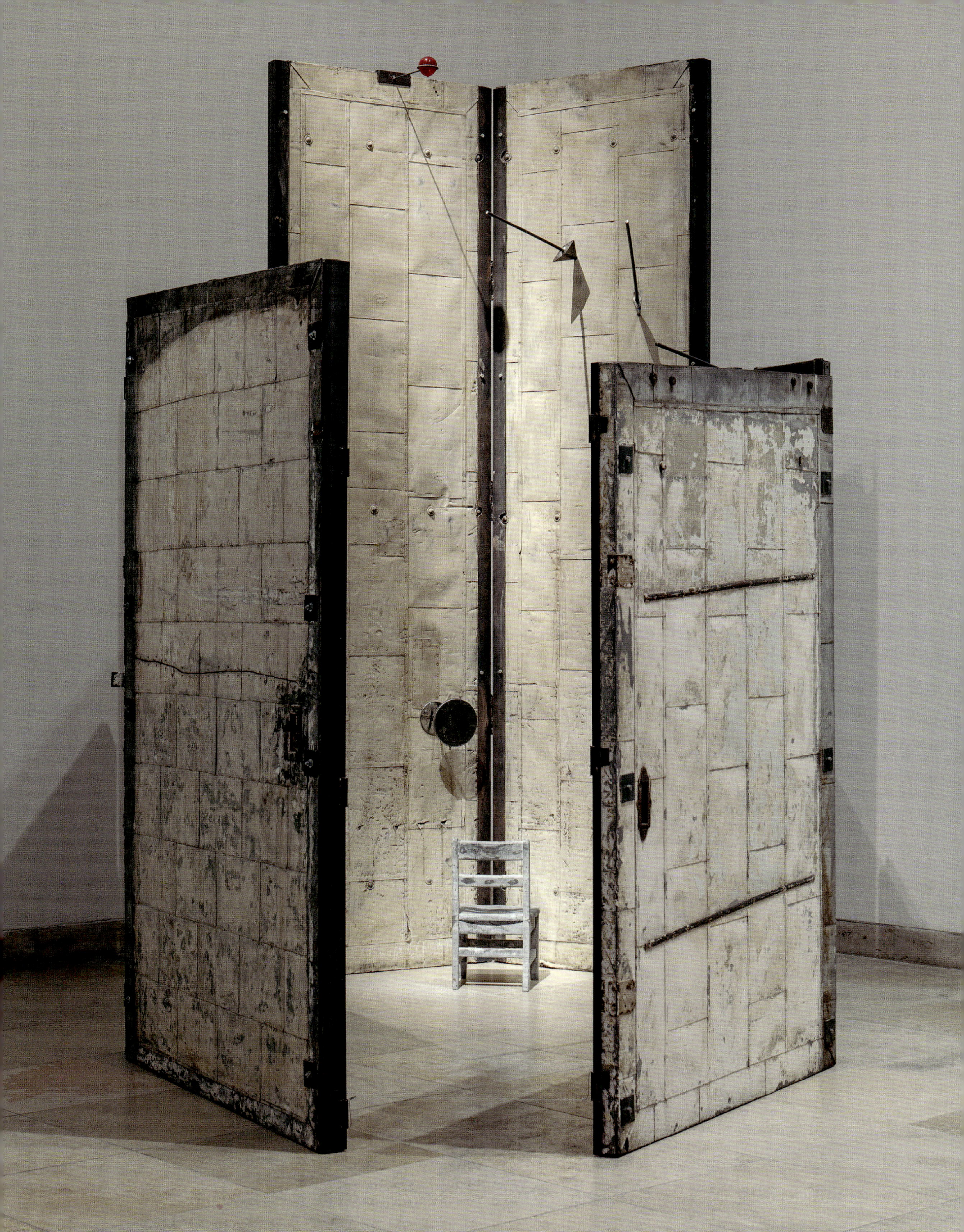

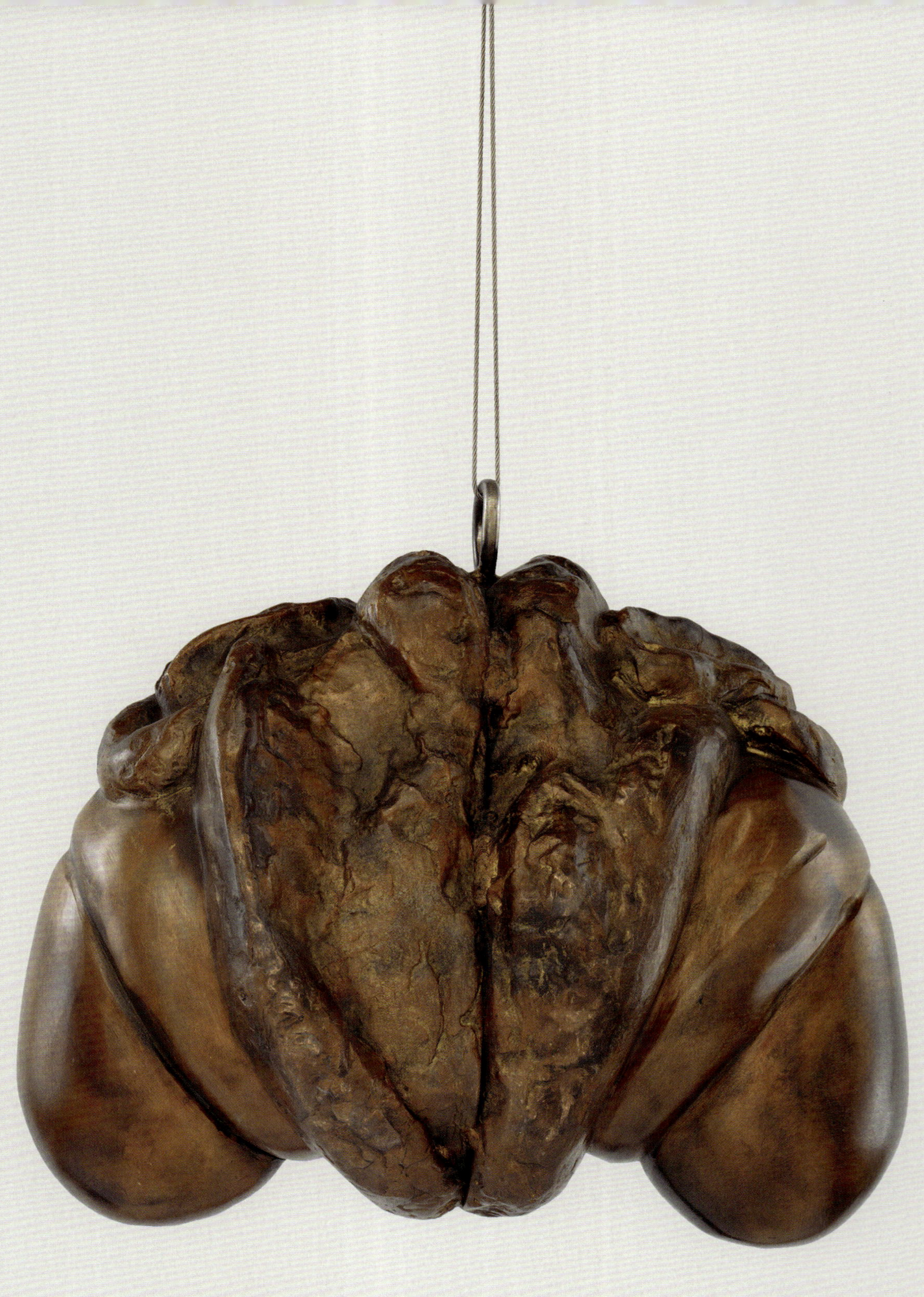

Janus fleuri 1968
Excerpt from *Louise Bourgeois: the spider, the mistress and the tangerine* 2008 projected in the Tank

following spread:
Arch of Hysteria 1993 in the Tank

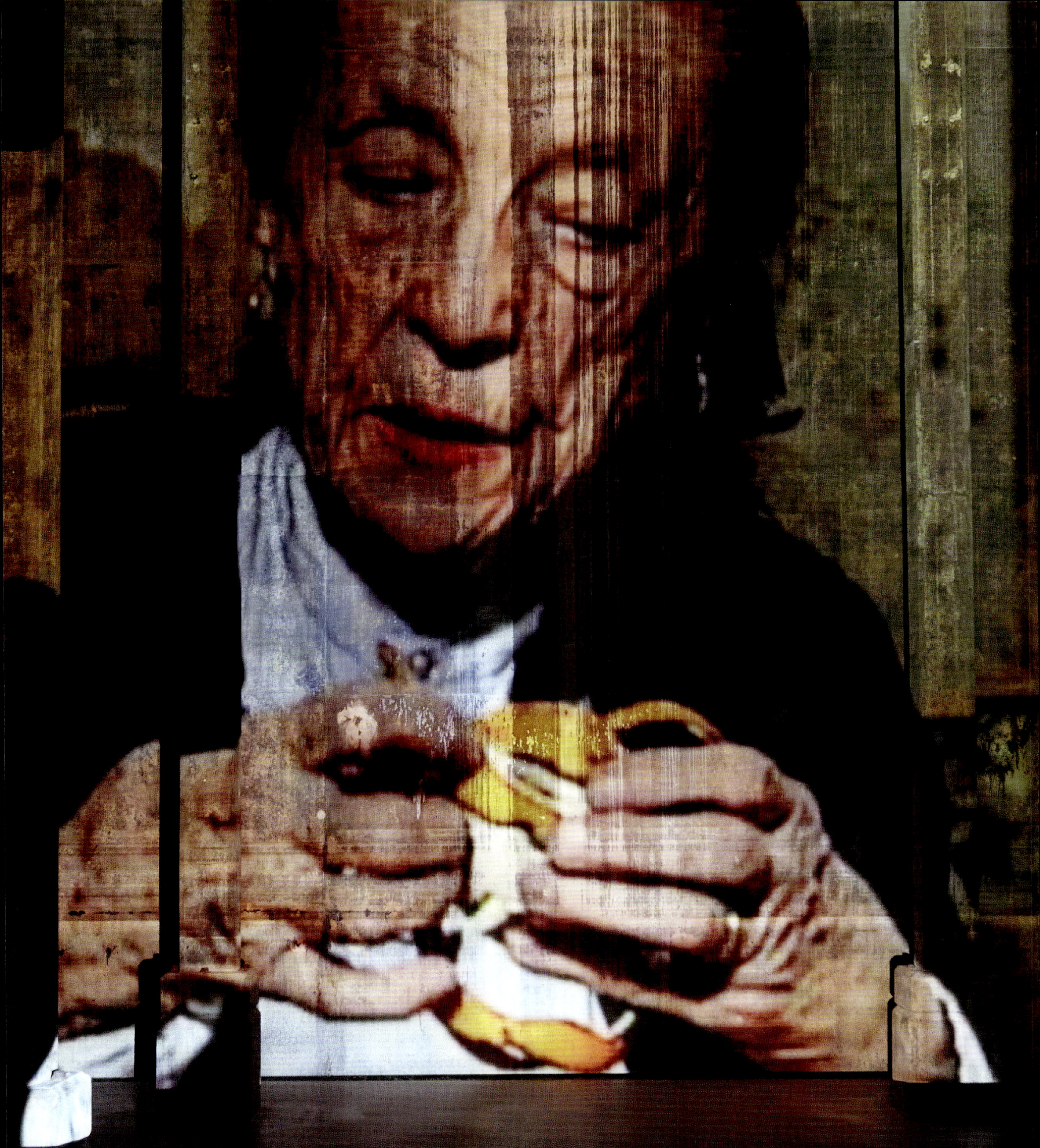

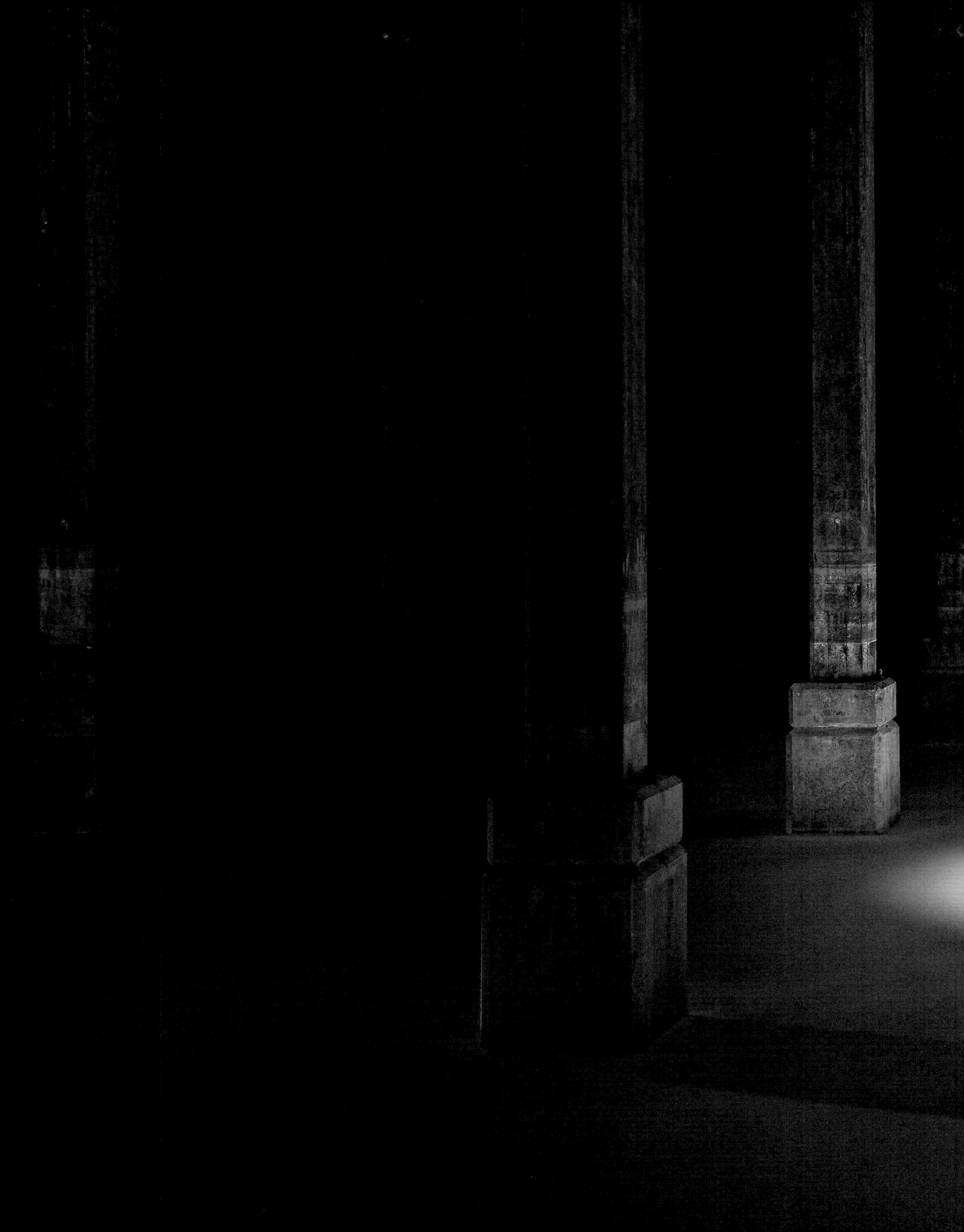

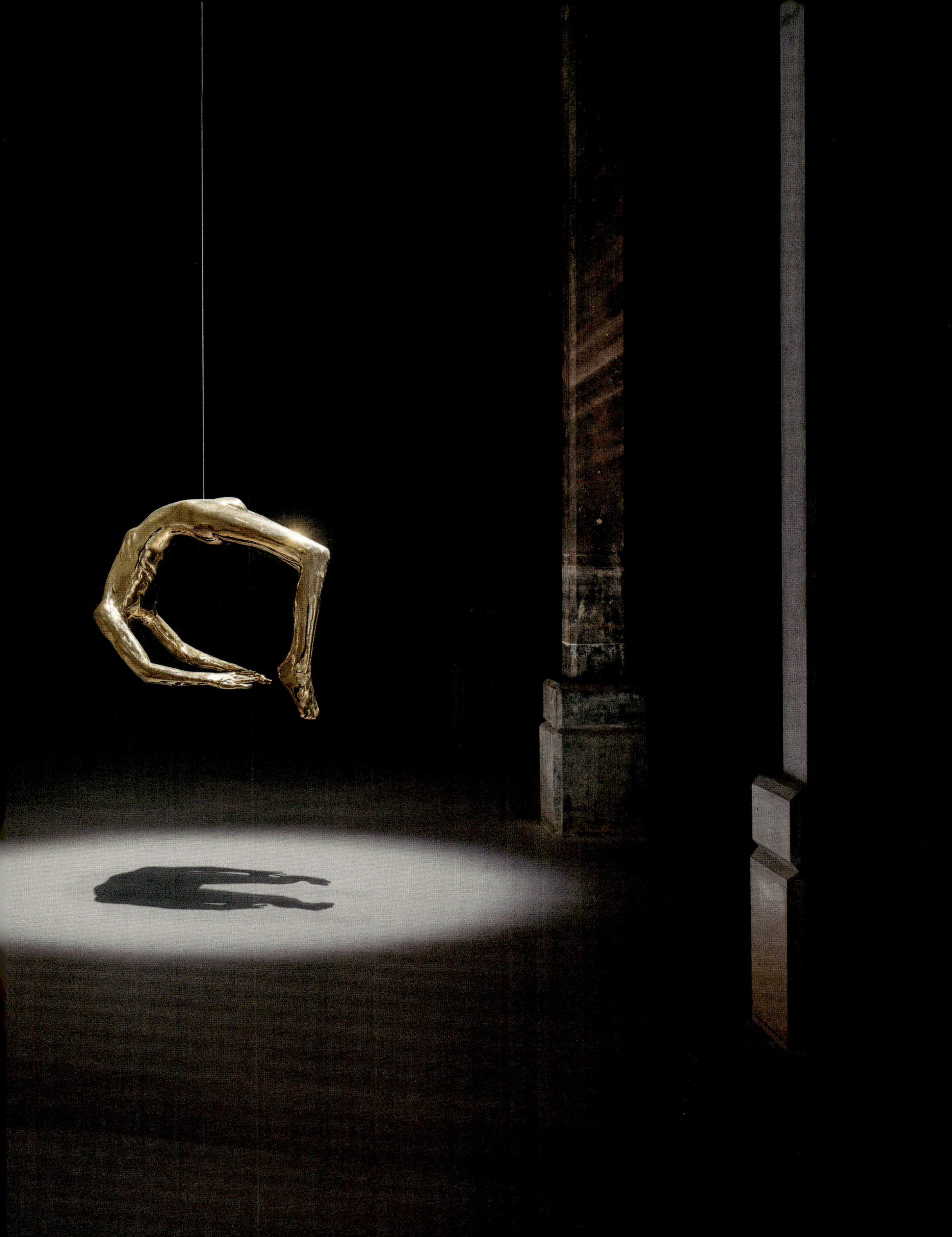

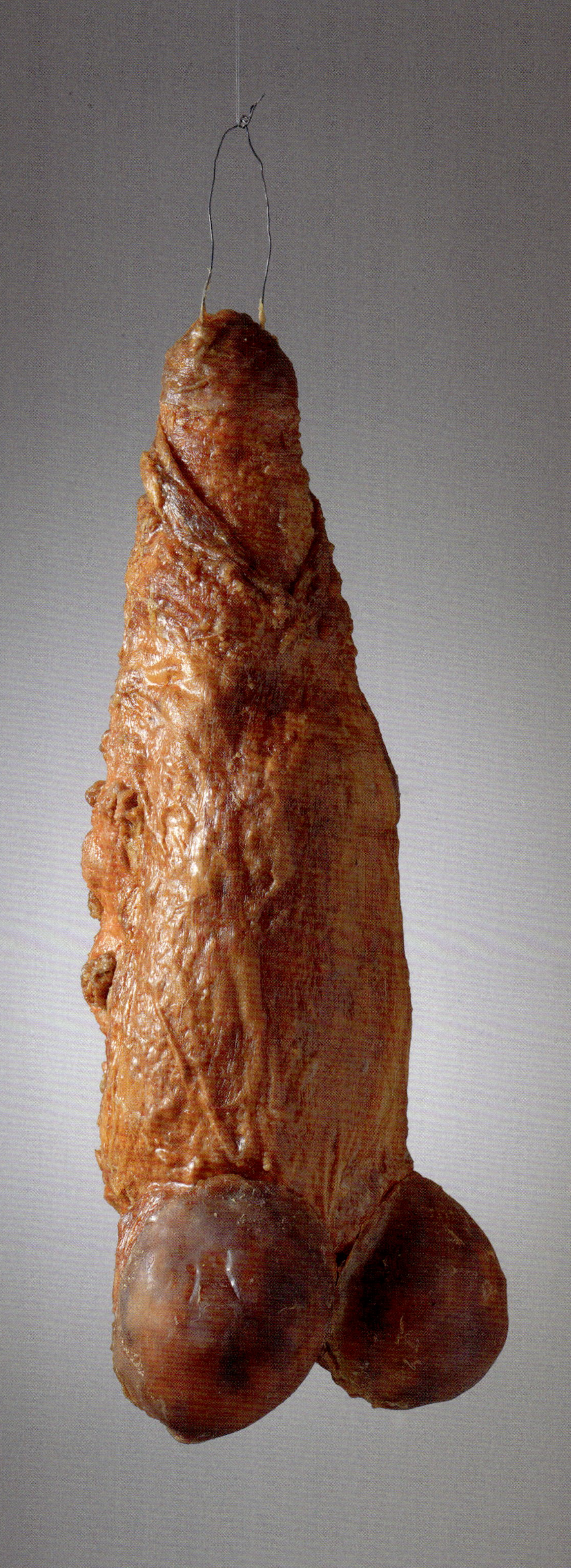

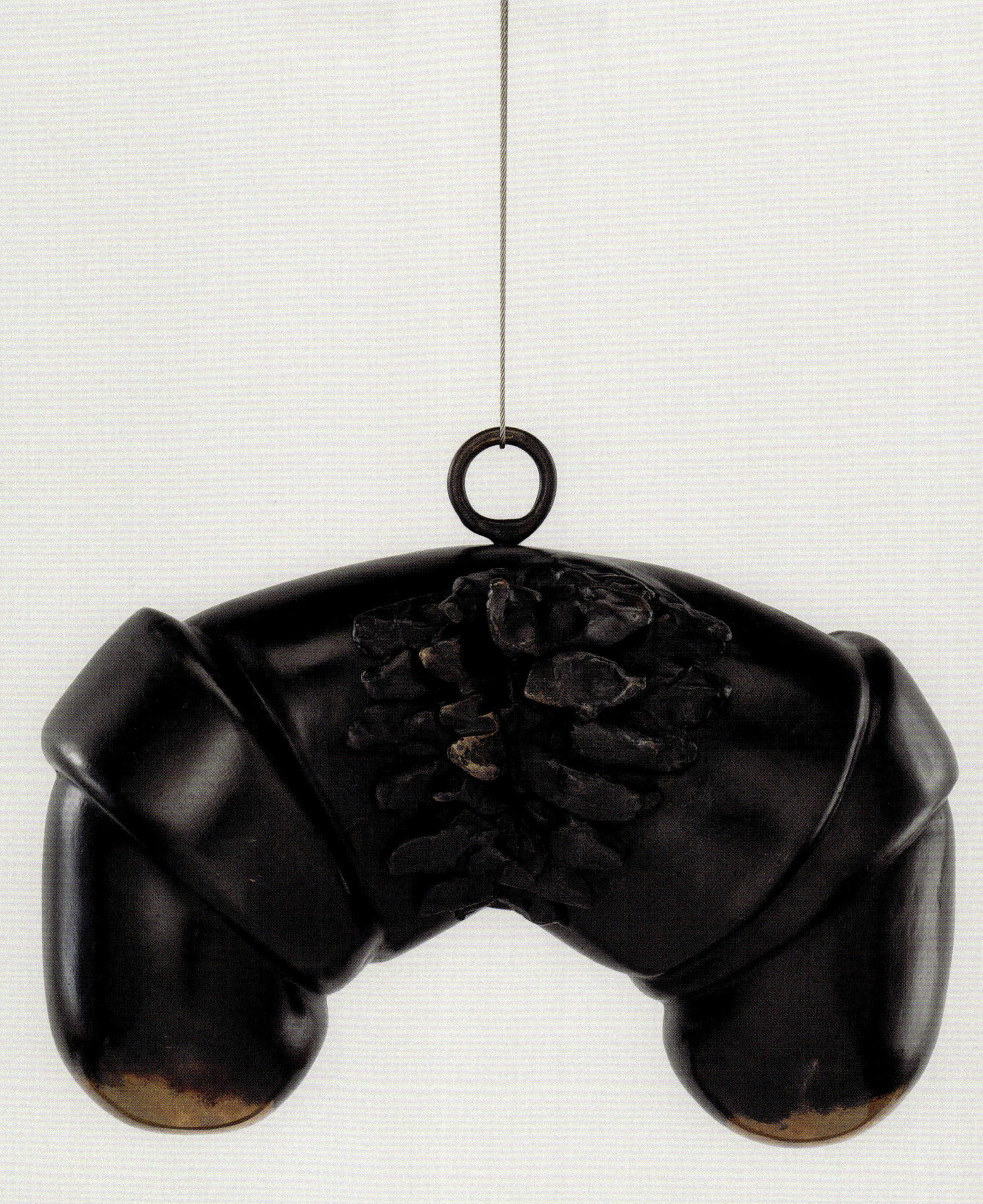

Fillette (Sweeter Version) 1968–99
Janus 1968

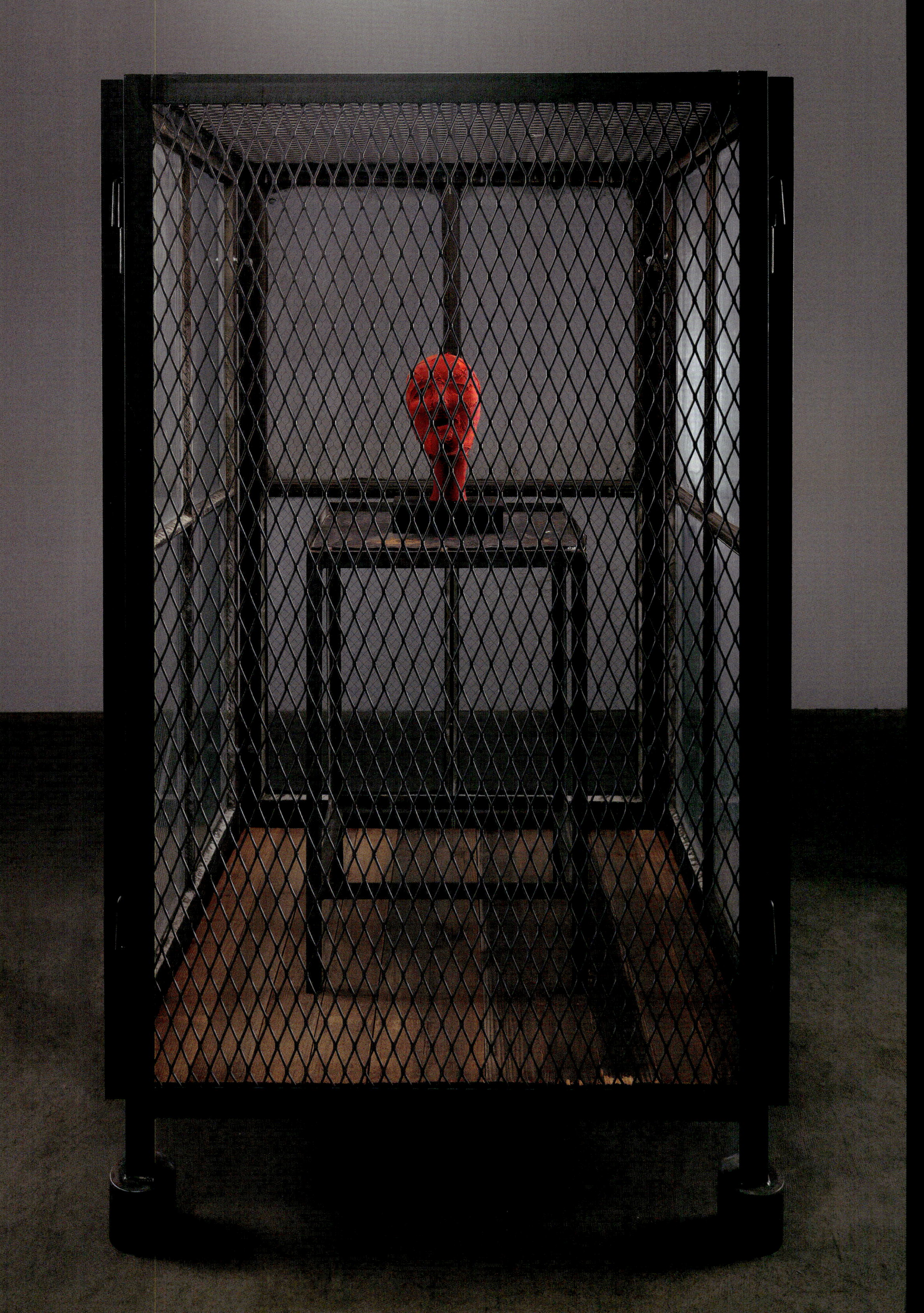

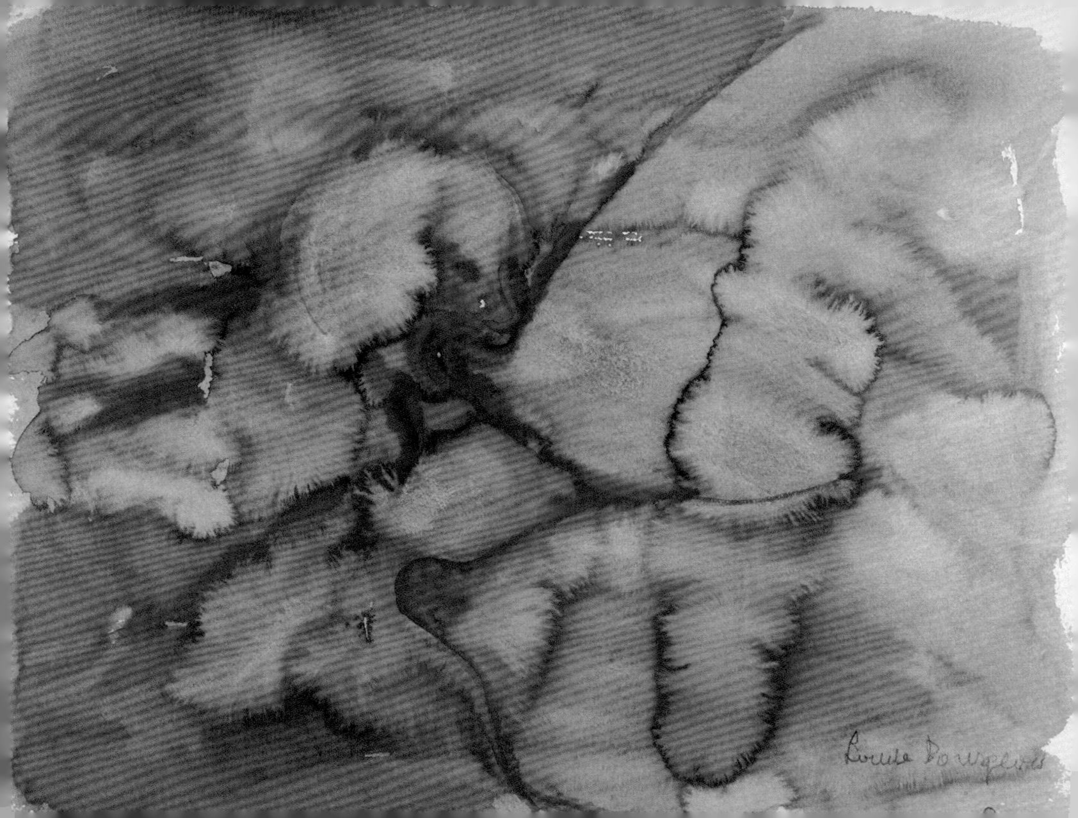
Louise Bourgeois

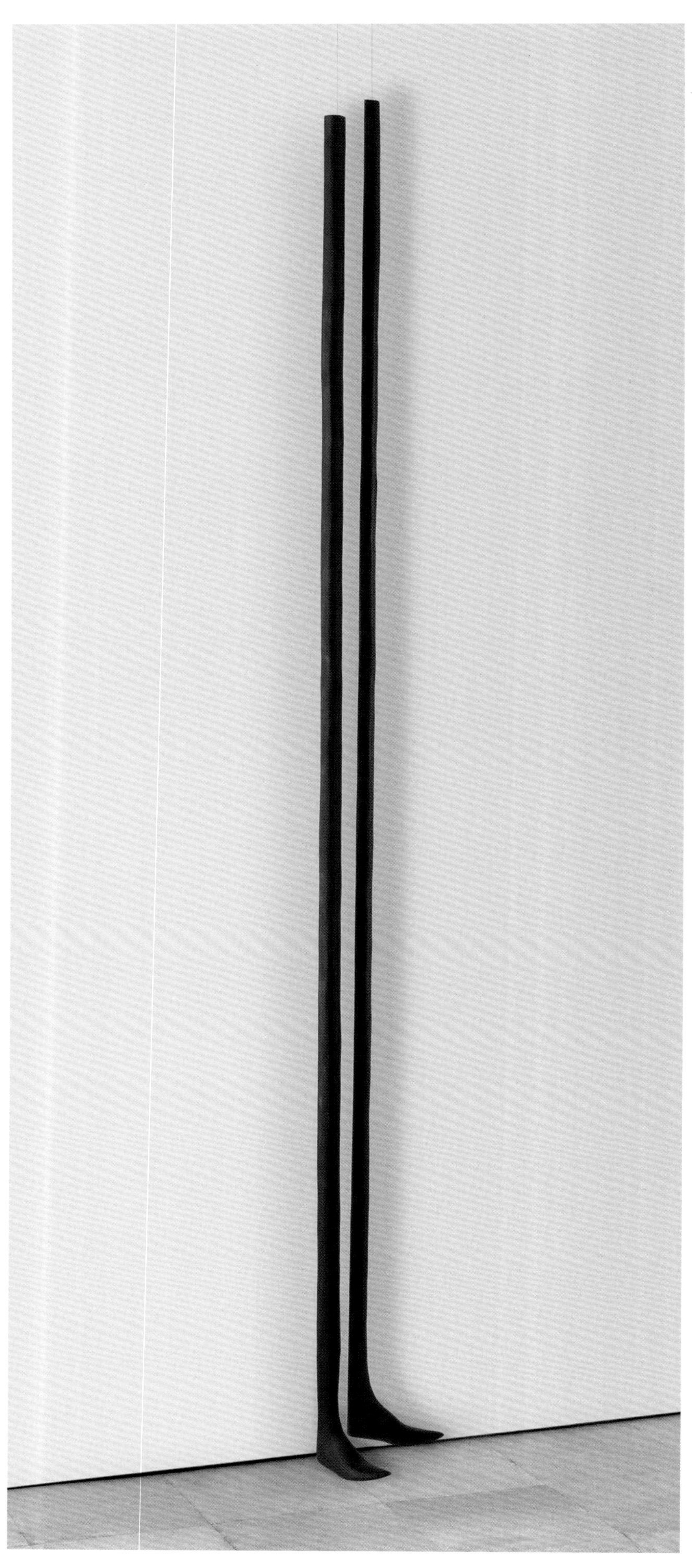

Legs 1986
Untitled 1999

following spread:
Self-portrait 2007 in the Tank

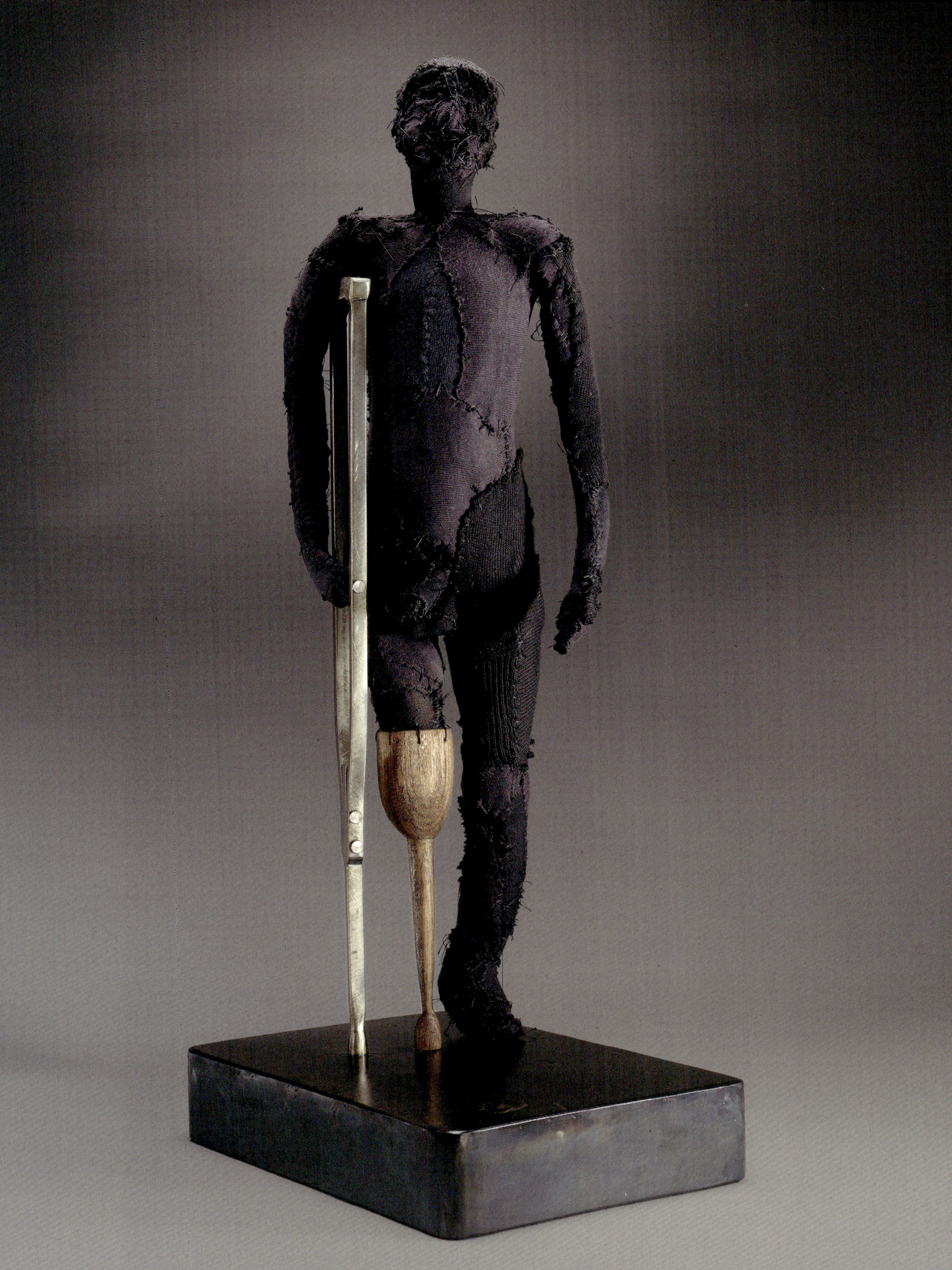

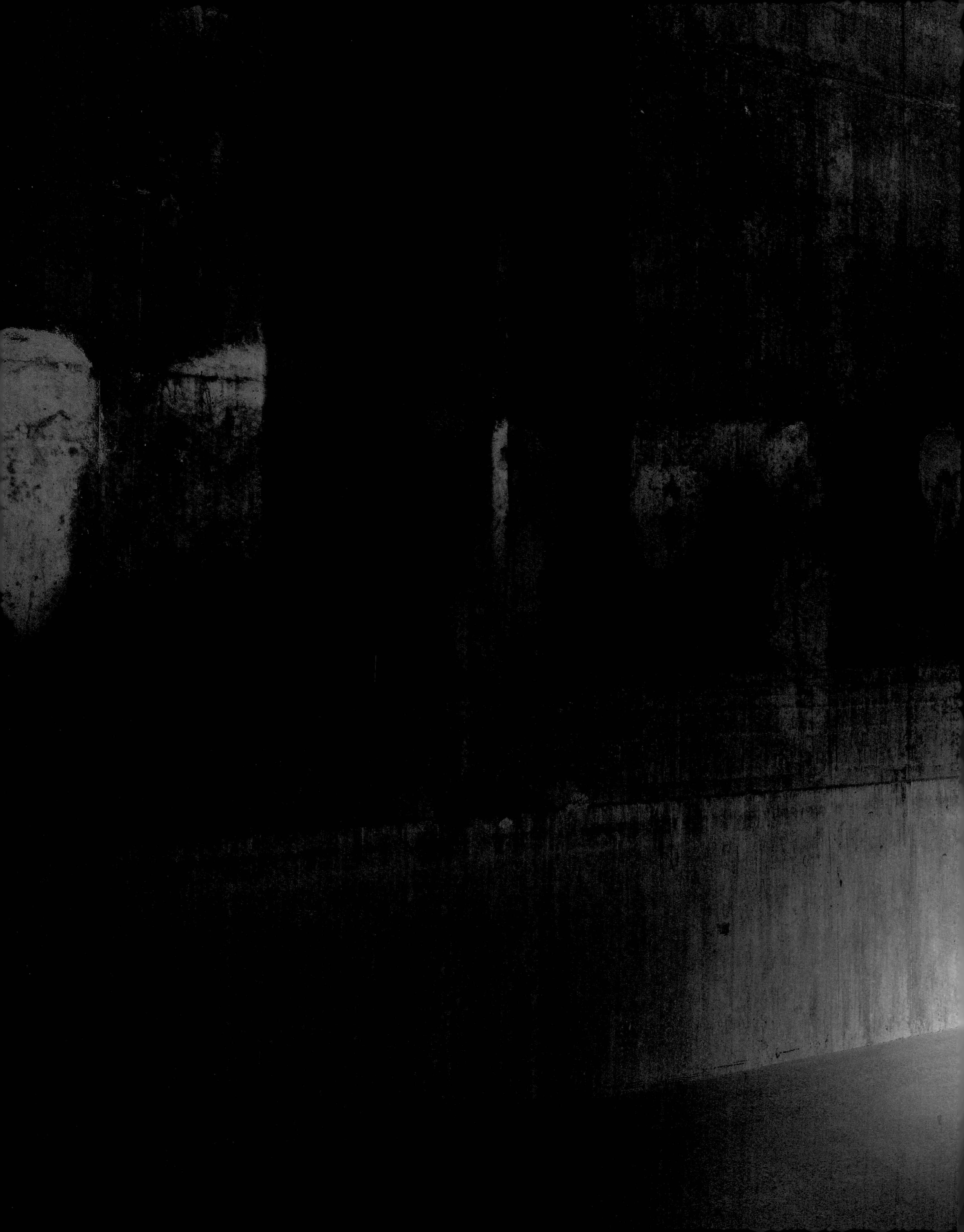

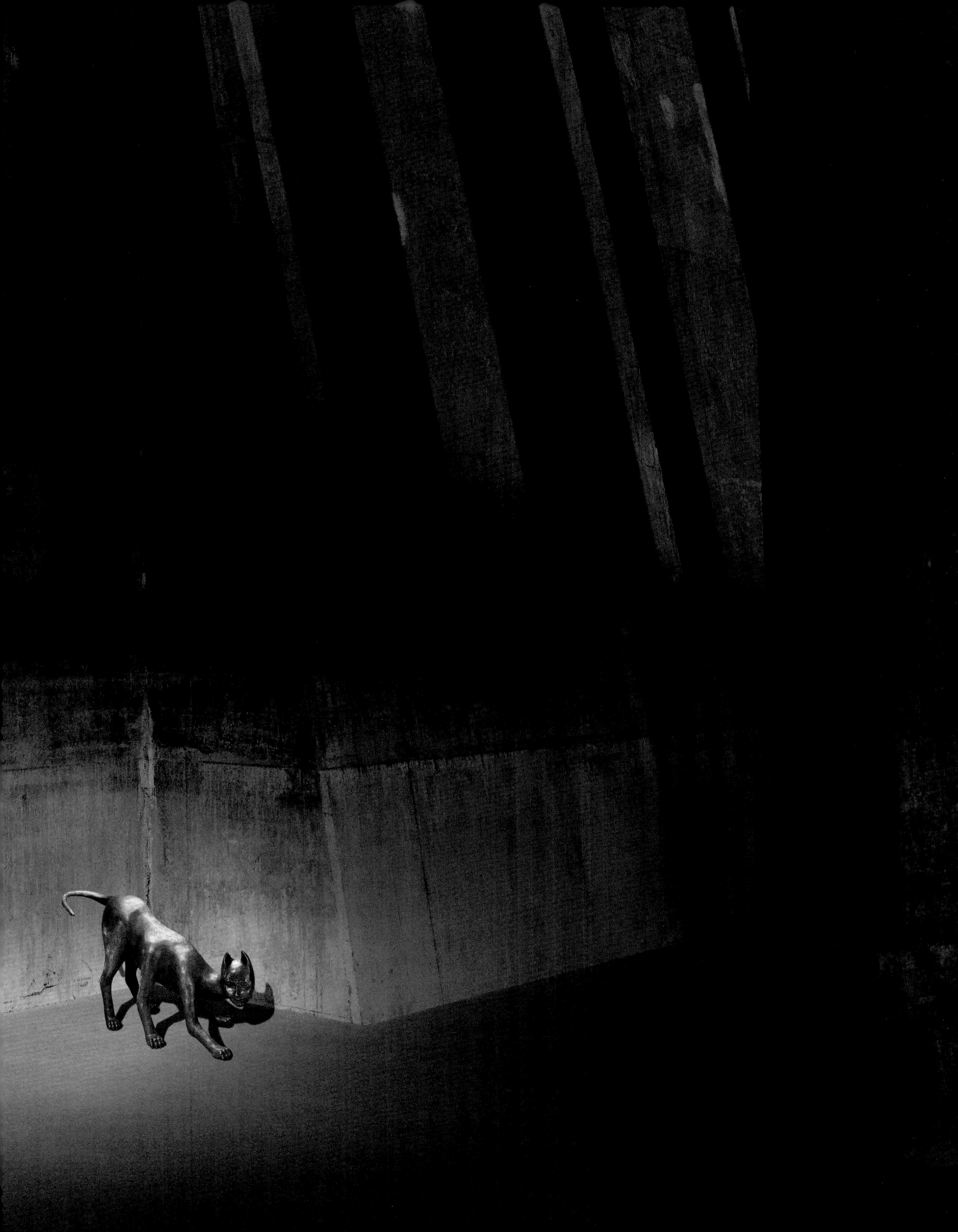

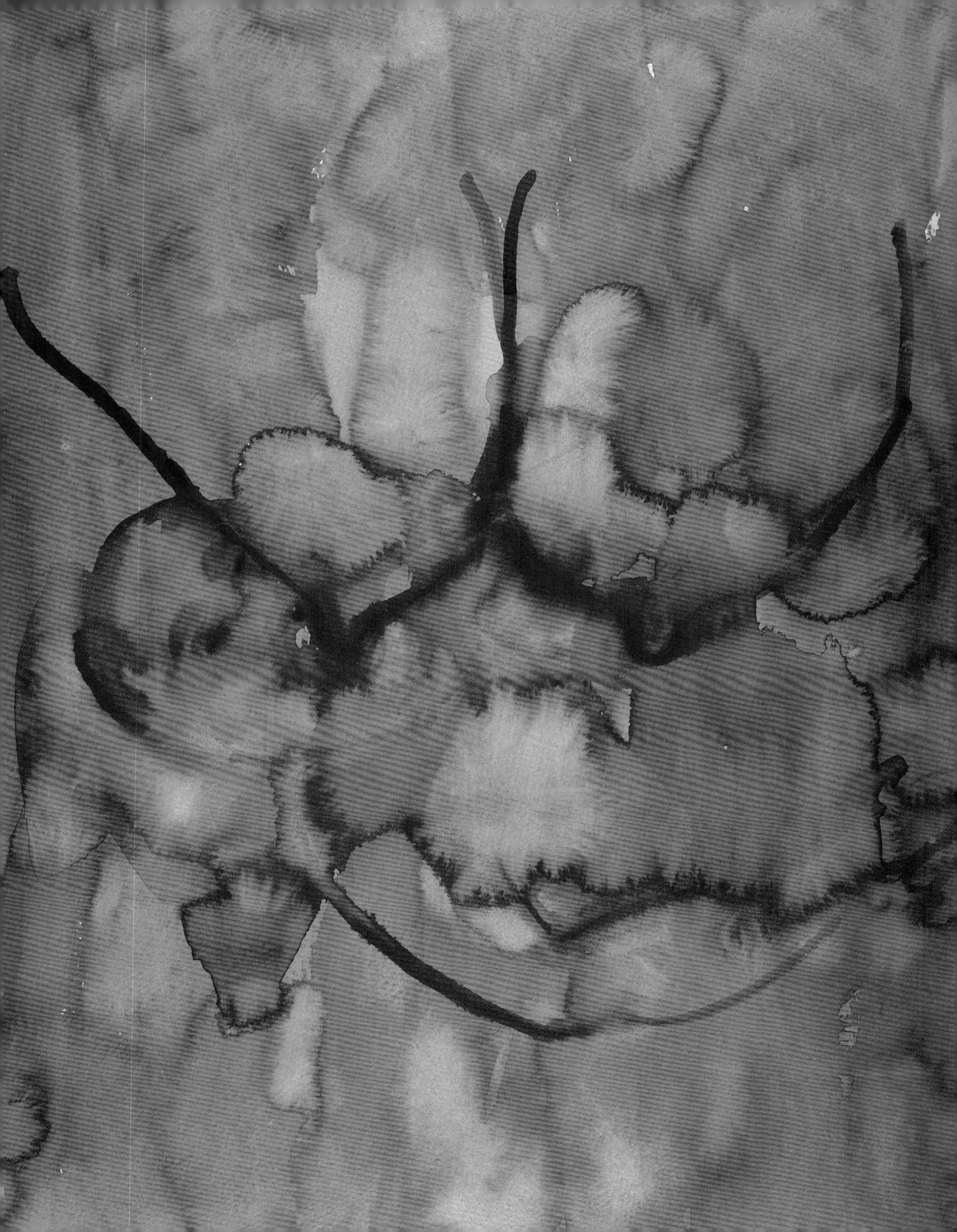

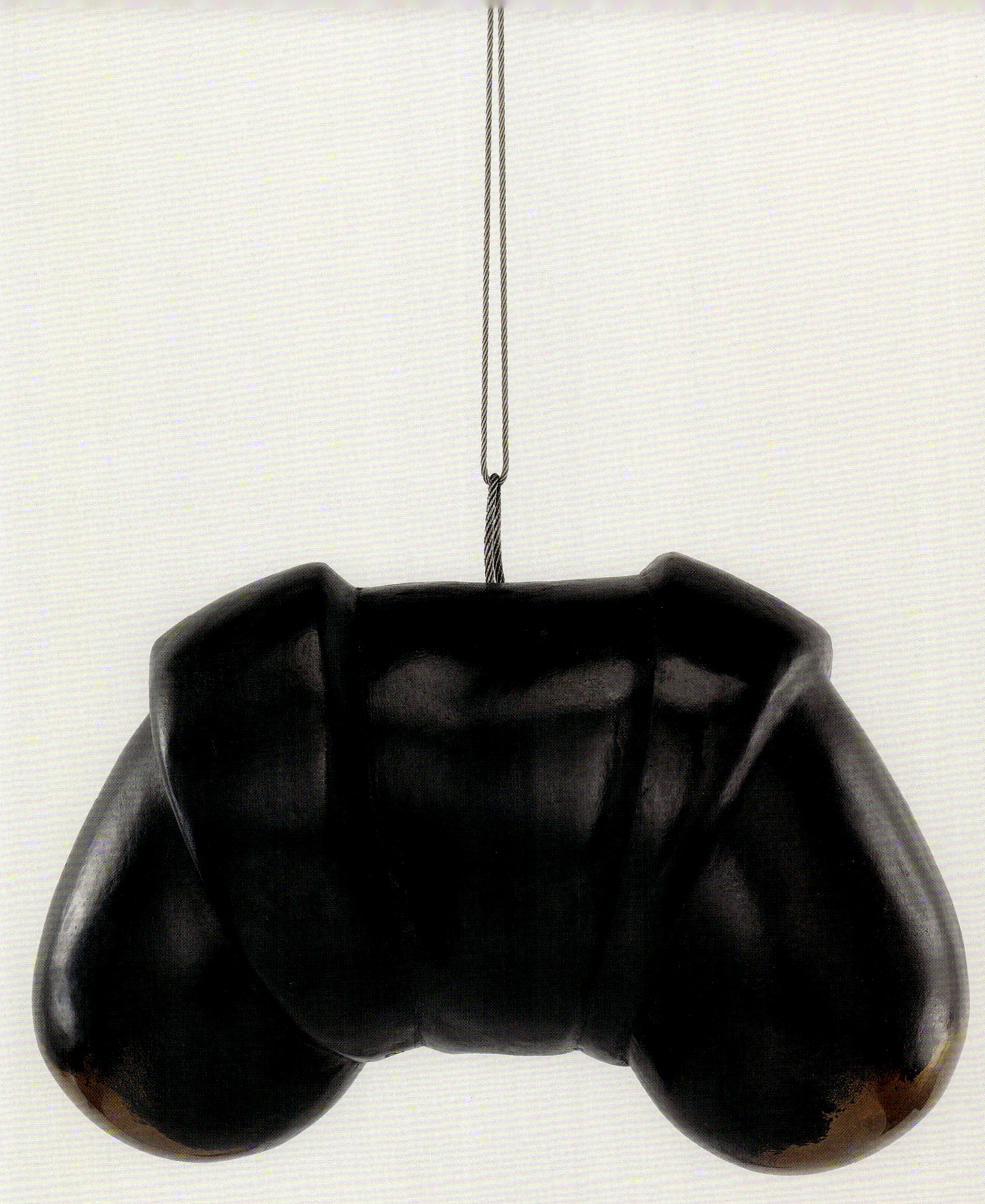

The Feeding 2007 (detail)
Hanging Janus 1968

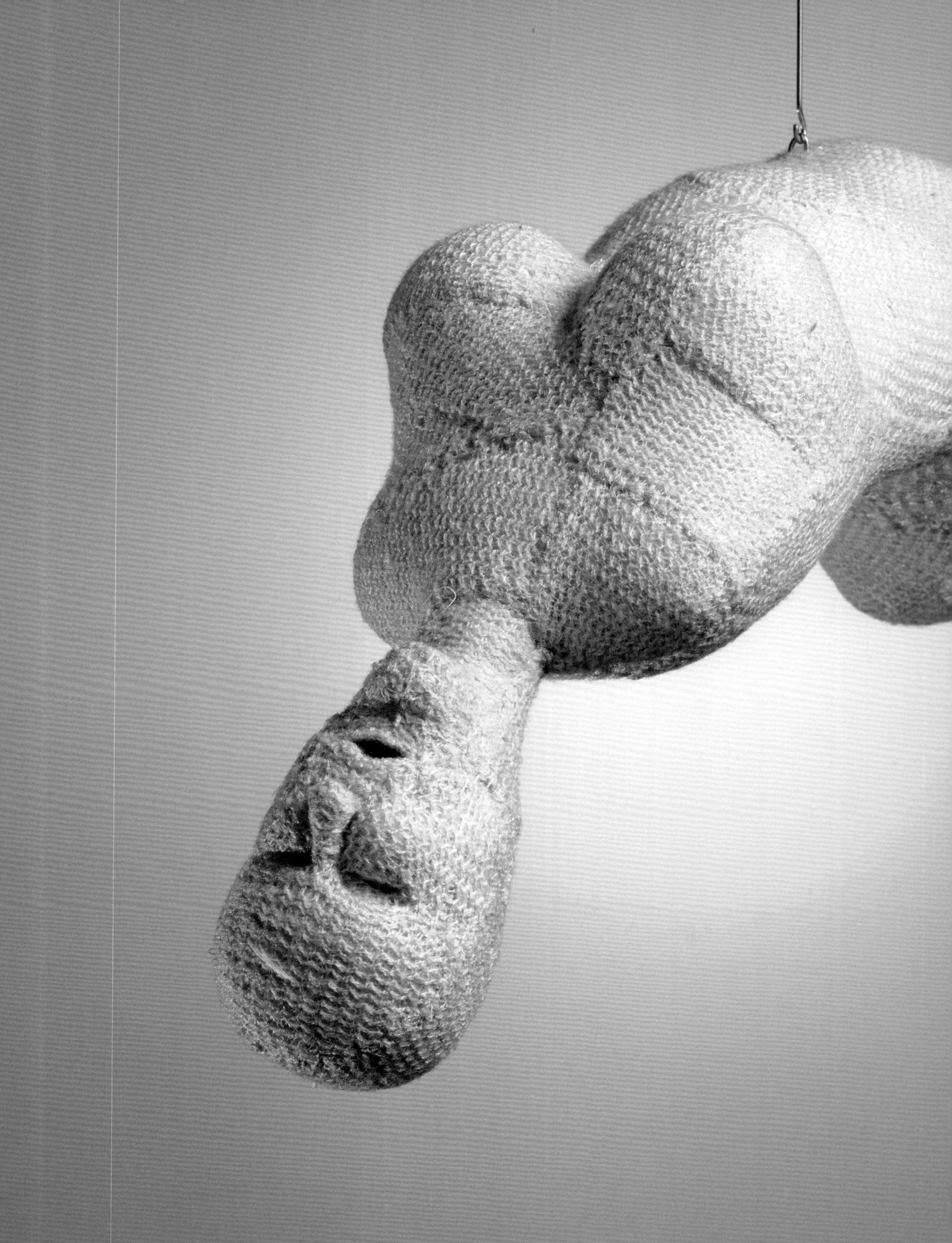

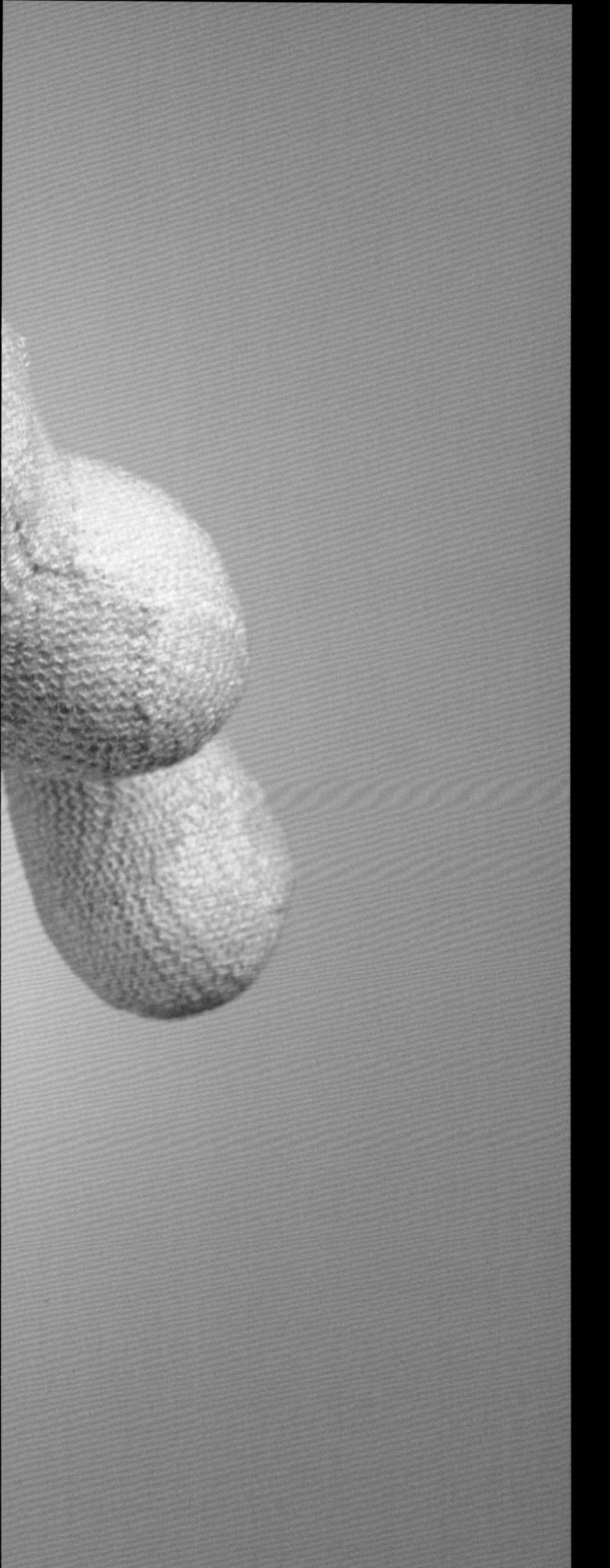

Arch of Hysteria 2004

following spread:
Twosome 1991 (detail) in

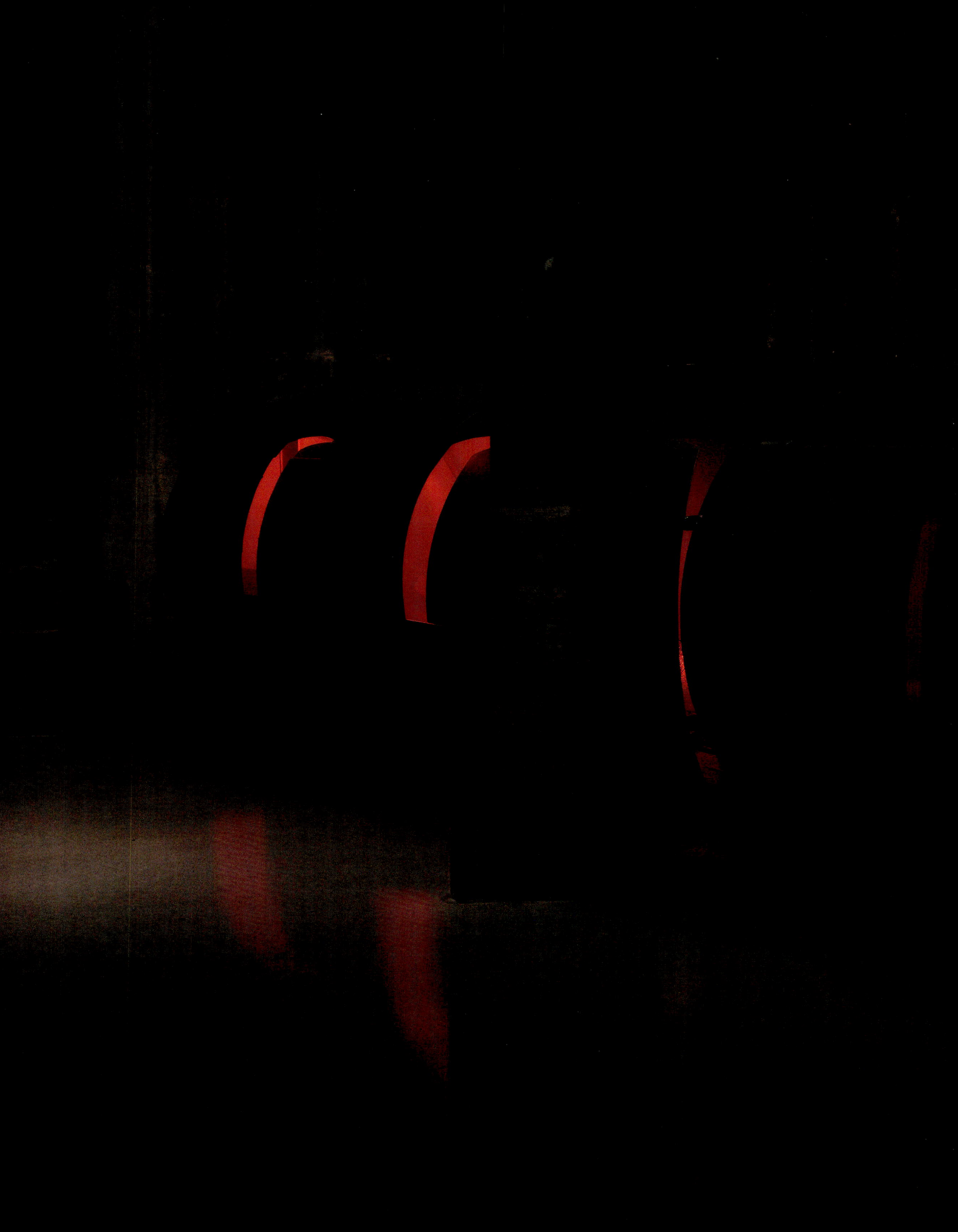

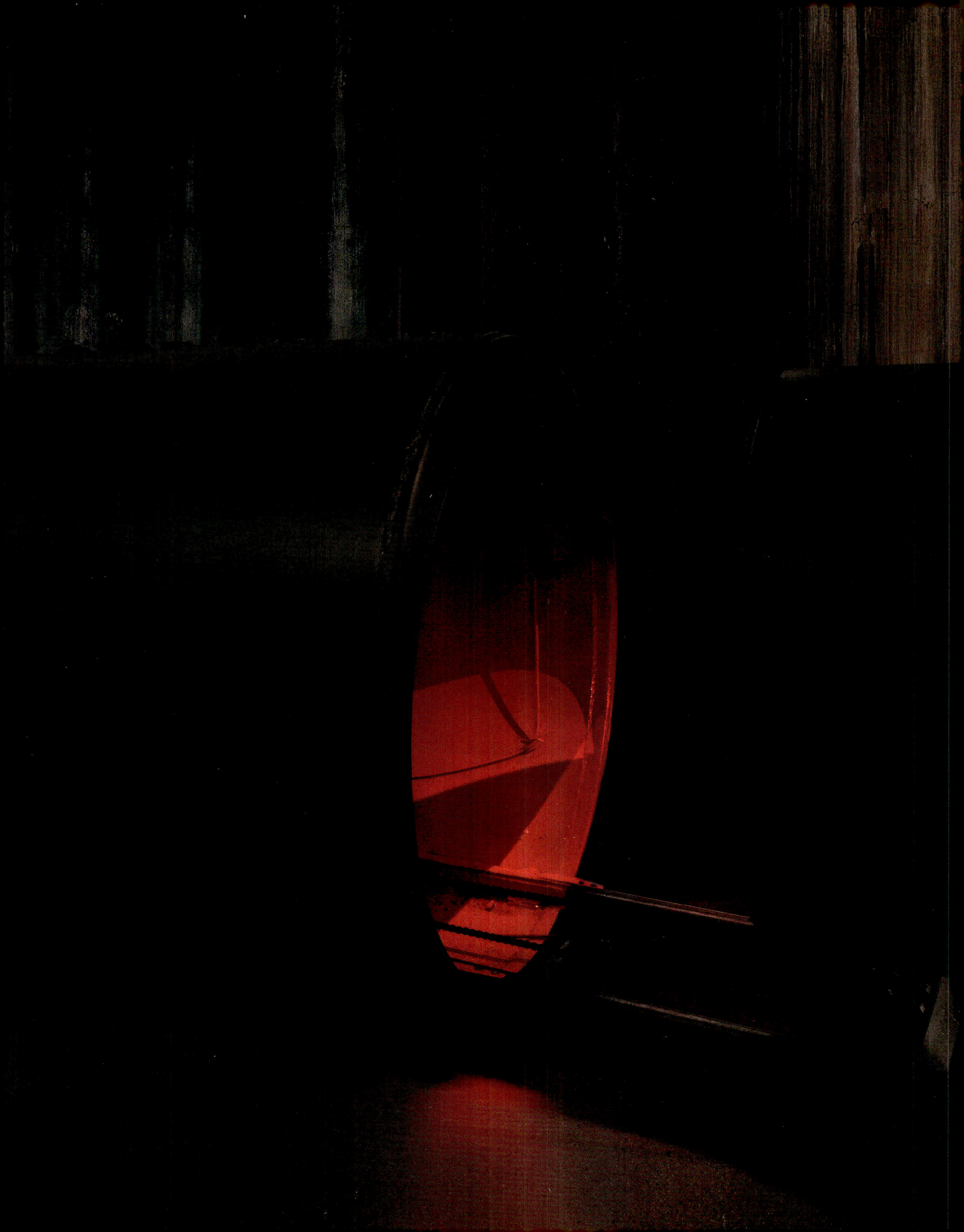

Coming into the dark roo
I put the light on
and saw 2 dogs making lov
on my bed – I said:
I am sorry
and closed the door softl
then I went down ~~the stai~~
across the street
and into Petes tavern
to sit and ~~wait~~ write
a letter

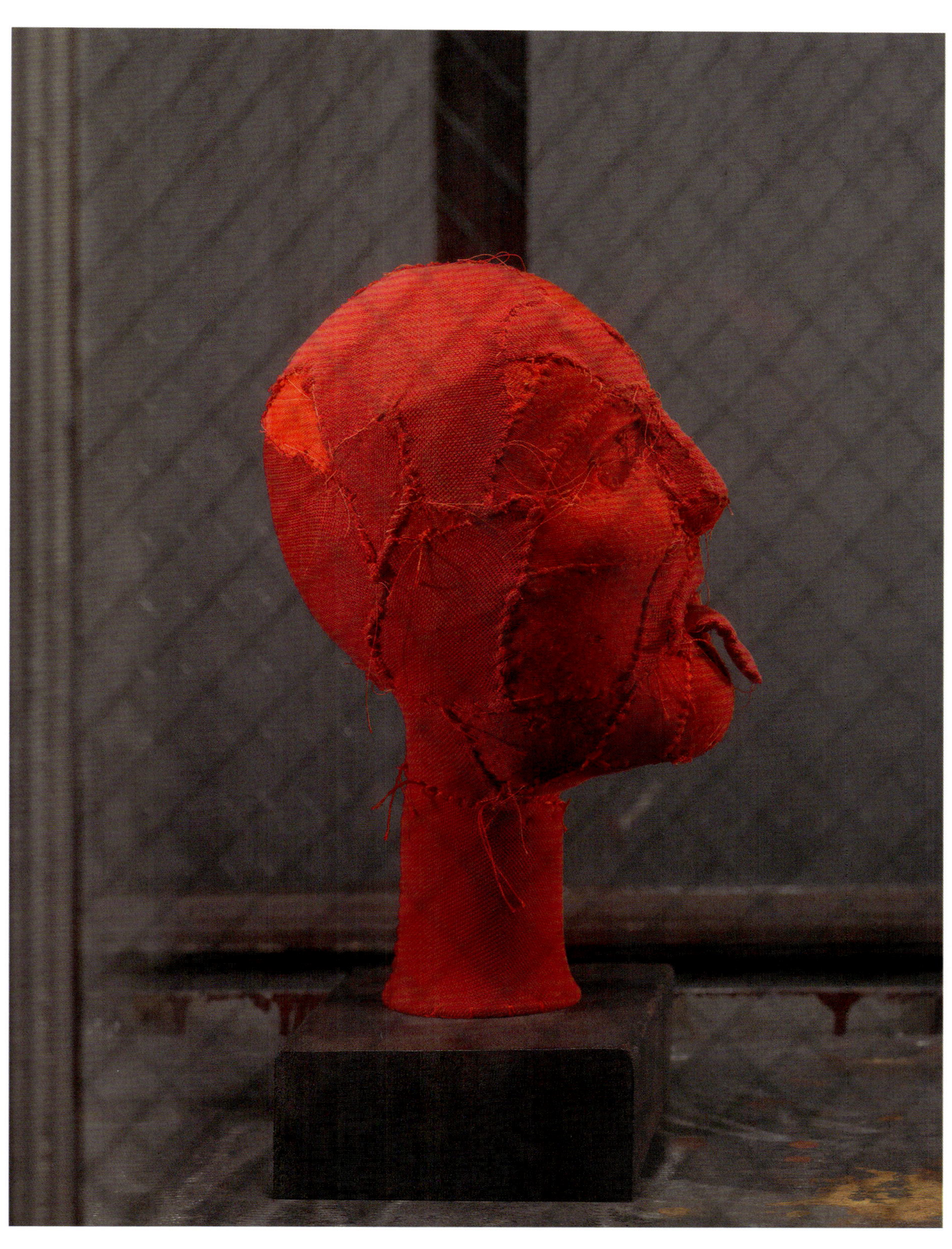

Jenny Holzer *Bourgeois X Holzer Projections* 2023 in the Tank
Cell X (Portrait) 2000 (detail)

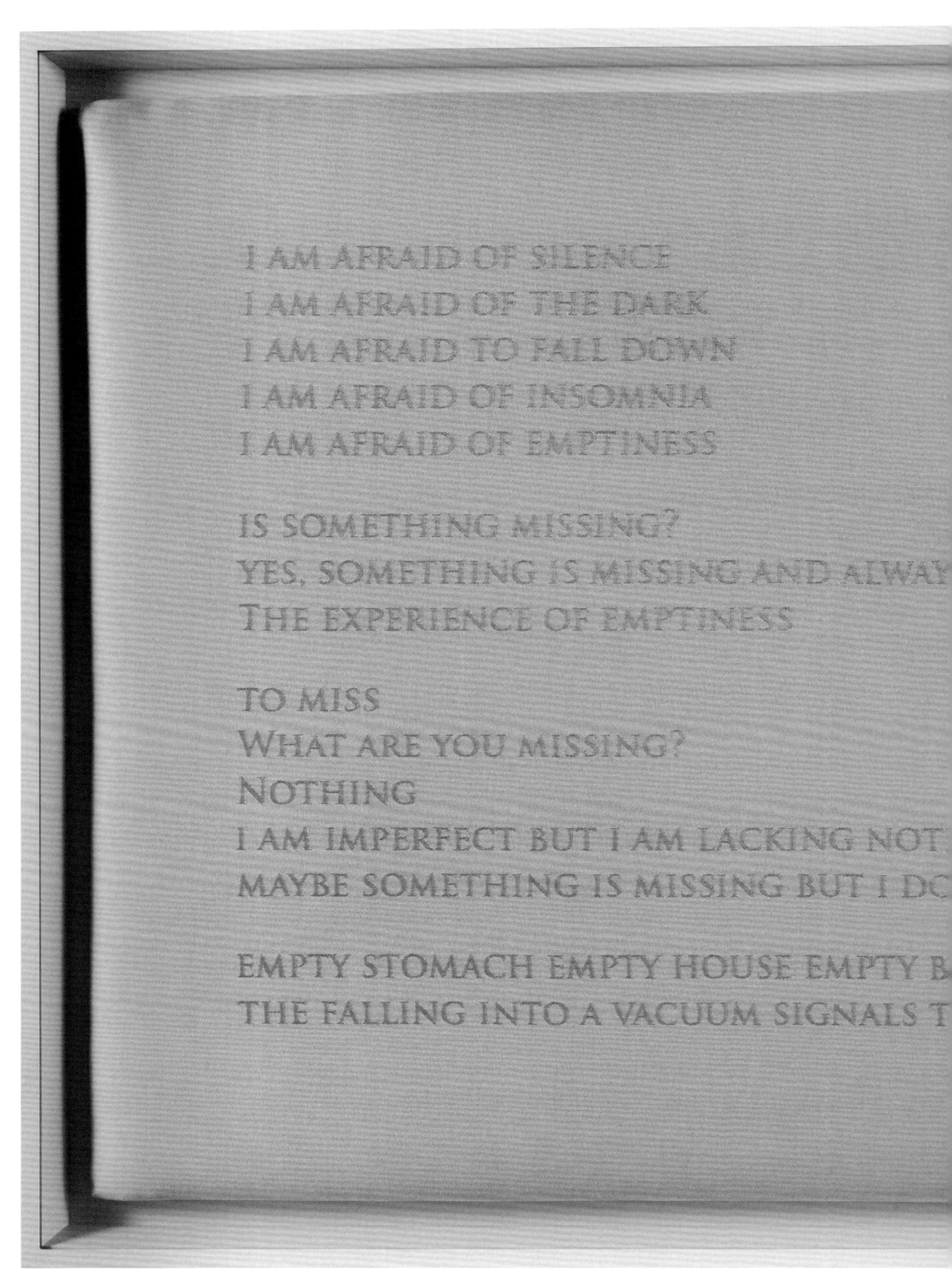

 I Am Afraid 2009

following spread:
Couple 2001 in the Tank

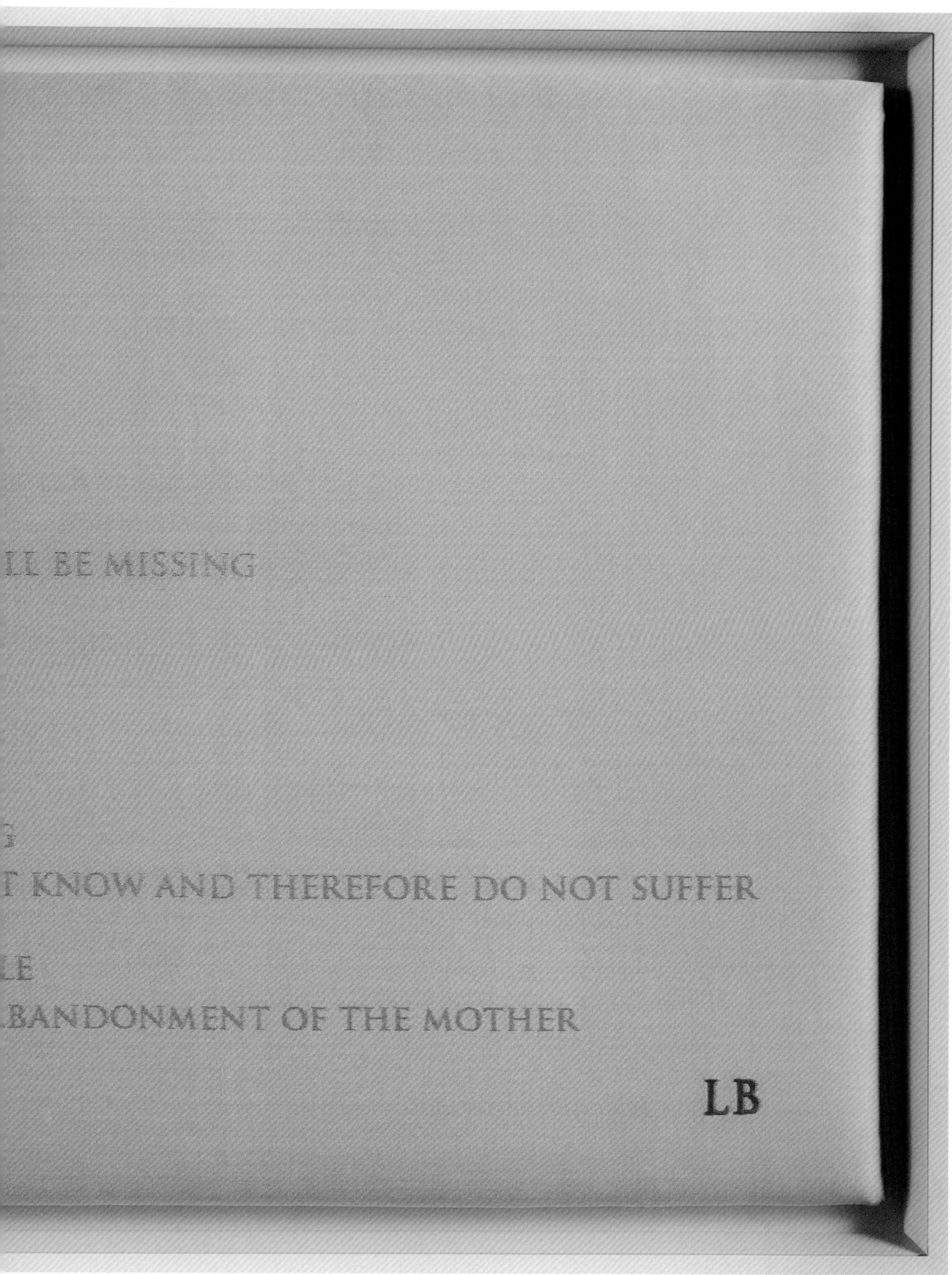
LL BE MISSING
T KNOW AND THEREFORE DO NOT SUFFER
LE
BANDONMENT OF THE MOTHER
LB

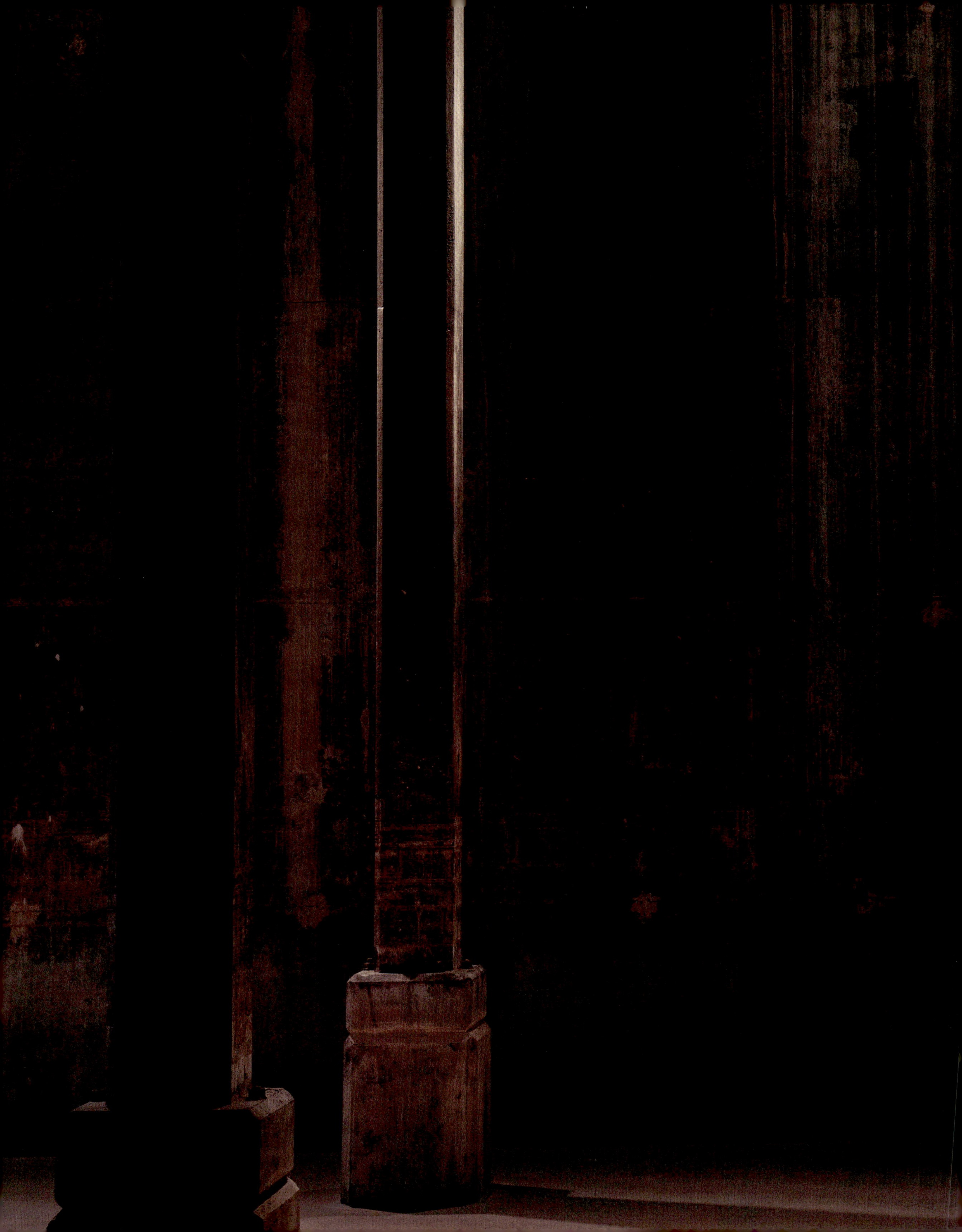

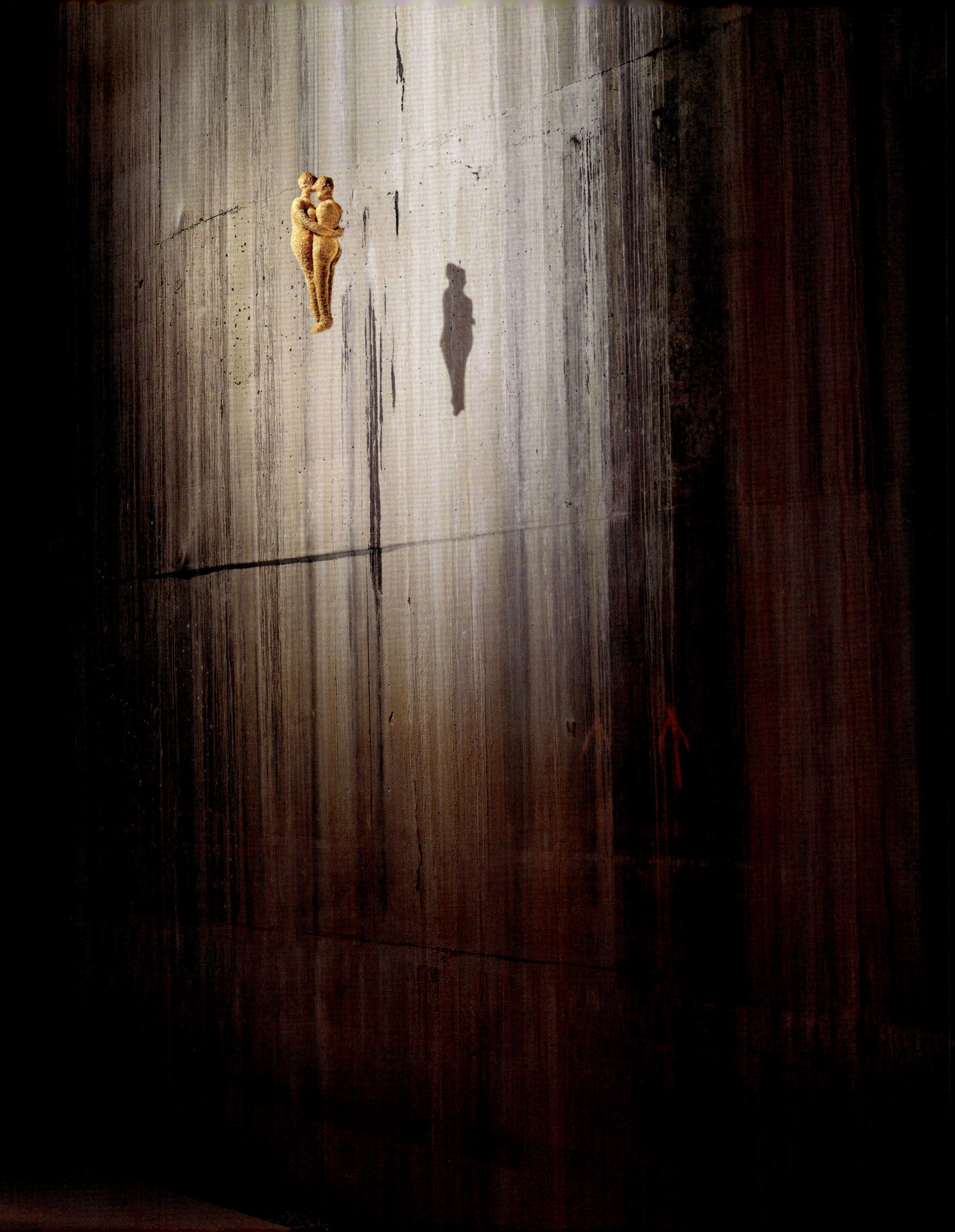

CHRONOLOGY

Louise Bourgeois in Cimiez, Nice, France, 1932

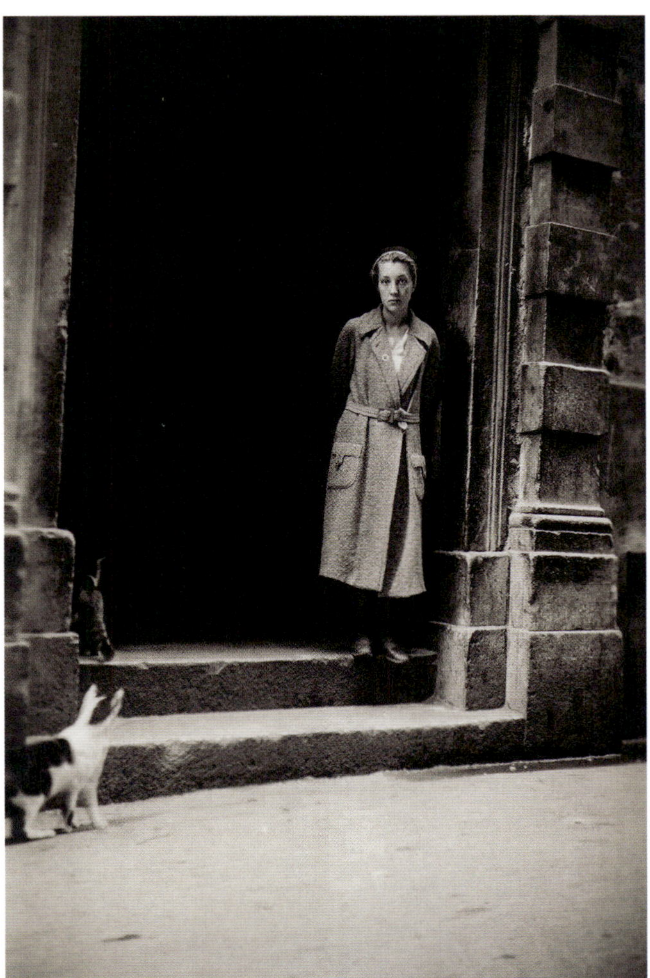

1911
Louise Joséphine Bourgeois is born on 25 December in Paris. Her parents, Louis and Joséphine, own a tapestry restoration business which includes a sales gallery at 174 boulevard Saint-Germain. The family (Bourgeois's sister Henriette was born in 1904 and her brother Pierre in 1913) resides in an apartment next door, at 172 boulevard Saint-Germain.

1912
The Bourgeois family rents a house in Choisy-le-Roi and lives there until 1917. The property includes a two-storey atelier for tapestry workers.

1914
Outbreak of the First World War. Bourgeois's uncle, Désiré Bourgeois, enlists and is killed on 21 September. His wife and two sons move into the Bourgeois home. During the war, the family often stays with relatives in Aubusson. Louis is mobilised to fight in late 1914.

1916
Louis is wounded; Bourgeois and her mother visit him in a war hospital in Chartres.

1918
Joséphine becomes ill, probably with Spanish influenza, and never fully recovers.

1919
The family acquires property and establishes a tapestry restoration atelier in Antony, a suburb of Paris. The Bièvre river, the subject of Bourgeois's *Ode à la Bièvre* 2002 and 2007 (pp 164–67), flows through the garden. Its tannin-rich waters are useful for rinsing dilapidated tapestries and fixing vegetable dyes used in the restoration process.

1921
Bourgeois starts attending the prestigious Lycée Fénelon in Paris.

1922
Joséphine's health deteriorates, and the family begins spending winters in the south of France. They will stay at various locations in the area through to 1932.

Sadie Gordon Richmond, a British woman hired as the children's English tutor, lives with the family, on and off, for almost a decade. During this time she and Louis have an affair – one of his many infidelities. The complex dynamics of Bourgeois's childhood and her subsequent feelings of abandonment and betrayal, further complicated by Joséphine's illness, will later find expression in her work.

Around this time, Bourgeois begins helping in the atelier by drawing missing elements for tapestries undergoing restoration. Due to wear and tear at the bottom of tapestries portraying figures, she becomes expert at drawing feet.

1927–1930
While Bourgeois's education is strongly supported by Joséphine, a feminist, it is frequently interrupted by her mother's illness. She withdraws from the Lycée Fénelon in 1927, though she returns for her *baccalauréat* in 1932. By 1928 she is Joséphine's primary caregiver, and pursues her education by correspondence with the École Universelle, studying mathematics, physics and chemistry.

1932
Visits Scandinavia and Leningrad (St Petersburg, Soviet Union).

On 14 September, Bourgeois's mother Joséphine dies at the age of fifty-three. Distraught, Bourgeois attempts suicide in the Bièvre and is saved by her father.

In November, she begins studying geometry and differential calculus at the Sorbonne.

1933–1935
Stops studying mathematics. Enrols in the Académie de la Grande Chaumière and begins oil painting with Yves Brayer. Studies with graphic designer Paul Colin, who encourages her second trip to the Soviet Union, where she sees the Moscow Art Theatre. Takes courses in Romanesque Art and Philosophy and Art at the Sorbonne, and studies painting with Roger Bissière and Othon Friesz, and sculpture with Robert Wlérick.

1936
Takes classes at the École des Beaux-Arts and attends the École du Louvre to study art history and train as a docent. Works as a teaching assistant for Yves Brayer at the Académie de la Grande Chaumière, a role that involves hiring nude life models.

1937
Gives tours as a docent at the Musée du Louvre. Her still-life painting is accepted by the Salon d'Automne.

1938
Studies with Fernand Léger, whom she credits with inspiring her to be a sculptor.

Opens a small art gallery in her father's tapestry sales gallery.

Meets Robert Goldwater, an American art historian, when he visits Bourgeois's gallery on 24 August. They marry in a civil service in Paris on 12 September, and on 12 October Bourgeois arrives in New York City.

1939
Returns to France with Goldwater during the summer. Visits family and friends and travels to Bordeaux, where they arrange to adopt Michel Olivier, an orphan (b1936).

1940
Michel Olivier Bourgeois arrives in New York on 21 May. Bourgeois gives birth to Jean-Louis Bourgeois on 4 July.

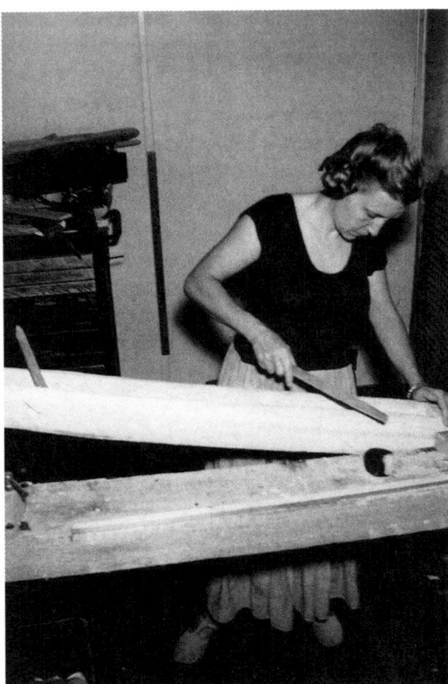

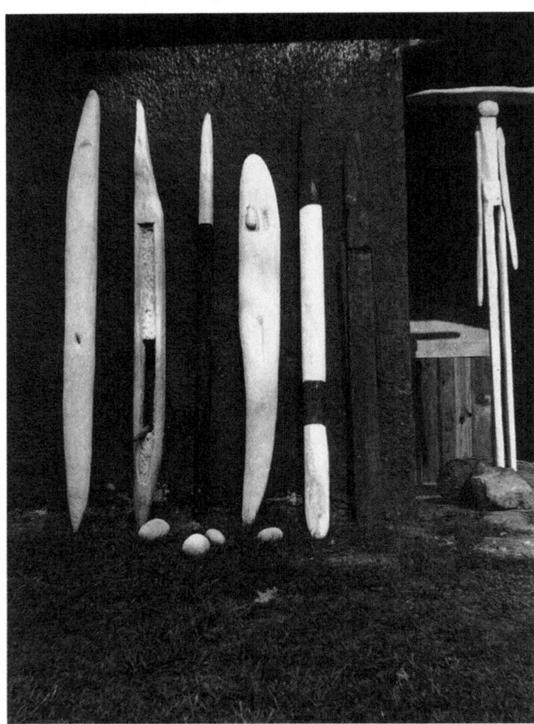

Bourgeois working on a Personage sculpture, 1949

Bourgeois's Personage sculptures in progress, including *Friendly Evidence* and *Observer* both 1947–49, outside her home in Easton, Connecticut, c1949

1941
The Bourgeois-Goldwater family purchases a country home in Easton, Connecticut, and moves to the Stuyvesant Apartments ('Stuyvesant's Folly') at 142 East 18th Street, New York. In the mid 1940s Bourgeois begins creating her first mature sculptures, the Personages, on the building's roof. She also works on these sculptures, including *Observer* (left and p 91) and *Woman in the Shape of a Shuttle* (left and p 95), both 1947–49, at the Easton property.

Bourgeois's third son, Alain Bourgeois, is born on 12 November.

1945
Paintings by Louise Bourgeois, Bourgeois's first solo exhibition, opens on 4 June at Bertha Schaefer Gallery, New York. Curates the exhibition *Documents France 1940–1944: Art–Literature–Press of the French Underground* at Norlyst Gallery, New York, with Marcel Duchamp's support. The exhibition includes anti-Nazi publications, art by Pierre Bonnard, Pablo Picasso and Jean Dubuffet, and writing by Louis Aragon, Jean-Paul Sartre and Gertrude Stein, among others.

Included in *The Women*, an exhibition of thirty women artists at Peggy Guggenheim's New York gallery, Art of This Century. Leonora Carrington, Lee Krasner, Hedda Sterne and others are also represented.

1947
Active at Atelier 17, Stanley William Hayter's renowned printmaking studio, which relocated to New York during the war years. Publishes *He Disappeared into Complete Silence* (pp 84–88), an illustrated book of nine engravings accompanied by short letterpress texts.

Presents seventeen paintings, including those later titled *Femme maison* (p 207), in her second solo exhibition, *Louise Bourgeois: Paintings*, at Norlyst Gallery.

1948
From May to July, Louis Bourgeois makes his only visit to New York. He and Bourgeois take an extended road trip through Quebec, Canada.

1949
Exhibits alongside Willem de Kooning, Hans Hoffman and others in a group exhibition at Peridot Gallery.

Has first solo exhibition of sculpture, *Louise Bourgeois, Recent Work 1947–1949: Seventeen Standing Figures in Wood* at Peridot Gallery, New York. Includes *Dagger Child* 1947–49, *Woman with Packages* 1949 (p 92) and a version of *The Blind Leading the Blind* 1947–49. The exhibition is conceived as an environmental installation, with sculptures installed directly into the floor and arranged in clusters as if at a cocktail party.

1950
Peridot Gallery presents *Louise Bourgeois: Sculptures*, which includes *Black Flames* 1947–49 (p 83), *The Winged Figure* 1948 (p 16) and *Knife Couple* 1949 (p 89).

Participates in 'Artists' Sessions at Studio 35', a closed-door symposium moderated by Alfred H Barr Jr, Richard Lippold and Robert Motherwell. Fourteen artists, most of whom are abstract expressionists, are invited to discuss contemporary American art.

Departs for a year-long stay in France with family, during which Goldwater conducts research for a Fulbright scholarship. Maintains a studio in Paris until 1955.

1951
The Personage *Sleeping Figure* 1950 is purchased for the Museum of Modern Art (MoMA) by Alfred H Barr Jr and shown soon after in a presentation of new acquisitions.

Bourgeois's father Louis dies in Paris on 9 April.

In June, travels with Goldwater to Antwerp, Belgium, where they see a James Ensor exhibition, and London, where art historian David Sylvester introduces them to Francis Bacon.

Suffers from deep depression precipitated by her father's death, and begins psychoanalysis in New York with Dr Leonard Cammer.

1952
Undergoes intensive analysis with Dr Henry Lowenfeld, a Freudian psychoanalyst, and begins writing what are now known as the psychoanalytic writings, an effort that effectively replaces her artistic practice for the following decade. Sees Lowenfeld regularly until 1967, then sporadically until his death in 1985.

Designs stage sets for *The Bridegroom of the Moon*, a dance performance by Erick Hawkins at the Hunter Playhouse, New York. Wallingford Riegger composes the music.

1953
Louise Bourgeois: Drawings for Sculpture and Sculpture is on view at Peridot Gallery; Bourgeois does not have another solo exhibition of new work until 1964.

The Fachetti Gallery in Paris organises an exhibition of Bourgeois's work, and Michel Seuphor writes an essay for the catalogue. Due to her worsening depression and anxiety, Bourgeois cancels the exhibition. Travels to various sites in Italy and France with her family, including the caves at Lascaux. Returns to France in 1955 and 1959.

1956
Establishes a bookstore, Erasmus Books and Prints, which closes in 1960.

Whitney Museum of American Art purchases *One and Others* 1955.

1957
Becomes an American citizen. Goldwater is appointed first director of the Museum of Primitive Art, New York, a position he holds until his death in 1973.

1958
Moves to an apartment at 435 West 22nd Street after Stuyvesant's Folly is slated to be demolished.

1960
Bourgeois's brother Pierre dies in a mental institution in Villejuif, France. He had suffered from what was likely schizophrenia since the mid 1940s.

1961
Travels with Goldwater to London and Paris and meets Belgian writer and artist Henri Michaux.

Experiments with new materials, such as plastic, latex and rubber, and begins developing a series of biomorphic sculptures informed by her psychoanalysis.

1962
Moves with Goldwater to 20th Street, where she lives for the rest of her life.

1963
Begins teaching at Brooklyn College; returns in 1968. Also teaches at Pratt Institute, Brooklyn in 1965 and 1967.

1964
The Stable Gallery, New York, presents Bourgeois's first solo exhibition of new work since 1953. Debuts several Lair sculptures, including *Labyrinthine Tower* 1962 (p 99) and *Fée couturière* 1963 (pp 16, 109). Almost simultaneously, a solo exhibition of drawings is on view at Rose Fried Gallery, New York.

1966
Travels with Goldwater to attend the First World Festival of Negro Arts in Dakar, Senegal. Also visits the Ivory Coast, Nigeria and Portugal.

Included in *Eccentric Abstraction*, a group exhibition curated by Lucy Lippard at Fischbach Gallery, New York. This seminal exhibition promoted formlessness, materiality and process (over then-dominant trends of minimalism) and presented Bourgeois's work in dialogue with a younger generation of artists, including Bruce Nauman and Eva Hesse.

1967
Travels to Italy to work in marble (including on *Sleep II,* left and p 227) and bronze. Stays primarily in Pietrasanta, and visits quarries and foundries in Carrara and other nearby towns.

1968
Creates the sculpture *Fillette* (pp 33, 244).

Returns to Italy from May to October. Creates *Colonnata* (p 105) and *Clamart* (pp 106–07) in marble and develops her Janus sculptures in bronze. Returns to Italy in 1969 and 1970.

1969
Goldwater's book *What is modern sculpture?* is published by MoMA. It includes an illustration and discussion of Bourgeois's *Quarantania I* 1947–53, acquired via donation by the museum in the same year.

'Some reflections prompted by the recent work of Louise Bourgeois' by William Rubin, then chief curator of painting and sculpture at MoMA, is published in *Art International*'s April issue.

The Quartered One 1964–65 (pp 17, 226) is included in *The New American Painting and Sculpture: The First Generation* at MoMA.

Signs a contract with Knoedler Gallery, New York, where she participates in two group exhibitions in 1970 and 1971.

Bourgeois working on *Sleep II* in Pietrasanta, Italy, 1967

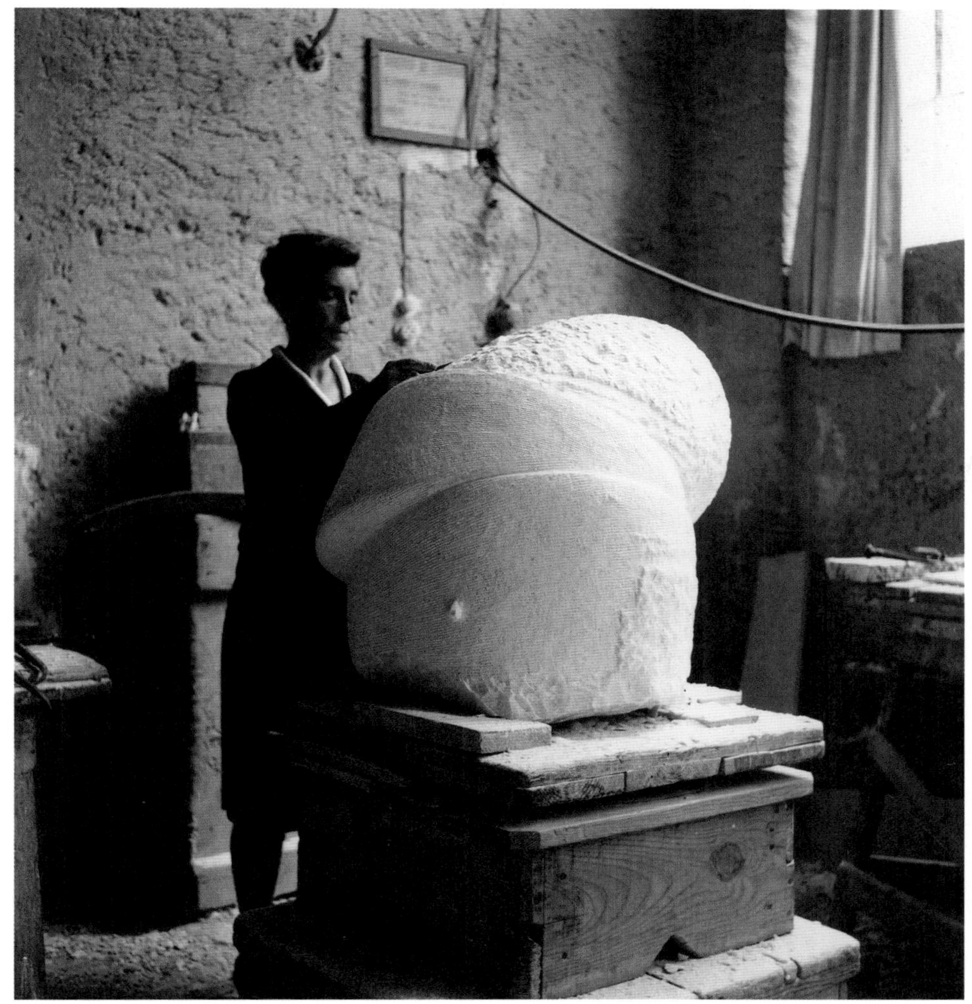

1970–1973
Gets involved in the feminist art movement, though never explicitly identifies as a feminist artist. Takes part in exhibitions, benefits, panel discussions and demonstrations. Protests against the under-representation of women at the Whitney Museum in 1970, and at MoMA in 1972, with Lee Krasner and Chryssa. In 1973, marches in support of MoMA employees on strike. Participates in *13 Women Artists*, organised by the Women's Ad Hoc Committee, New York, and several other exhibitions focusing on women artists.

1973
Robert Goldwater dies at home on 26 March.

In June, nineteen women artists and curators, including Lucy Lippard, Linda Nochlin, Howardena Pindell and Nancy Spero, write to William Rubin of MoMA, championing Bourgeois and expressing their strong support of a 'large scale museum exhibition' of her sculpture. The museum will not hold a retrospective exhibition until 1982.

Shows the large marble floor piece *Number Seventy-Two (The No March)* 1972 at the Whitney Museum. Creates sets, costumes and a poster for a production of two one-act plays, Tennessee Williams' *This property is condemned* (1966) and August Strindberg's *The stronger* (1889) at the Women's Interart Center, New York.

Musée National d'Art Moderne, Paris, purchases Bourgeois's marble *Cumul I* 1969, now part of the collection of Centre Georges Pompidou.

1974
Travels to France and Germany; visits her sister Henriette and cousin Jacques in Paris. Debuts *The Destruction of the Father* 1974 (pp 222–25) in her first solo exhibition in ten years, *Louise Bourgeois: Sculpture 1970–1974*, at 112 Greene Street Gallery, New York.

1975
Artforum publishes Lucy Lippard's important essay 'Louise Bourgeois: from the inside out', illustrating *The Destruction of the Father* on the cover.

1977
Receives an Honorary Doctorate of Fine Arts from Yale University.

Selected to participate in *From Women's Eyes* at the Rose Art Museum (Brandeis University, Massachusetts) by Deborah Wye, one of the exhibition's four curators. Wye becomes a leading scholar of Bourgeois's work, and editor of the online catalogue raisonné of prints and books published by MoMA in 2018.

1978
Meets the performer Suzan Cooper, whom she befriends along with the writer and performer Chris Kraus. Cooper performs in *A Banquet / A Fashion Show of Body Parts*.

Hamilton Gallery of Contemporary Art, New York, presents *Louise Bourgeois: New Work*. Stages the performance *A Banquet / A Fashion Show of Body Parts* on 21 October, closing day.

Louise Bourgeois: 'Triangles': New Sculpture and Drawings, 1978 is on view at Xavier Fourcade Gallery, New York. University Art Museum, Berkeley, presents *Louise Bourgeois: Matrix/Berkeley 17*, curated by Deborah Wye.

1979
Xavier Fourcade Gallery presents *Louise Bourgeois, Sculpture 1941–1953. Plus One New Piece*.

Repaints three sculptures titled *The Blind Leading the Blind* (all 1947–49) acid pink – 'an anti-artistic color statement' according to the artist – and renames one of them *C.O.Y.O.T.E.* (pp 96–97), an acronym for 'Call Off Your Old Tired Ethics', in honour of Margo St James's prostitutes' union.

1980
Receives the Award for Outstanding Achievement in the Visual Arts at the National Women's Caucus for Art conference in New Orleans, Louisiana. Other honours in this decade include an Honorary Doctorate of Fine Arts from Bard College in 1981; the French rank of Officer of the Order of Arts and Letters in 1983; and the College Art Association's Distinguished Artist Award for Lifetime Achievement in 1989.

Jerry Gorovoy, a young artist working at Max Hutchinson Gallery, New York, includes *C.O.Y.O.T.E.* 1947–49 in a group exhibition of abstract sculptures. James Mollison, director of the Australian National Gallery, Canberra, sees the exhibition and acquires Bourgeois's sculpture for the museum in 1981. By the end of the 1980s, Gorovoy will be Bourgeois's principal assistant and close confidant. He continues in that role until her death, and is now president of her foundation, The Easton Foundation.

Acquires a studio in an old garment factory at 475 Dean Street in Brooklyn. The added space allows Bourgeois to work on increasingly large-scale sculptures.

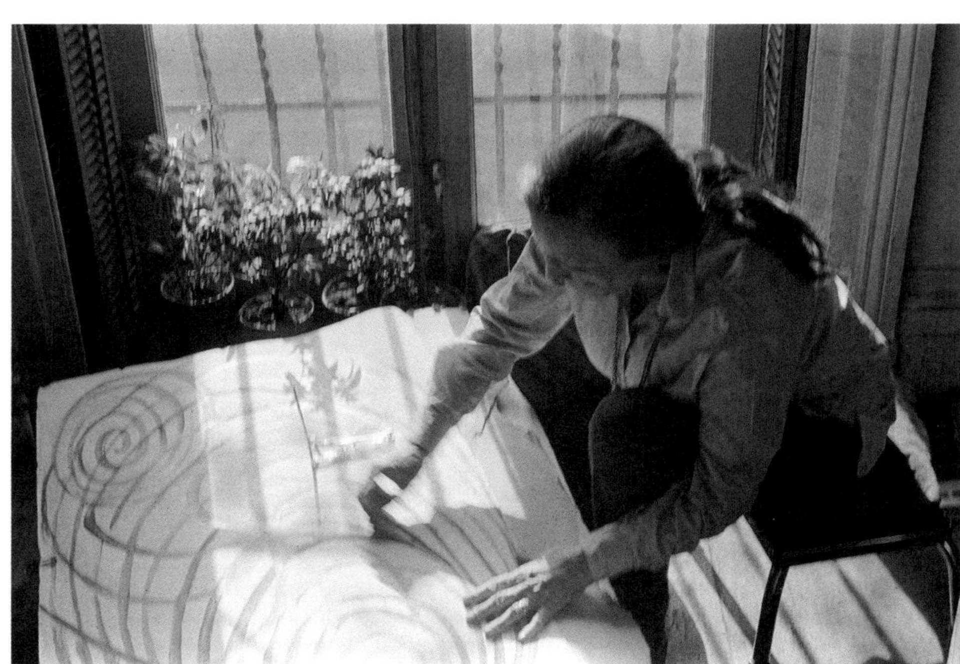

Bourgeois working on a spiral drawing in her home on 20th Street, New York, 1970

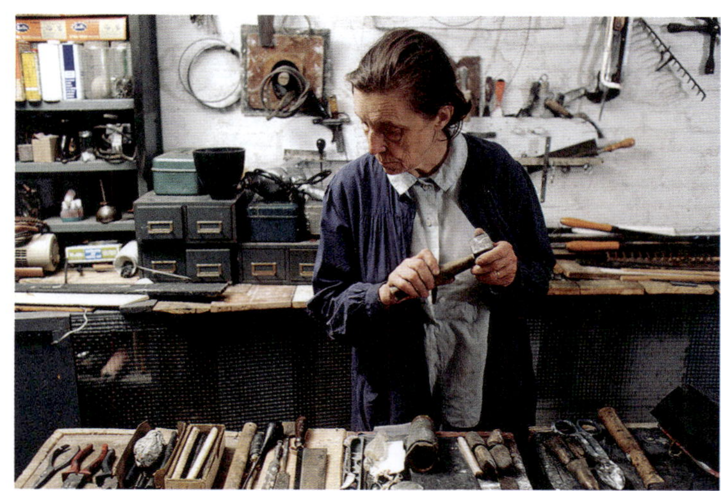

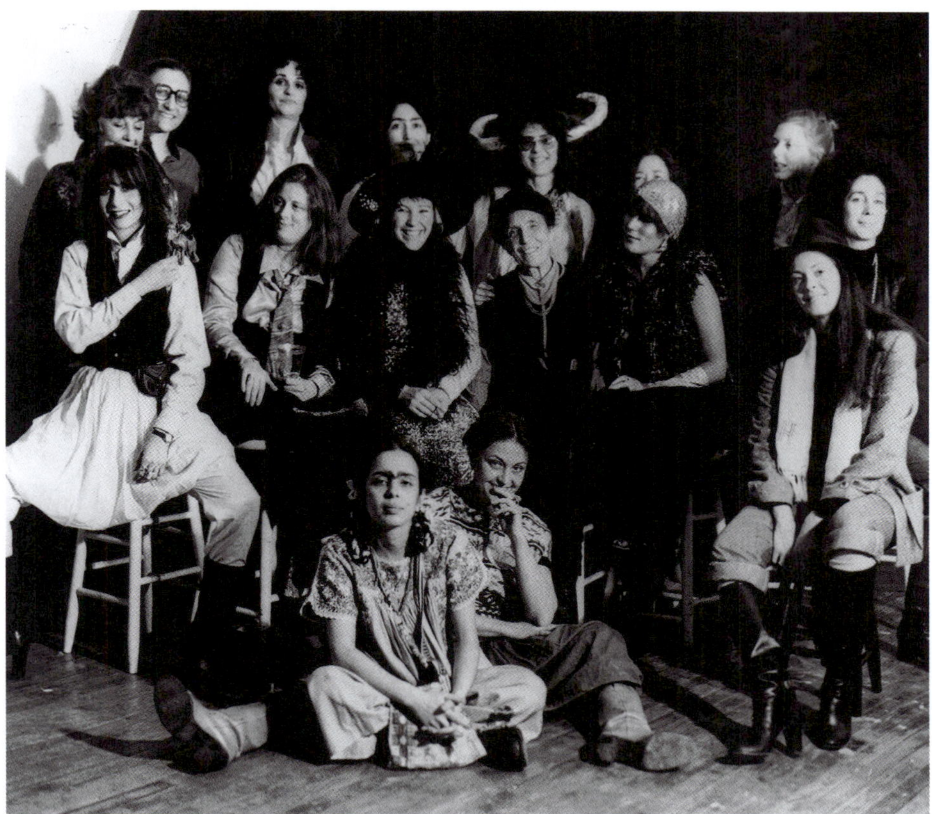

Bourgeois in the studio of her home on 20th Street, New York, 1974

Feminist dinner party given by Ana Mendieta and Mary Beth Edelson in honour of Louise Bourgeois, 14 March 1979. Guests were asked to come dressed as a famous historical or contemporary woman artist. From left, top row: Gloria MacDonald (as the Empress of China), Barbara Moore (as herself), Judith Bernstein (as herself), Joyce Kozloff (as one of 'the two Fridas' from Frida Kahlo's 1939 painting of the same name), Mary Beth Edelson (as Leonor Fini), Phyllis Krim (as herself) and Poppy Johnson (as a woman to be named by the group); middle row: Marcia Resnick (as Isabelle Eberhardt), Anne Sharp (as a woman astronaut), Pat Hamilton (as Mae West), Louise Bourgeois (as herself), Suzan Cooper (as Bourgeois's mother), Hannah Wilke (as herself) and Barbara Zucker (as herself); front row: Ana Mendieta (as Frida Kahlo) and Michelle Stuart (as the second of 'the two Fridas')

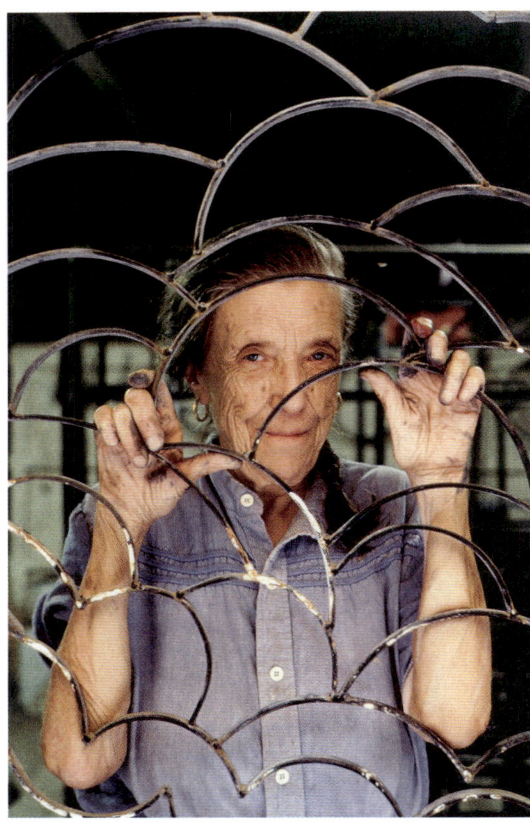

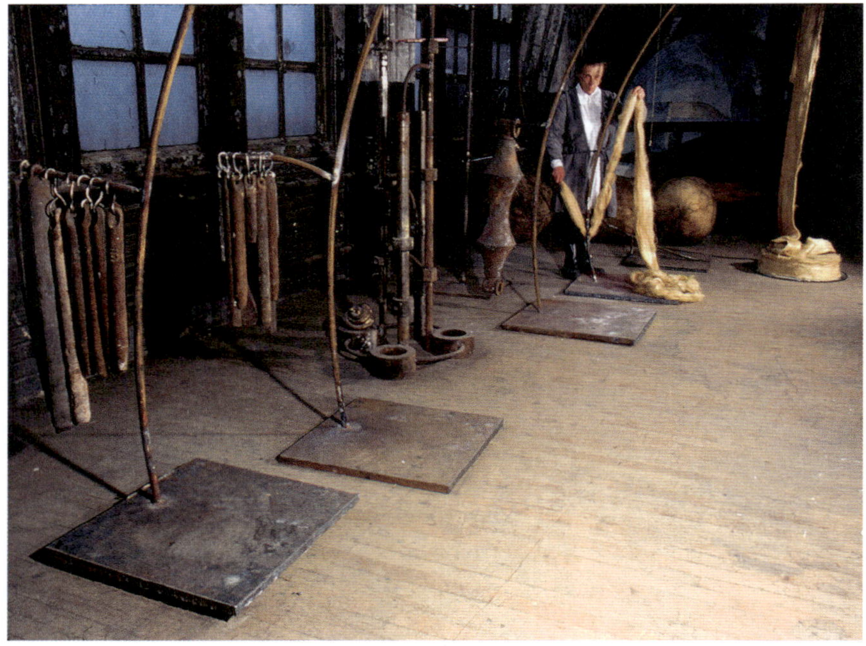

Bourgeois looking through the gate she designed for her Brooklyn studio, New York, 1982

Bourgeois in her Brooklyn studio, New York, 1992

On 9 July, Henriette Bonnotte, Bourgeois's sister, dies.

The Iconography of Louise Bourgeois, curated by Gorovoy at Max Hutchinson Gallery, presents many of Bourgeois's paintings for the first time in over thirty years. *Louise Bourgeois Sculpture: The Middle Years 1955–1970* is on view at Xavier Fourcade Gallery.

1981

Meets writer and curator Robert Storr, who becomes a leading commentator on her work. The Renaissance Society at the University of Chicago presents *Louise Bourgeois: Femme Maison*, curated by Patrice Marandel.

Returns to Italy with Jerry Gorovoy to work on a new marble sculpture.

Acquires an 1860s house on Staten Island, New York, for her son Michel. He never moves in and Bourgeois turns the empty house into the sculpture *Maison Vide* c1860–1981 (no longer extant).

1982

Louise Bourgeois: Retrospective opens at MoMA, and travels to Contemporary Arts Museum, Houston; Museum of Contemporary Art, Chicago; and Akron Art Museum, Ohio, through to 1983. Curated by Deborah Wye, it is the museum's first retrospective of a woman sculptor and marks the beginning of more widespread recognition of Bourgeois's art.

Robert Miller Gallery, New York, commissions Robert Mapplethorpe to take a portrait of Bourgeois for the MoMA retrospective catalogue. Written by Wye, it is the first monographic publication on the artist. Mapplethorpe photographs Bourgeois wearing a black monkey-fur coat and cradling her sculpture *Fillette* 1968. The museum crops the sculpture out in the catalogue.

Produces *Partial Recall* in conjunction with the MoMA exhibition, a slideshow with voiceover narrative recounting her childhood and early family life. In December, *Artforum* publishes the related photo essay, 'Child abuse: a project by Louise Bourgeois'.

Exhibits new marble and bronze works in *Bourgeois Truth*, her debut at Robert Miller Gallery, New York.

1985

Attends opening of her first solo exhibition in Europe, *Louise Bourgeois: Retrospektive 1947–1984*, at Galerie Maeght-Lelong, Paris. The exhibition travels to Zürich.

In London, the Serpentine Gallery presents *Louise Bourgeois*, curated by Stuart Morgan.

1986

Bourgeois's solo exhibition at Robert Miller Gallery features *Articulated Lair* 1986, an important precursor to her Cell series.

1988

Attends the opening of *Louise Bourgeois: Works on Paper 1939–1988* at the Museum Overholland, Amsterdam, and then travels to Carrara, Italy, to work on a series of sculptures in pink marble including *Untitled (with Hand)* (pp 210–11).

1989

Works with the lithographer Judith Solodkin of SOLO Impression. Meets intaglio printers Felix Harlan and Carol Weaver of Harlan & Weaver, New York, with whom she will create multiple print editions and illustrated books until the end of her life.

Solo exhibitions are held at Galerie Lelong, Paris (*Louise Bourgeois: Dessins 1940–1986*); Robert Miller Gallery (*Louise Bourgeois: Sculpture*); Sperone-Westwater Gallery, New York (*Louise Bourgeois: Works from the 50s*); and Dia Art Foundation, Bridgehampton, New York (*Louise Bourgeois: Works from the Sixties*).

Galerie Lelong, New York, exhibits the sculpture *Clouds and Caverns* 1982–89 (pp 19, 128–29) in *Louise Bourgeois: Progressions and Regressions*, along with two works featuring staircases, *No Escape* and *No Exit*, both 1989.

Centre Georges Pompidou includes *Articulated Lair* 1986 and *Henriette* 1985 (p 238) in *Magiciens de la terre* at the Grande Halle de La Villette.

Bourgeois's first retrospective in Europe, *Louise Bourgeois: A Retrospective Exhibition*, curated by Peter Weiermair, opens at the Frankfurter Kunstverein, Frankfurt, and travels throughout Europe until 1991.

1990

Receives several awards in this decade, including the MacDowell Medal from the MacDowell Colony, New Hampshire in 1990; the Grand Prix in Sculpture by the French Ministry of Culture, 1991; the Mayor's Award for Art & Culture, New York, 1993; and the 1995 Biennial Award from the Royal Museum, Tokyo and the Hakone Open-Air Museum, Hakone, Kanagawa Prefecture, Japan.

On 27 April, Bourgeois's son Michel dies.

Discovers a pair of large, steel gas tanks at an out-of-business gas station in Staten Island and appropriates them for her monumental, mechanised sculpture *Twosome* 1991 (pp 25, 256–57).

1991

Twosome 1991 is included in *Dislocations* at MoMA, curated by Robert Storr.

Debuts six Cells in the *Carnegie International*, organised by Lynne Cooke and Mark Francis for the Carnegie Museum of Art, Pittsburgh. This series will ultimately encompass sixty works.

1992

Shows the Cell *Precious Liquids* 1992 at Documenta IX in Kassel, Germany.

Presents the installation and related performance *She Lost It* at The Fabric Workshop, Philadelphia.

1993

Represents the United States at the American Pavilion of the 45th Venice Biennale. The exhibition includes *Cell (Glass Spheres and Hands)* 1990–93 (pp 141–43) and *Cell (Arch of Hysteria)* 1992–93.

Helping Hands, a sculptural installation in honour of social and political activist Jane Addams, is permanently installed in Chicago Women's Park and Gardens.

1994

Solo museum exhibitions are held at St Louis Art Museum (*Louise Bourgeois: The Personages*) and Kestner Gesellschaft, Hanover (*Louise Bourgeois: Sculptures*).

The Brooklyn Museum, in association with The Corcoran Gallery of Art, Washington, DC, presents *The Locus of Memory*, an expanded version of Bourgeois's 1993 exhibition at the Venice Biennale; it includes Bourgeois's first large-scale *Spider* 1994. The exhibition travels to venues in the United States, Europe and Canada until 1996.

MoMA opens *The Prints of Louise Bourgeois*, curated by Deborah Wye, accompanied by the first volume of Bourgeois's print catalogue raisonné.

Louise Bourgeois: The Red Rooms opens at Peter Blum's gallery Blumarts, New York. Blum also supports several print projects with Bourgeois during this period, including *Homely Girl: A Life* 1992, her two-volume collaboration with American playwright Arthur Miller.

Begins creating what will become *The Insomnia Drawings* 1994–95, a series of 220 mixed-media drawings, made while suffering from insomnia.

1995

Louise Bourgeois: Pensées-plumes, a retrospective of drawings curated by Marie-Laure Bernadac, is held at the Musée National d'art Moderne, Centre Georges Pompidou, Paris, and travels to Helsinki, Finland. Bernadac also includes Bourgeois's spoken word work, *Otte*, and several sculptures in *Feminin-Masculin: Le Sexe de l'Art*, a group exhibition organised with Bernard Marcadé at the Centre Pompidou. Bernadac becomes a leading French scholar on Bourgeois's work.

Otte is released as a CD, accompanied by music by Satch Hoyt and Ramuntcho Matta, and produced by Brigitte Cornand. Cornand directs *Chère Louise*, a film by Les Films Du Siamois, Paris, for Canal+, and goes on to make several more films about Bourgeois.

Louise Bourgeois is on view at Museo de Arte Contemporáneo de Monterrey (MARCO), Mexico, and travels to Seville and Mexico City.

The Musée d'Art Moderne de la Ville de Paris presents *Louise Bourgeois: Sculptures, environments, dessins 1938–1995*, curated by Suzanne Pagé and Béatrice Parent, as an extension of *The Locus of Memory*.

Bourgeois and her assistant Jerry Gorovoy preparing to make a mould for a sculpture in her Brooklyn studio, New York, 1995

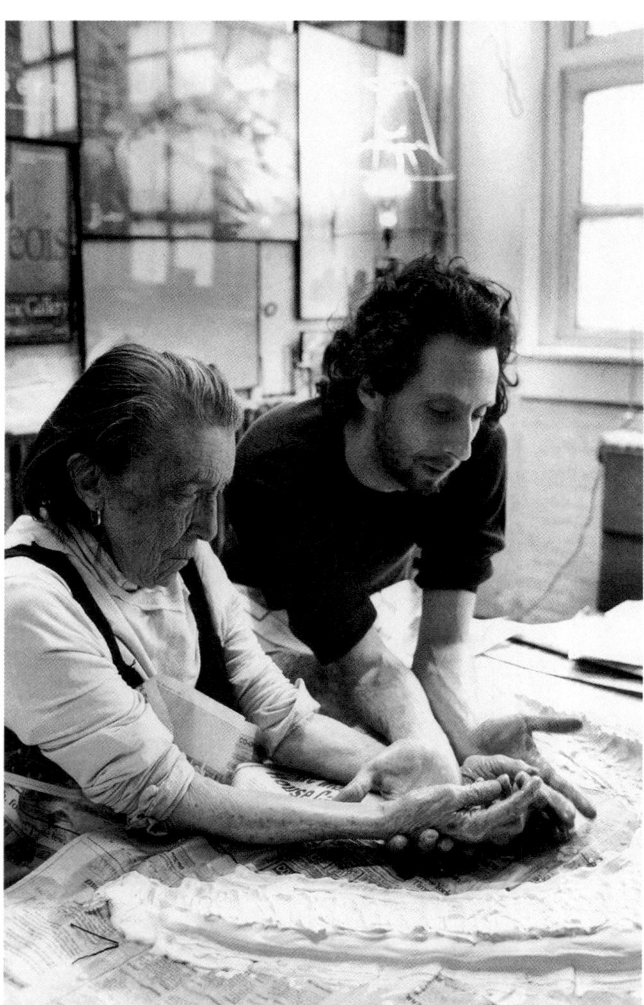

An exhibition of forty-six works by Bourgeois, curated by Jason Smith, opens at the National Gallery of Victoria, Melbourne, and travels to the Museum of Contemporary Art, Sydney.

Begins working extensively with fabric, incorporating clothing and textiles from throughout her life into her work. Garments which retain especially evocative memories of people, places or events are arranged inside the Cells and in a series of 'pole' works, in which clothes are hung at various points around a central axis. Other clothes and fabrics will be used in stuffed sculptures, such as the hanging *Couple* 2001 (pp 21, 262–63) and *Umbilical Cord* 2003 (pp 20, 189), or as pages of fabric books.

1996

Louise Bourgeois: Drawings, curated by Lawrence Rinder, is held at the Berkeley Art Museum and Pacific Film Archive of the University of California, Berkeley, and travels to The Drawing Center, New York, and the MIT List Visual Art Center, Boston. Included in *Inside the Visible*, curated by Catherine de Zegher, at The Institute of Contemporary Art, Boston. The exhibition travels to the Art Gallery of Western Australia, Perth, in 1997.

Installs four life-size fabric figures in the belltower of St Pancras Church, London, for the exhibition *The Visible and the Invisible: Re-presenting the Body in Contemporary Art and Society*, organised by the Institute of International Visual Arts.

Louise Bourgeois, curated by Paulo Herkenhoff, is presented at the XXIII International São Paulo Bienal, São Paulo. Sculptural installation *Les bienvenus* is inaugurated in a park in Choisy-le-Roi, France, where Bourgeois spent her early childhood.

Galerie Hauser & Wirth, Zurich presents *Louise Bourgeois: Red Room Installation/ Drawings*.

1997

Presented with the National Medal of Arts by President Bill Clinton at the White House; Bourgeois's son Jean-Louis accepts the award on her behalf.

Solo exhibitions are held at Fondazione Prada, Milan (*Louise Bourgeois: Blue Days and Pink Days*, curated by Pandora Tabatabai Asbaghi); and The Yokohama Museum, Japan (*Louise Bourgeois: Homesickness*, curated by Taro Amano).

Commissioned by the French Government to create a work for the new Bibliotheque Nationale de France, designed by architect Dominique Perrault. Creates *Toi et moi* 1997, a large aluminium wall relief that reflects and distorts viewers.

1998

The Musée d'Art Contemporain, Bordeaux, mounts *Louise Bourgeois*, curated by Marie-Laure Bernadac. It travels to the Belem Foundation, Lisbon; Malmö Konsthall, Sweden, and the Serpentine Gallery, London. Violette Editions, London, publishes *Louise Bourgeois: destruction of the father/reconstruction of the father, writings and interviews, 1923–1997*, edited and introduced by Bernadac and Hans Ulrich Obrist.

1999

Kunsthalle Bielefeld, Germany, presents *Louise Bourgeois*, curated by Thomas Kellein.

Participates in the 48th Venice Biennale, directed by Harald Szeemann, and is awarded the Golden Lion for a living master of contemporary art.

The Museo Nacional Centro de Arte Reina Sofía, Madrid, presents *Louise Bourgeois: Memory and Architecture*, curated by Jerry Gorovoy and Danielle Tilkin. The exhibition includes *Poids* 1992 (p 131), which will not be exhibited again until the exhibition at the Art Gallery of New South Wales in 2023.

2000

Receives several awards in this decade, including an Honorary Doctorate of Fine Arts from the Art Institute of Boston, 2000; the Wolf Prize in the Arts for Painting and Sculpture by the Wolf Foundation, Israel, 2003; the Österreichisches Ehrenzeichen für Wissenschaft und Kunst (Austrian Decoration for Science and Art), 2007; and the Aragon-Goya Award from the Goya Foundation of the Aragon Government in Zaragoza, Spain, 2008.

Commissioned by Frances Morris for the inaugural installation of Tate Modern's Turbine Hall in London. Debuts her monumental spider, *Maman* 1999, and three architectural towers: *I Do, I Undo* and *I Redo* 1999–2000, which incorporate mirrors, staircases and viewing platforms, along with smaller-scale sculptures (pp 204–06). The three towers are acquired by Château La Coste, France for permanent installation in a building designed by architect Jean Nouvel.

The Fonds National d'Art Contemporain acquires *The Welcoming Hands* 1996, for permanent installation in the Jardin des Tuileries, Paris.

The National Museum of Contemporary Art, Seoul, presents the retrospective, *Louise Bourgeois: The Space of Memory*.

2001

Exhibitions are held at the Akademie der bildenden Künste Wien, Vienna (*Louise Bourgeois: Reconstruction of the Past*); and the State Hermitage Museum, St Petersburg (*Louise Bourgeois at the Hermitage*, curated by

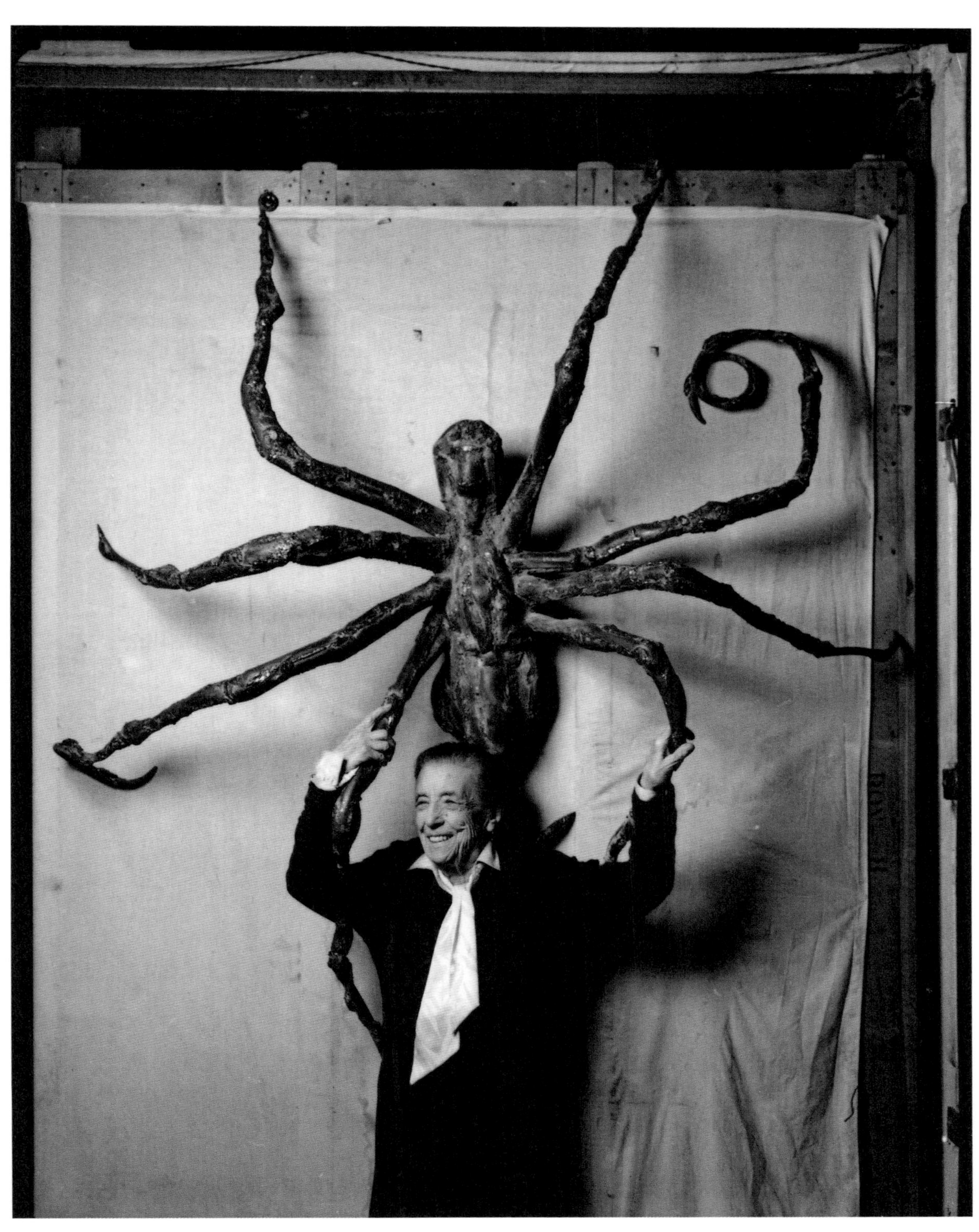

Bourgeois with *Spider IV* 1996, 1996

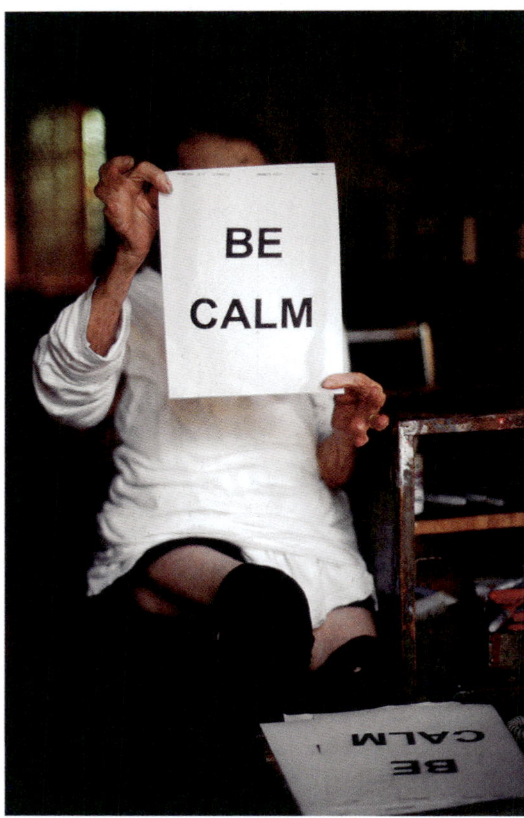

Bourgeois in her home on 20th Street, New York, 2004

Julie Sylvester). The latter exhibition travels, from 2002 to 2003, to Helsinki City Art Museum, Finland; Kulturhuset, Stockholm, Sweden; Museet for Samtidskunst, Oslo, Norway; and Louisiana Museum of Modern Art, Humlebæk, Denmark.

2002
Louise Bourgeois: The Early Work, curated by Josef Helfenstein, shows at Krannert Art Museum, University of Illinois at Urbana.

Four 'Portrait Cells' from 2000 and *The Insomnia Drawings* 1994–95 are shown at Documenta XI, Kassel.

Kunsthaus Bregenz, Austria, hosts a large presentation of drawings and sculptures, including *Spider* 1997 (pp 36, 161–63).

Palais de Tokyo, Paris, includes a sound piece, film viewing and artist's salon in *Louise Bourgeois: Le jour la nuit le jour*.

Creates the fabric book *Ode à la Bièvre* from her own clothes (pp 164–67). The abstract imagery and text reference the Bièvre river, which flowed through the garden of her childhood home. In 2007, an edition of the book is made with digital printing by Raylene Marasco of Dyenamix, New York. Works with Dyenamix on several fabric editions around this time, including the woven *I Am Afraid* 2009 (pp 260–61).

2003
Dia Center for the Arts inaugurates its new space in Beacon, New York, with a selection of Bourgeois's sculptures from the 1960s, along with *The Destruction of the Father* 1974 and *Spider* 1997. Solo exhibitions are held at the Sigmund Freud Museum, Vienna (*A View from the Outside, Louise Bourgeois: The Reticent Child*); and The Irish Museum of Modern Art, Dublin (*Louise Bourgeois: Stitches in Time*, curated by Frances Morris).

Begins working closely with Benjamin Shiff of Osiris, whom she first met in the late 1980s. Creates the first of several editions and unique printed works on large-scale printing plates designed to fit her worktable.

2004
A survey of fifty-three works is presented at Daros Exhibitions, Zürich, in *Louise Bourgeois: Emotions Abstracted*.

2005
Wifredo Lam Center, Havana, exhibits sculptures and prints in *Louise Bourgeois: One and Others*, curated by Philip Larratt-Smith. Two new hanging aluminum sculptures, both *Untitled* 2004 (p 220), and the sound piece *C'est le murmure de l'eau qui chante* 2001–03, are included in the 51st Venice Biennale. Kunshalle Wien, Vienna, presents *Louise Bourgeois: Back and Forth*.

Forced to vacate her Brooklyn studio in December. The building is demolished for redevelopment.

2006
Louise Bourgeois: Femme is presented by the Walters Art Museum in partnership with the Contemporary Museum in Baltimore, Maryland.

Kunsthalle Bielefeld, Germany, exhibits *Louise Bourgeois: La Famille*.

Bourgeois's monumental mirror work, *Art Is a Guaranty of Sanity*, is installed in the atrium of the Civic Plaza expansion, Phoenix, Arizona.

2007
Bourgeois's *Hold Me Close*, a memorial to victims of the 2004 Indian Ocean tsunami, made in collaboration with architect Alan Wanzenberg, is unveiled in Thailand's Hat Noppharat National Park.

Included in *WACK! Art and the Feminist Revolution* curated by Cornelia Butler at the Museum of Contemporary Art, Los Angeles. The exhibition travels to the National Museum of Women in the Arts, Washington, DC, PS1 Contemporary Art Center, Long Island City, New York, and Vancouver Art Gallery, British Colombia.

Louise Bourgeois: Retrospective, curated by Frances Morris, Marie-Laure Bernadac and Jonas Storsve, opens at Tate Modern, London. Travels to the Centre Pompidou, Paris; the Guggenheim Museum, New York; the Museum of Contemporary Art, Los Angeles; and the Hirshhorn Museum and Sculpture Garden, Washington, DC.

2008
Awarded the French medal of Commander of the Legion of Honour by President Nicolas Sarkozy at Bourgeois's home on 21 September.

The Museo Nazionale di Capodimonte, Naples, juxtaposes sixty of Bourgeois's works with art from its collection in *Louise Bourgeois for Capodimonte*.

Louise Bourgeois: the spider, the mistress and the tangerine, a film by Marion Cajori and Amei Wallach, debuts in the United States.

2010
Collaborates with artist Tracey Emin on a suite of fabric prints, *Do Not Abandon Me* 2009–10, and with writer Gary Indiana on a fabric book, *To Whom It May Concern* 2010.

Seven late bronzes from Bourgeois's Echo series (p 175) are included in the 17th Biennale of Sydney: *The Beauty of Distance: Songs of Survival in a Precarious Age*, curated by David Elliott.

On 31 May, Louise Bourgeois dies in New York City.

The Fondazione Vedova, Venice, presents *Louise Bourgeois: The Fabric Works*, curated by Germano Celant.

2011
Louise Bourgeois: The Return of the Repressed, curated by Philip Larratt-Smith, is shown at Fundación PROA, Buenos Aires, and travels to São Paulo and Rio de Janeiro, Brazil. The two-volume *Louise Bourgeois: the return of the repressed* is published; edited by Larratt-Smith, it features the artist's previously unpublished psychoanalytic writings.

The Damned, the Possessed and the Beloved 2007–10 is installed inside a glass pavilion designed by architect Peter Zumthor at The Steilneset Memorial in Vardø, Norway, a monument to the trial and execution of ninety-one people – mostly women – for witchcraft in the seventeenth century.

Fondation Beyeler, Basel, presents the exhibition *Louise Bourgeois: À l'infini*, curated by Ulf Küster, to mark 100 years since the artist's birth.

2012
The first survey of Bourgeois's work in the Middle East, *Louise Bourgeois: Conscious and Unconscious*, curated by Philip Larratt-Smith, opens at the Qatar Museums Authority Gallery, Doha. A condensed version of Larratt-Smith's South American exhibition *Louise Bourgeois: The Return of the Repressed* opens at the Freud Museum, London, and presents Bourgeois's artwork with an extensive selection of her psychoanalytic writings in the context of Freud's last home.

Bourgeois with her hand-coloured etching *La famille* (in progress) in her home on 20th Street, New York, 2009

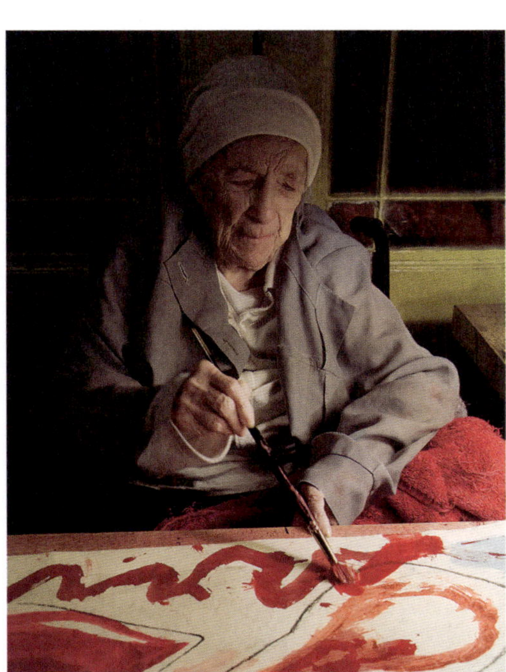

Louise Bourgeois: Late Works and *Louise Bourgeois and Australian Artists*, curated by Jason Smith and Linda Michael respectively, open as paired exhibitions at Heide Museum of Modern Art, Melbourne.

2013
The Scottish National Gallery of Art, Edinburgh, presents *Louise Bourgeois: A Woman Without Secrets*, featuring works from the ARTIST ROOMS collection assembled by Anthony D'Offay.

2015
Louise Bourgeois: I Have Been to Hell and Back, curated by Iris Müller-Westermann, opens at Moderna Museet, Stockholm and travels to Museo Picasso, Málaga, Spain.

Haus der Kunst, Munich, presents *Louise Bourgeois: Structures of Existence: The Cells*, curated by Julienne Lorz; the exhibition travels to Garage Museum of Contemporary Art, Moscow; Guggenheim Museum Bilbao, Spain; and Louisiana Museum of Modern Art, Humlebaek, Denmark.

2016
The critical biography *Intimate Geometries: The Art and Life of Louise Bourgeois* by Robert Storr is published.

2017
Solo exhibitions are held at the Tel Aviv Museum of Art, Israel (*Louise Bourgeois: Twosome*); the Museum of Modern Art, New York (*Louise Bourgeois: An Unfolding Portrait*, curated by Deborah Wye); and the San Francisco Museum of Modern Art, California (*Louise Bourgeois: Spiders*).

2018
Louise Bourgeois: To Unravel a Torment opens at Glenstone Museum, Potomac, Maryland, and travels to Museum Voorlinden, Wassenaar, Netherlands, and Fundação de Serralves, Porto, Portugal.

Solo exhibitions are presented by the Long Museum West Bund, Shanghai (*Louise Bourgeois: The Eternal Thread*, curated by Philip Larratt-Smith, travels to Beijing in 2019) and the Schinkel Pavillon, Berlin (*Louise Bourgeois: The Empty House*).

2019
The Rijksmuseum, Amsterdam, presents Bourgeois's sculptures in its gardens. *Louise Bourgeois and Pablo Picasso: Anatomies of Desire*, curated by Marie-Laure Bernadac, shows at Hauser & Wirth, Zürich.

The biography *Louise Bourgeois: Femme Couteau* by Bernadac is published.

2021
The exhibition *Louise Bourgeois: Freud's Daughter*, curated by Philip Larratt-Smith, is presented at The Jewish Museum, New York.

2022
Major exhibitions are held at the Hayward Gallery, London (*Louise Bourgeois: The Woven Child*, curated by Ralph Rugoff and Julienne Lorz; travels to Gropius Bau, Berlin); Kunstmuseum Basel, Switzerland (*Louise Bourgeois x Jenny Holzer: The Violence of Handwriting across a Page*, curated by Jenny Holzer and Anita Haldemann); and the Metropolitan Museum of Art, New York (*Louise Bourgeois: Paintings*, curated by Clare Davies, travels to the New Orleans Museum of Art, Louisiana).

On 8 December, Bourgeois's son Jean-Louis dies.

2023
In May, the National Museum, Oslo, presents *Louise Bourgeois: Imaginary Conversations*, curated by Briony Fer and Andrea Kroksnes.

In September, the Belvedere Museum, Vienna, opens *Louise Bourgeois, Persistent Antagonism*, curated by Sabine Fellner and Johanna Hofer.

On 25 November, *Louise Bourgeois: Has the Day Invaded the Night or Has the Night Invaded the Day?*, curated by Justin Paton, opens at the Art Gallery of New South Wales, Sydney. The sculpture *Maman* 1999 is presented in front of the Art Gallery's South Building.

LIST OF WORKS

Works are listed in chronological order, then alphabetical order for each year.

Dimensions are given in centimetres, height × width × depth

† Artworks exhibited but not illustrated

* Artworks in the Personages series

Bourgeois made the wood sculptures in the Personages series with the intention of later casting them in bronze. The wood versions date from 1946 to 1950; the bronze editions were cast between 1990 and 2010.

In the 1960s and later, Bourgeois made several sculptures in plaster, also with the intention of casting them in bronze. For such works, the date of creation is followed by the casting date.

Louise Bourgeois
France/USA 1911–2010

Self-portrait c1939
gouache on cardboard
44.5 × 21.6 cm
Collection The Easton Foundation, New York

Untitled 1940
oil and pencil on board
33.3 × 30.2 cm
Collection The Easton Foundation, New York

Femme maison 1946–47
oil and ink on linen
91.4 × 35.6 cm
Private collection, New York

* *Persistent Antagonism* 1946–48
painted bronze, metal, stainless steel
168.9 × 30.5 × 30.5 cm
Collection The Easton Foundation, New York

He Disappeared into Complete Silence 1947
illustrated book; nine engravings with letterpress text
25.4 × 35.6 cm each spread
Private collection, New York

St. Sébastienne 1947
watercolour and pencil on paper
27.9 × 18.4 cm
Collection The Easton Foundation, New York

C.O.Y.O.T.E. 1947–49
painted wood
137.4 × 214.5 × 28.9 cm
National Gallery of Australia, Canberra, purchased 1981

* *Black Flames* 1947–49
painted bronze, stainless steel
176.5 × 30.5 × 30.5 cm
Collection The Easton Foundation, New York

* *Corner Piece* 1947–49
painted bronze, stainless steel
217.8 × 30.5 × 30.5 cm
Collection The Easton Foundation, New York

* *Dagger Child* 1947–49
painted bronze, stainless steel
192.1 × 30.5 × 30.5 cm
Private collection, New York

* *Needle Woman* 1947–49
painted bronze, stainless steel
143.5 × 30.5 × 30.5 cm
Collection The Easton Foundation, New York

* *Observer* 1947–49
bronze, dark patina, stainless steel
193 × 71.1 × 30.5 cm
Collection The Easton Foundation, New York

* *Pillar* 1947–49
painted bronze, stainless steel
156.2 × 30.5 × 30.5 cm
Collection The Easton Foundation, New York

* *Portrait of C.Y.* 1947–49
painted bronze, nails, stainless steel
168.9 × 30.5 × 30.5 cm
Collection The Easton Foundation, New York

* *Untitled* 1947–49
painted bronze, stainless steel
162.6 × 30.5 × 30.5 cm
Collection The Easton Foundation, New York

* *Untitled* 1947–49
painted bronze, stainless steel
173.4 × 30.5 × 30.5 cm
Collection The Easton Foundation, New York

* *Woman in the Shape of a Shuttle* 1947–49
painted bronze, stainless steel
166.4 × 30.5 × 30.5 cm
Collection The Easton Foundation, New York

* *The Winged Figure* 1948
painted bronze, stainless steel
179.1 × 95.3 × 30.5 cm
Private collection, New York

* *Knife Couple* 1949
bronze, stainless steel
171.5 × 30.5 × 30.5 cm
Collection The Easton Foundation, New York

* *Quarantania III* 1949
bronze, stainless steel
151.1 × 37.5 × 34.9 cm
Private collection, New York

* *Woman with Packages* 1949
painted bronze, stainless steel
165.1 × 45.7 × 30.5 cm
Collection The Easton Foundation, New York

†* *Figure qui apporte du pain* 1950
bronze, stainless steel
154.3 × 30.5 × 30.5 cm
Collection The Easton Foundation, New York

Loose sheet of writing, c1958
printed translation of text originally written in French and English
27.9 × 21.6 cm; LB-0513
Collection Louise Bourgeois Archive, The Easton Foundation, New York

Labyrinthine Tower 1962, cast 2003
bronze
45.7 × 30.5 × 26.7 cm
Private collection, New York

Lair 1962, cast 2004
painted bronze
49.5 × 50.8 × 50.8 cm
Collection The Easton Foundation, New York

Fée couturière 1963, cast 2010
painted bronze
100.3 × 57.2 × 57.2 cm
Collection The Easton Foundation, New York

Le regard 1963
latex over fabric
12.7 × 39.4 × 36.8 cm
Collection The Easton Foundation, New York

Torso, Self-portrait 1963–64, cast 1999
painted bronze
62.9 × 40.6 × 20 cm
Collection The Easton Foundation, New York

The Quartered One 1964–65, cast 2010
bronze, dark patina
158.1 × 61 × 50.8 cm
Private collection, New York

End of Softness 1967, cast 1999
bronze, gold patina
17.8 × 51.8 × 38.7 cm
Collection The Easton Foundation, New York

Sleep II 1967
marble, wood
95.5 × 90.8 × 82 cm
Collection The Easton Foundation, New York

Unconscious Landscape 1967–68, cast 2010
bronze, black and polished patina
30.5 × 55.9 × 61 cm
Collection The Easton Foundation, New York

Clamart 1968
marble, wood
120.6 × 73.6 × 76.2 cm
Private collection, New York

Colonnata 1968
marble, wood
91.4 × 83.9 × 66 cm
Collection The Easton Foundation, New York

Hanging Janus 1968
bronze, dark and polished patina
17.5 × 27.9 × 15.9 cm
Collection The Easton Foundation, New York

Hanging Janus with Jacket 1968
bronze, dark and polished patina
27 × 52.4 × 16.2 cm
Collection The Easton Foundation, New York

Janus 1968
bronze, dark and polished patina
25.4 × 33 × 17.8 cm
Collection The Easton Foundation, New York

Janus fleuri 1968
bronze, gold patina
25.7 × 31.8 × 21.3 cm
Private collection, New York

Fillette (Sweeter Version) 1968–99
latex over fabric
55.9 × 21.6 × 22.9 cm
Collection The Easton Foundation, New York

Femme pieu c1970
painted wood, metal pins
6.4 × 6.4 × 16.5 cm
Private collection, New York

Mother and Child 1970
wax, metal pins, needles
19.1 × 12.7 × 12.7 cm
Collection The Easton Foundation, New York

Untitled c1970
paint on board
119.4 × 149.9 cm
Private collection, New York

Untitled (Hand) 1970
wax, fabric
4.4 × 19.1 × 12.7 cm
Collection The Easton Foundation, New York

Le Trani Episode 1971
plaster, latex
41.9 × 58.7 × 59.1 cm
Collection The Easton Foundation, New York

The Destruction of the Father 1974
archival polyurethane resin, wood, fabric, red light
237.8 × 362.3 × 248.6 cm
Glenstone Museum, Potomac, Maryland (exhibition copy shown; 2017)

Clouds and Caverns 1982–89
metal, wood
274.3 × 553.7 × 182.9 cm
Collection The Easton Foundation, New York, courtesy Kunstmuseum Den Haag

Shredder 1983
wood, metal, painted plaster
244 × 218.4 × 289.6 cm
Private collection, New York

Nature Study 1984–94
marble
91.4 × 40.6 × 32.4 cm
Collection The Easton Foundation, New York

Henriette 1985
bronze
152.4 × 33 × 30.5 cm
Private collection, New York

Legs 1986
rubber, steel
2 parts: 309.2 × 7.6 × 20.3 cm; 306 × 7.6 × 22.2 cm
Collection The Easton Foundation, New York

Nature Study 1986
bronze, silver nitrate patina
15.2 × 25.4 × 17.8 cm
Collection The Easton Foundation, New York

Untitled 1986
watercolour, ink, oil, charcoal and pencil on paper
60.3 × 48.3 cm
Collection The Easton Foundation, New York

Untitled (Scissors) 1986
watercolour and ink on blue paper
27.9 × 21.6 cm
Private collection, New York

I Love You 1987
ink on graph paper
26.7 × 20.3 cm
Private collection, New York

I Love You Do You Love Me 1987
ink on graph paper
26.7 × 20.3 cm
Private collection, New York

I Love You Do You Love Me? 1987
ink and pencil on paper
27.9 × 19.4 cm
Private collection, New York

I Love You Even If You Don't Love Me 1987
ink on graph paper
26.7 × 20.3 cm
Private collection, New York

Le Suicide Threat 1987
watercolour and ink on paper
30.5 × 15.2 cm
Collection The Easton Foundation, New York

Untitled (with Hand) 1989
marble
78.7 × 77.5 × 53.3 cm
Private collection, New York

My Blue Sky 1989–2003
gouache, watercolour, ink, pencil and coloured pencil on paper mounted to wood and glass window frame
70.5 × 58.4 × 15.9 cm
Private collection, New York

Ventouse 1990
marble, glass, electric light
86.4 × 198.1 × 81.3 cm
Collection The Easton Foundation, New York

Cell (Glass Spheres and Hands) 1990–93
glass, iron, wood, linoleum, canvas, marble
219.5 × 218.8 × 220 cm
National Gallery of Victoria, Melbourne, purchased with the assistance of the Leslie Moira Henderson Bequest, 1995

Breasts and Blade 1991
bronze, silver nitrate and polished patina
27.9 × 81.3 × 81.3 cm blade open
Private collection, New York

Le Trani Episode 1991
alabaster, electric light
25.4 × 40.6 × 38.1 cm
Collection The Easton Foundation, New York

Twosome 1991
painted steel, electric light, motor
190.5 × 1244.6 × 193 cm
Collection The Easton Foundation, New York

Le défi II 1992
steel, glass, electric light
200.7 × 179.7 × 59.7 cm
Collection The Easton Foundation, New York

Poids 1992
steel, glass, metal
485.1 × 327.7 × 61.6 cm
Private collection, New York

Arch of Hysteria 1993
bronze, polished patina
83.8 × 101.6 × 58.4 cm
Collection The Easton Foundation, New York

Arched Figure 1993, cast 2010
bronze, fabric, wood
116.8 × 193 × 99.1 cm
Art Gallery of New South Wales, purchased with funds provided by the Art Gallery of New South Wales Foundation 2016

Untitled (no. 7) 1993
bronze, silver nitrate patina
12.1 × 68.6 × 43.2 cm
Collection The Easton Foundation, New York

Spider IV 1996
bronze
203.2 × 180.3 × 53.3 cm
Collection The Easton Foundation, New York

Untitled (I Have Been to Hell and Back) 1996
embroidered handkerchief
49.5 × 45.7 cm
Private collection, New York

Spider 1997
steel, tapestry, wood, glass, fabric, rubber, silver, gold, bone
449.6 × 665.5 × 518.2 cm
Collection The Easton Foundation, New York

Untitled (Broom Woman) 1997
steel, steel welds, wood broom head, fabric
162.6 × 61 × 33 cm
Private collection, courtesy Hauser & Wirth Collection Services

Culprit Number Two 1998
painted steel, steel, wood, glass, lead, mirror
381 × 289.6 × 335.3 cm
Collection The Easton Foundation, New York

Merci Mercy 1999
lead, steel
26 × 21 × 1.3 cm
Private collection, New York

Repairs in the Sky 1999
lead, steel, fabric, thread
45.7 × 66 × 1.6 cm
Private collection, New York

Topiary IV 1999
steel, fabric, beads, wood
68.6 × 53.3 × 43.2 cm
Private collection, New York

Untitled 1999
fabric, wood, metal
64.8 × 20.3 × 30.5 cm
Private collection, New York

Maman 1999
bronze, silver nitrate patina, stainless steel, marble
927.1 × 891.5 × 1023.6 cm
Collection The Easton Foundation, New York

I Redo (interior element) 1999–2000
steel, glass, wood, tapestry
49.5 × 31.8 × 31.8 cm
Collection Château La Coste, France

I Undo (interior element) 1999–2000
steel, glass, wood, enamel
43.2 × 31.8 × 31.8 cm
Collection Château La Coste, France

Cell X (Portrait) 2000
steel, glass, wood, fabric
194.9 × 122.6 × 122.6 cm
Private collection, New York

Untitled 2000
fabric, stainless steel
154.9 × 30.5 × 30.5 cm
Private collection, New York

Couple 2001
fabric
50.8 × 16.5 × 7.6 cm
Private collection, New York

Hysterical 2001
fabric, stainless steel
45.7 × 20.3 × 15.9 cm
Collection The Easton Foundation, New York

The Cold of Anxiety 2001
fabric, steel
208.3 × 30.5 × 25.4 cm
Private collection, New York

The Found Child 2001
fabric
30.5 × 68.6 × 40.6 cm
Collection The Easton Foundation, New York

The Needle 2001
ink and pencil on paper
27.9 × 21.6 cm
Collection The Easton Foundation, New York

I Held His Eyes within My Gaze 2002
lithograph on fabric
15.2 × 15.2 cm
Collection The Easton Foundation, New York

Sublimation 2002
illustrated book; charcoal, pencil, coloured pencil, oil stick, acrylic, tempera, gouache, watercolour, ink, steel and paper collage, 15 pages
104.6 × 147.8 cm each
Collection The Easton Foundation, New York

The Couple 2002
glass, fabric, steel
41.9 × 43.2 × 33.7 cm
Collection The Easton Foundation, New York

The Woven Child 2002
fabric, steel, aluminium
23.5 × 20.3 × 20.3 cm
Private collection, New York

Crouching Spider 2003
bronze, brown and polished patina, stainless steel
270.5 × 835.7 × 627.4 cm
Collection The Easton Foundation, New York

The Couple 2003
aluminium
365.1 × 200 × 109.9 cm
Private collection, New York

The Good Mother 2003
fabric, thread, stainless steel, wood, glass
109.2 × 45.7 × 38.1 cm sculpture and stand;
196.9 × 106.7 × 86.4 cm vitrine
Collection The Easton Foundation, New York

Umbilical Cord 2003
fabric, stainless steel
44.8 × 30.5 × 30.5 cm
Private collection, New York

Arch of Hysteria 2004
fabric
12.7 × 51.4 × 22.9 cm
Collection Posten Moderne, Trondheim, Norway

Heart 2004
rubber, stainless steel, metal, thread, plastic, wood, cardboard
59.1 × 48.3 × 29.2 cm
Collection The Easton Foundation, New York

The Hidden Past 2004
fabric, wood, stainless steel
226.1 × 76.2 × 76.2 cm
Private collection, New York

Untitled 2004
aluminium
166.4 × 106.7 × 63.5 cm
Collection The Easton Foundation, New York

Untitled 2005
fabric, stainless steel
172.1 × 30.5 × 30.5 cm
Private collection, New York

Untitled 2006
fabric, fabric collage, embroidery
173.4 × 99.1 cm
Collection The Easton Foundation, New York

10 AM Is When You Come to Me 2007
etching suite with hand additions in watercolour, gouache and pencil, 40 sheets
38.1 × 91.4 cm each
Private collection, New York

Echo X 2007
painted bronze, steel
233.7 × 48.3 × 30.5 cm
Collection The Easton Foundation, New York

Has the Day Invaded the Night or Has the Night Invaded the Day? 2007
aluminium, stainless steel, steel, diodes
581.7 × 320 × 299.7 cm
Private collection, New York

Ode à la Bièvre 2007
illustrated book: digital prints and screenprint on fabric, 25 pages
29.2 × 38.1 cm each
Private collection, New York

Self-portrait 2007
bronze, silver nitrate patina
45.7 × 66.7 × 40.6 cm
Collection The Easton Foundation, New York

The Arrival 2007
fabric, glass, wood, stainless steel
10.2 × 29.8 × 12.1 cm sculpture;
30.5 × 41.9 × 34.3 cm glass dome
Collection The Easton Foundation, New York

† *The Feeding* 2007
gouache on paper
59.7 × 45.7 cm
Collection The Easton Foundation, New York

The Feeding 2007
gouache on paper
45.4 × 59.7 cm
Collection The Easton Foundation, New York

† *The Feeding* 2007
gouache on paper
59.7 × 45.7 cm
Collection The Easton Foundation, New York

† *The Feeding* 2007
gouache on paper
45.7 × 59.7 cm
Collection The Easton Foundation, New York

The Feeding 2007
gouache on paper
59.7 × 45.7 cm
Collection The Easton Foundation, New York

The Feeding 2007
gouache on paper
59.7 × 45.7 cm
Collection The Easton Foundation, New York

The Feeding 2007
gouache on paper
45.7 × 59.7 cm
Collection The Easton Foundation, New York

The Waiting Hours 2007
fabric collage, 12 parts
38.4 × 31.1 cm each
Sammlung Goetz, München

Where My Motivation Comes From 2007
etching with hand additions in ink and pencil
149.9 × 99.7 cm
Private collection, courtesy Hauser & Wirth

Conscious and Unconscious
2008
fabric, rubber, thread, stainless steel, wood, glass
175.3 × 94 × 47 cm sculpture and stand; 224.8 × 167.6 × 94 cm vitrine
Collection The Easton Foundation, New York

À l'infini 2008–09
etching suite with hand additions in watercolour, gouache, pencil, coloured pencil and ink on paper, 16 sheets
101.6 × 152.4 cm each
ARTIST ROOMS: Tate and National Galleries of Scotland
Lent by Artist Rooms Foundation 2013

Eugénie Grandet 2009
collage suite; embroidery, metal, plastic, glass, drypoint, aquatint and digital print on fabric, 16 sheets
30.5 × 21.6 × 1.9 cm each
Collection The Easton Foundation, New York

I Am Afraid 2009
woven fabric mounted on stretcher
110.5 × 182.9 cm
Private collection, New York

Untitled 2009
fabric, wood
44.5 × 27.9 × 24.1 cm
Collection The Easton Foundation, New York

Jenny Holzer
USA b1950

Bourgeois X Holzer Projections
2023
light projection
Commissioned by the Art Gallery of New South Wales with the support of The Easton Foundation for *Louise Bourgeois: Has the Day Invaded the Night or Has the Night Invaded the Day?* 2023
© Jenny Holzer/Artist Rights Society (ARS), New York/ Copyright Agency 2023

Excerpts from Louise Bourgeois's personal writings are used in *Bourgeois X Holzer Projections* 2023 with permission of the Louise Bourgeois Archive and © The Easton Foundation/VAGA at Artist Rights Society (ARS), New York. Projected writings reproduced in this catalogue: loose sheet of writing, c1959 (LB-0768) (p 214); loose sheet of writing, 29 Sep 1955 (LB-0126) (p 228); diary entry, 20 Sep 1947 (p 258).

Kali Malone
USA/Sweden b1994

The Spear 2023
sound recording
4:15 min
Recorded with the meantone baroque organ at Örgryte Nya Kyrka in Gothenburg, Sweden
Additional organ accompaniment by Anna Von Hausswolff

The Spiral 2023
sound recording
4:42 min
Recorded with the meantone baroque organ at Örgryte Nya Kyrka in Gothenburg, Sweden
Additional organ accompaniment by Anna Von Hausswolff

The Spider 2023
sound recording
8:51 min
Recorded with the meantone Düben organ at the German Church in Stockholm, Sweden

The Wheel 2023
sound recording
4:38 min
Recorded with the meantone St Petri Organ at Malmö Konstmuseum in Malmö, Sweden

The Ladder 2023
sound recording
3:44 min
Recorded with the meantone St Petri Organ at Malmö Konstmuseum in Malmö, Sweden

The Field 2023
sound recording
25 min
Recorded with the meantone St Petri Organ at Malmö Konstmuseum in Malmö, Sweden

Commissioned by the Art Gallery of New South Wales for *Louise Bourgeois: Has the Day Invaded the Night or Has the Night Invaded the Day?* 2023; *The Spear*, *The Spiral*, *The Spider*, *The Wheel* and *The Ladder* sound recordings presented in 'Day', *The Field* sound recording presented in 'Night'
© Kali Malone

Film and audio

The exhibition *Louise Bourgeois: Has the Day Invaded the Night or Has the Night Invaded the Day?* 2023 features excerpts from the following films:

Louise Bourgeois: on sublimation, 1991, dir Jacqueline Kaess-Farquet, courtesy Independent Art Films JKF

Louise Bourgeois: the spider, the mistress and the tangerine, 2008, dirs Marion Cajori & Amei Wallach © Art Kaleidoscope Foundation, New York

Louise Bourgeois: no trespassing, 1994, dir Nigel Finch, edited by Anthony Wall, produced by Arena Films, reproduced courtesy of the British Broadcasting Corporation

Excerpt from Louise Bourgeois's performance *A Banquet / A Fashion Show of Body Parts* (featuring Suzan Cooper), staged in the installation *Confrontation*, Hamilton Gallery of Contemporary Art, New York, 21 Oct 1978, filmed by Theresa LoSchiavo © The Easton Foundation, New York

The exhibition also includes sound recordings of Louise Bourgeois singing children's songs and melodies, including 'C'est le murmure de l'eau qui chante' and Brahms' 'Lullaby'.
Sound recordings, 5 Dec 2000 (AV.01058_01-02_s02; s03; s04)
Sound recordings, date unknown (AV.01246_01-02_s01; 02-02_s01)
Collection Louise Bourgeois Archive, The Easton Foundation, New York

CREDITS

Bourgeois's artworks are photographed by Christopher Burke, unless otherwise noted.

Works

dust jacket, pp 6–7, 210–11, 216–17, 222–23, 228, 230–31, 236–37, 242–43, 250–51, 256–57, 258, 262–63: Ring Studio (concepts)
pp 22, 36, 161–63, 239: Photos: Maximilian Geuter
pp 23, 211, 218–19: Photos: Peter Bellamy
p 25: Photo: Jiaxi Yang and Zhe Zho
pp 38, 139, 216–17: Photos: JJYPHOTO
pp 39, 145: Photos: Jonathan Leijonhufvud
pp 89–91, 94–95, 171–73, 222–25, 232–33: Photos: Ron Amstutz
pp 96–97: Photo: National Gallery of Australia
p 105: Photo: Robert Newcombe
pp 113, 115: Photos: Allan Finkelman
pp 120–21: Photo: François Fernandez
p 131: Photo: Georges Poncet
pp 141–43: Photos: National Gallery of Victoria
pp 176–83: Photos: Benjamin Shiff
pp 214, 228, 258: Artwork © Jenny Holzer, photos: Art Gallery of New South Wales, Felicity Jenkins
pp 221, 241: Photos: Art Gallery of New South Wales, Felicity Jenkins
p 227: Photo: Adam Rzepka
pp 256–57: Photo: Elad Sarig

Illustrations

p 1: Photo © Yann Charbonnier, ADAGP/Copyright Agency, 2023
p 23: Louise Bourgeois *The Trauma of Abandonment* 2001 (detail, no 1 of 12), illustrated book; digital prints on fabric with thread additions, 12 pages, 25.4 × 15.2 cm each (approx), private collection
p 26: Louise Bourgeois, diary entry, 7 February 1995, ink and pencil on bound page, 20 × 13.7 cm, Collection Louise Bourgeois Archive, The Easton Foundation, New York
p 39: Louise Bourgeois *Knife Figure* 2002, fabric, steel, wood, 22.2 × 76.2 × 19.1 cm, Collection The Easton Foundation, New York
p 45: Photo: Mark Setteducati
p 47: Louise Bourgeois, poster for *Scenes from an almost socialist marriage* by Suzan Cooper and Chris Kraus, Performing Garage, New York, 1978, 35.6 × 50.8 cm (LBE-0225), Collection Louise Bourgeois Archive, The Easton Foundation, New York
p 49: (top and bottom) Images © Charles Deering McCormick Library of Special Collections Northwestern University, photos: Peter Moore
p 50: Photo © Jean-François Jaussaud
p 53: Louise Bourgeois, loose sheet of writing, c2008, crayon on paper, 22.9 × 30.5 cm (LB-0516), Collection Louise Bourgeois Archive, The Easton Foundation, New York
p 54: Image courtesy Tate Modern, photo: Marcus Leith
p 57: (top) Courtesy Moviestore Collection Ltd/Alamy Stock Photo; (bottom) Courtesy Cross City Films Limited 2021/Netflix
p 58: (top) Courtesy Pathé Pictures International and Jan Chapman Films; (bottom) Louise Bourgeois *High Heels* 1998, fabric, steel, 35.6 × 74.9 × 20.3 cm, private collection
p 63: Louise Bourgeois, loose sheet of writing, 3 December 1951, typewritten in black ink on off-white paper, 27.9 × 21.6 cm (LB-0454), Collection Louise Bourgeois Archive, The Easton Foundation, New York
p 267: Photo: Studio Fotografico, I. Bessi, Carrara
p 269: (top) Photo: Mark Setteducati; (bottom) Courtesy the estate of Mary Beth Edelson and David Lewis Gallery, photo © Estate of Mary Beth Edelson
p 270: (top) Photo: Allan Finkelman; (bottom) Photo © Peter Bellamy
p 272: Photo © Jean-François Jaussaud
p 273: Photo © Peter Bellamy
p 274: Photo: Pouran Esrafily
p 275: Photo © Alex Van Gelder

'Has the day invaded the night or has the night invaded the day?': Louise Bourgeois's unending search
Justin Paton

1
Statements by Bourgeois drawn on in this paragraph include: 'We're made of completely contrary elements, opposed elements; and this produces formidable tensions', in Alain Kirili, 'The passion for sculpture: a conversation with Louise Bourgeois', *Arts*, vol 63, no 7, Mar 1989, reprinted in Marie-Lauer Bernadac & Hans Ulrich Obrist (eds), *Louise Bourgeois: destruction of the father/ reconstruction of the father, writings and interviews 1923–1997*, Violette Editions, London, 1998, p 183; 'I refuse to choose. I am a woman of emotion who still pines to be a woman of rationality – I am torn between the two, and I have learned to accept them both', in 'On beauty: a conversation with Bill Beckley', in Bernadac & Obrist, p 357; 'The purpose of sculpture is really self-knowledge', in *Louise Bourgeois: the spider, the mistress and the tangerine*, 2008, dirs Marion Cajori & Amei Wallach, film © Art Kaleidoscope Foundation, New York; 'My knives are like a tongue – I love you, I hate you. If you don't love me, I am ready to attack. They're very double-edged', in Bourgeois, 'Self-expression is sacred and fatal: statements' in Christiane Meyer-Thoss, *Louise Bourgeois: designing for free fall*, Amman Verlag, Zurich, 1992, p 178; 'The work is a pendulum and a guarantee that you are a sociable being', in *Louise Bourgeois*, video interview by Kate Horsfield & Lyn Blumenthal, Video Data Bank, School of the Art Institute of Chicago, 1975.

2
Louise Bourgeois, diary entry, 7 Feb 1995, Collection Louise Bourgeois Archive, The Easton Foundation, New York (hereafter cited as The Easton Foundation).

3
Bourgeois, in *Reclaiming the body: feminist art in America*, 1995, dir Michael Blackwood, film © Michael Blackwood Productions Inc, 1995.

4
Jerry Gorovoy, comment made during panel discussion, 'Knots and sutures', presented in association with the exhibition *Louise Bourgeois: The Eternal Thread*, Long Museum, Shanghai, 2 Nov 2018.

5
'Taking cover: interview with Stuart Morgan', *Artscribe*, Jan 1988, reprinted in Bernadac & Obrist, p 152. A lair, Bourgeois continued, 'is a place to go, a place you need to go, a transitory protection'.

6
'[Janus] is symmetrical, like the human body, and it has the scale of those various parts of the body to which it may, perhaps, refer: a double facial mask, two breasts, two knees. Its hung position indicates passivity but its low slung mass expresses resistance and duration. It is perhaps a self-portrait – one of many.' Bourgeois in *Art Now: New York*, vol 1, no 7, Sep 1969; LBE-0042, The Easton Foundation.

7
Bourgeois, diary entry, 14 Sep 1950, The Easton Foundation: 'Exile or alienation is a necessary (not sufficient tho) condition of work'; reprinted in Bernadac & Obrist, p 57.

8
Bourgeois, quoted in Susi Bloch, 'Interview with Louise Bourgeois', *The Art Journal*, vol 35, no 41, reprinted in Bernadac & Obrist, pp 106–07. The exhibitions referred to were: *Louise Bourgeois, Recent Work 1947–1949: Seventeen Standing Figures in Wood* (3–29 Oct) and *Louise Bourgeois: Sculptures* (2–28 Oct).

9
Bourgeois, quoted in 'Two conversations with Deborah Wye', in Bernadac & Obrist, p 123. In June 1945 Bourgeois organised the exhibition *Documents France 1940–1944: Art–Literature–Press of the French Underground* at Norlyst Gallery, New York.

10
For 'the tension of their relations', see Bourgeois, in '10 artists in the margin', *Design Quarterly*, no 30, Walker Art Center, Minneapolis, 1954, reprinted in Bernadac & Obrist, p. 66.

11
Bourgeois, loose sheet of writing, 29 Sep 1955, LB-0126, The Easton Foundation. Reproduced in Philip Larratt-Smith, *Louise Bourgeois: Freud's daughter*, Jewish Museum, New York & Yale University Press, New Haven & London, 2021, p 21.

12
Joan Acocella, 'The spider's web', *New Yorker*, 4 Feb 2002, p 75.

13
Lucy Lippard, 'Louise Bourgeois: from the inside out', *Artforum*, vol 13, no 7, Mar 1975, pp 26–33.

14
'The tailor-bird is a little bird. The title was French right from the start. It's a piece with holes, several floors, and is like a labyrinth. You can put your hand in it, and you don't know which is the entrance and which is the exit. It's a bird's nest hanging in a tree.' Bourgeois, quoted in Marie-Laure Bernadac, *Louise Bourgeois*, Flammarion, Paris, 2006, p 100.

15
Bourgeois, loose sheet of writing, c1968, LB-1187, The Easton Foundation, reprinted in Bernadac & Obrist, pp 75–76.

16
Bourgeois quoted in Kirili 1989, reprinted in Bernadac & Obrist, p 184.

17
This letter, written to Museum of Modern Art director William Rubin and dated 6 June 1973, states that 'In quality and in length of creative endeavor Bourgeois ranks with the best American sculptors.' Its nineteen signatories include Joyce Kozloff, Lucy Lippard, Mary Miss, Linda Nochlin, Howardena Pindell, Sylvia Sleigh and Joan Snyder. LL-0214, The Easton Foundation.

18
Kate Horsfield & Lyn Blumenthal, *Louise Bourgeois*, Video Data Bank, School of the Art Institute of Chicago, 1975.

19
Sylvia Plath, from 'Totem', in *Ariel*, Faber & Faber, London, 1965, p 76. The dinner party honouring Bourgeois took place at Mary Beth Edelson's loft at 110 Mercer Street, Soho, on 14 Mar 1979.

20
Bourgeois quoted in Cindy Nemser, 'Forum: women in art', *Arts Magazine*, Feb 1971, vol 15, p 18.

21
Bourgeois, quoted in 'Taking cover: interview with Stuart Morgan', reprinted in Bernadac & Obrist, pp 155–56.

22
Bourgeois, 'Self-expression is sacred and fatal: statements', in Meyer-Thoss 1992, p 178.

23
Bourgeois, in Kirili 1989, reprinted in Bernadac & Obrist, p 184.

24
Bourgeois, 'Freud's toys', in *Artforum*, vol 28, no 5, Jan 1990, p 113; reprinted in Larratt-Smith 2021, p 150.

25
Larratt-Smith, *Louise Bourgeois: the eternal thread*, The Long Museum & Shanghai Fine Arts Publishing, Shanghai, 2018, p 18.

26
'My mother would sit out in the sun and repair a tapestry or a petit point. She really loved it. This sense of reparation is very deep within me.' Bourgeois in 'Self-expression is sacred and fatal: statements' in Meyer-Thoss 1992, p 187.

27
Robert Storr discusses Bourgeois and Brâncuși, creator of the *Endless column*, in *Intimate geometries: the art and life of Louise Bourgeois*, Thames & Hudson, London, 2016, pp 35, 298.

28
Bourgeois, in *Louise Bourgeois: no trespassing*, 1994, dir Nigel Finch, Arena Films, BBC, quoted in Bernadac & Obrist, p 258.

29
Rachel Cusk, *A life's work*, Faber & Faber, London, 2001, p 101. Cusk's comment about motherhood as a primal version of all separations appears on p 3.

30
Bourgeois, loose sheet of writing, Apr–May 1959, LB-0877, The Easton Foundation; Bourgeois, loose sheet of writing, Jan 1961, LB-0668, The Easton Foundation; and Bourgeois, loose sheet of writing, 22 Dec 1963, LB-0302, The Easton Foundation. Italics used here and in later quotations indicate passages translated from French in Bourgeois's original.

31
Storr describes the congested basement studio in Storr 2016, p 305.

32
'So when I talk about storage, I mean that I have kept and taken care of these pieces for years and years, and I never left them, the way I left my family.' Bourgeois, in 'Interview with Trevor Rots', 1990, in Bernadac & Obrist, p 195.

33
In *Louise Bourgeois in New York* 1991, dir Jacqueline Kaess-Farquet, documentary film.

34
Bourgeois, in Donald Kuspit, *An interview with Louise Bourgeois*, Elizabeth Avedon Editions, Vintage Contemporary Artists, New York, 1988, pp 31–32: 'I don't dream. You might say I work under a spell. I truly value the spell. I have the privilege of being able to enter the spell, to enter this very arid land where you are likely to find your birthright ... The spell and the dream are not the same. The spell is more friendly than the dream. The "spell" is acted out on a physical level; it's not a passive state, like a dream. The dream blinds you; the spell does not. It is a friendly process.'

35
Bourgeois, 'Self-expression is sacred and fatal: statements', in Meyer-Thoss 1992, p 185.

36
Bourgeois, loose sheet of writing, c1965, LB-1441, The Easton Foundation, published as 'On the creative process' in Bernadac & Obrist, p 74.

37
Larratt-Smith 2021, p 112.

38
Adam Phillips, *Promises, promises: essays on literature and psychoanalysis*, Faber & Faber, London, 2000, p 322.

39
Bourgeois, in transcribed conversation with Jerry Gorovoy, c1990s, LB-0045, The Easton Foundation.

40
Bourgeois, quoted in 'Taking cover: interview with Stuart Morgan', in Bernadac & Obrist, p 154.

41
'My relation to the war appears in the work by the use of black, the black of the war, which was the black of mourning ... What the war meant to me was that suddenly ... I saw everything in black, black coffins, black legs, black people. It was the deep mourning of the war. It is as simple as that.' Bourgeois, quoted in 'Two conversations with Deborah Wye', in Bernadac & Obrist, p 123.

42
'My mother had emphysema, a chronic lung disease, and I treated her with cupping and poultices. Hence my obsession with the business of medical treatment.' Bourgeois, in conversation with Bernard Marcadé, in *Louise Bourgeois*, 1993, dir Camille Guichard, film, Terra Luna Productions, Paris, quoted in Bernadac & Obrist, p 249. Larratt-Smith's coffin comparison is in *Louise Bourgeois: Freud's daughter*, 2021, p 112.

43
'I have not failed as a truth seeker.' Bourgeois, loose sheet of writing, c1959, LB-0129, The Easton Foundation; Bourgeois, loose sheet of writing, Mar–Apr 1964, LB-0188, The Easton Foundation.

44
The sculptures *The She-Fox* 1985 and *Nature Study* 1984–94 (p 113) rework a plaster cast of a hunting dog that Bourgeois found in a dumpster near Modern Art Foundry in Queens. Jan Garden Castro makes the connection with the sphinxes that flank the marble Throne of Cérès in the collection of the Louvre Museum in 'Louise Bourgeois: turning myths inside out', *Sculpture*, 1 Jan 2000, sculpturemagazine.art/louise-bourgeois-turning-myths-inside-out. See also collections.louvre.fr/en/ark:/53355/cl010277577. Sites accessed 21 May 2023.

45
Bourgeois's self-portrait as cat is best savoured alongside her comment that 'In real life, I feel like the mouse behind the radiator.' Bourgeois in 'Self-expression is sacred and fatal: statements' in Meyer-Thoss 1992, p 195.

46
Bourgeois, in Eleanor Munro (ed), *Originals: American women artists*, Simon and Schuster, New York, 1979, pp 166–67.

47
Plath 1965, p 56.

48
On Bourgeois in the context of feminism and the women's art movement, see *WACK! art and the feminist revolution*, Museum of Contemporary Art, Los Angeles & MIT Press, Cambridge, MA & London, 2007.

49
Mary Beth Edelson, typewritten record of the guest list, menu and entertainment at the party in honour of Bourgeois on 14 Mar 1979. Thanks to Joyce Kozloff for providing a copy of this document.

50
Storr 2016, p 107.

51
Phyllida Barlow, 'The sneeze of Louise', in *Objects for, and other things: Phyllida Barlow*, Black Dog Publishing, London, 2004, pp 168–75.

52
Bourgeois, loose sheet of writing, c1961, LB-0019, The Easton Foundation.

53
'It is not conscious motivation. It is unconscious motivation. After a work is finished, then you say, Ah, my God! This is what I meant.' Bourgeois, in her illustrated book *Album* 1994, p 69.

54
Bourgeois, 'Freud's toys', *Artforum*, vol 28, no 5, Jan 1990, p 113, reprinted in Larratt-Smith 2021, p 151.

55
Bourgeois, loose sheet of writing, c1957, LB-0251, The Easton Foundation.

56
'Life force' is the artist's phrase. Of the raw block of stone, she said to Donald Kuspit, 'I take it over with my fantasy, my life force.' Kuspit 1988, p 59.

'It comes back again and again': on Louise Bourgeois and psychoanalysis
Jamieson Webster

1
Louise Bourgeois, in transcribed conversation with Jerry Gorovoy, c1992, LB-0837, Collection Louise Bourgeois Archive, The Easton Foundation, New York (hereafter cited as The Easton Foundation).

2
Bourgeois, loose sheet of writing, c1958, LB-0127, The Easton Foundation.

3
Bourgeois, in transcribed conversation with Gorovoy, Sep 1990, LB-0051, The Easton Foundation.

4
Bourgeois, loose sheet of writing, c1995, LB-2172, The Easton Foundation. The italics here and in later quotations indicate passages translated from French in Bourgeois's original; punctuation and line breaks have been retained as closely as possible. Translations from French to English are by Richard Sieburth and Françoise Gramet.

5
Bourgeois, in transcribed conversation with Gorovoy, c1992, LB-0837, The Easton Foundation.

6
For a full list of psychoanalytic thinkers read by Bourgeois, see Philip Larratt-Smith, 'The case of LB', in *Louise Bourgeois: Freud's daughter*, Jewish Museum, New York & Yale University Press, New Haven & London, 2021, p 105.

7
Bourgeois, in transcribed conversation with Gorovoy, Sep 1990, LB-0051, The Easton Foundation.

8
Bourgeois, diary entry, 2 Sep 1994, The Easton Foundation.

9
Bourgeois, in transcribed conversation with Gorovoy, 1994, LB-2191, The Easton Foundation. In a filmed interview by Kate Horsfield and Lyn Blumenthal in 1975, Bourgeois says of the surrealists: 'I objected to them violently ... I objected to their lordly manner, to their success, to their pontificality. Well, considering my running away from home, from my country and from my father, it was obvious that any father figures appearing from France onto these shores was going to rub me the wrong way.' Video Data Bank, School of the Art Institute of Chicago, 1975.

10
Unpublished interview with Nena Dimitrijević, 1994, The Easton Foundation.

11
Dimitrijević interview, 1994.

12
Bourgeois, excerpt from a notebook, p 1, 29 Oct 1995; LB-0827, The Easton Foundation.

13
Bourgeois, loose sheet of writing, 29 Jan 1958; LB-0272, The Easton Foundation.

14
Bourgeois, diary entry, 19 Jul 1988, The Easton Foundation.

15
Bourgeois, diary entry, 8 Mar 1985, The Easton Foundation.

16
Bourgeois, writing on verso of her 1947 Norlyst Gallery exhibition announcement, date unknown, LB-0689, The Easton Foundation.

The heart of something: an interview with Chris Kraus
Justin Paton

1
Bourgeois, loose sheet of writing, c2008, LB-0516, Collection Louise Bourgeois Archive, The Easton Foundation, New York.

Night mind: Louise Bourgeois's dream recordings
Selected by Philip Larratt-Smith

1
Bourgeois in Donald Kuspit, *An interview with Louise Bourgeois*, Elizabeth Avedon Editions, Vintage Contemporary Artists, New York, 1988, pp 31–32.

2
Louise Bourgeois, loose sheet of writing, 8 Feb 1952, LB-0467, Collection Louise Bourgeois Archive, The Easton Foundation, New York (hereafter cited as The Easton Foundation).

3
Christiane Meyer-Thoss, *Louise Bourgeois: designing for free fall*, Ammann Verlag, Zurich, 1992, p 122.

4
Bourgeois, diary entry, 11 Sep 1980, The Easton Foundation.

SELECTED BIBLIOGRAPHY

Bernadac, Marie-Laure. *Louise Bourgeois: femme couteau*, Flammarion, Paris, 2019

——— (ed). *Louise Bourgeois and Pablo Picasso: anatomies of desire*, exh cat, Hauser & Wirth Publishers, Zurich, 2019

Bernadac, Marie-Laure & Hans Ulrich Obrist (eds). *Louise Bourgeois: destruction of the father/reconstruction of the father, writings and interviews, 1923–1997*, Violette Editions, London, 1998

Celant, Germano. *Louise Bourgeois: the fabric works*, exh cat, Skira, Milan & New York, in association with Fondazione Emilio e Annabianca Vedova, Venice, 2010

Davies, Clare & Briony Fer. *Louise Bourgeois: paintings*, exh cat, The Metropolitan Museum of Art, New York, 2022

Fellner, Sabine & Johanna Hofer. *Louise Bourgeois, persistent antagonism*, exh cat, with texts by Bice Curiger, Sabine Fellner, Johanna Hofer, Ulf Küster and John Yau, Belvedere Museum, Vienna, 2023

Gorovoy, Jerry & Danielle Tilkin. *Louise Bourgeois: memory and architecture*, exh cat, with texts by Mieke Bal, Jennifer Bloomer, Beatriz Colomina, Lynne Cooke, Josef Helfenstein and Christiane Terrisse, Museo Nacional Centro de Arte Reina Sofía, Madrid, 1999

Holzer, Jenny & Louise Bourgeois. *The violence of handwriting across a page*, exh cat, JRP|Editions, Zurich & Kunstmuseum Basel, Basel, 2022

Kroksnes, Andrea & Briony Fer. *Louise Bourgeois: imaginary conversations*, exh cat, with texts by Jo Applin, Briony Fer, Alison Karasyk Hines, Andrea Kroksnes and Sérgio B Martins, The National Museum, Oslo, 2023

Kuspit, Donald. *An interview with Louise Bourgeois*, Elizabeth Avedon Editions, Random House, New York, 1988

Küster, Ulf. *Louise Bourgeois*, Hatje Cantz, Ostfildern, 2011

Larratt-Smith, Philip (ed). *Louise Bourgeois, Freud's daughter*, exh cat, with texts by Philip Larratt-Smith and Juliet Mitchell, Jewish Museum, New York & Yale University Press, New Haven & London, 2021

——— (ed). *Louise Bourgeois: the return of the repressed* (two volumes), with texts by Elisabeth Bronfen, Donald Kuspit, Philip Larratt-Smith, Juliet Mitchell, Mignon Nixon, Paul Verhaeghe & Julie De Ganck, and Meg Harris Williams, Violette Editions, London, 2012

Lorz, Julienne (ed). *Louise Bourgeois. structures of existence: the Cells*, exh cat, with texts by Bart De Baere, Lynne Cooke, Kate Fowle, Jerry Gorovoy, Julienne Lorz, Griselda Pollock, Dionea Rocha Watt, Nancy Spector and Ulrich Wilmes, Haus der Kunst, Munich & Prestel, Munich, London & New York, 2017

Meyer-Thoss, Christiane. *Louise Bourgeois: designing for free fall*, Ammann Verlag, Zurich, 1992

Morris, Frances (ed). *Louise Bourgeois*, exh cat, with essays by Paulo Herkenhoff, Julia Kristeva, Donald Kuspit, Elisabeth Lebovici, Mignon Nixon, Linda Nochlin, Alex Potts, Robert Storr et al, Tate Publishing, London, 2007

Morris, Frances & Marina Warner. *Louise Bourgeois*, Tate Publishing, London, 2000

Rales, Emily Wei & Ali Nemerov (eds). *Louise Bourgeois: to unravel a torment*, exh cat, with texts by Briony Fer, Philip Larratt-Smith and Emily Wei Rales, Glenstone Museum, Potomac, Maryland, 2018

Rugoff, Ralph & Julienne Lorz. *The woven child*, exh cat, with texts by Lynne Cooke, Rachel Cusk, Julienne Lorz and Ralph Rugoff, Hayward Gallery Publishing, London & Hatje Cantz, Osfildern, 2022

Smith, Jason & Linda Michael. *Louise Bourgeois in Australia*, exh cat, Heide Museum of Modern Art, Melbourne, 2012

Storr, Robert. *Intimate geometries: the art and life of Louise Bourgeois*, Thames & Hudson, London, 2016

Wye, Deborah. *Louise Bourgeois: an unfolding portrait*, exh cat, The Museum of Modern Art, New York, 2017

——— (ed). *Louise Bourgeois: the complete prints & books*, online publication, moma.org/bourgeoisprints, The Museum of Modern Art, New York, 2012–18

SELECTED FILMS

Louise Bourgeois, 1975, interview by Lyn Blumenthal and Kate Horsfield, Video Data Bank, School of the Art Institute of Chicago

Louise Bourgeois, 1993, dir Camille Guichard, Terra Luna Films, Paris

Louise Bourgeois: no trespassing, 1994, dir Nigel Finch, Arena Films, BBC, London

Louise Bourgeois: the spider, the mistress and the tangerine, 2008, dirs Marion Cajori & Amei Wallach © Art Kaleidoscope Foundation, New York

CONTRIBUTORS

Jane Campion is an award-winning New Zealand–born Australasian filmmaker. She is the writer and director of the internationally acclaimed films *The piano* (1993) and *The power of the dog* (2021), for which she has received two Academy Awards, two BAFTA Awards, and two Golden Globe Awards. Other films include *Sweetie* (1989), *An angel at my table* (1990) and *Holy smoke!* (1999). Her television work includes the miniseries *Top of the lake* (2013) and *Top of the lake: China girl* (2017). She is currently the director of a pop-up two-year film school aimed at emerging writer/directors and funded by Netflix.

Chris Kraus is the author of four novels, three essay collections and a literary biography of Kathy Acker. Her books include *Summer of hate* (2012), *Where art belongs* (2011), *Torpor* (2006), *Video Green: Los Angeles art and the triumph of nothingness* (2004), *Aliens and anorexia* (2000) and the acclaimed novel *I love Dick* (1997). She has written about art and culture for *The Guardian*, *The New Yorker*, *The Washington Post* and many other publications. She is a co-editor, alongside Hedi El Kholti, of the independent press Semiotext(e). She lives in Los Angeles and teaches writing at ArtCenter.

Philip Larratt-Smith is a curator and writer based in New York. Since 2019, he has been curator of The Easton Foundation in New York, which administers the legacy of Louise Bourgeois. In 2011, he presented Bourgeois's psychoanalytic writings in the exhibition and two-volume publication *Louise Bourgeois: The Return of the Repressed* (2012). His recent exhibitions of Louise Bourgeois's work include *Louise Bourgeois: Freud's Daughter* at the Jewish Museum, New York (2021).

Justin Paton is head curator of international art at the Art Gallery of New South Wales. His recent projects for the Art Gallery include *Francis Upritchard: Here Comes Everybody* and (with co-curator Lisa Catt) *Dreamhome: Stories of Art and Shelter* and the inaugural Tank project *Adrián Villar Rojas: The End of Imagination*. Paton's books include *How to look at a painting* (Awa Press, Wellington, 2005), *McCahon country* (Auckland Art Gallery Toi O Tāmaki & Penguin Random House New Zealand, Auckland, 2019) and, most recently, the book of the *Dreamhome* exhibition (Art Gallery of New South Wales, 2023).

Jamieson Webster is a psychoanalyst in New York City and teaches at The New School for Social Research. Webster is the author of *Conversion disorder* (Columbia University Press, New York, 2018) and *The life and death of psychoanalysis* (Karnac, London, 2011), and the co-author of *Stay, illusion! the Hamlet doctrine* (Pantheon and Vintage, New York, 2013). A collection of her writings, *Disorganisation and sex*, was published in 2022 (Divided Publishing, Brussels). She writes regularly for *Artforum*, *The New York Review of Books* and *The New York Times*.

ACKNOWLEDGEMENTS

'She created a kingdom in a way that very few people ever have,' Chris Kraus says of Louise Bourgeois in her interview in this book. For the challenge and privilege of exploring that realm and sharing it with audiences in Sydney, I and my colleagues offer thanks, first of all, to Jerry Gorovoy. His trust and support, in his capacity as president of The Easton Foundation, have made an ambitious exhibition possible. His intimate knowledge of Bourgeois's work, based on three decades as the artist's assistant and closest supporter ('Jerry who knows', as Bourgeois once put it), has been indispensable in the development and refinement of the exhibition concept and selection.

As curator of this exhibition, I also extend special thanks to Philip Larratt-Smith, curator at The Easton Foundation and advising curator for this exhibition, who has been an essential guide through Bourgeois's 'kingdom' – patiently fielding questions, drawing our attention to telling works and relationships, and advocating for an exhibition that discloses the tensions and complexities of Bourgeois's art. For their professionalism, remarkable attention to detail, and generously shared knowledge, thanks also go to Maggie Wright, executive director of The Easton Foundation and Louise Bourgeois Archive, Sewon Kang, Hera Kim and David Walker; and, at the Louise Bourgeois Studio, the team of Cait Schuyler, Kendal Grady, Beth Higgins, Richard Bruce, Johee Kim, David Baskin and Simon Rybansky.

Bourgeois's significance today is borne out in this exhibition by contributions by two women artists: renowned artist of words Jenny Holzer and composer and organist Kali Malone. Amplifying Bourgeois's concerns through their unmistakable visual and sonic languages, Holzer and Malone offer a complement and essential counterpoint to the more familiar forms of interpretation that accompany the exhibition. I thank Leah Hartman, Mengna Da and Jeff Lauber at the Jenny Holzer Studio for working so responsively on Holzer's projections of Bourgeois's writings; and Regina Greene and my colleague Jonathan Wilson, curator of music and community, for facilitating Malone's deeply considered and emotive compositions for the show. Thanks to Jacqueline Kaess-Farquet for kindly making available for the exhibition some memorable footage from a 1991 interview with Bourgeois. It is fitting here also to acknowledge the film program curated by Ruby Arrowsmith-Todd and EO Gill for the Art Gallery's cinema. Inspired by conversations with Jerry Gorovoy about Bourgeois's favourite films and directors, *Louise Bourgeois goes to the movies* brings together directors from Rainer Werner Fassbinder to Robert Altman in an exploration of love, psychoses, anxious desire and twisted relationships.

Further demonstrating the importance of Bourgeois for artists and writers today, Jane Campion, Chris Kraus and Jamieson Webster have contributed wonderfully to this publication. Bourgeois and her works come to life through their eyes. I also acknowledge the late Suzan Cooper, whose work as a performer is discussed by Chris Kraus in her interview and seen in the exhibition, and Cooper's daughter Sonia Goldberg. I offer congratulations and gratitude to colleagues at the Art Gallery of New South Wales whose combined talents have created a vital book that not only reflects but amplifies the exhibition's themes: graphic designer Mitch Brown and senior graphic designer Elliott Bryce Foulkes; Julie Donaldson, publishing manager (former); Faith Chisholm, publishing manager (acting); Lisa Girault, editor; Cara Hickman, production and studio manager; Polly Gillman, rights and licensing coordinator; Jenni Carter, photography manager; Felicity Jenkins, photographer; Emily Sullivan, assistant curator of contemporary international art; Linda Michael, independent editor; and Jacob Ring, Ring Studio.

Louise Bourgeois: Has the Day Invaded the Night or Has the Night Invaded the Day? is the first full monographic exhibition presented in the Art Gallery's new building on Gadigal Country. I thank Michael Brand, director, and Maud Page, deputy director and director of collections, for their conviction that the first such show, and one of the most extensive shows ever presented at the Art Gallery, should be by a great woman artist and, moreover, one whose work does not cease to challenge. Those thanks extend to Miranda Carroll, director of public engagement (former); Hakan Harman, chief operating officer; and John Richardson, director of development. John and his team, including Brontë Hock, major gifts manager, Michela Angeloni, campaign coordinator, Zoë Hart, senior manager, corporate partnerships, and Sarah Martin, senior manager, strategic partnerships, brought together an array of generous supporters. We also thank Destination NSW, supporters of the Sydney International Art Series, which connects so many Australian gallery-goers with compelling art and exhibitions.

Realising this exhibition in the year following the opening of a new building was bound to come with challenges. For meeting those challenges with characteristic focus, clarity, tenacity and good humour, I thank Danielle Earp, senior exhibitions manager, and Lauren Parker, senior registrar. I'm especially grateful to Emily Sullivan, who has, as assistant curator, brilliantly guided so many aspects of the project. In the wider team, thanks to Kate Beckingham, registrar; Phoebe Rathmell, projects coordinator of art, music, film; Lydia Dowman, assistant registrar; Chenoah Diagne, assistant registrar; Caroline Geraghty, head of registration; and Charlotte Cox, head of exhibitions. Thanks to Nicole Cusack and Aimee Jeffries, junior exhibition designers, and Jemima Woo, senior exhibition designer, for their tireless and detailed creative work. From our dedicated installation and audiovisual team, I thank Nik Rieth, installation manager; Jeremy Skellern, installation production coordinator; Tim Dale, senior installation officer; Monica Rudhar, senior installation officer; Mark Taylor, AV technician; Kane Hancock, AV services manager; Jaye Ottens, lighting technician; and Kate Brown, lighting technician. Sally Webster, head of sustainable campus development, and Daniel Griffin, senior project manager, exhibitions and capital works, provided crucial advice on build and install, with the support of Nicole Dahlberg, project assistant facilities; Darcy Whitlam, senior display technician; Gary Bennett, workshop coordinator; Katie Iveson, trades assistant; and Angelo Polizogopoulos, painting coordinator.

For their care for and advice about works in so many mediums, thanks to Carolyn Murphy, head of conservation; Kasi Albert, senior conservator, objects; Sarah Bunn, exhibitions conservator; Frances Cumming, exhibitions and loans conservator; Bronwyn Tulloh, conservator objects; and Lisa Mansfield, time-based art conservator. Thanks also to Sonja Falkiner, risk and safety manager, for her considered advice. For their work welcoming visitors and looking after the exhibition, thanks to Karl Robideau, head of visitor experience; Catherine Pye, visitor experience manager; Kuldeep Duhan, head of security and gallery services; Telly Linakis, security manager; Arthur Boucas, Tracey Keogh and Sheila Weir, team leaders, gallery services; and their teams. Samia Sayed, public programs producer, Jamie Khamphet, assistant programs producer, and Clare Willcox, public programs manager, have developed a rich accompanying public program. Leeanne Carr, creative learning manager, and Victoria Collings, family programs manager, have connected schools and younger audiences with Bourgeois's legacy. Francesca Ford, manager of digital projects, and Flora Suen, digital media coordinator, led the creation of the exhibition audio guide with the team from Art Processors. Thanks to Hannah McKissock-Davis, senior content editor; Holly Bennett, creative content producer; Kirsten Tilgals, online producer; Rachael Hammond, head of marketing and communications; Julieta Lopez, marketing manager; James Ricupito, communications specialist; and Sarah Shields, communications manager, for spreading the word about a singular exhibition.
For fostering appreciation of Bourgeois's life and art through lectures and programs, we extend our thanks to Robert Heather, executive director, and Yvette Pratt, chief operating officer, of the Art Gallery Society. Thanks also to Rebecca Allport, Maryanne Marsh, Daniel McCready, Toby Newell and Jason Lui of the Gallery Shop.

At the heart of the exhibition is an exceptional group of loans from The Easton Foundation and the Louise Bourgeois Trust. For lending these works and providing additional support for the exhibition in Sydney, the Art Gallery of New South Wales offers heartfelt thanks again to Jerry Gorovoy, president of The Easton Foundation, and his team. The Art Gallery joins with The Easton Foundation in thanking Hauser & Wirth (representatives of the Estate of Louise Bourgeois) and its presidents Marc Payot, Manuela Wirth and Iwan Wirth, for their support of the exhibition and key loans. From early sculptures to exquisite textile suites to haunting Cells, an array of extraordinary loans enriches this exhibition. For entrusting us with these works in Australia, we offer sincere thanks to: Artist Rooms Foundation, UK; Collection Château La Coste, France; Fondation Beyeler, Basel; Glenstone Museum, Potomac, Maryland; Hauser & Wirth Collection Services, New York; Hauser & Wirth Collection Services, Zurich; Kunstmuseum Den Haag; National Gallery of Australia, Canberra; National Gallery of Victoria, Melbourne; Peder Lund; Collection Posten Moderne, Trondheim, Norway; private collection, New York; Sammlung Goetz, München; Tate and National Galleries Scotland. The Easton Foundation also acknowledges More Specialized Transport and Acumen Fine Art Logistics.

Bourgeois's artworks are thrillingly physical, and none more so than her monumental sculpture *Maman* 1999. For helping us to bring many works – *Maman* chief among them – from around the world to Sydney, we sincerely thank the Neville Holmes Grace Exhibition Endowment Fund and the family of generous supporters named overleaf, chief among them John Grill AO and Rosie Williams. In a talk given to those supporters recently, Sydney artist Del Kathryn Barton testified to the power of her own first encounter, on overseas travels, with the mighty presence that is *Maman*. With the assistance of our exhibition patrons, we are honoured to set the stage locally for such transformative encounters with Louise Bourgeois's art.

Justin Paton
Head curator of international art
Art Gallery of New South Wales

SYDNEY INTERNATIONAL ART SERIES

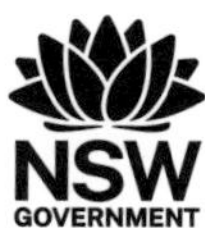

Strategic sponsor

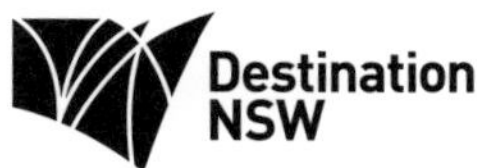

Major partners

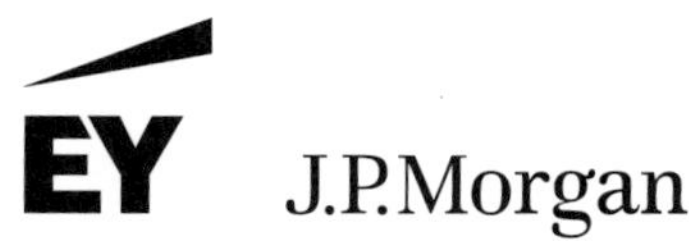

Media partners

JCDecaux The Saturday Paper

Hotel partner

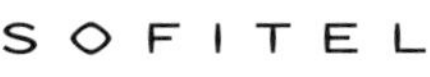

Principal exhibition patron

John Grill AO and Rosie Williams

Endowment patron

Neville Holmes Grace Exhibition Endowment Fund

Major exhibition patron

Victoria Taylor

Exhibition patrons

Alenka Tindale
Ginny and Leslie Green
Julie Green and Frans Vandenburg

Publication patrons

Anita Belgiorno-Nettis
Barbara Wilby
Women's Art Group
Yang Yang

Published by Art Gallery of New South Wales
on Gadigal Country
Art Gallery Road, The Domain
Sydney 2000, Australia
artgallery.nsw.gov.au

in association with the exhibition
Louise Bourgeois: Has the Day Invaded the Night or Has the Night Invaded the Day?
Art Gallery of New South Wales, Sydney
25 November 2023 – 28 April 2024

A catalogue record for this book is available from the National Library of Australia
ISBN 9781741741681

Publishing manager: Julie Donaldson/Faith Chisholm*
Text editing: Linda Michael
Design: Mitch Brown*, Elliott Bryce Foulkes*
Editorial support: Lisa Girault*, Emily Sullivan*
Rights and permissions: Polly Gillman*
Photography: as indicated in 'Credits'
Proofreading: Maggie Wright, Philip Larratt-Smith, Sewon Kang, The Easton Foundation; Kay Campbell, The Comma Institute
Production: Cara Hickman*
Typeface: Quadrant and Preston by Vincent Chan (Matter of Sorts)
Prepress: Spitting Image
Printed in China by the Australian Book Connection
*Art Gallery of New South Wales

The Art Gallery of New South Wales is a statutory body of the NSW State Government

Dust jacket: Louise Bourgeois *Arch of Hysteria* 1993 in the Tank

Distribution:
Thames & Hudson Australia
Thames & Hudson UK
University of Washington Press USA